Reading and Spelling: Development and Disorders

Reading and Spelling: Development and Disorders

Edited by

Charles Hulme
University of York

R. Malatesha Joshi
Oklahoma State University

LONDON AND NEW YORK

First published 1998 by Lawrence Erlbaum Associates, Inc., Publishers

2 Park Square, Milton Park, Abingdon, Oxon OX14 4RN
711 Third Avenue, New York, NY 10017, USA

Routledge is an imprint of the Taylor & Francis Group, an informa business

First issued in paperback 2016

Transferred to Digital Printing 2009 by Routledge

Copyright © 1998 Taylor & Francis.

All rights reserved. No part of this book may be reprinted or reproduced or utilised in any form or by any electronic, mechanical, or other means, now known or hereafter invented, including photocopying and recording, or in any information storage or retrieval system, without permission in writing from the publishers.

Notice:
Product or corporate names may be trademarks or registered trademarks, and are used only for identification and explanation without intent to infringe.

Library of Congress Cataloging-in-Publication-Data

Reading and spelling: development and disorders / edited by Charles Hulme, R. Malatesha Joshi.
    p. cm.
   Includes bibliographical references and index.
   1. Reading—Code emphasis approaches. 2. Reading—Remedial teaching. 3. English language—Orthography and spelling—Study of teaching. I. Hulme, Charles. II. Joshi, R. Malatesha.
   LB1050.22.R43 1998   372.43—dc21
   98-18656   CIP

Publisher's Note
The publisher has gone to great lengths to ensure the quality of this reprint but points out that some imperfections in the original may be apparent.

ISBN 978-1-138-98460-8 (pbk)
ISBN 978-0-8058-2773-6 (hbk)

Contents

I: The Development of Decoding Skills   1

1. Why Is Speech So Much Easier Than Reading?   5
   Alvin M. Liberman

2. The Decomposition of Decoding   19
   Philip B. Gough and Sebastian Wren

3. Language Prediction Skill, Phonological Recoding Ability, and Beginning Reading   33
   William E. Tunmer and James W. Chapman

4. Rime-Based Coding in Early Reading Development in English: Orthographic Analogies and Rime Neighborhoods   69
   Usha Goswami

5. Word Reading by Sight and by Analogy in Beginning Readers   87
   Linnea C. Ehri

6. Phonological Awareness: Its Nature and Its Influence Over Early Literacy Development   113
   Valerie Muter

7. Why and How Phoneme Awareness Helps Learning to Read   127
   José Morais, Phillipe Mousty, and Régine Kolinsky

8. Proto-Literate Knowledge: Antecedents and Influences on Phonological Awareness and Literacy   153
   Roderick W. Barron

II: Developmental Impairments of Decoding Skills — 175

9. Outcomes of Adults With Childhood Histories of Dyslexia — 179
Maggie Bruck

10. Development and Variation in Developmental Dyslexia — 201
Margaret Snowling, Nata Goulandris, and Neil Defty

11. The Development of Reading Skills in Poor Readers: Educational Implications — 219
Rebecca H. Felton

12. Normal and Dyslexic Reading Development: The Role of Formal Models — 235
Jamie L. Metsala and Gordon D. A. Brown

13. The Origin and Functions of Phonological Representations in Deaf People — 263
Jesus Alegria

14. The Role of Letter Learning in Developing Phonemic Awareness Skills in Preschool Children: Implications for Explanations of Reading Disorders — 287
Rhona S. Johnston

15. Fixed Reference Eye and Reading Disability: Is There a Connection? — 303
Nata K. Goulandris, Ann McIntyre, and Margaret Snowling

III: Reading Comprehension — 317

16. Predicting Reading Comprehension From Listening Comprehension: Is This the Answer to the IQ Debate? — 319
R. Malatesha Joshi, Katherine A. Williams, and Jackie R. Wood

17. Comprehension Skill and Inference-Making Ability: Issues of Causality — 329
Kate Cain and Jane Oakhill

18. Individual Differences in Children's Comprehension Skill: Toward an Integrated Model 343
Jane Oakhill, Kate Cain, and Nicola Yuill

IV: Spelling 369

19. Beginning to Spell in English 371
Rebecca Treiman

20. Phonological and Orthographic Processes in Good and Poor Spellers 395
Carolyn Lennox and Linda S. Siegel

21. The Anatomy of Word-Specific Memory 405
P.G. Aaron, Susan Wilczynski, and Victoria Keetay

22. Strategies Used by 9- to 12-Year-Old Children in Written Spelling 421
Che Kan Leong

23. The Role of Analogy in Early Spelling Development 433
Kate Nation and Charles Hulme

V: The Remediation of Reading Problems 447

24. What Kind of One-on-One Tutoring Helps a Poor Reader? 449
Connie Juel

25. Studies of Computer-Aided Remediation for Reading Disabilities 473
Barbara W. Wise and Richard K. Olson

Author Index 489

Subject Index 501

Part I

THE DEVELOPMENT OF DECODING SKILLS

One of the great discoveries in the study of reading in the last 25 years, is the realization that learning to read depends intimately on a child's phonological skills. This, like many other important ideas, is inherently simple, although it has some profound, and quite complex ramifications. The chapters in Part 1 explore the relationship between phonology and the development of reading skills from a variety of perspectives.

The realization that reading depends critically on phonology was first developed by the Haskins group. It is therefore most appropriate that this section should begin with a chapter by Alvin Liberman. In chapter 1, Liberman asks a disarmingly simple question: Why is speech so much easier than reading and writing? His persuasive, although controversial, answer is that speech is easy because we have evolved specialized neural mechanisms for perceiving and producing it. The nub of this argument is that speakers are endowed with a brain module specialized for controlling the production of speech gestures (the intricate patterns of movement of the vocal tract that allow us to produce the sounds of our language). A more controversial corollary of this view is that the perception of speech also depends on specialized neural structures that automatically transcode speech that we hear into a code for the gestures that were responsible for articulating it. According to this view, the process of gaining access to the small segments of speech, termed *phonemes*, is very difficult because phonemes are only abstractions from a more fundamental motor code. A child may learn to speak quite adequately without access to the nature of the motor code underlying the perception and production of speech. In learning to read however, the child is required to develop an explicit understanding of phonemes that, to quote a memorable phrase of another of our contributors, is an "unnatural act" (Gough & Hillinger, 1980).

The chapters by Gough and Wren (chap. 2) and by Tunmer and Chapman (chap. 3) both argue that adequate word recognition skills are fundamental to skilled reading. Gough and Wren develop the idea that word recognition, in turn, depends on learning to abstract the rule governed relationships between letters and sounds. They argue persuasively that this cipher underlies our ability to read both regular and irregular words in a language like English. Whereas the majority of studies of the development of children's word reading have concentrated on reading words in isolation, Tunmer and Chapman report studies that examine the way in which "bottom-up" decoding skills interact with the use of linguistic context. Their results show clearly that when reading an unfamiliar word children are able to benefit from the context provided by a sentence. However, even when the words have irregular spelling–sound correspondences (e.g., "biscuit"), the cues to their pronunciation contained in their spelling patterns are of crucial importance. Furthermore, variations in decoding skill (or *cipher knowledge*, in Gough's terms) are more important to success in reading unfamiliar words than are variations in sensitivity to sentential contexts.

The last five chapters in Part 1 address two central and interrelated theoretical issues: The level of phonological analysis that is most relevant to the child learning to read and the mechanisms underlying the association between phonological skill and reading. Goswami (chap. 4) reviews a large body of work relating to the child's use of analogies in learning to read (knowing how to read "beak" may help the child to read a similar, but unfamiliar word, such as "peak"). She argues that the process of making analogies is a powerful force in early reading development, and that this in turn is related to children's sensitivity to onset–rime units in words. (The onset of a syllable is the initial consonant or consonant cluster; the rime is the vowel and succeeding consonants in SPR-ING). This is an elegant theory that links together an idea about the level of phonological analysis that is crucial for learning to read (onset/rime units) with a mechanism (using analogies) Ehri's (chap. 5) chapter presents a rather different perspective in which she lays more emphasis on the importance of smaller units of speech (phonemes) as a foundation for the child's early reading skills, and although recognizing the role of analogies in reading, she sees this as a process that depends on prior learning of a basic stock of sight words and a degree of phonemic awareness. Both chapters argue for a role of analogies in early reading, but there is a difference of emphasis as to the level of phonological analysis that is important and the stage at which analogies come into play.

The level of phonological analysis that is important in early reading is also explored by Muter and Morais (chap. 6) and Morais, Mousty, and Kolinsky (chap. 7). Muter presents data from a longitudinal study that argue for the primacy of phonemic analysis rather than onset–rime analysis for early reading development. Morais and his colleagues argue that phonemic awareness is critical for learning to read effectively in an alphabetic language and that the relationship is a reciprocal one so that the development of reading skills are critical for a full development of phonemic awareness. Barron (chap. 8) also supports this interactive view. He presents the novel idea that young children's learning of letter names and sounds may be critical in facilitating their phonemic awareness. This awareness in turn, facilitates the process of learning to read. Barron's argument for the importance of letter knowledge is supported by evidence from a variety of sources, including the study reported by Muter, showing that early letter knowledge is an excellent predictor of the rate with which young children learn to read.

REFERENCES

Gough, P. B., & Hillinger, M. L. (1980). Learning to read: An unnatural act. *Bulletin of the Orton Society, 30,* 179–196.

Chapter 1

Why Is Speech So Much Easier Than Reading and Writing?

Alvin M. Liberman
Haskins Laboratories

About 25 years ago, some of my colleagues posed the question that was, in their view, basic to an understanding of the reading process and the ills that so frequently attend it: What must would-be readers know that mastery of speech will not have taught them? Drawing on a combination of common sense, old knowledge about language, and new knowledge about speech, they arrived at the hypothesis that a missing and necessary condition was what has come to be called *phonological awareness*—that is, a conscious understanding that words come apart into consonants and vowels. Research then demonstrated that such awareness is not normally present in preliterate children or illiterate adults; that measures of awareness provide, perhaps, the best single predictor of reading achievement; and that training designed to develop awareness has generally beneficial effects on learning to read.

However, the pioneers of phonological awareness rather neglected the flip side of their inquiry: Why is phonological awareness not necessary for speech? My aim is to repair that omission. To that end, I seek reasons, in addition to those my colleagues found, why the phonologic structures that are common to speaker and hearer are nevertheless not noticed by either. Beyond further rationalizing the hypothesis—now a fact—that phonological awareness is not a normal by-product of learning to speak, those reasons should lay bare the critical difference between speech and reading/writing, and thus let us see why the one is so much easier than the other. Moreover, when taken together with considerations having to do with the operation of the phonological faculty, they may enlarge our understanding of certain deficiencies that poor readers have, including even those that stand apart from the process of reading itself (Liberman, Shankweiler, & Liberman, 1989).

I begin, however, not with notions about why speech does not require awareness, but rather with some speculations about why that aspect of the issue was initially scanted. That is surely a chancy and presumptuous thing for me to do, for I cannot expect researchers to have written about the questions they never raised, so I cannot know whether my colleagues did not think to ask them, or did not think them fit to ask. I must therefore rely on what I know of the awareness issue as it developed in the thinking of Isabelle Liberman who, together with her colleagues Donald Shankweiler and Ignatius Mattingly at Haskins Laboratories, was among the pioneers of the awareness enterprise.

When Isabelle found herself responsible for teaching teachers how children learn to read, and why some do not, she had not yet done research in the field and was only minimally acquainted with the literature. She therefore undertook a two-part program. First, she took stock of what she, and presumably every other educated person, knew about speech and language that might be relevant, carefully selecting only those facts and generalizations that were firmly established. Then, given those pieces of secure and presumably pertinent knowledge, she measured their implications against the received wisdom about reading as it appeared in textbooks and the research literature. What Isabelle (and, as she thought, everybody else) knew that seemed relevant fell into two categories: the difference between language and all other forms of natural communication, and the difference between speech and reading/writing.

In regard to the difference between language and other natural modes of communication, Isabelle knew that the most important property of language is that it is open or productive, in contrast to all nonhuman, but equally natural, modes of communication, which are not.

This is to say that language can communicate an indefinitely large and varied set of messages, including many that are entirely novel. Human beings communicate in this wonderfully open way as easily and naturally as they walk, but only because they have ready access to the two productive devices—phonology and syntax—that their language faculty provides. Lacking both a phonology and a syntax, nonhuman animals have only such apparatus as is necessary to connect a few signals to an equal or smaller number of unchangeable messages. In light of this, the idea held by some reading specialists, that skilled readers should go directly from print to meaning, presumably bypassing their phonological and syntactic processes altogether (Smith, 1971), seemed distinctly odd. Surely, that would be to do in reading what is not normally done in speech, where phonologic

1. WHY IS SPEECH SO MUCH EASIER? 7

and syntactic processing are not a matter of choice but mandatory, and so to trade productivity for the severe constraints that characterize all other natural forms of communication. In opposition to this idea, it seemed to Isabelle that a writing system, as well as the manner of its use, must preserve generativity at all costs, and that our alphabetic system does it quite well, but only when properly used. Proper use requires that readers attach the artifacts of the alphabet to the natural structures of their language, taking care to make the connection at the earliest possible stage. That done, the readers get all the rest of the complex processing for free, courtesy of the biological specialization for language that they own simply by virtue of membership in the human race.

Thus, at the level of the word, the readers who have read it right can deploy their powerful phonologic resources, with the result that productivity is preserved and they are not reduced to treating words within the narrow limits that the nonhuman, nonphonologic modes allow. In this connection, it seemed to be little appreciated in the reading community that the phonology a reader can exploit is not merely a list of sounds—or letter–sound correspondences—but rather a marvelous combinatorial scheme, unique to speech, that comprehends all the words the readers already know, as well as those they have forgotten, and those they have yet to learn.

At the level of the sentence, no intellectual exertions are necessary once the readers have made proper contact with their natural language faculty, for then even the most complex sentences will be handled as easily as they are in speech, which is, more often than not, easy enough. It seemed wrong, therefore, that many reading specialists assumed the existence of a "visual" language, in which readers not only perceive the print visually, as they must, but also represent the words that way. For surely, the natural way of understanding the sentence would be entirely beyond the reach of such a visual reader, if only because the syntactic component of the biological specialization for language cannot have evolved to deal with anything but phonologic representations (together, of course, with their grammatical appendages); there is no reason to think it would know what to do with the outputs of the visual system. So if the representations were exclusively visual, readers would be required to develop a wholly new mechanism, and one for which they had no natural bent, simply to do what the old system, given a more propitious input, is adapted to do automatically. Since the most sophisticated scientists had been unable to figure out how the old system works, it seemed most unlikely that visual readers could succeed where the scientists had failed, and thus invent a new system just to meet the unnatural demands of the visual way they had unwisely chosen to read. In this connection, Isabelle and her colleagues came to think it seriously misleading to suppose that language can be visual *or* auditory when, in fact, it can be neither. For reasons I develop later, Isabelle and her colleagues were in the process of conceiving that language, including its phonological component, is a biologically coherent modality in its own right, possessed of its own uniquely linguistic structures and processes. They wondered, then, why it might be hard for someone who is perfectly at home in that modality to enter it by way of a seemingly simple transcription of its modality-specific structures. Just about everything Isabelle and her colleagues wanted to know about beginning reading was brought into sharp focus by that question.

As for the difference between speech and reading/writing, it is plain that the former is a species-typical product of biological evolution, arguably the most apparent and defining of our genetically determined characteristics, in contrast to the latter, which is an intellectual achievement of an apparently difficult sort. There is, then, a strong presumption that we have been talking ever since we emerged as a species (or, according to some, as a genus), which is somewhere from 200,000 to several million years ago; but it was less than 4,000 years ago that some of our fellow humans discovered the alphabetic principle and put it to practical use. What was truly unique about this discovery was not the idea that drawings can be used to represent speech instead of objects or ideas; that was of critical importance, to be sure, but it had been exemplified in the rebus, the first true (i.e., productive) writing system, and then elaborated several times independently in the syllabic or morphosyllabic scripts of, for example, Sumerian, Mayan, or Chinese. The unique discovery underlying the alphabet was neither more nor less than what I have already identified as segmental phonology, the part of grammar that generates all words by variously combining and permuting a small number of consonants and vowels. Seen that way, the alphabet was a triumph of applied linguistics. But why has it to be reckoned a triumph? Why has the discovery been made only once, all applications having been borrowed, in effect, from that first, seminal event? In short, why was it hard 4,000 years ago for all prealphabetic humans, and why is it hard now for the prealphabetic child?

Surely, reading teachers must have asked these questions, for they could hardly know what it is they have to teach, or how to teach it, without knowing what it is the student must learn, and why the learning might not be easy. But when Isabelle searched the textbooks and the research literature for the answers, she could not even find the questions. Nevertheless, ideas about reading were thick on the ground, and all did at least imply answers to her questions, answers that ranged, in her view, from the merely improbable to the seemingly impossible. At the latter end of the continuum was a notion, now in full flower as a basic assumption of Whole Language, that foreclosed almost all questions about the reading process by asserting that learning to read is just as easy and natural as learning to speak, or would be if only we taught reading the way we teach speech

1. WHY IS SPEECH SO MUCH EASIER? 9

(Goodman & Goodman, 1979). It seems shocking that this proposition, so obviously false in light of absolutely everything we know about language and its biology, should be taken seriously by so many, and should, indeed, have become the cornerstone of what is currently the most widely accepted theory of reading and how to teach it. A little closer to being merely improbable was the claim—made, incidentally, by a guiding spirit of Whole Language—that reading is a "psycholinguistic guessing game" (Goodman, 1976). But by far the most numerous theories located the difficulty somewhere in the eyes. Surely people cannot be expected to read if they cannot see the print. However, just as surely, it could hardly have been pandemic visual deficiencies that had so effectively blocked the development of an alphabet; hence, it can hardly be true, except in special cases, that rectifying such deficiencies is now the critical step in the development of the ability to use one.

Of course, some did make what seemed an appropriate obeisance to phonology by supposing that children had to learn the so-called letter–sound correspondences—the heart of phonics instruction. However, that emphasis on those correspondences rested uneasily on the false assumption that speech is an acoustic alphabet, for it is only on such an assumption that a child might have been able to "synthesize" a word out of its letter–sound constituents—that is, "sound it out." For reasons to be developed later, speech cannot be, and is not, an acoustic alphabet, so attempts to sound out a word from the sounds of its letters will typically produce an utterance—as often as not, a nonword—that has as many syllables as the target word has letters. However, learning the sounds of the letters might be of some help in moving the child to the right insight about the alphabet, which is that a printed word is a piece of language—actually, a phonologic structure—to which certain meanings may or may not be attached. But sounding out was not the only way to get the child to see what the game is all about, nor did it seem necessarily the best way.

All the foregoing is by way of telling why Isabelle Liberman, Donald Shankweiler, Ignatius Mattingly, and other early members of the Haskins reading group turned their attention to speech. That seemed the thing to do, because speech and an alphabetic writing system have the same primary function, which is to convey the internal structure of words. Therefore, one might hope to find in speech the key to understanding why that structure was so hard to get from the printed page.

Happily for the reading group, other Haskins colleagues had for some time been doing research on speech, and had uncovered a few characteristics that were possibly relevant to the reading problem. The one that seemed most likely was that speech is not the acoustic alphabet so many had assumed it to be, and thus it cannot be mapped directly onto the optical alphabet a reader must learn to use (Liberman, Cooper, Shankweiler, & Studdert-Kennedy, 1967). The reason is easily understood once one thinks about the requirements of phonologic communication. The most obvious of these is imposed by the generative combinatorial strategy that phonology exploits, for if words are to be formed by combining and permuting a set of meaningless units, then the units must be commutable, which is to say discrete, invariant, and categorical, just like the letters of the alphabet, indeed. But if those units were sounds, and the sounds had to have those characteristics, then the sounds could only be produced by articulatory maneuvers that also had them, too. In that case a speaker could not say [bag], but only [b'] [ə] [g'], and to say [b'] [ə] [g'] is not to speak, but to spell. Communication by spelling would, of course, be painfully slow, and the listener would presumably find it nearly impossible to organize the phonologic segments into the larger units of words and sentences. It is also relevant to the rate problem that even if it could somehow be solved in production, the result would defeat the ear. Speech delivers phonologic information at rates of 10 to 20 consonants and vowels per second. But if each consonant and vowel were a unit sound, as it would be in an acoustic alphabet, rates that high would strain the temporal resolving power of the ear and overreach its ability to keep sequential order straight. Thus, an acoustic alphabet is impossible if people are to speak and listen as fast as they must.

Some of Isabelle's speech-research colleagues had come to believe that nature solved the commutability and rate problems by defining the phonologic units not as sounds but as abstract motor structures that control the articulatory movements by which those sounds are made (Liberman & Mattingly, 1985). The critical advantage for the speaker is that unit gestures corresponding to the discrete, invariant, and categorical units of the phonology can be coarticulated—that is, overlapped and merged—with the further result that speakers can run them off at the high rates that characterize speech and make language possible. For the listener, coarticulation efficiently packs information about several phonological segments into the same piece of sound, thus loosening the constraints that are imposed by the temporal resolving power of the ear. As for the difficulty that auditory perception has with sequential order, coarticulation produces context-conditioned variations in the acoustic signal that mark order by the shape of the signal, not by some temporal sequence of its presumably discrete pieces. Thus, to perceive that [b] comes first in [ba] and second in [ab], the listener relies on the fact that the acoustic cues for the consonants are mirror images, reflecting the coarticulated gestures from consonant closure to vowel opening in the one case, and the reverse progression in the other. If such syllables are of relatively short duration, the acoustic signals will carry information about both consonant and vowel throughout their lengths, so acoustic shape can be the only basis for determining the order of the phonetic units. Given a linguistic specialization that recovers the gestures, the acoustically different signals will nevertheless evoke the same phonetic percept, accurately marked for its position in the sequence.

The general consequence of coarticulation is that almost any piece of sound, no matter how short, carries information about not one but several units in the phonologic string. Accordingly, the sounds of speech are not a substitution cipher on the phonologic structure, but a complex and specifically linguistic code in which there is simply no correspondence in segmentation between any delimitable acoustic segments and the segments of the phonology. This is not to say that the underlying phonology is not alphabetically segmented, only that the segmentation is not apparent at the acoustic surface.

It was, then, the foregoing facts and speculations that initially suggested to the Haskins reading group that children who had mastered speech might nevertheless be unaware of the discrete segments it conveys. In listening to a word, the children would not have heard a succession of discrete, segmented sounds. Moreover, as previously noted, it would have been hard to develop awareness in the children simply by showing them how to divide a word into, or synthesize it from, alphabet-size pieces of speech sound because, apart from vowels, such sounds do not exist.

As I earlier implied, our reading research colleagues did not have all the reasons why awareness is lacking, but they had at least one, and that was enough to head their enterprise in the right direction. They could take satisfaction in the fact that their reason was well grounded in the background science (Mattingly, 1971; Shankweiler & Liberman, 1971). Moreover, the hypothesis held up under empirical tests, and bent agreeably to necessary elaborations and amendments by such colleagues as Benita Blachman, Susan Brady, Anne Fowler, and Hyla Rubin. But most important was the practical application, which lay in the assumption that to help children learn to read someone should teach them how words come apart, because speech had not revealed to the children that they do, yet that was exactly what they needed to understand if they were to properly appreciate and apply the alphabetic principle. Once children had that principle, they would know what to look for, and thus further refinements in their understanding of the exact relation between the alphabetic script and the language could come with experience in reading, as the phonemic and morphophonemic regularities of the writing system revealed themselves. This would happen more readily, of course, if the teacher provided the right help by contriving exercises designed to make the regularities most apparent. As for the irregularities, enlightened instruction would introduce them gradually, while also showing that many were not so wholly irregular as they seemed.

Thus, given what the reading group had yet to do in the further development and testing of their fertile hypothesis, there was no compelling reason for them to wonder why awareness was not essential in learning to speak. Indeed, in the matter of speech, they had gone about as far as they could go, for even their speech research colleagues did not, at that time, have a firm grip on the rest of the story. We may not have that even now, but, as I dare to say later in this chapter, we may at least have it in hand.

To understand why speech is different in the matter of awareness, and so to close the circle, I observe again that, in spite of the complexly encoded nature of the speech signal, phonological structures are in fact contained within it. Those structures *must* be produced and received by the speaker and listener, whether they know it or not, for if the structures were not, language as it has come to be would not exist. Moreover, it *is* possible to become aware of those structures, for, if it were not, alphabetic reading and writing as they have come to be would not exist. No matter, then, that the speech process itself is fully automatic, hence unavailable to consciousness as a process; for the listener, that process must nevertheless produce phonologic representations of which the listener can be conscious. In that connection, Mattingly noted that the automatic process that derives meaning from speech need not, in principle, ever make available to consciousness the phonologic structures that are intermediate to its goal; and, alone among students of language, he speculated about the possible function that such representations might serve (Mattingly, 1990). For our purposes, however, it is enough to know that the representations are present and available. The previously noted bad fit in segmentation between those representations and the acoustic signal is but one reason (and not necessarily the most compelling one) why there is, nevertheless, no awareness; in any case, it can hardly account for the fact that, for speech, in contrast to reading and writing, awareness is not necessary. What, then, does account for that fact?

The easy answer is that speech is a kind of instinct, and therefore a thought-free process, whereas reading/writing is an intellectual achievement of sorts. But that is just to restate the question; I want, therefore, to try a possibly more satisfying answer. Unfortunately for that purpose, such an answer arises from an unconventional theory of speech that is probably not well known to students of the reading process. Worse yet, a proper account of the theory would require that I describe several experiments, and that would require, in turn, a quick tour through the most technical details of acoustic phonetics. To avoid that thicket I describe and support the theory on grounds of plausibility only, and, within those bounds, keep reading ever in view. However, even that oversimplified approach requires an initial detour.

Consider, then, how reading, writing, and speech meet a requirement that is imposed on all three. Indeed, this requirement is imposed on every kind of communication, easily qualifying as the most fundamental requirement there is. It is odd, then, that it appears not to enter into the calculations of researchers in speech or reading, the more so because it is easy to see and easy to understand. The requirement is simply that what counts for the sender must count for the receiver. For that requirement to be met, two closely related conditions must be fulfilled: Out of all possible signals, a certain few must be recognized as relevant to language; and the representations in the minds of sender and receiver must, at some point, be the same. On the assumption that a thing is more likely to be noticed if it has a name, Mattingly and I called this the requirement for "parity," and challenged theorists of any stripe to say how it was established and how maintained for whatever kind of communication they study (Liberman & Mattingly, 1989).

In the case of alphabetic reading and writing, it is easy to see exactly what the parity requirement is, and how it is met. Suppose, for example, that I write "P" and also "/." Every user of the Roman alphabet knows that the first character counts for language, but the second does not. Moreover, the writer of "P" is in league with the reader of "P," because they have a common understanding of what linguistic unit the "P" counts for: the bilabial voiceless stop consonant [p] that introduces the syllable [pat]. Thus parity exists, and the system will run. But we see immediately that parity, though real, is arbitrary; a user of the Cyrillic alphabet would agree that the character "P" counts, but insist that it counts not for a stop consonant but for the continuant [r], as in [rat]. Of course, parity has got to be arbitrary in writing systems, because it was established by agreement. Those who developed the Roman alphabet arrived at a compact that bound them to certain arbitrary decisions about which optical shapes would index which phonological units of the language. All who use that alphabet must become parties to that compact; adhering to its terms they can communicate; otherwise, not.

But what of speech? How is it that [p] became relevant to language and a snort did not? Surely, not by agreement, because nobody invented speech or somehow derived it as a secondary cipher on some more basic mode of communication; hence, nobody got everybody else to speak according to arbitrary decisions about which percepts count, and what they count for. To assume the contrary would be hardly less absurd than to assume divine intervention, as if there had been some extra commandments that Moses dropped on his way down from Sinai, one of which said, "Thou shalt not commit the phoneme [p], except as it is thy intention to communicate." No more is it plausible to suppose that speaker and listener have a common representation just because they both subscribe to an agreement that [p] is the name of some otherwise ordinary sound they both hear. As Studdert-Kennedy remarked to me some time ago, the thing about phonemes is that they "name themselves." My aim is to tease out the theoretical implications of that piece of wisdom.

But first, I would describe the conventional view of speech, just to show how the system it envisions fails to meet Studdert-Kennedy's requirement; how, in other words, it falls short in the matter of parity, and therefore cannot enlighten us about the most fundamental difference between speech and reading/writing. To simplify the matter, let us, for the moment, consider only speech perception. The view held explicitly by almost all researchers in speech—and, I should think, at least tacitly by people concerned about reading—goes as follows (for discussion, see Liberman, 1992; Liberman & Mattingly, 1985). The elements of speech are sounds, and their perception is as it would be for sounds of any other kind. All depend on the general processes of auditory perception, so all produce percepts of a generally auditory sort. Thus, the percepts evoked by a stop consonant and a squeaking door can differ only in the mix of auditory primitives—pitch, loudness, and timbre, for example—out of which they are presumably formed. They are made of the same perceptual stuff, as it were, which is to say that the percept evoked by the speech sound can be no more phonetic than the percept evoked by the squeaking door. In its most general form, this comes down to the assumption that language simply appropriated for its uses the most general processes and representations of the auditory modality. On that conventional assumption, however, the nonlinguistic auditory percepts would have somehow to be connected to language if they were to enjoy the very particular communicative privileges that linguistic status confers. According to the conventional theory, the necessary link is made at a cognitive stage, beyond perception, where the auditory percepts are associated with the phonetic units of language, and so, in effect, given phonetic names.

Of course, the percepts evoked in reading are just ordinarily visual in fact, as the percepts of speech are ordinarily auditory in theory, so it is a matter of fact, not theory, that the visual percepts have to be given phonetic names if they are to be used for linguistic purposes. No mystery there, however, because those percepts have only to be named after the perceivable phonetic units that are evoked by the sounds of speech, independently of the alphabetic shapes that were arbitrarily selected to stand in their stead. But what could the presumably auditory percepts of speech be named after? Surely, not themselves—the specifically phonetic names the conventional theorist would attach to them are neither primary acts nor percepts; accordingly, they must be in the nature of ideas, presumably innate, that are peculiar to language. However, even for the theorist who has a taste for such innate ideas, assuming their existence does not settle the parity issue because it still remains to explain how particular auditory percepts came to be connected to them. Presumably, many were called, but few were chosen. How, then, were the choices made, who made them, and what guaranteed that all would choose the same way? The seemingly inescapable conclusion is that, on the conventional view, parity in speech must have been established by agreement. But that's no way to run a natural communication system—parity by agreement is acceptable, even necessary, for a biologically secondary process like reading, but not for the primary processes of speech. To say otherwise is to claim that speech is an artifact, like the alphabet, and that does violence to the facts.

It has simply got to be, I think, that the percepts evoked by the sounds of speech, in contrast to those evoked by the alphabet, are phonetic, not by virtue of having been given phonetic names, but *ab initio*, by their very nature. That is, they cannot be commonly auditory, as the conventional view would have it, but must rather belong to a phonetic modality that is as different from auditory as auditory is from visual. The primary perceptual response to speech would then be recognized as phonetic in the same way that a visual percept is recognized as visual; there is no need for some cognitive process to endow it with phonetic significance by giving it a phonetic name. On this unconventional view, what evolved was a communicative modality. Unlike the communicative modalities that evolved in other animals, this one was linguistic in nature, and therefore had a phonetic component. Given the functional requirements of phonological communication, the constituents of the phonetic component were, as I've already said, not sounds but gestures. That these gestures are specifically, distinctly, and exclusively phonetic is not just a matter of plausibility, but of fact: They are a distinct set, different from those we make with the same organs when we swallow, move food around in the mouth, or lick our lips. Having evolved to have a phonetic function, they serve no other. As for parity, it is built into the very bones of the phonetic modality, for the speaker produces specifically phonetic gestures, and the listener perceives them. Thus, the acts and percepts of speaker and listener do not have to be arbitrarily connected to language or to each other. The gestures provide a common phonetic currency, good for all linguistic transactions.

Also specialized for phonetic communication is the manner in which the gestures are controlled, since in the elaborate overlapping and merging that I called coarticulation, they are required, as other kinds of action are not, to preserve and transmit information about the discrete string of (phonetic) control structures that are their distal sources. Mattingly and I proposed that all of this is managed by what we have called a "phonetic module," a biological specialization that, like all such specializations, has its own domain, its own mode of automatic signal processing, and its own primitives. The consequence for the purposes of this chapter is that speakers do not have to know how to spell a word in order to say it. Indeed, they do not even have to know that it has a spelling. They have only to think of the word, whatever that means; the phonetic module then spells it for them, automatically selecting and coordinating the gestures that form the phonologic structure. Small wonder the speakers do not notice that the structure is spelled, or how.

Listeners are in a similar case. Presented with the speech signal, they need not puzzle out the complex relation between it and the segmented phonetic structure it conveys. That, too, can be left to the phonetic module, because its complementary perceiving face is specifically adapted to parsing the signal so as to represent phonetic structure by recovering the underlying gestures that are its elements.

It is also relevant here to say again that the phonetic module is but one component of the larger specialization for language, because then we see that syntax, the other major component, must have evolved to work in close harmony with its phonetic partner; theirs would have been a marriage made in heaven. We should expect, then, that the representations produced as the output of the phonetic component would be grist for the syntactic mill, precisely adapted to what syntax wants and needs to do its job. Hence, those representations would pass through to syntax exactly as they came out of the phonetic module. They would not call attention to themselves because they would not require attention, and they would not require attention because they would not have to be made into something that they originally were not. That is the reason why experience in perceiving speech does not automatically produce awareness of its essential phonologic constituents.

Perhaps this story also redeems the claim I made at the outset about the various deficiencies that poor readers might have. The point is that the phonetic module cannot be expected to work equally well for everybody. It would follow then that the phonetic representations produced by a faulty module would be less than normally distinct and therefore that much harder to bring into conscious awareness. For much the same reason, there would presumably be an impairment of working memory for verbal material, which would surely cause reading difficulties. Indeed, we should expect that all phonetically dependent abilities would be, in some degree, impaired, whether they were directly related to reading. But, given that the module works only in the phonetic domain, the consequences, whatever they are, should be found there and nowhere else.

I must not suppose that all I have said here is what Studdert-Kennedy meant when he said that phonemes "name themselves," but it's the only case I am able to make, and until I think of a better one, I am happy to be stuck with it. I like it, even as it is, because, aside from its fit to experimental results I have not presented here, it enables me to see why phonological awareness is neither a precondition nor a result of learning to speak. More generally, it tells me how speech differs from reading and writing, why it is easier, and, not least, what is wrong with the conventional story about how it works.

REFERENCES

Goodman, K. S. (1976). Reading: A psycholinguistic guessing game. In H. Singer & R. Ruddell (Eds.), *Theoretical models and processes of reading* (2nd ed.). Newark, DE: International Reading Association.

Goodman, K. S., & Goodman, Y. M. (1979). Learning to read is natural. In L. B. Resnick & P. A. Weaver (Eds.), *Theory and practice of early reading* (Vol. 1, pp. 137–154). Hillsdale, NJ: Lawrence Erlbaum Associates.

Liberman, A. M. (1992). The relation of speech to reading and writing. In L. Katz & R. Frost (Eds.), *Orthography, phonology, morphology, and meaning* (pp. 167–178). Amsterdam: Elsevier.

Liberman, A. M., Cooper, F. S., Shankweiler, D. D., & Studdert-Kennedy, M. (1967). Perception of the speech code. *Psychological Review, 74*, 431–461.

Liberman, A. M., & Mattingly, I. G. (1985). The motor theory of speech perception revised. *Cognition, 21*, 1–36.

Liberman, A. M., & Mattingly, I. G. (1989). A specialization for speech perception. *Science, 243*, 489–494.

Mattingly, I. G. (1971). Reading, the linguistic process, and linguistic awareness. *Haskins Laboratories Status Report on Speech Research, SR27*, 23–24.

Mattingly, I. G. (1990). Reading and the biological function of linguistic representation. In I. G. Mattingly & M. Studdert-Kennedy (Eds.), *Modularity and the motor theory of speech perception* (pp. 339–346). Hillsdale, NJ: Lawrence Erlbaum Associates.

Shankweiler, D. P., & Liberman, I. Y. (1971). Misreading: A search for causes. *Haskins Laboratories Status Report in Speech Research, SR27*, 35–38.

Smith, F. (1971). *Understanding reading* (1st ed.). New York: Holt, Rinehart & Winston.

Chapter 2

The Decomposition of Decoding

Philip B. Gough
Sebastian Wren
University of Texas at Austin

Decoding—the recognition of the printed word—is an important part of reading. There is, of course, much more to reading than decoding, but without decoding there could be no reading. Decoding is necessary, but not sufficient. As we (Gough & Tunmer, 1986; Hoover & Gough, 1990) like to put it, reading (R) equals the product of decoding (D) and comprehension (C): $R = D \times C$.

In children, the ability to decode accounts for most of the variance in reading ability. Firth (1972) reported a correlation of .92 between pseudoword naming and reading. Hoover and Gough (1990) found that the ability to name pseudowords correlated .84, .80, .75, and .84 with the ability to comprehend text in the first, second, third, and fourth grades, respectively.

In adults, it accounts for much less of the variance. However, we must not let this mislead us into thinking it is any the less important. Breathing may not account for much of the variance in the quality of life, but life without it would not be possible. The same can be said of decoding: We could not read without it.

The reason why decoding accounts for a smaller proportion of reading variance in college students is, we presume, restriction of range. College students are, in the main, good decoders; people who cannot decode are seldom admitted to college. On a hypothetical scale ranging from 0 to 1, college students presumably score .5 or above, but even though the range is severely restricted, decoding still accounts for a significant proportion of reading variance (Cunningham, Stanovich, & Wilson, 1990).

The question, then, is what is this skill? In reading a newspaper or a novel, the skilled reader recognizes a word or more every quarter of a second. That is, in a mental lexicon containing upwards of 25,000 entries, the reader finds (or activates) exactly the right one in something on the order of 180 milliseconds.

What knowledge does the reader need in order to accomplish this feat? In the case of an alphabetic orthography like English, we (Gough, Juel, & Griffith, 1992; Gough & Walsh, 1991) argued that the reader needs two kinds of information. One is knowledge of the spelling–sound correspondences of the language, or what we have called the *orthographic cipher*.

The cipher of English is very complex. The letters of English do not stand in one-to-one correspondence with their phonemes. They could not—the English alphabet has only 26 letters, whereas spoken English contains over three dozen phonemes. Thus, either some letters must represent more than one phoneme, or some phonemes must be represented by combinations of letters.

Both things have happened. Nearly every letter in English corresponds to more than one phoneme, as illustrated in Table 2.1. Five phonemes

TABLE 2.1
Some Examples of the Polyphony of English Letters

ace	act
curb	comb
cat	city
fed	fudge
el	eel
off	of
gum	gym
hoar	hour
ice	in
jet	juan
kit	knit
cold	could
memory	mnemonic
fun	hymn
on	own
pill	philip
queen	Iraq
rub	Perrier
sin	shin
tin	thin
us	use
vex	
wen	when
xerox	xerox
youth	silly
crazy	nazi

(/č, š, θ, ð, ɔ′) are regularly represented by pairs of letters (*ch, sh,* and *th*). Also, virtually every correspondence is context dependent: The reader cannot tell which phoneme a letter represents without knowledge of the surrounding letters, often as many as two or three, sometimes as many as five (compare *chore* and *choreography*).

How is this knowledge represented? We don't yet know. Some (e.g., Coltheart, 1978; Coltheart, Curtis, Atkins, & Haller, 1993) hold that it is embodied in a set of rules. Others (e.g., Glushko, 1979; Goswami, 1988; Marcel, 1980) argue that it is generated by analogy. Still another view (Plaut, McClelland, Seidenberg, & Patterson, 1996; Seidenberg & McClelland, 1989) holds that the cipher consists of sets of connections between orthographic, hidden, and phonological units.

Which view of the cipher is correct? Despite the fact that hundreds of studies have attacked this question, we don't yet have a definitive answer. However, for our purposes, we don't need to know, because we do know how to assess the reader's mastery of the cipher: We can measure the reader's ability to decode pseudowords. Skilled readers can easily name (or make phonological decisions about) pseudowords like *grisk* and *clard* and *spiffle*; those who have no knowledge of the cipher cannot.

Where does this knowledge come from? We're not certain, but we're confident that it does not result from direct instruction (at least it does not result *directly* from direct instruction). For one thing, the rules the child is taught in phonics are too few. Moreover, the rules of phonics are context-free rules, whereas nearly every spelling–sound correspondence in English depends on its context. The rules of the cipher, if they exist, are context-dependent rules.

Why is the cipher important? In the young reader, the answer is obvious. The child comes to the reading task with a vocabulary far in excess of his or her sight vocabulary. Thus, almost every time the child reads, he or she will come across words that he or she has never seen before in print. The child needs some way of identifying those words.

Some (e.g., Goodman & Goodman, 1979) have argued that context will provide the means. Context may indeed help, but context is a false friend. The effect of a context depends on the predictability of the target word, and the predictability of most content words is effectively zero (Gough, 1983). Moreover, the effect of context increases with word frequency and decreases with word length (Alford, 1980). Thus, context will help the child most with words the child already knows (e.g., the function words, which are 4 times as predictable as content), but least with long, unfamiliar words with which he or she most needs help.

The child needs the cipher to deal with novel words; the child also needs the cipher to hold words in memory after they are recognized. It is easy to learn to distinguish a handful of words, because one can find something distinctive about each one. However, with each additional word it becomes harder to find something distinctive about that word. If the child is trying to memorize each word, each new word is harder than the last.

We are not sufficiently aware that most words the child (or the adult) encounters are met infrequently. The distribution of word frequencies is exponential (Carroll, Davies, & Richman, 1971), and the modal frequency in any corpus is one; with respect to any text, most of its words are *hapax legomena.*

From the fact that the child constantly encounters rare and novel words, it follows that the child who has internalized the cipher, the child who can make use of a system that will automatically and effortlessly transform the printed word into phonological form, will be at an advantage. Our research has supported this hypothesis. Much of our research over the last 15 years has been dedicated to demonstrating the importance of the cipher. The child who has internalized the cipher reads (and spells) in a different way than he or she did before.

How does the child who has the cipher differ from the child who doesn't? We (Gough, Juel, & Roper-Schneider, 1983) identified five ways.

First, they read better. That is, a child who has the cipher reads faster and more accurately than a child who has not yet acquired the cipher.

Second, although all readers manifest the word frequency effect (we all decode common words more accurately and rapidly than rare ones), the magnitude of that effect varies with knowledge of the cipher. Children who have the cipher show a smaller frequency effect than children who have not yet acquired the cipher.

Third, children who have mastered the cipher exhibit a regularity effect, but no such effect is seen in a child who has not yet acqured the cipher. For the child who has not yet mastered the cipher, there is no such thing as an irregular word; all words are simply sight words. In the absence of the cipher, there is no difference between regular and irregular words.

Fourth, children who have the cipher make different kinds of errors. Children who have the cipher create neologisms; they might misread *sugar* as /səgr/. But children who don't have the cipher make only word substitutions (*sugar* as *super*).

Finally, when they do make substitutions, cipher readers make a different kind of substitution than do those who don't have the cipher. The cipher reader's substitutions tend to be new; they are created on the spot. However, the noncipher reader draws his or her substitutions from the previous text.

Acquisition of the cipher not only changes the child's reading ability, it also changes the child's spelling. The cipher reader spells phonetically (*camel* as *kaml*), whereas the child who does not have the cipher seldom does (*camel* as *qzmny*). In keeping with this, the cipher reader's spellings

2. THE DECOMPOSITION OF DECODING

correspond in length to the target word, whereas the noncipher reader's errors are only loosely related in length (*rain* might be misspelled with eight letters). Most dramatically, the cipher reader spells only with letters, whereas the child without the cipher may insert nonalphabetic matter into his or her spellings.

It may not seem so obvious that the adult also needs the cipher, because the skilled adult reader rarely encounters novel words (and when he or she does, they are probably not in his or her oral lexicon). Most words the skilled reader encounters are already recognizable in print. For some of these words, recognition is easy, because the reader will have practiced their recognition thousands of times. For example, if a 21-year-old college student had read one hour a day for 15 years, he or she would have seen the word *the* almost 6 million times. However, the majority of words we see, we see only rarely, perhaps no more than once or twice a year. The cipher facilitates the recognition of these rarely encountered words, because it reduces the burden on memory: What is regular need not be remembered at all, because it can be reconstructed. This is reflected in the fact that low-frequency irregular words are the slowest of all to retrieve from memory. Clearly, the cipher is also important to the adult. Skilled adults' mastery of that cipher is reflected in the fact that they can name pseudowords nearly as rapidly as they can pronounce their own names.

The cipher, then, is of central importance to both the child and the adult, but it is not enough. Students of English orthography (notably spelling reformers) have noted that there are many exception or irregular words in our language, words that depart from the regularities of the orthography. However, we should note that even more numerous than the irregular words are what might be called *polyphonic words*—words containing letter sequences that can be pronounced in more than one way. Consider, for example, words containing the vowel sequence *ea* (like *heat, head, heart, steak, area, theatrical, pineapple*). What these examples show is that *ea* takes on a variety of phonological forms; only occasionally does the first vowel do the talking. However, which form it takes can seldom be determined by any sublexical sequence. For instance, the fact that *head* is pronounced /hɛd/ cannot be derived from any sublexical sequence. Neither *hea* nor *ead*, both of which are polyphonic, will determine the choice of vowel; only the entire word will do that. What this means is that child (and adult) readers need an abundance of lexical knowledge, that is, knowledge about specific words.

Thus, both the child and the adult need two kinds of information. The question, then, is how are these two kinds of knowledge represented? Are they stored separately, as a dual-route hypothesis (e.g., Coltheart, 1978) would propose? Or are they stored in a single system, as recent connectionist models would maintain?

Almost 20 years ago, Baron (1979) suggested a psychometric approach to this problem. Baron observed that a child (or, for that matter, an adult) could recognize both pseudowords and regular words using what he called an *orthographic mechanism*, which makes use of "such general and productive relations between letter patterns and sounds as exist" (Baron, 1979, p. 386), or, in short, what we have called the cipher. However, this mechanism would not enable the correct pronunciation of exception or irregular words. For that, Baron proposed that the reader could employ a lexical mechanism, which relies instead on word-specific knowledge. This mechanism could also be employed to regular words.

Thus, by Baron's model, depicted in Fig. 2.1, the naming of both regular and exception words should be based on one mechanism (a lexical mechanism), whereas the naming of regular and pseudowords must be based on another (i.e., the cipher). Baron shrewdly observed that this model predicts that there should be correlations between regular word and exception word naming, and between regular and pseudoword naming. However, the model would not predict a strong correlation (only that resulting from the reader's general competence) between exception and pseudoword naming.

In a series of studies, Baron and his collaborators asked children to read lists of regular (R), exception (E), and pseudowords (N). In every instance, they found higher correlations between R and E and between R and N than between E and N (see Fig. 2.2).

At first blush, these results clearly corroborate the proposal that the two kinds of information are stored in separate representations, but we (Gough & Walsh, 1991) were troubled by Baron's data. For one thing, although the correlations between R and E, and between R and N, were always consistently higher than that between E and N, the latter correlations were very substantial. It did not seem as if this correlation was spurious, as if these two skills were dissociated.

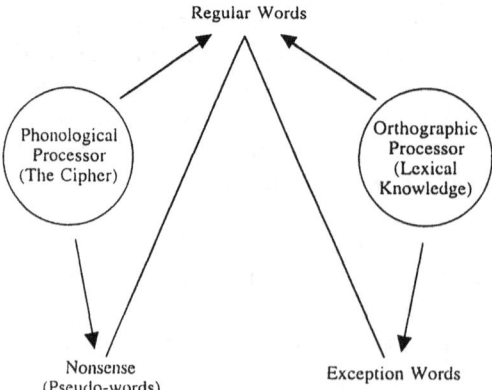

FIG. 2.1. The dual processor model.

2. THE DECOMPOSITION OF DECODING

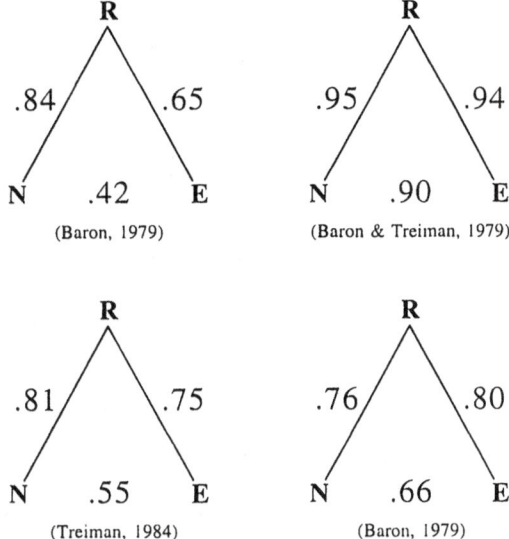

FIG. 2.2. Intercorrelations of the naming accuracy between regular, exception, and pseudowords.

Gough and Walsh developed their own version of the regular-exception-nonword (REN) test. Their aim was to discover whether lexical knowledge could be dissociated from cipher knowledge. Could they find children who had managed the one without the other?

It seemed entirely possible that one could find children who had the cipher but had not yet mastered much lexical knowledge, but are there any children who had acquired lexical knowledge without the cipher? To measure knowledge of the cipher, Gough and Walsh used the child's ability to name pseudowords (N); to measure lexical knowledge, they used the child's ability to name exception words (E). In order to make the two scales commensurate, Walsh had the idea of making the pseudowords homophones of the exception words. Thus, the exception word *tongue* would be presented to the child as *tung*. This allowed testers to ask, if this word had been regular, could the child have read it?

We followed Walsh's suggestion and asked 104 ex-first graders to read 75 items: 25 exception words, 25 regular words yoked in length and frequency to the exceptions, and 25 pseudowords that were homophones of the exception words.

Our results did not conform to the pattern of previous REN studies. Where previous studies had, without exception, found the EN correlation lower than the other two, this one did not. Moreover, more important than the magnitude of these correlations was the bivariate nature of the distribution. The scatterplot is shown in Fig. 2.3. These results clearly indicated that knowledge of the cipher was necessary but not sufficient for the acquisition of lexical knowledge. For only 6 of 104 children did their lexical knowledge

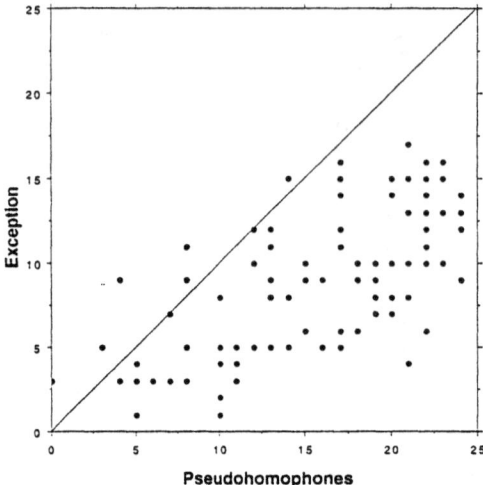

FIG. 2.3. The relation between knowledge of the cipher and lexical knowledge.

exceed their cipher knowledge, and then only slightly. These were simply no "Chinese" readers, that is, children who could read many exception words without mastering the cipher.

In a subsequent study, Gough and Walsh (1991) even found that children who had internalized the cipher could learn to read and spell new exception words better (i.e., more rapidly and accurately) than children who had not yet acquired the cipher; as Stanovich (1986) might have described it, the rich get richer. Gough and Walsh concluded, then, that the cipher and lexical information are not stored in separate mechanisms. Instead, the lexical knowledge is assembled on top of the cipher. The cipher is the foundation, and lexical knowledge the superstructure, of the reading lexicon.

Recently, a number of investigators (e.g., Cunningham & Stanovich, 1993; Olson, Wise, Conners, Rack, & Fulker, 1989; Stanovich & West, 1989) revived Baron's idea. They proposed that skilled reading involves two kinds of processing, which they called *phonological processing* and *orthographic processing*. Phonological processing is used to describe things like the ability to name pseudowords, or to decide which of two pseudowords sounds like a real word—in short, tasks that require knowledge and use of the spelling-sound correspondences of English, or what we have called the cipher. Orthographic processing, in contrast, is defined by tasks like choosing between homophones or reading irregular words, tasks in which knowledge of the cipher alone will not lead to success.

As we see it, both processes have been mislabeled. What is called phonological processing does not involve the processing of phonology; this term would be better used to describe speech, or speech recognition. Instead, phonological processing is used to describe the translation of print into phonological form. What it must involve is knowledge of the letter–sound correspondences of English, or what we have called the orthographic cipher. It would be more accurate to call this *orthographic processing*. Indeed, that is exactly what Baron and Strawson (1976) called it, but we prefer to call it *deciphering*.

The term *orthographic processing* is used to describe performance on tasks that could not be accomplished using only the cipher. What these tasks require is knowledge of the spelling or pronunciation of a specific word. For example, in Richard Olson's (Olson, Kliegl, Davidson, & Foltz, 1985) orthographic task, the subjects had to decide which of two homophonic strings (e.g., *rane–rain*) was actually the word. Or in Stanovich and West's (1989) homophone choice task, the subjects had to decide which of two homophones was semantically related to a third word (e.g., *rose: flour* or *flower?*). In neither task does deciphering yield the answer, because instead it yields two identical phonological forms; something more, namely knowledge of how that specific word is spelled, is required.

These tasks themselves make the point that the reader needs more than the cipher to read and write, that there is more to skilled reading and spelling than what has been called *phonological processing*. Two kinds of information are clearly needed to be a skilled reader of a deep orthography like English, but the unanswered question is, how are those two types of information represented?

It occurred to us that we could use Baron's psychometric approach to this problem. We could develop three versions of each of the tasks that have been used to tap phonological and orthographic processing. In one version, the cipher alone would enable a correct response; this would tap phonological processing. In another, the cipher would not suffice—only word-specific information would lead to a correct response; this would tap orthographic processing. Finally, in a third (duplex) version, either kind of information would suffice.

The first of these tasks was a naming task. Following Baron, we asked subjects to name regular, exception, and pseudowords, and measured their latencies. In a second task, we used the same three kinds of words in a task we called *spelling verification*: Each subject heard a word, then saw a spelling of that word and decided whether it was correct or incorrect. The task was performed three times, once with regular words, once with exception words, and once with pseudowords.

The third task was lexical decision. The word-specific or orthographic version of this task asked subjects to compare words with pseudohomophones. (This task is a serial version of Olson's orthographic task.) In the phonological or cipher version of this task, subjects compared pseudohomophones with nonhomophonic pseudowords. (This task is a modification of Olson's phonological task.) The duplex version of this task was standard lexical decision, which can be solved using either orthographic or phonological processing.

The final task, modeled after Stanovich and West's homophone choice task, we called *semantic choice*: The subject saw a target word, followed by a pair of items; each subject was asked to decide which of the latter two was semantically related to the target. The orthographic version of this task was the homophone choice task used by Stanovich and West (e.g., *metal* followed by *steel* vs. *steal*): The two words were homophones, so only orthographic knowledge would enable a correct response. In the phonological version, the choice was between two pseudohomophones (e.g., *cloud* followed by *rane* vs. *jale*): Because neither was a real word, only phonological recoding could lead to a correct response. In the duplex version, the choice was between two real words (e.g., *salt* followed by *pepper* vs. *yellow*): These might be distinguished either phonologically or orthographically.

One hundred UT undergraduates participated in this series of tasks. They did one version of each of the four tasks during each of three laboratory sessions. Median latency in each task was computed for each subject; means of these medians are presented in Table 2.2. Analysis of variance revealed significant main effects of both task and materials. Spelling verification proved to be the fastest task, followed by naming, then lexical decision; semantic choice was the slowest. A significant interaction evidently arose from the exceptional difficulty of the pseudoword semantic choice task.

Our primary interest is not in the comparison of the 12 tasks, but rather their interrelations. The intercorrelation matrix is presented in Table 2.3. An exploratory factor analysis revealed only two factors with Eigenvalues greater than one. All 12 tasks were loaded with the first factor, which accounted for 58% of the variance. The second factor had large positive loadings only on the three naming tasks, with modest negative loadings on the the other nine.

TABLE 2.2
Means and Standard Deviations for Subjects' Latencies in Four Tasks

	Mean	*Standard Deviation*
WC	820	163
CC	1003	215
PC	1150	253
WS	538	105
OS	641	140
PS	751	176
WD	634	95
CD	670	121
PD	1284	330
WN	579	88
ON	669	98
PN	782	173

TABLE 2.3
Intercorrelations of Measures of Phonological and Orthographic Processing

	NP	NX	NO	SP	SX	SO	DP	DX	DO	CP	DX	CO
NP	1.000											
NX	.785	1.000										
NO	.827	.833	1.000									
SP	.481	.396	.448	1.000								
SX	.419	.406	.423	.600	1.000							
SO	.348	.430	.434	.687	.652	1.000						
DP	.377	.359	.412	.533	.362	.468	1.000					
DX	.438	.464	.487	.625	.658	.667	.476	1.000				
DO	.449	.438	.468	.536	.716	.581	.500	.797	1.000			
CP	.556	.445	.488	.511	.634	.439	.389	.565	.630	1.000		
CX	.530	.537	.556	.596	.614	.634	.496	.614	.626	.650	1.000	
CO	.482	.413	.529	.551	.590	.509	.260	.545	.545	.720	.677	1.000

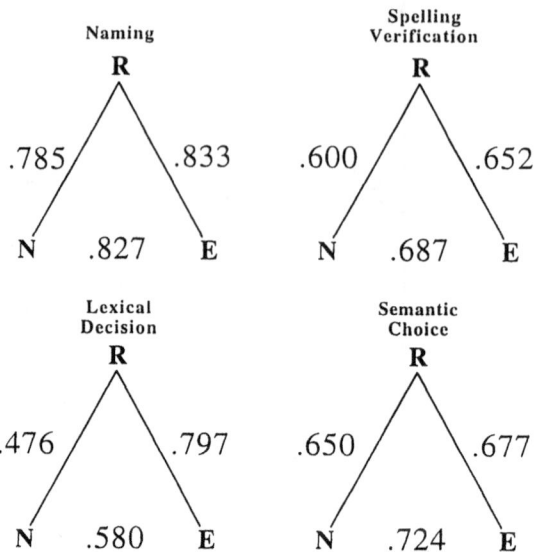

FIG. 2.4. Intercorrelations of response latencies on tasks involving regular, exception, and pseudowords.

The purpose of this study was to evaluate the dual processor hypothesis. Accordingly, we designed a confirmatory factor analysis. We assessed the fit of a model that contained four task factors, and two independent processing components. The model failed miserably, yielding a Bentler-Bonnett normed fit index of .82 and a chi square (with 38 degrees of freedom) of 173.9. The model simply failed to account for the intercorrelations.

Why does the model fail? The answer is clear if we examine Baron's triangles. Remember Baron's argument: If regular words and pseudowords rely on knowledge of the orthographic cipher, they should be strongly correlated. If regular words and exception words rely on lexical knowledge, they should be strongly correlated. However, if exception words and pseudowords rely on separate mechanisms, they should be less strongly correlated.

The present study offered four separate tests of this prediction, one for each task. The correlation triangles are presented in Fig. 2.4. Not one of the four tests was consistent with the two-factor proposal. In both spelling and semantic choice, the correlation between N (based on the presumed phonological processor) and E (based on a presumably different, orthographic processor) was the highest correlation, not the lowest, and in the other two tests it was intermediate.

There is no doubt that skilled decoding of English requires two sorts of knowledge, both knowledge of the regularities of English spelling-sound correspondences (or what we have called the *cipher*), and knowledge of the spelling and pronunciation of particular words. However, the present data provide little support for the proposal that these two kinds of knowledge reside in separate mechanisms.

It appears to us that word-specific knowledge is constructed on a frame built by the regular, systematic correspondences. In our metaphor, knowledge of the cipher is the foundation, and word-specific or lexical knowledge is the superstructure, of decoding. And, of course, the cornerstone is phonemic awareness.

REFERENCES

Alford, J. A., Jr. (1980). *Lexical and contextual effects on reading time*. Unpublished doctoral dissertation, University of Texas at Austin.

Baron, J. (1979). Orthographic and word-specific mechanisms in children's reading of words. *Child Development, 50*, 60–72.

Baron, J., & Treiman, R. (1980). Use of orthography in reading and learning to read. In J. F. Kavanagh & R. L. Venezky (Eds.), *Orthography, reading, and dyslexia* (pp. 171–189). Baltimore: University Park Press.

Carroll, J. B., Davies, P., & Richman, B. (1971). *The word frequency book*. New York: Houghton Mifflin.

Coltheart, M. (1978). Lexical access in simple reading tasks. In G. Underwood (Ed.), *Strategies of information processing* (pp. 151–216). London: Academic Press.

Coltheart, M., Curtis, B., Atkins, P., & Haller, M. (1993). Models of reading aloud: Dual-route and parallel-distributed-processing approaches. *Psychological Review, 100*, 589–608.

Cunningham, A. E., & Stanovich, K. E. (1993). Children's literacy environments and early word recognition skills. *Reading and Writing: An Interdisciplinary Journal, 5*, 193–204.

Cunningham, A. E., Stanovich, K. E., & Wilson, M. R. (1990). Cognitive variation in adult students differing in reading ability. In T. Carr & B. A. Levy (Eds.), *Reading and its development: Component skills approaches* (pp. 129–159). New York: Academic.

Firth, I. (1972). *Components of reading disability*. Unpublished doctoral dissertation, University of New South Wales, Kensington, N.S.W., Australia.

Glushko, R. J. (1979). The organization and activation of orthographic knowledge in reading aloud. *Journal of Experimental Psychology: Human Perception and Performance, 5*, 674–691.

Goodman, K. S., & Goodman, Y. M. (1979). Learning to read is natural. In L. B. Resnick & P. A. Weaver (Eds.), *Theory and practice of early reading* (Vol. 1, pp. 137–154). Hillsdale, NJ: Lawrence Erlbaum Associates.

Goswami, U. (1988). Orthographic analogies and reading development. *Quarterly Journal of Experimental Psychology, 40*, 239–268.

Gough, P. B. (1983). Context, form, and interaction. In K. Rayner (Ed.), *Eye movements in reading: Perceptual and language processes* (pp. 203–210). New York: Academic.

Gough, P. B., Juel, C., & Griffith, P. L. (1992). Reading, spelling, and the orthographic cipher. In P. B. Gough, L. C. Ehri, & R. Treiman (Eds.), *Reading acquisition*, (pp. 35–48). Hillsdale, NJ: Lawrence Erlbaum Associates.

Gough, P. B., Juel, C., & Roper-Schneider, D. (1983). A two-stage model of initial reading acquisition. In J. A. Niles & L. A. Harris (Eds.), *Searches for meaning in reading/language processing and instruction* (pp. 207–211). Rochester, NY: National Reading Conference.

Gough, P. B., & Tunmer, W. E. (1986). Decoding, reading and reading disability. *Remedial and Special Education, 7*, 6–10.

Gough, P. B., & Walsh, M. A. (1991). Chinese, Phoenicians, and the orthographic cipher of English. In S. Brady & D. Shankweiler (Eds.), *Phonological processes in literacy* (pp. 199–209). Hillsdale, NJ: Lawrence Erlbaum Associates.

Hoover, W. A., & Gough, P. B. (1990). The simple view of reading. *Reading and Writing: An Interdisciplinary Journal, 2,* 127–160.

Marcel, T. (1980). Phonological awareness and phonological representation: Investigation of a specific spelling problem. In U. Frith (Ed.), *Cognitive processes in spelling* (pp. 373–403). San Diego, CA: Academic.

Olson, R., Kliegl, R., Davidson, B., & Foltz, G. (1985). Individual and developmental differences in reading disability. In G. E. MacKinnon & T. Waller (Eds.), *Reading research: Advances in theory and practice* (Vol. 4, pp. 1–64). London: Academic.

Olson, R. K., Wise, B., Conners, F., Rack, J., & Fulker, D. (1989). Specific deficits in component reading and language skills: Genetic and environmental influences. *Journal of Learning Disabilities, 22,* 339–348.

Plaut, D. C., McClelland, J. L., Seidenberg, M., & Patterson, K. (1996). Understanding normal and impaired word reading: Computational principles in quasi-regular domains. *Psychological Review, 103*(1), 56–115.

Seidenberg, M. S., & McClelland, J. L. (1989). A distributed, developmental model of word recognition and naming. *Psychological Review, 96,* 523–568.

Stanovich, K. E. (1986). Matthew effects in reading: Some consequences of individual differences in acquisition of literacy. *Reading Research Quarterly, 21,* 360–406.

Stanovich, K. E., & West, R. F. (1989). Exposure to print and orthographic processing. *Reading Research Quarterly, 24,* 402–433.

Treiman, R. (1984). Individual differences among children in spelling and reading styles. *Journal of Experimental Child Psychology, 37,* 463–477.

Chapter 3

Language Prediction Skill, Phonological Recoding Ability, and Beginning Reading

William E. Tunmer
James W. Chapman
Massey University

There are at least three strategies that beginning readers can use to identify unfamiliar words in connected text (Ehri, 1991; Ehri & Robbins, 1992). They can use their developing knowledge of correspondences between subcomponents of written and spoken words to generate the word's pronunciation, they can analogize to known words that are stored in lexical memory, and they can use the constraints of sentence context to narrow the possibilities of what the word might be. This chapter is concerned with three questions relating to the use of the latter strategy. First, what role, if any, does language prediction skill (i.e., the ability to use the constraints of sentence context) play in the development of word recognition skill? Second, if language prediction skill does indeed make a contribution to the development of word recognition skill, is it a source of individual differences in learning to read? And third, how important is language prediction skill in relation to other skills, such as phonological recoding (i.e., the ability to translate letters and letter patterns into phonological forms)?

There are two strongly opposing views on the role of language prediction skills in beginning reading (Adams & Huggins, 1985; Tunmer & Hoover, 1992). The first derives largely from the work of Goodman (1967, 1982, 1986) and Smith (1973, 1979, 1988), according to whom skilled reading is primarily an activity of using the syntactic and semantic redundancies of language to generate hypotheses, or guesses, about the text yet to be encountered. On the basis of this claim, Goodman and Smith argued that unlike fluent readers, poor and beginning readers are less able to make use of contextual redundancy in ongoing sentence processing. From this assumption and the further assumption that the ability to read evolves naturally and spontaneously out of children's prereading experiences in much the same way that their oral language develops (Goodman & Goodman, 1979), "whole language" theorists like Goodman and Smith concluded that reading instruction should be modeled on first language acquisition, where the focus is on meaning construction, not on the abstract structural units by which meaning is conveyed. Children should therefore be taught to use sentence context cues as the primary strategy for recognizing words in text. They should be encouraged to monitor for meaningfulness and engage in "risk taking" (i.e., guessing what the word might be), and to make corrections only when necessary to make sense.

Children should also be taught to use graphophonemic cues, but only very sparingly and only as backup support to confirm language predictions. Explicit and systematic instruction in letter–sound correspondences is discouraged for three reasons. First, concentrating too heavily on learning letter–sound correspondences may result in children losing the natural insight that print is meaningful. Second, the small amount of letter–sound knowledge that beginning readers need can, in any event, be acquired through writing activities. Third, English orthography contains so many irregularities anyway that focusing too much attention on teaching letter–sound correspondences will not only waste valuable time but possibly even confuse children and impede progress. Instead, whole language proponents hold that instruction in letter–sound correspondences should almost always arise *incidentally* in the context of reading connected text.

In opposition to the whole language view is the claim that language prediction skill is not important in either learning to read or skilled reading. According to this claim, reliance on contextual guessing to identify unfamiliar words will result in little progress because the average predictability of content words in running text is about 10%, compared to about 40% for function words (e.g., *on, the, to*), which are typically short, high-frequency sight words that beginning readers can already recognize (Gough, 1983). The meaning of text therefore depends disproportionately on the meanings of its *least* familiar and predictable words. Consequently, unless children are reading very low-level texts with repeated sentence structures, a high degree of predictability, and a large amount of picture support, they will have a 1 in 10 chance of guessing the correct word.

Consistent with this finding and contrary to the claim that poor and beginning readers are less able to use sentence context to identify words as they read, research has shown that the effect of context on speed of ongoing word recognition during reading *decreases* with increasing age, grade level, reading ability, word familiarity, and stimulus quality (see

Stanovich, 1980, 1984, 1986, for reviews). Studies that have examined accuracy of recognizing words in isolation and in context report a similar pattern of results (e.g., Nicholson, 1991). On the basis of such findings, Stanovich (1980) concluded that poor readers compensate for difficulties in word recognition by relying more on sentence context to facilitate ongoing word recognition. In contrast, good readers are less reliant on syntactic and semantic information because they are more proficient in using word-level information. Because poor readers do not seem less likely to use sentence context to facilitate word recognition when the context is adequately understood, Stanovich (1986) concluded that "compared to other prerequisite skills—such as phonological awareness—the variability in the ability to use context to facilitate word recognition is so relatively low that it may not be a major determinant of individual differences in reading acquisition" (p. 369).

According to this view, then, less skilled readers should be discouraged from compensating for poor word recognition skill by relying on context. Instead, they should be encouraged to take advantage of the systematic mappings between subcomponents of written and spoken words. Sublexical analyses involving phonological information will then result in positive learning trials (i.e., correct word identifications), which in turn lead to the amalgamation of orthographic and phonological representations in semantic memory (Ehri, 1991, 1992). These amalgamated representations are thought to provide the basis for rapid and efficient access to the mental lexicon, which in turn frees up cognitive resources for allocation to comprehension and text integration processes. In summary, as Adams and Huggins (1985) pointed out, "The didactic recommendations following from either of [the two opposing views on the role of language prediction skill in beginning reading] are counterproductive from the perspective of the other" (p. 264).

An alternative view to the two just described proposes that language prediction skill enables beginning readers to *combine* knowledge of the constraints of sentence context with incomplete graphophonemic information to identify unfamiliar words (including irregularly spelled ones) and thus increase both their word-specific knowledge and their knowledge of grapheme–phoneme correspondences (Tunmer, Herriman, & Nesdale, 1988; Tunmer & Hoover, 1993). The ability to use contextual information allows beginning readers to monitor accuracy in word identification by providing them with immediate feedback when their attempted responses to unfamiliar words in text fail to conform to the surrounding grammatical context, such as when a candidate word from the mental lexicon results in either a violation of a strict subcategorization rule, which governs the syntactic structures into which a word can enter (e.g., The boy *slept* the bed), or a violation of a selectional restriction rule, which places constraints on how words of different form classes can be combined (e.g., The cage *slept*). Because grammatical rules of this nature apply mostly to structures within sentences, the effects of contextual constraint generally do not extend beyond the sentence boundary, as demonstrated in studies by Miller and Coleman (1967) and Kibby (1980).

If children are aware of the nature of the alphabetic code—that is, if they are aware that "there is a system of correspondences to be mastered," which Gough and Juel (1991) referred to as "cryptanalytic intent" (p. 51)—then the use of sentence context as backup support to confirm hypotheses about what unfamiliar words might be, based on incomplete spelling–sound knowledge, will help children to increase their word-specific knowledge from which additional spelling–sound correspondences can be induced. According to this view, then, children who have become "active problem solvers" with regard to graphic information (Juel, 1991, p. 782) will use contextual cues to supplement word-level information rather than to substitute for it. As Adams and Huggins (1985) argued, "On encountering a visually new word, [the child can] create a representation for it using the decoded information and the surrounding context to deduce its lexical identity" (p. 276). Identifying unfamiliar words by using the constraints of sentence context in conjunction with gradually improving phonological recoding skills will in turn enable beginning readers to accumulate even more spelling–sound knowledge, which, according to Ehri (1991, 1992), provides the basic mechanism for acquiring word-specific knowledge. Ehri (1992) argued that the development of word-specific knowledge depends centrally on recoding knowledge because "it is this knowledge that allows readers to establish the network of [visual–phonological] connections leading from a word's spelling to its pronunciation in memory when the word is established as a sight word" (p. 138).

Support for the suggestion that language prediction skill and phonological recoding ability make important contributions to the development of word-specific knowledge comes from studies by Gough and Walsh (1991) and Adams and Huggins (1985). Because no word in English is completely phonologically opaque, even exception words provide accurate phonological cues to the word's identity (Ehri, 1992; Gough & Hillinger, 1980). When beginning readers apply their developing knowledge of grapheme–phoneme correspondences to unfamiliar irregular words, the result will often be close enough to the correct phonological form that sentence context cues can be used to arrive at a correct identification (Gough & Hillinger, 1980; Jorm & Share, 1983). In a study of word recognition skills in beginning readers, Gough and Walsh (1991) found the standard positive correlation between pseudoword naming (a measure of phonological recoding ability) and exception word naming ($r = .66$). Of greater interest, a scatterplot of their data revealed that there were many children who performed reasonably well on the pseudoword naming test but recognized few exception words. However, there were no children who performed poorly on the pseudoword naming test and well on the exception word naming test. These findings suggest that phonological recoding ability is necessary but not sufficient for the development of word-specific knowledge. Consistent with this interpretation, Gough and Walsh also found that beginning readers with higher levels of phonological recoding ability required fewer trials to learn unfamiliar exception words than did children with lower levels of phonological recoding ability.

If phonological recoding ability is indeed necessary but not *sufficient* for the development of word-specific knowledge, then what other skills or experiences are required? Multiple successful identifications facilitated in part by contextual information (at least in the early stages) would appear to be the most likely possibility. Adams and Huggins (1985) asked good and poor readers in Grades 2 through 5 to read a frequency-graduated (from high to low) series of 50 irregularly spelled words, first in isolation, and then in underdetermining contexts (e.g., "The football hit him in the stomach," in which the target word was *stomach*). They found that accuracy of recognizing irregular words of "intermediate familiarity" (which varied with age and ability) improved markedly with context for *every* age and ability group, and concluded that "the facilitative potential of context is a function of the subjective familiarity of the word to be recognized" (p. 274).

From an analysis of the children's responses as they progressed through the list, Adams and Huggins identified three stages in the development of word-specific knowledge. Words at the beginning of the list were read quickly and accurately, even in the absence of context. This reflects the most advanced stage of development. The orthographic representations of these words have become fully consolidated in the mental lexicons of the readers. During the second or transitional stage of development, a point was reached in the list (which varied across children) at which the words were recognized with hesitation or not at all in isolation but were read correctly in context. It is at this stage that beginning readers are able to combine partial word-level information with sentence context cues to identify unfamiliar words. As the children progressed beyond this section of the list (which lasted for a span of 5 to 10 words) to the more difficult words of lower frequency, they began making more errors, until eventually most of their responses were incorrect with or without context. This reflects the first stage of development of word-specific knowledge. A defining characteristic of this stage was the strong tendency for children to pronounce words in accordance with canonical spelling-to-sound rules. As Adams and Huggins (1985) pointed out, "Although distinctly incorrect, such responses can also be seen as not-so-distant approximations to the correct words" (p. 276). This finding is consistent with Gough and Walsh's (1991) claim that phonological recoding ability is essential for acquiring word-specific knowledge.

Adams and Huggins also found that for words of lower frequency, the younger and poorer readers did not derive as much benefit from context as did the older and better readers. They suggested that multiple encounters are probably required before these words are recognized by less skilled readers, at which point the words enter the children's mental lexicons with Stage 2 status. With further successful identifications facilitated by contextual information, the orthographic representations of these words become more fully consolidated in semantic memory, eventually reaching Stage 1 status. Consistent with this suggestion, Cunningham and Stanovich (1990) found that for third- and fourth-grade children, exposure to print accounts for independent variance in word-specific knowledge even after variance due to phonological coding is partialed out.

Although the findings of the Adams and Huggins study suggest that language prediction skill may contribute to the development of word-specific knowledge, there remains the question of whether the ability to use the constraints of sentence context is a source of individual differences in learning to read. That is, are differences in language prediction skill related to differences in the rate at which children progress through the stages of sight word acquisition identified by Adams and Huggins? Some suggestive evidence comes from studies reporting positive correlations between measures of grammatical sensitivity (or awareness) and context-free word recognition and/or phonological recoding (Bowey, 1986; Bowey & Patel, 1988; Bryant, Maclean, & Bradley, 1990; Fowler, 1988; Siegel & Ryan, 1988; Stanovich, Cunningham, & Feeman, 1984; Tunmer, 1989; Tunmer et al., 1988; Willows & Ryan, 1986). Research further indicates that grammatical sensitivity typically correlates more strongly with context-free word recognition than with reading comprehension (Bowey, 1986; Bowey & Patel, 1988; Siegel & Ryan, 1988; Stanovich et al., 1984; Tunmer, 1989; Willows & Ryan, 1986).

The most direct measure of language prediction skill is the oral cloze task, in which the child is asked to listen to incomplete sentences and to supply the missing word. Willows and Ryan (1986) found that performance on the oral cloze task was significantly related to reading achievement in a sample of first-, second-, and third-grade children even after the effects of age, general cognitive development, short-term memory, and vocabulary knowledge were statistically controlled. Using a reading-level match design in which good, younger readers were matched with poor, older readers on several measures of reading ability and on verbal intelligence, Tunmer, Nesdale, and Wright (1987) found that the good readers scored significantly better than the poor readers on two measures of grammatical sensitivity, an oral cloze task and a word-order correction task. However, because of the correlational nature of the Willows and Ryan (1986) and Tunmer et al. (1987) studies, it is possible that the strong relationships observed between grammatical sensitivity and reading simply reflect the indirect contribution of some third factor such as phonological sensitivity, which has been shown to be related to both grammatical sensitivity and reading ability (Tunmer et al., 1988).

Elsewhere we (Tunmer & Hoover, 1993) have suggested that the tasks devised to measure phonological and grammatical sensitivity require *metalinguistic operations*, which we defined as mental operations performed on the outputs of the modular subsystems involved in sentence comprehension. We also suggested that these operations require control (or executive) processes. Measures of phonological and grammatical sensitivity may therefore require component operations that are similar in character. However, if grammatical sensitivity facilitates the development of word recognition skill by enabling beginning readers to use context to identify unfamiliar words, which, in turn, increases their word-specific knowledge and knowledge of grapheme–phoneme correspondences, then grammatical sensitivity should make a contribution to the development of word recognition ability that is distinct from that made by phonological sensitivity. In support of this claim, Tunmer (1989) found in a longitudinal study that grammatical sensitivity in first grade was significantly related to phonological recoding in second grade after the effects of verbal intelligence, general cognitive ability, and phonological sensitivity were partialed out.

So far no evidence has been cited showing that either language prediction skill or phonological recoding ability is directly related to the use of context in reading. We are aware of only one study that has attempted to address this issue. In a longitudinal study, Rego and Bryant (1993) tested children at two points during their first year of schooling, when the mean ages of the children were 5 years, 6 months and 5 years, 11 months. Contextual facilitation in reading was assessed by the number of words that the children were able to read correctly when the first 10 words that they missed on a standardized test of context-free word recognition were placed in sentence contexts read aloud by the experimenter. Rego and Bryant found that each of three measures of grammatical sensitivity (one of which was an oral cloze task) taken in the first session predicted contextual facilitation in the second session, even after controlling for the effects of age, general intelligence, vocabulary knowledge, and verbal memory. However, two measures of phonological sensitivity failed to make an independent contribution to later contextual facilitation in reading. A possible explanation of the latter finding is that most of the children tested might not have reached the stage in the development of their word recognition skills during which they would have begun relying more heavily on phonological skills, even though they were making use of these skills in their preconventional spellings. In the second session the children performed at floor levels on a pseudoword naming test (Rego, 1991), and in the standardized test of context-free word recognition, 30 of the 54 children tested could not read a single word. The mean number of words read correctly was 0.35. It is therefore possible that phonological skills may contribute to the use of context in reading at a somewhat later stage of reading development.

To explore these issues further, we carried out two experiments. The purpose of the first experiment was to examine the potential contribution of phonological recoding skill to reading exception words in isolation and in context, and the purpose of the second experiment was to determine more precisely the nature of the relation of language prediction skill and phonological recoding ability to the identification of unfamiliar words in context.

EXPERIMENT 1

As noted earlier, Gough and Hillinger (1980) suggested that the mispronunciations resulting from the application of letter–sound rules to unfamiliar exception words will often be sufficiently close to the correct phonological forms that the words can be correctly identified in context. Groff (1983) attempted to test this claim by asking 49 second-grade children to listen to a passage and to detect and correct words that sounded "funny." Fourteen sentences in the passage contained a regularized pronunciation of an exception word (e.g., "Do you *have* a headache?", where *have* was pronounced /hāv/). In support of Gough and Hillinger's (1980) hypothesis, Groff found that the children were able to correctly identify 93% of the mispronounced words.

There are, however, three difficulties with Groff's study. First, the regularized pronunciations of the exception words were presented only in context, not in isolation. It is therefore possible that the children would have performed almost as well when the mispronounced words were presented without context, which would indicate that context was not particularly important in identifying the words. Second, Groff appears not to have taken any steps to ensure that the sentence contexts selected for the stimulus items were underdetermining ones. In the example given previously ("Do you /hāv/ a headache?"), the word *have* is highly predictable from the context alone. The high levels of performance achieved by beginning readers on Groff's mispronunciation correction task might therefore be attributable to the use of highly predictable contexts in the test materials rather than to children's ability to use context as an aid to identifying mispronounced words. Third, for reasons that are unclear, Groff decided to select only stimulus words that occur with high frequency in written materials. However, because words of higher print frequency are more likely to be words that beginning readers can already recognize (Gough, 1983), the ability of children to identify mispronounced words of lower frequencies would be of greater interest. Experiment 1 was designed to overcome the methodological shortcomings of Groff's study.

Method

Subjects

Sixty-seven children participated in the first experiment: 34 Year 2 and 33 Year 3 children drawn from two primary schools located in middle-class neighborhoods in a large New Zealand provincial city. The mean ages of the Year 2 and Year 3 children were 6 years, 8 months and 7 years, 7 months, respectively (children in New Zealand begin formal schooling on or close to their fifth birthday). Only native speakers of English were chosen. Children with known hearing, language, or intellectual impairment were excluded.

Materials

A mispronunciation correction task was developed that comprised 80 regularized pronunciations of exception words that were first presented in isolation and then, on another occasion, in context. Half the words were the first 40 words of the list of 50 irregularly spelled words used by Adams and Huggins (1985), with one exception. Because New Zealand has converted to a metric system of measurement, the word *pint* and its associated sentence context (i.e., "We both wanted ice cream so we bought a *pint*") were replaced with a stimulus item that appeared later in Adams and Huggins' list (viz., "Lifting heavy boxes will make your back *ache*"). The words in Adams and Huggins' list, which are arranged in decreasing order of print frequency according to Carroll, Davies, and Richman (1971), were divided into four groups of 10 words each (i.e., Items 1 through 10, Items 11 through 20, Items 21 through 30, and Items 31 through 40). The remaining 40 words used as stimulus items were selected from a word frequency count based on New Zealand materials (Elley & Croft, 1989). Elley and Croft's norms are regarded by the authors as more appropriate for use in New Zealand but include only nouns. The list contains 2,050 nouns graded into eight levels of decreasing frequency. Ten irregularly spelled nouns were selected from each of four levels (Levels 2, 4, 6, and 8), and an underdetermining sentence context was created for each word (see Appendix A). The reason that the 40 additional words were incorporated into the mispronunciation correction task was that they were judged to be less difficult than the words from the Adams and Huggins' test, which was developed for an age range (7 to 10 years) that extended well beyond the age of the children in the present study.

The list of 80 test items comprised 10 blocks of eight words each. Each block included four words from Adams and Huggins' list of 40 words (one word randomly selected from each of the four frequency groups within the list, as specified earlier) and four words from the 40 words selected from the Elley and Croft (1989) noun frequency count (one word randomly selected from each of the four frequency levels). The complete list of 80 exception words used in the mispronunciation correction task is presented in Appendix B.

To ensure that the sentence contexts for the 80 mispronounced test items were underdetermining ones, the contexts were presented as an oral cloze task to a separate sample of 31 Year 2 children (with a mean age of 6 years, 5 months) and 32 Year 3 children (with a mean age of 7 years, 3 months). The contexts were presented individually to the children using a hand-held puppet. The children were told that the puppet "forgets to say all the words" and that their task was to guess what word was left out of each sentence. The results indicated that the average predicability of the 80 target words was 8.05%, which is below the naturally occurring rate of predictability of 10% for content words in running text (Gough, 1983). The results further indicated that the average predictability of the contexts created for the words selected from the Elley and Croft (1989) noun frequency count was less than that of the contexts for the words from the Adams and Huggins' (1985) list (3.68% vs 12.42%).

Procedure

The children were tested individually in two sessions during the middle term of the school year. Each session lasted 15 to 30 minutes. During the first session the children were presented with the regularized pronunciations of the 80 test items. For example, *tongue* was pronounced /tŏngū/, *stomach* was pronounced /stōmăch/ (as in *stow-match*), *wasp* was pronounced /wăsp/, *devil* was pronounced /dēvəl/, *pudding* was pronounced /pŭdding/, and *castle* was pronounced /căstəl/. The written form of some of the test items contained homographic spelling patterns, which are letter sequences that have different pronunciations in different words (e.g., *ove* as in *love* and *clove*; *ead* as in *head* and *bead*). In such cases the nonstandard pronunciation was used. That is, *bread* was pronounced /brēd/ and *glove* was pronounced /glōv/.

The items were presented to the children in the form of a game involving a hand-held puppet. The following instructions were given in the first session:

> Today we're going to play a word game with Alice. In this game Alice tries to say a word but she says it the wrong way. You have to figure out what Alice is trying to say. Alice says, "/brĕkfăst/" [*breakfast*]. What word do you think she is trying to say? [If the child failed to respond or responded incorrectly, the correct pronunciation was provided.] Good. Let's try another one. Alice says, "/mŏther/" [*mother*]. What word do you think she is trying to say? [Corrective feedback was provided, if necessary.] Okay, now let's see if you can play the game. When Alice says a word, you try to guess what she is trying to say. [Encouragement was provided throughout the test, but no corrective feedback was given. If the child failed to respond after 5 to 10 seconds, the item was repeated. If the child still failed to respond after another 5 to 10 seconds, the next item was presented.] Okay, let's try this one.

In the second session, which occurred one to two weeks after the first session, the children were presented with the same items as before but this time in underdetermining sentence contexts (e.g., "The football hit him in the /stōmăch/"). The following instructions were given:

> In this game Alice says a sentence but says one of the words the wrong way. You have to figure out what Alice is trying to say. Listen carefully. One of the words in the sentence that Alice says will sound funny. Alice says, "I like to go camping with my /făther/ [*father*]." What word do you think she is trying to say? [If the child failed to respond or responded incorrectly, the correct pronunciation was provided.] Okay, now let's see if you can play the game. When Alice says a sentence with a funny word, you try to guess what she is trying to say. [At this point the procedure was identical to that followed when the words were presented in isolation.]

The order of presentation of the items under both conditions was counterbalanced across children at each year level. Scoring was based on the number of words correctly identified at each of the four frequency levels for each list under each presentation condition.

A potential risk in using the same words in isolation and in context was that the effects of context might be inflated because of prior exposure of the items. To rule out this possibility when the 40 items from the Adams and Huggins (1985) study were presented as a *reading* task, Adams and Huggins carried out a separate study and found that the effects, if any, of prior exposure were quite small. Because the children in Adams and Huggins' study showed a strong tendency to regularize the pronunciations of unfamiliar exception words, it seems reasonable to generalize their findings regarding prior exposure of items to the mispronunciation correction task, which involves the presentation of the regularized pronunciations of the same items.

Results and Discussion

Children's performance in the mispronunciation correction task was expressed as the percentage of correct responses. Table 3.1 presents the mean percentages of correctly identified words as a function of presentation condition (isolation vs. context), frequency level, stimulus materials (List A vs. List B), and year of schooling (Year 2 vs. Year 3). List A comprised the 40 test items from Adams and Huggins' (1985) materials, and List B comprised the 40 items based on words drawn from Elley and Croft's (1989) noun frequency count. As discussed previously, the four levels of decreasing frequency for each list were based on different frequency counts.

Figure 3.1 presents the mean percentages of correctly identified words for both lists under each presentation condition, collapsing across year levels and frequency levels. A 2 (Year: Year 2 vs. Year 3) × 2 (Materials: List A vs. List B) × 2 (Condition: isolation vs. context) analysis of variance revealed significant main effects for Year, $F(1, 65) = 6.90$, $p < .05$; Materials, $F(1, 65) = 789.36$, $p < .001$; and Condition, $F(1, 65) = 1563.58$, $p < .001$. As expected, the children found the materials from the Adams and Huggins' (1985) study more difficult. In addition, the mispronounced words were easier to identify when presented in context than in isolation. No interactions reached significance. As can be seen in Fig. 3.1, the overall improvement with context was the same for both sets of stimulus items.

Separate 2 (Year) × 2 (Condition) × 4 (Frequency) analyses of variance were carried out on the data from each list. The analysis of variance of the scores from List A revealed significant main effects for Year, $F(1, 65)$

TABLE 3.1
Mean Percentages of Correctly Identified Words on the Mispronunciation Correction Task as a Function of Presentation Condition, Frequency Level, Stimulus Materials, and Year of Schooling[a]

	Presentation Condition							
	Isolation				Context			
Materials	1	2	3	4	1	2	3	4
List A								
Year 2	20.29	12.94	25.00	2.06	61.18	65.59	59.71	18.82
	(13.14)	(15.86)	(16.19)	(5.92)	(12.74)	(20.03)	(20.22)	(15.33)
Year 3	26.36	23.03	26.97	3.94	66.36	74.55	66.97	31.52
	(15.17)	(19.92)	(20.99)	(7.47)	(12.45)	(20.78)	(18.45)	(19.70)
List B								
Year 2	26.76	33.53	40.88	25.88	75.59	69.41	76.76	63.58
	(18.21)	(14.75)	(19.13)	(18.11)	(17.61)	(15.94)	(21.28)	(22.00)
Year 3	42.12	42.12	50.61	35.45	84.24	72.73	87.88	73.94
	(18.33)	(15.76)	(20.61)	(19.70)	(12.26)	(14.42)	(14.31)	(20.76)

[a]Standard deviations in parentheses.

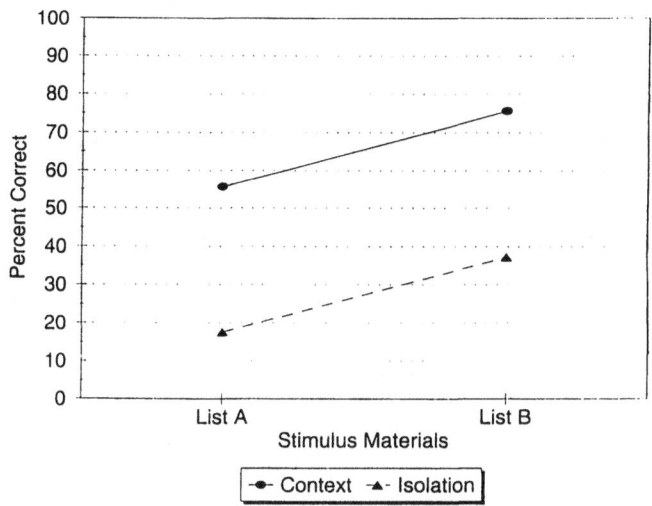

FIG. 3.1. Mean percentages of correctly identified words on the mispronunciation correction task as a function of stimulus materials and presentation condition.

= 5.09, $p < .05$; Condition, $F(1, 65) = 868.30$, $p < .001$; and Frequency, $F(3, 195) = 213.07$, $p < .001$. The Year 3 children performed better than the Year 2 children, mispronounced words were easier to identify when presented in context than in isolation, and mispronounced words of higher print frequency tended to be easier to identify than words of lower frequency. Regarding the latter effect, the words of lowest frequency (Level 4) were particularly difficult for the children, with scores approaching floor levels when the regularized pronunciations of these words were presented in isolation (see Table 3.1). It is possible that some of the words in this group (which included *rely, ninth, react, recipe, ache, deny, vague, tomb, drought,* and *trough*) were not in the children's listening vocabularies. The only interaction to reach significance was the Condition x Frequency interaction, $F(3, 195) = 46.55$, $p < .001$. The improvement in performance with context was much lower for Level 4 words than for words of higher frequency, most likely because the children's scores on the Level 4 words were at floor levels when these words were presented in isolation.

The analysis of variance of the scores from List B again showed main effects for Year, $F(1, 65) = 8.12$, $p < .01$; Condition, $F(1, 65) = 1274.97$, $p < .001$; and Frequency, $F(3, 195) = 25.23$, $p < .001$, and also a significant Condition × Frequency interaction, $F(3, 195) = 7.68$, $p < .001$. Figure 3.2 presents the mean percentages of correctly identified words as a function of frequency level and presentation condition, collapsing across year levels. As can be seen in the figure, improvement in performance with context was relatively greater with Level 1 words, which would account for the

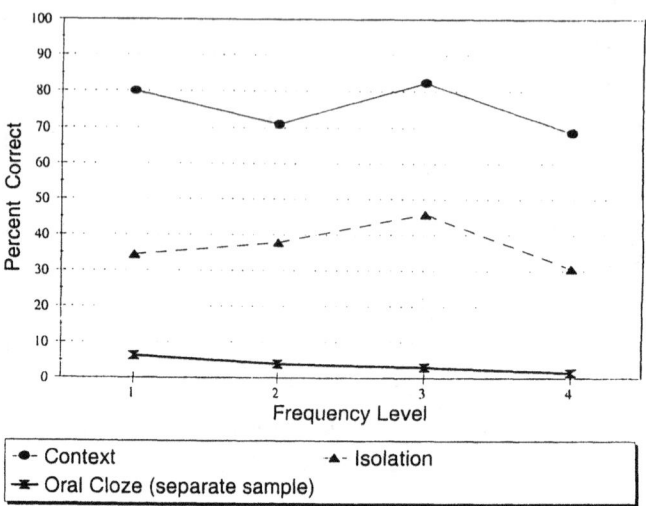

FIG. 3.2. Mean percentages of correctly identified words on the mispronunciation correction task as a function of frequency level and presentation condition (List B words only).

Condition × Frequency interaction. The reason for this difference is unclear and could be due to any number of factors: degree of similarity between the regularized pronunciations of Level 1 words and their correct pronunciations, the number of words with similar pronunciations to the target words, the degree of contextual constraint provided by the sentence contexts, or random fluctuation. Regarding the first possibility, Stanovich (1991) pointed out that "the issue of how best to define regularity is maddeningly complex and contentious" (p. 435). In selecting the irregularly spelled words at each frequency level, no attempt was made to control for *degree* of irregularity because there appears to be no clear procedure for doing so. Of greater importance, the data presented in Fig. 3.2 indicate that there was only a slight decline in performance with decreasing print frequency, which suggests that the words from List B were aurally familiar to the children.

Figure 3.2 also presents the mean predictability of the target words when the sentence contexts were presented as an oral cloze task to a separate sample of children (see previous discussion). Overall, the mean predictability of the target words was 3.7%. However, when the regularized pronunciations of the target words were presented in isolation to the children of the present experiment, the mean percentage of correctly identified words was 37.2%. Even without context, the potentially available graphophonemic information in the irregularly spelled words was sufficient to enable the children to identify over one third of the words. When the same regularized pronunciations were presented in underdetermining contexts, overall performance increased to 75.5%, a twofold increase in the number of words correctly identified. Although this level of performance is not as high as the mean score of 92.3% reported by Groff (1983), it does suggest that his general conclusion was correct, namely, that the mispronunciations resulting from the application of grapheme–phoneme correspondence rules to unfamiliar exception words will often be close enough to the correct phonological forms that the words can be correctly identified in context. The results of the present study are important because they demonstrate that Groff's findings generalize to exception words of lower frequency, that sentence context makes a contribution to the identification of mispronounced exception words beyond that provided by graphophonemic information alone (as estimated by presenting the regularized pronunciations of the words in isolation), and that sentence context greatly improves children's ability to identify mispronounced exception words, even when the contexts are underdetermining ones.

In summary, the results of Experiment 1 indicate that the graphophonemic information contained in irregularly spelled words is *potentially* very useful in acquiring word-specific knowledge, especially when combined with sentence context cues.

EXPERIMENT 2

The purpose of Experiment 2 was to examine more directly the contributions of phonological recoding ability and language prediction skill to the identification of unfamiliar exception words in underdetermining sentence contexts.

Method

Subjects

The initial sample comprised 305 Year 2 and Year 3 children who were individually administered four tests over four sessions. However, because not all children were able to complete all four sessions (due to their being absent or transferring to another school), the sample size decreased to 289 children: 157 Year 2 children (with a mean age of 6 years, 6 months) and 132 Year 3 children (with a mean age of 7 years, 6 months). The children were drawn from three schools and came from a wide range of social backgrounds. Only native speakers of English were chosen. Children with known hearing, language, or intellectual impairment were excluded from the study.

The method of reading instruction to which all children were exposed strongly adhered to the "whole language" philosophy of teaching reading. When confronted with an unfamiliar word, children in New Zealand schools are encouraged to use prior sentence context to guess what the word might be, or, if necessary, to skip the word and read to the end of the sentence, and then reread the sentence and put in a word that makes sense. If these two strategies fail, the child is encouraged to name the initial letter of the word and guess. Children are not encouraged to pronounce the sounds of isolated letters and overtly blend the subsyllabic sound units together.

Materials

Four tests were administered to the children: the Burt Word Reading Test, an oral cloze task, a contextual facilitation task, and a pseudoword naming task.

Burt Word Reading Test. The Burt Word Reading Test, New Zealand Revision (Gilmore, Croft, & Reid, 1981) is a standardized test of context-free word recognition. The children were presented with a list of words of increasing difficulty and asked to look at each word carefully and say it aloud. Testing continued until 10 successive words were read incorrectly or were not attempted. Scoring was based on the number of words read correctly.

Oral Cloze Task. Language prediction skill was assessed by means of an oral cloze task similar to one developed by Siegel and Ryan (1988). Each child was presented with 25 test items that varied in the form class and location of the missing word (e.g., "Sam _____ Jane went swimming"; "The little _____ put on their dresses"; "John buys lollies at the _____"). The task was presented to the children in the form of a game with a hand-held puppet. The following instructions were given:

> Today we're going to play a word guessing game with Peter. This is Peter. Peter says, "Hello, how are _____?" Peter sometimes forgets to say all the words. Can you say what word Peter left out? [If the child failed to respond, the missing word was provided.] Peter should have said, "Hello, how are *you*?" [The tester placed heavy emphasis on the word *you*.] Peter forgot to say the word *you*. When Peter leaves something out, you see if you can tell Peter what word he should have said, okay? Peter says, "The teacher read a _____." [The tester moved the puppet's mouth for each word and stopped for the deleted word. If the child responded incorrectly, corrective feedback was provided. If the child failed to respond, the item was repeated. If the child continued to fail to respond, different words were

offered as possibilities, with the first one being unsuitable.] Could Peter say, "The teacher read a *tree?*" [When the child completed four practice items, the test items were given but without corrective feedback.] Okay, now let's see if you can play the game. When Peter forgets a word, you try to guess what the word is. [General encouragement was given throughout the testing, but no corrective feedback was provided. However, if the child failed to respond after a pause of 10 seconds or asked for the sentence to be said again, the item was repeated.]

For many items there were alternative words that could be supplied that would yield semantically and syntactically well-formed sentences. Children's responses were therefore scored as correct if the word they provided was appropriate to the sentence context.

Contextual Facilitation Task. The purpose of this task was to assess children's ability to read irregularly spelled words in isolation and in context. The materials were the same as those used in the mispronunciation correction task of Experiment 1. However, to increase children's motivation to complete the task when the words were presented in isolation and to lessen poor readers' sense of failure, 20 words from the New Zealand Basic Word List (Elley, Croft, & Cowie, 1977) were interspersed among the original list of 80 exception words (see Appendix B) such that every fifth word in the new list of 100 words was a high-frequency sight word. The New Zealand Basic Word List comprises the 300 most frequently occurring words in the 195 most widely used beginning reading books in New Zealand. It was therefore anticipated that most of the children would be able to recognize these 20 basic sight words, which were: *in, they, of, at, said, he, you, she, for, on, it, was, and, mother, the, I, look, a, to,* and *is.*

The children were individually administered the contextual facilitation task in two sessions that were separated by one to two weeks. During the first session, the children were asked to read aloud the list of 100 words according to the following instructions:

Today I'm going to show you some words I'd like you to read. Some of the words will be easy words, but some will be hard. Try your best to work out what each word is. [The child was encouraged to attempt every word on the list. If the child did not attempt a response within 10 to 15 seconds, the next word was presented. General encouragement was given throughout the testing, but no corrective feedback was provided.]

During the second session, the children were asked to read aloud the same 80 exception words that were presented in the first session, but on this occasion the words were primed by orally presented sentence contexts (the same underdetermining contexts that were used in the mispronunciation correction task of Experiment 1). The following instructions were given to the children:

> Here are some sentences. I want you to read silently along with me as I read the sentences to you. In each sentence there is going to be one word that I am going to point to and ask you to read. [At this point the procedure was identical to that followed when the words were presented in isolation.]

Unlike Adams and Huggins (1985), who asked their children to read the sentence contexts as well as the target words, the preceding contexts in the present study were presented orally to the children. As Stanovich (1984) pointed out, the inefficient word recognition processes of less skilled readers may degrade the contextual information that they receive, rendering it less useful. Although Adams and Huggins used sentence contexts that comprised words of substantially higher frequencies than the target words, and instructed their testers to help children over any difficulties they had in reading the contexts, we wanted to make doubly sure that all readers of the present study had the same opportunity to make use of prior sentence context in identifying target words, especially because a major aim of the study was to determine whether differences in language prediction skill accounted for differences in acquiring word-specific knowledge.

The order of presentation of the items under both conditions of the contextual facilitation task was counterbalanced across children at each year level. Scoring was based on the number of words correctly read at each of the four frequency levels for each list (List A vs. List B; see Materials section of Experiment 1) under each presentation condition (isolation vs. context).

Pseudoword Naming Test. Thirty monosyllabic pseudowords from Section 3 of the Decoding Skills Test (Richardson & DiBenedetto, 1985) were used to measure phonological recoding ability. The pseudowords were presented in order of increasing difficulty, ranging from simple consonant-vowel-consonant patterns (e.g., *jit, med, dut*) to blends, digraphs, and vowel variations (e.g., *prew, thrain, fruice*). The original instructions for the test were piloted with a separate sample of children who were told that the items were not real words and had no meaning but could be pronounced like real words. However, many of the children were very resistant to reading "words" that had no meaning, most likely because of the heavy emphasis on meaning construction in their reading programs. The instructions to the pseudoword naming test were therefore modified as follows:

> Today I'm going to show you some funny sounding names. They are the names of children who live in a faraway land. Let's pretend that we are going to visit these children and want to learn to say their names the way

they do. You can read their names only if you sound them out. Remember, do not try to make them into real words. Let's try this one. [The first practice item, *ez*, was presented and the child was encouraged to sound it out. If the child failed to respond correctly, or failed to respond after 5 to 10 seconds, the tester demonstrated how to sound out the item.] This letter makes an /e/ sound and this letter makes a /z/ sound, so the name is /e/-/z/, *ez*. [The tester then presented the second practice item and, if necessary, demonstrated how to sound it out.] Okay, now let's see if you can play the game. I'm going to show you some names and I want to see if you can tell me how to say them. [The child was encouraged to sound out each name. If the child made a real word response, he or she was reminded that the right answer could not be a real word. If the child read a name in syllables (e.g., *juh -i- tuh* for *jit*), he or she was asked to say what name it made.] Okay, what name does that make? [General encouragement was given throughout the test session but no corrective feedback was provided.]

When the child incorrectly pronounced an item, the mispronunciation was recorded using the pronunciation key provided by Richardson and DiBenedetto (1985). Items were scored according to the number of sounds in the items that were correctly pronounced. For example, if *jit* was correctly pronounced, three points were given. However, if *jit* was pronounced "jat" or "jid," only two points were given. If *jit* was pronounced "jad," only one point was given. The total number of possible points was 101.

Procedure

The four tests were administered to the children in four sessions over a 4-week period during the middle term of the school year. The children were tested individually in a quiet withdrawal room in their school. The Burt Word Reading Test and oral cloze task were administered in the first session, the contextual facilitation task was administered in the second and third sessions, and the pseudoword naming test was administered in the fourth session. Each session lasted 15 to 30 minutes.

Results and Discussion

Contextual Facilitation Task. Children's performance in the contextual facilitation task was expressed as the percentage of correct responses. Table 3.2 presents the mean percentages of correctly read words as a function of presentation condition, frequency level, stimulus materials, and year of schooling. The four independent variables are defined in the same manner as in the mispronunciation correction task of Experiment 1. As before, the four levels of decreasing frequency for each list are based on different frequency counts. For the isolation presentation condition, a separate analysis of the 20 high-frequency sight words that were interspersed among

TABLE 3.2
Mean Percentages of Correctly Read Words on the Contextual
Facilitation Task as a Function of Presentation Condition,
Frequency Level, Stimulus Materials, and Year of Schooling[a]

	Presentation Condition							
	Isolation				Context			
Materials	1	2	3	4	1	2	3	4
List A								
Year 2	20.60	16.39	11.02	4.64	53.86	41.39	34.22	13.31
	(29.96)	(24.05)	(20.56)	(10.19)	(26.42)	(30.71)	(26.79)	(17.73)
Year 3	48.99	35.32	29.21	12.09	76.98	68.99	60.07	30.36
	(34.58)	(30.86)	(27.30)	(16.92)	(19.77)	(28.67)	(27.12)	(23.45)
List B								
Year 2	38.98	33.19	15.18	20.66	60.96	50.84	34.34	40.54
	(38.50)	(34.17)	(26.02)	(26.63)	(33.76)	(35.80)	(31.80)	(31.61)
Year 3	71.51	61.01	37.55	45.47	87.12	80.00	62.95	67.55
	(33.45)	(34.40)	(33.45)	(29.59)	(20.96)	(27.82)	(30.87)	(26.86)

[a]Standard deviations in parentheses.

the 80 exception words indicated that the children performed at ceiling levels, as expected. The mean percentage of correctly read sight words was 93.3% for the Year 2 children and 97.9% for the Year 3 children.

Figure 3.3 presents the mean percentages of correctly read words as a function of presentation condition, frequency level, and stimulus materials, collapsing across year levels. As can be seen in the figure, the children tended to perform better on the List B materials than on the List A materials. A 2 (Year) × 2 (Materials: List A vs. List B) × 2 (Condition: isolation vs. context) analysis of variance indicated that this difference was significant, $F(1,303) = 582.87$, $p < .001$. As in the mispronunciation correction task of Experiment 1, the children found the words from the Adams and Huggins' (1985) study more difficult to identify than the words drawn from the Elley and Croft (1989) noun frequency count.

Separate 2 (Year) × 2 (Condition) × 4 (Frequency) analyses of variance were carried out on the data from each list. The analysis of variance of the scores from List A revealed significant main effects for Year, $F(1,303) = 67.07$, $p < .001$; Condition, $F(1,303) = 1449.82$, $p < .001$; and Frequency, $F(1,909) = 632.60$, $p < .001$. The Year 3 children outperformed the Year 2 children, the 80 exception words were easier to read when presented in context than in isolation, and words of higher frequency were easier to read than words of lower frequency. All interactions were significant: Year × Condition, $F(1,303) = 15.35$, $p < .001$; Year × Frequency, $F(3,909) = 25.37$, $p < .001$; Condition × Frequency, $F(3,909) = 86.42$, $p < .001$; and

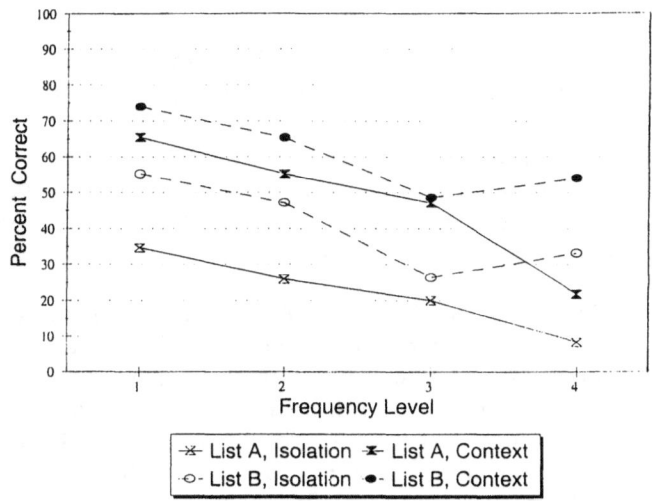

FIG. 3.3. Mean percentages of correctly read words on the contextual facilitation task as a function of presentation condition, frequency level, and stimulus materials.

Year × Condition × Frequency, $F(3,909) = 16.96$, $p < .001$. The effects of Condition and Frequency on word recognition accuracy were each relatively greater for Year 3 children, most likely because the performance of the younger children approached floor levels when the more difficult words were presented in isolation (see Table 3.2). Similarly, the effect of Condition on word recognition accuracy was relatively greater for words of higher frequency, again because the performance of the children approached floor levels when the words of lower frequency were presented in isolation. This tendency was greater among the younger children, which would account for the Year × Condition × Frequency interaction.

The analysis of variance of the scores from List B again showed main effects for Year, $F(1,303) = 67.78$, $p < .001$; Condition, $F(1,303) = 830.18$, $p < .001$; and Frequency, $F(3,909) = 412.28$, $p < .001$. Regarding the frequency effect, a comparison of Figs. 3.2 and 3.3 reveals that the effect of *print* frequency on performance was much greater (for the words from List B) when the children were asked to read the words than when they were asked to identify the mispronounced forms of the words, as would be expected. Only two interactions reached significance: the Condition × Frequency interaction, $F(3,909) = 5.84$, $p < .001$; and the Year × Condition × Frequency interaction, $F(3,909) = 11.74$, $p < .001$. The Year 3 children made greater gains from context when reading words of lower frequency than when reading words of higher frequency (see Table 3.2), most likely because they performed reasonably well when the words of higher frequency were presented in isolation. These results are similar to those reported by Adams and Huggins (1985), who found that contextual facilitation effects were greatest for words of intermediate difficulty.

Burt Word Reading Test, Oral Cloze Task, Pseudoword Naming Test. The means and standard deviations for the remaining measures of Experiment 2 are displayed in Table 3.3. As expected, the Year 3 children outperformed the Year 2 children on all three measures.

Analyses of Contextual Facilitation Variable. A new variable, contextual facilitation, was created by computing the difference between each child's performance in the contextual facilitation task when the 80 exception words were presented in isolation and in context. If better readers rely less on context to identify words because they are more proficient in using word-level information, then contextual facilitation should be negatively correlated with performance on the Burt Word Reading Test and the pseudoword naming test. However, the magnitude of both correlations was weak and failed to reach significance ($r = -.04$, $p > .05$, and $r = .11$, $p > .05$, respectively). If language prediction skill enables children to use sentence context to narrow the possibilities of what an unfamiliar word might be, then performance on the oral cloze task should be positively correlated with contextual facilitation scores. Although the correlation between language prediction skill (as measured by the oral cloze task) and contextual facilitation was positive, the magnitude of the correlation was low, $r = .15$, $p < .05$.

To investigate further this pattern of results, a scatterplot of the pseudoword naming and contextual facilitation scores was generated. The scatterplot revealed an inverted U-shaped configuration. A very similar configuration was obtained when the Burt Word Reading Test and con-

TABLE 3.3
Tests of Differences Between Means of
Year 2 and Year 3 Children on Experimental Measures[a]

Variable	Maximum Score	Year Level		$t(287)$
		Year 2	Year 3	
Burt Word Reading Test	110	24.94 (12.27)	36.01 (11.59)	7.83*
Oral cloze task	25	15.64 (3.65)	17.94 (3.70)	5.30*
Pseudoword naming test	101	55.92 (23.52)	72.31 (19.35)	6.56*

[a]Standard deviations in parentheses.
*$p < .001$.

textual facilitation scores were plotted. These results would explain the lack of a significant linear relationship between contextual facilitation and either pseudoword naming or real word recognition (as measured by the Burt Test). Table 3.4 presents the mean percentages of correctly read words for all children as a function of presentation condition (isolation vs. context) and percentile rank on the pseudoword naming test, and Fig. 3.4 displays the mean percentages of contextual gain as a function of percentile rank on the pseudoword naming test.

An important pattern in the data presented in Fig. 3.4 can be observed when the children are divided into three groups on the basis of their percentile scores on the pseudoword naming test: poor decoders (0–30), moderate decoders (31–70), and good decoders (71–100). The isolated word scores (see Table 3.4) and contextual facilitation scores of the poor decoders were relatively low, suggesting that if beginning readers are unable to take advantage of the graphophonemic information provided in irregular words, context will be of little or no help. For example, when presented with a sentence like, "He ran away from the *wasp*," beginning readers will not be able to derive much benefit from the prior sentence context unless they are able to identify some of the letter sounds in the target word.

The contextual facilitation scores of the good decoders were also low, but this was because their ability to decode words in isolation was so high (see Table 3.4). This finding is consistent with research described earlier indicating that contextual dependency declines with reading ability. Good readers rely less on context to identify difficult words because of their superior decoding skills. The low contextual facilitation scores of the poor

TABLE 3.4
Mean Percentages of Correctly Read Words on the Contextual Facilitation Task as a Function of Presentation Condition and Percentile Rank on the Pseudoword Naming Task

Percentile Rank on Pseudoword Naming Task	Pseudoword Naming Score Range	n	Presentation Condition	
			Isolation	Context
0–10	≤30	30	1.0	11.9
11–20	31–39	29	5.1	24.1
21–30	40–49	32	5.7	28.6
31–40	50–59	31	14.1	41.1
41–50	60–65	31	20.8	52.3
51–60	66–71	29	27.0	56.4
61–70	72–78	31	34.0	62.6
71–80	79–85	31	51.0	74.6
81–90	86–93	36	66.9	85.3
91–100	≥94	25	79.6	91.6

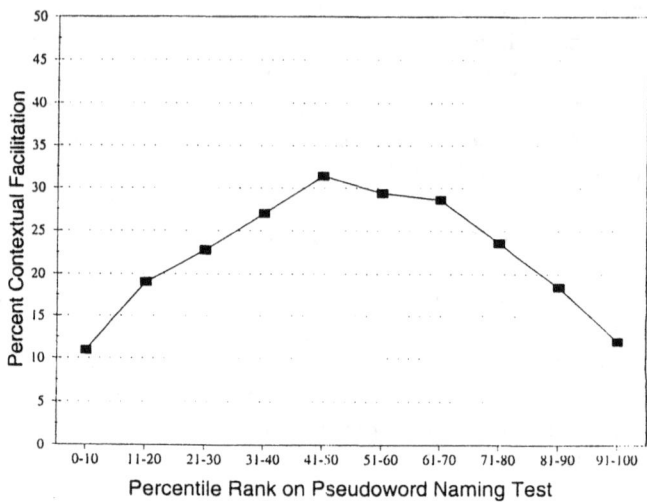

FIG. 3.4. Mean percentages of contextual facilitation as a function of percentile rank on pseudoword naming task.

and good decoders would explain the failure to find a stronger correlation between language prediction skill and contextual facilitation, which, as noted earlier, was only .15. The poor decoders did not possess a sufficiently high level of decoding skill to enable them to take full advantage of their language prediction skills, whereas the decoding skills of the good decoders were so advanced that they were less reliant on their language prediction skills in identifying difficult words.

Interestingly, the children classified as having moderate or emerging decoding skills had the highest contextual facilitation scores. The ability of these children to take advantage of the available graphophonemic cues in irregular words was not sufficiently advanced that they could identify many of the words in isolation (see Table 3.4). However, when the words appeared in context, the performance of these children improved considerably. These results suggest that beginning readers of moderate decoding ability can combine knowledge of the constraints of sentence context with incomplete graphophonemic information to identify unfamiliar words. This in turn would increase these children's word-specific knowledge and provide them with the basis for inducing further spelling–sound relationships. Individual differences in language prediction skill may therefore be particularly important during this phase of reading development.

Analyses of New Contextual Facilitation Variable. To explore this possibility further, a different scoring procedure was used following the work of Rego and Bryant (1993). Contextual facilitation (now referred to as "priming by context") was assessed by the number of words that the children were able to read correctly when the first 15 words that they missed in the contextual facilitation task under the isolation presentation condition were presented in context. Scores therefore ranged from 0 to 15. The scores of 21 children were so high when the words were presented in isolation that their opportunity for improvement was restricted. These children's scores were therefore excluded from further analyses, which reduced the sample size by approximately 7%. The mean contextual facilitation score was 4.61 ($SD = 2.94$) for the Year 2 children and 6.81 ($SD = 3.09$) for the Year 3 children, a difference that was significant, $t(256) = 5.79$, $p < .001$. The ability of children to take advantage of context in identifying unfamiliar words improves with schooling.

Displayed in Table 3.5 are the partial correlations among all experimental measures, controlling for age and amount of schooling (because children in New Zealand enter formal schooling on or close to their fifth birthday, controlling for children's age also controls for amount of schooling). All intercorrelations were significant, with magnitudes ranging from moderate to strong. The correlation between pseudoword naming and priming by context was greater than that between language prediction skill and priming by context (.60 vs. .45). Similarly, the correlation between pseudoword naming and exception word naming (isolation) was greater than that between language prediction skill and exception word naming (.78 vs .42). Both differences were significant ($p < .01$). Phonological recoding ability appears to be more important than language prediction skill in learning to recognize unfamiliar exception words, even when the words are presented in context. Not surprisingly, the ability to read exception words in isolation was highly correlated with the ability to read the same words in context, and both measures were highly correlated with overall reading ability as measured by the Burt Word Reading Test. The Burt Test includes a large number of irregularly spelled words, especially toward the beginning of the test.

TABLE 3.5
Partial Correlations Among Experimental Measures With the Effects of Age and Amount of Schooling Controlled

Variable	1	2	3	4	5	6
1. Priming by context	—	.55	.75	.61	.45	.60
2. Exception words (isolation)		—	.91	.88	.42	.78
3. Exception words (context)			—	.90	.51	.84
4. Burt Word Test				—	.45	.80
5. Oral cloze					—	.45
6. Pseudoword naming						—

Note. $N = 256$. All partial correlations were significant at the .001 level.

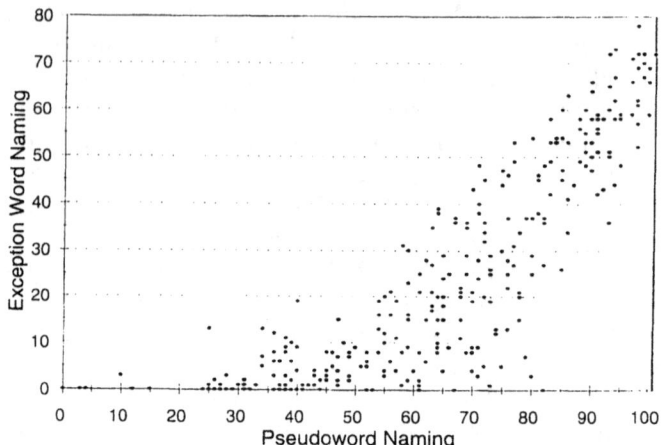

FIG. 3.5. Scatterplot of pseudoword naming and exception word naming.

Consistent with the findings of others (e.g., Gough & Walsh, 1991), there was a strong positive correlation between reading exception words in isolation and pronouncing pseudowords ($r = .78$). A scatterplot of the data revealed a pattern of results very similar to that reported in the study by Gough and Walsh (1991) described previously. Although many children performed reasonably well on pseudoword naming and poorly on exception word naming, no children performed poorly on pseudoword naming and well on exception word naming (see Fig. 3.5). Phonological recoding ability (as measured by pseudoword naming) appears to be necessary but not sufficient for acquiring word-specific knowledge.

To determine whether language prediction skill and phonological recoding ability make independent contributions to variance in reading unfamiliar exception words primed by context, hierarchical multiple regression analyses were carried out with age/amount of schooling entered as the first predictor variable (see Table 3.6). From the first two analyses presented in Table 3.6 it is apparent that, although both language prediction skill and phonological recoding ability account for significant independent variance in beginning readers' ability to read unfamiliar words in context, the independent variance due to phonological recoding ability is over four times as large as that due to language prediction skill. The standardized beta weights indicate that phonological recoding ability has the greatest impact on children's performance, even greater than age/amount of schooling. However, it is clear that language prediction skill makes an important contribution to reading unfamiliar words in context.

As argued previously, language prediction skill may interact with phonological recoding ability such that only children who have begun to acquire knowledge of letter–sound correspondences will be able to make

TABLE 3.6
Summary of Multiple Regression Analyses With Number of Unfamiliar
Exception Words Correctly Read in Context as Criterion Variable

Step	Predictor	R	R^2 Change	Standardized Beta Weights
	(A)			
1	Age/amount of schooling	.436	.190**	.191**
2	Oral cloze	.598	.167**	.220**
3	Pseudoword naming	.716	.155**	.477**
	(B)			
1	Age/amount of schooling	.436	.190**	.191**
2	Pseudoword naming	.691	.287**	.477**
3	Oral cloze	.716	.036**	.220**
	(C)			
1	Age/amount of schooling	.436	.190**	.183**
2	Oral cloze	.598	.167**	.000
3	Pseudoword naming	.716	.155**	.166
4	Oral cloze X Pseudoword naming	.721	.007*	.476*

*$p < .05$. **$p < .001$.

use of context in identifying (partially decoded) unfamiliar words (see Fig. 3.4). Exclusive reliance on context to identify unfamiliar words will not result in progress because the predictability of content words in connected text is so low. To test the hypothesis that the effects of language prediction skill on reading unfamiliar word in context interacts with phonological recoding ability, the product of oral cloze performance and pseudoword naming was entered as the last predictor variable, as shown in the final analysis of Table 3.6. In support of the hypothesis, the results indicate that the product of the two variables account for a significantly greater amount of variance than the linear combination of the two variables alone. Further support for the hypothesis comes from a scatterplot of the relation of phonological recoding ability to priming by context. As can be seen in Fig. 3.6, there were no children who performed poorly on the pseudoword naming test and well on the contextual priming task. Only children who had begun to acquire phonological recoding ability were able to use context to identify unfamiliar words, suggesting that phonological recoding ability is necessary (but not sufficient) for taking advantage of sentence context.

At first glance the superior performance of the good decoders in Fig. 3.6, and the corresponding positive correlation of .60 between pseudoword naming and priming by context shown in Table 3.5, would appear to contradict the data presented in Fig. 3.4, which indicate that contextual facilitation declines at higher levels of decoding ability. However, the data presented in Fig. 3.4 merely show the *absolute* gains made when words first

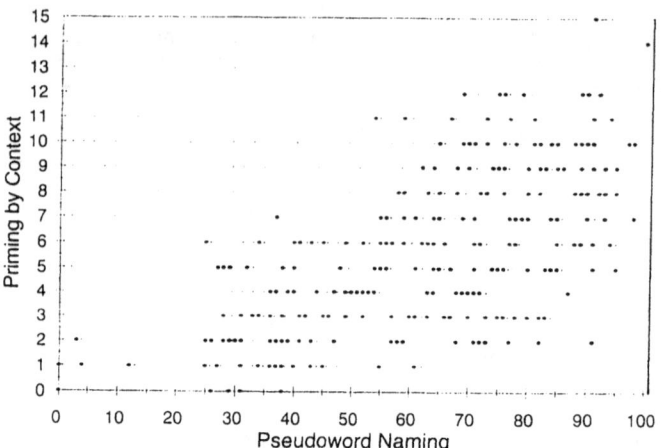

FIG. 3.6. Scatterplot of pseudoword naming and priming by context.

presented in isolation are presented in context. At increasing levels of decoding skill, the opportunity for improvement with context decreases because, as noted previously, the better decoders were able to recognize a higher proportion of the words in isolation. Interestingly, when contextual facilitation is recalculated as the ratio of contextual gain (i.e., number of words recognized in context minus number of words recognized in isolation) to *potential* improvement (i.e., number of words presented in isolation minus number of words recognized in isolation), the relationship between pseudoword naming and contextual facilitation (now referred to as "relative contextual gain") is linear (see Fig. 3.7).[1] What these data clearly indicate is that, although good decoders do not need to rely on context as often because of their superior ability to recognize words in isolation, when they do rely on context they are much more likely to identify unfamiliar words than are less skilled readers.

When the partial correlations between relative contextual gain and the other experimental variables were computed, a pattern of correlations was obtained that was very similar to that shown in Table 3.5, but with relative contextual gain substituted for priming by context (the variables relative contextual gain and priming by context were themselves highly correlated, $r = .87$). However, the magnitudes of the correlations involving relative contextual gain were somewhat larger. For example, the correlations of relative contextual gain with pseudoword naming and language prediction skill (as measured by the oral cloze task) were .68 and .51, respectively. Of greater interest, a scatterplot of the relation of pseudoword naming to relative contextual gain produced a pattern almost identical to that shown

---

[1]We wish to thank Philip Gough for bringing this data analysis procedure to our attention.

3. LANGUAGE PREDICTION SKILL AND READING

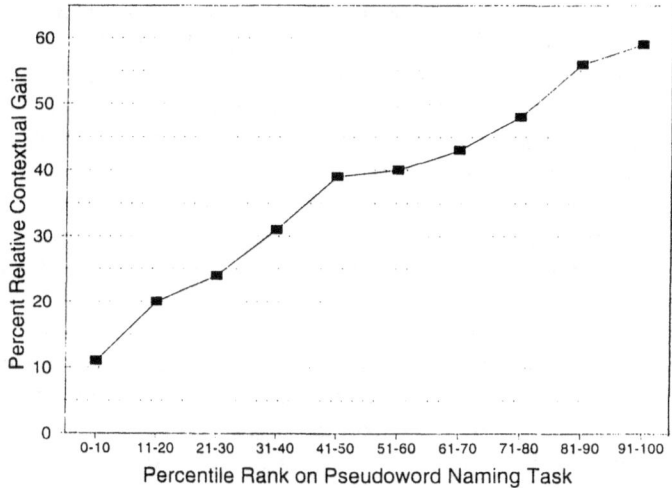

FIG. 3.7. Mean percentages of relative contextual gain as a function of percentile rank on pseudoword naming task.

in Fig. 3.6. Obtaining highly convergent results with two different scoring procedures provides additional support for the major findings of Experiment 2.

In summary, the data presented in Experiment 2 indicate that the ability to make use of contextual information is important. However, context can only be used as backup support to confirm hypotheses about what unfamiliar words might be based on available word-level information. Context cannot be used as a substitute for word-level information.

GENERAL DISCUSSION

This study was concerned with three questions. First, what role, if any, does language prediction skill play in the development of word-specific knowledge? Second, if language prediction skill does indeed make a contribution to the development of word recognition ability, is it a source of individual differences in learning to read? And third, how important is language prediction skill in relation to phonological recoding ability?

With regard to the first question, we hypothesized that language prediction skill facilitates the development of word recognition ability by enabling beginning readers to combine sentence context cues with incomplete graphophonemic information to identify unfamiliar words. This in turn increases children's word-specific knowledge from which additional spelling-to-sound patterns can be induced. Two experiments were carried out to test this hypothesis. In Experiment 1, a mispronunciation correction task was used to determine the potential contribution of phonological recoding ability to reading exception words in isolation and in underdetermining contexts. When the regularized pronunciations of irregularly spelled words (e.g., *stomach* pronounced as "stow-match") were presented in isolation, the potentially available graphophonemic information in the words enabled the children to identify many of them (see Fig. 3.2). When these same mispronounced words were presented in underdetermining contexts (e.g., "The football hit him in the /stōmăch/"), there was a twofold increase in children's performance. These results demonstrate that the graphophonemic information contained in irregularly spelled words can be very useful, especially when combined with sentence context cues.

The purpose of Experiment 2 was to examine more directly the relative contributions of phonological recoding ability and language prediction skill to the identification of unfamiliar exception words in underdetermining contexts. The results of the contextual facilitation task showed that, as expected, the accuracy of recognizing irregular words improved with context, a finding consistent with earlier studies (e.g., Adams & Huggins, 1985). Of greater interest was the finding that children with moderate or emerging phonological recoding skills showed the greatest absolute gains with context (see Fig. 3.4). It appears that the ability of these children to take advantage of the available graphophonemic cues in irregular words was not sufficiently advanced that they could identify many of the words in isolation. However, when the words were presented in underdetermining contexts, the performance of these children greatly improved. In contrast, the contextual facilitation scores of the poor decoders were relatively low, suggesting that if beginning readers are unable to make use of the graphophonemic information provided in irregular words, context will be of little or no benefit to them. A scatterplot of the relation of phonological recoding ability to reading words primed by context (as assessed by the number of words that the children were able to read correctly when the first 15 words that they missed in isolation were presented in context) supported this interpretation (see Fig. 3.6). Only children who had begun to acquire phonological recoding ability were able to use context to identify unfamiliar words.

Although the results of the second experiment suggest that the ability to make use of context may be particularly important for beginning readers with emerging phonological recoding skills, there remains the question of whether language prediction skill accounts for individual differences in children's ability to use context to identify unfamiliar words. Multiple regression analyses of the data indicated that, although language prediction skill made an independent contribution to variance in recognizing unfamiliar words in context, phonological recoding ability accounted for a much greater amount of independent variance (see Table 3.6). That is, even in the extreme case of learning to recognize irregularly spelled words, phonological recoding ability was much more important than language prediction skill. These results are consistent with the claim that phonological recoding ability provides the basic mechanism for acquiring word-specific knowledge (Ehri, 1991, 1992; Gough & Walsh, 1991). A scatterplot of the scores from the pseudoword naming test and exception word naming test provided additional support for this claim (see Fig. 3.5). The data indicated that phonological recoding ability is necessary but not sufficient for the development of word-specific knowledge, a finding similar to that reported by Gough and Walsh (1991).

The results of the study have important implications for educational practice. Although most practitioners argue that beginning readers should be encouraged to make use of both sentence context and letter–sound cues in recognizing unfamiliar words, the critical question is this: What relative emphasis should be placed on each? Put simply, if a child is reading aloud and comes across a word that he or she does not know, what is the first thing the teacher should tell the child to do? Proponents of the whole language approach to beginning reading instruction argue that children should be taught to use sentence context cues as the primary strategy for recognizing words in text. Graphophonemic cues should only be used very sparingly and only as backup support to confirm language predictions. The results of the present study support the opposite view, namely, that children should be encouraged to look for familiar spelling patterns first and to use context only as backup support to confirm hypothesis about what unfamiliar words might be based on available word-level information.

ACKNOWLEDGMENTS

This research was funded by a grant from the New Zealand Ministry of Education, Contract No. ER35/299/5.

We wish to thank Julie Russell and Johanna van Laar-Veth for their professionalism and competence in collecting and scoring the data.

Correspondence concerning this article should be addressed to William E. Tunmer, Faculty of Education, Massey University, Private Bag 11222, Palmerston North, New Zealand.

REFERENCES

Adams, M. J., & Huggins, A. (1985). The growth of children's sight vocabulary: A quick test with educational and theoretical implications. *Reading Research Quarterly, 20,* 262–281.

Bowey, J. A. (1986). Syntactic awareness in relation to reading skill and ongoing reading comprehension monitoring. *Journal of Experimental Child Psychology, 41*, 282–299.

Bowey, J. A., & Patel, R. K. (1988). Metalinguistic ability and early reading achievement. *Applied Psycholinguistics, 9*, 367–383.

Bryant, P., Maclean, M., & Bradley, L. (1990). Rhyme, language and children's reading. *Applied Psycholinguistics, 11*, 237–252.

Carroll, J. B., Davies, P., & Richman, B. (1971). *Word frequency book*. New York: American Heritage.

Cunningham, A. E., & Stanovich, K. E. (1990). Assessing print exposure and orthographic processing skill in children: A quick measure of reading experience. *Journal of Educational Psychology, 82*, 733–740.

Ehri, L. C. (1991). Development of the ability to read words. In R. Barr, M. L. Kamil, P. B. Mosenthal, & P. D. Pearson (Eds.), *Handbook of reading research* (Vol. 2, pp. 383–417). New York: Longman.

Ehri, L. C. (1992). Reconceptualizing the development of sight word reading and its relationship to recoding. In P. Gough, L. Ehri, & R. Treiman (Eds.), *Reading acquisition* (pp. 107–143). Hillsdale, NJ: Lawrence Erlbaum Associates.

Ehri, L. C., & Robbins, C. (1992). Beginners need some decoding skill to read by analogy. *Reading Research Quarterly, 27*, 13–26.

Elley, W., & Croft, C. (1989). *Assessing the difficulty of reading materials: The noun frequency method*. Wellington, New Zealand: New Zealand Council for Educational Research.

Elley, W., Croft, C., & Cowie, C. (1977). *A New Zealand basic word list*. Wellington, New Zealand: New Zealand Council for Educational Research.

Fowler, A. E. (1988). Grammaticality judgements and reading skill in grade 2. *Annals of Dyslexia, 38*, 73–94.

Gilmore, A., Croft, C., & Reid, N. (1981). *Burt Word Reading Test New Zealand Revision*. Wellington, New Zealand: New Zealand Council for Educational Research.

Goodman, K. S. (1967). Reading: A psycholinguistic guessing game. *Journal of the Reading Specialist, 6*, 126–135.

Goodman, K. S. (1982). Miscue analysis: Theory and reality in reading. In F. K. Gollasch (Ed.), *Language and literacy: The selected writings of Kenneth S. Goodman*. Boston: Routledge & Kegan Paul.

Goodman, K. S. (1986). *What's whole in whole language: A parent–teacher guide*. Portsmouth, NH: Heinemann.

Goodman, K. S., & Goodman, Y. M. (1979). Learning to read is natural. In L. B. Resnick & P. A. Weaver (Eds.), *Theory and practice of early reading* (Vol. 1, pp. 137–154). Hillsdale, NJ: Lawrence Erlbaum Associates.

Gough, P. B. (1983). Context, form and interaction. In K. Rayner (Ed.), *Eye movements in reading: Perceptual and language processes* (pp. 203–211). San Diego, CA: Academic.

Gough, P. B., & Hillinger, M. (1980). Learning to read: An unnatural act. *Bulletin of the Orton Society, 30*, 179–196.

Gough, P., & Juel, C. (1991). The first stages of word recognition. In L. Reiben & C. Perfetti (Eds.), *Learning to read: Basic research and its implications* (pp. 47–56). Hillsdale, NJ: Lawrence Erlbaum Associates.

Gough, P. B., & Walsh, M. (1991). Chinese, Phoenicians, and the orthographic cipher of English. In S. Brady & D. Shankweiler (Eds.), *Phonological processes in literacy* (pp. 199–209). Hillsdale, NJ: Lawrence Erlbaum Associates.

Groff, P. (1983). A test of the utility of phonics. *Reading Psychology: An International Quarterly, 4*, 217–225.

Jorm, A., & Share, D. (1983). Phonological recoding and reading acquisition. *Applied Psycholinguistics, 4,* 103–147.
Juel, C. (1991). Beginning reading. In R. Barr, M. L. Kamil, P. B. Mosenthal, & P. D. Pearson (Eds.), *Handbook of reading research* (Vol. 2, pp. 759–788). New York: Longman.
Kibby, M. W. (1980). Intersentential processes in reading comprehension. *Journal of Reading Behavior, 12,* 299–312.
Miller, G. R., & Coleman, E. B. (1967). A set of thirty-six passages calibrated for complexity. *Journal of Verbal Learning and Verbal Behavior, 6,* 851–854.
Nicholson, T. (1991). Do children read words better in context or in lists? A classic study revisited. *Journal of Educational Psychology, 83,* 444–450.
Rego, L. (1991). *The role of early linguistic awareness in children's reading and spelling.* Unpublished doctoral dissertation, University of Oxford, England.
Rego, L., & Bryant, P. (1993). The connection between phonological, syntactic and semantic skills and children's reading and spelling. *European Journal of Psychology of Education, 8,* 235–246.
Richardson, E., & DiBenedetto, B. (1985). *Decoding skills test.* Parkton, MD: York.
Siegel, L., & Ryan, E. (1988). Development of grammatical-sensitivity, phonological, and short-term memory skills in normally achieving and learning disabled children. *Developmental Psychology, 24,* 28–37.
Smith, F. (1973). *Psycholinguistics and reading.* New York: Holt, Rinehart & Winston.
Smith, F. (1979). *Reading without nonsense.* New York: Teachers' College Press.
Smith, F. (1988). *Understanding reading* (4th ed.). Hillsdale, NJ: Lawrence Erlbaum Associates.
Stanovich, K. (1980). Toward an interactive-compensatory model of individual differences in the development of reading fluency. *Reading Research Quarterly, 16,* 32–71.
Stanovich, K. (1984). The interactive-compensatory model of reading: A confluence of developmental, experimental and educational psychology. *Remedial and Special Education, 5,* 11–19.
Stanovich, K. E. (1986). Matthew effects in reading: Some consequences of individual differences in the acquisition of literacy. *Reading Research Quarterly, 21,* 360–406.
Stanovich, K. E. (1991). Word recognition: Changing perspectives. In R. Barr, M. L. Kamil, P. B. Mosenthal, & P. D. Pearson (Eds.), *Handbook of reading research* (Vol. 2, pp. 418–452). New York: Longman.
Stanovich, K. E., Cunningham, A. E., & Feeman, D. J. (1984). Intelligence, cognitive skills and early reading progress. *Reading Research Quarterly, 19,* 278–303.
Tunmer, W. (1989). The role of language-related factors in reading disability. In D. Shankweiler & I. Liberman (Eds.), *Phonology and reading disability: Solving the reading puzzle* (pp. 91–131). Ann Arbor: University of Michigan Press.
Tunmer, W. E., Herriman, M. L., & Nesdale, A. R. (1988). Metalinguistic abilities and beginning reading. *Reading Research Quarterly, 23,* 134–158.
Tunmer, W., & Hoover, W. (1992). Cognitive and linguistic factors in learning to read. In P. Gough, L. Ehri, & R. Treiman (Eds.), *Reading acquisition* (pp. 175–214). Hillsdale, NJ: Lawrence Erlbaum Associates.
Tunmer, W., & Hoover, W. (1993). Components of variance models of language-related factors in reading disability: A conceptual overview. In R. M. Joshi & C. K. Leong (Eds.), *Reading disabilities: Diagnosis and component processes* (pp. 135–173). Dordrecht, The Netherlands: Kluwer.
Tunmer, W. E., Nesdale, A. R., & Wright, A. D. (1987). Syntactic awareness and reading acquisition. *British Journal of Developmental Psychology, 5,* 25–34.
Willows, D. M., & Ryan, E. B. (1986). The development of grammatical sensitivity and its relationship to early reading achievement. *Reading Research Quarterly, 21,* 253–266.

APPENDIX A:
The Sentence Contexts for the 40 Words Selected from Elley and Croft (1989)[2]

Group 1
1. Her granny is very *kind*.
2. He got mud on his *shoe*.
3. The dog had to have a *wash*.
4. He put suntan lotion on his *body*.
5. He couldn't find his *money*.
6. In Auckland they have great *weather*.
7. The man repaired the broken *watch*.
8. He spilt spaghetti all down his *front*.
9. The children's granny baked some *bread*.
10. We got very cold swimming in the *river*.

Group 2
11. They searched for the *treasure*.
12. The friends shared a *biscuit*.
13. The child used the blocks to build a *castle*.
14. The cake was shaped like a *heart*.
15. He washed the plastic *bowl*.
16. For a snack he ate a *banana*.
17. Last year there was a big *flood*.
18. The dog chased the *lamb*.
19. He lost his *glove*.
20. The farmer dug a hole for the *post*.

Group 3
21. He pushed the door with his *shoulder*.
22. She put her glass on top of the *piano*.
23. They could not solve the *mystery*.
24. The queen lived in a large *palace*.
25. The man argued with the *referee*.
26. When they went tramping, they used a *compass*.
27. At the zoo we saw a *camel*.
28. The toy boat was made of *metal*.
29. He came to the party dressed as a *devil*.
30. The children collected the *scissors*.

Group 4
31. My brother likes *spinach*.
32. On the rock there was a *lizard*.
33. She was sick with the *measles*.
34. We always like to eat *pudding*.
35. The cat chased the *pigeon*.
36. He cut up the *onion*.
37. Mum paid the *chemist*.
38. For lunch we had some *soup*.
39. Sam has big *muscles*.
40. He ran away from the *wasp*.

[2]When these sentences were presented in the contextual facilitation task of Experiment 2, the target words were not italicized on the children's copy of the test items.

APPENDIX B:
The 80 Exception Words Used in the Mispronunciation Correction Task

1. treasure	31. palace	61. blind
2. wounded	32. body	62. vague
3. spinach	33. bowl	63. lamb
4. tomb	34. pigeon	64. soup
5. deaf	35. recipe	65. sword
6. none	36. rhythm	66. devil
7. kind	37. referee	67. ocean
8. shoulder	38. money	68. bread
9. island	39. guitar	69. rely
10. echo	40. break	70. glove
11. piano	41. trough	71. tongue
12. shoe	42. sweat	72. muscles
13. prove	43. onion	73. scissors
14. biscuit	44. banana	74. heights
15. lizard	45. whom	75. river
16. react	46. compass	76. mechanic
17. veins	47. weather	77. post
18. wash	48. dough	78. drought
19. mystery	49. ninth	79. wasp
20. busy	50. flood	80. calf
21. measles	51. chemist	
22. castle	52. lose	
23. ache	53. iron	
24. truth	54. anchor	
25. deny	55. watch	
26. heart	56. camel	
27. pudding	57. scent	
28. stomach	58. touch	
29. sugar	59. front	
30. chorus	60. metal	

Chapter 4

Rime-Based Coding in Early Reading Development in English: Orthographic Analogies and Rime Neighborhoods

Usha Goswami
Institute of Child Health, London

A remarkable number of research studies have now found evidence for a strong link between phonological knowledge and reading development (e.g., Bradley & Bryant, 1983; Fox & Routh, 1975; Juel, 1988; Lundberg, Frost, & Petersen, 1988; Lundberg, Olofsson, & Wall, 1980; Maclean, Bradley, & Bryant, 1987; Perfetti, Beck, Bell, & Hughes, 1987; Snowling, 1980; Stanovich, Cunningham, & Cramer, 1984; Tunmer & Nesdale, 1985; Vellutino & Scanlon, 1987; Wagner, 1988). The research discussed in this chapter focusses on one aspect of phonological knowledge—knowledge of the units that linguists call *onsets* and *rimes* (e.g., Treiman, 1988, 1992)—and discusses the role that these phonological units may play in the reading development of young children. It is argued that rime-based coding is clearly evident in the reading strategies adopted by young children who are learning to read English, and that this rime-based coding offers a number of advantages in decoding the English orthography. In particular, rime-based coding allows children to make analogies to new words that share rimes with familiar words, and it also significantly reduces the ambiguity of written English.

THE DEVELOPMENTAL PRIORITY OF ONSETS AND RIMES

Even preschoolers show knowledge of onsets and rimes. The onset of a spoken word corresponds to the initial consonant/s in the written form of the word. The onset of *cup* is "c," the onset of *tree* is "tr," and the onset of *spread* is "spr." The rime of a spoken word corresponds to the vowel/s and any final consonants in the written form of the word. The rime of *cup* is "up," the rime of *tree* is "ee," and the rime of *spread* is "ead." Most of these onsets and rimes correspond to more than one phoneme. A phoneme is the smallest unit of sound that changes the meaning of a word. *Cup* and *cut* differ by a final phoneme, and *cup* and *cap* differ by a medial phoneme. Although the onset of *cup* and the rime of *tree* are single phonemes, the onset of *tree* and the rimes of *cup* and *spread* correspond to two phonemes, and the onset of *spread* corresponds to three phonemes.

Studies that have compared onset-rime awareness with phonemic awareness suggest that onsets and rimes are the more accessible linguistic units for young children. For example, Treiman and Zukowski (1991) used a "same-different" task to compare phonological judgments at either the onset-rime or the phonemic level. Children aged 4, 5, and 6 years were asked whether words like *plea* shared a beginning sound with *plank* (onset) or with *pray* (initial phoneme), and whether words like *rat* shared a final sound with *bat* (rime) or with *wit* (final phoneme). The 4- and 5-year-old children were significantly better at making judgments about shared onsets and rimes than about phonemes. Only the 6-year-olds, who had been learning to read for about a year, showed equivalent performance in both tasks. Converging evidence that onsets and rimes are easier than phonemes comes from a study by Kirtley, Bryant, Maclean, and Bradley (1989). They devised a version of the "oddity task" that could either be solved using onsets and rimes, or phonemes. In the oddity task, children must choose the odd word out from a set of three on the basis of a difference in sound. For word triples like *top, rail,* and *hop*, the odd word can be selected on the basis of the whole rime, whereas for triples like *mop, lead,* and *whip*, the odd word out must be chosen on the basis of the final phoneme. Kirtley et al. found that 4-, 5-, and 6-year-olds were all significantly better in spotting the odd word out in the rime task than in the task that required judgments about final phonemes.

One interpretation of these studies is that an awareness of onsets and rimes emerges *prior* to an awareness of phonemes, and is present in preschoolers. In fact, most of the phonological awareness literature can be interpreted as showing a developmental priority for onsets and rimes in children learning to read English (Goswami & Bryant, 1990). Phonemic awareness seems to emerge largely as a *consequence* of learning to read an alphabetic orthography. Although this idea is by no means universally accepted (see Carlisle, 1991; Morais, 1991; Morais, Alegria, & Content, 1987; Seymour & Evans, 1994), it generates an interesting hypothesis about initial reading acquisition. The hypothesis is that rime-based coding might be very important in initial reading, at least for children who are learning to read a nontransparent orthography such as English. This idea is supported by the literature on phonological awareness, which has demonstrated that children do not embark on the task of learning to read as blank slates with no prior knowledge relevant to the new task of understanding print. Instead, they have a fair amount of knowledge about the phonology of their language as well as about its semantics, and the phonological knowledge that they have is largely about onsets and rimes. If we assume that children actively try to use their phonological knowledge to make sense of the orthography when they begin to learn to read, then it follows that we should be able to find evidence for rime-based coding in early reading.

STUDIES OF ORTHOGRAPHIC ANALOGIES IN CHILDREN'S READING

One way of examining whether there is a correspondence between children's phonological knowledge and their reading behavior is to investigate how children use their knowledge of the spelling–sound correspondences in one word when reading another. This question can be studied by looking at the kinds of *analogies* that children make between words when they are reading. If children are taught to decode one word, such as *beak*, and are then shown new words that share part of the same spelling pattern, such as *peak, bean,* and *bark*, the resulting pattern of transfer can help to establish the way in which the clue word (*beak*) has been coded. In a number of clue word analogy studies using a variety of different words, it has consistently been shown that children prefer to use analogies between *rimes* in words. Even though *beak* and *peak* share the same number of letters as *beak* and *bean*, children consistently make more analogies when the spelling segment that is shared between two words reflects the rime (Goswami, 1986, 1988, 1991). The rime effect is not due to phonological priming, because similar levels of transfer do not occur when two words share a rhyming sound but differ in rime orthography (as in *head* and *said*, or *most* and *toast*; Goswami, 1990a).

Furthermore, children in the earliest stages of learning to read, even those who cannot yet decode many words reliably, only make analogies between shared rimes. Analogies that reflect the onset and part of the rime, as in *beak* → *bean*, or *trim* → *trip*, usually emerge slightly later than rime analogies, after about 6 months of reading progress (Goswami, 1993). Analogies that depend on single phonemes that do not correspond to either onset or rime units, such as analogies between vowel digraphs in single-syllable words (*beak* → *heap*), also depend on some reading development, emerging at around the same point as analogies that reflect the onset and part of the rime. Analogies between singleton vowels (*trim* →

slit) appear to be rare. This pattern of transfer supports the idea that when children use one word as a basis for reading another, spelling sequences that reflect rimes are most salient. Although children use analogies between onsets in reading, too (*trim* → *trot*), the developmental sequence of onset analogies has not yet been studied in any detail.

If the use of rime analogies depends on an active attempt to link orthographic patterns with phonological knowledge, then there should also be individual differences in children's ability to use rime analogies in reading, just as there are individual differences in their phonological awareness. Indeed, this is the case. Children with better onset-rime skills make more rime analogies in the clue word task (Goswami, 1990b). Furthermore, the link between onset-rime awareness and rime analogies seems to be a highly specific one. Analogies that depend on the onset and part of the rime, as in *beak* → *bean*, are most strongly linked to an awareness of phonemes (Goswami & Mead, 1992). The finding that individual differences in phonemic knowledge are related to the use of onset-and-part-of-the-rime analogies, and individual differences in onset-rime awareness are linked to the use of rime analogies, is not really surprising. Whereas rime analogies require children to segment words into onset-rime units, onset-and-part-of-the-rime analogies require segmentation of the rime, and this requires phonemic knowledge.

Dyslexic children, who have poor phonological skills, do not show a spontaneous use of rime analogies (e.g., Lovett, Warren-Chaplin, Ransby, & Borden, 1990). A dyslexic child who is taught to read the word *part* does not show transfer to the analogous written word *cart*, despite showing clear evidence of having learned the spelling pattern of *part*. However, even dyslexic children can be helped to use analogies in instructional programs that provide phonological input as well as training in analogy (e.g., Gaskins et al., 1988; Gaskins, Downer, & Gaskins, 1986). This finding suggests that it is the impoverished phonological skills of dyslexic children, rather than any difficulties in using analogies per se, that underlie their inability to use rime analogies spontaneously in reading.

AN INTERACTIVE ANALOGY MODEL OF READING DEVELOPMENT

The pattern of analogy transfer described previously can be used to suggest a model of reading development that is at variance with traditional stage models of learning to read. In these traditional models, children are thought to pass from an initial stage of logographic recognition, through an alphabetic stage of grapheme–phoneme reading, to a final stage of orthographic word recognition that involves the use of larger graphemic sequences in words (e.g., Frith, 1985; Marsh, Friedman, Welch, & Desberg, 1981). In contrast to this view, an *interactive analogy* model of reading development can be proposed that argues that the phonological knowledge that children *bring with them* to reading plays an important role in establishing orthographic recognition units from the earliest phases of development (Goswami, 1993). This model entails the assumption that the early visual analysis of words is *founded* in phonological knowledge (Goswami, 1991; Stuart & Coltheart, 1988).

According to the interactive analogy model of reading development, children begin learning to read English by establishing direct recognition units for words that are phonologically underpinned at the onset-rime level. As reading develops, grapheme clusters and graphemes other than those corresponding to onsets and rimes are also underpinned phonologically, supplementing the original onset-rime coding with a full phonemic specification of the graphemes in the words. Other recent interactive models of reading development have argued that early orthographic recognition units code initial and final *phonemes* (e.g., Ehri, 1992; Perfetti, 1992; Stuart & Coltheart, 1988). According to these other models, words like *net* and *plum* are represented as *n-t* and *p-m*, whereas according to the interactive analogy model, the recognition units that children establish for these words code phonology in the form *n-et* and *pl-um*. Whereas the partial phonemic coding view entails the belief that young children have only a sketchy knowledge of the full orthographic forms of the words that they are learning to read, the interactive analogy model assumes fairly detailed orthographic knowledge on the part of the beginning reader.

How sketchy is young children's initial learning about the orthography? In fact, Reitsma (1983) showed that explicit orthographic learning in children can be very rapid. Reitsma found that Dutch 7-year-olds could visually memorize a new spelling pattern in only three exposures, and that this learning was orthographically based: The children remembered whether they had learned *vabriek* or *fabriek* (which are phonologically equivalent). The assumption that young children lack detailed orthographic knowledge of the words that they can read may thus be wrong.

In addition, Treiman and her colleagues recently showed that there is less orthographic redundancy at the onset-rime juncture than elsewhere in the letter string in English (Treiman, Mullennix, Bijeljac-Babic, & Richmond-Welty, 1995). They noted that the characteristics of the orthography itself could encourage readers to use an onset-rime parsing when reading words. This suggestion can be extended to propose that, for young children, *automatic* visual learning about orthographic rime units might occur simply from print exposure. Such automatic learning does not necessitate any *explicit* awareness of orthographic rime units on the part of the child, as visual knowledge about orthographic structure could be *implicit* for the young learner (see Brooks, 1977; Reber, 1967, for related evidence from adults). It would only be when phonological knowledge was brought into play and children actively began to try to link orthography with phonology that orthographic rime units would increase in salience for reading, because early phonological knowledge is about rimes.

The idea that orthographic redundancy drives automatic and implicit rime learning may not be true in other orthographies, however. Other orthographies represent the phonology of their respective languages differently, and thus print exposure in these orthographies might be expected to have different effects. In orthographies with a very *transparent* relationship between spelling and sound, such as Spanish, German, and Serbo-Croat, once a child has learned the relevant grapheme–phoneme correspondences then any word can be decoded. The relationship between orthography and phonology at the phonemic level is highly predictable. Consequently, the *nature* of the orthographic units that are important to beginning readers of these transparent orthographies may be different from those used by beginning readers of less transparent orthographies, such as English (Wimmer & Goswami, 1994). Early rime skills may be less intimately connected to early reading in these transparent orthographies, and there is at least some evidence to support this view (Wimmer, Landerl, & Schneider, 1994). In English, by contrast, a focus on rimes reflects the structure of the orthography, and markedly reduces the irregularity of spelling–sound correspondences (Stanback, 1992), making reading acquisition easier for the child.

NEIGHBORHOOD EFFECTS IN CHILDREN'S READING

How can we test the proposal that rimes are important units for children learning to read English? One way is to study *neighborhood* effects in children's reading. The orthographic neighbors of a given word are usually defined in terms of the graphemes that they share with the target word. According to the traditional neighborhood measure, Coltheart's (1978) 'N' measure, a word's neighbors are derived by replacing each of the letters of a letter string with every other alphabet letter. Words like *buck*, *bank*, and *pack* are all equally strong neighbours of *back*. Studies relying on the N measure have suggested that rime-based coding only emerges gradually in children as reading develops, after knowledge of grapheme–phoneme correspondences (GPCs) has been established (e.g., V. Colheart & Leahy, 1992; Laxon, V. Coltheart, & Keating, 1988; Laxon, Masterson, & V. Coltheart, 1991; Laxon, Masterson, Pool, & Keating, 1992; although see Brown & Watson, in preparation). However, as children's early learning about the orthography seems to focus on *rimes*, the N measure may not be the best measure to choose when studying neighborhood effects in children's reading.

A better approach for developmental studies may be to define a word's neighborhood in terms of its *rime* neighbors. Evidence for early rime-based coding can then be sought by giving children nonsense words to read that either share rimes with many real words, or that share rimes with very few or no real words. This method was used by Treiman, Goswami, and Bruck (1990), who gave first- and third-grade children nonsense words to read that either had many rime neighbors (such as *tain—main, rain, lain, gain, plain*) or very few (*goan—moan, groan*). Matched pairs of each nonsense word type were created to equate the two lists for the constituent GPCs of the nonsense words (e.g., *tain, goach/goan, taich*). Treiman et al. found that rime familiarity significantly affected reading success at both ages. However, their methodology did not enable them to make a direct comparison of children's use of rime-based coding with children's use of GPCs.

One way of making such a comparison is to try to study *regularity* and *consistency* effects in children's nonsense word reading. Regular words have traditionally been used as an index of grapheme–phoneme coding (Coltheart, 1978). For example, the regular word *back* is assumed to be read by combining the phonemes for the graphemes "b," "a," and "ck." More recently, consistency has also been recognised as an important variable in studies of skilled reading (Andrews, 1982). The word *back* is both regular *and* consistent, because all its rime neighbors (*rack, sack, black*) are pronounced in the same regular way. The word *hear* is regular and *inconsistent*, because some of its rime neighbors, like *dear*, are regular in GPC terms, whereas others, like *bear*, are not. Words can also be *irregular* and consistent, like the word *talk*. Although words like *talk* are irregularly pronounced according to GPC rules, all of their rime neighbors are consistently pronounced in the same way (*walk, balk, stalk*).

Developmental studies that have used regularity and consistency measures to try to compare the use of rimes with GPCs have been interpreted as showing that rime-level units are acquired *later* than GPCs by young readers of English. A good example is a study by Coltheart and Leahy (1992), who compared children's ability to read three kinds of nonsense words: nonsense words analogous to regular and consistent words, like *dack;* nonsense words analogous to regular and inconsistent words, like *kear;* and nonsense words analogous to irregular and consistent words, like *nalk*. They found that first-, second-, and third-graders produced more "regular" pronunciations for the regular-consistent nonsense words (*dack/back*) than for the regular-inconsistent nonsense words (*kear/hear/bear*) or the irregular-consistent nonsense words (*nalk/talk*). Although Coltheart and Leahy had predicted that *all* nonsense words should be equally likely to yield regular pronunciations on a GPC model, they argued that the production of a significant number of regular pronunciations for the irregular-consistent nonsense words (*nalk* pronounced to rhyme with *talc*), coupled with the much higher success rate in reading the regular consistent nonsense words (*dack*), nevertheless showed that the children were relying on GPCs, and were failing to use rime units in their reading.

This conclusion is too simple, however. First, it is wrong to assume that the production of regular pronunciations for nonsense words like *dack* is evidence for the use of GPCs. These pronunciations could equally be due to the use of rime-based analogies to other regular words, for example using the rime unit from *back* to read *dack*. Second, the comparison between regular consistent (*dack*) and irregular consistent (*nalk*) nonsense words ignores the total number of available rime neighbors for each nonsense word type. In Coltheart and Leahy's study, the number of real word rime neighbors was significantly greater for the regular consistent nonsense words (140 rime neighbors) than for the irregular consistent nonsense words (68 rime neighbors), some of which additionally had regular neighbors, and so were not really irregular-consistent nonsense words at all. Once these factors are taken into account, then the results could be argued to provide support for early rime-based coding. According to an analogy model of reading development, which gives early priority to rimes, reading success will depend on the availability of analogous neighbors in the mental lexicon. The greater the number of available neighbors, the greater the accuracy with which children should read analogous nonsense words.

RIMES VERSUS GRAPHEME–PHONEME CORRESPONDENCES

The problems with Coltheart and Leahy's study highlight the fact that it is difficult to use nonsense words to contrast children's use of rime-based correspondences with their use of GPCs. However, it might be possible to overcome the methodological problems associated with such comparisons by using nonsense words that are equated for *phonology*. Consider the two phonologically equivalent nonsense words *dake* and *daik*. *Dake* shares a rime with many neighbors (*cake, bake, make*, etc.), and *daik* shares a rime with no neighbors. This difference enables the comparison of rime-based coding with GPC knowledge, because the former category of nonsense words (*dake*) has familiar rimes and familiar GPCs, whereas the latter category (*daik*) only has familiar GPCs. The two types of nonsense word can be approximately equated for the familiarity of their constituent GPCs by matching them for conditional bigram frequency. Because the phonological matching ensures that both types of nonsense word require the same output phonology, any speed or accuracy differences that arise in reading the two types of nonsense word cannot be due to articulatory differences or to GPC familiarity, but must necessarily be due to *rime* familiarity.

We have just carried out a study based on the contrast described previously. For this study, we designed lists of both monosyllabic and bisyllabic nonsense words that had either many or no neighbors at the level of the rhyme. The inclusion of bisyllabic words in such studies may be very important. For monosyllabic words, rhyme and rime are the same, but for multisyllabic words, rhyme and rime can differ. For example, the words *mountain* and *fountain* share their entire orthography apart from the onset: They rhyme with each other and they share the same rimes for each syllable. The words *behind* and *unwind* also rhyme, but the rime of the first syllable in each word differs: Only the rime of the second syllable is the same. The words *wagon* and *melon* share a final rime, but they do not rhyme because the stress is on the first syllable. Brady, Fowler, and Gipstein (in preparation) found that, in oral tasks using such multisyllabic words, rhyme awareness precedes rime awareness for 4- and 5-year-old children. It is thus quite possible that, when children are reading multisyllabic words, rhymes are more important than rimes.

Our experiment compared children's speed and accuracy in reading nonsense words like *dake, daik, bomic* (comic), and *bommick*. We called the *dake/bomic* word lists O+P+ words, because these nonsense words possess *both* orthographic (O+) and phonological (P+) rhyme neighbors. We called the *daik/bommick* lists O–P+ words, because although these nonsense words have phonological rhyming neighbors (P+), they do not have orthographic neighbors for the spelling pattern that represents the entire rhyme (O–).[1] We were only able to equate the monosyllable lists for GPC familiarity. The mean positional bigram frequency of the O+P+ words (*dake*) was 2875, and the mean positional bigram frequency of the O–P+ list (*daik*) was 3025.

Seven-, 8-, and 9-year-old children were tested, and they showed a remarkably consistent pattern of performance with the two types of nonsense word that was maintained across both the speed and the accuracy measures. The O+P+ monosyllabic nonsense words like *dake* were read significantly faster and more accurately than the O–P+ monosyllabic nonsense words like *daik* by children of all ages, and a group of Cambridge students tested as an adult control group (mean age 23 years) showed the same significant pattern. The accuracy data are shown in Table 4.1, and provide clear evidence for the use of rime-based orthographic coding by children as young as 7 years of age.

Table 4.1 also shows children's performance with the lists of O+P+ and O–P+ bisyllabic stimuli. Because real-word monosyllabic analogues exist

---

[1]The bisyllabic words do, however, have orthographic rime neighbors for each of their constituent *syllables*, such as *bommick—Tom, kick.*

TABLE 4.1
Accuracy of Nonsense Word Reading:
O+P+ Words Versus O–P+ Words

	Monosyllables		Bisyllables		Age
List type	O+P+	O–P+	O+P+	O–P+	
Example	Dake	Daik	Bomic	Bommick	
	Murn	Mirn	Rillow	Rilloe	
% correct	56 >	36	65 >	50	7 yrs.
	64 >	48	79 >	61	8 yrs.
	92 >	79	95 >	85	9 yrs.
	94 >	85	100 >	98	23 yrs.

for each syllable of both of these types of nonsense word, enhanced reading time and accuracy would only be predicted for the O+P+ words if the orthography of the entire letter string apart from the onset was used as a basis for pronunciation. To our surprise, we found exactly the same pattern of performance with the bisyllabic stimuli as with the monosyllabic stimuli. Seven, 8-, and 9-year-old children and college students were significantly faster and more accurate at reading the O+P+ nonsense words (*bomic*) than the O–P+ nonsense words (*bommick*). In fact, both accuracy and speed were significantly higher with the bisyllabic stimuli than with the monosyllabic stimuli. This finding implies that there is a strong effect of the orthographic familiarity of word segments larger than the rime in pronouncing print, even by 7 years of age (it also accords with the findings of Reitsma, 1983).

TRAINING CHILDREN TO USE RIME ANALOGIES IN READING

According to converging evidence from children's reading analogies and from studies of nonsense word reading, rime-based coding is used by young readers. These findings have a clear implication for teaching. Methods of teaching children to read that focus on rhyme and on rimes should be beneficial for reading progress. A number of training studies have recently been published that study the effects of rime analogy training on reading development, with mixed results. Rime analogy training appears to help young children only when the analogy training is accompanied by phonological training, when a number of exemplars of the analogy are provided, and when a reasonable depth of training is given by the teacher. These conclusions are speculative, however, because longer-term training studies that avoid the problem of unseen control groups have yet to be carried out.

Training studies that use short and intensive periods of rime training have in general found correspondingly short-term gains in reading. Two examples of such studies are provided by the work of Wise, Olson, and Treiman (1990), and Bruck and Treiman (1992).

Wise et al. (1990) used a computerized system for teaching reading called DECtalk in their studies. In this system, a single word appears on the computer screen, and the computer then pronounces either the whole word, the individual phonemes in the word, the onset and rime units, or two units corresponding to a postvowel segmentation, highlighting the corresponding orthographic units as it does so. For example, if the word is *clap*, the computer could highlight and pronounce the *cl* segment followed by the *ap* segment (onset-rime segmentation), the *cla* segment followed by the *p* segment (postvowel segmentation), each individual phoneme, or the entire syllable.

In Wise et al.'s study, postvowel segmentation was compared to onset-rime segmentation in a design that equated these two units for the number of constituent letters across trials. For example, if the target word was *clap*, then onset-rime segmentation led to two units of two letters each (cl-ap) whereas post-vowel segmentation led to one three-letter unit and a single letter (cla-p). If the target word was *dish*, then the reverse was true (d-ish, di-sh). Six-year-old children were given three trials with each word, their task being to produce a blended pronunciation from the sounds generated by the computer. Retention was measured immediately after receiving a block of 8 words (immediate posttest), and also after the presentation of 32 words (delayed posttest). Wise et al. found that word learning was better in the onset-rime condition than in the postvowel condition at immediate posttest, but that this was only sometimes true at delayed posttest. The benefits of onset-rime segmentation on word learning thus appeared to be short-lived. Wise et al. suggested that this could have been because learning to read 32 new words in a half-hour session with a computer is a difficult and unusual task for young children.

Bruck and Treiman reached a similar conclusion about the short-term gains of rime-based training in a study based on clue words. They compared performance in three segmentation conditions: a rime condition, a postvowel condition, and a phoneme condition. The 6-year-old children in their study first learned to read a list of 10 words written on cards, such as *pig* and *hop*. A rime group was then trained to read 10 new words that shared rimes with the taught list (*big*, *top*), a postvowel group was trained to read 10 new words that shared consonant-vowel (CV) units with the taught list (*pin*, *hot*), and a phoneme group was trained to read 10 new words that shared vowels with the taught list (*rib*, *got*). Training consisted of showing the children the new words, also written on cards, with the shared orthographic segment either highlighted in colored pen (color trials), or simply printed in black and white. The child first had to pronounce the shared orthographic segment, and then derive the pronunciation for the whole word. Most children received three or four such training sessions, lasting about 10 minutes each, which continued until they could pronounce the 10 new words correctly twice in succession.

Learning and transfer were measured on the fifth day. Bruck and Treiman found that, although the rime group learned the new words in significantly fewer trials than the other two groups, they also remembered significantly fewer of the trained words on the fifth day (recalling on average 5.3 words correctly, compared to 5.8 words for the CV group and 6.1 words for the vowel group). They also showed poorer generalization to some previously unseen nonsense words (like *nig* and *pim*) than did the other two groups. Bruck and Treiman concluded that the benefits of rime-based training are relatively short-lived. However, there is a problem with their study: The children in their rime group received significantly less training than the other two groups overall. Because the children in the rime group learned to read the new words more quickly than the children in the other two training groups, their learning may have been relatively shallow, and thus Bruck and Treiman's result may be due to differences in training time rather than to differences in training unit.

Training studies that have provided rime training over longer periods of time, and especially studies that have paired orthographic rime training with phonological training, have generally found much stronger results than these short-term studies. So far, however, these longer-term training studies have relied on unseen control groups, who were given only normal classroom teaching over the training period. This omission of treated control groups makes it difficult to draw any firm conclusions about the long-term benefits of rime analogy training. Nevertheless, the pedagogical importance of such studies is indisputable, and two longer-term training studies are discussed next: that of Peterson and Haines (1992), who provided rime-based training for a period of a month; and that of White and Cunningham (1990), who provided rime-based training to two different school populations for a period of a year each.

Peterson and Haines studied a kindergarten group of 5- to 6-year-olds. They used a rime training method based on word families. Each child was given individual training with the 10 rime families being used, in sessions lasting approximately 15 minutes each. In a given session, one word from the family being studied would be introduced (e.g., *ball*), and segmented into its onset and rime (b-all). The onset-rime units were pronounced separately, and a new word from the family was then added, also segmented into its onset and rime (e.g., f-all). The rime similarity was pointed out to the child and emphasized, and four more analogous words were gradually added in the same fashion (*mall, wall, hall, gall*). This word family approach, which entails the inclusion of more than one example of a rime-analogous word, may be important for the depth of learning attained. Research in problem solving by analogy has found that the provision of multiple example analogies significantly benefits learning (e.g., Brown & Kane, 1988; Goswami, 1992).

Peterson and Haines assessed the effects of rime analogy training in a posttest that involved reading new words by analogy to new clue words. This analogy test was given to control children from the same classrooms who had not received analogy training. Although the two groups of children had shown equivalent performance in this test prior to training, at posttest the rime-trained group significantly outperformed the control group in their reading performance. Peterson and Haines also found that the children with better segmentation skills benefited most from the analogy training. Analogy training in turn helped the development of segmentation skills. Similar findings have been reported by Ehri and Robbins (1992), in a study that found that children who were good segmenters benefited more from rime analogies when trying to read words written in an artificial orthography than children who were poor segmenters.

White and Cunningham (1990) also used a word family approach to analogy training (multiple examples), but they included phonological training in their study as well. The subjects in their study were 290 six- and seven-year-old children in a particular school district in Hawaii, whose teachers had been trained to use an analogy reading programme based on onsets and rimes. A group of children from comparable schools in the same district, whose teachers had not received this analogy training, acted as controls. In addition to the analogy training, which was based on learning 200 clue words and their rime families, the children also worked intensively with rhyming words at an oral level. The training period lasted for an entire year, the first 4 months being spent in phonological training, and the next 8 months in linking phonology and orthography via analogy. At the end of this year, the children in the analogy classrooms were significantly ahead of the children in the control classrooms in standardized measures of *both* decoding and comprehension. These results were replicated in a follow-up study conducted a year later, involving an equally large group of children (305). The children in the analogy classrooms clearly benefited from a rime-based training program. The success of this program may be partly due to the explicit emphasis that was placed on linking orthographic and phonological information at the level of the rime. Similar results concerning the linkage of orthographic and phonological information (using plastic letters) were reported by Bradley and Bryant (1983), and by Hatcher, Hulme, and Ellis (1994).

CONCLUSIONS

Studies investigating transfer in reading (analogies), nonsense word reading, and the effects of training reading at different phonological levels have all produced evidence for the notion that the rime is a crucial unit for the beginning reader of English. This conclusion is certainly consistent with the data on young children's orthographic analogies (Goswami, 1986, 1988, 1990b, 1991, 1993). Analogies depend crucially on the richness of the relevant knowledge base, and the data on children's reading analogies suggest that different representations of the orthography are available at different points in development. In particular, early representations depend on onsets and rimes. The patterns of orthographic transfer found in the analogy studies appear to be intimately connected with the developmental pattern of phonological awareness, because rimes seem to be more accessible than phonemes for young children. Children's initial orthographic representations might thus be driven by phonological knowledge. This idea has important implications for the design of connectionist models of reading development, both in terms of the level of representation that is specified in the models, and in terms of how this relates to phonology.

Regularity and consistency effects in children's nonsense word reading were then examined, and were shown to support the notion that orthographic rime units have special developmental salience. It was argued that if orthographic neighborhoods were defined in terms of shared rimes rather than according to Coltheart's (1978) N, existing data was consistent with the idea that young children use rime-based coding from the beginning of learning to read. In particular, it was shown that when monosyllabic words were equated for the familiarity of their constituent grapheme–phoneme correspondences, children showed a clear advantage in reading nonsense words that had many rime neighbors (O+P+ words) compared to nonsense words that had no rime neighbors (O–P+ words). This finding may imply that the notion that children can choose between a direct and an indirect route in learning to read is too simplistic (see Barron, 1986, for a review). Although the developed system may have access to these two routes to reading, for the developing system the acquisition of orthographic knowledge seems to be founded in phonological skills.

Finally, studies that have provided rime-based training in reading were considered (Bruck & Treiman, 1992; Ehri & Robbins, 1992; Peterson & Haines, 1992; White & Cunningham, 1990; Wise, Olson, & Treiman, 1990). It was found that rime analogy training benefited reading development most when the training lasted for a reasonable length of time (at least a month), when it involved multiple examples of analogy (the word family approach), and when it included phonological as well as orthographic training (explicitly linking shared rhyme to shared spelling patterns for rimes). The latter finding is entirely predictable from the notion that reading development depends on the active use of phonological knowledge to understand the orthography. Although different orthographies may be most usefully analyzed at different phonological levels, for young children learning to read English it can be concluded that the rime is a critical functional unit in this interactive process.

ACKNOWLEDGMENTS

I would like to thank the head teachers, teachers, and children of the many schools in Oxford and Cambridge who took part in these studies. Support for this research was partly provided by a Medical Research Council Project Grant (G9326935N).

REFERENCES

Andrews, S. (1982). Phonological recoding: Is the regularity effect consistent? *Memory & Cognition, 10,* 565–575.
Barron, R. (1986). Word recognition in early reading: A review of the direct and indirect access hypotheses. *Cognition, 24,* 93–119.
Bradley, L., & Bryant, P. E. (1983). Categorising sounds and learning to read: A causal connection. *Nature, 310,* 419–421.
Brady, S., Fowler, A., & Gipstein, M. (in preparation). *Questioning the role of syllables and rimes in early phonological awareness.* Manuscript in preparation.
Brooks, L. (1977). Visual pattern in fluent word identification. In A. S. Reber & D. L. Scarborough (Eds.), *Towards a psychology of reading* (pp. 88–114). Hillsdale, NJ: Lawrence Erlbaum Associates.
Brown, A. L., & Kane, M. J. (1988). Preschool children can learn to transfer: Learning to learn and learning by example. *Cognitive Psychology, 20,* 493–523.
Brown, G. D. A., & Watson, F. L. (1993). *The development of alphabetic reading in children.* Manuscript submitted for publication.
Bruck, M., & Treiman, R. (1992). Learning to pronounce words: The limitations of analogies. *Reading Research Quarterly, 27,* 374–389.
Carlisle, J. F. (1991). Questioning the psychological reality of onset-rime as a level of phonological awareness. In S. A. Brady & D. P. Shankweiler, (Eds.), *Phonological processes in literacy* (pp. 85–95). Hillsdale, NJ: Lawrence Erlbaum Associates.
Coltheart, M. (1978). Lexical access in simple reading tasks. In G. Underwood (Ed.), *Strategies in information processing* (pp. 151–216). San Diego, CA: Academic.
Coltheart, V., & Leahy, J. (1992). Children's and adult's reading of nonwords: Effects of regularity and consistency. *Journal of Experimental Psychology, Learning, Memory, and Cognition, 18,* 718–729.
Ehri, L. C. (1992). Reconceptualising sight word reading. In P. B. Gough, L. C. Ehri, & R. Treiman (Eds.), *Reading acquisition* (pp. 107–143). Hillsdale, NJ: Lawrence Erlbaum Associates.

Ehri, L. C., & Robbins, C. (1992). Beginners need some decoding skill to read words by analogy. *Reading Research Quarterly, 27*, 12–28.
Fox, B., & Routh, D. K. (1975). Analysing spoken language into words, syllables and phonemes: A developmental study. *Journal of Psycholinguistic Research, 4*, 331–342.
Frith, U. (1985). Beneath the surface of developmental dyslexia. In K. Patterson, M. Coltheart, & J. Marshall (Eds.), *Surface dyslexia* (pp. 301–330). Cambridge, England: Academic.
Gaskins, I. W., Downer, M. A., Anderson, R. C., Cunningham, P. M., Gaskins, R. W., & Schommer, M. (1988). A metacognitive approach to phonics: Using what you know to decode what you don't know. *Remedial & Special Education, 9*, 36–41.
Gaskins, I. W., Downer, M. A., & Gaskins, R. W. (1986). *Introduction to the Benchmark School word identification/vocabulary development program*. Media, PA: Benchmark.
Goswami, U. (1986). Children's use of analogy in learning to read: A developmental study. *Journal of Experimental Child Psychology, 42*, 73–83.
Goswami, U. (1988). Orthographic analogies and reading development. *Quarterly Journal of Experimental Psychology, 40A*, 239–268.
Goswami, U. (1990a). Phonological priming and orthographic analogies in reading. *Journal of Experimental Child Psychology, 49*, 323–340.
Goswami, U. (1990b). A special link between rhyming skills and the use of orthographic analogies by beginning readers. *Journal of Child Psychology and Psychiatry, 31*, 301–311.
Goswami, U. (1991). Learning about spelling sequences: The role of onsets and rimes in analogies in reading. *Child Development, 62*, 1110–1123.
Goswami, U. (1992). *Analogical reasoning in children*. Hillsdale, NJ: Lawrence Erlbaum Associates.
Goswami, U. (1993). Toward an interactive analogy model of reading development: Decoding vowel graphemes in beginning reading. *Journal of Experimental Child Psychology, 56*, 443–475.
Goswami, U., & Bryant, P. E. (1990). *Phonological skills and learning to read*. Hillsdale, NJ: Lawrence Erlbaum Associates.
Goswami, U., & Mead, F. (1992). Onset and rime awareness and analogies in reading. *Reading Research Quarterly, 27*, 152–162.
Hatcher, P. J., Hulme, C., & Ellis, A. W. (1994). Ameliorating early reading failure by integrating the teaching of reading and phonological skills: The phonological linkage hypothesis. *Child Development, 65*, 41–57.
Juel, C. (1988). Learning to read and write: A longitudinal study of 54 children from first through fourth grades. *Journal of Educational Psychology, 80*, 437–447.
Kirtley, C., Bryant, P., Maclean, M., & Bradley, L. (1989). Rhyme, rime and the onset of reading. *Journal of Experimental Child Psychology, 48*, 224–245.
Laxon, V., Coltheart, V., & Keating, C. (1988). Children find friendly words friendly too. *British Journal of Educational Psychology, 58*, 103–119.
Laxon, V., Masterson, J., & Coltheart, V. (1991). Some bodies are easier: The effects of consistency and regularity on children's reading. *Quarterly Journal of Experimental Psychology, 43A*, 793–825.
Laxon, V., Masterson, J., Pool, J., & Keating, C. (1992). Nonword naming: Further exploration of the pseudohomophone effect in terms of orthographic neighbourhood size, grapheme changes, spelling–sound consistency, and reader accuracy. *Journal of Experimental Psychology, Learning, Memory, and Cognition, 18*, 730–748.
Lovett, M. W., Warren-Chaplin, P. M., Ransby, M. J., & Borden, S. L. (1990). Training the word recognition skills of dyslexic children: Treatment and transfer effects. *Journal of Educational Psychology, 82*, 769–780.
Lundberg, I., Frost, J., & Petersen, O. (1988). Effects of an extensive programme for stimulating phonological awareness in pre-school children. *Reading Research Quarterly, 23*, 163–284.

Lundberg, I., Olofsson, Å., & Wall, S. (1980). Reading and spelling skills in the first school years predicted from phonemic awareness skills in kindergarten. *Scandinavian Journal of Psychology, 21,* 159–173.

Maclean, M., Bryant, P.,E., & Bradley, L. (1987). Rhymes, nursery rhymes and reading in early childhood. *Merrill-Palmer Quarterly, 33,* 255–282.

Marsh G., Friedman, M. P., Welch V., & Desberg P. (1981). A cognitive-developmental approach to reading acquisition. In G. E. MacKinnon & T. G. Waller (Eds.), *Reading research: Advances in theory and practice* (Vol. 3, pp. 199–221). New York: Academic.

Morais, J. (1991). Constraints on the development of phonemic awareness. In S. A. Brady & D. P. Shankweiler (Eds.), *Phonological processes in literacy* (pp. 5–27). Hillsdale, NJ: Lawrence Erlbaum Associates.

Morais, J., Alegria, J., & Content, A. (1987). The relationships between segmental analysis and alphabetic literacy: An interactive view. *Cahiers de Psychologie Cognitive, 7,* 415–438.

Perfetti, C. (1992). The representation problem in reading acquisition. In P. B. Gough, L. C. Ehri, & R. Treiman (Eds.), *Reading acquisition* (pp. 145–174). Hillsdale, NJ: Lawrence Erlbaum Associates.

Perfetti, C., Beck, I., Bell, L., & Hughes, C. (1987). Phonemic knowledge and learning to read are reciprocal: A longitudinal study of first grade children. *Merrill-Palmer Quarterly, 33,* 283–319.

Peterson, M. E., & Haines, L. P. (1992). Orthographic analogy training with kindergarten children: Effects on analogy use, phonemic segmentation, and letter–sound knowledge. *Journal of Reading Behaviour, 24,* 109–127.

Reber, A. S. (1967). Implicit learning of artificial grammars. *Journal of Verbal Learning and Verbal Behaviour, 6,* 855–863.

Reitsma, P. (1983). Printed word reading in beginning readers. *Journal of Experimental Child Psychology, 36,* 321–339.

Seymour, P. K., & Elder, L. (1986). Beginning reading without phonology. *Cognitive Neuropsychology, 3,* 1–36.

Seymour, P. K., & Evans, H. M. (1994). Levels of phonological awareness and learning to read. *Reading and Writing, 6,* 221–250.

Snowling, M. J. (1980). The development of grapheme–phoneme correspondence in normal and dyslexic readers. *Journal of Experimental Child Psychology, 29,* 294–305.

Stage, S. A., & Wagner, R. K. (1992). Development of young children's phonological and orthographic knowledge as revealed by their spellings. *Developmental Psychology, 28,* 287–296.

Stanback, M. L. (1992). Syllable and rime patterns for teaching reading: Analysis of a frequency-based vocabulary of 17,602 words. *Annals of Dyslexia, 42,* 196–221.

Stanovich, K. E., Cunningham, A. E., & Cramer, B. R. (1984). Assessing phonological awareness in kindergarten: Issues of task comparability. *Journal of Experimental Child Psychology, 38,* 175–190.

Stuart, M., & Coltheart, M. (1988). Does reading develop in a sequence of stages? *Cognition, 30,* 139–181.

Treiman, R. (1988). The internal structure of the syllable. In G. Carlson & M. Tanenhaus (Eds.), *Linguistic structure in language processing* (pp. 27–52). Dordrecht, The Netherlands: Kluwer.

Treiman, R. (1992). The role of intrasyllabic units in learning to read and spell. In P. B. Gough, L. C. Ehri, & R. Treiman (Eds.), *Reading acquisition* (pp. 65–106). Hillsdale, NJ: Lawrence Erlbaum Associates.

Treiman, R., Goswami, U., & Bruck, M. (1990). Not all nonwords are alike: Implications for reading development and theory. *Memory and Cognition, 18,* 559–567.

Treiman, R., Mullennix, J., Bijeljac-Babic, R., & Richmond-Welty, E. D. (1995). The special role of rimes in the description, use and acquisition of English orthography. *Journal of Experimental Psychology: General, 124,* 107–136.

Treiman, R., & Zukowski, A. (1991). Levels of phonological awareness. In S. Brady & D. Shankweiler (Eds.) *Phonological processes in literacy* (pp. 67–83). Hillsdale, NJ: Lawrence Erlbaum Associates.

Tunmer W. E., & Nesdale A. R. (1985). Phonemic segmentation skill and beginning reading. *Journal of Educational Psychology*, 77, 417–527.

Vellutino, F. R., & Scanlon, D. M. (1987). Phonological coding, phonological awareness and reading ability: Evidence from a longitudinal and experimental study. *Merrill-Palmer Quarterly*, 33, 321–363.

Wagner, R. K. (1988). Causal relations between the development of phonological processing abilities and the acquisition of reading skills: A meta-analysis. *Merrill-Palmer Quarterly*, 34, 261–279.

Wagner, R. K., & Torgeson, J. K. (1987). The nature of phonological processing and its causal role in the acquisition of reading skills. *Psychological Bulletin*, 101, 192–212.

White, T. G., & Cunningham, P. M. (1990, April). *Teaching disadvantaged students to decode by analogy*. Paper presented at the annual meeting of the American Educational Research Association, Boston, MA.

Wimmer, H., & Goswami, U. (1994). The influence of orthographic consistency on reading development: Word recognition in English and German children. *Cognition*, 51, 91–103.

Wimmer, H., Landerl, K., & Schneider, W. (1994). The role of rhyme awareness in learning to read a regular orthography. *British Journal of Developmental Psychology*, 12, 469–484.

Wise, B. W., Olson, R. K., & Treiman, R. (1990). Subsyllabic units as aids in beginning readers' word learning: Onset-rime versus post-vowel segmentation. *Journal of Experimental Child Psychology*, 49, 1–19.

Wylie, R. E., & Durrell, D. D. (1970). *Elementary English*, 47, 787–791.

Yopp, H. K. (1988). The validity and reliability of phonemic awareness tests. *Reading Research Quarterly*, 23, 159–177.

Chapter 5

Word Reading by Sight and by Analogy in Beginning Readers

Linnea C. Ehri
City University of New York Graduate School

The focus of my chapter is on the beginning period when children first learn to read print.[1] My purpose is to portray the processes that they use to read words. It is clear from various lines of research (Adams, 1990; Perfetti, 1985; Rayner & Pollatsek, 1989) that the core of acquiring reading skill is learning to read individual words in a way that floods the reader's consciousness with meanings as his or her eyes fixate successively on individual words in lines of text.

Let me remind you that there are various ways to read words (Ehri, 1992, 1994). Words that have been read several times might be read by sight; that is, by remembering how they were read before and accessing this representation in lexical memory (Adams & Huggins, 1985; Ehri, 1980, 1992; Ehri & Saltmarsh, 1995; Reitsma, 1983). Less familiar words might be read by phonological recoding; that is, by transforming graphemes into phonemes and blending the phonemes into pronunciations with recognizable meanings (Carnine, 1977; Chall, 1983; Feitelson, 1988). Alternatively, less familiar words might be read by analogy; that is, by recognizing

---

[1]Information in this chapter was originally presented at a NATO institute in Portugal. The institute was attended by many language and reading researchers from around the world. Participants were grateful that everyone was able to spend 2 weeks sharing their ideas and findings and that NATO was willing to sponsor this very important meeting of minds.
    This work was supported in part by Grant No. HD-23719 awarded by the U.S. National Institute of Child Health and Human Development.

how they resemble known sight words (Glushko, 1979, 1981; Goswami, 1986; Marsh, Freidman, Welch, & Desberg, 1981). Or less familiar words might be read by relying on context cues or a combination of context and graphic cues to predict what the word might be (Goodman, 1976).

In case you doubt that word reading lies at the core of text reading skill, let me explain what has convinced me. I became interested in word reading when I attempted to study children's comprehension of text and how it might be improved (Ehri & Wilce, 1974). I tried to select text that I thought children in second through fourth grades would find interesting and comprehensible. However, there were always some words that some children did not read accurately in any story we picked, and this thwarted our efforts to measure how rapidly they read and what they understood about the text. I began to realize that the secret to adequate reading comprehension in beginning readers was competent word reading. If they could read the words, then they could comprehend the meaning of text (provided it made sense at their level of intelligence, vocabulary, and world knowledge). Thus, I turned my attention to a study of how children learn to read words.

Measures of word recognition and reading comprehension are very highly correlated, for example, $r = .74$ among first graders, $r = .69$ among second graders, as reported in a study by Juel, Griffith, and Gough (1986). Very high levels of word reading accuracy are required in order for texts to be readable. According to Clay (1985), word accuracy levels between 95% and 100% define a text as easy reading. Accuracy levels between 90% and 94% designate texts at a reader's instructional level. Accuracy levels between 80% and 89% indicate a hard text. In short, high levels of word reading accuracy are required to support adequate reading comprehension.

What enables readers to read words accurately as their eyes fixate on successive words during text reading? The commonly held view is that multiple sources operate to support word reading (Rumelhart, 1977). An interactive view of word reading is portrayed in Fig. 5.1. The multiple sources of information that contribute to text reading are portrayed as boxes surrounding the space where text is processed. Readers possess a lexicon of words (see bottom of Fig. 5.1), that is, a mental dictionary where sight words are stored in memory. When words that are known by sight appear in print, readers' brains access the words quickly and automatically with little attention or effort.

To experience what it means to recognize words automatically, perform the exercise in Fig. 5.2. Look at each picture of an object, proceed from left to right across each row, name the pictures as quickly as you can, and ignore the words printed on the pictures. You will find that it is not easy to name the pictures, that the words interfere and slow you down despite

5. WORD READING IN BEGINNERS

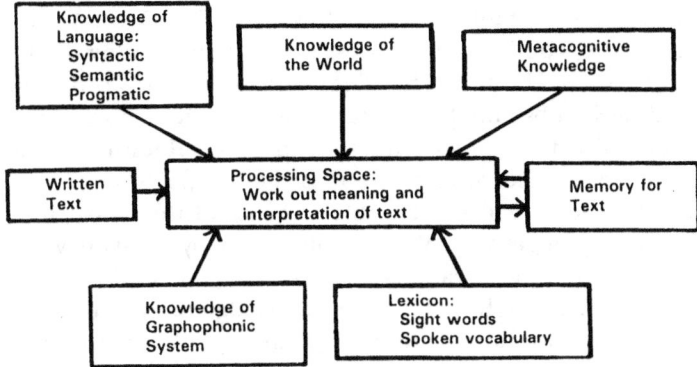

FIG. 5.1. Interactive model specifying sources of knowledge that contribute to the text reading process.

FIG. 5.2. Pictures printed with semantically related words that create interference in a task requiring subjects to name the pictures as rapidly as possible and to ignore the printed words. From "Learning to Read and Spell Words" by L. C. Ehri, 1987, *Journal of Reading Behavior, 19*, 5–31. Reprinted by permission of L. C. Ehri and the National Reading Conference.

your intention to ignore them. You suffer interference not only from competing pronunciations of the printed words but also from their meanings, which are activated automatically when the words are seen. Interference from meanings is evidenced by the fact that words in the same semantic category as the pictures ("cow" printed on the horse) slow readers down more in naming the pictures than words in different semantic categories ("cow" printed on the table) (Golinkoff & Rosinski, 1976). As early as the end of first grade, children can process words they know by sight automatically (Guttentag & Haith, 1978). The contribution of word automaticity to text reading is substantial. If most words in a text are recognized automatically by sight, this allows readers to proceed fluently and to devote full attention to the meaning of the text (Perfetti, 1985).

Of course, readers will not be able to read all the words in a text by sight, particularly beginners. Words not known by sight may be read in other ways, although these ways require attention and consume more processing time. Readers might apply their knowledge of grapheme–phoneme relations (i.e., graphophonetic knowledge in Fig. 5.1) to convert the spelling into a pronunciation that they recognize as a word, referred to as *phonological recoding*. They might pronounce a word by recognizing how it is analogous to a word they already know by sight. They might use context clues alone or in combination with letter–sound clues to guess what the word is.

Contextual support for word identification comes from several sources identified in Fig. 5.1. Readers have memory for the text read up to that point. They have knowledge of the world. These sources create expectations for readers about the meanings of words being read. Also, readers' linguistic knowledge yields expectations about the form class (syntactic function) of words occurring in specific positions within sentences. Several studies indicate that words are read more accurately in context than in isolation (Ehri & Wilce, 1980a; Goodman, 1965; Nicholson, 1991), showing that contextual expectations enhance the accuracy of word identification, particularly when readers do not know the words by sight or when they have difficulty decoding the words.

An important outcome of the interactive processes involved in text reading is redundancy, according to Perfetti (1985). Each word is processed not just in one or another single way but in multiple ways operating simultaneously. A word may be identified through one source but its identity may be confirmed by other sources, thus creating redundancy in the system. For example, a particular word may be identified by sight because lexical access is fast operating. World knowledge and linguistic knowledge may immediately confirm that the word fits syntactic and semantic expectations. Graphophonic knowledge may verify that the word's pronunciation corresponds to its spelling pattern. In this way, readers' text reading accuracy is maintained at a high level by multiple sources of knowledge operating in parallel.

Reading educators such as Goodman (1972, 1976) have been critical of claims that readers read individual words when they read text. This is because individual word reading is regarded as requiring too much attention and effort, and hence disrupting comprehension. According to Goodman, graphic cue sampling combined with contextual guessing are the primary means used to read words.

I hope it is already apparent why Goodman's view is faulty. Automatic access of sight words in lexical memory requires little attention and effort, probably much less than the procedure of guessing words. Because the written forms of sight words are represented fully in memory, there is no need to sample graphic cues and guess words. Moreover, the most important words in text are too unpredictable to be guessed accurately (Gough & Walsh, 1991). Eye movement studies have shown that readers look at most words in text. They do not skip words that can be predicted from context clues (McConkie & Zola, 1981). Skilled readers are highly adept at automatic lexical access and decoding, and they expend little attention or effort performing these processes (Ehri & Wilce, 1983; Guttentag & Haith, 1978). This allows them to devote their full attention to comprehending meaning.

In sum, I hope it is clear that learning to read words in multiple ways accurately and automatically is fundamental to acquiring text reading skill. This is why I have concentrated on studying how beginners learn to read words.

LEARNING TO READ WORDS BY SIGHT

Sight word reading involves the process of reading words that have been read several times before, by accessing information about the words in memory. The term *sight* indicates that sight of the word triggers that word in memory, including information about its spelling, pronunciation, and meaning.

Misconceptions about sight word reading persist. One is that only irregularly spelled words are read by sight. This is not true—all words, once they have been read a few times, become sight words, even easily decoded words. Another confusion is between process and instructional method. Some educators regard sight word reading as the method of teaching students to read words printed in isolation on flashcards. This also is not true—sight word reading refers to the *process* of reading words via lexical access. Readers acquire sight words mainly by reading words in context rather than in isolation. Another misconception is that sight word learning is governed by very different processes from phonological recoding, and that acquisition involves rote memorizing the visual forms of words, including their shapes. This too is not true—the research we have conducted over the years reveals that sight word learning is phonological at root (Ehri, 1978, 1980, 1984, 1987, 1992).

How are sight words stored in memory? The key capability to explain is how readers can look at any printed word on a page and locate that particular word in memory. Requirements for an adequate explanation are stiff. The nature of the *connection* that links the written form of the word to its lexical entry in memory must be explained. The connection must be one that enables the reader to distinguish among thousands of words in the lexicon; that leads to one particular word including its pronunciation and meaning quickly, accurately, and automatically; and that enables readers to ignore all the many other similarly spelled words. Also, the connection must be easy to learn. According to Reitsma's (1983) study, only four exposures to words are needed for beginning readers to retain information about sight words in memory.

There are two competing views about the nature of the connections that are formed. According to the traditional *visual-route* view, connections are formed between the visual features of words and their meanings (Coltheart, 1978). These relationships are unsystematic and arbitrary, and so they must be rote memorized through repeated practice. According to the alternative *visual-phonological* route view, connections are formed between letters in the spellings of specific words and phonemes detected in their pronunciations (Ehri, 1980, 1987, 1992). Readers utilize their knowledge of the graphophonic system to form these connections for specific words. These connections are stored in memory and provide the lexical access path to read the word.

This difference can be illustrated with the following example. If sight words are learned by rote, then it should not matter whether the spelling LFT stands for the word *elephant* or the word *monkey*. Both should be equally easy to learn with repetition and practice. In actuality, it does matter. LFT as a symbol for *elephant* is much easier to learn provided the learner knows that the letters *L, F,* and *T* typically symbolize the sounds /l/, /f/, and /t/, respectively, and provided the learner can detect these three sounds in the word's pronunciation. With this knowledge, connections can be formed between the printed form of the word and the word's pronunciation stored in memory. These connections are illustrated in Fig. 5.3. In contrast to LFT-*elephant* connections that are systematic because they conform to the reader's knowledge of grapheme–phoneme correspondences, the connections formed between LFT and *monkey* are arbitrary, unsystematic, and must be memorized on their own without help from any mnemonic system. Such connections take longer to learn, they are harder to remember, and hence are less reliable.

Although easier to learn and remember, connections such as LFT for *elephant* present one problem: There are other words that LFT might also symbolize, such as *left* or *lift*. LFT as a spelling of *elephant* does not exclude these other words, and hence is not fully reliable. However, if a fuller spelling symbolizing all phonemes were provided, then the spelling would be completely reliable because it would fully specify that word and exclude

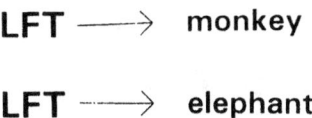

FIG. 5.3. Illustration of possible connections formed between written words and their pronunciations by readers to store sight words in lexical memory.

all other words. Such a fully connected spelling is illustrated in Fig. 5.3. For readers who apply their knowledge of the spelling system to interpret all of the graphemes as symbols for phonemes in the word, they may even conclude that certain ambiguous sounds such as the "schwa" vowels occurring in unstressed syllables are really the short vowel sounds suggested by letters, *-eph*, and *-ant*. I have suggested that this process of optimizing the correspondences between letters seen in spellings of words and sounds detected in pronunciations is the way that sight words are stored fully in memory (Ehri, 1984, 1992; Ehri & Wilce, 1980b, 1986).

When do beginning readers become able to use their alphabetic knowledge to learn sight words by forming graphophonic connections? We reasoned that before children know much about letters and phonemic segmentation, they probably learn sight words by forming connections between salient visual features of written words and their meanings, referred to as *visual cue reading*. Frith (1985) referred to this early period as the *logographic phase* of word reading, but more recently I have relabeled this the *pre-alphabetic phase*. The reason for changing the label is to distinguish visual cue reading, which involves the selection of one or another cue, from true logographic reading such as that performed by readers of Chinese who process words as visual Gestalts (Ehri, 1995).

Gough, Juel, and Griffith (1992) have provided examples of visual cue reading. If a thumbprint happens to appear next to a word such as *wagon*, visual cue readers ignore the letters and remember the thumbprint. Visual cue readers may remember that *camel* has two humps in the middle, or that *look* has two eyes in the middle. Visual cue reading is how emergent readers are able to read environmental print, by noting salient visual features accompanying the print, such as the arches behind McDonalds (Masonheimer, Drum, & Ehri, 1984). They learn to read the environment, not the print (Mason, 1980). (For more information on this phase of word reading, see Ehri, 1991, 1994.)

Once children learn about letter–name or letter–sound relations and how to use this knowledge to link letters seen in spellings of words to sounds heard in their pronunciations, they should be capable of forming connections between salient letters and sounds in order to remember how to read the words by sight. We have called this *phonetic cue reading*.

We performed a study to examine whether visual cue reading and phonetic cue reading characterize how beginners remember how to read words at different phases of reading development, and to determine what capabilities might account for the shift from one approach to the other (Ehri & Wilce, 1985). We selected six words and created two different kinds of spellings: a set of visually distinctive spellings and a set of simplified phonetic spellings. These are shown in Fig. 5.4. The set of visually salient spellings consisted of letters that varied in size, thus creating words with distinctive shapes. None of the letters corresponded to any sounds in the words. The set of phonetic spellings consisted of letters that corresponded to some sounds in the words. The visual forms of these words were less distinctive, with all letters uniform in size. Children were given several trials to learn to read the two types of spellings. On the first trial, we told them how to read the words. On subsequent trials, they tried to remember how to read the words and were given feedback if incorrect. We measured the number of words read correctly on each trial.

Nouns	Phonetic Spelling	Visual Spelling
GIRAFFE SET		
knee	NE	Fo
giraffe	JRF	WBC
balloon	BLUN	xGsT
turtle	TRDL	yMp
mask	MSK	uHe
scissors	SZRS	qDjK
ELEPHANT SET		
arm	RM	Fo
diaper	DIPR	xGsT
elephant	LFT	WBC
comb	KOM	uHe
pencil	PNSL	qDjK
chicken	HKN	yMLp

FIG. 5.4. Visual and phonetic spellings that children were taught to read in the word learning task.

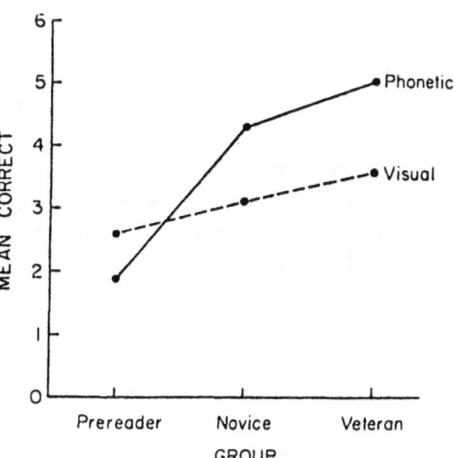

FIG. 5.5. Mean number of phonetic and visual spellings read correctly in the word learning task as a function of beginning reader group. From "Movement into Reading: Is the First Stage of Printed Word Learning Visual or Phonetic?" by L. C. Ehri and L. S. Wilce, 1987, *Reading Research Quarterly, 20*, 163–179. Reprinted with permission of the International Reading Association. All rights reserved.

We reasoned that if beginners look for salient visual features to remember how to read words, then they should learn to read the visual spellings more readily than the phonetic spellings. However, if they are capable of forming connections between letters and sounds to remember how to read words, then they should learn the phonetic spellings more readily than the visual spellings.

To examine whether beginners at different points in their reading development find one type of spelling easier to learn than the other type, we selected kindergarteners and divided them into three reading ability groups: Prereaders who had not mastered letters and could read few if any preprimer words; novices who knew all the letters and read a few preprimer words; veterans who knew letters and read several preprimer words. We expected that the prereaders would be visual cue readers and would remember how to read the visual spellings more easily than the phonetic spellings, whereas the novices and veterans, having knowledge of letters, would find the phonetic spellings easier to learn. This is what we found. Mean scores are depicted in Fig. 5.5. These findings support the concepts of visual cue reading and phonetic cue reading as two different ways in which beginners remember how to read sight words, and they indicate that the shift from visual to phonetic cues happens very early in development, as soon as beginners learn the alphabet and before they acquire phonological recoding skill. (See Byrne, 1992; Byrne & Fielding-Barnsley, 1989, 1990; Scott & Ehri, 1989, for additional evidence bearing on this issue.)

The idea that novice beginning readers utilize phonetic cues to remember how to read sight words was pursued by Rack, Hulme, Snowling, and Wightman (1994). Their purpose was to verify that novice beginners were indeed reliant on phonetic relations linking spellings of words to their pronunciations. In our study, many of the letters in our phonetic spellings were present in conventional spellings of the words, so our subjects might have learned them more easily because they were familiar with the conventional spellings.

To explore sight word learning in beginners, Rack et al. (1994) created two types of simplified spellings of words. Both types consisted of three or four letters, and all but one of the letters in each spelling symbolized sounds detectable in the word's pronunciation. It was the odd letter that distinguished the two sets of spellings. In one set of spellings, the odd letter was phonetically close to a sound in the pronunciation because it was the *voicing mate* of the sound; for example, the P in TPL spelling *table*, the K in KDN spelling *garden*. Voicing mates have identical places of articulation but differ in whether or not the vocal cords vibrate to produce the sound; for example, /p/ and /b/, /k/ and /g/. In the other set of spellings, the odd letter was phonetically more distant; for example, the G in TGL (*table*), the B in BDN (*garden*). Neither odd letter was found in the correct spellings of the words. These odd letters occurred either in initial or medial positions of the spellings.

Novice beginners who knew most letters but could read only a few words and could not decode any words were selected for the study. They were given several trials to learn to read the two kinds of spellings. The authors reasoned that if novices were indeed using phonetic cues to remember how to read the words, they should learn the phonetically close spellings more easily than the distant spellings. This is what they found in two replications of the experiment.

These findings provide support for the concept of phonetic cue reading as a way of reading words that is distinct from phonological recoding. The words that subjects learned to read could not be read by sounding out and blending, but instead had to be accessed from memory (e.g., BFR, KVI, GRFI, PTL, TKT to symbolize *beaver, coffee, gravy, puddle,* and *target,* respectively). There were enough letters to enable learners to form connections between spellings and pronunciations to store specific words in memory, but not enough letters to support phonological recoding. Subjects were able to make use of the letters that were phonetically close to sounds in the words but were phonemically inaccurate (i.e., voicing mates), indicating that beginning readers are sensitive to phonetic relations between spellings and pronunciations of words.

Findings challenge the idea proposed by Frith (1985) and Gough and Hillinger (1980) that beginners are limited to using visual information to read words prior to the time they acquire phonological recoding skill. These findings, combined with those of our studies (Ehri & Wilce, 1985; Scott & Ehri, 1989), show that children who lack phonological recoding skill can nevertheless use their alphabetic knowledge to read words. In other words, there is an intermediate phase in the development of word reading that comes between visual cue reading and mature alphabetic recoding, a rudimentary alphabetic phase consisting of phonetic cue reading.

Rack et al. (1994) performed a third experiment to show that the same processes enable beginners to remember how to read conventional spellings of real words. Two kinds of words were selected: words with transparent spellings exhibiting straightforward correspondences between letters and sounds (e.g., *march, garden, nose*); and words with opaque spellings containing at least one phonetically atypical letter (e.g., *bomb, island, knee*). Novice beginning readers were given several trials to learn to read these words. It was expected that transparent spellings would permit readers to form more direct connections than would opaque spellings, and thus they would learn to read transparent spellings more easily than opaque spellings. This is what was found. These results support the idea that sight word learning involves a process of forming connections between spellings and pronunciations of words, and that beginning readers use this process not simply in the laboratory when they learn to read simplified spellings invented by us, but also when they learn to read the conventional spellings of real words.

READING WORDS BY ANALOGY

I have shown you how beginning readers are thought to learn to read words by sight, according to our theory and research. Another way to read words involves applying one's knowledge of sight words to read unfamiliar words that are analogous to the sight words; for example, having the word *beak* in your lexicon, encountering *peak* for the first time, and reading the new word by recognizing how it is similar to the known word. One issue that has divided researchers centers on the question of when beginning readers become able to read unfamiliar words by analogy to known sight words. What capabilities enable them to read words in this way?

Goswami (1986) proposed that reading words by analogy is one of the earliest methods used, one that appears even before beginners are able to phonologically recode words (Goswami & Bryant, 1990). One reason why this method is more accessible to beginners is that it is easier for them to segment and blend subsyllabic units consisting of onsets and rimes (e.g., /p/-/ik/ in *peak*) than to segment and blend phonemic units (e.g., /p/-/i/-/k/) (Treiman, 1985, 1986, 1992). Rimes are defined as the pronounced vowel and all that follows it in the syllable; onsets consist of anything that precedes the rime in the syllable.

In several studies, Goswami (1986, 1988, 1990a, 1990b) showed that reading words by analogy is performed more easily by beginners than reading words by phonological recoding. In her studies, beginners were taught to read a clue word, such as *beak*. The clue word was kept in view, and subjects were shown and asked to read several unfamiliar words and nonwords, some analogous to the clue (e.g., *bean, beal, peak, neak*), and some not (e.g., *lake, pake*). She observed that more analogs were read correctly than were control words. Analogs sharing rimes with clue words were correct most often. Even children who could read no words on a standardized word reading test were observed to read a few words by rime analogy.

However, a task analysis of what is required to read monosyllabic words by analogy raises doubt that analogizing is possible without rudimentary decoding skill. In order to read *peak* by analogy to *beak*, readers must be able to do several things:

1. They must recognize how the two words are both similar and different.
2. They must be able to segment the spoken and written words into onsets and rimes, and recognize how letters match up to spoken segments.
3. They must recognize what sound the onset letter in the unfamiliar word symbolizes (P = /p/), and they must be able to blend the new onset with the old rime to say the new word.
4. In addition, if the clue word is not present during the reading task but must be accessed in memory as a sight word, then readers must posess sufficient memory for letters in the sight word to recognize the partial correspondence between the known and new words.

This analysis makes it apparent that analogizing requires several aspects of decoding skill: knowledge of letter–sound correspondences, onset-rime segmentation and blending skill, and sufficient knowledge of the graphophonic system to retain a letter-analyzed representation of sight words in memory.

According to our research (Ehri & Wilce, 1985, 1987a, 1987b), nonreaders and novice beginning readers would not be expected to succeed at reading new words by analogy to known words because they lack some of the requisites. They lack the blending skill needed to combine new onsets with old rimes. They lack sufficient memory for letters in sight words. Being phonetic cue readers, they possess only partial knowledge of letters in sight words, so when they see new words sharing letters with known sight words, they mistake the new words for the known words, hence misreading *peak* as *beak*.

We performed a study to examine whether some decoding skill was required to read words by analogy (Ehri & Robbins, 1992). We selected

5. WORD READING IN BEGINNERS

kindergartners and first graders and gave them a nonword reading task to distinguish those who could decode at least a couple words from those who could not. We reasoned that decoders would possess the requisite skills needed to read words by analogy, whereas nondecoders would not. Subjects were assigned either to an experimental or to a control group. Both groups were taught to read a set of five words. On reaching criterion, they were shown five new transfer words and asked to read them. For the experimental subjects, the words were analogous to words they had learned. For control subjects, they were not analogous but contained the same letter–sound relations found in training words. The words learned in the various conditions are presented in Table 5.1. The words had novel (nonstandard) but systematic spellings, and the system was explained to children when they learned the words: "The middle two letters have a line over them. The line tells you that the letters say their own name in the word."

We created spellings for words that we thought would be easy for novice beginners to analyze graphophonically. The letters in spellings all had names that included the relevant sounds (e.g., RĀĀN for *rain*, consisting of R whose name "ar" includes /r/, A saying its own name, and N whose name "en" includes /n/). The letters were printed in capitals, which are more familiar to beginners than lower-case letters. (The only exception was lower case *i*, to avoid confusion between *I* and *l*.) The transfer words were made easier to read by including continuant /s/ at the beginning of all the words.

Pretests verified that the analogy and control groups did not differ in their reading ability. After subjects reached criterion in reading the training words, they received a transfer task in which they attempted to read the transfer words without any help. They were told, "Now I am going to show you some new words. These words all begin with the letter S. The letters that come after S will be the same as you saw before in the other words. Look at each word and try to read it by remembering how you read the other words. If you don't know what it says, try to figure it out." This yielded a measure of their ability to attack new words by analogizing.

TABLE 5.1
Words Read in the Analogy and Control Conditions
During Training and in the Transfer Tasks

Analogy Words	Control Words	Transfer Words
KĀĀV (cave)	RĀĀN (rain)	SĀĀV (save)
FĒĒL (feel)	KĒĒP (keep)	SĒĒL (seal)
MĪĪN (mine)	FĪĪT (fight)	SĪĪN (sign)
RŌŌP (rope)	BŌŌL (bowl)	SŌŌP (soap)
BŪŪT (boot)	MŪŪV (move)	SŪŪT (suit)

Note. Spellings are printed in capital letters, pronunciations in parentheses.

Results revealed that analogizing benefited decoders but it did not benefit nondecoders. Among decoders, the analogy group read significantly more words correctly than the control group, $M = 1.84$ versus 0.84 words correct (5 words maximum). Among nondecoders, most subjects (90%) failed to read any words correctly in both conditions. Analysis of nondecoders' errors revealed that they tended to misread new words as old words when the words shared letters, indicating the use of phonetic cue reading. For example, the transfer word SiiN (*sign*) was misread as the training word MiiN (*mine*). Decoders never made this error. Rather, most of their misreadings began with /s/, which precluded the training words.

From an analysis of subjects' misreadings, it was apparent that the most salient cues used by phonetic cue readers were the vowels consisting of doubled letters topped by a horizontal bar. Some nondecoders exhibited attempts to delete and blend sounds in reading the transfer words, but without complete success. For example, one child looked at SAAV, responded with the training word "cave," and then modified his answer to "scave." Another child noticed the difference between training and transfer words but could not read the new word, saying "It's like FiiT with two i's but it starts with S."

Our results supported Goswami's (1986) assertion that it is easier for beginners to read new words by analogy than by phonological recoding. However, our findings did not support her claim that analogizing is the earliest form of word reading and that even nonreaders and novice beginners can do it. Rather, our findings indicated that beginners must possess rudimentary decoding skill to be able to analogize in reading new words.

One difference between our study and Goswami's studies is that we required children to access the clue words *in memory,* whereas Goswami kept the clue words *in view* as her beginners read the transfer words. Clearly our task was harder than hers. The reason we imposed a memory requirement on readers was because this is closer to what they must do when they analogize in their reading outside the laboratory. It may be that nondecoders, when relieved of this memory requirement, can analogize easily. To examine this possibility, we extracted the relevant data from a study by Goswami and Mead (1992). In their study, children were divided into decoders and nondecoders based on their performance on a nonword reading task, with decoders defined as those reading more than one nonword and nondecoders defined as those reading one or zero nonwords, the same criteria we used. Subjects had the clue words to look at when they read analogous and control words. Of interest was how well nondecoders read analogous words when they had the clue words in view. We reasoned that if graphophonic analytic skill is central to analogizing, then novice readers should not do much better with base words in view.

5. WORD READING IN BEGINNERS

To review the details of this study, children were first pretested for their ability to read analogous and control word sets. Then they were taught to read a clue word, for example, *beak*, which they were told could help them read some of the words they had just tried to read in the pretest. Then the analogous and control words were presented for reading. To illustrate, for the clue word *beak*, the test words presented were *peak, weak, speak, bask, bank,* and *lake*. Results revealed that nondecoders read many fewer words by analogy than decoders: $M = 1.7$ versus 6.2 correct (9 maximum). In fact, nondecoders' scores were not far above zero. They read slightly more words by analogy when the clue words were present than when the clue words were not present (on the pretest): $M = 1.67$ versus 0.75 words correct. Nondecoders read few if any control words.

Goswami and Mead (1992) interpreted their findings to indicate that nondecoders did exhibit analogizing. However, there is room for doubt. The mean was quite low. We are not told what proportion of the subjects failed to read any words by analogy, thus making it unclear how representative the mean is for the sample. The difference between the pretest and transfer test means involving analogous words was not tested for significance by itself, but only as part of a more complex ANOVA that included performances of decoders as well as nondecoders reading various types of analogous and control words on both pretests and transfer tests. Given the low mean scores, it is very likely that most nondecoders received zero scores on the pretest, and many may have scored zero on the experimental task as well. With so many zero scores, an ANOVA that included the nondecoders may have been less appropriate for testing effects of the variables than a nonparametric test. These uncertainties raise doubt about whether Goswami and Mead (1992) really showed what they claimed to have shown regarding the analogizing ability of nondecoders. From mean performances, it is apparent that, even with clue words in view, nondecoders did surprisingly little analogizing when they attempted to read the unfamiliar words. Our explanation is that nondecoders do not possess the analytic skills needed to match up, segment, and recombine the relevant parts of the clue and test words.

TRAINING NONDECODERS TO READ WORDS BY ANALOGY

We conducted a study to examine whether we could improve nondecoders' ability to read words by analogy by giving them specific forms of training. This study was an extension of the one described earlier by Ehri and Robbins (1992). We used similar nonstandard spellings of training and transfer words. We selected kindergartners and first graders ($N = 52$) who could name most of the uppercase target letters used to spell our words. Children were divided into decoders and nondecoders based on a nonword reading pretest ($N=41$ nondecoders, 19 decoders) and randomly assigned to either of two training conditions, a segmentation condition and a multiple word condition.

In the segmentation condition, students were taught to divide the training or base words into onsets and rimes as they learned to read them. For example, they would look at FEEL, read it as *feel*, then point to the two parts of the spelling and say "f" - "eel." This training procedure was expected to benefit readers by familiarizing them with the spelling–sound units shared by base and transfer words. In a previous study by Wise, Olson, and Treiman (1990), first graders remembered how to read a set of words better after they practiced reading the words by blending onsets and rimes than after they practiced reading the words by blending word parts segmented after the vowel.

In the multiple word condition, we taught children to read three sets of analogous training words containing rime subunits that were spelled and sounded the same. For example, Set 1 included *mine*, Set 2 included *fine* and Set 3 included *line*. This procedure was expected to set up in lexical memory multiple instances of sight words all sharing rime units.

To evaluate children's ability to analogize at the end of training, they were shown eight transfer words, half analogous to the training words they learned to read, and half nonanalogous but containing the same letter–sound relations. To illustrate, the training words were: KAAV, FEEL, MiiN, BUUT (*cave, feel, mine, boot*); the analogous transfer words were SAAV, SEEL, SiiN, SUUT (*save, seal, sign, suit*); the nonanalogous transfer words were: SAAL, SEEN, SiiT, SUUP (*sail, seen, sight, soup*). Students in the multiple word training condition learned to read the set listed above plus the following sets: DAAV, PEEL, LiiN, TUUT (*Dave, peel, line, toot*); BRAAV, MEEL, FiiN, RUUT (*brave, meal, fine, root*).[2] After reaching criterion with each set, they attempted to read the eight transfer words. Of interest was whether nondecoders in the two training conditions would reveal much ability to read any transfer words, and if so, whether they would read the analogous transfer words better than the nonanalogous transfer words.

For the 23 nondecoders who received segmentation training, results revealed that the majority failed to read any transfer words: 87% scored zero on the analogous words, and 91% scored zero on the nonanalogous

---

[2]Actually, the set of words contained one additional item, base words ROOP (*rope*), NOOP (*nope*), DOOP (*dope*), and transfer words SOOP (*soap*) and SOOV (*sove*, a nonword). We suspected that the analogous and nonanalogous transfer words might not be comparable in terms of learning ease, so we taught another group of subjects (not those included in the main study) to read the transfer words. We found that SOOP was much easier to learn to read than SOOV, and thus performances with these items were not scored in the main study.

words. Among the 18 nondecoders who learned to read multiple sets of training words, their failure rate was almost as high. After learning Set 1 training words, 78% failed to read any analogous transfer words and 78% failed to read any nonanalogous words. After learning Set 2, the proportions were 83% and 83%, respectively. After learning Set 3, the proportions were 67% and 78%, respectively. Thus, it is clear that the two forms of training did not improve nondecoders' ability to read words by analogy. In contrast, the training methods were effective with the 19 decoders. Far fewer received scores of zero reading analogous and nonanalogous transfer words, and performance with analogous words was superior to performance with nonanalogous words.[3]

These results indicate that our training procedures did not provide nondecoders with sufficient graphophonic analytic skill to analogize. One reason why the onset-rime segmentation training may not have been effective is that it did not teach students how to blend onsets and rimes but only how to segment them, and instruction was limited only to the five training words. Establishing multiple sight words with the same rime units in memory also did not exert much impact on analogizing among nondecoders. Our explanation is that, being phonetic cue readers, nondecoders stored only partial representations of the base words in memory when they learned to read them, so they lacked the letter knowledge about known words to recognize that they shared rime spellings with unfamiliar words.

CONTRIBUTION OF ANALOGIZING TO SIGHT WORD LEARNING

In the study by Ehri and Robbins (1992) and its extension described previously, we assessed the contribution of analogizing in two ways: one involving children's ability to attack new words, the other involving their sight word learning. To test sight word learning, students were told how to read the transfer S-words and were given several practice trials with feedback to see whether analogizing helped them remember how to read the words. This process of lexically accessing familiar words in memory we have called *sight word learning* (Ehri, 1991).

Let me review findings in the Ehri and Robbins (1992) study. Students learned to read the set of five training words to criterion and then were given five transfer words all beginning with S to read. Following this, they were given a word learning task in which they were shown each S-word and told how to read it. Then they were given five trials in which they

---

[3]There were too few decoders in each of the training conditions to determine whether one training method was more effective than the other.

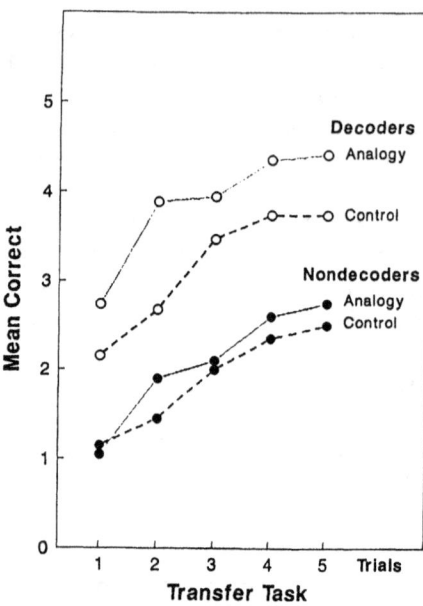

FIG. 5.6. Mean number of words read correctly in the transfer task by decoders and nondecoders in the analogy and control conditions. From "Beginners Need Some Decoding Skill to Read Words by Analogy" by L. Ehri and C. Robbins, 1992, *Reading Research Quarterly*, 27, 13–26. Reprinted with permission of the International Reading Association. All rights reserved.

practiced reading the S-words. If wrong, they were told the correct reading. Results are presented in Fig. 5.6, where it is apparent that children reading words analogous to training words outperformed children reading control words as the trials proceeded. The difference was statistically significant for decoders, but it fell short of significance for nondecoders. These findings reveal a second way that analogizing may benefit word reading—by helping beginners establish sight words in lexical memory when those words are analogous to words already known by sight.

In the follow-up study in which students received either onset-rime segmentation training or multiple base word training, we gave students practice reading the transfer S-words also. In this case, transfer words were practiced for three trials. Half of the words were analogous to training words and half were not. Results revealed that most nondecoders learned to read some of the words. By the third trial, 76% of the subjects read at least one word successfully. Nondecoders read significantly more analogous than control transfer words correctly, and their performance improved with practice. By Trial 3, the nondecoders were reading a mean of 1.4 analogous words but only 0.8 control words correctly (4 maximum).

These findings reveal that nondecoders did benefit from analogous relations between words in their ability to remember how to read new words with practice. That this benefit can be attributed to the training procedures is suggested by the fact that in our previous study where no special training was provided (Ehri & Robbins, 1992), nondecoders did not benefit from analogies in the word learning transfer task (see Fig. 5.6).

5. WORD READING IN BEGINNERS

As we have found in previous studies, remembering how to read words is an easier task than attacking new words to decode them. Apparently, analogizing can contribute to word memory processes at an earlier point in development than it can contribute to word decoding processes. Perhaps both training procedures made nondecoders sufficiently aware of sublexical rime units recurring in words, so that these units could be used for storing new words in lexical memory. This possibility awaits further study.

ISSUE: RELATIONSHIP OF ANALOGIZING TO INSTRUCTION

What is the relationship between analogizing and beginning reading instruction? Alternative views have been proposed and have stirred some controversy. These views differ in terms of whether instruction in analogizing is seen as preparation for explicit instruction in phonological recoding, whether analogizing instruction is seen as supplanting recoding instruction, or whether recoding instruction precedes analogizing instruction.

One view is the *bridge* view, in which teaching beginners to read by analogy provides a bridge easing the task of teaching them how to phonologically recode. In learning to analogize, children are taught how to segment and pronounce subsyllabic units, which include single graphophonic units appearing at the beginning or ending of syllables. Also in learning to analogize, children are taught to combine and recombine subsyllabic units, principally onsets and rimes (e.g., f-an, t-an, m-an, p-an). This provides instruction in blending. Learning grapheme–phoneme relationships and learning to blend are two essential ingredients that bring children partway in learning how to sound out and blend grapheme-phoneme units (i.e., phonological recoding). Having this partial, preparatory knowledge may better enable learners to benefit from recoding instruction. They will know some of the components, and the recoding operations will make more sense to them.

Another view of the relationship between analogizing and phonological recoding is that analogizing instruction is an alternative way of teaching children to use alphabetic relations in their reading and can supplant explicit recoding instruction. According to the *replacement view*, teaching children to process print–speech units larger than grapheme–phoneme correspondences is sufficient for enabling them to build a lexicon of words. They do not need to be taught to break the alphabetic system down into grapheme–phoneme units. One reason is that the system is less predictable at the graphophonic level than at a subsyllabic level. For example, the vowel O by itself may be pronounced in many ways, whereas the vowel O in the rime -OCK is pronounced one way. Teaching children to analogize serves to introduce them to print–speech mapping relations and the blending process. As they learn to process a greater variety of onsets and rimes within words, they are able to figure out on their own the rest of the system including those grapheme–phoneme-size units that are needed to work out mapping relations between print and speech.

A third view is the traditional *phonics* approach, previously cited. Chew (1994), a proponent of this view, challenged the claim that because children have difficulty segmenting and blending words using phoneme-size units, they should be taught first with larger subsyllabic units, principally onsets and rimes. Chew claimed that children may have difficulty segmenting and blending in the absence of instruction, but with adequate explicit instruction they can easily be taught letter–sound correspondences and how to blend them into words. Given adequate graphophonic instruction there is no need to begin with larger units.

One piece of evidence can be interpreted as bearing on this issue. Whereas our attempts to prompt analogizing in novice beginning readers yielded meager effects as reported previously, we performed another study with novices that exerted a huge impact on their ability to read new words as well as to remember how to read words with practice (Ehri & Wilce, 1987a). In this study, nondecoders were selected and assigned either to an experimental or a control group. The experimental group was taught to read several sets of similarly spelled words to criterion, mostly nonsense syllables including those with consonant clusters, such as BLUT, DRUB, SPUM, and LUND. Words were spelled using nine consonant letters and four short vowels. Similar spellings forced students to decode all the letters as they symbolized sounds in the words. The control group practiced letter–sound relations in isolation. At the end of training, students were given various posttests, including a nonword decoding test to verify effects of training and a task in which students practiced remembering how to read 15 real words.

We expected that the experimental group would function as *cipher readers* (a term coined by Gough & Hillinger, 1980) and would read words and nonwords skillfully because they had learned to phonologically recode print. In contrast, the control subjects would function as phonetic cue readers, they would have difficulty reading nonwords, and they would process only partial letter–sound cues in learning to read words. Our predictions were confirmed. As evident in Fig. 5.7, the cipher readers decoded many more nonsense words (not those they had studied during training) than did the cue readers, verifying that the cipher readers had much better phonological recoding skill. In the word learning task, subjects practiced reading a set of 15 similarly spelled real words such as DRIP, DRUM, DUMP, STAB, and STAMP for several trials. From Fig. 5.7, it is apparent

5. WORD READING IN BEGINNERS 107

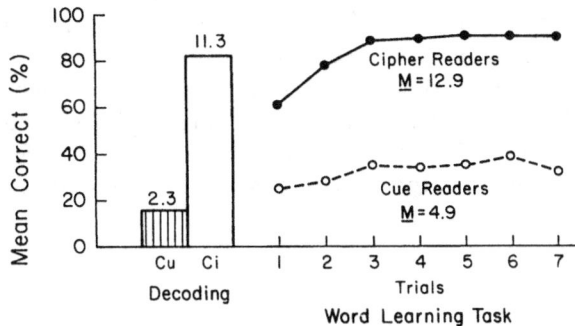

FIG. 5.7. Mean performances in the decoding and word learning posttests by novices after they received training as cipher (Ci) readers or cue (Cu) readers.

that cipher readers mastered the list within three trials, whereas cue never averaged more than 40% correct in reading the words. Analysis of cue readers' errors revealed that they were mixing up words with similar letters, indicating memory for partial cues in the words. These results reveal how powerful phonological recoding training is for enabling novice beginners to read words effectively.

I should point out that there were some subjects (i.e., 6 out of 15) who were not successful in acquiring recoding skill from our training procedure. However, the instruction we provided was neither extensive nor optimum. If we had spent more time with subjects and had given them more practice with a greater assortment of letter combinations in several different kinds of tasks that were more intrinsically motivating, we probably would have been more successful. Another limitation of the study was that the subjects who did learn to decode had above-average IQs. Whether improved instructional procedures would enable average children to acquire decoding skill as well awaits study. However, evidence from studies by Wallach and Wallach (1976), Williams (1980), and others who provided decoding training to average and at-risk beginning readers indicate that it is very possible.

The point of mentioning my study was to contrast its strong impact on the reading ability of novice readers with the weak showing apparent in studies of analogizing in novice readers discussed previously. I am concerned about the abandonment of direct code instruction in favor of analogy instruction. Standing alone, analogy instruction may be little more than another form of whole-word instruction if teachers never get around to teaching the code directly and if learners are not taught to analyze larger subsyllabic units into grapheme–phoneme correspondences. As Liberman pointed out in his chapter (see chap. 1, this volume), grapheme–phoneme correspondences are very hard to discover, even in transparent orthographies (which English is not). Thus, to expect average beginning readers to make this discovery in the course of being taught to read by analogy may be unrealistic and destined to failure for many children. The fact that phonological recoding is not easy to teach to beginners is further evidence that children are not going to pick it up on their own, and shows that we need to try even harder to develop effective instructional approaches that are classroom-friendly and can be incorporated easily by teachers into their instructional routines.

CONCLUSION

Learning to read words is fundamental for acquiring reading proficiency in English. Recent research on beginning reading has advanced our understanding about the acquisition of word reading skill. Our knowledge about how beginners learn to read sight words has been revised. Rather than rote memorizing sight words as visual Gestalts, students remember how to read sight words by forming connections between letters seen in the spellings of words and sounds detected in pronunciations of the words. In order for learners to establish complete representations of sight words in memory, they need to know how to segment pronunciations into phonemes and which graphemes typically symbolize phonemes in words. Without such knowledge, it is very difficult to remember how to read words by sight and to become a skilled reader.

The second advance in our knowledge of word reading involves the use of analogizing to read words. Students read unknown words by recognizing how the words have similar spelling patterns and pronunciations to words they already know how to read. Findings indicate that beginners can use an analogy strategy early in their development as readers. However, they need to have some analytic recoding skill to perform the operations involved in analogizing. Novices who lack sufficient recoding skill are less apt to read new words by analogy to known words, and are more apt to apply a phonetic cue reading strategy and mistake new words for known words because the two words share some letter cues. In order for analogizing to operate as an effective reading strategy, students must acquire a sizable store of sight words whose constituent letters are fully represented in memory. As children build larger lexicons of fully represented sight words, they will have more words available for analogizing, as Bowey and Hansen (1994) showed.

These advances in our understanding of how beginners learn to read words convey one very important implication for instruction: They show that grapheme–phoneme correspondences and phonological recoding skill are essential for students to acquire at the outset of their development as readers. This knowledge is needed to build a vocabulary of fully remembered sight words as well as to attack new words successfully, by either graphophonic recoding or analogizing. The acquisition of graphophonic analytic skill should not be left up to chance or to self-discovery; it should be taught systematically by first-grade teachers. Their classroom instruction should include informal testing to verify that these essential skills are being acquired, and extra tutorial steps should be taken with students who are failing to respond.

REFERENCES

Adams, M. (1990). *Beginning to read: Thinking and learning about print.* Cambridge, MA: MIT Press.
Adams, M., & Huggins, A. (1985). The growth of children's sight vocabulary: A quick text with educational and theoretical implications. *Reading Research Quarterly, 20,* 262–281.
Bowey, J., & Hansen, J. (1994). The development of orthographic rimes as units of word recognition. *Journal of Experimental Child Psychology, 58,* 465–488.
Byrne, B. (1992). Studies in the acquisition procedure for reading: Rationale, hypotheses and data. In P. Gough, L. C. Ehri, & R. Treiman (Eds.), *Reading acquisition* (pp. 1–34). Hillsdale, NJ: Lawrence Erlbaum Associates.
Byrne, B., & Fielding-Barnsley, R. (1989). Phonemic awareness and letter knowledge in the child's acquisition of the alphabetic principle. *Journal of Educational Psychology, 81,* 313–321.
Byrne, B., & Fielding-Barnsley, R. (1990). Acquiring the alphabetic principle: A case for teaching recognition of phoneme identity. *Journal of Educational Psychology, 82,* 805–812.
Carnine, D. (1977). Phonics versus look-say: Transfer to new words. *Reading Teacher, 30,* 636–640.
Chall, J. S. (1983). *Stages of reading development.* New York: McGraw-Hill.
Chew, J. (1994). *Professional expertise and parental experience in the teaching of reading, or Mother often knows best.* York, England: Campaign for Real Education.
Clay, M. (1985). *The early detection of reading difficulties* (3rd ed.). Auckland, New Zealand: Heinemann.
Coltheart, M. (1978). Lexical access in simple reading tasks. In G. Underwood (Ed.), *Strategies of information processing* (pp. 151–216). London: Academic.
Ehri, L. C. (1978). Beginning reading from a psycholinguistic perspective: Amalgamation of word identities. In F. B. Murray (Ed.), *The development of the reading process* (pp. 1–33). Newark, DE: International Reading Association.
Ehri, L. C. (1980). The development of orthographic images. In U. Frith (Ed.), *Cognitive processes in spelling* (pp. 311–338). London: Academic.
Ehri, L. C. (1984). How orthography alters spoken language competencies in children learning to read and spell. In J. Downing & R. Valtin (Eds.), *Language awareness and learning to read* (pp. 119–147). New York: Springer-Verlag.
Ehri, L. C. (1987). Learning to read and spell words. *Journal of Reading Behavior, 19,* 5–31.
Ehri, L. C. (1991). Development of the ability to read words. In R. Barr, M. Kamil, P. Mosenthal & P. Pearson (Eds.), *Handbook of reading research* (Vol. II, pp. 383–417). New York: Longman.
Ehri, L. C. (1992). Reconceptualizing the development of sight word reading and its relationship to recoding. In P. Gough, L. C. Ehri, & R. Treiman (Eds.), *Reading acquisition* (pp. 107–143). Hillsdale, NJ: Lawrence Erlbaum Associates.
Ehri, L. C. (1994). Development of the ability to read words: Update. In R. Ruddell, M. Ruddell, & H. Singer (Eds.), *Theoretical models and processes of reading* (4th ed., pp. 323–358). Newark, DE: International Reading Association.

Ehri, L. C. (1995). Phases of development in learning to read words by sight. *Journal of Research in Reading, 18*, 116–125.

Ehri, L. C., & Robbins, C. (1992). Beginners need some decoding skill to read words by analogy. *Reading Research Quarterly, 27*, 12–26.

Ehri, L. C., & Saltmarsh, J. (1995). Beginning readers outperform older disabled readers in learning to read words by sight. *Reading and Writing: An Interdisciplinary J., 7*, 295–326.

Ehri, L. C., & Wilce, L. S. (1974). Research in brief: Printed intonation cues and reading in children. *Visible Language, 8*, 265–274.

Ehri, L. C., & Wilce, L. S. (1980a). Do beginners learn to read function words better in sentences or in lists? *Reading Research Quarterly, 15*, 451–476.

Ehri, L. C., & Wilce, L. S. (1980b). The influence of orthography on readers' conceptualization of the phonemic structure of words. *Applied Psycholinguistics, 1*, 371–385.

Ehri, L. C., & Wilce, L. S. (1983). Development of word identification speed in skilled and less skilled beginning readers. *Journal of Educational Psychology, 75*, 3–18.

Ehri, L. C., & Wilce, L. S. (1985). Movement into reading: Is the first stage of printed word learning visual or phonetic? *Reading Research Quarterly, 20*, 163–179.

Ehri, L. C., & Wilce, L. S. (1986). The influence of spellings on speech: Are alveolar flaps /d/ or /t/? In D. Yaden & S. Templeton (Eds.), *Metalinguistic awareness and beginning literacy.* (pp. 101–114). Portsmouth, NH: Heinemann.

Ehri, L. C., & Wilce, L. S. (1987a). Cipher versus cue reading: An experiment in decoding acquisition. *Journal of Educational Psychology, 79*, 3–13.

Ehri, L. C., & Wilce, L. S. (1987b). Does learning to spell help beginners learn to read words? *Reading Research Quarterly, 22*, 47–65.

Feitelson, D. (1988). *Facts and fads in beginning reading: A cross-language perspective.* Norwood, NJ: Ablex.

Frith, U. (1985). Beneath the surface of developmental dyslexia. In K. E. Patterson, J. C. Marshall, & M. Coltheart (Eds.), *Surface dyslexia: Neuropsychological and cognitive studies of phonological reading* (pp. 301–330). London: Lawrence Erlbaum Associates.

Glushko, R. J. (1979). The organization and activation of orthographic knowledge in reading aloud. *Journal of Experimental Psychology: Human Perception and Performance, 5*, 674–691.

Glushko, R. J. (1981). Principles for pronouncing print: The psychology of phonography. In A. M. Lesgold & C. A. Perfetti (Eds.), *Interactive processes in reading* (pp. 61–84). Hillsdale, NJ: Lawrence Erlbaum Associates.

Golinkoff, R., & Rosinski, R. (1976). Decoding, semantic processing and reading comprehension skill. *Child Development, 47*, 252–258.

Goodman, K. S. (1965). A linguistic study of cues and miscues in reading. *Elementary English, 42*, 639–643.

Goodman, K. S. (1972). Orthography in a theory of reading instruction. *Elementary English, 49*, 1254–1261.

Goodman, K. S. (1976). Reading: A psycholinguistic guessing game. In H. Singer & R. Ruddell (Eds.), *Theoretical models and processes of reading* (2nd ed., pp. 497–508). Newark, DE: International Reading Association.

Goswami, U. (1986). Children's use of analogy in learning to read: A developmental study. *Journal of Experimental Child Psychology, 42*, 73–83.

Goswami, U. (1988). Orthographic analogies and reading development. *Quarterly Journal of Experimental Psychology, 40*, 239–268.

Goswami, U. (1990a). Phonological priming and orthographic analogies in reading. *Journal of Experimental Child Psychology, 49*, 323–340.

Goswami, U. (1990b). A special link between rhyming skill and the use of orthographic analogies by beginning readers. *Journal of Child Psychology and Psychiatry, 31*, 301–311.

Goswami, U., & Bryant, P. (1990). *Phonological skills and learning to read.* Hillsdale, NJ: Lawrence Erlbaum Associates.

Goswami, U., & Mead, F. (1992). Onset and rime awareness and analogies in reading. *Reading Research Quarterly, 27,* 152–162.

Gough, P. B., & Hillinger, M. (1980). Learning to read: An unnatural act. *Bulletin of the Orton Society, 30,* 180–196.

Gough, P. B., Juel, C., & Griffith, P. (1992). Reading, spelling and the orthographic cipher. In P. Gough, L. C. Ehri, & R. Treiman (Eds.), *Reading acquisition* (pp. 35–48). Hillsdale, NJ: Lawrence Erlbaum Associates.

Gough, P. B., & Walsh, S. (1991). Chinese, Phoenicians, and the orthographic cipher of English. In S. Brady & D. Shankweiler (Eds.), *Phonological processes in literacy: A tribute to Isabelle Y. Liberman* (pp. 199–209). Hillsdale, NJ: Lawrence Erlbaum Associates.

Guttentag, R., & Haith, M. (1978). Automatic processing as a function of age and reading ability. *Child Development, 49,* 707–716.

Juel, C., Griffith, P., & Gough, P. (1986). Acquisition of literacy: A longitudinal study of children in first and second grade. *Journal of Educational Psychology, 78,* 243–255.

Marsh, G., Freidman, M., Welch, V., & Desberg, P. (1981). A cognitive-developmental theory of reading acquisition. In G. Mackinnon & T. G. Waller (Eds.), *Reading research: Advances in theory and practice* (Vol. 3, pp. 199–221). New York: Academic Press.

Mason, J. (1980). When *do* children begin to read: An exploration of four-year-old children's letter and word reading competencies. *Reading Research Quarterly, 15,* 203–227.

Masonheimer, P. E., Drum, P. A., & Ehri, L. C. (1984). Does environmental print identification lead children into word reading? *Journal of Reading Behavior, 16,* 257–272.

McConkie, G. W., & Zola, D. (1981). Language constraints and the functional stimulus in reading. In A. M. Lesgold & C. A. Perfetti (Eds.), *Interactive processes in reading* (pp. 155–175). Hillsdale, NJ: Lawrence Erlbaum Associates.

Nicholson, T. (1991). Do children read words better in context or in lists? A classic study revisited. *Journal of Educational Psychology, 83,* 444–450.

Perfetti, C. (1985). *Reading ability.* New York: Oxford University Press.

Rack, J., Hulme, C., Snowling, M., & Wightman, J. (1994). The role of phonology in young children learning to read words: The direct-mapping hypothesis. *Journal of Experimental Child Psychology, 57,* 42–71.

Rayner, K., & Pollatsek, A. (1989). *The psychology of reading.* Englewood Cliffs, NJ: Prentice-Hall.

Reitsma, P. (1983). Printed word learning in beginning readers. *Journal of Experimental Child Psychology, 75,* 321–339.

Rumelhart, D. (1977). Toward an interactive model of reading. In S. Dornic (Ed.), *Attention and performance VI* (pp. 573–603). Hillsdale, NJ: Lawrence Erlbaum Associates.

Scott, J. A., & Ehri, L. C. (1989). Sight word reading in prereaders: Use of logographic vs. alphabetic access routes. *Journal of Reading Behavior, 22,* 149–166.

Treiman, R. (1985). Onsets and rimes as units of spoken syllables: Evidence from children. *Journal of Experimental Child Psychology, 39,* 161–181.

Treiman, R. (1986). The division between onsets and rimes in English syllables. *Journal of Memory and Language, 25,* 476–491.

Treiman, R. (1992). The role of intrasyllabic units in learning to read and spell. In P. Gough, L. C. Ehri, & R. Treiman (Eds.), *Reading acquisition* (pp. 65–106). Hillsdale, NJ: Lawrence Erlbaum Associates.

Wallach, M., & Wallach, L. (1976). *Teaching all children to read.* Chicago: University of Chicago Press.

Williams, J. (1980). Teaching decoding with an emphasis on phoneme analysis and phoneme blending. *Journal of Educational Psychology, 72,* 1–15.

Wise, B., Olson, R., & Treiman, R. (1990). Subsyllabic units in computerized reading instruction: Onset rime vs. postvowel segmentation. *Journal of Experimental Child Psychology, 49,* 1–19.

Chapter 6

Phonological Awareness: Its Nature and Its Influence Over Early Literacy Development

Valerie Muter
Institute of Child Health, London

It is well-documented that phonological awareness and knowledge of letter names are very strong predictors of early reading success (see Adams, 1990, for a review). Large-scale studies of beginning reading, conducted in the United States in the 1960s, found prereaders' letter knowledge to be the best predictor of first-grade reading, followed by their ability to discriminate phonemes auditorally, with mental age coming in third (Bond & Dykstra, 1967; Chall, 1967). This chapter describes the results of a longitudinal study in which 38 British children were followed from nursery school through their first two years at primary school. It focuses on the nature of phonological awareness, its interaction with letter knowledge, and its contribution to beginning reading and spelling.

Correlational and longitudinal research has established that phonological awareness, even when assessed in preschoolers, is a powerful predictor of progress in beginning reading. Adams (1990) divided tasks that measure phonological awareness into four main types. First, there are tasks of syllable and phoneme segmentation in which the child identifies, taps, or counts the constituent syllables or phonemes of presented words. Second, sound blending tasks require the child to put together strings of phonemes provided by the examiner. Third come tests of rhyme detection and production. Finally, there are phoneme manipulation tasks that require the child to add, delete, or transpose syllables or phonemes within words. All of these tasks will predict subsequent reading and spelling progress, although more difficult and later-acquired skills (like phoneme segmentation and manipulation) tend to yield stronger predictions than do earlier acquired skills (like syllable segmentation and rhyming; Adams, 1990).

An important question to raise is whether the different types of phonological awareness tasks are all measuring essentially the same single global skill, or whether phonological awareness comprises a number of constituent subskills, each of which plays a different role in early literacy development. Stanovich, Cunningham, and Cramer (1984) carried out a factor analysis of 10 different phonological awareness tasks that had been administered to kindergartners. This revealed only one factor on which all the nonrhyming tests loaded highly. Yopp (1988) uncovered two factors from her principal components analysis (with oblique rotation) of 10 phonological awareness tasks given to 96 kindergarten children. The first factor, on which the tests of segmentation, blending, and isolation loaded highly, required only one cognitive operation, and was termed *simple phonological awareness*. The second factor, *compound phonological awareness*, on which the tests of phoneme manipulation loaded highly, involved two cognitive operations and placed a heavier load on memory.

Although both of these studies employed tests of rhyming, this skill did not load significantly on the factors derived by Stanovich et al. (1984) or Yopp (1988). Goswami and Bryant (1990) argued that segmentation, deletion, and similar tasks are measures of phonemic awareness, whereas rhyming tests are sensitive, not to individual phonemes within words, but to their onset-rime units. Stahl and Murray (1994) agreed that level of subsyllabic unit (onset, rime, phoneme) is more important in defining level of phonological awareness than task difficulty. Goswami and Bryant (1990) would, therefore, have predicted that rhyming and segmentation skills should exert different influences over reading and spelling development.

Correlational and longitudinal studies of contributors to early literacy development have been complemented by training studies in which phonological skills (or less frequently, letter names) have been taught to children on the assumption that this will lead to an improvement in their reading and spelling achievements. The early, well-controlled, and large-scale training studies failed to establish a statistically reliable link between phonological awareness (or letter knowledge) developments and subsequent improvements in literacy skill (Adams, 1990; Bradley & Bryant, 1983; Lundberg, Frost, & Petersen, 1988; Olofsson & Lundberg, 1985). However, recent training studies have resolved this apparent paradox by showing that it may not be viable to separate phonological awareness training from within the context of reading instruction (Ball & Blachman, 1988; Cunningham, 1990; Hatcher, Hulme, & Ellis, 1994). These studies have shown that training in phonological skills that is isolated from reading, and spelling is demonstratably less effective than training that forms explicit links between children's underlying phonological skills and their experiences in learning to read. Thus, phonological processes influence reading through their interaction with other reading-relevant skills, a perspective that Hatcher et al. termed the *phonological linkage hypothesis.*

Experimental training studies have helped to make more explicit the interaction of phonological awareness with other reading components. Byrne and Fielding-Barnsley (1989) studied acquisition of the alphabetic principle in preliterate children aged 3 to 5 years. They defined this principle as "a usable knowledge of the fact that phonemes can be represented by letters, such that whenever a particular phoneme occurs in a word, and in whatever position, it can be represented by the same letter" (p. 313). The children were first taught how to read the words *mat* and *sat*; they were then asked to decide whether the printed word *mow* should be pronounced as "mow" or "sow." Reliable performance on this transfer task was achieved only by those children who could phonemically segment the speech items, who identified the initial sound segments, and who had learned the graphic symbols for the sounds "m" and "s." Thus, phoneme awareness *and* grapheme–phoneme knowledge are needed in combination for successful acquisition of the alphabetic principle.

In the present study, tests of phonological awareness, which included rhyming and segmentation tasks, were administered longitudinally to 38 children at ages 4, 5, and 6. Principal components analyses were conducted in order to determine whether the different tasks were assessing a single global skill, or whether there existed within the phonological domain demonstrably separate and independent subskills. The children were also administered tests of letter name knowledge in each year of the study, standardized tests of reading and spelling at ages 5 and 6, and tests of oral and written arithmetic at age 6. The relative contributions of phonological awareness and letter knowledge (and of their interactive "product" term) to early reading and spelling were studied within a longitudinal perspective through path analysis.

METHODOLOGY

Subjects. Thirty-eight nonreading children were selected from nursery schools in North London. At the outset of the study, the mean age of the children was 4 years, 3 months (range 3 years, 10 months to 4 years, 9 months). The subjects were determined to be of normal intelligence; their mean IQ on the Wechsler Preschool and Primary Scale of Intelligence (Wechsler, 1967), administered in Year 1 of the study, was 114.67.

Design. A longitudinal paradigm was adopted. All subjects underwent testing at three equidistant points in time over a 2-year period, initially while at nursery school and during each of their first 2 years at primary school. There was no subject attrition during the course of the study.

Independent Measures. The following tests of phonological awareness were administered in each year of the study (with the exception of Sound Blending, given in only Years 2 and 3):

1. *Rhyme detection,* consisting of 10 items, in which the subject selected from an array of three words and found the one that rhymed with the stimulus word.
2. *Rhyme production,* which required the child to produce as many rhyming words as possible during 30 seconds in response to two separate stimulus words (*day* and *bell*).
3. *Phoneme identification,* in which the child supplied the final sound for each of eight "unfinished" single-syllable words.
4. *Phoneme deletion,* which required the child to delete the initial sound of each of 10 single syllable words.
5. *Sound blending,* from the Illinois Test of Psycholinguistic Ability (Kirk, McCarthy, & Kirk, 1968), which required the child to blend or put together strings of phonemes in single-syllable words, multisyllable words, and nonwords.

All the words used for the experimental tests were selected from Bridie Raban's corpus of spoken vocabulary in 5-year-old British children (Raban, 1988). The items in the tests of phoneme identification, phoneme deletion, and rhyme detection benefited from picture support.

In addition to the phonological tests, a test of *letter knowledge* was given in which the children were asked to name the 26 alphabetic letters written in lower case on individual flashcards and presented in random order.

Outcome Measures

These were obtained in Years 2 and 3 of the study, and comprised the following tests:

1. *Single word reading*—the British Abilities Scales (BAS) Reading Test (Elliott, Murray, & Pearson, 1983).
2. *Continuous prose reading*—the Neale Analysis of Reading Ability–Revised (Neale, Christophers, & Whetton, 1989).
3. *Single word spelling*—the Schonell Graded Word Spelling Test (Schonell & Schonell, 1956).
4. *Tests of oral and written arithmetic*—the arithmetic subtest from the Wechsler Intelligence Scale for Children–Revised (Wechsler, 1976), and a pencil-and-paper arithmetic test derived from the Basic Number Screening Test (Gillham & Hesse, 1976)—given only in Year 3 of the study.

RESULTS

Part 1: The Nature of Phonological Awareness

The children's phonological scores were entered into a series of principal components analyses, with orthogonal rotation, conducted separately for each year of the study. Two independent (uncorrelated) factors emerged:

- A segmentation factor, on which the tests of phoneme identification, deletion, and sound blending loaded highly.
- A rhyming factor, on which the tests of rhyme detection and production loaded highly.

The phonological awareness tests and their loadings on the segmentation and rhyming factors are presented in Table 6.1.

Part B: The First Year of Reading and Spelling

Path analyses were conducted in order to chart the relationships between the reading-related measures from nursery through the first and then the second year at primary school. The cumulative series of multiple regression analyses resulted in path diagrams for which the standardized path coefficient, β, denoted the strength of the relationship for a given path. The

TABLE 6.1
Summary of the Principal Components Analyses:
Loadings of the Phonological Awareness Tests on the
Derived Factors, Segmentation, and Rhyming

	Segmentation		
Test	Year 1	Year 2	Year 3
Phoneme identification	0.81	0.84	0.91
Phoneme deletion	0.86	0.77	0.60
Sound blending		0.69	0.72
Rhyme detection	0.32	0.29	0.16
Rhyme production	−0.06	0.06	0.07
	Rhyming		
Test	Year 1	Year 2	Year 3
Phoneme identification	0.20	−0.01	−0.02
Phoneme deletion	−0.01	0.26	0.64
Sound blending		0.40	0.50
Rhyme detection	0.82	0.75	0.84
Rhyme production	0.91	0.90	0.85

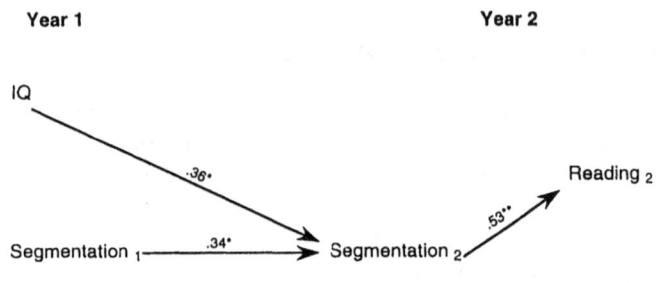

*Significant at .05 level.
**Significant at .01 level.
***Significant at .001 level.

Fig. 6.1. Path diagram depicting the contribution of segmentation and IQ to BAS Reading during the first year at school.

measures entered into the path analyses were IQ, factor scores for rhyming and segmentation (as derived by the principal components analyses), letter name knowledge, reading, and spelling. The raw scores for each variable were converted into z scores; the purpose of "centering" the scores in this way was to ensure comparability of measurement scales across all the variables for all the analyses.

The path diagram in Fig. 6.1 depicts the relative contribution of rhyming and segmentation skills (and of IQ) to BAS reading during the children's first year at school. Segmentation ability at nursery school contributed to segmentation skill a year later, which in turn influenced the children's performance in reading in that year. Rhyming, however, failed to make a significant contribution to reading skill ($\beta = -0.20$, ns). IQ exerted an indirect influence on reading via segmentation ability. Segmentation (in Year 2) also significantly contributed to Schonell spelling performance ($\beta = 0.66$, $p < .001$), whereas rhyming did not ($\beta = 0.12$, ns).

The path diagrams of Fig. 6.2 depict the relationships among segmentation, letter knowledge, and reading and spelling during the first year at school. Segmentation and letter knowledge made separate and specific contributions to both early reading and spelling, with an additional significant contribution from the product term, letter knowledge × segmentation, which reflected the interaction or "linkage" of the two component skills. The product term exerted a small additional influence on reading, and a massive effect on spelling. The linear combination of segmentation and letter knowledge in Year 2 plus the product of these variables accounted for 60% of the variance in reading and 70% of the variance in spelling.

6. PHONOLOGICAL AWARENESS 119

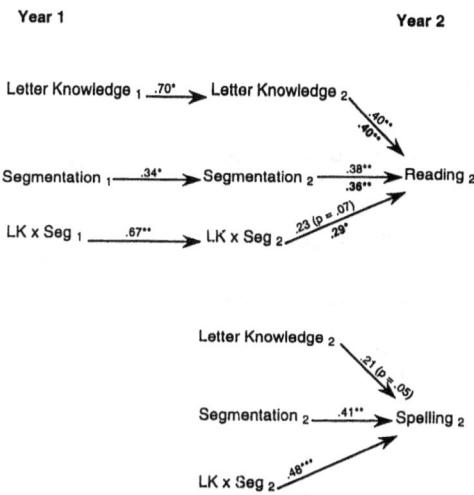

*Significant at .05 level.
**Significant at .01 level.
***Significant at .001 level.

FIG. 6.2. Path diagram depicting the contribution of letter knowledge, segmentation, and their product term (LK × Seg) to BAS and Neale Reading and to Schonell Spelling during the first year at school.

Part C: Reading and Spelling Into the Second Year at School—The Complete Picture

The path diagram of Fig. 6.3 charts the relationships among the reading-related variables as the children proceeded from nursery school through their first 2 years at primary school. The right-hand portion of the diagram depicts the influences over reading as the children completed their second year at school. Although segmentation ability had a profound effect on reading during the first year at school, it failed to continue its contribution into the following year ($\beta = 0.17$, ns, for BAS reading; and $\beta = 0.19$, ns, for Neale reading). Nor did rhyming ability influence reading development in Year 3 ($\beta = 0.13$, ns, for BAS reading; and $\beta = 0.19$, ns, for Neale reading). The major contributors to reading progress in the last year of the study were reading vocabulary from the previous year and concurrent letter knowledge.

In contrast to the findings in reading, phonological awareness continued to exert a powerful influence on spelling throughout the first 2 years at primary school. Figure 6.4 depicts the relationships among the spelling-related variables in Years 1 through 3. In the right-hand portion of the diagram,

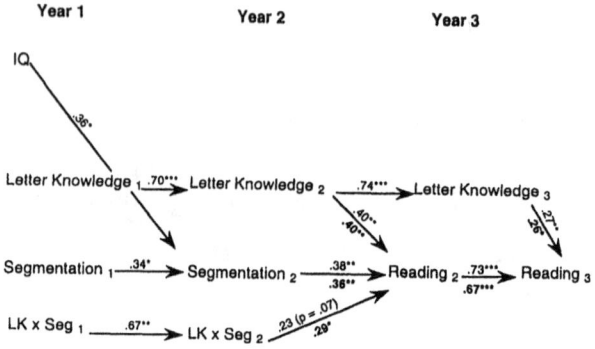

FIG. 6.3. Path diagram depicting the relationships among letter knowledge, segmentation, and their product term (LK × Seg) and reading (BAS and Neale) during the first 2 years at school.

both segmentation and rhyming can be seen to contribute to spelling in the last year of the study. Neither concurrent letter knowledge nor the product variable contributed to final year spelling ($\beta = 0.14$, ns, for letter knowledge; and $\beta = 0.12$, ns, for the product term). Second-year spelling did not contribute to spelling ability in the following year ($\beta = 0.16$, ns).

In order to demonstrate that the effects of phonological awareness are specific to literacy progress and not to educational ability in general, it was necessary to analyze the contributions of the segmentation and rhyming

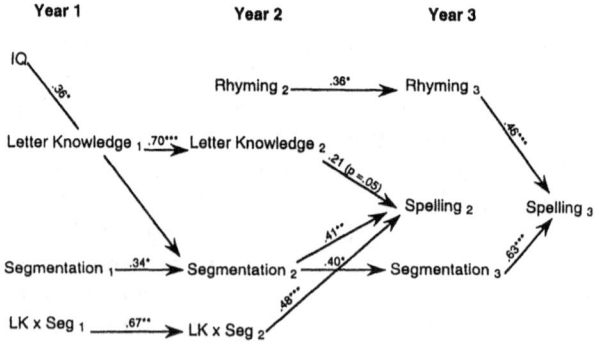

FIG. 6.4. Path diagram depicting the relationships among letter knowledge, rhyming, segmentation, their product term (LK × Seg), and Schonell Spelling during the first two years at school.

scores to arithmetic knowledge. Multiple regression analyses demonstrated that neither the concurrent segmentation nor rhyming scores significantly contributed to the children's third-year scores on the WISC-R Arithmetic subtest, after controlling for the effects of IQ ($\beta = 0.30$, ns, for segmentation; and $\beta = 0.28$, for rhyming). What was (initially) surprising, however, was that the third-year segmentation and rhyming scores made a significant contribution to the children's performance on the written arithmetic test ($\beta = 0.33$, $p < .05$; $\beta = 0.42$, $p < .05$, respectively). However, it could be argued that the ability to complete a written arithmetic test is dependent on reading skill, because children who read letters and words well presumably also read and interpret numbers and arithmetical operation signs with greater ease than do nonreaders. To test out this hypothesis, a further multiple regression analysis was carried out entering the children's BAS reading scores in Year 3 ahead of the phonological awareness measures. Segmentation and rhyming skills no longer contributed to written arithmetic performance ($\beta = 0.18$, ns; and $\beta = 0.12$, ns, respectively), but BAS reading did so at a significant level ($\beta = 0.52$, $p < .01$).

DISCUSSION

The Nature of Phonological Awareness

The principal components analyses of the phonological tests given in each year of the study consistently uncovered two independent factors, specifically phoneme segmentation and rhyming. This study is thought to be among the first to demonstrate the existence of two essentially independent subskills (or perhaps more accurately, levels of subsyllabic unit) underlying phonological awareness. The present results provide empirical support for Goswami and Bryant's (1990) model of early reading development, which assumed that rhyming ability and phoneme awareness constitute separate and distinct subskills or levels within the phonological domain. In their model, rhyming reflects children's awareness of onset-rime boundaries within words, which in turn forms a basis for their ability to make use of analogical strategies in reading and spelling. Tests of phoneme segmentation reflect children's awareness of smaller phonemic units within words which they use, not so much in early reading, but certainly in the "sounding out" of words they are asked to spell.

The First Year of Reading and Spelling

Rhyming and segmentation not only constitute separate phonological subskills, but they also exert differential effects over early literacy development. During the first year of learning to read, segmentation significantly contributed to both early reading and spelling, whereas rhyming did not. The effect of IQ on reading was an indirect one, exerting its influence through its contribution to segmentation ability. Thus, bright children find segmenting words into phonemes easier than less bright children, and it is this skill in segmentation that promotes reading development.

Segmentation ability had a powerful effect on the first year of learning to read and spell, and so, to a roughly equal extent, did letter knowledge. It seemed probable that the present study was capturing the majority of children at that point in their literacy development when they were beginning to acquire the "alphabetic principle," that is, the knowledge that particular phonemes in words are represented systematically by particular letters (Byrne & Fielding-Barnsley, 1989). This knowledge is achieved when children have had sufficient exposure to letters in graphemic form, and after they have attained a level of phonological awareness that enables them to split words into their component sounds (Ehri, 1992). It is the acquisition of the alphabetic principle that enables the child to proceed from the logographic to the alphabetic stage in reading development (Byrne & Fielding-Barnsley, 1989).

However, it is not just a question of children achieving the reading-related skills of phonological awareness and graphemic knowledge in a purely additive fashion. Training studies (Ball & Blachman, 1988; Cunningham, 1990; Hatcher, Hulme, & Ellis, 1994) have shown that children make most progress in reading when phonological awareness training is combined in a meaningful way with the learning of letter names and sounds. It is this combination that is reflected in the product term, letter knowledge × segmentation. Phonological awareness training and teaching letter–sound relationships may help improve children's reading, but when they are both taught, or even better taught in combination, the effect on progress is significantly enhanced. The clear demonstration of positive contributions from segmentation and letter knowledge to early literacy progress, and more important, the additional influence of the interactive effect of the two skills, supports the phonological linkage hypothesis proposed by Hatcher, Hulme, and Ellis (1994). Thus, in order to optimize progress in reading, it is necessary to teach children in such a way that explicit links are formed between children's underlying phonological awareness and their experiences in learning to read. The extent to which linkage has occurred, as measured by the additional variance accounted for by the product term in this study, predicts success in early reading and, more particularly, spelling development.

Reading and Spelling Into the Second Year at School

Reading and spelling were affected by different cognitive processes during the second year at primary school. Second-year reading was significantly influenced by reading vocabulary from the previous year and concurrent letter knowledge, not by phonological awareness per se. These results appeared to capture the consolidation of a sight-reading vocabulary very much along the lines proposed by Ehri (1992). In her view, children set up connections between sequences of letters in printed words and the phonemes that represent them. The connections are formed out of readers' knowledge of sound–letter correspondences and of orthographic regularities abstracted through their reading experiences. Children use these connections that have been set up in memory in order to directly access the pronunciations of words. This process omits the intermediate stage of applying grapheme-to-phoneme correspondence rules, and is consequently faster and more direct. The path diagram of Fig. 6.3 indicated that the major contributors to reading progress in the final year of the study were reading vocabulary from Year 2 and concurrent letter knowledge. Consistent with Ehri's model is the view that the children are continuing to make improvements in their letter-to-sound knowledge (letter knowledge 3) and using their established reading lexicon to draw inferences about orthographic regularities (reading 2). These two processes in combination fuel further reading development, but without a direct phonological component. The time course of influences over reading supports the view that more advanced orthographic reading skill is underpinned by phonological knowledge through a direct mapping process (Rack, Hulme, Snowling, & Wightman, 1994). This core knowledge, reflected in the establishment of the alphabetic principle, is developed in the first year at school through the interactive influence of phonological segmentation skill and exposure to letters in graphemic form.

Spelling, however, appears to remain phonologically and phonemically bound, with both segmentation and rhyming influencing the second year of learning to spell. Although segmentation significantly contributed to spelling, the letter knowledge × segmentation product term did not. It seemed as though, once the alphabetic principle had been established through reading and writing experience in Year 2, the children proceeded to a subsequent stage in which segmentation skills continued to exert an effect but not in relation to simple letter–sound knowledge. Unlike the pattern of influence in reading, spelling from Year 2 did not influence spelling in the following year. It may be that the children's spelling vocabulary during their first year at school was more limited and idiosyncratic than their reading vocabulary, and thus could not form a sufficiently usable base on which to build a more advanced vocabulary in the following year. It seems likely that rhyming and segmentation contribute to quite different aspects of the spelling process. In line with the Goswami and Bryant (1990) model, it could be hypothesized that rhyming skills promote the awareness of the onset-rime distinction within words, which may in turn influence children's use of analogy in spelling. In contrast, segmentation abilities promote the awareness of phonemes within words, which then facilitate the children's ability to make use of phonemic encoding principles in spelling. The present findings support the view that children apply grapheme-to-phoneme correspondences in their early spelling attempts, but then later on begin to take note of larger segments in words, probably of analogy/onset-rime units.

The present study demonstrated that the effects of phonological awareness are specific to reading and spelling, and that they do not exert a generalized influence over educational development. Neither segmentation nor rhyming contributed to oral arithmetic skills at age 6. These phonological skills appeared to influence written arithmetic, but this effect disapppeared after the children's reading skills were entered into a multiple regression ahead of segmentation and rhyming. It seems plausible that reading ability would significantly influence progress in written arithmetic, because one would expect a strong correlation between children's knowledge of and ability to read letters and words, and their proficiency in "reading" numbers and arithmetical symbols.

CONCLUSION

The present study has shown that phonological awareness comprises independent subskills that reflect children's awareness of different units of sound (i.e., of phonemes in segmentation tasks and of onset-rime units in rhyming tasks). There is growing evidence to show that these skills exert differential influences over early reading and spelling development. Segmentation, in interaction with letter knowledge, makes a powerful contribution to beginning reading and spelling. This stage of explicitly applying grapheme-to-phoneme correspondence rules is rapidly succeeded in reading by a faster and more direct process in the form of visual–phonological connections. Spelling, however, remains more explicitly phonologically driven; segmentation skills appear to promote phoneme awareness as children "sound out" words they are asked to spell, whereas rhyming skills draw attention to onset-rime units and thus encourage the adoption of analogical strategies in spelling.

ACKNOWLEDGMENTS

The author is grateful to Sara Taylor for her assistance in data collection, to Dr. Jim Stevenson for his advice on statistical analysis, and to Professor Margaret Snowling for her many useful suggestions and her support.

REFERENCES

Adams, M. J. (1990). *Beginning to read: Thinking and learning about print.* Cambridge, MA: MIT Press.

Ball, E. W., & Blachman, B. A. (1988). Phoneme segmentation training: Effect on reading readiness. *Annals of Dyslexia, 38,* 208–225.

Bond, G. L., & Dykstra, R. (1967). The cooperative research programme in first grade reading instruction. *Reading Research Quarterly, 2,* 5–142.

Bradley, L., & Bryant, P. E. (1983). Categorising sounds and learning to read—a causal connection. *Nature, 301,* 419–521.

Byrne, B., & Fielding-Barnsley, R. (1989). Phonemic awareness and letter knowledge in the child's acquisition of the alphabetic principle. *Journal of Educational Psychology, 82,* 805–812.

Chall, J. S. (1967). *Learning to read: The great debate.* New York: McGraw-Hill.

Cunningham, A. E. (1990). Explicit versus implicit instruction in phonemic awareness. *Journal of Experimental Child Psychology, 50,* 429–444.

Ehri, L. C. (1992). Reconceptualising the development of sight word reading and its relationship to recoding. In P. B. Gough, L. C. Ehri, & R. Treiman (Eds.), *Reading acquisition* (pp. 107–143). Hillsdale, NJ: Lawrence Erlbaum Associates.

Elliott, C. D., Murray, D. J., & Pearson, L. S. (1983). *British Abilities Scales.* Windsor, England: NFER-Nelson.

Gillham, W. E. C., & Hesse, K. A. (1976). *Basic Number Screening Test.* Sevenoaks, Kent, England: Hodder and Stoughton Educational.

Goswami, U., & Bryant, P. E. (1990). *Phonological skills and learning to read.* London: Lawrence Erlbaum Associates.

Hatcher, P., Hulme, C., & Ellis, A. W. (1994). Ameliorating reading failure by integrating the teaching of reading and phonological skills: The phonological linkage hypothesis. *Child Development, 65,* 41–57.

Kirk, S. A., McCarthy, J. J., & Kirk, W. D. (1968). *Illinois Test of Psycholinguistic Abilities.* Urbana: University of Illinois Press.

Lundberg, I., Frost, J., & Petersen, O.-P. (1988). Effects of an extensive programme for stimulating phonological awareness in pre-school children. *Reading Research Quarterly, 23,* 264–284.

Neale, M. D., Christophers, U., & Whetton, C. (1989). *Neale Analysis of Reading Ability—Revised British edition.* Windsor, England: NFER-Nelson.

Olofsson, A., & Lundberg, I. (1985). Evaluation of long-term effects of phonemic awareness training in kindergarten: Illustrations of some methodological problems in evaluation research. *Scandinavian Journal of Psychology, 26,* 21–34.

Raban, B. (1988). *The spoken vocabulary of five-year-old children.* Reading, England: The Reading and Language Information Centre, University of Reading.

Rack, J., Hulme, C., Snowling, M., & Wightman, J. (1994). The role of phonology in young children learning to read words: The direct mapping hypothesis. *Journal of Experimental Child Psychology, 57,* 42–71.

Schonell, F. J., & Schonell, F. E. (1956). *Diagnostic and attainment testing: Including a manual of tests, their nature, use, recording and interpretation.* London: Oliver and Boyd.

Stahl, S. A., & Murray, B. A. (1994). Defining phonological awareness and its relationship to early reading. *Journal of Educational Psychology, 86,* 221–234.

Stanovich, K. E., Cunningham, A. E., & Cramer, B. R. (1984). Assessing phonological awareness in kindergarten children: Issues of task comparability. *Journal of Experimental Child Psychology, 38,* 175–190.

Wechsler, D. (1967). *Wechsler Preschool and Primary Scale of Intelligence.* San Antonio, TX: The Psychological Corporation.

Wechsler, D. (1976). *Wechsler Intelligence Scale for Children–Revised.* London: Harcourt Brace Jovanovich.

Yopp, H. K. (1988). The validity and reliability of phonemic awareness tests. *Reading Research Quarterly, 13,* 159–177.

Chapter 7

Why and How Phoneme Awareness Helps Learning to Read

José Morais
Philippe Mousty
Régine Kolinsky
Université Libre de Bruxelles, Belgium

By the middle of the 1980s, the great majority of cognitive psycholinguists concerned with the acquisition of literacy skills agreed that phoneme awareness and learning to read an alphabetic script are related in a theoretically interesting way. This claim was based on an impressive amount of experimental data accumulated over a period of more than 15 years. Researchers such as Isabelle Liberman, Paul Rozin, Philip Gough, and Harry Savin argued that if literacy acquisition was to be understood, it was necessary to take into account the links between written and spoken language (cf. chapters by these authors in Kavanagh & Mattingly, 1972; Reber & Scarborough, 1977).

We believe that the relationship between the acquisition of phoneme awareness and the acquisition of alphabetic literacy is one of reciprocal causation. As both skills develop over an extended period of time, in principle, mutual causal influences can take place between them. Phoneme awareness begins developing when and because children have to learn what letters stand for. At the same time, children need to master both the simple and complex (i.e., context-dependent) graphophonological conversion rules necessary for phonological decoding.

More recently, however, authors such as Giuseppe Cossu and John Marshall proposed that phoneme awareness may be a mere epiphenomenon. In addition, more substantive suggestions concerning the involvement of an implicit or "direct" learning of graphophonological correspondences have also been put forward. Thus, it appears that the role of phoneme awareness in alphabetic literacy acquisition is still a matter for debate.

In the first part of this chapter, we take issue with Cossu and Marshall's argument that phonological decoding capacities can develop in the complete absence of phoneme awareness. We also review the main empirical evidence supporting the notion that phoneme awareness plays a causal role in alphabetic literacy acquisition. In the second part, we examine data suggesting that implicit or direct learning of grapho-phonological correspondences occurs early in development. We address the question of whether or not phoneme awareness plays any role in the learning of these correspondences. The hypothesis that phoneme awareness plays a causal role in literacy acquisition is, in our view, compatible with the assumption (shared by Cossu and Marshall) that the acquisition of literacy depends in a crucial way on the availability of biologically determined capacities used in spoken language. Finally, in the third part, we suggest that future research on alphabetic literacy acquisition should be concerned with sublexical orthographic representations that are larger than the single letter. Ways in which phoneme awareness might contribute to the development of these representations should also be considered. Moreover, future research needs to investigate how these processes may differ across different languages that have different phonological structures.

DOES PHONEME AWARENESS PLAY A CAUSAL ROLE IN ALPHABETIC LITERACY ACQUISITION? EVIDENCE FROM TRAINING STUDIES AND FROM STUDIES WITH SPECIAL GROUPS

Cossu, Rossini, and Marshall (1993a, 1993b, the latter paper being a reply to published comments on the first one; cf. Bertelson, 1993; Byrne, 1993a; Morton & Frith, 1993) claimed that the explicit, conscious recognition of phonemes "is irrelevant to the acquisition of literacy" (Cossu et al., 1993b, p. 300). From this idea, they derived the implication that rather than teaching phonological awareness, "The time might be better spent in teaching reading (where reading, of course, includes implicit knowledge of grapheme–phoneme correspondences)" (Cossu et al., 1993a, p. 135).

Two preliminary remarks are worth making. Cossu et al. are, in all likelihood, right when they say that the metaphonological games used to assess phoneme awareness are not crucial per se for reading acquisition. Some of these games, such as phoneme inversion, involve procedures that are never used in reading or spelling. However, the purpose of these tasks is merely to verify whether the subjects possess conscious representations of phonemes. One cannot conclude that phoneme awareness itself is irrelevant simply because the particular operations involved in the tasks are irrelevant for reading and spelling.

Another preliminary remark concerns the nature of the conscious representations of phonemes that are activated as children begin to read and spell. Our attempts to look introspectively into our own representations may be misleading. The phonological processes that we as skilled readers resort to are mainly automatic and unconscious and, moreover, our conscious representations of phonemes may be much more conceptualized than children's are. On the other hand, trying to obtain verbal reports from children may be very difficult, and may be more a reflection of reconstructive processes than of the representations they actually use. We believe that knowing exactly what conscious representations of phonemes used in reading and spelling look like is not a necessary precondition for studying them. To draw an analogy, we do not know exactly what attention is, yet, nevertheless, a great deal has been discovered about the role of attentional processes.

If we understand Cossu et al.'s line of reasoning correctly, to put the child in a reading setting is all that matters for reading acquisition; thus, any method allowing exposure to alphabetic writing should work equally well. However, the reading performance of children does vary as a function of instructional method. Whatever the long-term effects of whole-word and phonics methods, it is commonly observed that a phonic method (which attempts to promote the discovery and understanding of the alphabetic code) leads to much faster acquisition of word and pseudoword reading and spelling than a whole-word method. For example, in one of our studies (Alegria, Morais, D'Alimonte, & Seyll, unpublished data), we found that more than half of the first graders who were learning to read with whole-word teaching read fewer words correctly than the worst reader among the children who were learning to read with a phonics method. Moreover, about one third of the "phonics" children read more words than the best reader among the "whole-word" children. Perhaps even more impressively, we did not find a single child who could read a substantial number of novel words without having received some explicit instruction in the alphabetic code. We are convinced that trying to provide children with an explicit knowledge of grapheme–phoneme correspondences does not have the same effects on the development of literacy as simply giving them the opportunity to extract these correspondences from alphabetic material.

It is difficult to understand how it is possible to have an explicit knowledge of grapheme–phoneme correspondences without being aware of the phonemes involved in these correspondences. Accordingly, grapheme–phoneme correspondences cannot be taught in a explicit way without teaching phonemic segmentation at the same time. In the absence of phonemic segmentation, teaching grapheme–phoneme correspondences means, in fact, teaching letter–sound correspondences. As we see later on, the fact that in many studies it was necessary to combine teaching of letter–sound correspondences with phonemic segmentation instruction in order to improve reading and spelling skills implies that learning letter–sound correspondences does not necessarily mean becoming aware of phonemes. Learning that the letter *b* corresponds to the sound [b'] is not the same as discovering that it corresponds to the initial phoneme of the sound [b']. By simply learning letter–sound correspondences, children will not have learned how to identify the individual phonemes in a syllable. Unfortunately, in most experimental studies, knowledge of letter–sound correspondences and knowledge of grapheme–phoneme correspondences are confounded. Most authors indicate that they have tested knowledge of grapheme–phoneme correspondences, whereas in fact they have only tested knowledge of letter–sound correspondences.

The distinction between knowledge of grapheme–phoneme correspondences and knowledge of letter–sound relations may have important implications. One is that the progress obtained in literacy skills from teaching children by a phonics method might not depend in any significant way on the children's phoneme awareness, especially when the method emphasises letter–sound correspondences rather than grapheme–phoneme ones. Teaching in this way might lead to an implicit learning of grapheme–phoneme correspondences, which in turn might be followed by some intuition about the phonemic structure of spoken language. If this were the case, it is possible that, even in children learning to read via a phonics method, phoneme awareness may be a mere epiphenomenon.

However, it is possible to demonstrate in a compelling way that phoneme awareness plays an important role in literacy acquisition. Many studies have shown that teaching phonemic skills (either alone, or in conjunction with teaching grapheme–phoneme correspondences) has positive effects on reading and spelling performance. Therefore, contrary to Cossu et al.'s proposition, the development of phoneme awareness is relevant to literacy acquisition. Because this point is so crucial, we now present a short review of the main research findings.

The well-known study by Lundberg, Frost, and Petersen (1988) is probably one of the most impressive in this area. These authors used an 8-month program to develop phonological awareness skills in preschool children. At the end of the school year, although the trained children were no better than controls in either letter knowledge or higher-order language comprehension, they were, as expected, superior to the controls on metaphonological tests, especially on phonemic segmentation. When reassessed in first grade, the trained subjects were no better than controls at either mathematics or Raven's Progressive Matrices. However, they were better at both word recognition and spelling. At the end of the second grade, there was a tendency for their superiority in reading and spelling to have increased. This result is sometimes interpreted as meaning that extended training on phonemic segmentation may itself promote literacy skills. However, this interpretation ignores the fact that, during the same period, the children may have gained some letter knowledge from their relatives or in school. Thus, it may be the combination of phoneme and letter training that contributed to the progress made in reading and spelling.

Several lines of evidence suggest that a combination of training in phonemic awareness and training in letter knowledge may have a causal influence. Williams (1980) observed that children who had received training in phonemic analysis and synthesis made greater progress in word and pseudoword reading across a school year than children who did not receive this twofold instruction. Ball and Blachman (1988, 1991) observed that training letter–sound knowledge alone had no impact on word reading and spelling, whereas training both letter–sound knowledge and phonemic segmentation had a strong effect. Similarly, in Bradley and Bryant's (1983) study, the group of children who received only metaphonological instruction did not show improvements in reading and spelling compared to controls. As in Ball and Blachman's study, only those children who received a combination of phonological awareness and letter–sound training showed gains in reading and spelling. Thus, it seems likely that training in both letter–sound correspondences and phoneme awareness is crucial to facilitating the development of reading and spelling abilities.

Two recent studies support this conclusion. Hatcher, Hulme, and Ellis (1994) found that the greatest progress in reading was obtained by a group of 7-year-old poor readers who received special training in both metaphonological awareness and reading. Secondly, Defior and Tudela (1994) found that only the group of first graders who were taught phonemic abilities using plastic letters as an aid showed significant improvements in reading and spelling. In addition, because the Hatcher et al. study was conducted in English (a deep orthography) and the Defior and Tudela study was conducted in Spanish (a shallow orthography), the degree of transparency of the language may be irrelevant.

One apparent exception to the superiority of combined training on phonemic abilities and letter knowledge over phonemic training alone is a result reported by Bentin and Leshem (1993). In this study, both types of training led to a similar improvement in reading relative to controls. However, it should be noted these children were tested at the end of their school year. Thus, consistent with our previous comment on Lundberg et al.'s study, it may be that the children who received only phonemic training in the context of the study also received (at the same time) some information concerning letter–sound associations from their families.

A further interesting finding was reported by Cunningham (1990). She taught kindergarten and first-grade children to associate the phonemic constituents of words with wooden chips, to delete a phoneme from an utterance, and to categorize utterances according to a common phoneme. She found that this instruction had a positive influence on reading ability, compared with a control group. This positive effect was magnified if the program also included conceptual training in which the relevance and use of phonemic abilities in reading was stressed. This finding is difficult to reconcile with Cossu and Marshall's position.

We now turn to examine Cossu and Marshall's finding that phonological decoding abilities can develop in the complete absence of phoneme awareness in more detail. They are inspired by the logic of dissociation, which is currently used in neuropsychology to tease apart different processes in the cognitive system. In the same way as brain-damaged patients displaying selective cognitive deficits may provide evidence for the existence of separate capacities, children may be examined for possible dissociations between the acquisition of phoneme awareness and the acquisition of phonological transcoding in reading and spelling.

Cossu and Marshall (1990) and Marshall and Cossu (1990, 1991) argued that if children exist who show evidence of phonological decoding in reading while displaying no sign of phoneme awareness, then one should not consider phoneme awareness to be a crucial factor in the acquisition of phonological decoding procedures. Let us assume for now that such children do exist. One would be allowed, indeed, to claim that phonological decoding abilities can develop in the complete absence of phoneme awareness. However, the limitations of this conclusion must also be emphasized. The fact that there may be some children who are able to acquire phonological decoding despite lacking phoneme awareness is not inconsistent with the idea that, for the large majority of children, phoneme awareness is crucial to developing decoding skills. Moreover, if the minority of children who display the dissociation develop poorer decoding skills than children who do not show a dissociation, one would still conclude that phoneme awareness makes a crucial contribution to the development of decoding skills.

Keeping these caveats in mind, it is time to evaluate the empirical evidence reported by Cossu and Marshall. They presented the case of a child, TA, who displayed excellent phonological transcoding abilities yet, according to Cossu and Marshall, had not developed phoneme awareness. They concluded from this apparent dissociation that *implicit* operations resulting from experience with an alphabetic script may be sufficient to establish phonological transcoding.

We disagree with this conclusion, because we think that TA's lack of phoneme awareness was not demonstrated. First of all, one should notice that TA had a full-scale IQ of 47 and a digit span of only two items. Thus, in all likelihood, his cognitive impairments prevented him from fully understanding the instructions provided in the metalinguistic tests. Marshall and Cossu (1990) rejected this objection by arguing that TA's cognitive limitations did not prevent him from acquiring literacy skills. However, as we mentioned earlier, the games used to assess phoneme awareness may involve operations that go beyond those required by phoneme awareness per se.

As we see later in the chapter, this is particularly true for the tests designed by Cossu and Marshall. For instance, correctly counting two, three, or four phonemes in an utterance demands a counting ability that is not inherent to the capacity to represent phonemes explicitly. Perhaps even more demanding was a test that required the deletion of the first two phonemes from words up to nine phonemes long. Unexpectedly, TA obtained 43% correct responses in this test. This seems an excellent score for a mentally impaired child with a digit span of only two items! Let us consider one of the easier items: *mela.* Here, TA was supposed to focus on the first phoneme, then to identify it as m, then to think that *mela* without *m* yields *ela*, then to focus on the first phoneme of *ela* and to identify it as *e*, then to think that *ela* without *e* yields *la*, and finally to check that he has not subtracted exactly two phonemes, neither more nor less.

It does not necessarily follow however, that performing this task requires phoneme awareness. First, we have no information about the items on which TA succeeded, nor about the nature of his errors. It is possible that he succeeded only on those items in which the first two phonemes corresponded to a syllable. Second, it is plausible that he succeeded by mentally writing the spoken word, then deleting the first two letters, and finally mentally reading the remaining part.

Alternatively, it is also possible that TA had assimilated the link between graphemes and phonemes without being able to separate the successive phonemes of an utterance. It might be possible to attend to the phonemic constituents of speech without developing a concept of a phoneme. It is this concept that is needed in any kind of mental manipulation, such as deletion or reversal, both of which require the creation of a new sound. In Brazil, we (Scliar-Cabral, Morais, Nepomuceno, & Kolinsky, submitted) tested a group of adults who had 4 years of normal schooling when they were children but nevertheless remained rudimentary readers. They failed a test of phoneme deletion that required them to delete the initial consonant of a three-phoneme utterance. However, they performed above chance on a classification task that required them to focus attention selectively on the initial consonant. They were, for example, able to focus on the /b/ in *bat*, yet at the same time they were unable to think about the /b/ in isolation. Focusing attention on a phoneme without representing it in isolation might be an early, rudimentary form of phoneme awareness.

There are very few published reports that examine both reading and phonemic awareness in children with general cognitive deficits such as

Down syndrome. A recent study by Vallar and Papagno (1993) on a young woman with Down syndrome with an IQ of 71 indicated that her reading was accurate but extremely slow. She performed well on a test of initial phoneme judgment (39 correct responses out of 40). She was, however, completely unable to perform spoonerisms (e.g., saying "Zino Doff" in response to "Dino Zoff"). This dissociation between judgment of initial phoneme identity and exchange of initial phoneme shows quite clearly the importance of the cognitive demands of the task.

Cossu et al. (1993a) found that although a group of 10 Down syndrome children were able to read to some extent, they were unable either to count phonemes or delete the first two phonemes from an utterance. We decided that it would be informative to test a similar group of children using phoneme awareness tests that are cognitively less demanding than those used by Cossu et al. The characteristics of our subjects are described in Table 7.1. There were five girls and three boys taken from two schools for mentally impaired children. They came from families of low income. Their IQs ranged from 40 to 66 (mean: 52.5), and their ages ranged from 10 to 20 years (mean: 13.3). Only one of these subjects, P.G., was a child with Down syndrome.

We gave these children two reading tests from the BELEC battery (Mousty, Leybaert, Alegria, Content, & Morais, 1994). One of these (MIM test) included 12 high-frequency words, 12 low-frequency words, and 12 pseudowords. All items were regular, half being short (5-letters long) and half long (at least 4-syllables long, 10 to 12 letters) in each category. The second test (REGUL test) included 24 words, all short (3 to 6 letters) but half of them were regular (such as *ami, caisse*), and half were irregular (such as *faisan, femme, porc, echo*).

TABLE 7.1
Characteristics of the Subjects

	Experimental Group					Control Group			
	Gender	Age (Years)	IQ	Words Read (n = 24)		Gender	Age (Years)	Grade	Words Read (n = 24)
1.	F	15	42	22	1.	F	8	3	23
2.[a]	F	13	50	21	2.	F	8	3	21
3.	F	11	65	21	3.	F	9	4	22
4.	F	20	40	20	4.	F	8	3	19
5.	F	14	40	13	5.	F	8	3	13
6.	M	10	54	15	6.	M	8	3	15
7.	M	12	66	20	7.	M	8	3	19
8.	M	12	63	22	8.	M	8	3	23
Mean		13.4	52.5	19.3			8.1	3.1	19.4

[a] Down syndrome.

Reading-age control subjects were selected from normal schools and were individually matched to an experimental subject for the number of regular and short words read correctly (out of 24). Both groups read 80% of these words. The controls were 8 or 9 years old and matched to the experimental group for gender.

The results are presented in Table 7.2. Both the cognitively impaired and the control children read more regular words correctly on the REGUL test than irregular words. On the MIM test, the experimental (but not the control children) read the short items better than the long ones. This interaction between group and length was particularly strong for pseudoword reading: The two groups did not differ on the short pseudowords, but a large group difference was found for the long items. One possible interpretation of this difference is that both groups were reading, at least partly, using phonological decoding. It is likely, however, that the control children had reached a higher level of automatization. P.G., the only Down child, displayed a pattern of results entirely consistent with the overall trend of her group.

The error analysis is consistent with the notion that phonological decoding was the dominant strategy used by our subjects. Most of the errors were limited to one phoneme, for instance *doper* was read as /dOpεR/ by two experimental and three control subjects, *caler* as /kalεR/ by three experimental and one control, and *laver* as /lavεR/ by one experimental

TABLE 7.2
Reading Tests: Number of Correct Responses for Each Experimental Subject, and Mean Percentages of Correct Responses for the Experimental and the Control Groups

Experimental Group	High-Frequency Words		Low-Frequency Words		Pseudowords		Words	
	Short (/6)	Long (/6)	Short (/6)	Long (/6)	Short (/6)	Long (/6)	Regular (/12)	Irregular (/12)
1.	6	5	4	4	5	5	12	11
2.[a]	5	5	6	4	5	4	10	6
3.	6	3	5	2	5	1	10	0
4.	5	3	5	3	6	3	10	5
5.	4	1	2	0	3	3	7	5
6.	4	5	2	2	5	4	9	5
7.	6	5	5	3	5	3	9	6
8.	6	5	6	2	4	2	10	4
	88%	67%	73%	42%	79%	52%	80%	44%
Control Group								
	77%	85%	69%	67%	81%	79%	90%	61%

[a]Down syndrome.

and two controls. Errors on irregular words generally consisted of regularizations. For example, the final *c* of *porc* was pronounced by five experimental subjects and one control. Likewise, the *ch* of *echo* was pronounced /ʃ/ by five experimental and six controls. These results suggest very clearly that both groups of children were reading mainly on the basis of correspondence rules, and that both had an insufficient knowledge of orthographic patterns.

The metaphonological tests were:

1. A test of rhyme judgment, in which the subjects had to say whether or not two pseudowords rhymed.
2. A test of syllabic fusion, in which they had to fuse V + CV.
3. A test of phonemic fusion, in which they had to fuse C + V.
4. A test of syllabic deletion, in which they had to delete the initial V from a VCV.
5. A test of phonemic deletion, in which they had to delete the C of a CV.
6. A test of segmentation of CVC words.
7. A test of segmentation of CVC pseudowords.

In Tests 6 and 7, the subjects were required to attempt to pronounce separately the initial consonant, the vowel, and the final consonant. Later on, the same subjects were tested on the deletion of the first two phonemes from either two- or three-syllable words under three separate conditions: In one condition, the two phonemes were an initial CV syllable; in another condition, they belonged to a CVC syllable; and in the last condition, the first two phonemes belonged to a CCV syllable. Four examples were given before each set of trials. Corrective feedback was given after the subject's response on each experimental trial.

The mean scores for each group of subjects are shown in Table 7.3. The control subjects were better than the experimental subjects on all tests. This was expected, because the control children had superior general cognitive ability and better short-term memory skills. Nevertheless, it is important to note that although they made some errors, the cognitively impaired children were able to perform these metaphonological tasks. In both groups, fusing and deleting syllables were easier than fusing and deleting phonemes.

Contrary to what we might expect, the poor scores obtained by the subjects of Cossu et al. (1993a) were not replicated here (although in our experiment, we did observe some very low scores in the two-phoneme deletion test only). A number of methodological differences may account for the discrepancy between Cossu et al.'s results and ours. First, unlike

TABLE 7.3
Mean Percentage and Range of Correct Responses in
Each Metaphonological Test for Each Group (the Range of
Results for the Experimental Group as Well as the Results
of the Child With Down Syndrome Are Also Indicated)

	Experimental Group	Control Group	Down
Rhyme judgment	80% (54%–100%)	98%	54%
Fusion:			
Syllable	87% (70%–100%)	99%	75%
Phoneme	73% (25%–90%)	92%	70%
Deletion:			
Syllable	91% (75%–95%)	100%	90%
Phoneme	68% (45%–95%)	87%	65%
Segmentation of CVC:			
Words	80% (50%–100%)	90%	90%
Pseudowords	66% (30%–100%)	93%	70%
Deletion of first two phonemes:			
Syllable CV	83% (30%–100%)	90%	80%
CV (in CVC$ . . .)	68% (0%–100%)	89%	50%
CC (in CCV$ . . .)	59% (10%–90%)	74%	80%

Cossu et al., in our materials phonological structure was consistent across all items in each trial. Second, we gave the subjects corrective feedback throughout testing. Finally, the reading skills of our subjects was approximately at the 8-year-old level, whereas Cossu et al.'s subjects were reading at about the 7-year-old level.

The message from these results, contrary to those presented by Cossu et al. (1993a), is that it is possible to observe clear signs of phoneme awareness in children of low cognitive ability. At first glance, we thought that the tasks used by Cossu et al. were too difficult, thus explaining their failure to observe phoneme awareness. However, this explanation may not be sufficient, given that we obtained relatively good scores on tests almost as difficult as theirs. The discrepancy between findings might be related to the tasks, the cognitive level of the subjects, their reading level, or to any combination of these factors. It would be possible to continue experimental investigations in order to obtain a clear dissociation between easy and difficult tasks. However, to do so would be a waste of time from our point of view. Instead, it is the responsibility of Cossu and his collaborators to present clear evidence that cognitively impaired children—who are able to read and spell using a phonological procedure—do not possess phoneme awareness when tested using appropriate tasks.

RECENT STUDIES OF THE IMPLICIT LEARNING OF PHONOLOGICAL DECODING AND SUBLEXICAL RELATIONS

Several recent studies have investigated implicit learning of grapheme–phoneme correspondences. The critical notion is of self-generated associations. For example, Thompson and Fletcher-Flinn (1993) suggested that a sublexical relation between the orthographic component in final position -*t* and the phonological component /-t/ may be formed through the occurrence of -*t* in the written representation of several items from the reader's phonological lexicon (/nɔt/, /gɛt/, /kat/, etc.). These sublexical relations constitute a source of knowledge that can be used when reading, if recall procedures are insufficient. Until now, these claims have been considered consistent with the hypothesis that phonemic awareness is crucial to the establishment of sublexical relations.

However, Thompson and Fletcher-Flinn added the following assertion: "Unlike independent letter–phoneme correspondences for which much of the information can be provided through direct teaching, sublexical relations cannot be provided in direct teaching" (1993, pp. 31–32). We should examine these two claims carefully. Clearly, some sublexical relations are taught in the context of reading and spelling instruction using a phonics method. However, we would agree that not all sublexical relations above the grapheme–phoneme level can be provided through direct teaching. The other claim, concerning the issue of whether or not letter–phoneme correspondences can be provided through direct teaching, constitutes a more important source of disagreement.

Isabelle Liberman (see, e.g., Liberman, 1991) often stressed the dilemma facing teachers of reading. To tell the child that the letter *t* represents the sound [t'] is to tell him or her something wrong, and to tell the child that it represents a phoneme is to tell him or her something right but that does not help the child. In other words, there can be no direct teaching of phonemes. Some people use the term *implicit phonics* to refer to a technique in which the child is led to pay attention to what, for example, *bat, bet,* and *bit* have in common. This is simply phonics, because phonics cannot be more explicit than that. Teaching the sounds of consonants is also an indirect way of conveying the notion of phoneme; one hopes that the child will finish by ignoring the neutral vowel and discovering the consonant. The important point is that recognizing phoneme invariance is not a matter of discriminating sounds; to reach the phoneme requires a process of abstraction. Although one can begin phonic teaching by using vowels or consonants that can be pronounced in isolation, "indirect" teaching is required for the more encoded phonemes.

Thompson and Fletcher-Flinn (1993) argued that, according to their theory about sublexical relations, the children's use of such relations would be affected by the differential characteristics of print word experience. In English, *b* is very frequent in word initial position but rare in final position, whereas *t* appears at least as often in final as in initial position. Consistent with this distribution, they found that beginning readers reading CV or VC pseudowords more often omitted the final *b* than the final *t*, whereas no such difference appeared at initial position. Following this demonstration, their subjects were assigned to an experimental condition in which they were trained to read words containing a final *b*, and a control condition in which the same words were presented but only orally. The children's pseudoword reading was also tested. Only the children from the experimental group pronounced the final *b* in the pseudowords more often after training than before training. This suggests that procedures based on sublexical relations, in this case on a grapheme–phoneme relation, may be generated. Unfortunately, the data available from this study does not allow us to conclude to what extent this process corresponds to implicit learning. The children were in first grade and had not received instruction in letter–sound correspondences at school. However, neither their knowledge of these correspondences nor their ability to pay attention to the phonemic constituents of speech utterances were checked.

The set of graphophonological relations used by the skilled reader is probably very large and it may include several levels of structure (graphemes, nuclei and codas, onsets and rimes, syllables, etc.). Therefore, the process of learning these relations may be—to a large extent—implicit. However, this is not the issue under debate; the question is whether or not phonological decoding can be completely learned implicitly. Conversely, it may be the case that an initial impulse given by the awareness of phonemes and the conscious knowledge of their relation to graphemes is necessary.

The well-known experiments of Brian Byrne (e.g., Byrne, 1993b) suggest that grapheme–phoneme correspondences cannot be learned implicitly from simple exposure to an alphabetic notation. Although the print exposure the children received may have been insufficient to show an effect, Byrne also showed that, given the same amount of print experience, kindergarten children trained in phoneme awareness and letter–sound associations were able to recognize short written words that contained those components. Moreover, no further phonemic training was necessary to recognize previously untrained phonemes and their graphemic counterparts, or to recognize already trained phonemes in novel word positions—the children had learned a general principle.

Recently, Rack, Hulme, Snowling, and Wightman (1994) questioned the role that sequential decoding may play in beginning reading. In their experiments, better learning was obtained when a critical letter was changed in such a way that the phoneme corresponding to that letter only differed from the phoneme corresponding to the *replaced* letter in voicing (d/t) than when it differed either in place of articulation (d/b) or in both features (d/p). Rack et al. argued that, in the early stages of learning to read, a process of direct mapping between cues for pronunciation (which are present in the letters of the word) and the pronunciation of the corresponding word occurs automatically and unconsciously. However, it is difficult to separate the implicit learning process from the role of conscious knowledge. Although the subjects were only 5 years old, they had been taught letter–sound relations at school and they displayed considerable knowledge of these relations. This conscious knowledge may have increased the children's sensitivity to the phonological proximity of the target and its replacement.

Discussing this effect of phonological proximity, Rack et al. used the term *implicit awareness of the structure of speech sounds.* We find it difficult to understand this paradoxical notion of implicit awareness. That people are sensitive to phonological similarity has been documented many times. Therefore, one expects that it will be easier to associate a letter representing one sound with a letter that represents a similar sound than to associate it with a letter that represents a less similar sound. In addition, we are skeptical about the role of such partial cues in written word recognition after the very initial stages of learning to read. The paradigm used by the authors, of associative learning with sequences of consonants, is one in which the subjects can benefit from such a strategy. However, it is probably not akin to the normal situation of learning to read.

Sensitivity to phonological relations has been observed in young children's spontaneous or invented spelling, but this may reflect explicit knowledge of letter–sound or grapheme–phoneme relations rather than implicit knowledge. In a study in which kindergarten pupils were taught phoneme awareness (Blachman, Ball, Black, & Tangel, 1994), a large improvement in invented spelling was observed. For instance, although none of the children were able to spell the word *sick* correctly, about one third of the children trained in phoneme awareness spelled all the phonemes with conventional letters, whereas none of the controls demonstrated this level of representation. Interestingly, the invented spellings of the trained subjects were much more accurate than those of the controls, even for letters that had not been included in the training. This is a further demonstration that acquiring phoneme awareness provides a general principle that can then be applied to new phonemes and new situations.

All people who can read an alphabetic script are aware of the phonemic structure of language. If phoneme awareness were an epiphenomenon, it would constitute a very extraordinary case of universal insight following implicit learning. In artificial grammar learning, subjects show only partial knowledge of the rules and often report incorrect rules (Reber, 1989; Reber & Lewis, 1977). In the implicit learning of dynamic systems, the explicit knowledge reported by the subjects is also frequently incorrect (Berry & Broadbent, 1984). In the Hebb digits task, which shows a facilitatory effect of repetition, the subjects may remain unaware of the repetition (McKelvie, 1987). In a similar vein, subjects are unaware of the contingency (Lewicki, Hill, & Biziot, 1988) following the implicit learning of responses contingent on previously presented items, and, in implicit learning of sequences in reaction times tasks, only some subjects become aware of the sequences (Willingham, Nissen, & Bullemer, 1989). Thus, in most situations of implicit learning there seems to be no insight into the learned pattern. It is worth noting, however, that the very notion of learning without concurrent awareness is still a matter for debate. Shanks and St. John (1994) offered the conclusion that there is "little actual support for unconscious rule induction (i.e., for implicit learning), or for the unconscious learning of any other type of information" (p. 368).

In the studies mentioned here, no attempt was made to provide a precise index of awareness either before or during learning. Therefore, it is difficult to claim that the learning demonstrated was independent of awareness. Similarly, a precise inquiry into the degree of conscious awareness of sublexical relations that children develop as they acquire the phonological decoding mechanism has not yet been made. We have observed that first-grade children who already know some grapheme–phoneme correspondences can use their experience of decoding new words to discover contextual and positional rules. After a few months of reading instruction, D. noticed that (in French) *in* is only read as /ɛ̃/ when it is followed by a consonant. The comments made by this child clearly suggested that he had realized that the pronunciation of this letter string depends on syllabic units. He also realized that *er* is pronounced as /ɛR/ when it occurs within a word and precedes a consonant, but as /e/ when it occurs at the end of a word.

A more fundamental question to ask is why explicit learning is necessary for the acquisition of the phonological transcoding procedures. When one considers the cases of implicit learning mentioned previously, one notices that what has to be learned is a set of rules governing the relations between a set of already individualised elements. This is not the case when learning an alphabet. The elements—the phonemes—are still to be discovered. An explicit knowledge of these elements may be required before contextual and positional rules can be learned, perhaps implicitly. In learning to read and write an alphabetic script, implicit and explicit learning may have specific and complementary roles.

Emphasis on implicit learning in learning to read, especially when coupled with a disregard for the importance of learning through awareness, is more consistent with whole-word teaching than with a phonic method. As Adams and Bruck (1993) documented, the whole-language approach to teaching reading is based on the idea that the best way to learn to read is to read. The title of the paper by Cossu et al. (1993b), "Reading Is Reading Is Reading," suggests that they share this view.

Cossu and his colleagues went a step further when they claimed that learning to read is a natural biological process. Is it because we have tested and talked with more than 100 illiterate adults that we argue that learning to read cannot be a biological process? Were we wrong believing, as we assumed everybody believed, that literacy is a cultural phenomenon based partly on the biological capacities that enable us to process speech?

The fact that alphabetic literacy depends on biological capacities must be recognized. We ourselves have argued that the specific phonological deficits evident in many dyslexics and poor readers may result from some anomaly in their speech processing systems (see, for a review, Morais & Mousty, 1992). This is not inconsistent with the idea that phoneme awareness plays a causal role in the acquisition of phonological transcoding procedures. Phoneme awareness makes explicit some of the structural units that are involved in speech production and perception. This allows a writing system to be based on these units. Phoneme awareness is difficult to achieve because these units are hidden both in the acoustic stream of speech and in our conscious percept of speech. Although phoneme awareness requires teaching (it is not spontaneous—it can appear at 5 years of age, at 60 years, or never), it depends ultimately on our biological predisposition for language. However, to depend on and to be part of something are not the same thing: Phoneme awareness and literacy are not biological achievements.

SUBLEXICAL ORTHOGRAPHIC REPRESENTATIONS AND THE POSSIBLE ROLE OF DIFFERENCES AMONG DIFFERENT LANGUAGES

Phoneme awareness can help children to develop a knowledge of orthographic units larger than the letter, and children who have learned a set of simple grapheme–phoneme correspondences will soon meet many deviations from these simple rules as their experience with written language grows. They will notice that the simple rule only applies in some cases and discover (or be told) that adjacent letters in the word are also important. Thus, beginning readers and spellers inevitably supplement simple correspondence rules with an increasingly sophisticated set of rules about exceptions.

Deviations from simple grapheme–phoneme correspondences are of two types. First, deviations may reflect contextual and positional dependence. Our informal observations suggest that explicit knowledge of these deviations is dependent on the development of phoneme awareness. Unfortunately, published studies do not yet provide us with any systematic evidence on this.

Second, deviations may stem from local irregularities. There is increasing correlational evidence that children learn irregular words as deviations from rules. Indeed, several studies indicate that knowledge of irregular words and knowledge of grapheme–phoneme correspondences are highly correlated. Byrne, Freebody, and Gates (1992) found that second-grade poor readers with good decoding ability but below-average recognition of irregular words had better reading of both regular *and* irregular words when tested 1 year later compared with their peers who had the reverse pattern of skills (i.e., poor decoding but average irregular word recognition). Gough and Walsh (1992) examined individual differences in pseudoword and irregular word reading. They found subjects with good pseudoword reading and poor irregular word reading, but no subjects with the reverse pattern. This supports the idea that decoding skills are necessary to learn to read irregular words. Moreover, their subjects with good decoding skills learned new irregular words quicker than did poorer decoders. Foorman, Francis, Novy, and Liberman (1991) compared children who had received a large amount of instruction in letter–sound correspondences with those who had received only a small amount of such instruction. They found that the more highly trained children showed greater gains in reading and spelling both regular and irregular words. In a similar vein, Leybaert and Content (1995) compared second-grade children learning to read with either a whole-word or a phonics approach. The children taught by phonic methods were better at reading and spelling irregular words than were those taught by whole-word methods. Finally, Bradley (1988) found that metaphonological skill measured at 6 years predicted irregular word retention at 7 years, even after variations in irregular word retention at 6 years were taken into account. Interestingly, irregular word retention at 6 years did not predict metaphonological skill at 7 years.

This evidence suggests that the construction of an orthographic lexicon depends—both for regular and irregular words—on the use of a phonological decoding procedure that incorporates more and more rules as a function of reading experience. In the early stages, this phonological decoding procedure will depend on explicit knowledge of simple grapheme–phoneme correspondences and hence also on phoneme awareness. With development, contextual and positional correspondence rules are acquired and the learner gains representations of orthographic units that are larger than the single letter. This is related to the important role that intermediate units play in skilled reading—a topic that has been disregarded in some of the most important models of skilled reading (Coltheart, 1978; Coltheart, Curtis, & Atkins, 1993; McClelland & Rumelhart, 1981; Seidenberg & McClelland, 1989). None of these models represent units that are intermediate in size between letters and words. However, there is increasing evidence, both from experimental and neural imagery studies, that intermediate units play an important role in skilled reading. Next, we list only a few examples.

Radeau, Morais, Mousty, Saerens, and Bertelson (1991, 1992; see also Mewhort & Beale, 1997) used an incremental presentation procedure to examine the uniqueness point for written word recognition. They found that grouping letters by syllable affects the size of the uniqueness point effect. Other studies also illustrate the perceptual role of the syllable. Prinzmetal, Treiman, and Rho (1986) found that subjects are more likely to erroneously combine the identity of one letter and the color of an adjacent letter if the two letters belong to the same syllable rather than to different syllables. As subsequently suggested by Prinzmetal, Hoffman, and Vest (1991) and by Rapp (1992), this effect could be both prelexical and lexical in origin. The effect does not seem to be confounded with bigram frequency: In Spanish, Carreiras, Alvarez, and de Vega (1993) obtained an effect of syllable frequency on lexical decision responses even when bigram frequency was equated both within and across syllable boundaries. In addition to syllables, intrasyllabic units such as onset and rime might also constitute units of perceptual analysis in written word recognition. For example, Treiman and Chafetz (1987) found that skilled readers responded faster in a lexical decision task when an extraneous symbol separated the onset and the rime than when it occurred within the rime.

Neural imagery data show that strings of consonants and words activate an occipitotemporal area in the right hemisphere (Compton, Grossenbacher, Posner, & Tucker, 1991). However, only words and orthographically legal pseudowords, but not strings of consonants, activate a prestriate area in the internal part of the left hemisphere (Compton et al., 1991; Petersen, Fox, Snyder, & Raichle, 1990). These data do not provide evidence for a particular intermediate unit, but they do suggest that some intermediate unit or units may be relevant.

Given the relevance of intermediate units in written word recognition, it is important to consider how awareness of these units may develop during literacy acquisition. In doing so, one should not overlook the potential importance of differences between different languages. Orthographic structures correspond to phonological structures, and these differ across languages. A cross-language approach is thus necessary, at both the phonological and orthographic levels.

On the orthographic side, there are some conflicting results between English and French and between English and Dutch that may reflect genuine differences between the orthographic structures of these languages. Taft and Radeau (1995) found that skilled readers of French, contrary to skilled readers of English, use the syllable but not the BOB (rime of the first syllable plus the initial consonant of the next syllable) in a naming task. As indicated previously, there is evidence from native speakers of English that orthographic units correspond to onset and rime. In contrast, van Daal, Reitsma, and van der Leij (1994), testing Dutch disabled readers, found no evidence to suggest that reading was based on onset-rime segmentation. Whether this discrepancy is related to reading level or to genuine language differences obviously needs to be clarified.

Turning to the phonological structure of different languages and to the speech segmentation processes adopted by native speakers of different languages, there is already clear-cut evidence that both structures and processes are language dependent. Using a monitoring paradigm, Mehler, Dommergues, Frauenfelder, and Segui (1981) manipulated the relationship between the phonological structure of the target (e.g., /ba/ or /bal/) and the phonological structure of the carrier word (e.g., the French words *ba.lance* or *bal.con*). French native speakers needed more time when there was no exact correspondence between the target and the initial syllable of the carrier word than when there was such a correspondence. This interaction suggests that a syllabification procedure was operating during the process of word recognition. However, Cutler, Mehler, Norris, and Segui (1983, 1986) observed that this interaction was absent when English listeners were tested, regardless of whether English or French materials were used. In contrast, French listeners still displayed the interaction when tested using English materials. Listeners thus seem to use fixed strategies that depend on their native language. Differences have now been shown for many other languages, including Spanish, Catalan (Sebastián-Gallés, Dupoux, Segui, & Mehler, 1992), and Japanese (Cutler & Otake, 1994; Otake, Hatano, Cutler, & Mehler, 1993).

We have developed another paradigm that probably taps deeper perceptual processes than that used by Mehler et al. (1981). In their monitoring task, the language effects might stem from the format of the phonological representations involved in the matching operation in different languages rather than from perception itself. Moreover, it is possible that some subjects may rely on lexical or orthographic representations, even though these are not particularly useful. It seems possible, therefore, that factors outside the perceptual system may provide the basis on which responses are made in the monitoring task (see discussions, e.g., in Bradley, Sánchez-Casas, & García-Albea, 1993; Dupoux & Mehler, 1992; Eimas, Marcovitz Hornstein, & Payton, 1990; Frauenfelder, Segui, & Dijkstra, 1990).

In a recent paper, we argued that illusory speech conjunctions may constitute a technique for examining early, unconscious word representations (Kolinsky, Morais, & Cluytens, 1995). One advantage of this technique is that no intentional retrieval of word constituents is required, because both the stimuli and the responses are at the word level. The procedure was inspired both by dichotic phonetic feature blending experiments (e.g., Cutting, 1976) and by the visual "illusory conjunctions" phenomenon (e.g., Treisman & Paterson, 1984; Treisman & Schmidt, 1982). The paradigm consists of eliciting illusory words that are created by blending two dichotic stimuli. We compared experimental trials in which the two stimuli contain all the information necessary for the illusory perception of a French target word (e.g., target *bijou*, /biʒu/ in /kiʒu-bɔtõ/), to *control* trials, in which the dichotic pair lacks the critical linguistic property that would allow the illusion to occur (e.g., /kiʒu-dɔtõ/). The distribution of information between the two stimuli was manipulated experimentally in order to test the relevance of different constituents of words for spoken word recognition: the initial consonant, as already illustrated; the place of articulation or the voicing of the initial consonant; the first vowel; or the syllables (e.g., /bitõ-koʒu/). We observed that, in French, illusory words were more frequently experienced if the distribution corresponded to syllables rather than other linguistic properties (e.g., /bɔtu-kiʒõ/). Furthermore, syllabic migration errors were still observed in a ear-oriented naming task. The dominant role of the syllable in French was thus strongly supported by our findings.

Using this paradigm, differences between languages have also been observed. For example, we found that the initial consonant is more prevalent in the migration errors of Portuguese than French speakers (Kolinsky & Morais, 1993). A similar pattern of results was found for illiterate adults (Morais & Kolinsky, 1994) and preliterate children (Castro, Vicente, Morais, Kolinsky, & Cluytens, 1995). This perhaps suggests that the phenomenon reflects early unconscious codes, unaffected by orthographic representations. We believe that the relationship between these speech perception findings and reading mechanisms should be examined. For a long time the study of speech and the study of reading have been separated, which is unfortunate given the theoretical and empirical links that exist between them.

We have examined a few patients who, interestingly, displayed correlated deficits across speech perception, reading mechanisms, and metaphonological tasks. A surface dyslexic, J.S., displayed no effect of lexicality in either reading or writing, but did show a large effect of regularity. He was only slightly impaired in his conscious phonemic abilities (in reading, too, there were a number of single consonant confusions, suggesting a slight impairment in his graphophonological conversion procedure, besides his impairment in the addressing procedure).

Two phonological dyslexics, P.R. and S.A., and a deep dyslexic, V.D., were extremely poor at nonword reading, but none of them displayed a regularity effect. Interestingly, all were also extremely poor at the phonemic tests, performing at around chance level, although two of them performed much better on rhyme judgments and a syllable test than on phoneme tests. Thus, when the reading deficit spares the mechanism of phonological assembly (i.e., surface dyslexia), phonemic awareness is still present. However, in those cases where phonological assembly is dramatically damaged, the patients behave almost like illiterate people in tests of metaphonological ability. The assembly procedure in reading may therefore depend on the same phoneme representations that are evoked for the purpose of intentional, conscious manipulations of phonemes.

More recently, we tested these subjects on a new set of metaphonological tasks and on the speech dichotic test designed to induce attribute migration errors (unpublished data). Their results were compared to those of four control subjects of the same age and educational level, and to 36 younger undergraduate students. We wanted to know if individuals with impaired phonemic analysis and phonological assembly in reading would show the same pattern of attribute migrations in speech recognition as would normal listeners.

The results were very clear. J.S. (whose reading had improved but who still displayed a strong surface dysgraphia) performed as poorly as the phonological dyslexics in the dichotic task. However, he was the only patient who showed both a reasonable level of performance on phonemic metaphonological tests and the normal pattern of migrations for French listeners (i.e., a high rate of migrations for syllables). The deep dyslexic and the two phonological dyslexics failed to show migrations. It should be noted that, with the exception of J.S., who was relatively good at repeating both words and nonwords, all the other patients displayed good word repetition but relatively poor nonword repetition. However, because the phonological dyslexics V.D. and P.R. had been diagnosed as Broca's aphasics, whereas S.A. had been diagnosed as a Wernicke's aphasic, there was not a clear association with one type of aphasia.

Do these data suggest that the distinction between conscious and unconscious phonological representations has to be questioned? We do not believe so. Indeed, this distinction was clearly supported by the dissociation observed in illiterate people: Whereas Portuguese illiterate adults were unaware of phonemes, these units did participate in the migration errors they experienced, just as they did in literate controls (Morais & Kolinsky, 1994). In addition, inspection of the neuroanatomical and neuropsychological data available up to now suggests that conscious and unconscious representations of phonemes rely on different—although, as it could be expected, relatively close—brain areas (see discussion in Morais & Kolinsky, 1994). Of course, a trivial interpretation of our correlational data may be that the cerebral damage experienced by our patients was wide enough to affect two closely localized systems of representation: the representations used in speech perception, and those used in phonological assembly and conscious operations. We do not have neuroanatomical data precise enough to answer this. However, an alternative and much more interesting interpretation of our observations is that conscious and unconscious phonological representations are functionally dependent. If the elaboration of conscious segmental representations of speech depends on the quality of the global speech percept, then damage to the structures involved in the perceptual processing of speech may lead not only to a perceptual deficit, but also to an impairment of both metaphonological and decoding skills. Thus, although we argue that phonemic awareness plays a crucial role in learning to read an alphabetic orthography, we do not deny the importance of implicit phonological representations. In particular, in languages in which perceptual processing at the phonemic level may be crucial for the quality of the global conscious speech percept, the loss of unconscious phonemic representations may prevent the speaker from activating the corresponding conscious representations.

ACKNOWLEDGMENTS

Our work reported here has been supported by the Belgian "Fonds National de la Recherche Scientifique-Loterie Nationale" (convention 8.4505.92), and "Ministère de la Communauté française" ("Action de recherches concertée," 91/96–148), as well as by the Human Frontiers of Science Program (Research project entitled "The processing consequences of contrasting language phonologies") and the European Communities ("Human Capital & Mobility," Research project entitled "Language as cognitive capacity: Perception and acquisition"). The third author is Research Associate of the Belgian Fonds National de la Recherche Scientifique (F.N.R.S.). Eva Debaix and Stéphanie Remy took part in the collection of the data and deserve our gratitude.

REFERENCES

Adams, M. J., & Bruck, M. (1993). Word recognition: The interface of educational policies and scientific research. *Reading and Writing: An Interdisciplinary Journal, 5,* 113–139.

Alegria, J., Morais, J., D'Alimonte, G., & Seyll, S. *The development of speech analysis and reading acquisition in a whole-word setting.* Manuscript submitted for publication.

Ball, E. W., & Blachman, B. A. (1988). Phoneme segmentation training: Effect on reading readiness. *Annals of Dyslexia, 38,* 208–225.

Ball, E. W., & Blachman, B. A. (1991). Does phoneme segmentation training in kindergarten make a difference in early word recognition and developmental spelling? *Reading Research Quarterly, 26,* 49–66.

Bentin, S., & Leshem, H. (1993). On the interaction between phonological awareness and reading acquisition: It's a two-way street. *Annals of Dyslexia, 43,* 125–148.

Berry, D. C., & Broadbent, D. E. (1984). On the relationship between task performance and associated verbal knowledge. *Quarterly Journal of Experimental Psychology, 36A,* 209–231.

Bertelson, P. (1993). Reading acquisition and phonemic awareness testing: How conclusive are data from Down's syndrome? (Remarks on Cossu, Rossini, and Marshall, 1993). *Cognition, 48,* 281–283.

Blachman, B. A., Ball, E. W., Black, R. S., & Tangel, M. (1994). Kindergarten teachers develop phoneme awareness in low-income, inner-city classrooms. Does it make a difference? *Reading and Writing: An Interdisciplinary Journal, 6,* 1–18.

Bradley, D. C., Sánchez-Casas, R. M., & García-Albea, J. E. (1993). The status of the syllable in the perception of Spanish and English. *Language and Cognitive Processes, 8,* 197–233.

Bradley, L. (1988). Making connections in learning to read and to spell. *Applied Cognitive Psychology, 2,* 3–18.

Bradley, L., & Bryant, P. (1983). Categorizing sounds and learning to read—a causal connection. *Nature, 310,* 419–421.

Byrne, B. (1993a). Learning to read in the absence of phonemic awareness? A comment on Cosu, Rossini, and Marshall (1993). *Cognition, 48,* 285–288.

Byrne, B. (1993b). Studies in the acquisition procedure for reading: Rationale, hypotheses, and data. In P. B. Gough, L. C. Ehri, & R. Treiman (Eds.), *Reading acquisition* (pp. 1–34). Hillsdale, NJ: Lawrence Erlbaum Associates.

Byrne, B., Freebody, P., & Gates, A. (1992). Longitudinal data on the relations of word-reading strategies to comprehension, reading time, and phonemic awareness. *Reading Research Quarterly, 27,* 141–151.

Carreiras, M., Alvarez, C. J., & de Vega, M. (1993). Syllable frequency and visual word recognition in Spanish. *Journal of Memory and Language, 32,* 766–780.

Castro, S.-L., Vicente, S., Morais, J., Kolinsky, R., & Cluytens, M. (1995). Segmental representation of Portuguese in 5- and 6-year-olds: Evidence from dichotic listening. In I. HubFaria & J. Freitas (Eds.), *Studies of the acquisition of Portuguese* (pp. 1–16). Lisbon: Colebrei.

Coltheart, M. (1978). Lexical access in simple reading tasks. In G. Underwood (Ed.), *Strategies of information processing* (pp. 151–216). New York: Academic.

Coltheart, M., Curtis, B., & Atkins, P. (1993). Models of reading aloud: Dual-route and parallel-distributed-processing approaches. *Psychological Review, 100,* 589–608.

Compton, P., Grossenbacher, P., Posner, M., & Tucker, D. M. (1991). A cognitive anatomical approach to attention in lexical access. *Journal of Cognitive Neuroscience, 3,* 304–312.

Cossu, G., & Marshall, J. C. (1990). Are cognitive skills a prerequisite for learning to read and write? *Cognitive Neuropsychology, 7,* 21–40.

Cossu, G., Rossini, F., & Marshall, J. C. (1993a). When reading is acquired but phonemic awareness is not: A study of literacy in Down's syndrome. *Cognition, 46,* 129–138.

Cossu, G., Rossini, F., & Marshall, J. C. (1993b). Reading is reading is reading. *Cognition, 48,* 297–303.

Cunningham, A. E. (1990). Explicit versus implicit instruction in phonemic awareness. *Journal of Experimental Child Psychology, 50,* 429–444.

Cutler, A., Mehler, J., Norris, D., & Segui, J. (1983). A language specific comprehension strategy. *Nature*, *304*, 159–160.
Cutler, A., Mehler, J., Norris, D., & Segui, J. (1986). The syllable's differing role in the segmentation of French and English. *Journal of Memory and Language*, *25*, 385–400.
Cutler, A., & Otake, T. (1994). Mora or phoneme? Further evidence for language-specific listening. *Journal of Memory and Language*, *33*, 824–844.
Cutting, J. E. (1976). Auditory and linguistic processes in speech perception: Inferences from six fusions in dichotic listening. *Psychological Review*, *83*, 114–140.
Defior, S., & Tudela, P. (1994). Effect of phonological training on reading and writing acquisition. *Reading and Writing: An Interdisciplinary Journal*, *6*, 299–320.
Dupoux, E., & Mehler, J. (1992). Unifying awareness and on-line studies of speech: A tentative framework. In J. Alegria, D. Holender, J. Morais, & M. Radeau (Eds.), *Analytic approaches to human cognition* (pp. 59–75). Amsterdam: North-Holland.
Eimas, P. D., Marcovitz Hornstein, S. B., & Payton, P. (1990). Attention and the role of dual codes in phoneme monitoring. *Journal of Memory and Language*, *29*, 160–180.
Foorman, B. R., Francis, D. J., Novy, D. M., & Liberman, D. (1991). How letter–sound instruction mediates progress in first-grade reading and spelling. *Journal of Educational Psychology*, *83*, 459–469.
Frauenfelder, U. H., Segui, J., & Dijkstra, T. (1990). Lexical effects in phonemic processing: Facilitatory or inhibitory? *Journal of Experimental Psychology: Human Perception and Performance*, *16*, 77–91.
Gough, P. G., & Walsh, M. A. (1992). Chinese, Phoenicians and the orthographic cipher of English. In S. Brady & D. Shankweiler (Eds.), *Phonological processes in literacy. A tribute to Isabelle Y. Liberman* (pp. 199–209). Hillsdale, NJ: Lawrence Erlbaum Associates.
Hatcher, P. J., Hulme, C., & Ellis, A. W. (1994). Ameliorating early reading failure by integrating the teaching of reading and phonological skills: The phonological linkage hypothesis. *Child Development*, *65*, 41–57.
Kavanagh, J. F., & Mattingly, I. G. (1972). *Language by ear and by eye*. Cambridge, MA: MIT Press.
Kolinsky, R., & Morais, J. (1993). Intermediate representations in spoken word recognition: A cross-linguistic study of word illusions. In *Proceedings of the 3d European Conference on Speech Communication and Technology*, 731–734.
Kolinsky, R., Morais, J., & Cluytens, M. (1995). Intermediate representations in spoken word recognition: Evidence from word illusions. *Journal of Memory and Language*, *34*, 19–40.
Lewicki, P., Hill, T., & Biziot, E. (1988). Acquisition of procedural knowledge about a pattern of stimuli that cannot be articulated. *Cognitive Psychology*, *20*, 24–37.
Leybaert, J., & Content, A. (1995). Reading and spelling acquisition in two different teaching methods: A test of the independence hypothesis. *Reading and Writing: An Interdisciplinary Journal*, *7*, 65–88.
Liberman, I. Y. (1991). Phonology and beginning reading revisited. In C. von Euler (Ed.), *Wenner-Gren International Symposium Series: Brain and reading* (pp. 207–220). Hampshire, England: Macmillan.
Lundberg, I., Frost, J., & Petersen, O. (1988). Effects of an extensive program for stimulating phonological awareness in pre-school children. *Reading Research Quarterly*, *23*, 263–284.
Marshall, J. C., & Cossu, G. (1990). Is pathological development part of normal cognitive neuropsychology? A rejoinder to Marcel. *Cognitive Neuropsychology*, *7*, 49–55.
Marshall, J. C., & Cossu, G. (1991). Poor readers and black swans. *Mind and Language*, *6*, 135–139.
McClelland, J. L., & Rumelhart, D. E. (1981). An interactive activation model of context effects in letter perception: Part I. An account of basic findings. *Psychological Review*, *88*, 375–407.

McKelvie, S. J. (1987). Learning and awareness in the Hebb digits task. *Journal of General Psychology, 114,* 75–88.
Mehler, J., Dommergues, S., Frauenfelder, U. H., & Segui, J. (1981). The syllable's role in speech segmentation. *Journal of Verbal Learning and Verbal Behavior, 20,* 298–305.
Mewhort, D. J. K., & Beale, A. L. (1977). Mechanisms of word identification. *Journal of Experimental Psychology: Human Perception and Performance, 3,* 629–640.
Morais, J., & Kolinsky, R. (1994). Perception and awareness in phonological processing: The case of the phoneme. *Cognition, 50,* 287–297.
Morais, J., & Mousty, P. (1992). The causes of phonemic awareness. In J. Alegria, D. Holender, J. Morais, & M. Radeau (Eds.), *Analytic approaches to human cognition* (pp. 93–212). Amsterdam: North-Holland.
Morton, J., & Frith, U. (1993). What lesson for dyslexia from Down's syndrome? Comments on Cossu, Rossini, and Marshall (1993). *Cognition, 48,* 289–296.
Mousty, P., Leybaert, J., Alegria, J., Content, A., & Morais, J. (1994). BELEC: Une batterie d'évaluation du langage écrit et de ses troubles. In J. Grégoire & B. Piérart (Eds.), *Evaluer les troubles de la lecture: Les nouveaux modèles théoriques et leurs implications diagnostiques* [Evaluating reading difficulties: The new theoretical models and their diagnostic implications] (pp. 127–145). Brussels: De Boeck.
Otake, T., Hatano, G., Cutler, A., & Mehler, J. (1993). Mora or syllable? Speech segmentation in Japanese. *Journal of Memory and Language, 32,* 258–278.
Petersen, S. E., Fox, P. T., Snyder, A. Z., & Raichle, M. E. (1990). Activation of extrastriate and frontal cortical areas by visual words and word-like stimuli. *Science, 249,* 1041–1044.
Prinzmetal, W., Hoffman, H., & Vest, K. (1991). Automatic processes in word perception: An analysis from illusory conjunctions. *Journal of Experimental Psychology: Human Perception and Performance, 17,* 902–923.
Prinzmetal, W., Treiman, R., & Rho, S. H. (1986). How to see a reading unit. *Journal of Memory and Language, 25,* 461–475.
Rack, J., Hulme, C., Snowling, M., & Wightman, J. (1994). The role of phonology in young children learning to read words: The direct-mapping hypothesis. *Journal of Experimental Child Psychology, 57,* 42–71.
Radeau, M., Morais, J., Mousty, P., Saerens, M., & Bertelson, P. (1991, November). *The effect of the uniqueness point in processing printed words.* Spoken communication at the 32nd Annual Meeting of the Psychonomic Society, San Francisco.
Radeau, M., Morais, J., Mousty, P., Saerens, M., & Bertelson, P. (1992). A listener's investigation of printed word processing. *Journal of Experimental Psychology: Human Perception and Performance, 18,* 861–871.
Rapp, B. C. (1992). The nature of sublexical orthographic organization: The bigram trough hypothesis examined. *Journal of Memory and Language, 31,* 33–53.
Reber, A. S. (1989). Implicit learning and tacit knowledge. *Journal of Experimental Psychology: General, 118,* 219–235.
Reber, A. S., & Lewis, S. (1977). Implicit learning: An analysis of the form and structure of a body of tacit knowledge. *Cognition, 5,* 333–361.
Reber, A. S., & Scarborough, D. L. (1977). *Toward a psychology of reading.* Hillsdale, NJ: Lawrence Erlbaum Associates.
Scliar-Cabral, L., Morais, J., Nepomuceno, L., & Kolinsky, R. *Phonemic awareness versus phonemic sensitivity: A study of Brazilian adults of different levels of literacy.* Manuscript submitted for publication.
Sebastián-Gallés, N., Dupoux, E., Segui, J., & Mehler, J. (1992). Contrasting syllabic effects in Catalan and Spanish. *Journal of Memory and Language, 31,* 18–32.
Seidenberg, M. S., & McClelland, J. L. (1989). A distributed, developmental model of word recognition and naming. *Psychological Review, 96,* 523–568.

Shanks, D. R., & St. John, M. F. (1994). Characteristics of dissociable human learning systems. *Behavioral and Brain Sciences, 17,* 367–447.

Taft, M., & Radeau, M. (1995). The influence of the phonological characteristics of a language on the functional units of reading: A study in French. *Canadian Journal of Psychology, 49,* 330–346.

Thompson, G. B., & Fletcher-Flinn, C. M. (1993). A theory of knowledge sources and procedures for reading acquisition. In G. B. Thompson, W. E. Tunmer, & T. Nicholson (Eds.), *Reading acquisition processes* (pp. 20–73). Clevedon, Avon, England: Multilingual Matters.

Treiman, R., & Chafetz, J. (1987). Are there onset- and rime-like units in printed words? In M. Coltheart (Ed.), *Attention and performance XII. The psychology of reading* (pp. 281–298). Hillsdale, NJ: Lawrence Erlbaum Associates.

Treisman, A., & Paterson, R. (1984). Emergent features, attention, and object perception. *Journal of Experimental Psychology: Human Perception and Performance, 10,* 12–32.

Treisman, A., & Schmidt, H. (1982). Illusory conjunctions in the perception of objects. *Cognitive Psychology, 14,* 107–141.

Vallar, G., & Papagno, C. (1993). Preserved vocabulary acquisition in Down's syndrome: The role of phonological short-term memory. *Cortex, 29,* 467–483.

van Daal, V. H. P., Reitsma, P., & van der Leij, A. (1994). Processing units in word reading by disabled readers. *Journal of Experimental Child Psychology, 57,* 180–210.

Williams, J. P. (1980). Teaching decoding with a special emphasis on phoneme analysis and phoneme blending. *Journal of Educational Psychology, 72,* 1–15.

Willingham, D. B., Nissen, M. J., & Bullemer, P. (1989). On the development of procedural knowledge. *Journal of Experimental Psychology: Learning, Memory, and Cognition, 15,* 1047–1060.

Chapter 8

Proto-Literate Knowledge: Antecedents and Influences on Phonological Awareness and Literacy

Roderick W. Barron
University of Guelph, Ontario, Canada

Understanding the acquisition of literacy can be regarded as an attempt to understand the nature of the mental representations that underlie the relationship between print and speech, and how these representations are modified during the course of the acquisition of reading and spelling skills. These changing mental representations have been examined most closely during and following the period of time that children receive formal instruction (e.g., Brown & Loosemore, 1994; Hulme, Snowling, & Quinlan, 1991; Plaut, McClelland, Seidenberg, & Patterson, 1996; Seidenberg & McClelland, 1989), but there is increasing interest in the nature of print–speech representations before children have learned to read or spell any words accurately (e.g., Barron, 1986, 1991, 1994; Bowey, 1994; Byrne, 1992; Ehri 1978, 1979, 1983, 1984, 1992, 1993; Perfetti, 1992; Rack, Hulme, Snowling, & Wightman, 1994; Stahl & Murray, 1994). Attempts to characterize these early, proto-literate representations may play a role in identifying the specific knowledge about print and speech that predicts successful acquisition of reading and spelling skill, and may also assist in efforts to resolve a controversy that is a central issue in this chapter—the nature of the relationship between phonological awareness and literacy.

There are two commonly held views about the causal connection between phonological awareness and literacy. The first can be summarized by this statement: Phonological awareness causes literacy. According to this view, phonological awareness emerges spontaneously during the course of normal language development, and it has a subsequent causal influence on the acquisition of reading and spelling skill (e.g., Bradley & Bryant, 1983; Bryant, Maclean, Bradley, & Crossland, 1990; Cunningham, 1990; Goswami & Bryant, 1990; Lundberg, Frost, & Petersen, 1988). Knowledge of print, whether acquired informally or formally, does not influence the causal link going from phonological awareness to literacy.

The second view can be summarized by this statement: Literacy causes phonological awareness. According to this view, phonological awareness is a by-product of having learned to read and spell, and it does not emerge spontaneously during the course of language development (e.g., Bertelson, Morais, Alegria, & Content, 1985; Morais, Cary, Alegria, & Bertelson, 1979). Instead, literacy is regarded as a foundation skill on which phonological awareness is based and, as literacy skill increases, phonological awareness skill is further refined.

Of course, the relationship between phonological awareness and literacy is much more complex and interactive than is indicated by these two extreme statements (e.g., Morais, 1991a, 1991b; Morais, Alegria, & Content, 1987), and efforts to understand the precise nature of that relationship should begin with an attempt to define what is meant by the terms *phonological awareness* and *literacy*. In pursuit of this understanding, I discuss each of these terms with the goal, in each case, of offering definitions that may provide a basis for specifying the nature of print–speech representations, particularly those that might be available to children before they can read and spell. I begin with phonological awareness.

PHONOLOGICAL AWARENESS: UNITS AND TASKS

Stanovich (1986) provided a widely cited working definition in which he described phonological awareness as "conscious access to the phonemic level of the speech stream (i.e., individual speech sounds) and some ability to cognitively manipulate representations at this level" (p. 362). Since that time, however, he has modified the definition in order to avoid potential ambiguities associated with the term *consciousness* and to counteract the fact that some investigators use the term *phonological awareness* to refer specifically to manipulations at the phonemic level, whereas others use it to refer to any task that involves sensitivity to units of speech. Stanovich (1992) proposed that the term *phonological sensitivity* replace phonological awareness and that phonological sensitivity should be seen as being on a continuum. He argued that tasks involving explicit reports of analyses of smaller-sized units (e.g., phoneme deletion tasks) should be regarded as reflecting deep phonological sensitivity, whereas tasks involving less explicit reports of larger, unanalyzed units (e.g., rhyme matching tasks) should be regarded as reflecting shallow sensitivity.

Stanovich's (1992) reconsideration of the definition of phonological awareness functions to highlight several fundamental questions about the nature of that skill. First, what are the units of speech of which children are aware? Second, how does phonological awareness change with development? Third, what are the task parameters that might influence children's awareness of phonological units? There is broad consensus in the literature that changes in phonological awareness are associated with changes in awareness of the units making up the syllable. Treiman, in a set of seminal papers (see Treiman, 1992, for a review), identified units within the syllable that are arranged hierarchically, and found that children are more likely to demonstrate awareness of units at the top of the hierarchy before they are aware of units at the bottom. According to Treiman, syllables (e.g., *top, stamp*) can be segmented into onset and rime units in which the onset consists of an initial consonant (/t/) or consonant cluster (/st/), whereas the rime consists of a vowel (/ɑ/ or /æ/) and an optional following consonant (/p/) or consonant cluster (/mp/). The onsets and rimes can be further segmented into individual phonemes (e.g., /s/, /t/, /æ /, /m/, /p/). Treiman and others showed that syllable segmentation is easier at the onset-rime boundary than elsewhere in the syllable and that manipulating an onset (e.g., /st/) is easier than manipulating a phoneme embedded within an onset (e.g., /s/ within /st/). Children appear to be aware of rime units before they are aware of onset units (e.g., Maclean, Bryant, & Bradley, 1987), and this awareness can be facilitated through early language experiences involving rhyming (e.g., Bryant, Bradley, Maclean, & Crossland, 1989; Bryant et al., 1990).

Children who are aware of rime units may not show a similar level of awareness for the individual phonemes making them up. In fact, several investigators have proposed that children may not analyze rimes into their component phonemes; instead, they treat them as global units (Bertelson & deGelder, 1989; Cardoso-Martins, 1994). Finally, awareness of phonemes within a syllable may depend on their serial position (some final phonemes seem to be easier to delete than initial phonemes; e.g., Content, Kolinsky, Morais, & Bertelson, 1986; Stahl & Murray, 1994) and their degree of attachment to surrounding phonemes (e.g., liquids and nasals seem to be more closely attached to their preceding vowels than are obstruents; see Treiman, 1984).

Phonological awareness also depends on the tasks that children are required to perform. Stanovich, Cunningham, and Cramer (1984) found that phonological awareness tasks tended to load on a common factor. The one exception to this conclusion was rhyming task performance, which was at ceiling in their experiment. Yopp (1988) also used a factor analytic approach, but identified two factors, with one factor involving tasks that were similar to those used by Stanovich et al. (1984) and the other involving tasks that were more complex and had higher memory loads according to task analyses. Stahl and Murray (1994) pointed out that Yopp (1988) may have confounded level of subsyllabic unit with task difficulty. These investigators varied level of subsyllabic unit (onsets, rimes, phonemes) and task (isolation, blending, deletion, segmentation) independently. Although one factor accounted for a substantial percentage of the variance in analyses of subsyllabic unit (the scores were summed over task) and task (the scores were summed over subsyllabic unit), the percentage value was slightly higher for subsyllabic unit (81.7%) than for task (72.6%). Their results suggest that level of subsyllabic unit may be somewhat more important in defining level of phonological awareness than task difficulty.

It is important to note, however, that phonological awareness tasks can vary substantially in memory demands, and some investigators have proposed that there may be some that are nothing more than working memory tasks (e.g., Wagner & Torgesen, 1987), and that phonological awareness and working memory draw on the same underlying phonological ability. This possibility was recently investigated by Hansen and Bowey (1994). Measures of memory and phonological awareness shared a great deal of common variance, but according to Hansen and Bowey's (1994) hierarchical regression results, each made independent contributions to predicting several measures of word reading performance of Grade 2 subjects. In addition, measures of phonological awareness (but not measures of working memory) predicted performance on a nonword reading task. Finally, McDougall, Hulme, Ellis, and Monk (1994) showed that individual differences in speech rate (a measure of rate of rehearsal) may underlie differences in working memory. They found that measures of working memory did not account for any additional significant variance in predicting word reading performance in children once the variance associated with speech rate was removed statistically. Measures of phonological awareness (onset and phoneme deletion), however, continued to account for significant variance in word reading following the removal of variance associated with speech rate.

Reducing the memory demands of phonological awareness tasks can influence the age at which children show evidence of awareness of phonological segments. Bowey (1994) required children to decide, for example, which one of two pictures (e.g., a picture of a crab and a picture of a skate) began with the same phoneme (e.g., /s/) as a target picture (e.g., a picture of a sock). Following extensive feedback during practice sessions, Bowey (1994) found that 5-year-olds were above chance on this phonological identity task (taken from Wallach, Wallach, Dozier, & Kaplan, 1977) but at chance on a more memory-demanding oddity task (e.g., based on Bradley & Bryant, 1983) in which classification was based on the medial phoneme.

Taken together, these results suggest that phonological awareness is a very heterogeneous skill despite the fact that a large proportion of the variance is accounted for by one or two factors in several studies (e.g., Stahl & Murray, 1994; Stanovich et al., 1984; Yopp, 1988; see also Carrillo, 1994). First, the position of a subsyllabic unit in the hierarchical structure of the syllable influences subjects' ability to manipulate it. Children can manipulate higher-order onset and rime units more easily than the phonemes of which they consist. Second, the articulatory classification of the phoneme and its position in the syllable influence performance. Third, task variables influence the likelihood of showing phonological awareness for a particular subsyllabic unit. Fourth, although phonological awareness and working memory (or speech rate) make independent contributions to predicting reading performance, tasks with lower memory demands may be more likely to reveal awareness of subsyllabic units than those with higher demands. Fifth, as is discussed later, different levels of orthographic units can influence, and be influenced by, different levels of phonological units both before and after children can actually read or spell any words.

PROTO-LITERACY AND THE ONSET OF LITERACY

There have been two primary approaches to investigating the hypothesis that literacy causes phonological awareness. The first comes from the landmark research by Morais et al. (1979) showing that adult illiterates are not aware of units at the phonemic level. The advantage of this approach is that the causal influence of literacy on phonological awareness is relatively clear. Individuals deprived of the opportunity to learn to read as children are still not aware of phonemes as adults; however, they are able to acquire phonemic awareness skill when, as adults, they learn to read (Morais, Bertelson, Cary, & Alegria, 1986).

The second approach comes from examining children who have ample opportunity to learn to read. The evidence from this approach is less clear. First, although performance on phonological awareness tests is a strong predictor of subsequent success in reading skill in longitudinal studies, it is not clear how well the children could read and spell when they initially performed the phonological awareness tasks (e.g., Mann & Liberman, 1984; Stanovich et al., 1984) or, if known, the influence of initial reading level was not removed statistically (e.g., see Wagner & Torgesen's 1987 reanalysis of Lundberg, Olofsson, & Wall, 1980). Second, when very young children are used in longitudinal studies on reading in order to remove the influence of reading experience, the phonological awareness task performance that successfully predicts subsequent success in reading may involve subsyllabic units, such as rimes, that may not be influenced by literacy (e.g., Maclean et al., 1987). Third, even when investigators assess children who cannot read on tasks that involve awareness of subsyllabic units that may be more likely to be influenced by literacy (e.g., onsets and phonemes), they often fail to take into account what children know about print before they learn to read and spell (e.g., Kirtley, Bryant, Maclean, & Bradley, 1989).

The onset of literacy is typically defined with reference to performance on standardized psychometric tests in which children are required to read aloud single words out of context and to spell such words to dictation (e.g., Jastak & Wilkinson, 1984 [Wide Range Achievement Test–Revised]; Woodcock, 1987 [Woodcock Reading Mastery Tests–Revised]). More recently, the additional requirement of reading aloud nonwords has been added because nonwords require the children to decode the word rather than just look up a memorized pronunciation (e.g., Rack, Snowling, & Olson, 1992). This is a very stringent definition of literacy, and it ignores the fact that children who obtain very low scores on such tests may know a great deal about print and the relationship between print and speech, even though what they know does not qualify as "literacy" based on performance in these difficult, resource-demanding tasks.

Adams (1990) suggested that activities such as being read to aloud, watching educational television programs such as *Sesame Street*, and playing word and letter games may give middle-class children thousand of hours of exposure to printed words and their corresponding phonological representations before they are formally taught reading and spelling skills. Although much of this exposure is passive, requiring minimal interaction by the child, the amount of effective exposure may still be substantial and have the potential of influencing the development of literacy skill. Furthermore, research on children's emergent literacy suggests that literacy-related knowledge is gradually acquired during the course of language development and is facilitated by environments that offer many opportunities to interact with printed information (e.g., Clay, 1985, 1991; Ferreiro, 1986; Hiebert, 1993; Mason, 1992; Teale, 1986; Wells, 1985).

The literacy-related knowledge that prereaders acquire as a result of being exposed to printed information appears to be quite diverse. Ferreiro (1986) suggested that repeated exposure to print in stories provides children with a basis for distinguishing print from pictures as sources of information about the content of written stories. Gibson and Levin (1975) argued that print exposure fosters recognition of the distinctive graphic features of print (see also Hiebert, 1978, 1981; Hiebert, Cioffi, & Antonak, 1984; Lavine, 1977). Masonheimer, Drum, and Ehri (1984) suggested that print exposure is involved in children's learning to recognize printed words that occur frequently in the environment (e.g., advertising logos such as K-Mart and Coke) and in gradually acquiring the ability to recognize them independently of the graphic context in which they are usually seen. Although there is some evidence that children's knowledge of the graphic features of print may be related to subsequent reading and spelling acquisition, the relationship may be mediated by other variables (e.g., letter–name and letter–sound associations; Lomax & McGee, 1987), and there is not much evidence that environmental print recognition or logographic word recognition are strong predictors of subsequent reading skill (e.g., Ehri, 1992; Mason, 1992; Wimmer & Hummer, 1990).

Finally, Scarborough and Dobrich (1994a, 1994b) recently reviewed three decades of research examining the effect of parents reading to preschoolers (shared reading) on the acquisition of language and literacy skills. Their surprising finding was that this widely valued procedure for exposing prereaders to printed information yielded only modest relationships with outcome measures of reading achievement, emergent literacy skill, and oral language, even in studies in which shared reading was used as a deliberate intervention (the estimated median of the correlation coefficients did not exceed .28 across five sets of studies; but see Bus, van IJzendoorn, & Pellegrini, 1995; Dunning, Mason, & Stewart, 1994; Lonigan, 1994; Whitehurst et al., 1994, for critical reactions to Scarborough & Dobrich's 1994a, 1994b, review).

There may, however, be other types of knowledge acquired by prereaders that make more direct and substantial contributions to reading and spelling skill acquisition. Children often know the associations between letters and their names (*g*—pronounced "gee") and letters and their sounds (*g*—/g/ pronounced "guh") before they can read any words aloud accurately or generate any accurate spellings. I have referred to this knowledge as *proto-literate knowledge* because it may represent the first evidence that children have made a connection between print and speech at the subsyllabic level—the level that is essential for understanding the alphabetic principle (e.g., Barron, 1986, 1991, 1994; Barron et al., 1992).

Letter–name and letter–sound knowledge appear to be acquired at different rates. In a cross-sectional study of middle-class children in Southern California, Worden and Boettcher (1990) found that 3-year-old children could report about four letter names but could not report any letter sounds. By age 5 they could report almost all of the letter names (22 out of 26) but only about one third of the letter sounds. It was not until age 7 that letter–sound knowledge equaled letter–name knowledge in their study. Although letter–name and letter–sound performance were highly correlated overall ($r = .72$ uppercase and .83 lowercase), the correlation values were low for 4- and 5-year-olds between the letters they could name and those for which they could supply a sound. Among 6-year-olds, however, the correlation was higher, at least for uppercase letters ($r = .49$), suggesting that by this time the partial letter–sound information contained in some letter names had begun to influence the generation of letter–sound associations (e.g.,

Ehri, 1983). It should be noted, however, that these data are in sharp contrast to evidence for proto-literate knowledge in, for example, Europe, where Lundberg et al. (1988) reported that at age 7 the Danish children in their longitudinal training study knew only about four letter names. Similarly, Wimmer, Landerl, Linortner, and Hummer (1991) and Hoien, Lundberg, Stanovich, and Bjaalid (1995) reported relatively low letter–name knowledge for Austrian and Norwegian children, respectively, compared to Worden and Boettcher's (1990) North American sample.

Although letter–name and letter–sound knowledge are related to the acquisition of reading skill (e.g., see Adams, 1990; Bradley & Bryant, 1991; Ehri, 1983), there is also evidence that this information is involved in the acquisition of phonological awareness and, therefore, may be implicated in initial print–sound representations that are formed by prereaders. First, Stuart and Coltheart (1988) and Vellutino and Scanlon (1987) reported simple correlations between letter–sound knowledge and measures of phonological awareness ranging from $r = .60$ to .80 for prereaders. Similarly, letter–name knowledge also yields substantial, although somewhat smaller correlations with phonological awareness performance of nonreaders (e.g., Bowey, 1994, $r = .49$ to .59; see also Bowey & Francis, 1991; Wagner, Torgesen, & Rashotte, 1994).

Second, letter–name and letter–sound knowledge are strongly implicated in prereaders' performance in several production and recognition tasks that involve processing print. Read (1986) demonstrated that prereaders employ letter–name and letter–sound associations to represent the phonetic structure of spoken words in their invented spellings (e.g., *wtr* for the word *water*), although the names of some letters are more likely to be employed than others (e.g., Treiman, 1993, 1994; Treiman, Tincoff, & Richmond-Wetley, 1996; Treiman, Weatherston, & Berch, 1994). Ehri and Wilce (1985) found that prereaders who had high letter–name and letter–sound association knowledge were better able to learn and remember nonsense words consisting of letters whose sounds and names could be blended into real words (e.g., *szrs* = *scissors*) than visually distinctive nonwords whose constituent letter names and letter sounds could not be so blended (e.g., *qDjK*). Rack et al. (1994) recently showed that this result is also obtained when visual similarity to the conventional spelling of the word is controlled.

Byrne and Fielding-Barnsley (1989, 1990, 1993) showed that high letter–sound knowledge was critical in prereaders' success in learning a small set of words (e.g., *mat*, *sat*) and then transferring their knowledge to the "reading" task of deciding that "mow" rather than "sow" is the correct pronunciation of the printed word *mow*. Stuart (1990) demonstrated that prereaders with high letter–sound knowledge are above chance in choosing between a printed word (e.g., *pan*) that corresponded to a target picture (picture of a pan) and a printed distracter word (e.g., *cut*), whereas children

8. PROTO-LITERATE KNOWLEDGE

with low letter–sound knowledge performed at chance on this task. Finally, Muter (1994) found that prereaders' letter–sound knowledge and phoneme segmentation skill made independent contributions to reading and spelling skill 1 year later, whereas rhyming skill was not a significant predictor.

RELATIONSHIPS BETWEEN PROTO-LITERACY AND PHONOLOGICAL AWARENESS: HIERARCHICAL REGRESSION AND TRAINING STUDIES

In order to examine more directly the relationship between proto-literate knowledge and phonological awareness, Barron, Seldon, Golden, Marmurek, and Haines (1991) identified 112 kindergarten children (mean age = 5 years, 6 months) who could not read or spell any more than one or two words based on the sum of their performance across three standardized reading tests and one standardized spelling test. These tests consisted of the Woodcock Word Identification Test (raw score mean = 0.96); the Slosson Oral Reading Test (raw score mean = 0.28); the WRAT-R Reading Test (raw score mean = 23.6), and the WRAT-R Spelling Test (raw score mean = 17.35). In addition, they could not decode any nonwords on the Word Attack subtest of the Woodcock Reading Mastery Test–Revised (raw score mean = 0.04). The children varied, however, in their knowledge of the sounds associated with letters as measured by two tasks. In the letter–sound naming task, the experimenter pointed to an uppercase letter (e.g., *D*) and asked what sound it made. In the letter–sound recognition task, the experimenter pointed to an uppercase letter (e.g., *D*) and asked which of the following three spoken words (e.g., "bed," "day," "fit") began with the sound that went with the letter.

These measures of letter–sound proto-literate knowledge were entered last (sixth) in a hierarchical multiple regression. The phonological awareness outcome measures consisted of several tasks. In the first task, children deleted onsets (say "top" without the /t/ sound) and in the second task they deleted a phoneme from a consonant cluster (say "stop" without the /s/ sound) in one-syllable words. The remaining tasks were the Bradley and Bryant (1983, 1985) rhyme and alliteration oddity tasks. In the rhyme task, the children were required to decide which one of three words had an odd sound in the middle (e.g., *leg, bag, rag*) or final (*nut, fun, cut*) position in the word. In these two cases, the rime unit could be used as the basis of classification. In the alliteration oddity, however, the onset was used as the basis of classification (e.g., *bus, rug, bun*). The first four predictor measures, in their order of entry, were chronological age, I.Q. (estimated from the vocabulary, information, geometric and block design subtests of the WPSSI), arithmetic knowledge (WRAT-R arithmetic test), and memory ability (recall sequences of three words in order).

The fifth (second to last) measure was referred to as *task specific variance* and it consisted of performance on a task that was very similar to an outcome measure but involved a different phonological unit. A syllable deletion task was the source of task specific variance for the onset and phoneme deletion tasks, because it involved the same task demands but required awareness of syllables rather than onset and phoneme subsyllabic units. A score based on the sum of the two oddity rhyming tasks was used as a measure of task specific variance for the oddity alliteration task, because they involved the same task demands as the alliteration task but required awareness of different subsyllabic units (i.e., rimes rather than onsets). Finally, the alliteration oddity task was used as a measure of task specific variance for the two oddity rhyme tasks, because it involved the same task demands as the rhyme task but required awareness of different subsyllabic units (i.e., onsets rather than rimes).

Following removal of the variance associated with the first five predictive measures, the two measures of letter–sound knowledge accounted for significant proportions of the variance in subjects' performance on the oddity alliteration task (3% and 5% of the variance, respectively), which involved onset units, but these measures of proto-literate knowledge did not account for any remaining variance in subject performance on either of the oddity rhyme tasks. The multiple Rs for the regressions ranged from .77 to .84. In addition, the letter–sound recognition measure accounted for significant variance in the onset deletion task (5%, multiple $R = .63$) and the letter–sound naming measure accounted for significant variance in the phoneme deletion task (9%, multiple $R = .50$)

These results are consistent with a bidirectional relationship between phonological awareness and literacy because they show that proto-literacy, in the form of letter–sound knowledge, accounted for a significant proportion of the variance in onset and phoneme phonological awareness tasks for children who were unable to read or spell. They also show that letter–sound measures of proto-literacy do not account for subjects' awareness of rime units, a result that is consistent with the view that literacy does not influence awareness of rhymes (e.g., Bertelson & deGelder, 1989). Instead, rhyming skill appears to emerge earlier during the course of language development (Maclean et al., 1987) and is related to the acquisition of literacy, possibly because awareness of phonological rime units facilitates sensitivity to corresponding orthographic rime units, allowing new words to be read by analogy between identical orthographic/phonological units (e.g., Goswami & Mead, 1992).

The Barron et al. (1991) results are also consistent with several recent studies. Carrillo (1994), Stahl and Murray (1994), and Wimmer et al. (1991, experiment 3) found that letter–name and letter–sound knowledge are related to kindergarten children's ability to segment syllables into onsets and rimes, and to detect phonemes within onset and rime units. Using latent variable causal modeling procedures on longitudinal data, Wagner et al. (1994) found that letter–name and letter–sound knowledge in kindergarten was related to children's phonological awareness performance in Grade 1, even though the variance associated with phonological awareness performance in kindergarten was removed. This pattern was repeated the following year, as letter–name and letter–sound knowledge in Grade 1 was related to phonological awareness in Grade 2; again, phonological awareness performance measured a year earlier (in Grade 1) was removed. Furthermore, Bowey (1994) showed that 4-year-olds with high letter–name knowledge, who were clearly nonreaders, were more accurate at detecting onsets and phonemes in a phoneme identity task than those with low letter–name knowledge. She also found, however, that vocabulary knowledge accounted for some of the variance in the performance of these young nonreaders.

Training phonological awareness skill may also provide a way of evaluating the role of proto-literate knowledge in the acquisition of phonological awareness. Bradley and Bryant (1983), in their pioneering study, demonstrated that letter-sound-based training of phonological awareness facilitated subsequent acquisition of reading skill (see Defior & Tudela, 1994, for recent confirmation of their results). Unfortunately, Bradley and Bryant (1983, 1985) did not measure the effects of such training on phonological awareness. Hohn and Ehri (1983) and Ball and Blachman (1991), however, combined letter–sound knowledge with phonological awareness in training with nonreaders, and both studies showed that phoneme segmentation performance was facilitated relative to their control groups.

Based on these findings, Barron et. al (1992) investigated the role of level of letter–sound knowledge and print-based feedback in a phonological awareness training experiment that involved kindergarten children who could not yet read or spell. Sixty-six nonreaders (5½ years of age) were divided into two groups that were equated on measures of IQ, memory, and arithmetic knowledge but who differed in letter–name and letter–sound knowledge. The children were trained using the Bradley and Bryant (1983) oddity task with both word and nonword items. As training progressed, the basis of the oddity decision was shifted from rime identity (e.g., *map, ham, cap*) to consonant onsets (*bet, bag, cow*), then to consonant phonemes embedded in a rime (e.g., *log, dip, bag*) and, finally, to vowel phonemes embedded in a rime (e.g., *sit, kid, cap*).

The words were spoken by a DECtalk speech synthesizer (e.g., Lovett, Barron, Forbes, Cuksts, & Steinbach, 1994; Olson, Foltz, & Wise, 1986) and, as each word was generated, a small white square appeared on the color video monitor of a microcomputer. Once the series of three items was presented, the children used a light pen to touch the square on the monitor that corresponded to the odd word or nonword they had heard in the series. Immediately afterward, DECtalk told the child whether or not the answer was correct and then pronounced the correct item. At the same time that DECtalk gave this oral feedback, the children in the speech and print feedback group also saw the three words or nonwords; each item was printed in blue above its corresponding white square. In addition, the letter corresponding to the critical phoneme in the "odd" word or nonword was printed in red. The children in the speech-only feedback group saw the same blue and red display, but no print feedback was presented; instead, the letters making up the words were replaced by asterisks. Finally, in the semantic category control group, the children were given spatial (asterisks) and auditory feedback that was similar to the children in the speech-only feedback group, but their oddity decisions were based on semantic rather than phonological information. The training lasted approximately 3 hours, and the pretest and posttest measures consisted of rime oddity and phoneme deletion tasks.

Only the children with low letter–sound knowledge demonstrated pretest to posttest gains in rhyming task performance when compared to the control group, and these gains were not influenced by exposure to print feedback. Essentially, the phonological awareness training was effective in moving the rhyming performance of the low letter–sound groups up to the level of the high letter–sound groups. In contrast, the children who had both high letter–sound knowledge and were given print feedback during learning were the only group to show pretest to posttest gains in phoneme deletion task performance compared to the control group. These results indicate that awareness of phonemes is facilitated among children who cannot yet read or spell when high letter–sound knowledge and print feedback are combined during training.

In addition to examining pretest to posttest changes on phonological awareness measures, Barron et al. (1992) also examined the effect of level of letter–sound knowledge on subjects' performance during the acquisition phase of the training experiment. They found that children with high and low letter–sound knowledge were equally proficient at oddity task performance involving rime units (e.g., *cat, tap, fat*). Children with low letter–sound knowledge, however, dropped to chance level of performance when the basis of the oddity tasks was shifted from rimes to onsets (e.g., *bet, bag, cow*). The high letter–sound children continued to perform well above chance.

Although these results appear to implicate proto-literate knowledge in the acquisition of phonological awareness, they differ substantially from the findings of Lundberg et al. (1988), who successfully trained phonological awareness skills without letter–sound training and without prior knowledge of letter sounds or letter names. Although Lundberg et al.'s (1988) subjects were more than a year older than the children in Barron et al.

(1992) and in other studies (e.g., Bowey, 1994), their results indicate that proto-literate knowledge may not be necessary in order to acquire awareness of onsets and phonemes. Instead, proto-literate knowledge, particularly letter–sound knowledge, may function as a facilitator in the process of becoming aware of onsets and phonemes in words.

MENTAL SPELLINGS FOR SPEECH

The specific manner in which letter–sound knowledge functions to facilitate phonological awareness might involve reciprocal activation between letters and sounds whereby at least some phonemic units in words activate the letters to which they are associated when the word is processed auditorially. The resulting letter activation may enhance phonological awareness performance by providing at least a partial "mental spelling" of the word. These early print–speech representations may not represent complex orthographic information (e.g., *-tion, ph,* etc.); instead, they may be the reverse of the one-to-one, letter-to-sound representations proposed by Ehri (1992) in her description of phonetic cue reading and by Rack et al. (1994) in their description of the direct-mapping hypothesis. These representations may involve only initial and final letters and may or may not represent vowel information. Accordingly, they may not be as complete as the representations involved in cipher reading (e.g., Gough & Hillinger, 1980; Gough, Juel, & Griffith, 1992) and, therefore, are not sufficient to support an accurate oral reading or spelling response for a word presented out of context, or for a nonword.

There is evidence that both children and adults activate and use orthographic representations of words in auditory word recognition and in phonological awareness tasks (e.g., see Barron, 1994, for a review). Dijkstra, Frauenfelder, and Schreuder (1993), for example, employed a *go, no go* priming task with adults and found that phonemes activate letters as readily as letters activate phonemes. Seidenberg and Tanenhaus (1979) found that adults' auditory word recognition is influenced by a word's spelling. They required subjects to decide whether or not two spoken words rhymed. In their task, subjects heard two words, such as *tune* and *dune,* and then indicated their yes/no rhyme decision by pressing a button. Recording of response time commenced with the onset of the second spoken word. Seidenberg and Tanenhaus (1979, experiment 3) found that subjects were faster on pairs of words like *tune* and *dune* that rhymed and had the same spelling for their rimes than on pairs of words that rhymed, but had different rime spellings (e.g., *moon, dune*). Similarly, they were slower on pairs of words whose rimes were spelled the same but did not rhyme (e.g., *cough, tough*) than on pairs of words that did not rhyme and had different rime spelling (e.g., *stuff, tough*). This auditory orthographic effect is similar in magnitude to that obtained when the word pairs are presented visually (e.g., Meyer, Schvaneveldt, & Ruddy, 1974; Seidenberg & Tanenhaus, 1979, experiment 1).

In the area of phonological awareness, Bruck (1992) reported that although normal readers have higher scores on phonological awareness tasks than do dyslexic readers, they also make more orthographic "overshoot" errors. The normal readers are more likely to report that digraphic words have as many phonemes as they have letters (e.g., they incorrectly report that a nonword like *leem* has four rather than three phonemes). Bruck's (1992) normal readers were also more likely to report that the nonword *thoace* was pronounced as *hoace* rather than *oace* following instructions to delete the first sound (e.g., $th = /\theta/$). Ehri and Wilce (1980) reported that children tend to make orthographic overshoot errors by treating "silent letters" as has having phonemic correspondences in a phoneme counting task (e.g., *pitch* is counted as having five phonemes, whereas *rich* is counted as having four phonemes, even though both items actually consist of only three phonemes). Similarly, Tunmer and Nesdale (1982, 1985) found that kindergarten and Grade 1 children make overshoot errors because they count out four rather than three taps to items like *them* and the nonword *theb*.

These results suggest that orthographic information is activated during auditory word recognition and that it is used in phonological awareness tasks by beginning readers as well as adults. One question arising from these findings is whether or not children who are just beginning to read would show any evidence of activating orthographic representations of words automatically, even when it was not required by the demands of the task or the product of a deliberately chosen strategy (e.g., children in Tumner & Nesdale's [1982, 1985] studies appear to have intentionally activated a word's spelling in order to facilitate their phoneme tapping performance).

In order to explore this possibility, Pearson and Barron (1986) investigated the auditory orthographic effect obtained by Seidenberg and Tanenhaus (1979), using children who were just learning to read. We used two groups of children who corresponded to the novice and veteran groups identified by Ehri and Wilce (1985). The 18 novices were all in Grade 1 (6 years, 4 months) and had good letter–sound (73%) and letter–name (94%) knowledge, but could read aloud accurately only 6% and spell 7% of the words employed in the rhyming task. The 20 veterans were all in Grade 2 (7 years, 2 months) and also had good letter–sound (95%) and letter–name (100%) knowledge, but they could read aloud 85% of the words used in the rhyming task and spell 61%. We found that both groups of subjects were faster on orthographically similar (*far, car*) than dissimilar

8. PROTO-LITERATE KNOWLEDGE 167

(*tea, key*) rhyming pairs and slower on orthographically similar (*low, cow*) than dissimilar (*face, ring*) nonrhyming pairs. The magnitude of this auditory orthographic effect was the same for both groups, and the errors (less than 5%) and response times were correlated positively.

Pearson and Barron (1989) replicated these results with different words and subjects, including a group of adults. We also used pictures rather than spoken words as the second item in each rhyming pair (the first item was always a spoken word) in order to explore the generality of the phenomenon. The subjects heard the first word and then saw a picture and were instructed to decide whether or not the word and the name of the picture rhymed (e.g., similar rhyme = *band*, picture of a hand; dissimilar rhyme = *chew*, picture of a shoe; similar nonrhyme = *gone*, picture of a bone; dissimilar nonrhyme = *rule*, picture of a bell). The 20 novices were all in Grade 1 (6 years, 4 months) and could give 76% of the sounds and 91% of the names of the letters of the alphabet, but they could read aloud only 3% of the rhyming task words. The 20 veterans were in Grade 2 (7 years, 2 months), could produce 96% of the sounds and 100% of the names of the letters of the alphabet, and could read 92% of the words. The 35 adults were all university students and fluent readers.

The previous pattern of results was replicated when the members of the rhyme pair were both presented auditorially and when the second member of the pair was a picture, because both the novices and the veterans showed an auditory orthographic effect that was the same magnitude for both groups. In addition, the adult group produced an auditory orthographic activation effect in both the word–word and word–picture conditions. These results indicate that the orthographic representations of words are activated by children (novice readers) who were only able to read aloud and spell about 5% of the words used in the rhyming tasks.

CONCLUSIONS AND SPECULATIONS

The evidence just presented can be used in constructing a framework for understanding the nature of print–speech representations before children can read and spell, and the nature of the relationship between phonological awareness and literacy. Early print–speech representations may consist of letter–name and letter–sound associations. Letter–sound association knowledge is often imprecise (e.g., giving the response "buh" to the letter *b* involves producing the phoneme /b/ as well as a following neutral vowel, e.g., /ə/, but there may be sufficient overlap between a "phoneme plus neutral vowel sound" and actual phonemes that hearing a phoneme embedded in a word is sufficient to activate the letter to which it is associated, particularly when the phoneme is in the initial or final position in the word. Once initially constructed, these representations might be consolidated through a mechanism that involves reciprocal activation between graphemes and phonemes. This activation may initially involve single phonemes and single letters but, as print exposure increases, more complex orthographic units may be involved (e.g., *th*, vowel digraphs, *-tion*).

Although these print–speech representations may not be sufficient to generate an accurate reading or spelling, they may be sufficient to influence rhyming decisions. In addition, they may influence phonological awareness performance by providing nonspeech (i.e., graphemic and orthographic) information that may assist children in isolating and manipulating individual phonemes and, ultimately, in further refining their phonological awareness skills as literacy is acquired. The letter–sound effects in phonological awareness performance and training with nonreaders and the auditory orthographic activation effect with novice readers can be considered as an early indication that initial print–sound representations have been formed and have the potential of enhancing phonological awareness skills and promoting the acquisition of literacy skills.

REFERENCES

Adams, M. J. (1990). *Beginning to read: Thinking and learning about print.* Cambridge, MA: MIT Press.

Ball, E. W., & Blachman, B. A. (1991). Does phoneme segmentation training in kindergarten make a difference in early word recognition and developmental spelling? *Reading Research Quarterly, 26,* 49–66.

Barron, R. W. (1986). Word recognition in early reading: A review of the direct and indirect access hypotheses. *Cognition, 24,* 93–119.

Barron, R. W. (1991). Proto-literacy, literacy, and the acquisition of phonological awareness. *Learning and Individual Differences, 3,* 243–255.

Barron, R. W. (1994). The sound-to-spelling connection: Orthographic activation in auditory word recognition and its implications for the acquisition of phonological awareness and literacy skills. In V. W. Berninger (Ed.), *The varieties of orthographic knowledge I: Theoretical and developmental issues* (pp. 219–242). Dordrecht, The Netherlands: Kluwer.

Barron, R. W., Golden, J. O., Seldon, D. M., Tait, C. F., Marmurek, H. H. C., & Haines, L. C. (1992). Teaching prereading skills with a talking computer: Letter-sound knowledge and print feedback facilitate nonreaders' phonological awareness training. *Reading and Writing: An Interdisciplinary Journal, 4,* 179–204.

Barron, R. W., Seldon, D. M., Golden, J. O., Marmurek, H. H. C., & Haines, L. P. (1991, April). *Proto-literacy and nonreaders' acquisition of phonological awareness.* Paper presented at the meeting of the Society for Research in Child Development, Seattle, WA.

Bertelson, P., & deGelder, B. (1989). Learning about reading from illiterates. In A. M. Galaburda (Ed.), *From neurons to reading* (pp. 1–23). Cambridge, MA: MIT Press.

Bertelson, P., Morais, J., Alegria, J., & Content, A. (1985). Phonetic analysis capacity and learning to read. *Nature, 313,* 73–74.

Bowey, J. A. (1994). Phonological sensitivity in novice readers and nonreaders. *Journal of Experimental Child Psychology, 58,* 134–159.

Bowey, J. A., & Francis, J. (1991). Phonological analysis as a function of age and exposure to reading instruction. *Applied Psycholinguistics, 12*, 91–121.
Bradley, L., & Bryant, P. E. (1983). Categorizing sounds and learning to read: A causal connection. *Nature, 301*, 419–421.
Bradley, L., & Bryant, P. E. (1985). *Rhyme and reason in reading and spelling* (IARLD Monographs, No. 1). Ann Arbor: University of Michigan Press.
Bradley, L., & Bryant, P. (1991). Phonological skills before and after learning to read. In S. A. Brady & D. P. Shankweiler (Eds.), *Phonological processes in literacy: A tribute to Isabelle Y. Liberman* (pp. 37–45). Hillsdale, NJ: Lawrence Erlbaum Associates.
Brown, G. D. A., & Loosemore, R. L. (1994). A computational approach to dyslexic reading and spelling. In C. K. Leong & R. M. Joshi (Eds.), *Developmental and acquired dyslexia: Neuropsychological and neurolinguistic perspectives* (pp. 195–219). Dordrecht, The Netherlands: Kluwer.
Bruck, M. (1992). Persistence of dyslexics' phonological awareness deficits. *Developmental Psychology, 28*, 874–886.
Bryant, P. E., Bradley, L., Maclean, M., & Crossland, J. (1989). Nursery rhymes, phonological skills, and reading. *Journal of Child Language, 16*, 407–428.
Bryant, P. E., Maclean, M., Bradley, L., & Crossland, J. (1990). Rhyme and alliteration, phoneme detection, and learning to read. *Developmental Psychology, 26*, 429–438.
Bus, A. G., van IJzendoorn, M. H., & Pellegrini, A. D. (1995). Joint book reading makes success in learning to read: A meta-analysis of intergenerational transmission of literacy. *Review of Educational Research, 65*, 1–21.
Byrne, B. (1992). Studies in the acquisition procedure for reading: Rationale, hypotheses, and data. In P. B. Gough, L. C. Ehri, & R. Treiman (Eds.), *Reading acquisition* (pp. 1–34). Hillsdale, NJ: Lawrence Erlbaum Associates.
Byrne, B., & Fielding-Barnsley, R. (1989). Phonemic awareness and letter knowledge in the child's acquisition of the alphabetic principle. *Journal of Educational Psychology, 81*, 313–321.
Byrne, B., & Fielding-Barnsley, R. (1990). Acquiring the alphabetic principle: A case for teaching recognition of phoneme identity. *Journal of Educational Psychology, 82*, 805–812.
Byrne, B., & Fielding-Barnsley, R. (1993). Evaluation of a program to teach phonemic awareness to young children: A one-year follow up. *Journal of Educational Psychology, 85*, 104–111.
Cardoso-Martins, C. (1994). Rhyme perception: Global or analytical? *Journal of Experimental Child Psychology, 57*, 26–41.
Carrillo, M. (1994). Development of phonological awareness and reading acquisition: A study in Spanish language. *Reading and Writing: An Interdisciplinary Journal, 6*, 279–298.
Clay, M. (1985). *The early detection of reading difficulties.* Auckland, New Zealand: Heinemann.
Clay, M. (1991). *Becoming literate: The construction of inner control.* Auckland, New Zealand: Heinemann.
Content, A., Kolinsky, R., Morais, J., & Bertelson, P. (1986). Phonetic segmentation in prereaders: Effect of corrective information. *Journal of Experimental Child Psychology, 42*, 49–72.
Cunningham, A. E. (1990). Explicit versus implicit instruction in phonemic awareness. *Journal of Experimental Child Psychology, 50*, 429–444.
Defior, S., & Tudela, P. (1994). Effect of phonological training on reading and writing acquisition. *Reading and Writing: An Interdisciplinary Journal, 6*, 299–320.
Dijkstra, T., Frauenfelder, U. H., & Schreuder, R. (1993). Bidirectional grapheme–phoneme activation in a bimodal detection task. *Journal of Experimental Psychology: Human Perception and Performance, 19*, 931–950.
Dunning, D. B., Mason, J. A., & Stewart, J. P. (1994). Reading to preschoolers: A response to Scarborough and Dobrich (1994) and recommendations for future research. *Developmental Review, 14*, 324–339.

Ehri, L. C. (1978). Beginning reading from a psycholinguistic perspective: Amalgamation of word identities. In F. B. Murray (Ed.), *The recognition of words: IRA series on the development of the reading process* (pp. 1–33). Newark, DE: International Reading Association.

Ehri, L. C. (1979). Linguistic insight: Threshold of reading acquisition. In T. G. Waller & G. E. MacKinnon (Eds.), *Reading research: Advances in theory and practice* (Vol. 1, pp. 63–114). New York: Academic.

Ehri, L. C. (1983). A critique of five studies related to letter-name knowledge and learning to read. In L. Gentile, M. Kamil, & J. Blanchard (Eds.), *Reading research revisited* (pp. 143–153). Columbus, OH: Merrill.

Ehri, L. C. (1984). How orthography alters spoken language competencies in children learning to read and spell. In J. Downing & R. Valtin (Eds.), *Language awareness and learning to read* (pp. 119–147). New York: Springer-Verlag.

Ehri, L. C. (1992). Reconceptualizing the development of sight word reading and its relationship to decoding. In P. B. Gough, L. C. Ehri, & R. Treiman (Eds.), *Reading acquisition* (pp. 107–143). Hillsdale, NJ: Lawrence Erlbaum Associates.

Ehri, L. C. (1993). How English orthography influences phonological knowledge as children learn to read and spell. In R. J. Scholes (Ed.), *Literacy: Linguistic and cognitive perspectives* (pp. 21–43). Hillsdale, NJ: Lawrence Erlbaum Associates.

Ehri, L. C., & Wilce, L. S. (1980). The influence of orthography on readers' conceptualization of the phonemic structure of words. *Applied Psycholinguistics, 1*, 371–385.

Ehri, L. C., & Wilce, L. S. (1985). Movement into reading: Is the first stage of printed word learning visual or phonetic? *Reading Research Quarterly, 20*, 163–179.

Ferreiro, E. (1986). The interplay between information and assimilation in beginning literacy. In W. Teale & E. Sulzby (Eds.), *Emergent literacy* (pp. 15–49). Norwood, NJ: Ablex.

Gibson, E. J., & Levin, H. (1975). *The psychology of reading.* Cambridge, MA: MIT Press.

Goswami, U., & Bryant, P. (1990). *Phonological skills and learning to read.* East Sussex, England: Lawrence Erlbaum Associates.

Goswami, U., & Mead, F. (1992). Onset and rime awareness and analogies in reading. *Reading Research Quarterly, 27*, 152–162.

Gough, P. B., & Hillinger, M. L. (1980). Learning to read: An unnatural act. *Bulletin of the Orton Society, 30*, 179–196.

Gough, P. B., Juel, C., & Griffith, P. L. (1992). Reading, spelling, and the orthographic cipher. In P. B. Gough, L. C. Ehri, & R. Treiman (Eds.), *Reading acquisition* (pp. 35–48). Hillsdale, NJ: Lawrence Erlbaum Associates.

Hansen, J., & Bowey, J. A. (1994). Phonological analysis skills, verbal working memory, and reading ability in second-grade children. *Child Development, 65*, 938–950.

Hiebert, E. (1978). Preschool children's understanding of written language. *Child Development, 49*, 1231–1234.

Hiebert, E. (1981). Developmental patterns and interrelationships of preschool children's print awareness. *Reading Research Quarterly, 16*, 236–260.

Hiebert, E. H. (1993). Young children's literacy experiences in home and in school. In S. R. Yussen & M. C. Smith (Eds.), *Reading across the life span* (pp. 33–55). New York: Springer-Verlag.

Hiebert, E., Cioffi, G., & Antonak, R. F. (1984). A developmental sequence in preschool children's acquisition of reading readiness skills and print awareness concepts. *Journal of Applied Developmental Psychology, 5*, 115–126.

Hohn, W. E., & Ehri, L. C. (1983). Do alphabetic letters help prereaders acquire phonemic segmentation skill? *Journal of Educational Psychology, 75*, 752–762.

Hoien, T., Lundberg, I., Stanovich, K. E., & Bjaalid, I.-K. (1995). Components of phonological awareness. *Reading and Writing: An Interdisciplinary Journal, 7*, 171–188.

Hulme, C., Snowling, M. J., & Quinlan, P. (1991). Connectionism and learning to read: Steps towards a psychologically plausible model. *Reading and Writing: An Interdisciplinary Journal, 3*, 159–168.

Jastak, S., & Wilkinson, G. S. (1984). *Wide Range Achievement Test–Revised.* Wilmington, DE: Jastak Associates.

Kirtley, C., Bryant, P. E., Maclean, M., & Bradley, L. (1989). Rhyme, rime, and the onset of reading. *Journal of Experimental Child Psychology, 48,* 224–245.

Lavine, L. O. (1977). Differentiation of letter-like forms in prereading children. *Developmental Psychology, 13,* 89–94.

Lomax, R. G., & McGee, L. M. (1987). Young children's concepts about print and reading: Toward a model of word reading acquisition. *Reading Research Quarterly, 22,* 237–256.

Lonigan, C. J. (1994). Reading to preschoolers exposed: Is the emperor really naked? *Developmental Review, 14,* 303–323.

Lovett, M. W., Barron, R. W., Forbes, J. E., Cuksts, B., & Steinbach, K. A. (1994). Computer speech-based training of literacy skills in neurologically-impaired children: A controlled evaluation. *Brain and Language, 47,* 117–154.

Lundberg, I., Frost, J., & Petersen, O.-P. (1988). Effects of an extensive program for stimulating phonological awareness in preschool children. *Reading Research Quarterly, 23,* 263–284.

Lundberg, J., Olofsson, A., & Wall, S. (1980). Reading and spelling skills in the first school years predicted from phonemic awareness skills in kindergarten. *Scandinavian Journal of Psychology, 21,* 159–173.

Maclean, M., Bryant, P. E., & Bradley, L. (1987). Rhymes, nursery rhymes, and reading in early childhood. *Merrill-Palmer Quarterly, 33,* 255–281.

Mann, V. A., & Liberman, I. Y. (1984). Phonological awareness and verbal short-term memory. *Journal of Learning Disabilities, 17,* 592–599.

Mason, J. M. (1992). Reading stories to preliterate children. In P. B. Gough, L. C. Ehri, & R. Treiman (Eds.), *Reading acquisition* (pp. 215–241). Hillsdale, NJ: Lawrence Erlbaum Associates.

Masonheimer, P. E., Drum, P. A., & Ehri, L. C. (1984). Does environmental print identification lead children into word reading? *Journal of Reading Behavior, 16,* 257–271.

McDougall, S., Hulme, C., Ellis, A., & Monk, A. (1994). Learning to read: The role of short-term memory and phonological skills. *Journal of Experimental Child Psychology, 58,* 112–133.

Meyer, D. E., Schvaneveldt, R. W., & Ruddy, M. (1974). Functions of graphemic and phonemic codes in visual word recognition. *Memory & Cognition, 2,* 309–321.

Morais, J. (1991a). Constraints on the development of phonemic awareness. In S. A. Brady & D. P. Shankweiler (Eds.), *Phonological processes in literacy: A tribute to Isabelle Y. Liberman* (pp. 5–27). Hillsdale, NJ: Lawrence Erlbaum Associates.

Morais, J. (1991b). Phonological awareness: A bridge between language and literacy. In D. J. Sawyer & B. J. Fox (Eds.), *Phonological awareness in reading: The evolution of current perspectives* (pp. 31–71). New York: Springer-Verlag.

Morais, J., Alegria, J., & Content, A. (1987). The relationships between segmental analysis and alphabetic literacy: An interactive view. *Cahiers de Psychologie Cognitive, 7,* 415–438.

Morais, J., Bertelson, P., Cary, L., & Alegria, J. (1986). Literacy training and speech segmentation. *Cognition, 24,* 45–64.

Morais, J., Cary, L., Alegria, J., & Bertelson, P. (1979). Does awareness of speech as a series of phones arise spontaneously? *Cognition, 7,* 323–331.

Muter, V. (1994). The influence of phonological awareness and letter knowledge on beginning reading and spelling development. In C. Hulme & M. Snowling (Eds.), *Reading development and dyslexia* (pp. 45–62). London: Whurr.

Olson, R. K., Foltz, G., & Wise, B. (1986). Reading instruction and remediation with the aid of computer speech. *Behavior Research Methods, Instruments, and Computers, 18,* 93–99.

Pearson, L. L., & Barron, R. W. (1986, June). *Activation of orthography by beginning readers in an auditory rhyme task.* Paper presented at the Canadian Psychological Association meetings, Toronto, Ontario, Canada.

Pearson, L. L., & Barron, R. W. (1989, March). *Orthography influences beginning readers' auditory rhyme judgments.* Paper presented at the American Educational Research Association meetings, San Francisco, CA.

Perfetti, C. A. (1992). The representation problem in reading acquisition. In P. B. Gough, L. C. Ehri, & R. Treiman, (Eds.), *Reading acquisition* (pp. 145–174). Hillsdale, NJ: Lawrence Erlbaum Associates.

Plaut, D. C., McClelland, J. L., Seidenberg, M. S., & Patterson, K. E. (1996). Understanding normal and impaired word reading: Computational principles in quasi-regular domains. *Psychological Review, 103,* 56–115.

Rack, J., Hulme, C., Snowling, M., & Wightman, J. (1994). The role of phonology in young children's learning to read words: The direct-mapping hypothesis. *Journal of Experimental Child Psychology, 57,* 42–71.

Rack, J. P., Snowling, M. J., & Olson, R. K. (1992). The nonword reading deficit in developmental dyslexia: A review. *Reading Research Quarterly, 27,* 29–53.

Read, C. (1986). *Children's creative spelling.* London: Routledge & Kegan Paul.

Scarborough, H. S., & Dobrich, W. (1994a). On the efficacy of reading to preschoolers. *Developmental Review, 14,* 245–302.

Scarborough, H. S., & Dobrich, W. (1994b). Another look at parent–preschoolers' book reading: How naked is the emperor? *Developmental Review, 14,* 245–302.

Seidenberg, M. S., & McClelland, J. L. (1989). A distributed, developmental model of word recognition and naming. *Psychological Review, 96,* 523–568.

Seidenberg, M. S., & Tanenhaus, M. K. (1979). Orthographic effects of rhyme monitoring. *Journal of Experimental Psychology, 5,* 546–554.

Stahl, S. A., & Murray, B. A. (1994). Defining phonological awareness and its relationship to early reading. *Journal of Educational Psychology, 86,* 221–234.

Stanovich, K. E. (1986). Matthew effects in reading: Some consequences of individual differences in the acquisition of literacy. *Reading Research Quarterly, 21,* 360–407.

Stanovich, K. E. (1992). Speculations on the causes and consequences of individual differences in early reading acquisition. In P. B. Gough, L. C. Ehri, & R. Treiman (Eds.), *Reading acquisition* (pp. 307–342). Hillsdale, NJ: Lawrence Erlbaum Associates.

Stanovich, K. E., Cunningham, A. E., & Cramer, B. (1984). Assessing phonological awareness in kindergarten children: Issues of task comparability. *Journal of Experimental Child Psychology, 38,* 175–190.

Stuart, M. (1990). Factors influencing word recognition strategies in prereading children. *British Journal of Psychology, 81,* 135–146.

Stuart, M., & Coltheart, M. (1988). Does reading develop in a sequence of stages? *Cognition, 30,* 139–181.

Teale, W. H. (1986). Home background and young children's literacy development. In W. H. Teale & E. Sulzby (Eds.), *Emergent literacy: Writing and reading* (pp. 173–206). Norwood, NJ: Ablex.

Treiman, R. (1984). On the status of final consonant clusters in English. *Journal of Verbal Learning and Verbal Behavior, 23,* 343–356.

Treiman, R. (1992). The role of intrasyllabic units in learning to read and spell. In P. B. Gough, L. C. Ehri, & R. Treiman (Eds.), *Reading acquisition* (pp. 65–106). Hillsdale, NJ: Lawrence Erlbaum Associates.

Treiman, R. (1993). *Beginning to spell.* New York: Oxford University Press.

Treiman, R. (1994). Use of consonant letter names in beginning spelling. *Developmental Psychology, 30,* 567–580.

Treiman, R., Tincoff, R., & Richmond-Wetley, E. D. (1996). Letter names help children to connect print and speech. *Developmental Psychology, 32,* 505–514.

Treiman, R., Weatherston, S., & Berch, D. (1994). The role of letter names in children's learning of grapheme–phoneme relations. *Applied Psycholinguistics, 15,* 97–122.

Tunmer, W. E., & Nesdale, A. R. (1982). The effects of digraphs and pseudowords on phoneme segmentation in young children. *Applied Psycholinguistics, 3*, 299–311.

Tunmer, W. E., & Nesdale, A. R. (1985). Phonemic segmentation skill and beginning reading. *Journal of Educational Psychology, 77*, 417–427.

Vellutino, F. R., & Scanlon, D. M. (1987). Phonological coding, phonological awareness, and reading ability: Evidence from a longitudinal and experimental study. *Merrill-Palmer Quarterly, 33*, 321–363.

Wagner, R. K., & Torgesen, J. K. (1987). The nature of phonological processing and its causal role in the acquisition of reading skill. *Psychological Bulletin, 101*, 192–212.

Wagner, R. K., Torgesen, J. K., & Rashotte, C. A. (1994). Development of reading-related phonological processing abilities: New evidence of bi-directional causality from a latent variable longitudinal study. *Developmental Psychology, 30*, 73–87.

Wallach, L., Wallach, M. A., Dozier, M. G., & Kaplan, N. E. (1977). Poor children learning to read do not have trouble with auditory discrimination but do have trouble with phoneme recognition. *Journal of Educational Psychology, 69*, 36–39.

Wells, G. (1985). Preschool literacy-related activities and success in school. In D. R. Olson, N. Torrance, & A. Hildyard (Eds.), *Literacy, language, and learning* (pp. 229–255). New York: Cambridge University Press.

Whitehurst, G. J., Epstein, J. N., Angell, A. L., Payne, A. C., Crone, D. A., & Fischel, J. E. (1994). Outcomes of emergent literacy intervention in Headstart. *Journal of Educational Psychology, 86*, 542–555.

Wimmer, H., & Hummer, P. (1990). How German first graders learn to read and spell: Doubts about the importance of the logographic stage. *Applied Psycholinguistics, 11*, 349–368.

Wimmer, H., Landerl, K., Linortner, R., & Hummer, P. (1991). The relationship of phonemic awareness to reading acquisition: More consequence than precondition. *Cognition, 40*, 219–249.

Woodcock, R. W. (1987). *Woodcock Reading Mastery Tests–Revised*. Circle Pines, MN: American Guidance Service.

Worden, P. E., & Boettcher, W. (1990). Young children's acquisition of alphabetic knowledge. *Journal of Reading Behavior, 22*, 277–295.

Yopp, H. K. (1988). The validity and reliability of phonemic awareness tests. *Reading Research Quarterly, 23*, 159–177.

Part II

DEVELOPMENTAL IMPAIRMENTS OF DECODING SKILLS

Studies of both normal and abnormal development have contributed to understanding the central importance of phonological skills for learning to read. Part II develops some of the issues raised in Part I, and explores the roles of phonological and visual deficits as possible causes of difficulties in learning to read.

Bruck (chap. 9) and Snowling, Goulandris, and Defty (chap. 10) focus on dyslexia. Bruck describes one of just a handful of studies that have examined adults who were diagnosed as dyslexic in childhood. The majority of these individuals show persisting problems with reading in adulthood and, as has been shown in many studies of dyslexic children, they also show marked difficulties in reading nonwords. In contrast to some other recent work in this area, Bruck finds no difference on some low-level visual tasks between dyslexic adults and controls. This leads her to question the suggestion that dyslexia is characterized by a deficit in the visual transient subsystem. However, in line with many other studies, Bruck reports evidence that the adult dyslexics she studied show persisting phonological difficulties. She argues persuasively that dyslexic reading difficulties are best interpreted within a single route framework, and that the difficulty for dyslexics is in creating mappings between representations of orthography and phonology. Her arguments lend further weight to those advanced by Gough and Wren and Ehri in Part I, and Metsala and Brown (chap. 12) in this section, all of whom also advocate a unitary mechanism for mapping between spelling patterns and sound.

Bruck's ideas from studies of adults are nicely complemented by studies of dyslexic children described by Snowling, Goulandris, and Defty. They show that dyslexic children have phonological deficits that appear to become more severe as they get older. In the early stages of learning to read, the reading and spelling strategies of their dyslexic sample did not differ from those of younger children of the same reading age, but their development was constrained, and as time proceeded significant problems in nonword reading and phonological spelling strategies emerged. These findings are consistent with the idea discussed by Bruck and by Metsala and Brown that a phonological processing deficit affects the way in which children establish mappings between orthography and phonology. Snowling et al. (chap. 10) go on to discuss individual differences in the reading strategies used by dyslexic children, and hypothesize that these may depend on differences in the severity of their underlying phonological deficit at the time at which they come to learn to read.

Felton (chap. 11) reports the results of a longitudinal study of poor readers between the third and eighth grades. She finds that reading deficits persist over time in spite of children having received remedial teaching, and that nonword reading deficits are particularly severe. She suggests that as poor readers progress through school there may be a failure to appreciate that some of them continue to need teaching that is directed at overcoming their decoding difficulties.

In a theoretical chapter, Metsala and Brown go on to show how computational models can provide powerful explanations of the patterns of reading difficulties observed in dyslexia, such as those described by Bruck and Snowling et al. They explore the effects of impairing the phonological representations embodied in a connectionist model on its ability to learn the mappings between orthography and phonology. A striking finding is that a phonological impairment in the model mimics the pattern of difficulties in learning to read found in dyslexic children.

In chapter 13, Alegria describes studies of the phonological skills of deaf children. As we would expect, the deaf typically experience severe phonological difficulties and consequent problems in learning to read. The chapter reviews evidence that, in the deaf, the availability of lip-read information has a large effect on the development of phonological representations. Such findings are consistent with evidence that, for hearing people, lip-read information gains automatic access to a phonetic "speech" module. Recent studies by Alegria and his colleagues have explored the effects of a system known as *cued speech* on the phonological development of the deaf. In cued speech, hand shapes and positions, which are designed to disambiguate the phonetic information conveyed by lip-read cues, are formed in synchrony with speech. Most impressively, and surprisingly, the use of cued speech to deaf children from an early age facilitates their language comprehension and phonological skills. These findings, of course, are very much in line with the central role assigned by Liberman to gestural information for speech perception. A full integration of this research with the development of phonological skills in normal children should have important implications for our understanding of phonological development, which, it has been argued, provides the foundation for reading development.

Although there is an enormous body of evidence pointing to the importance of phonological difficulties as a cause of children's problems in learning to decode, there remains strong interest in the possibility that at least some cases of reading difficulties depend on visual problems. The chapters by Johnston (chap. 14) and by Goulandris, McIntye, and Snowling (chap. 15) examine this possibility from two different perspectives.

Johnston argues that difficulties in learning letter names and sounds may be crucial for dyslexics, and that these difficulties may in turn compromise the development of their phonological skills. She also argues, more controversially, that differences between the relative strengths of visual and phonological skills in dyslexic children may determine their subsequent pattern of reading and development. According to this idea, children with relatively strong visual skills may, in the face of phonological weaknesses, develop atypical reading strategies that do not emphasize the creation of systematic mappings between print and sound in the normal way. This atypical pattern of learning, it is hypothesized, may over time lead to further deficiencies in reading and phonological skills.

The chapter by Goulandris et al. explores a simpler hypothesis about the possible nature of visual difficulties in dyslexic children. They report a study that examined the incidence of "unstable ocular dominance" in dyslexic children and control children. Their results failed to support earlier suggestions that dyslexia may be caused by problems of ocular dominance. Although many dyslexic children show unstable ocular dominance, so too do many children who are learning to read normally, and difficulties in ocular dominance were not predictive of either the severity or pattern of reading difficulties that the dyslexic children showed. It would seem that this particular hypothesis about the source of dyslexic children's reading difficulties can, and should, be laid to rest!

Chapter 9

Outcomes of Adults With Childhood Histories of Dyslexia

Maggie Bruck
McGill University, Quebec

Although developmental dyslexia is diagnosed in childhood, follow-up studies indicate that this condition is not specific to childhood but persists into adulthood. According to interview and standardized test data, although many are educationally and occupationally successful, adults with histories of childhood diagnoses of dyslexia continue to exhibit significant reading and spelling disabilities (Bruck, 1985; Finucci, Gottfredson, & Childs, 1986; Labuda & DeFries, 1988; Rawson, 1968). However, little is known about the source or nature of these problems. In the past 10 years, I have conducted several studies on the reading and spelling profiles as well as on the cognitive profiles of adults with childhood histories of dyslexia. These studies are of interest for several reasons. First, on the applied level, the results of these studies provide important information on the prognosis of childhood dyslexia. Second, on a theoretical level, these studies contribute to a unified and extensive account of the basic symptoms and cognitive deficits that underlie developmental dyslexia. Specifically, if the same difficulties that characterize dyslexic children also characterize this population as it reaches adulthood, this indicates that the conceptualization of dyslexia that has been derived from childhood data is developmentally invariant. On the other hand, if dyslexic adults and children show different profiles of difficulties, these data provide a framework for understanding how cognitive profiles may change as a function of experience and development. The data presented in this chapter consistently support the first view—that reading and cognitive profiles of dyslexics remain constant from childhood to adulthood. I argue that phonological processing deficits account for a large proportion of the difficulties encountered by dyslexic children and adults.

In this chapter, I discuss a number of studies that have examined reading profiles, component word recognition skills, visual processing, and phonological processing skills of adult dyslexics (I use this abbreviated term to refer to adults with childhood diagnoses of dyslexia). Although other researchers have engaged in similar endeavors, I focus on studies carried out in my laboratory. I summarize the results of a number of published studies and present in greater detail the results of some recently conducted studies that are reported for the first time in this chapter.

Although the studies reported in this chapter include different samples of adults, and although they do address different issues, they share the following methodological framework. First, subject selection procedures were identical across all studies. Adult dyslexics were identified from the patient files of a clinic that specialized in the assessment and treatment of childhood reading disabilities. Childhood file information was used to identify patients who met the following exclusionary definition of dyslexia: The child experienced difficulty in learning to read despite at least average intelligence; reading problems could not be explained on the basis of social, emotional, cultural, pedagogical, or medical factors; and childhood reading difficulties were associated with word recognition problems, as evidenced by clinical judgments and by performance on standardized word recognition tasks. Averaging across studies, the children were 9 years old when first assessed in the clinic. Patients who met these criteria, and who were older than 17 and no longer attending high school at the time of follow-up, were located and asked to participate in a research project.

Although the studies that I describe in this chapter include three different samples of dyslexic adults, the profiles of these adults are similar across studies. The average age of these samples ranged from 21 to 24 years of age. IQ, as assessed by the PPVT and Cattell Culture Fair Test, was in the normal range. The adult dyslexics represented a range of educational achievements: At the time of follow-up testing, many were in college or had graduated from college; but at the same time, there were as many subjects who had not continued their education after high school, or who had not finished high school.

It is important to note that by virtue of the subject selection procedures, these studies differ from other studies of poor adult readers or of adult dyslexics (e.g., Byrne & Ledez, 1983; Mason, 1978; Read & Ruyter, 1985) in which subjects were selected on the basis of their reading levels at the time of testing. In contrast, in my studies the major criterion used for subject selection was childhood diagnosis of dyslexia. As a result, in each study there were several dyslexics (approximately 5%) who would not be classified as poor readers in other studies. (Some researchers have labeled these subjects "recovered dyslexics," but it is also possible that they may have been improperly diagnosed in childhood.) As a result, the focus of my studies differs from that of previous studies: It examines the hypothesis that regardless of follow-up standardized test scores, adults with childhood diagnoses of dyslexia experience persisting deficits.

A second common feature of the studies reported in this chapter is that the dyslexics are compared to age-matched adults and, in some studies, they are also compared to younger normal readers who are matched for reading or spelling skills. In some cases, normal children who were much poorer readers than the dyslexics served as the comparison group. These comparisons with younger but normal learners were carried out to evaluate the developmental level of the processes or component skills of the dyslexics (see Backman, Mamen, & Ferguson, 1984; Stanovich & Siegel, 1994, for a discussion of reading-matched level designs).

Finally, a common objective in all my studies was to determine if dyslexic adults showed the same pattern of deficits as dyslexic children. By implication, the adult work was an extension of a previously researched domain of skills or difficulty associated with childhood reading disabilities.

READING PROFILES OF ADULTS WITH CHILDHOOD DIAGNOSES OF DYSLEXIA

It is now well established that dyslexic children's major difficulty involves recognition of single words (for reviews, see Gough & Tunmer, 1986; Stanovich, 1982; Vellutino, 1979). Poor word recognition diverts resources from the processes that are necessary for comprehension.

Similar deficits are also found in adult dyslexics as indicated by their scores on standardized reading tests that were administered to all our subjects at the time of follow-up testing. Standardized word recognition scores were very low for most subjects, and these were associated at times with impaired comprehension skills (for similar results, see Felton, Naylor, & Wood, 1990; Labuda & DeFries, 1988). Scores on standardized comprehension tasks were always higher than those on standardized word recognition tasks. On the word recognition tasks, only 5% of all the tested subjects scored above the 50th percentile, whereas on the comprehension standardized tests 22% of the subjects scored above the 50th percentile. The highest word recognition scores were obtained in one study that exclusively focused on dyslexics with college education (Bruck, 1989); the average word recognition score for the dyslexics was at the 32 percentile. When educational achievement was not a criterion for study entry, the word recognition percentile scores were lower (e.g., 21% in Bruck, 1990; 11% in Hayduk, Bruck, & Cavanagh, 1996).

Performance on a number of experimental tasks highlight adult dyslexics' word recognition deficits: They are not merely inaccurate, they are also extremely slow to accurately recognize words. For example, in one study (Bruck, 1989), I compared the word recognition skills of a group of educationally successful adult dyslexics (they had continued into university programs after leaving high school) to that of Grade 6 students matched on a standardized word recognition task. The dyslexics made the same number of errors as the Grade 6 children on a variety of experimental word recognition tasks, a validation of the matching procedure. However, the dyslexics were uniformly and substantially slower than the Grade 6 students in their recognition of these words.

Interactive-compensatory models of word recognition stipulate that when lower-level word recognition skills are deficient, higher-level sources of knowledge (e.g., contextual knowledge) become important (e.g., Stanovich, 1986, for a review). Specifically, it is hypothesized that the word recognition skills of good readers are so fast and automatic that conscious use of contextual information is not used to assist word recognition. Dyslexic children, however, with poor word recognition skills, rely on context to a greater degree than good readers to assist word recognition (Bruck, 1988; Bruck & Waters, 1990b). I have also found a similar pattern in adult dyslexics (Bruck, 1989). I measured the accuracy and latency of word recognition when words were read in a neutral context and when the same words were read in a meaningful passage of prose. Adult dyslexics (compared to age-matched normal readers and reading-matched Grade 6 students) showed much larger context facilitation effects. This pattern was particularly striking in terms of the latency measures.

It should be pointed out that reliance on context for word recognition is not an entirely satisfactory compensatory strategy for weak word recognition skills, for several reasons. First, even though adult dyslexics were much faster when reading words in meaningful sentences, they were still much slower than the normal readers by approximately 100 msec, not a trivial amount. Second, the reliance on context to assist word recognition may not necessarily increase comprehension; reliance on conscious predictions may reduce working memory capacity that holds sequences of words, while comprehension processes integrate them into meaningful conceptual structures (e.g., Stanovich, 1986). Finally, reliance on context to aid word recognition is often a liability in that the predictability of words in actual texts tends to be quite low (Gough, Alford, & Holley-Wilcox, 1981).

COMPONENT WORD RECOGNITION SKILLS

Some researchers have attempted to identify the defective components of dyslexics' word recognition mechanisms that might account for their poor word recognition skills. It is a widely held view that dyslexic children have a deficit in their knowledge of spelling–sound correspondences as reflected in their relatively poor performance on nonword pronunciation tasks (Rack, Snowling, & Olson, 1992, for a review). This pattern is so consistent that some researchers have suggested that it is the characteristic signature of dyslexia. Although there is a debate concerning when spelling–sound knowledge is important in word recognition, most agree that it is critically important during acquisition; it assists the beginning reader to recognize printed words that are in the child's vocabulary but have never been seen before (e.g., Jorm & Share, 1983). Poor knowledge of the correspondences between spelling and sounds is thus thought to impede dyslexic children's ability to read a wide variety of words.

Adult dyslexics also show poor performance on nonword tasks. In my own studies, adult dyslexics made more errors reading nonwords than age- and reading-matched normal subjects (Bruck 1989; see Felton et al., 1990, for similar results). But even when they generated the correct pronunciation of nonwords, adult dyslexics were extremely slow. For example, in my study of dyslexic college students, dyslexics' average latency to pronounce a nonword was 2019 msec, compared to 882 for age-matched control subjects and 839 for reading-matched control subjects. These data reflect the extreme difficulty that dyslexic adults have when pairing spellings with sounds.

It has been suggested that if spelling–sound knowledge is weak, then dyslexics may rely on another strategy to recognize words. For example, it has been suggested that perhaps they do not use spelling–sound information but instead recognize words on the basis of their visual properties only. To some extent this view is based on the dual-route model of word recognition that postulates two primary[1] independent procedures or routes through which words can be recognized (Coltheart, 1978; Coltheart, Curtis, Atkins, & Haller, 1993). One route is called a nonlexical route: The reader uses grapheme–phoneme correspondence (GPC) rules to translate the written word into an internal phonological representation that is then used to access the meaning of the word. This route, which is also called the *phonological route*, is used to pronounce nonwords and regular words—those that conform to GPC rules (e.g, *must* or *gave*). Words such as *have* or *yacht*, whose pronunciations violate these procedures, must be recognized by a second route. The second route is a lexical route: Words are directly recognized on the basis of their orthographic patterns. This involves using the orthographic pattern to directly retrieve the phonological form of the word from the mental lexicon. This route is used to recognize exception words such as *have* that violate GPC rules; as well, this route can also be used to recognize regular words. However, this route cannot be used to

---

[1]There is a third route in some models. Because it is rarely elaborated in reference to developmental dyslexia, it is not discussed in this chapter.

pronounce nonwords such as *lup*, because these are not represented in mental lexicon. According to the dual-route model, poor nonword performance is a direct indication that the phonological route is impaired. Because dyslexics have such difficulty reading nonwords, perhaps they rely on the lexical route to a greater degree than do normal subjects.

One common paradigm that has been used to examine the relative use of these two routes involves comparing the recognition of regular words whose pronunciations can be generated by applying spelling–sound correspondences (e.g., *must*) with exception words whose pronunciations cannot be derived on the basis of spelling–sound correspondences (e.g., *have*). According to a compensatory hypothesis, if dyslexics rely on a lexical route because of a sublexical route impairment, then one would expect that their relative performance on exception words versus regular words would be the same if not better than that of normal subjects. This pattern has not been obtained in dyslexic children. Rather, the differences in favor of regular words is sometimes larger in dyslexics than in age-matched normal readers (Backman et al., 1984; Murphy, Pollatsek, & Well, 1988; Seidenberg, Bruck, Fornarolo, & Backman, 1985), although the size of the difference is sometimes the same in dyslexics and reading-level matched readers.

Dyslexic adults continue to show the same pattern as dyslexic children (Bruck, 1989). Compared to normal readers, they do particularly poorly on high- and low-frequency exception words (in reference to regular words). It is important to note, however, that although adult dyslexics' recognition of regular words is better than their recognition of exception words, they are substantially slower than normal readers in their recognition of regular words.

If performance on exception words or the relative difficulty of exception to regular words is an index of the use of the lexical route, then these data suggest that dyslexics do not use the lexical route efficiently. If performance on nonwords is an index of the use of the nonlexical route, then dyslexics do not use the nonlexical route efficiently either. Adopting a dual-route view, these data imply that there is damage to both routes.

There is another interpretation of these data: Perhaps we are masking intragroup variability. Perhaps, in each study, there are some dyslexics with primary damage to the phonological route (as indexed by poor nonword performance and good exception word performance) and some with primary damage to lexical route (as indexed by poor exception word performance and good nonword performance). Castles and Coltheart (1993) and Manis and his colleagues (Manis, Seidenberg, Doi, McBride-Chang, & Petersen, 1996) addressed these issues with children. In both studies, these researchers counted the number of dyslexic children whose error scores on nonwords and exception words were greater than 1 standard deviation above the mean for the normal age-matched subjects in their samples. For both studies, the most predominant pattern was children with poor scores on both measures, so-called "mixed" subjects (60% Castles & Coltheart; 77% for Manis et al.). There were approximately equal numbers of children with normal nonword but poor exception word scores (so-called "pure surface" dyslexics) and with poor nonword but normal exception word scores (so-called "pure phonological" dyslexics). Further analyses were carried out on the mixed groups in each study. Here, a regression method was used to identify dyslexics with large discrepancies between poor nonword and poor exception word scores. Although there were a substantial proportion of subjects in each study that did show these discrepancies (yielding a number of children who could be labeled phonological dyslexics and surface dyslexics), nevertheless the important point is that these subjects were poor on both nonwords and exception words.

My analyses of data from 40 adult dyslexics and 24 age-matched normal readers yielded very similar patterns to those obtained by Castles and Coltheart and by Manis et al. In my adult dyslexic sample, 8% were classified as pure surface dyslexics and 15% were classified as pure phonological dyslexics, whereas 75% of the adult dyslexics showed the mixed profile—they were poor on both exception and nonwords. Thus, the majority of dyslexics show deficits to the lexical and nonlexical routes.

The issue that is important to address is how does one account for these deficits? Does one have to accept the dual-route explanation that there is damage to two independent routes? After all, as Manis et al. pointed out, the dual-route model does not provide any basis for predicting that most dyslexics will be impaired on both types of stimuli.

Another conceptual framework for understanding these data and for considering the sources of impairment is offered by computational and connectionist models, particularly the models developed by McClelland, Seidenberg, Patterson, and Plaut. There are several important features of the Seidenberg and McClelland model (1989; hereafter termed SM89) that distinguish it from strict dual-route models. First, lexical information is represented by patterns of activation over units encoding distributed representations of orthography, phonology, and semantics; there are no entries for single words. Second, whereas the dual-route model has two procedures for computing from orthography to phonology (the lexical and nonlexical routes), the SM89 model collapses these into one. A single processing mechanism generates pronunciations for "rule-governed" words such as *must*, exceptions such as *have*, and nonwords such as *mave*. This is because the learning algorithm picks up on the systematic aspects of the correspondences between spelling and pronunciation and, at the same time, encodes exceptions to these patterns. Third, there are no rules in the model—a single set of weights generates pronunciations for words, nonwords, and exceptions. Finally, whereas the dual-route model is based on the dichotomy between rule-governed words and exceptions, in the connectionist models there is a continuum of spelling–sound consistency. The rule-governed items and exceptions are at opposites of the continuum.

Because the model uses the same set of weights to pronounce regular words, exception words, and nonwords, it cannot account for the surface and phonological dyslexic patterns in terms of damage to independent naming mechanisms such as proposed by the dual-route model. In their recent paper, Manis et al. (1996) attempted to demonstrate how the model can account for these pure cases as well as for the more common mixed pattern; they did this by considering three types of anomalies that could cause the system to develop abnormally. These anomalies with relevant evidence from my own studies of dyslexics are presented in the following three sections of this chapter.

VISUAL DEFICITS ACCOUNT FOR WORD RECOGNITION DEFICITS

Developmental dyslexia could result from impairments in the visual system that would impair input to the reading system. Seidenberg (1992) simulated the effects of a visual impairment by degrading the orthographic representations of the model. He found that performance was poorer than in the nondegraded simulation. Although the impaired model had some difficulty reading regular words, it was most impaired on exception and nonwords. This pattern is consistent with the behavioral evidence on the reading profiles of dyslexic children and adults.

Despite this computational demonstration, the degree to which visual impairments actually are associated with developmental dyslexia is a recurrent controversy in the field. The hypothesis that was made popular by Orton in the 1920s and lost favor in the 1970s has recently been revived due to a focus on new models of visual processing. One of these influential models is the transient-sustained model (e.g., Breitmeyer, 1984, 1991; Breitmeyer & Ganz, 1976; Lovegrove, Garzia, & Nicholson, 1990; Lovegrove, Martin, & Slaghuis, 1986). According to the model, the visual system consists of two neuro-anatomical channels: the transient and the sustained pathways. The transient pathway is sensitive to the temporal qualities of stimuli (i.e., to movement and flicker) and is most sensitive to low spatial frequency stimuli and to high temporal frequency stimuli. In contrast, the sustained pathway is involved in pattern perception and is most sensitive to high spatial frequency stimuli; this pathway is characterized by a slow, sustained response to stimuli, a response that persists after the removal of the stimuli.

Lovegrove and his colleagues have conducted a number of studies examining the low-level visual processes of dyslexic children (for detailed reviews, see Hayduk et al., 1996; Lovegrove et al., 1986). Based on children's performance on visible persistence, pattern contrast sensitivity, flicker contrast sensitivity, and flicker masking tasks, Lovegrove and his colleagues concluded that developmental dyslexia arises from the failure of the transient pathway to effectively inhibit the sustained pathway. They proposed that the continued sustained channel activity results in poor integration of visual information, and confused perception of the words of a sentence. These perceptual deficits may result in deficits in the representation of orthographic components of words and, probably, in phonological deficits as well (Lovegrove et al., 1986, 1990). Finally, it is important to point out that transient system impairment may not be limited to a small proportion of the dyslexic population; Slaghuis and Lovegrove (1985) claimed that 75% of all their dyslexic subjects exhibited transient pathway deficits.

Studies supporting transient channel deficits have mainly included children between the ages of 8 and 14 years. This raises the question of whether transient pathway deficits persist beyond childhood into adulthood. Given the persisting word recognition deficits of this population, if visual deficits are indeed major determinants of developmental dyslexia, then transient deficits might persist into adulthood. It is also possible that these deficits may eventually dissipate with maturation and learning, leaving behind the continued signature symptoms of reading disabilities.

In order to test these hypotheses, we examined the low-level visual skills of 20 dyslexic adults and 20 age-matched normal readers (Hayduk, Bruck, & Cavanagh, 1993, and Hayduk et al., 1996). At the time of testing the adults were between the ages of 18 and 35 years; the average standardized word recognition score for the dyslexic group was at the 11th percentile.

Two different tasks were administered. The first task was a counterphase flicker contrast threshold task that was very similar to the one used by Martin and Lovegrove (1987). Their finding, that the largest between-group differences in threshold levels were obtained at the highest temporal frequencies, provides one of the strongest pieces of evidence for a transient deficit. There are several problems, however, with threshold tasks. First, because visual processing during reading generally does not involve threshold performance, the validity of these tasks for assessing reading relevant visual deficits is questionable. Second, psychophysical tasks such as threshold level tasks place heavy demands on attention, memory, and a variety of other factors. As a result, it is difficult to collect reliable data from subjects, especially dyslexics who often exhibit attentional or performance problems.

Because of these concerns, and as a next logical extension of this line of study, a second set of tasks, Treisman's visual search tasks were administered in order to measure transient pathway performance. Suprathreshold tasks such as the Treisman paradigm come closer to mapping low-level visual processing during reading than do traditional threshold measures.

In addition, the Treisman visual search paradigm is sensitive to signal strength (Treisman, 1991), but avoids the limitations of conventional psychophysical tasks by placing minimal demands on attention and memory, and by readily capturing the attention and interest of subjects. Thus, suprathreshold tasks such as Treisman's visual search tasks are automatic and engaging rather than attention demanding—a true test of early visual processing rather than a measure of attentiveness.

We failed to find any evidence for transient channel deficits in dyslexic adults. Their performance was similar to that of the normal readers on all conditions of the threshold tasks. On the visual search tasks, the dyslexics' performance (as measured by latency to detect a target) was poorer than that of normal readers on a number of tasks. However, these group differences occurred for tasks measuring transient as well as sustained channel processing, suggesting that there is not a specific transient deficit. Furthermore, although the model predicts that changes in contrast levels or in temporal frequency levels should selectively affect the performance of the dyslexics, this pattern was never obtained.

One interpretation of these data is that the visual deficits reported by Lovegrove and his colleagues do not persist into adulthood and are only detectable in dyslexic children. According to this explanation, transient channel deficits in childhood disrupt critical stages of development in the acquisition of reading. This disruption results in a permanent arrest in skill development; that is, even with the maturity of the transient system, dyslexics show persistent reading disabilities that are nonreversible. One difficulty with a maturational-lag interpretation is that Lovegrove and his colleagues reported transient system deficits in all their dyslexic samples. Even 14-year-old dyslexic children showed transient system deficits. Furthermore, Brannan and Williams (1988) found that although flicker thresholds decreased with age, the magnitude of the difference between good and poor readers remained constant as age increased. These data provide support for a persisting visual deficit through to at least 14 years of age.

In our study, the subjects were between the ages of 18 and 35 years. Thus, our youngest subjects were 4 years older than Lovegrove's oldest subjects. It is possible that transient system deficits subside only after the first 14 years of life. However, there is no empirical or theoretical basis for this predicted developmental spurt. The adult data raise the possibility that perhaps the previous results do not accurately reflect low-level visual processing of dyslexic children. Because there is a high comorbidity between reading disabilities and attentional deficit disorder (August & Garfinkel, 1990; Bruck, 1989), the assessment of visual processing in previous studies of dyslexic children may have been confounded by performance factors such as fatigue, boredom, and distractibility. In other words, perhaps previous studies on the visual processing skills of dyslexic children included a large proportion of children with attentional problems; it is attentional rather than visual problems that account for differences between normals and dyslexics on psychophysical tasks that require a substantial degree of vigilance and attention.

In order to test these hypotheses, we carried out four separate experiments to compare the visual processing skills of dyslexic children and age-matched normal readers (Hayduk et al., 1996). The characteristics of the subjects were similar across experiments: Their average age was 10.5 years; the average standardized word recognition scores for normal and dyslexic children were 75% and 11%, respectively. Finally, pooling across samples, only 10% of the dyslexic children met one of the traditional criteria for attentional disorder deficit. Counterphase flicker threshold tasks were administered in two experiments and suprathreshold visual search tasks were administered in another two experiments. For the most part, these tasks were similar to those administered to the adults, except that some of the procedures were changed to more effectively eliminate the potentially confounding effects of attention, eye movements, and memory. Dyslexic children performed comparably to age-matched normal readers. In the few cases when systematic differences occurred, this was for tasks that measured sustained channel functioning; the results of follow-up analyses that compared dyslexic children to reading-matched control subjects suggest that these differences may reflect reading experience rather than primary visual deficits.

Thus, the major impact of these studies with adults was to force a reevaluation of the position that transient system deficits underlie the problems of a substantial proportion of dyslexic children. Our data indicate that, with appropriate control procedures that reduce the role of attentional and memory problems, visual deficits are not observed.

Of course it could be argued that there are visual deficits that could be detected by other types of methodologies or other models (e.g., the parvomagno model that was tested by Livingstone, Rosen, Drislane, & Galaburda, 1991), or perhaps there are visual deficits that arise for higher-level processing. This is all possible. But regardless of the model adopted, it is important to assess the degree to which any of the obtained results may reflect other deficits rather than a primary deficit in vision. To our knowledge, this has not been done.

It also seems that if there are deficits in visual processing, this would affect dyslexics' performance on certain kinds of tasks. For example, one would predict that dyslexics would have difficulty attending to fine visual details required for spelling-check tasks. I found, however, that both children and adults perform similarly to level-matched controls on these tasks.

In one study, dyslexic college students, age-matched normal readers, and spelling-matched Grade 6 students selected the correct spelling of a word from among two foils (e.g., *balconey, balcony, balcuny*). On some trials none of the items was correct. The foils were phonologically as well as orthographically acceptable misspellings, thus eliminating the possibility of rejection of foils on the basis of phonological or orthographic acceptability. Therefore, correct performance required some fine visual perceptual skills. Although dyslexics took longer than the two control groups to select the correct match, their accuracy was the same as that of the reading-matched control group. Thus, dyslexics are as able as level-match controls to make use of visual information when there are no time constraints. It is possible that dyslexics' relatively good levels of performance on the recognition task reflect the contributions of print exposure and reading experiences (Bruck, 1992).[2]

To conclude, although visual deficits could lead to patterns of reading profiles that are characteristic of dyslexic children, the behavioral evidence to support this conceptualization is weak.

RESOURCE/COMPUTATIONAL LIMITATIONS ACCOUNT FOR DYSLEXICS' WORD RECOGNITION DEFICITS

According to SM89, the capacity of their model to learn the pronunciations of exception words depended on the computational resources (i.e., the number of hidden units). When the number of hidden units in the model was reduced, it was still able to learn many of the spelling–sound correspondences, especially for high-frequency words, but it performed poorly on irregular words and nonwords even after extensive training. That is, it allocated the limited resources for solving the problem to the patterns that occurred most frequently and consistently. These simulations suggest that some dyslexics may have a limitation in terms of the computational resources available for word recognition.

The behavioral evidence is consistent with these patterns. Specifically, not only are dyslexics poor on exception and nonwords, but the frequency effects are quite dramatic when compared to those of normal learners. Although dyslexics do have problems with recognizing even high-frequency words compared to normals, the differences are much greater in the case of low-frequency words (see Bruck, 1989). Although this is an interesting

---

[2]Similar results were obtained for a group of younger children. For the purposes of this chapter, I reanalyzed some data that I had published with Gloria Waters. I matched a group of Grade 6 poor readers–poor spellers (described in Bruck & Waters, 1990a) with a younger group of Grade 3 children who were good readers–good spellers (described in Waters, Bruck, & Malus-Abramowitz, 1988) on the basis of spelling test scores. These two groups of subjects performed similarly on a spelling-check task.

hypothesis, more work is required to directly demonstrate the resource limitations of dyslexics.

PHONOLOGICAL DEFICITS ACCOUNT FOR DYSLEXICS' WORD RECOGNITION DEFICITS

A third anomaly that could cause the system to develop abnormally is the inadequate representation of phonological knowledge. In alphabetic languages such as English, one of the first tasks facing the young learner is to figure out the correspondences between written forms (graphemes) and their phonemic segments. If the child has poor phonological representations to begin with, then the task of hooking up the visual symbols to the phonological representations will be quite difficult.

According to SM89, a nonword deficit reflects a phonological representation deficit, and this affects the single orthography to phonology conversion. But because the impairment that affects orthographic to phonological conversion is not specific to nonwords, it can also account for the fact that phonological dyslexics tend to be impaired in reading exception words as well as nonwords. In fact, introducing a phonological deficit in the model has the biggest effect on nonwords, less of an effect on exceptions, and less still on regulars.

Interestingly enough, it appears that the SM89 model could be characterized as having a phonological representation deficit. One result of the installation of an imperfect system for representing phonological segments in the SM89 model was that although the phonological representations were rich enough to allow the model to learn the pronunciations of the words in the training corpus and to generate plausible pronunciations for simple nonwords such as *nust*, the model did poorly on difficult nonwords such as *faije* or *tunce*. The model was limited by two major factors. First, the model was trained on a limited corpus of words that did not contain the unusual spelling patterns found in many of the nonwords. Nonword generalization is a more difficult task than merely producing the pronunciations of words in the training set. The model had not been exposed to the nonwords before, and therefore it had to piece together their pronunciations on the basis of exposure to other items. Second, the poor performance also reflected the degraded phonological representations. When these were improved in the next generation of the model (Plaut, McClelland, Seidenberg, & Patterson, 1996), there was improved performance on nonword generalization for difficult words such as *faije*.

I have recently collected some nonword data that are consistent with Manis and Seidenberg's hypothesis of dyslexics' degraded phonological representations. The study is an extension of previous work that I conducted with Treiman and Goswami (Treiman, Goswami, & Bruck, 1990). Subjects pronounced a list of 48 CVC nonwords. The rimes of half of the nonwords contained frequent spelling patterns, such as *tain* and *goach*; these rimes occur in a number of English words. The remaining nonwords, such as *goan* and *taich* shared their rimes with few or no real words. The graphemes in the high-frequency nonwords were the same as the graphemes in the low-frequency nonwords.

Normal readers of various ages read these nonwords. We found that even after 1 year of reading, Grade 1 children make fewer errors when pronouncing high- versus low-frequency nonwords. This same pattern was found for Grade 3 students and adults. These data are similar to the findings that frequency and consistency of spelling–sound correspondences affect performance on word tasks (e.g., Jared, McRae, & Seidenberg, 1990). We also tested a group of Grade 3 poor readers; there was a trend for Grade 3 poor readers to show a larger frequency effect than did good readers. This pattern is exactly what would be predicted from the phonological impairment hypothesis proposed by Manis and Seidenberg and on the basis of the SM89 model's nonword pronunciation. That is, one would expect larger frequency effects when phonological features are not adequately represented. However, because the Grade 3 poor readers were not carefully screened for dyslexia (i.e, they were selected from a classroom sample, solely on the basis of their poor word recognition scores), it is possible that the pattern might be clearer if a pure sample of dyslexics were included.

In the next study, I tested 29 dyslexic children and 21 dyslexic adults on the same nonwords. There was a control group of 24 children matched on age to the dyslexic children, and a control group of 20 adults age-matched to the dyslexic adults. The average age of the children was 10 years and the average age of the adults was 24 years. The dyslexic children and adults were equally impaired relative to their age group. On a standardized word recognition test, the children scored at the 9th percentile and adults scored at the 11th percentile. It also was the case that the normal child readers were at the same reading level as the adult dyslexic subjects.

A three-way analysis of variance was carried out on the number of correct responses on the nonword reading task. The independent variables were age group (children vs. adults), reader group (dyslexic vs. normal), and type of nonword (high frequency vs. low frequency), which served as a repeated measure. For the purposes of this discussion, the most important finding was an interaction between group and type of nonword, $F(1, 89) = 10.69$, $p < .001$ (see Fig. 9.1). The three way interaction missed traditional levels of significance, $F(1, 89) = 3.28$, $p = .07$. As can be seen from Fig. 9.1, although all groups of subjects showed significant frequency effects,

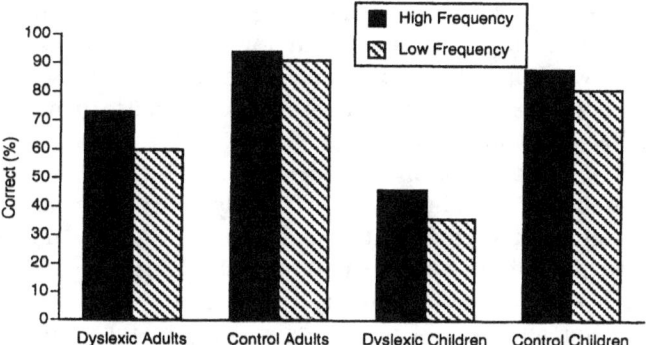

FIG. 9.1. Percentage correct nonwords—four groups.

the dyslexics showed larger effects than did the normal readers. The difference between familiar nonwords and unfamiliar nonwords was 13% for the dyslexic adults, 10% for the dyslexic children, 7% for the normal children, and 3% for the normal adults.

Reaction time data were collected for the adult sample only. These data are shown in Fig. 9.2. The pattern of results is consistent with that reported for the error data, although the interaction between group and type of nonword just failed to meet traditional standards of significance, $F(1, 39) = 3.82$, $p = .057$. That is, the dyslexics tended to show larger frequency effects than did the normal readers.

There are two explanations for the higher-than-expected frequency effect obtained by the dyslexics. First, this pattern reflects the poor phonological representations of the dyslexics. As can be remembered, the SM89 model's poor performance on difficult nonwords such as *kede* or *faije* relative to its better performance on nonwords such as *nust* or *fike* reflected

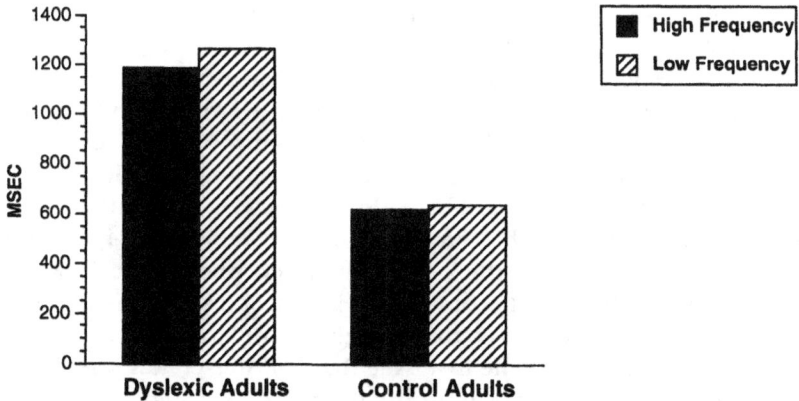

FIG. 9.2. High and low frequency nonwords: RT data.

in part its poor representation of phonological segments. (These nonwords are similar to the high-frequency and low-frequency items used in the present study.) With the evolution of newer models with improved phonological representations there is improved performance, especially on unfamiliar nonwords (Plaut et al., 1996).

Another explanation for my nonword findings is that they merely reflect the consequences of reading failure. The dyslexics were not exposed to the same number of words with the same frequency as the normal readers (see Stanovich, 1986, for an explanation of the Matthew effect). Similarly, the model had problems producing difficult nonwords as a result of a limited training set that did not contain many of the nonword spelling patterns. Although this might explain the pattern for the dyslexic children (i.e., they may have had much less training and exposure to words than their age-matched controls), this seems an unlikely explanation for the dyslexic adults. This is because they show larger frequency effects on the nonword task than level-matched normal children who were 14 years younger than the dyslexic adults. One might safely assume that these two groups have had at least equivalent exposure to a large corpus of words. Thus, the pattern obtained for the adult dyslexics is consistent with a phonological representation impairment.

Although the reading data strongly suggest that dyslexics suffer from primary phonological deficits, more direct evidence from nonreading tasks is required. This evidence is available. The strongest evidence is based on dyslexic children's performance on phonological awareness tasks (e.g., Bradley & Bryant, 1978; Bruck & Treiman, 1990; Manis, Szeszulski, Holt, & Graves, 1988; Olson, Wise, Connors, & Rack, 1990). Compared to reading- and age-matched control subjects, dyslexic children show deficits on a variety of tasks. They have difficulty segmenting, blending, deleting, and counting sublexical units. They show impairments in their awareness of onsets and rimes, as well as in their awareness of phonemes (e.g., Bruck, 1992; Bruck & Treiman, 1990).

Most researchers agree that poor phonological awareness is one of the core deficits that accounts for dyslexics' initial word recognition deficits and for their poor ability to learn the relationships between spellings and sounds, a critical component of word recognition (e.g., Bradley & Bryant, 1978, 1983; Lundberg, 1987; Share, Jorm, Maclean, & Matthews, 1984; Stanovich, 1992; Stanovich, Cunningham, & Cramer, 1984). However, there is little research on the degree to which phonological awareness skills improve as dyslexics become older and acquire some reading skill.

I have examined the degree to which these impairments persist beyond childhood (Bruck, 1990). The first issue that I addressed was whether adult dyslexics eventually attain age-appropriate levels of phonological awareness. Forty dyslexic adults were administered a battery of tasks to measure their awareness of syllables, onsets, and phonemes. Their performance was poorer than that of 20 age-matched normal readers on all tasks except one that reflected awareness of simple onsets. But these comparisons do not sufficiently highlight the extent of these adults' impairments; these are best seen in comparisons of the performance of the most proficient adult dyslexic subjects, all of whom read above the Grade 7 level, to that of Grade 3 children. Not only were the adults 13 years older than the normal readers, but the adults' reading and spelling levels were also substantially higher. Although dyslexic adults and Grade 3 children performed similarly on the syllable- and onset-awareness tasks, the Grade 3 children performed better than the adult dyslexics on the two phoneme segmentation tasks.

In summary, the results of the age-matched and reading-matched comparisons show that although some dyslexic adults do eventually acquire appropriate levels of onset awareness, they do not acquire appropriate levels of phoneme awareness, regardless of their age or their reading levels. This was a most unexpected pattern, because there is substantial evidence that normal readers' phoneme awareness is greatly promoted by the acquisition of alphabetic literacy skills (e.g., Bowey & Francis, 1991; Goswami & Bryant, 1990; Morais, 1987; Perfetti, Beck, Bell, & Hughes, 1987). However, the results of my studies indicate that for dyslexics there is little influence of orthographic knowledge on the growth of phonological skills.

One important issue that arises from the work on phonological awareness deficits is the degree to which dyslexics' phonological impairments are solely metalinguistic. In other words, does the major difficulty involve explicit segmentation or manipulation or retrieval, for example, or does it reflect more automatic phonological processes that are involved in language comprehension? In order to begin to address this issue, I examined the routines that dyslexic children and adults use for speech segmentation.

This work is based on previous work that we conducted with English-speaking adults (Bruck, Treiman & Caravolas, 1995). We developed a procedure to assess English-speaking adults' use of syllable representations versus smaller units in performing a nonword comparison task. In one condition, subjects heard a two-syllable nonword and, after a brief pause, a second two-syllable nonword. They were asked to judge as quickly as possible whether the two nonwords sounded the same at the beginning. For half the trials, the answer was "no"; the pairs did not share any phonemes (e.g., /glIpvʌk/-/trɛtnod/). For the other pairs the answer was "yes." Some of the "yes" pairs shared the entire first syllable (e.g., /kIpkæst/-/kIpbɛld/); these are called *whole* items. Other "yes" pairs only shared the onset and vowel of the first syllable (e.g., /flIgmIl/-/flIkboz/); these are called *part* items. All nonwords contained stress on the first syllable.

If people compare the nonwords on a phoneme-by-phoneme basis, response times should not differ for whole pairs and part pairs. However, if people compare syllabified representations of the stimuli, the whole-syllable pairs should be faster than the part-syllable pairs. Because the part-syllable pairs do not share their initial syllables, additional processing would be necessary to detect their similarity. The latter pattern was found: There was a substantial syllable effect. This pattern is interesting because, in theory, the most efficient way to perform this task is merely to listen to the first phoneme and to make a judgment; this strategy would result in the fastest reaction times, because subjects do not have to wait to listen to the whole syllable. However, it seemed that the more natural routine of initial syllable segmentation prevailed.

In order to obtain a more automatic measure of phonological processing than that obtained from phonological awareness tasks, I administered the same–different nonword task to dyslexics. If dyslexics performed differently than normals, then this would provide some evidence that phonological deficits are not specific to metacognitive tasks. As was the case in the previous research, I also included dyslexics of various ages because it is possible that speech processing routines may initially be delayed in children, but may mature by adulthood.

The same–different nonword task was given to 31 dyslexic children, 17 dyslexic adults, 28 normal children, and 18 normal adults. Normal and dyslexic subjects were matched on age. All dyslexics scored below the 32nd percentile on a standardized word recognition task and all normal readers scored above the 50th centile.

A three-way analysis of variance was carried out on the error and reaction time data. The independent variables were age (child vs. adult), reader group (dyslexic vs. control), and unit size (whole vs. part). There were no significant between group differences on the number of errors made on the "yes" pairs. Thus, the dyslexics were as accurate as the normal subjects. However, analysis of the reaction time data for the "yes" items yielded a significant reader group by unit size interaction, $F(1, 92) = 4.73$, $p < .03$ (see Fig. 9.3). Post-hoc analyses revealed that although normal and dyslexic subjects both made faster judgments for whole items than for part items, the effect was much larger for the normal than for the dyslexic subjects. It is also interesting to note that the dyslexics were significantly slower than the normals on the whole items, although they were similar on the part items. These results reflect the fact that there were a significant proportion of dyslexics in the sample who did not use syllable segmentation routines for this task—they processed the units on a phoneme by phoneme basis. The use of the latter strategy would have the effect of decreasing reaction times on part items, and thus they were able to make these judgments as quickly as normals, who were more likely to first use a syllable

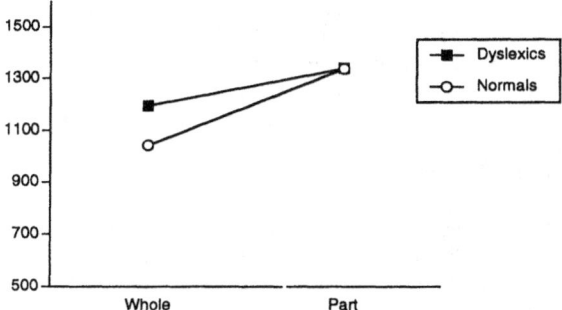

FIG. 9.3. Reaction times on same–different tasks.

routine and next a further parsing mechanism to isolate the correct phonemic units. Of course, there were some dyslexics who did show the normal pattern, but just not as many as found in the normal group. Also, the proportion of dyslexics who did not use a syllable segmentation routine was similar for the child sample (47%) and for the adult sample (47%).

Therefore, it appears that indeed phonological deficits associated with dyslexia are not specific to metalinguistic tasks but operate at more automatic levels as well for both children and adults. Presumably, deficits on these various tasks reflect the same representational deficits.

CONCLUSIONS

The patterns of deficits that characterize dyslexic children are the very same patterns that characterize adults with these childhood histories. Despite the fact that many of the subjects have been educationally successful, and despite the fact that as adults they have increased their level of word recognition skills, these data suggest that the primary deficits have not dissipated. The mechanisms and the processes do not seem to change or to mature. My work, along with that of many others in the field, implicates a core phonological deficit. This deficit can account for the various types of reading errors made by dyslexics both in childhood and in adulthood.

REFERENCES

August, G., & Garfinkel, B. (1990). Comorbidity of ADHD and reading disability among clinic-referred children. *Journal of Abnormal Child Psychology, 18,* 29–45.
Backman, J., Mamen, M., & Ferguson, H. B. (1984). Reading level design: Conceptual and methodological issues in reading research. *Psychological Bulletin, 96,* 560–568.

Bowey, J., & Francis, J. (1991). Phonological analysis as a function of age and exposure to reading instruction. *Applied Psycholinguistics, 12*, 91–122.

Bradley, L., & Bryant, P. (1978). Difficulties in auditory organization as a possible cause of reading backwardness. *Nature, 271*, 746–747.

Bradley, L., & Bryant, P. (1983). Categorizing sounds and learning to read—a causal connection. *Nature, 301*, 419–421.

Brannan, J., & Williams, M. (1988). The effects of age and reading ability on flicker threshold. *Clinical Vision Science, 3*, 137–142.

Breitmeyer, B. (1984). *Visual masking: An integrative approach.* Oxford, England: Clarendon.

Breitmeyer, B. (1991). Reality and relevance of sustained and transient channels in reading and reading disability. In R. Schmidt & D. Zambarbieri (Eds.), *Oculomotor control and cognitive processes.* North Holland: Elsevier.

Breitmeyer, B., & Ganz, L. (1976). Implications of sustained and transient channels for theories of visual pattern masking, saccadic suppression, and information processing. *Psychological Review, 83*, 1–36.

Bruck, M. (1985). The adult functioning of children with specific learning disabilities. In I. Sigel (Ed.), *Advances in applied developmental psychology* (pp. 91–129). Norwood NJ: Ablex.

Bruck, M. (1988). The word recognition and spelling of dyslexic children. *Reading Research Quarterly, 23*, 51–69.

Bruck, M. (1989). Prevalence and etiology of adjustment problems of children with learning disabilities. In J. J. Dumont & H. Nakken, (Eds.), *Learning disabilities: Cognitive, social and remedial aspects* (pp. 73–86). Amsterdam: Swets & Zeitlinger.

Bruck, M. (1990). Word recognition skills of adults with childhood diagnoses of dyslexia. *Developmental Psychology, 26*, 439–454.

Bruck, M. (1992). Persistence of dyslexics' phonological awareness deficits. *Developmental Psychology, 28*, 874–886.

Bruck, M., & Treiman, R. (1990). Phonological awareness and spelling in normal children and dyslexics: The case of initial consonant clusters. *Journal of Experimental Child Psychology, 50*, 156–178.

Bruck, M., Treiman, R., & Caravolas, M. (1995). The syllable's role in the processing of spoken English: Evidence from a nonword comparison task. *Journal of Experimental Psychology: Human Perception and Performance, 21*, 469–479.

Bruck, M., & Waters, G. (1990a). An analysis of the component spelling skills of good readers–poor spellers. *Applied Psycholinguistics, 11*, 425–437.

Bruck, M., & Waters, G. (1990b). A component skills analysis of the reading and spelling skills of children who show significant discrepancies in their reading and spelling abilities. In T. Carr & B. A. Levy (Eds.), *Reading and its development: Component skills approaches* (pp. 161–206). San Diego: Academic.

Byrne, B., & Ledez, J. (1983). Phonological awareness in reading-disabled adults. *Australian Journal of Psychology, 35*, 185–197.

Castles, A., & Coltheart, M. (1993). Varieties of developmental dyslexia. *Cognition, 47*, 149–180.

Coltheart, M. (1978). Lexical access in simple reading tasks. In. G. Underwood (Ed.), *Strategies of information processing* (pp. 151–216). New York: Academic.

Coltheart, M., Curtis, B., Atkins, P., & Haller, M. (1993). Models of reading aloud: Dual route and parallel-distributed-processing approaches. *Psychological Review, 100*, 589–608.

Felton, R., Naylor, C., & Wood, F. (1990). Neuropsychological profile of adult dyslexics. *Brain and Language, 39*, 485–497.

Finucci, J. M., Gottfredson, L. S., & Childs, B. (1986). A follow-up study of dyslexic boys. *Annals of Dyslexia, 35*, 117–136.

Goswami, U., & Bryant, P. (1990). *Phonological skills and learning to read.* Hillsdale, NJ: Lawrence Erlbaum Associates.

Gough, P., Alford, J., & Holley-Wilcox, P. (1981). Words and contexts. In O. Tzeng & H. Singer (Eds.), *Perception of print* (pp. 85–102). Hillsdale NJ: Lawrence Erlbaum Associates.
Gough, P., & Tunmer, W. (1986). Decoding, reading, and reading disability. *Remedial and Special Education, 7,* 6–10.
Hayduk, S., Bruck, M., & Cavanagh, P. (1993). Do adult dyslexics show low level visual processing deficits? *Annals of the New York Academy of Sciences, 682,* 351–353.
Hayduk, S., Bruck, M., & Cavanagh, P. (1996) Low level visual processing skills of adults and children with dyslexia. *Cognitive Neuropsychology, 13,* 975–1015.
Jared, D., McRae, K., & Seidenberg, M. S. (1990). The basis of consistency effects in word naming. *Journal of Memory and Language, 29,* 687–715.
Jorm, A. F., & Share, D. (1983). Phonological recoding and reading acquisition. *Applied Psycholinguistics, 4,* 103–147.
Labuda, M., & DeFries, J. C. (1988). Cognitive abilities in children with reading disabilities and controls: A follow-up study. *Journal of Learning Disabilities, 21,* 562–566.
Livingstone, M., Rosen, G., Drislane, F., & Galaburda, A. (1991). Physiological and anatomical evidence for a magnocellular defect in development dyslexia. *Proceedings of the National Academy of Sciences USA, 88,* 7943–7947.
Lovegrove, W., Garzia, R., & Nicholson, S. (1990). Experimental evidence for a transient system deficit in specific reading disability. *Journal of the American Optometric Association, 61,* 137–146.
Lovegrove, W., Martin, R., & Slaghuis, W. (1986). At theoretical and experimental case for a visual deficit in specific reading disability. *Cognitive Neuropsychology, 3,* 225–267.
Lundberg, I. (1987). Are letters necessary for the development of phonemic awareness? *European Bulletin of Cognitive Psychology, 5,* 472–475.
Manis, F., Seidenberg, M., Doi, L., McBride-Chang, C., & Petersen, A. (1996). On the bases of two subtypes of developmental dyslexia. *Cognition, 58,* 157–195.
Manis, F. R., Szeszulski, P., Holt, L., & Graves, K. (1988). A developmental perspective on dyslexic subtypes. *Annals of Dyslexia, 37,* 139–153.
Martin, F., & Lovegrove, W. J. (1987). Flicker contrast sensitivity in normal and specifically disabled readers. *Perception, 16,* 215–221.
Mason, M. (1978). From print to sound in mature readers as a function of reader ability and two forms of orthographic regularity. *Memory & Cognition, 6,* 568–581.
Morais, J. (1987). Segmental analysis of speech and its relation to reading ability. *Annals of Dyslexia, 37,* 126–141.
Murphy, A., Pollatsek, A., & Well, A. (1988). Developmental dyslexia and word retrieval deficits. *Brain and Language, 35,* 1–23.
Olson, R., Wise, B., Conners, F., & Rack, J. (1990). Organization, heritability, and remediation of component word recognition and language skills in disabled readers. In T. Carr & B. A. Levy (Eds.), *Reading and its development: Component skills approaches* (pp. 261–322). San Diego: Academic.
Perfetti, C. A., Beck, L., Bell, L., & Hughes, C. (1987). Phonemic knowledge and learning to read are reciprocal: A longitudinal study of first grade children. *Merrill-Palmer Quarterly, 33,* 283–319.
Plaut, D. C., McClelland, J. L., Seidenberg, M. S., & Patterson, K. E. (1996). Understanding normal and impaired word reading: Computational principles in quasi-regular domains. *Psychological Review, 103,* 56–115.
Rack, J. P., Snowling, M., & Olson, R. (1992). The nonword reading deficit in developmental dyslexia: A review. *Reading Research Quarterly, 27,* 28–53.
Rawson, M. (1968). *Developmental language disability.* Baltimore, MD: Johns Hopkins Press.
Read, C. R., & Ruyter, L. (1985). Reading and spelling skills in adults of low literacy. *Remedial and Special Education, 6,* 43–52.

Seidenberg, M. S. (1992). Dyslexia in a computational model of word recognition in reading. In P. Gough, R. Treiman, & L. Ehri (Eds.), *Reading acquisition* (pp. 243–274). Hillsdale, NJ: Lawrence Erlbaum Associates.

Seidenberg, M. S., Bruck, M., Fornarolo, G., & Backman, J. (1985). Word recognition skills of poor and disabled readers: Do they necessarily differ? *Applied Psycholinguistics, 6,* 161–180.

Seidenberg, M. S., & McClelland, J. L. (1989). A distributed developmental model of word recognition and naming. *Psychological Review, 96,* 447–452.

Share, D. L., Jorm, A. F., Maclean, R., & Matthews, R. (1984). Sources of individual differences in reading acquisition. *Journal of Educational Psychology, 76,* 1309–1324.

Slaghuis, W., & Lovegrove, W. (1985). Spatial-frequency- dependent visible persistence and specific reading disability. *Brain and Cognition, 4,* 219–240.

Stanovich, K. E. (1982). Individual differences in the cognitive processes of reading I: Word decoding. *Journal of Learning Disabilities, 15,* 485–493.

Stanovich, K. E. (1986). Explaining the variance in reading ability in terms of psychological processes: What have we learned. *Annals of Dyslexia, 35,* 67–96.

Stanovich, K. E. (1992). Speculations on the causes and consequences of individual differences in early reading acquisition. In P. Gough, L. Ehri, & R. Treiman (Eds.), *Reading acquisition* (pp. 307–342). Hillsdale, NJ: Lawrence Erlbaum Associates.

Stanovich, K. E., Cunningham, A. E., & Cramer, B. (1984). Assessing phonological awareness in kindergarten children: Issues of task comparability. *Journal of Experimental Child Psychology, 38,* 175–190.

Stanovich, K. E., & Siegel, L. S. (1994). Phenotypic performance profile of children with reading disabilities: A regression-based test of the phonological-core variable-difference model. *Journal of Education Psychology, 86,* 24–53.

Treiman, R., Goswami, U., & Bruck, M. (1990). Not all nonwords are alike: Implications for reading development and theory. *Memory & Cognition, 18,* 559–567.

Treisman, A. (1991). Search, similarity, and integration of features between and within dimensions. *Journal of Experimental Psychology: Human Perception and Performance, 17,* 652–676.

Vellutino, F. (1979). *Dyslexia: Theory and research.* Cambridge, MA: MIT Press.

Waters, G., Bruck, M., & Malus-Abramowitz, M. (1988). The role of linguistic and visual processes in spelling: A developmental study. *Journal of Experimental Child Psychology, 45,* 400–421.

Chapter 10

Development and Variation in Developmental Dyslexia

Margaret Snowling
University of York

Nata Goulandris
University College London

Neil Defty
University of Durham

Although from time to time new theories of dyslexia emerge, the most widely accepted view remains that dyslexic children are subject to verbal deficits and, more specifically, that they experience phonological processing difficulties. In contrast, there is less consensus about two issues with which this chapter is concerned. The first of these is the extent to which dyslexia can be characterized as a disorder of development. The second is the question of whether there are subtypes of dyslexia. The data that we use to debate these issues come from a 2-year longitudinal study of dyslexic children. We begin by focusing on whether it is more appropriate to consider dyslexia as reflecting atypical development or as a developmental delay in the acquisition of reading.

THE NATURE OF DEVELOPMENT IN DYSLEXIA

It has been a tradition in developmental psychology to draw a distinction between children who follow a normal course of development, albeit slowly, and children whose development is atypical or disordered. In the field of reading disabilities, the "delay" versus "difference" debate has not been fully resolved. From a neurodevelopmental perspective, Satz and his colleagues argued that dyslexic children suffer from a developmental delay or lag in the maturation of the central nervous system; initially they exhibit immaturities of visuoperceptual and motor development, skills that develop early, whereas later-developing skills are more delayed in older children, for example, language skills (e.g., Satz, Rardin, & Ross, 1971). On the basis of epidemiological data, Rutter and his colleagues argued against a distinctive "dyslexic" profile, reporting few signs or symptoms that differentiated children with specific reading retardation from generally backward readers (Rutter & Yule, 1975). Additionally, Bryant (1985), arguing from a cognitive perspective, proposed that the phonological skills of poor readers were at the lower end of the normal distribution, but dyslexics were not otherwise "different" from normal readers.

In contrast, a number of theorists have argued that dyslexia should be considered a specific developmental disorder (Frith, 1981; Miles, 1983). By implication, the development of dyslexic children is different. Evidence from a variety of sources has been used to support this "difference" view. Thus, when dyslexic readers have been compared with appropriately matched normal readers who read at a similar level, they have been found to have difficulties with phonological awareness (Bradley & Bryant, 1978), naming (Snowling, van Wagtendonk, & Stafford, 1988) and nonword repetition (Snowling, Goulandris, Bowlby, & Howell, 1986). There is also evidence that the reading strategies they adopt are different and, typically, they show nonword reading deficits (Rack, Snowling, & Olson, 1992). Findings such as these suggest that the development of different cognitive processes is out of step in dyslexia. Thus, the development of dyslexic children is qualitatively different from that of normal readers.

As is clear from this brief discussion, acceptance of the "difference" view hinges on the logic that finding differences between groups of dyslexic children and appropriately matched controls, studied at one point in time, constitutes sufficient evidence that the dyslexics are *developing* abnormally. Conversely, the failure to find differences constitutes evidence that dyslexic readers are developmentally delayed. A wide range of issues could be raised in objection to this logic. At the simplest and perhaps least interesting level, sampling differences between studies might account for some disparities in results. A number of studies, for example, have failed to find nonword reading deficits in dyslexic children when compared to reading-level-matched controls (Beech & Harding, 1984; Treiman & Hirsh-Pasek, 1985). Rack et al. (1992) suggested that possible reasons might be found in sample differences in IQ, age, and reading instruction. Younger children, particularly those who have been remediated, tend to do less poorly in nonword reading than do older dyslexics. Furthermore, a reading of the literature suggests almost certainly there are differences between clinically referred and school-based samples.

Second, an overreliance on data from one domain of processing may be misleading; Johnston and her colleagues argued that, because dyslexic children show verbal short-term memory deficits only in relation to age-matched and not in relation to reading-level-matched controls, they suffer from a delay in development (e.g., Johnston, Rugg, & Scott, 1987). However, if atypical development equates with uneven development, then finding dissociations between skills during development might be the hallmark of developmental disorder—for instance, delays in memory development may coexist with differences in language processing (e.g., van der Lely & Howard, 1994).

Finally, a delay at one stage in development might well produce a disorder later; children who are slow in their language development and show a delay in the development of phonology may develop a disorder of reading because of the ways in which emergent literacy skills are dependent on phonology (Snowling, 1987, p. 101).

One of the best ways to find out about the development of dyslexic children is by studying them as they develop. It is indeed surprising, given the wealth of research on the cognitive impairments associated with dyslexia, that the majority of studies have been carried out at one point in time. Such studies can provide only a snapshot of the problems experienced by dyslexic children and cannot throw light on how their underlying cognitive deficits change over time. One exception is a recent study by Manis, Custodio, and Szeszulski (1993) who followed a group of 21 dyslexic children over a 2-year period. At the beginning of the study the dyslexics were reading at the second-grade level, and they were compared with both reading-level- and age-level-matched controls. At the end of the study, they were reading at the third or fourth grade levels and again were compared with reading- and age-level controls. During the 2-year period, the dyslexics had progressed at a normal rate, making an average gain of 2.2 grade points on the Woodcock Word Identification Test. Nevertheless, they fell relatively further behind their peers in decoding nonwords that did not have orthographic neighbors, in phoneme deletion, and in irregular word spelling. The study that we report here took place within a similar time frame to that of Manis et al. (1993). However, the majority of our dyslexics were less advanced in their reading at the beginning of the study and they made substantially less progress over time (Snowling, Goulandris, & Defty, 1996).

The Dyslexic Sample

Twenty dyslexic children, aged between 7 years, 7 months and 12 years, 7 months, were recruited to this project via local health and education authorities. All of the children in our sample were of normal intelligence, their first language was English, and they were reading at least 18 months below age expectation on a single-word reading test. In addition, the usual exclusionary criteria were applied: None of the dyslexic children had a primary emotional disturbance nor a serious language impairment, they all had normal hearing and vision, and they attended school regularly.

Twenty reading-age-matched (RA) controls were selected from a London Primary School. These children formed the longitudinal control group and ranged in age from 5 years, 7 months to 8 years, 4 months. A third comparison group consisted of 20 normal readers who were of similar chronological age (CA) to the dyslexics at Time 1. These CA controls ranged in age from 7 years, 7 months to 12 years, 7 months, and were only tested at the beginning of the study.

Design of the Longitudinal Study

Our study was designed to elucidate the ways in which dyslexic children develop. Extensive data were therefore collected from each dyslexic child to form a series of case studies. We return to these later. For the moment, we concentrate on the status of the dyslexic children as a group. At Time 1 we present comparisons of the dyslexic children with age- and reading-level-matched controls and, at Time 2, we examine the progress of the dyslexic children in relation to that of the children who started out at a similar level of performance to them (the longitudinal comparison group).

The reading, spelling, and phonological processing skills of the dyslexic children were examined using a battery of tests, most of which have been used previously by our group to differentiate dyslexic from normal readers. To assess lexical and sublexical (phonological) reading skills, each child read 31 regular (e.g., *dance, bitter*) and 31 irregular words (e.g., *sign, biscuit*), matched for frequency and word length (Snowling, Stackhouse, & Rack, 1986). They also read 22 nonwords of one and two syllables (e.g., *smade, rept, tegwop, holtcom*). Both tests were untimed. To assess the use of spelling strategies, each child was asked to write 10 words of one, two, three, and four syllables (e.g., *pet, fish, trumpet, polish, membership, adventure*). In addition to recording the number of words spelled correctly, a qualitative analysis of each child's spelling errors was carried out and the number of phonetic, semiphonetic, and dysphonetic spelling errors was calculated.

To assess phonological skills, two rhyming tests were used. The first was derived from the rhyme oddity task of Bradley (1981). Children were required to decide which was the odd one out (the one that differed by the rime segment) from a string of spoken words (e.g., *cot, hot, fox, pot; hug, dig, pig, wig*). In the second rhyming task, they were required to generate strings of words to rhyme with a spoken target. The test comprised 20 words and the children were given 30 seconds per item. Word and nonword responses were both allowed.

In addition, two tests requiring the use of phonological codes (but not at a metalinguistic level) were administered. In a verbal repetition test, the children were asked to repeat a series of 12 words (e.g., *eskimo, statistics*) and 12 matched nonwords (e.g., *istebo, spapispics*) presented in blocks of six, with words and nonwords counterbalanced within the list (after Snowling, Stackhouse, et al., 1986). The children were also administered the Digit Span subtest from the Wechsler Intelligence Scale for Children–Revised, to assess verbal short-term memory. Finally, to assess the ability of the children to retrieve lexical phonology, they were required to name 40 pictures depicting objects such as a puppet or an escalator. All of these tasks were administered both at Time 1 and, 2 years later, at Time 2.

Dyslexic Deficits at Time 1

It can be recalled that, at the start of the study, we matched our dyslexic subjects on an individual basis for reading age and IQ with a group of normally developing readers who were younger than them, and we also included a group of age-level-matched controls who were individually matched for chronological age. Naturally, we anticipated that the dyslexics would perform significantly less well overall than the CA controls on the tests requiring reading, and this was indeed the case. Dyslexic children performed worse than their age-matched peers when reading regular, irregular, and nonwords, but similarly to younger RA controls. All groups showed a significant regularity effect. Thus, they read more regular than irregular words.

It turned out that matching the groups for reading level also equated them for spelling skills, as measured by a standardized spelling test. In turn, the CA controls were better spellers than were the dyslexics. Analysis of the children's performance when spelling words varying in word length indicated that group differences were smaller when spelling one- and four-syllable words that were, respectively, relatively easy or relatively hard. The qualitative nature of the spelling errors made by the dyslexic and the normal readers was also analyzed. This analysis used the spelling errors made on one-, two-, and three-syllable words only because performance on four-syllable words was generally very poor. The dyslexic readers made on average 5.2 phonetic, 4.7 semiphonetic, and 9 dysphonetic errors, and the performance of the RA controls was broadly similar. The CA controls performed differently, however, making a higher proportion of phonetic errors, 12.4 on average, compared with 3 semiphonetic and 1.5 dysphonetic errors.

Taken together, our data provided no evidence of any qualitative difference between dyslexic and normal readers in their reading or spelling strategies. Contrary to the results of previous studies of our own, the dyslexics appeared to be delayed in the acquisition of reading and spelling processes, performing less well than children of similar age but similarly to children of the same reading level. When we turned to examine their underlying phonological skills the picture was very similar. On both of the rhyming tests, the CA controls performed better than the dyslexics and, in the rhyme oddity task, the dyslexics performed like younger RA controls (rhyme production data were not available from the younger subjects). Similarly, the dyslexics performed as expected, taking account of reading age on digit span, a test of verbal short-term memory. An unexpected finding was that the dyslexics performed as well as CA controls on the picture naming task.

Thus, although the dyslexic children were generally weaker than their age-matched peers in reading, spelling, and phonological processing skills, they presented a pattern of performance closely similar to that of younger children matched on reading level. Our findings suggested that, by and large, the dyslexic children were following a normal but delayed course of development. Confidence in these findings would be strengthened if, over the following years, the dyslexic children continued to develop normally. Although such a course of development is entirely possible, it seemed to us unlikely given the frequently reported deficits in dyslexia (Hulme & Snowling, 1992a, for a review).

Dyslexic Deficits at Time 2

We reassessed the dyslexic children and their reading-age-matched controls 2 years after they had initially been seen. The CA controls were not retested. The normal readers had progressed in reading at greater-than-average expected rate over the 2-year period, and they had gained between 1.4 and 5 years on the B.A.S. Reading Test, a test of single-word reading. The dyslexics had made much less progress, with outcome scores ranging from just below that recorded at Time 1 to 3 years above in the case of two boys who had made good progress. An interaction between group and time indicated that the dyslexics made less progress than the controls and, although the two groups had been matched at Time 1, they differed at Time 2. A similar picture emerged when spelling progress was examined. Once again, the normal readers had made greater than the average expected rate over the 2-year period, between 1.8 and 6.3 years on the Vernon Graded Spelling Test. The dyslexics had made comparatively less progress, with outcome scores ranging from 6 months below that initially recorded to 3.6 years above. Again, there was an interaction between group and time. Moreover, an analysis of covariance with reading age at Time 1 and Time 2 as covariates indicated that their slower rate of progress in spelling was greater than would be predicted from their reading age.

Considering that the dyslexic children in our sample had made poorer progress than the younger children who had started out matched with them, it seemed incorrect to describe their difficulty simply as a delay in development, because this delay was increasing over time. We examined their performance on tests of regular, irregular, and nonword reading once again, to find out whether their pattern of performance would throw light on why the gap between their expected and actual achievement was widening. In these analyses we examined group differences in performance at Time 1 and Time 2.

Analysis of the regular and irregular word reading data revealed that the dyslexic children read the irregular words less well than did the controls, and they also progressed less well over time so that, by Time 2, the dyslexics read fewer words correctly. They also progressed less well in nonword reading and, here, a striking interaction was found: Although the dyslexics were no worse at nonword reading than were the normal RA controls at Time 1, by Time 2 they were significantly poorer.

In spelling, we found that the dyslexic children had more difficulty with the words of two and three syllables than did the normal readers, and more important, they progressed less well than them over time. The spelling errors made by the dyslexic and the normal readers were again classified. This time, there was a difference in the quality of responses made by children in the two groups. In particular, the dyslexic readers made a higher proportion of dysphonetic errors than controls at Time 2, suggesting problems in the use of phonological spelling strategies.

The data on reading and spelling at Time 2 produced a picture more in keeping with a "classic" picture of dyslexia. The poorer progress of the dyslexic children over time, particularly in reading irregular words, was associated with emerging deficits in nonword reading and in phonetic spelling. Why, then, were these deficits not evident at Time 1? We propose that, at the beginning of our study, the children in the normal control group who were quite young had not yet mastered the use of phonological reading and spelling strategies (cf. Ehri, 1992). The dyslexic children, by contrast, had already been identified at the time they were first seen and many were already receiving remediation to promote phonological skills. The fact that they ultimately made less progress than the normal children who had no special attention is salutary. Arguably, their relatively poor levels of alphabetic competence might explain their difficulty.

Was the dyslexics' poorer performance on reading and spelling tasks at Time 2 a consequence of difficulties in phonological processing? To examine this question, we reassessed the children on rhyming, repetition, verbal short-term memory, and naming tasks, replacing the rhyme oddity task used previously with a more difficult version (Snowling, Hulme, Smith, & Thomas, 1994). We found significant group differences this time on both the harder rhyme oddity task and on the rhyme production task in which the dyslexics produced fewer rhyming responses to the target words in the time allowed. In addition, they also performed worse than controls when repeating words and nonwords on the repetition task. Moreover, their difficulty in nonword repetition was confirmed by their relatively poor performance on a more difficult nonword repetition task in which nonwords of one to four syllables had to be repeated (Gathercole & Baddeley, 1989).

Finally, there was a significant interaction between group and time of test in picture naming. Although both groups had improved between Time 1 and Time 2, the progress of the normal readers was greater. Once again, the dyslexics' rate of progress over time was slower than to be expected.

Conclusions: The Progress of Dyslexic Children Over Time

At Time 1, the dyslexic children in our study appeared to be showing a delay in the development of phonological awareness and in short-term memory. They produced a poorer performance than did age-level-matched peers on tests of rhyme oddity, rhyme production, and verbal short-term memory, although they performed normally on nonmetalinguistic tasks including verbal repetition and picture naming. Two years later, their performance on the metalinguistic tasks and also in verbal repetition was not as good as that of younger children who had started out matched with them in reading skill and equated on these tasks. It also appeared that they had been developing more slowly in their picture naming ability, and they showed a dissociation between word and nonword reading performance over time. We would argue, tentatively, that the dyslexics' development of phonological abilities was delayed and, although their weaknesses were not discernible in relation to younger controls of between 6 and 8 years, they were significant 2 years further on when the normal children were becoming proficient in these skills. Even in an untimed picture naming task the dyslexics appeared to be experiencing an increasing problem, perhaps as the words on the test became more complex and difficult to retrieve. Their phonological difficulties were associated with a failure to develop proficient reading and spelling strategies, at least when these were compared with those of younger, normally developing children.

A strong interpretation of the cross-over interaction in nonword reading skill over time would be that the dyslexic children's development is atypical. Although they started out marginally better at reading nonwords than did controls, they ended up significantly worse. A similar gloss could be placed on their repetition abilities. In other areas of performance, for example, on verbal short-term memory tasks—their performance remained similar to that of controls over time. The picture that emerges, therefore, is one of uneven development in dyslexia, with the most striking finding being their poor progress over time in reading and spelling.

It is important to be cautious in the interpretation placed on these results. Following the same children through time has highlighted a number of methodological difficulties. The first problem that we alluded to is that of range effects on the tasks used. Conceivably, the nonword reading test that we used was insensitive to group differences between children in the early stages of reading development and, equally, the rhyme oddity task used at Time 1 was not suitable for assessing performance of more advanced readers at Time 2. Of equal concern are variations in the reliability of the tasks used, not assessed in the present study. Theoretically, however, it seems to us that one of the main factors that should be seriously considered is the possible heterogeneity of the groups under study. It has long been thought that there may be subtypes of dyslexia (Boder, 1971; Castles & Coltheart, 1993; Johnson & Myklebust, 1967) or, even when subtypes have been rejected, significant individual variation within the population of dyslexic readers was proposed (Seymour, 1986). We therefore need to consider the extent to which our interpretation must be tempered by evidence of individual differences amongst the dyslexic readers in our study.

INDIVIDUAL DIFFERENCES IN DYSLEXIC AND NORMAL READERS

The existence of children who show extreme variants of developmental dyslexia has led cognitive neuropsychologists to reject the group comparison approach, as exemplified by the first part of this chapter. Thus, in the UK, Temple and Marshall (1983) were the first to report a single-case study of a developmental "phonological dyslexic," HM, who could read words significantly better than nonwords. As well, Coltheart, Masterson, Byng, Prior, and Riddoch (1983) reported a single-case study of CD, a developmental "surface dyslexic" who read irregular words significantly less well than regular words.

These early case studies were severely criticized by Bryant and Impey (1986) because they lacked comparisons with normal controls. Replicating their techniques, Bryant and Impey showed that it was possible to find children who read like HM and like CD in a sample of normal readers of similar reading age. Notwithstanding these criticisms, single-case studies published later, including some of our own, have reported children who do appear to be characterized by reliance on one or other subcomponent of reading, and have attempted to relate their reading deficit to aspects of their cognitive profile. JM, a developmental "phonological dyslexic" whom we studied longitudinally, had severe nonword reading deficits that persisted over time in relation to reading-age-matched controls (Snowling & Hulme, 1989). We argued that his difficulties with phonological reading and spelling strategies were the consequence of phonological processing deficits at the level of output phonology, and he has had to learn to read in an atypical manner (Hulme & Snowling, 1992b; Snowling, Hulme, & Goulandris, 1994).

In contrast, JAS was a dyslexic undergraduate who read irregular words poorly and could be characterized as a developmental "surface dyslexic" (Goulandris & Snowling, 1991). She performed normally on phonological tasks but exhibited severe impairments of visual memory, suggesting that these had forced her to learn to read (and to spell) by relying on phonology. Might it be the case, therefore, that the existence of children at these two extremes of variation within our dyslexic sample obscured the true nature of the performance of dyslexic children over time?

To investigate this question, we first had to examine the dyslexic readers as individuals. To do this we used a technique advocated by Seymour (1990). We plotted for each child in the dyslexic and control groups their position on a graph relating nonword reading performance to irregular word reading skill. When plotting children's data in this way, those who fall within the upper-left quadrant of the graph are children who make a relatively high number of errors on irregular words compared to their performance on nonwords. These children might be considered to be surface dyslexic in their profile. Children who fall within the lower-right quadrant make a relatively high number of nonword and a relatively low number of irregular word reading errors. These children can, therefore, be considered phonological dyslexic in profile. We did this twice, once using data collected at Time 1 and once using the Time 2 data. Our most striking observation was the extensive overlap between the dyslexic children and their RA controls. In fact, the similarity of our two groups forced us to conclude that the majority of dyslexic readers read in a qualitatively similar manner to younger children of the same reading level (cf. Bryant & Impey, 1986), and it is rare to find the extreme variation that is seen in children who have been the subject of single-case studies. Nonetheless, such children have been reported and do exist; the important question of what causes them to read as they do may throw light on the determinants of variation in normal reading.

We reasoned that in order to make a valid comparison between children who manifested a phonological dyslexic profile in our study and those that had a surface dyslexic pattern of reading, we needed to choose rigorous and replicable procedures for defining such children. Because we believe

TABLE 10.1
Details of the Two "Phonological" and Two "Surface"
Dyslexic Readers at Time 1 and Time 2

	WISC-R IQ	Age Time 1	Reading Age Time 1	Reading Age Time 2
Phonological dyslexics				
EC	103	8.67	6.67	7.92
TO	116	7.58	6.08	7.67
Surface dyslexics				
JMc	101	9.83	6.42	7.83
DL	109	8.92	7.08	8.5

that it is only relevant to speak of a dyslexic profile if a child shows a pattern of performance outside of that normally expected, given their reading level (see also Bryant & Impey, 1986), we chose to define such children in the following way. First, using data from our RA controls at Time 1, we regressed reading age on nonword reading performance. We proceeded to predict, on the basis of this regression equation, the nonword reading score expected of every child in our dyslexic sample, given their reading age. Similarly, following the regression of reading age on irregular word reading in the normal readers, we were able to predict irregular word reading score from reading age. The next step was to examine the discrepancy between expected and actual achievement in nonword reading and in irregular word reading for each child, looking for children who showed extreme forms of variation from the expected pattern.

We defined as phonological dyslexic any child whose nonword reading was at least 25% behind expectation at Time 1 and at least 15% lower at Time 2. We defined as surface dyslexic any child whose irregular word reading was at least 20% behind expectation at Time 1 and at least 15% lower at Time 2. To an extent these cutoff points were arbitrary, but they defined the extremes of the distributions with which we were working. Using these definitions, we identified two phonological dyslexics and two surface dyslexic children in our sample of 20 dyslexic readers. The other 16 children exhibited a pattern of performance at one or both points in time that could be regarded as normal for reading age. The two phonological dyslexic children were TO (a boy) and EC (a girl). The two surface dyslexics were JMc and DL, (both boys); JMc's nonword reading was above average, DL's was average for his reading age.

Table 10.1 shows the details of the subjects TO, EC, JMc and DL at Time 1 and Time 2. It is revealed that all four children were significantly poorer than to be expected in reading and spelling skill at both points in time, and that they made less than the average expected rate of progress.

Comparing Phonological and Surface Dyslexia and Time 1

We began our exploration of the cognitive differences that underlie phonological and surface dyslexia by comparing the two pairs of children we had designated as such on the phonological processing tasks described previously. On most of these tasks, there was overlap between the scores gained by the two phonological and the two surface dyslexics. The tasks that failed to discriminate between the two pairs of children were WISC-R Digit Span, rhyme oddities, word repetition, and naming. However, the phonological dyslexics did worse than the surface dyslexics in rhyme production and in nonword repetition. TO's spelling had been so poor at Time 1 that a spelling analysis was not viable. However, we felt it relevant that EC made fewer phonetic and a greater proportion of dysphonetic spelling errors than the two surface dyslexic, JMc and DL, whose pattern of performance was within the normal range.

Comparing Phonological and Surface Dyslexia at Time 2

Two years later, at Time 2, we proceeded to examine the performance of the two "pairs" of dyslexic children on tests of phonological processing, similar to those given at Time 1, and additionally to observe their performance on a number of visual processing tasks. As at Time 1, relatively few of our tasks discriminated TO and EC from JMc and DL. This time they performed similarly on WISC-R Digit Span, rhyme production, rhyme oddity, and naming. We also administered Gathercole and Baddeley's (1989) nonword repetition test. The phonological dyslexics did worse on this test than did the surface dyslexics and, as before, they made more dysphonetic spelling errors.

Thus, relatively few measures differentiated the phonological and the surface dyslexic children, although we did find the phonological dyslexics to be relatively weaker on rhyming tasks and in nonword repetition, and the surface dyslexics made more phonetically acceptable spelling errors than did their phonological dyslexic counterparts. These findings suggest that developmental phonological dyslexics have weaker phonological processing skills than those designated surface dyslexic. But what of their visual processing abilities? A commonly voiced hypothesis is that children whose reading difficulties have their primary focus in reading irregular words are likely to have visual difficulties, forcing them to read phonologically. However, with the exception of some work by Seymour and Evans (1993) that contradicts it, there is as yet little empirical evidence bearing on this popular hypothesis. In this study, we too looked for visual processing differences between EC and TO, and JMc and DL. The children were all assessed using three tests of visual sequential memory for abstract forms, a visuomotor memory test requiring the reproduction of designs, letter and symbol-cancellation tasks, and the Children's Embedded Figures Test. None of these tests discriminated the two pairs of dyslexics, and there was considerable overlap in the scores they achieved.

Cognitive Differences Between Developmental Phonological and Developmental Surface Dyslexia: A Summary

Before taking stock of the evidence, it is relevant to report how the performance of the dyslexic cases reported here compared with that of normal readers. The comparison groups we chose were comprised of normal readers of similar reading age to the dyslexics at the two points in time (i.e., at between the 6- and the 7-year levels at Time 1 and between the 7- and the 8-year levels at Time 2). The focus of our interest was on how these children performed on the tasks that differentiated EC and TO from JMc and DL, namely on tests of rhyme processing, nonword repetition, and in the types of spelling errors they made. On all of these tasks, we found that the surface dyslexic children performed at the normal level for reading age, whereas the phonological dyslexics showed deficits.

Thus, our findings are consistent with the view that dyslexic children who have specific difficulty with nonword reading have more significant phonological processing difficulties than do dyslexic children whose difficulty is primarily in decoding irregular words (surface dyslexics). In turn, the processing difficulties of these children are in line with those of reading-level-matched controls. Contrary to prediction, we did not find data in this study to suggest that the two types of dyslexics differ in visual processing skill.

We have proposed elsewhere that the severity of an individual's phonological processing deficit determines the severity and indeed the nature of his or her reading and spelling difficulties, with more pervasive difficulties being associated with difficulties in nonword reading and in phonetic spelling (Snowling, Goulandris, & Stackhouse, 1994). The current findings are in line with this theory, because JMc and DL (the surface dyslexics) were better on the phonological processing tasks than were EC and TO. Moreover, because JMc and DL performed within the normal range for their reading level on the phonological tasks (but, by implication, less well than children of the same age), we propose tentatively that they might be characterized as being delayed in their phonological development. As a direct consequence, their reading development has been slow. In contrast, EC and TO have shown deficits in phonological processing relative to reading-level controls, and their reading development appears to have followed an atypical course as a consequence.

CONCLUSIONS

In this chapter, we have attempted to address two questions that have long been asked in the field of dyslexia. The first is the extent to which dyslexia can be considered a delay in development; the second, the question of subtypes. We would like to suggest that there is a related answer to both of these questions and, as evidence, we presented the data from a longitudinal study of dyslexic children. Before discussing our proposal, we argue that data from groups of dyslexic children studied at one point in time may be misleading and cannot provide definitive answers regarding the course of dyslexic development. Indeed, we have seen in our study of dyslexic children followed over 2 years that patterns of performance can change with time, and what at one point may appear to represent slow or delayed development may at a later point in time represent a developmental disorder. Early in the present study, for example, the dyslexic children performed like younger children of similar reading level in nonword reading, whereas later on they performed significantly worse than them, showing a discrepancy between word and nonword reading.

Moreover, at the level of individuals it is wrong to assume homogeneity in development. Rather, there is variation between children both in normal and dyslexic populations. When strict criteria are applied in order to identify children who show extreme variations in their pattern of performance, we argue that single-case exploration is warranted. Such single-case studies have allowed us to investigate cognitive differences between children who, in their reading, have specific nonword deficits (phonological dyslexia) and those who have specific difficulty reading irregular words (surface dyslexia). The main difference between these children, as far as we can determine, is in the severity of their phonological processing difficulties. We suggested that these are greater in the case of developmental phonological dyslexia; the corollary of this is that surface dyslexics perform at the level to be expected given their reading level, though less well than expected for their age. Put another way, surface dyslexics are delayed in their development but follow a normal pathway; phonological dyslexics may have a more specific phonological disorder. However, the possibility that surface dyslexics may have additional deficits, perhaps in visual processing, remains open (but see Hanley, Hastie, & Kay, 1992).

Our previous work led us to conclude that learning to read depends on the integrity of phonological representations (Hulme & Snowling, 1992b). The present data are in line with an extension of this idea that individual differences in dyslexia are the consequence of variation in the severity of phonological processing deficits. Our suggestion is that when phonological processing skills are impaired, the development of phonological or alphabetic reading and spelling strategies is compromised. The dyslexic profile that results has been described as developmental phonological dyslexia and shown by EC and TO here, as well as by our case JM, reported elsewhere (Snowling, Hulme, et al., 1994). When phonological processing skills are weak considering a child's age—that is, they are developmentally delayed but not severely impaired—phonological reading and spelling strategies can develop, albeit slowly, as was the case for JM and DL, who were able to use phonology in reading and in spelling. However, we would stress that, in this view, phonological and surface dyslexic profiles are *symptoms* of underlying cognitive differences between individuals. The reading patterns that we see at the behavioral level are the consequence of an interaction between a basic deficit at the cognitive level (we would argue in phonological processing), the child's cognitive strengths, and the environmental experiences he or she receives, for instance, through teaching (Snowling, 1987).

ACKNOWLEDGEMENTS

This research was supported by grant G8801538 from the Medical Research Council to the first author. We thank John Armstrong for his assistance and all of the children who participated.

REFERENCES

Beech, J. R., & Harding, L. M. (1984). Phonemic processing and the poor reader from a developmental lag viewpoint. *Reading Research Quarterly, 19*, 357–366.

Boder, E. (1971). Developmental dyslexia: Prevailing diagnostic concepts and a new diagnostic approach. In H. R. Myklebust (Ed.), *Progress in learning disabilities* (pp. 293–321). New York: Grune & Stratton.

Bradley, L. (1981). *Assessing reading difficulties.* Oxford, England: Heinemann.

Bradley, L., & Bryant, P. E. (1978). Difficulties in auditory organisation as a possible cause of reading backwardness. *Nature, 301*, 419.

Bryant, P. E. (1985). The question of prevention. In M. Snowling (Ed.), *Children's written language difficulties* (pp. 43–56). Windsor, England: NFER-Nelson.

Bryant, P. E., & Impey, L. (1986). The similarities between normal readers and developmental and acquired dyslexics. *Cognition, 24*, 121–137.

Castles, C., & Coltheart, M. (1993). Varieties of developmental dyslexia. *Cognition, 47*, 149–180.

Coltheart, M., Masterson, J., Byng, S., Prior, M., & Riddoch, J. (1983). Surface dyslexia. *Quarterly Journal of Experimental Psychology, 35A*, 469–496.

Ehri, L. C. (1992). Reconceptualising the development of sight word reading and its relationship to decoding. In P. B. Gough, L. C. Ehri, & R. Treiman (Eds.), *Reading acquisition* (pp. 107–144). Hillsdale: NJ: Lawrence Erlbaum Associates.

Frith, U. (1981). Experimental approaches to developmental dyslexia: An introduction. *Psychological Research, 43*, 97–109.

Gathercole, S. E., & Baddeley, A. D. (1989). Evaluation of the role of phonological STM in the development of vocabulary in children: A longitudinal study. *Journal of Memory and Language, 28,* 200–213.

Goulandris, A., & Snowling, M. (1991). Visual memory deficits: A plausible cause of developmental dyslexia? Evidence from a single case study. *Cognitive Neuropsychology, 8,* 127–154.

Hanley, J. R., Hastie, K., & Kay, J. (1992). Developmental surface dyslexia and dysgraphia: An orthographic processing impairment. *Quarterly Journal of Experimental Psychology, 44A,* 285–320.

Hulme, C., & Snowling, M. (1992a). Phonological deficits in dyslexia: A "sound" reappraisal of the verbal deficit hypothesis? In N. Singh & I. Beale (Eds.), *Progress in learning disabilities* (pp. 270–301). New York: Springer-Verlag.

Hulme, C., & Snowling, M. (1992b). Deficits in output phonology: An explanation of reading failure? *Cognitive Neuropsychology, 9,* 47–72.

Johnson, D. J., & Myklebust, H. (1987). *Learning disabilities: Educational principles and practices.* New York: Grune & Statton.

Johnston, R., Rugg, M., & Scott, T. (1987). Phonological similarity effects, memory span and developmental reading disorders: The nature of the relationship. *British Journal of Psychology, 78,* 205–211.

Manis, F. R., Custodio, R., & Szeszulski, P. A. (1993). Development of phonological and orthographic skill: A 2-year longitudinal study of dyslexic children. *Journal of Experimental Child Psychology, 56,* 64–86.

Miles, T. R. (1983). *Dyslexia: The pattern of difficulties.* London: Granada.

Rack, J. P., Snowling, M. J., & Olson, R. K. (1992). The nonword reading deficit in dyslexia: A review. *Reading Research Quarterly, 27,* 29–53.

Rutter, M., & Yule, W. (1975). The concept of specific reading retardation. *Journal of Child Psychology and Psychiatry, 16,* 181–197.

Satz, P., Rardin, D., & Ross, J. (1971). An evaluation of a theory of specific developmental dyslexia. *Child Development, 42,* 2009–2021.

Seymour, P. H. K. (1986). *Cognitive analysis of dyslexia.* London: Routledge & Kegan Paul.

Seymour, P. H. K. (1990). Developmental dyslexia. In M. W. Eysenck (Ed.), *Cognitive psychology: An international review* (pp. 135–196). Chichester, England: Wiley.

Seymour, P. H. K., & Evans, H. M. (1993). The visual (orthographic) processor and dyslexia. In D. M. Willows, R. S. Kruk, & E. Corcos (Eds.), *Visual processes in reading and reading disabilities* (pp. 317–346). Hillsdale, NJ: Lawrence Erlbaum Associates.

Snowling, M. (1987). *Dyslexia: A Cognitive developmental perspective.* Oxford, England: Basil Blackwell.

Snowling, M., Goulandris, N., Bowlby, M., & Howell, P. (1986). Segmentation and speech perception in relation to reading skill: A developmental analysis. *Journal of Experimental Child Psychology, 41,* 489–507.

Snowling, M., Goulandris, N., & Defty, N. (1996). A longitudinal study of reading development in dyslexic children. *Journal of Educational Psychology, 88,* 653–669.

Snowling, M., Goulandris, N., & Stackhouse, J. (1994). Phonological constraints on learning to read: Evidence from single-case studies. In C. Hulme & M. Snowling (Eds.), *Reading development and dyslexia* (pp. 86–104). London: Whurr.

Snowling, M., & Hulme, C. (1989). A longitudinal case study of developmental phonological dyslexia. *Cognitive Neuropsychology, 6,* 379–401.

Snowling, M., Hulme, C., & Goulandris, N. (1994). Word recognition in developmental dyslexia: A connectionist interpretation. *Quarterly Journal of Experimental Psychology, 47A,* 895–916.

Snowling, M., Hulme, C., Smith, A., & Thomas, J. (1994). The effects of phonetic similarity and word length on children's sound categorisation performance. *Journal of Experimental Child Psychology, 58,* 160–180.

Snowling, M., Stackhouse, J., & Rack, J. (1986). Phonological dyslexia and dysgraphia: A developmental analysis. *Cognitive Neuropsychology, 3,* 309–339.

Snowling, M., van Wagtendonk, B., & Stafford, C. (1988). Object-naming deficits in developmental dyslexia. *Journal of Research in Reading, 11,* 67–85.

Temple, C., & Marshall, J. C. (1983). A case study of developmental phonological dyslexia. *British Journal of Psychology, 74,* 517–533.

Treiman, R., & Hirsh-Pasek, K. (1985). Are there qualitative differences in reading behaviour between dyslexics and normal readers? *Memory & Cognition, 13,* 357–364.

van der Lely, H., & Howard, D. (1994). Specifically language impaired children: Linguistic impairment or short-term memory deficit? *Journal of Speech and Hearing, 36,* 1193–1207.

Chapter **11**

The Development of Reading Skills in Poor Readers: Educational Implications

Rebecca H. Felton
Bowman Gray School of Medicine, Winston–Salem, North Carolina

Failure to fully appreciate the alphabetic code is a primary deficit in poor readers in the English language system, where the orthography is shallow. In research studies this failure is operationalized by measuring the ability to read phonetically regular nonsense words. Studies also indicate that many reading-disabled individuals are able to acquire higher levels of sight-word recognition skills than would be predicted from their phonological reading skills (although sight-word reading remains impaired in comparison to nondisabled readers). A review of such research by Rack, Snowling, and Olson (1992) indicates that most dyslexics have specific deficits in nonword (phonological) reading, although several factors may impact the degree of such difficulty and its impact on overall reading skills. Such factors include the age of students when tested, the types of reading measures used, the instruction to which they have been exposed, the amount of exposure to print, and the degree to which students have compensated for their reading difficulties. Rack and colleagues agreed with the hypothesis (Stanovich, 1988) that students whose reading is poor in spite of average verbal intelligence are more likely to show more severe and more focal deficits in nonword reading than are children whose verbal skills are lower ("garden variety" poor readers, as described by Gough & Tunmer, 1986).

Felton and Wood (1992) utilized a reading-level-match design to test the nonword reading deficit hypothesis from a longitudinal perspective and to evaluate some of the questions raised by previous studies. One question concerned the Stanovich hypothesis predicting differential severity of nonword reading deficit in students with higher levels of verbal ability. To study the relationship between IQ/reading discrepancy and severity of deficits in phonological coding (nonword reading), samples were selected that represented a wide range of normal intellectual abilities. Third- and fifth-grade poor readers were matched to nondisabled first graders on measures of word identification (see Felton & Wood, 1992, for a detailed description of these procedures). Third-grade poor readers were divided into high- and low-IQ groups based on their verbal IQ (above or below 92), and matched on word identification scores. Using these criteria, in the high-IQ group the average discrepancy between verbal IQ and reading standard score was 18.9 with 71% of the sample having discrepancies greater than or equal to 15. For the low-IQ group the average discrepancy was 8.6, although three students (9%) did have discrepancies of at least 15 points.

The Felton and Wood study (1992) yielded strong evidence for pervasive nonword reading deficits in poor readers across a wide range of ages and levels of reading disability. Third- and fifth-grade poor readers were significantly impaired on nonword reading tasks in comparison to nondisabled first-grade students who were matched on word identification. In addition, although the poor readers showed some improvement in nonword reading skills from third to fifth grade, this improvement was slight, and some students failed to make any meaningful gains during this time. Furthermore, low-IQ poor readers (most of whom did not show IQ/reading discrepancies) were slightly more impaired on nonword reading than were students in the high-IQ group. Thus, these results failed to support the hypothesis proposed by Stanovich of greater difficulty in nonword reading in students with higher verbal intellectual skills. Review of studies by Stanovich and colleagues suggested that the sample characteristics (i.e., the greater severity of the poor readers in the nondiscrepant groups utilized by Felton & Wood) may have been a major factor in the differential findings.

In the current study, a subset of the poor readers described previously were retested at the end of the eighth grade in order to determine the development of reading skills, including nonword reading and sight-word identification, from the third through the eighth grade. The development of phonological processing skills were also measured. In addition, the impact of educational intervention on the outcome as well as the relationship of IQ/reading discrepancy to the development of reading and phonological awareness skills were evaluated.

METHOD

Subjects and Procedures

All of the subjects were students in the local school system who were participating in a longitudinal study of reading disability in which a large group of students who were initially defined as poor readers based on second-grade group achievement (California Achievement Test—CAT, 1985) test scores were tested. To qualify for the pool of potentially reading-disabled subjects, the students had to meet one of the following criteria: a reading score on the CAT below the 16th percentile in absolute terms—nondiscrepant poor readers, or a CAT reading score below the 16th percentile of the "scatter" around the IQ–reading regression line (Guilford & Fruchter, 1987)—discrepant poor readers. As expected, there was an overlap between these groups (23%). These procedure resulted in the identification of an original sample of 296 students (87 discrepant and 209 nondiscrepant) who were tested in the third grade with a battery of cognitive and educational tests. In the fifth grade, 213 of these subjects (59 discrepant and 154 nondiscrepant) were available for testing. For the present longitudinal study, a sample of 80 students were selected (from the original group of poor readers) who met the following criteria: participation in the full battery of tests at third and fifth grades, IQ within the normal range (operationalized as Full Scale IQ score $\geq$ 76 at third grade), and word identification skills at or below the 11.5 percentile for age and grade (based on local norms) in the third grade. The purpose of these criteria was to identify students who were clearly reading disabled in spite of intellectual abilities within the average range. Our research indicates that the 11.5 percentile is an appropriate cut point for identifying individuals with distinctly different profiles of behavioral and physiological characteristics related to reading (see Wood & Felton, 1994, for a full discussion of this issue).

Of these 80 students, 64 were available for testing at the end of eighth grade. These students were predominantly male (40 male, 24 female) and there were more non-White (primarily African American) than White students (40 non-White, 24 White). The mean age at time of testing was 14.9 (14.0 to 15.9). SES scores obtained using the Hollingshead four factor index (Hollingshead, 1975) indicated scores ranging from the lowest level of social strata (unskilled laborer, menial service worker) to the upper level (medium business and professional workers). The average SES score for the group was in the level of semiskilled workers.

For purposes of this study, students were classified as discrepant or nondiscrepant using the criteria most often employed in determining eligibility for learning disability services in the United States. That is, students were classified as discrepant if their standard score on the reading cluster of the Woodcock-Johnson Psycho-Educational Battery was 15 or more points lower than their full-scale IQ on the Wechsler Intelligence Scale for Children–Revised (WISC–R). Eighth grade reading standard scores were compared to third grade WISC–R scores (more recent IQ scores were not available on all students). Using this operational definition, 23 students were classified as discrepant and 41 as nondiscrepant. See Table 11.1 for information concerning scores obtained on the WISC–R for these two groups.

TABLE 11.1
Wechsler Intelligence Test Scores for
Discrepant and Nondiscrepant Poor Readers[a]

Variables	Nondiscrepant			Discrepant		
	x	(SD)	range	x	(SD)	range
Verbal IQ	87.56	(7.14)	74–105	96.70	(7.20)	82–113
Performance IQ	90.00	(9.65)	74–117	101.04	(7.66)	84–120
Full-scale IQ	87.66	(6.36)	78–101	98.26	(5.90)	88–108

[a]IQ scores based on WISC–R administered to students in third grade.

In order to evaluate the possible impact of intervention on reading outcome, information was obtained for all students concerning whether or not they had been identified as learning disabled by the school system. In this school system, certification as learning disabled is based on a discrepancy between IQ and achievement of at least 15 points. Of the total group of poor readers ($N = 64$), 30 had been so identified by eighth grade. Students were identified as early as kindergarten and as late as eighth grade. Months of service ranged from 8 to 90 (approximately 1 to 9 years). Data were not available concerning the amount of service actually delivered to each child (e.g., number of hours per week). Of the 23 students classified as discrepant using the criteria described previously, 15 (65%) were identified by the school system as learning disabled. Of greater interest, 15 students (37%) of the nondiscrepant group were also identified as learning disabled. This implies that these students were tested at some point in their school career and found to have IQ/achievement discrepancies. This could have occurred if their reading skills failed to improve at a rate comensurate with their peers, so that they had discrepancies later in their academic career. It is also possible that they received services based on an "alternative to discrepancy" option, which allows for certification without meeting the discrepancy criteria; however, this option is infrequently utilized.

Each student was tested individually (with the battery described next) during the summer prior to entry into high school (Grade 9). This battery included measures of reading skills that the students had been tested with in the third and fifth grades, so that their progress over time could be charted.

Assessment Instruments

Woodcock-Johnson Psycho-Educational Battery (WJPB)-Reading Cluster (Woodcock & Johnson, 1977). The Reading Cluster includes word identification, word attack, and passage comprehension. Word identification measures the ability to read words in isolation. Passage comprehension is measured using a cloze procedure in which the student reads paragraphs silently and determines which words are missing. The word attack subtest requires untimed reading of a list of words defined as "letter combinations that are not actual words or are extremely low frequency words in the English language" (Woodcock, 1978, p. 34). Thus, this is a measure in which the nonwords are less analogous to real words than are the nonwords on the Decoding Skills test. Raw scores are reported for word identification, passage comprehension, and word attack. The reading cluster includes the three components of reading and a standard score for age and a grade equivalent score are generated for each student.

Decoding Skills Test (Richardson & DiBenedetto, 1985). The Decoding Skills Test (DST) is a criterion-referenced test developed as a research tool for use in studies of reading disability. Reliability coefficients range from .95 to .99, and the DST is strongly ($p < .001$) correlated with other tests of reading. For this study, we administered Part 2 (Phonic Patterns), which requires untimed reading of graded lists of phonetically regular real words selected to represent common orthographic patterns, and nonwords that are analogous to the real words. Scores are generated for four types of words: monosyllabic real words, polysyllabic real words, monosyllabic nonsense words, and polysyllabic nonsense words. These raw scores are used to compute phonic transfer index (PTI) scores, which are calculated by dividing the number of pairs of correctly read real and nonsense words by the number of real words the child could read. Thus, the PTI is an indicant of the ability to apply known phonic patterns (from real words) to decoding nonwords (i.e., to read by analogy).

Sight Word Vocabulary (Adams & Huggins, 1985). This test measures an individual's sight word vocabulary both in and out of context. Fifty words with irregular spelling-to-sound correspondences are presented to the subject, who is then asked to read them aloud. About 20 minutes later, after other tests have been given, the same words are presented in a sentence. The words are presented in order of frequency. Two scores are generated: the number correct, and the number incorrect.

Lindamood Auditory Conceptualization Test (Lindamood & Lindamood, 1979). The student manipulates different-colored blocks to indicate conceptualization of the speech sound patterns presented by the examiner. Raw scores are converted to scores ranging from 0 to 100.

Test of Auditory Analysis (Rosner, 1979). Students are asked to segment words into syllables or phonemes (deletion of initial and final consonants as well as parts of consonant blends).

RESULTS

Development of Reading Skills From Third to Eighth Grade

In these analyses, we used point biserial correlations to compare the development of a variety of reading skills from third to eighth grade in poor readers with and without IQ/reading discrepancies. Table 11.2 presents the scores obtained on a standardized test (WJPB) of word identification and passage comprehension. These results clearly indicate that students who were poor readers in third grade continued to be below average in comparison to their peers in fifth and eighth grades—group standard scores for age do not show improvement over time with group performance below the 10th percentile of a national sample of students at each grade level tested. Eighth-grade performance of individual students ranged from below the 6th percentile to the 31st percentile (grade equivalents ranged from 2.2 to 7.0). Thus, even within this group of poor readers, there was a range of reading skills, with a few students improving into the low-average range (only eight students earned standard scores above the 20th percentile at the eighth grade).

Although the differences between discrepant and nondiscrepant students on the WJPB are small, differences in word identification at Grades 5 and 8 as well as the eighth-grade reading standard score and grade equivalent are statistically significant. That is, students with IQ/reading discrepancies are more impaired on word identification than are nondiscrepant readers, and this difference is reflected in measures of overall reading ability by the eighth grade.

Nonword reading scores for discrepant and nondiscrepant readers are shown in Table 11.3. Word attack as measured by the WJPB as well as nonword reading of monosyllabic and polysyllabic words as measured by the Decoding Skills Test (DST) are presented as raw scores. The mean word attack scores at third, fifth, and eighth grades for both discrepant and nondiscrepant poor readers were below the mean score earned by a sample of good first-grade readers (utilized in the Felton & Wood, 1992, study). Nondiscrepant students earned slightly higher scores on word attack but these differences were not statistically significant.

On the DST, poor readers also performed below the level of good first-grade readers on reading monosyllabic nonwords at third, fifth, and eighth grades, and were only slightly better than the first graders on polysyllabic nonwords by fifth to eighth grade. Again, nondiscrepant readers performed better on reading nonwords than did discrepant readers. These differences were particularly striking, and statistically significant, for reading polysyllabic nonsense words in the fifth and eighth grades.

Another measure of nonword reading ability within the poor-reader group involves the Phonic Transfer Indices (PTI), which are measures of

TABLE 11.2
Scores on Standardized Test of Reading in Third, Fifth, and Eighth Grades[a]

Variable	Nondiscrepant			Discrepant		
	Grade 3 x (Range)	Grade 5 x (Range)	Grade 8 x (Range)	Grade 3 x (Range)	Grade 5 x (Range)	Grade 8 x (Range)
Word identification (raw scores)	23.0 (19–26)	29.9 (24–36)	33.2 (25–39)	23.2 (18–26)	28.1 (20–33)	31.2 (21–36)
Passage comprehension (raw scores)	9.5 (5–13)	13.4 (7–18)	16.1 (12–21)	9.8 (5–15)	13.2 (8–17)	15.2 (9–19)
Reading standard score for age	79.7 (69–87)	80.3 (65–92)	80.4 (67–92)	79.3 (65–88)	78.3 (65–87)	77.1 (64–84)
Grade equivalent	2.1 (1.6–2.6)	3.3 (2.0–5.1)	4.2 (2.4–7.0)	2.1 (1.5–2.6)	3.0 (2.0–4.1)	3.6 (2.2–4.9)

[a]Scores based on Woodcock-Johnson Psycho-Educational Battery (WJPB).

TABLE 11.3
Scores on Nonword Reading Measures in Third, Fifth, and Eigth Grades

Variable	Nondiscrepant			Discrepant		
	Grade 3 x (Range)	Grade 5 x (Range)	Grade 8 x (Range)	Grade 3 x (Range)	Grade 5 x (Range)	Grade 8 x (Range)
WJPB Word Attack	4.2 (0–9)	9.1 (1–20)	9.2 (2–18)	3.2 (0–10)	7.6 (1–18)	7.7 (2–18)
DST Nonword–Monosyllabic	5.3 (0–14)	14.7 (1–24)	15.8 (1–27)	4.9 (0–14)	11.9 (0–23)	13.1 (0–22)
DST Nonword–Polysyllabic	1.1 (0–7)	11.6 (0–24)	13.2 (1–24)	1.2 (0–6)	6.1 (0–19)	9.7 (0–21)
DST PTI Monosyllabic	.29 (.0–.71)	.53 (.0–.53)	.56 (.11–.90)	.23 (.0–.53)	.48 (.0–.79)	.46 (.0–.77)
DST PTI Polysyllabic	.08 (.0–1.0)	.44 (.0–.78)	.48 (.06–.82)	.08 (.0–.38)	.27 (.0–.67)	.37 (.0–.79)

Note. WJPB = Woodcock-Johnson Psycho-Educational Battery; DST = Decoding Skills Tests; PTI = Phonic Transfer Index.

TABLE 11.4
Scores on Irregular Word Reading
(With and Without Context) in Eighth Grade

Variable	Nondiscrepant			Discrepant		
	x	(SD)	Range	x	(SD)	Range
Irregular words/out of context	26.0	(7.7)	8–41	23.1	(8.0)	4–37
Irregular words/in context	38.1	(5.2)	24–47	36.7	(6.6)	22–47

the ability to read nonwords by analogy to real words. According to Richardson and DiBenedetto (1985), Phonic Transfer Indices of .70 or above indicate good ability to read by analogies. As a group, the poor readers performed well below this standard for good application of phonetic knowledge by the eighth grade. Only 13 eighth graders earned PTI indices of .70 or greater for single-syllable words and only 6 reached this criteria for multisyllable words. In comparison to nondiscrepant poor readers, discrepant readers earned significantly lower PTI scores on monosyllabic words at eighth grade, and significantly lower PTI scores on polysyllabic words at fifth and eighth grades. Visual analysis of the data indicates that nondiscrepant readers made their greatest gains in nonword reading between third and fifth grades; the gains for the discrepant group during this same time period were not as great, and neither group showed much improvement from fifth to eighth grade.

Results of a second measure (in addition to the word identification subtest of the WJPB) of sight-word reading (Adams & Huggins, 1985) are presented in Table 11.4. These words were given as a measure of the students' ability to read words with very irregular spelling-to-sound correspondences. This test was not part of the battery prior to the eighth grade testing, so results are compared to subjects reported by Adams & Huggins ($N = 106$ good and poor readers in Grades 2 through 5). Eighth-grade poor readers in the current study earned scores on reading irregular words out of context that were at, or slightly below, the level that Adams and Huggins reported for good fourth-grade readers ($x = 26.92$). Consistent with the findings of Adams and Huggins, meaningful context was an aid to reading irregular words for the poor readers. Although the pattern of discrepant readers performing more poorly than nondiscrepant continued for this measure, the differences were not statistically significant.

Development of Phonological Awareness Skills From Third to Eighth Grade

Two measures of phonological awareness were given at third, fifth, and eighth grades (see Table 11.5). On the Test of Auditory Analysis Skills—TAAS (Rosner, 1979), students were asked to segment words into syllables

TABLE 11.5
Scores on Phonological Awareness Tests in Third, Fifth, and Eighth Grades

Variable	Nondiscrepant			Discrepant		
	Grade 3 x (Range)	Grade 5 x (Range)	Grade 8 x (Range)	Grade 3 x (Range)	Grade 5 x (Range)	Grade 8 x (Range)
Lindamood Test of Auditory Conceptualization Converted Score	39.6 (6–88)	58.3 (31–88)	62.1 (33–94)	48.1 (23–82)	63.0 (34–82)	69.9 (47–93)
Test of Auditory Analysis	7.4 (1–13)	9.4 (5–13)	9.8 (5–13)	7.3 (1–13)	9.3 (2–13)	10.2 (3–13)

or phonemes. There are 13 items on the test and, according to Rosner, students in third grade are typically able to perform all 13 items. There were no significant differences between discrepant and nondiscrepant groups on this measure, with students in both groups improving over time. At each grade level there were students who performed very poorly (at levels of segmentation considered optimal for students in the primary grades) and, as a group, the eighth-grade poor readers performed below the level considered optimal for third graders. It is also interesting to note that each group contained a few children who performed well on this test, even in the third grade.

The second measure of phonological awareness, the Lindamood Test of Auditory Conceptualization, measures several aspects of phonological processing (discrimination of sounds, ability to hold strings of sound in short-term memory, and the ability to sequence and manipulate sounds within syllables). Raw scores on the Lindamood are converted to scores that range from 0 to 100, with good readers reaching the ceiling of the test by seventh grade. As on the TAAS, both groups of poor readers improved in their performance on this test from third to eighth grade, but failed to achieve optimal levels of performance. Unlike the pattern seen on the reading tests, discrepant students' scores were higher than nondiscrepant, and these differences were statistically significant for third and eighth grades.

Relationship of Intervention to Outcome

For the poor readers in this sample, neither certification as learning disabled nor the length of certification (months of services) were significant factors in the level of reading skills in eighth grade. This was a finding across both discrepant and nondiscrepant groups, even though a higher percentage of children in the discrepant group received services. Using point biserial correlations controlling for both third-grade reading level (standard score on the WJPB) and for length of service, the differences in eighth-grade reading for discrepant versus nondiscrepant readers remained significant (.006). That is, neither the third-grade level of reading ability nor the length of time the student received learning disability services accounted for the differences between the discrepant and nondiscrepant readers.

DISCUSSION

These results clearly indicate that students who are very poor readers in the third grade remain poor readers in the eighth grade. Although a few students' overall reading scores improved into the low average range, the majority of the students remained below the 10th percentile in comparison to their peers at the end of eighth grade. It is also apparent that poor readers made more gains in all aspects of reading from third to fifth grades than from fifth to eighth grades. This was particularly true for decoding skills, in which the improvements were extremely small during the fifth to eighth grade period. Consistent with this finding, poor readers were more impaired, in comparison to nondisabled students, on nonword reading than on reading irregular words. As a group, the poor readers performed below the level of a sample of good first-grade readers on measures of nonword reading. In addition, none of the poor readers demonstrated good ability to apply knowledge of phonetic patterns to reading unfamiliar words. On a measure of sight-word reading (highly irregular words that cannot be read using standard spelling-to-sound correspondences), the poor readers performed at levels consistent with that reported for good fourth-grade readers.

Although these findings are consistent in both discrepant and nondiscrepant readers, there are some differences. For all measures of fifth- and eighth-grade reading (sight-word identification, passage comprehension, decoding), discrepant readers performed more poorly than did nondiscrepant readers. These differences were statistically significant for word identification (WJPB) at fifth and eighth grades, and for reading polysyllabic nonwords at the fifth and eighth grades. Thus, although the discrepant and nondiscrepant readers did not differ in word identification or nonword reading ability at third grade, readers in the discrepant group made less progress in word identification and much less progress in decoding skills from third to fifth grade than did the nondiscrepant readers.

Given these findings, the logical expectation would be that the students in the discrepant group had more severe problems in phonological awareness skills, because these language processing skills have been found to be strongly correlated with nonword reading ability (Torgesen, Wagner, & Rashotte, 1994). However, results of two measures of phonological awareness indicate that this is not the case. In fact, discrepant readers performed better on the Lindamood Test of Auditory Conceptualization, although these differences were statistically significant only at third grade. Discrepant and nodiscrepant readers performed almost identically on the Test of Auditory Analysis at third, fifth, and eighth grades.

To summarize, students whose eighth-grade reading scores were discrepant from their IQ as measured in the third grade made much smaller gains in nonword reading than did their nondiscrepant peers. This finding was true in spite of the fact that the two groups were not different on nonword reading ability in the third grade, and it was not explainable by the level of phonological awareness ability. These results are in particularly interesting in comparison to the findings reported by Felton and Wood

(1992), in which third-grade poor readers, divided into high- and low-IQ groups, showed the opposite pattern—the low-IQ group (nondiscrepant) showed slightly lower nonword reading scores than did the high-IQ group (discrepant). It is important to note that the poor readers in the current study are a subset of the students reported in the Felton and Wood study (those who were available for testing at the fifth and eighth grades). Other than the current sample being smaller due to attrition over time, the only difference was in the method used to divide the groups into discrepant and nondiscrepant. In the 1992 study, third graders were divided according to verbal IQ score alone (above or below 92) without regard to IQ/achievement discrepancies. However, most of the high-IQ students did show IQ/achievement discrepancies, and most of the low-IQ students did not. In the current study, students were divided according to actual full-scale IQ/achievement discrepancies based on eighth-grade achievement. These two procedures for determining discrepant versus nondiscrepant status resulted in nondiscrepant groups that were quite similar in verbal IQ ($\bar{x}$ = 87.0 for the original third-grade low-IQ group, and $\bar{x}$ = 87.6 for the eighth-grade nondiscrepant group). However, verbal IQ scores for the discrepant groups differed with the eighth-grade group having lower scores than did the third-grade group ($\bar{x}$ of 96.7 and 100.2, respectively).

The current findings provide some support for the Stanovich hypothesis of greater deficits in nonword reading in students with higher verbal IQ scores. However, these differences are not evident at third grade and are not explainable by phonological awareness skill as measured in this study. Given that the greatest differences in nonword reading skill occur between third grade and fifth grade, the question is raised concerning the impact of educational intervention. In the public school system, instruction in reading is provided more systematically in elementary school (through fifth grade) than in middle school (sixth to eighth grades). Thus, the finding that all of the poor readers made less progress in middle school than in elementary school is most likely related to the level of direct instruction they received. However, this does not explain the differences between discrepant and nondiscrepant readers. Given that a much higher percentage of students in the discrepant group received services as learning-disabled students, it would be reasonable to expect that this intervention would have resulted in higher levels of reading skills. Unfortunately, this was not the case—months of learning disability service did not predict reading outcome for either the discrepant or the nondiscrepant readers.

In conclusion, these results further support the nonword reading deficit in poor readers and indicate that nonword reading skills show even less improvement over time in some readers than others. Progress in all aspects of reading, but particularly for decoding skills, improves very little during the middle school years, when instruction in basic reading skills decreases.

Even when students are identified as learning disabled and receive direct intervention (often continuing into middle school), overall reading scores improve very little and decoding skills remain extremely impaired. These findings strongly indicate the need for early recognition of nonword reading deficits and the implementation of effective instructional interventions early in the students' school career. In addition, some poor readers will need continued direct instruction in word identification and decoding skills in the middle school years (and beyond) if these are not well developed during elementary school.

The relationship of IQ/achievement discrepancies must be studied further. Perhaps other measures of phonological processing skills are implicated in the differential improvement of some students, and these differences may or may not be related to the IQ/achievement discrepancy. The critical difference may be in the combination and/or the severity of a set of phonological processing weaknesses (e.g., phonological awareness, word finding and automaticity in naming, verbal short-term memory), which interact with instructional factors (onset and duration of instruction, type of reading methods used and the ways these are delivered) to determine outcome for individual students. In-depth, longitudinal studies of individual children who are provided different types and levels of intervention at different stages of their educational career will be necessary to answer the questions raised by this study.

ACKNOWLEDGMENT

This research was supported by PHS Grant HD 21887 to Bowman Gray School of Medicine.

REFERENCES

Adams, M. J., & Huggins, A. W. F. (1985). The growth of children's sight vocabulary: A quick test with educational and theoretical implications. *Reading Research Quarterly, 20*(3), 262–281.

California Achievement Test. (1985). Monterey, CA: CTB/McGraw-Hill.

Felton, R. H., & Wood, F. B. (1992). A reading level match study of nonword reading skills in poor readers with varying IQ. *Journal of Learning Disabilities, 25,* 318–326.

Gough, P. B., & Tunmer, W. E. (1986). Decoding, reading, and reading disability. *Remedial and Special Education, 7,* 6–10.

Guilford, J. P., & Fruchter, B. (1987). *Fundamental statistics in psychology and education.* New York: McGraw-Hill.

Hollingshead, A. B. (1975). *Four factor index of social status.* Unpublished manuscript. (Available from PO Box 1965, Yale Station, New Haven, CT 06520)

Lindamood, C. H., & Lindamood, P. C. (1979). *Lindamood auditory conceptualization test.* Boston: Teaching Resources Corporation.

Rack, J. P., Snowling, M. J., & Olson, R. K. (1992). The nonword reading deficit in developmental dyslexia: A review. *Reading Research Quarterly, 27,* 29–53.

Richardson, E., & DiBenedetto, B. (1985). *Decoding skills test.* Los Angeles: Western Psychological Services.

Rosner, J. (1979). *Helping children overcome learning difficulties.* New York: Walker and Company.

Stanovich, K. E. (1988). Explaining the differences between the dyslexic and the garden-variety poor reader: The phonological-core variable difference modes. *Journal of Learning Disabilities, 21,* 590–612.

Torgesen J. K., Wagner, R. K., & Rashotte, C. A. (1994). Longitudinal studies of phonological processing and reading. *Journal of Learning Disabilities, 27,* 276–286.

Wood, F. B., & Felton, R. H. (1994). Separate linguistic and attentional factors in the development of reading. *Topics in Language Disorders, 14,* 42–57.

Woodcock, R. W. (1978). *Development and standardization of the Woodcock-Johnson Psycho-Educational Battery.* Hingham, MA: Teaching Resources.

Woodcock, R. W., & Johnson, M. B. (1977). *Woodcock-Johnson Psycho-Educational Battery.* Allen, TX: DLM.

Chapter 12

Normal and Dyslexic Reading Development: The Role of Formal Models

Jamie L. Metsala
University of Maryland

Gordon D. A. Brown
University of Warwick

In this chapter we show that the use of formal models can enhance our understanding of both reading development and skilled adult reading. We argue that several empirical phenomena in the study of reading, including some that have been seen as highly significant, cannot be understood without careful consideration of the properties of the psychological mechanisms that are assumed to give rise to the relevant behavior. Such a claim, in itself, is surely unexceptionable. However, we suggest that appropriately detailed consideration of the properties of cognitive models may, in many cases, be impossible unless the models in question have received a formal expression of some kind. This formal expression will most often take the form either of a mathematical formulation of the model, or of a computer program that implements the cognitive model. We substantiate these claims with examples, each of which is designed to show how a formal analysis of, or formal model of, some aspect of reading behavior has led to insights and understandings that might not have emerged in the absence of formal modeling.

One example that we examine concerns the predictions of the phonological deficit account of dyslexia. Computational models have recently provided a possible explanation of why it is that the observed phonological processing deficits associated with reading disability lead to a selective difficulty in nonword reading alongside "normal" effects of spelling-to-sound regularity on reading accuracy. These empirical data had proved difficult to explain within the standard information-processing account of disabled-reading development. We also describe a framework for conceptualizing the development of phonological representations, and suggest that formal approaches may be necessary if we are to understand this development. A further example concerns skilled adult reading. Specifically, we suggest that the effects of spelling-to-sound regularity can be explained by viewing single-word reading as a simple statistical process, one that skilled readers can perform optimally.

The plan of the chapter is as follows. We first review several general advantages of formal approaches, and then show how formal analyses of the structure of the orthography-to-phonology mapping system in English shed important light on the nature of the task facing readers. Second, we describe some of the basic properties of connectionist models and review the type of data that they account for well. Next, seemingly paradoxical patterns of reading in dyslexic children are explained through comparing different connectionist models of the reading process. We then examine a framework for studying the development of phonological representations. A computational-level understanding of the principles that underlie the development of these representations will, we suggest, be a necessary step towards a complete explanation of reading difficulties. We also review ways in which formal approaches to the nature of the mental lexicon have constrained psychological models.

ADVANTAGES OF FORMAL ANALYSES

We begin by examining some of the general reasons for adopting a formal approach to modeling reading and its development. Most formal models of reading have been expressed in the form of computer programs, although mathematical models, which do not refer directly to underlying mechanisms, are also possible. In this chapter we adopt a broad interpretation of formal approaches, and include formal analyses of the statistical nature of the task facing beginning readers.

Perhaps the most important advantage of implementing models in a formal way is that it becomes possible to derive predictions from the models in an unambiguous way. The behavior of an implemented model can be examined under varying simulated conditions, enabling its predictions to be determined. These predictions can then be tested empirically, thus ensuring that the model is falsifiable. When a model has not been implemented, as for example with early versions of both "dual-route" and "analogy" models of reading, we may not be sure that the model can really perform the task(s) it is designed for (e.g., the reading of regular and irregular words, and nonwords). Thus, an early connectionist model of reading (Seidenberg & McClelland, 1989) was criticized for its inability to read nonwords as accurately as humans (Besner, Twilley, McCann, & Seergobin, 1990), and useful subsequent developments of the model have been motivated by this aspect of the model's behavior (e.g., Plaut, McClelland, Seidenberg, & Patterson, 1996).

We now have a much greater understanding of the kinds of psychological mechanisms that are needed for reading nonwords (see Brown, in press; Norris 1994; Plaut et al., 1996). If the model proposed by Seidenberg and McClelland (1989) had not been implemented, and its behavior examined through simulation, it would have been difficult if not impossible to deduce that it would perform relatively poorly on nonword reading. The complexity of the interactions between the many constituents of the model meant that the behavior of the system as a whole could only be examined through simulation. Thus, one primary reason for implementing models of human behavior is simply the complexity of the underlying processes. This illustrates the point that psychologists need to model psychological mechanisms for the same reason as weather forecasters need to model changing weather patterns: The behavior of the system as a whole is otherwise too complex to predict.

There are many other reasons for constructing formal models of psychological processes (see Brown & Loosemore, 1994). These include the need to ensure that one's model is truly explanatory. A verbally specified model may be merely a disguised redescription of the observed behavior that is to be explained. Novel predictions from a formal model can subsequently be tested empirically—thus, there are multiple checks on the explanatory adequacy of formal models that may not be available from verbal explanations. We now go on to illustrate the advantages of formal approaches with some concrete examples.

FORMAL ANALYSIS OF THE TASK OF READING

In this section we aim to show how a formal analysis of the language, and the task facing the reader, can lead to a better understanding of the strategies that we might expect skilled adult readers to adopt in reading the printed word. Here there are two different approaches that can be taken. On the one hand, a consideration of the properties of the spelling-to-sound mapping system in English may constrain our models of the mechanisms assumed to underpin spelling-to-sound decoding. On the other hand, we can adopt a mechanism-independent view, and ask a different question: Given the statistical structure of the English spelling-to-sound mapping system, what is the optimal strategy for subjects to adopt, independent of the mechanisms used to implement this strategy? We now briefly illustrate the application of each of these approaches.

First, a statistical analysis of the language can provide clues as to the type of mechanism that would provide efficient processing and generalization (Stanback, 1992; Treiman, Mullennix, Bijeljac-Babic, & Richmond-Welty, 1995). For example, Treiman et al. (1995) examined the consistency with which different orthographic segments are pronounced in English. They found that the most reliable sublexical unit for pronouncing a monosyllabic word is the orthographic rime of the word (we follow common practice in defining the *orthographic rime* of a word to be the letters that correspond to the phonological rime of the word; e.g., the *-ing* of *sing*). For example, the consistency of pronunciation (i.e., the percentage of words in which the orthographic rime in question received a consistent pronunciation) was 80% for VC units compared with 62% for the medial vowel in isolation, and 55% for CV units. (This particular analysis examined consistency over word "types" rather than word "tokens"; similar results were obtained in a number of different analyses.)

On the basis of this kind of formal analysis of language, it seems reasonable to expect that skilled adult readers, who have presumably learned the most reliable method of translating written representations into phonological ones, would make particular use of spelling-to-sound correspondences between orthographic and phonological rimes. There is considerable evidence that this is indeed the case, and that skilled adult readers mainly use rime-level correspondences (e.g., Treiman et al., 1995). Thus, although young children will make use of lower-level spelling-to-sound correspondences, such as those between graphemes and phonemes (Coltheart & Leahy, 1992), and although adults exhibit strategic flexibility and are more likely to use grapheme–phoneme-level correspondences (rather than rime-level correspondences) to read nonwords, especially if they appear in the context of other nonwords (Brown & Deavers, 1997), it now appears that skilled adults will make considerable use of rime-level correspondences in the reading of words (as might be expected on the basis of the analysis in Treiman et al., 1995). In support of this, many studies have found that the speed and accuracy with which skilled adults read monosyllabic words aloud is determined by the consistency with which the orthographic rime, such as the *-ave* in *have*, is produced (e.g., Brown, 1987; Glushko, 1979; Jared, McRae, & Seidenberg, 1990; Seidenberg, Waters, Barnes, & Tanenhaus, 1984; Taraban & McClelland, 1987).

Treiman et al. (1995) recently showed that no additional pronunciation latency variance is accounted for by measures of the consistency with which medial vowels (the *-a-* in *have*) or onset + medial vowel (the *ha-* in *have*) are pronounced. Consistent with this, Norris (1994) found that performance in a multiple-level computational model of reading was more severely impaired when correspondences between orthographic and phonological rimes were removed than when correspondences between graphemes and phonemes were removed. This provides further evidence for the importance of rime-level correspondences in the spelling-to-sound translation of English.

The previous discussion is intended to exemplify how a careful consideration of the statistical nature of the task can lead to constraints on theories of the underlying psychological mechanisms. However, the same consideration of the statistical properties of the spelling-to-sound mapping system in English may allow us to answer quite a different question: the question of what is the optimal or "adaptively rational" way to make use of the statistical constraints in the system to be learned.

This approach is different from formal modeling of the *mechanisms* hypothesized to underlie reading, because it assumes that it is possible to specify the optimal strategy of reading independent of consideration of the mechanism assumed to implement the processing. This is the approach of *rational analysis* as developed by Anderson (e.g., Anderson 1990; see also Shepard, 1987) and applied by him to the analysis of human memory (see especially Anderson & Milson, 1989; Anderson & Schooler, 1991). A central assumption is that human cognitive mechanisms are optimally adapted to the statistical nature of the environment in which they operate. The methodology involves independently examining the statistical properties of the relevant environment, and then deriving a function that would describe optimal behavior in the context of that environment. It then becomes possible to determine whether observed human behavior in the relevant domain can be described by this optimal function. We recently (Brown, 1997) applied this approach to the study of reading. We assumed that single-word reading could be viewed as a statistical process, in which the reader must compute the most probable pronunciation of a given orthographic string in light of the known statistical properties of the spelling-to-sound mapping system. The probability of a given pronunciation being the correct one for an orthographic-rime segment can be shown to be equal to the ratio of *consistent* pronunciations to *all* pronunciations of the orthographic segment in question. This ratio would be low for an exception word, and 1.0 for a word with a completely consistent pronunciation.

We examined the assumption that the time taken (by skilled adult readers) to name words would, if the underlying process adaptively reflected the statistics of the language, reflect this "consistency ratio." Brown (1997) demonstrated that skilled adult naming latencies, as obtained in many different experiments, could indeed be predicted on the assumption that latencies simply reflected the consistency of pronunciation of the orthographic rimes segments within the word in exactly the way predicted by the optimal reading hypothesis. In other words, the analyses supported the suggestion that readers are behaving in a statistically optimal way given the structure of the English spelling-to-sound mapping system. This probabilistic approach also provides a successful account of the widely observed frequency × consistency interaction; that is, the fact that effects of spelling-to-sound consistency are reduced or absent for high-frequency words (e.g., Seidenberg et al., 1984). According to the optimal reading hypothesis, this interaction follows straightforwardly from the fact that high-frequency exception words are, simply by virtue of their higher frequency, more consistent in their pronunciation than are low-frequency exception words. The analyses in Brown (1997) demonstrated that this factor alone is sufficient to explain the observed data.

Thus, the rational analysis of reading provides one example of the virtues of a formal analytic approach. Reading can be seen as statistically optimal or adaptively rational (Anderson, 1990), in that it reflects the probabilistic characteristics of the mapping between spelling and sound in English. This provides an important metric against which to judge the performance of mechanisms proposed to underlie word reading. The suggestion is that any such mechanism will only be successful if it approximates optimal reading. In the light of this suggestion, we now turn to a discussion of some specific computational mechanisms that have been proposed as accounts of reading.

CONNECTIONISM: WHAT IS IT?

Over the past decade, interest has grown in connectionist or parallel distributed processing accounts of behavior. These systems provide an alternative to traditional cognitive-level approaches that focus on the use of rules and strategies. Connectionism challenges some core assumptions of traditional models; specifically, the assumption that the basic unit of information processing is the symbol and the assumption that knowledge is represented in a propositional framework, with the corollary view that cognitive behavior is rule based (see Pylyshyn, 1984). Within this relatively new framework for explaining cognitive processes the association between input and output pairs is emphasized, without making reference to explicit rules. For example, Rumelhart and McClelland (1986) simulated the acquisition of the past-tense forms in English, employing a simple pattern associator that learned associations between verb stems and past tense verbs. This is in contrast to psycholinguistic approaches that make reference to underlying competence (i.e., rule-based knowledge). This early model provides one demonstration of how a simulation could generate rulelike behavior through learning regularities of the environment, without the explicit incorporation of rules into the system. Although recent research has cast doubt on the ability of simple models to capture the relevant behavior (e.g., Marcus, 1995; Prince & Pinker, 1988), the attempt to build implemented models of verb-tense learning has undoubtedly led to a considerably enhanced understanding of the kinds of mechanisms that must be postulated to explain different types of low-level language learning.

Connectionist systems, sometimes referred to as *neural networks*, are viewed as more compatible with the computational constitution of the human brain. These networks consist of many individual (subsymbolic) computing units that are heavily interconnected. Importantly, these closer approximations to "brainlike" architectures give rise to many behavioral qualities that are typical of human cognition; these include learning capacity, graceful degradation of performance under less than optimal conditions, use of a single mechanism to process regular and exceptional instances of a phenomenon, and flexible access to memory content as a natural outcome of distributed knowledge (see, e.g., Bechtel & Abrahamsen, 1991; Rumelhart & McClelland, 1986).

How do these connectionist systems work? We embed this explanation in terms of the operation of networks constructed to simulate reading behavior, although similar principles apply to many connectionist architectures. Within a network, individual units may be clustered to form a separate layer (i.e., a subpopulation of units)—for example, input (orthographic patterns), output (phonological patterns), and hidden layers (computational resource). Figure 12.1 displays this type of three-layer network. Units have associated with them an "activation value," often between 0 and 1, or a binary value of 0 or 1. A pattern of activity across a layer of units

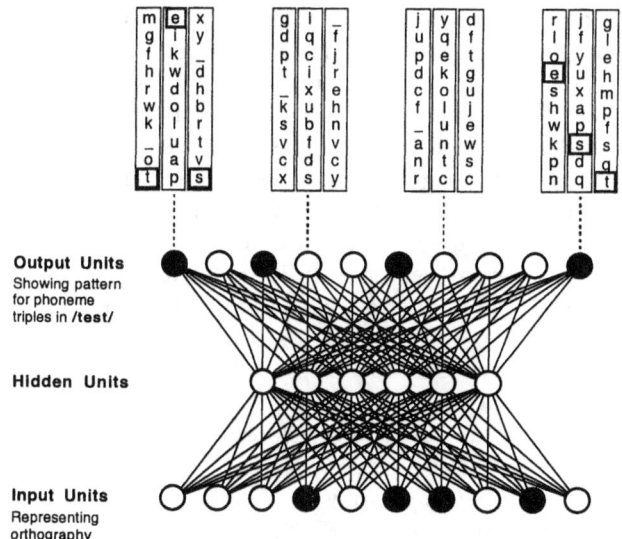

FIG. 12.1. A small three-layer connectionist reading architecture, illustrating the use of triple-based representations.

will be associated with a unique output, such as the pronunciation of a word. For example, a specified pattern of activity such as 101100011 might represent the word *mint*, and the pattern 000101011 the word *soap*.

Units in these networks are interconnected within and between layers, with connections of variable strengths. These multiple connections allow the activity value of one unit both to influence, and be influenced by, the activity value of other units in the network. It is the adjustment of connection strengths in proportion to the discrepancy between an actual pattern of activity and the desired (target) pattern that underlies learning (instantiated by an appropriate learning algorithm). In this way, the patterns of activity across one layer of the network (e.g., input—written words) can become associated with specific patterns of activity across a second layer (e.g., output—pronunciations). The network comes to learn the statistical properties of the associations between input and output activation patterns, giving rise to rulelike behavior, without explicit rules being built into the network.

Because connectionist systems gradually learn the statistical regularities of a system—such as the orthographic-to-phonological mapping system, or the regularities between present and past tense forms of verbs—they can be used to model the gradual emergence of the knowledge of such a system. This means that they have the potential to provide *developmental* accounts of performance in domains such as reading (see Seidenberg & McClelland, 1989). At all stages of the learning process, connectionist models are likely to be most successful at capturing the results of experiments that examine children's or adults' sensitivity to the statistical relationships that hold between orthographic and phonological representations. Such phenomena include the effects of word frequency, spelling-to-sound regularity (correspondences between graphemes and phonemes) and spelling-to-sound consistency (correspondences between orthographic and phonological rimes). Connectionist models have indeed been successful at reproducing such effects, and at explaining the interaction between spelling-to-sound consistency and frequency in reading for both adults and children (Seidenberg, 1985; Seidenberg et al., 1984; Taraban & McClelland, 1987; Waters & Seidenberg, 1985; Waters, Seidenberg, & Bruck, 1984).

Connectionist models embody simple principles of associative learning, and the fact that they provide a good account of empirical results that demonstrate readers' sensitivity to the statistical associations between spelling and sound in English lends support to the conclusions that: (a) The reading of single words can usefully be viewed as a statistical process, with much of the variance in human performance on single-word reading tasks being explicable in terms of the statistical relationship between spelling and sound representations; and (b) connectionist models of reading have been successful to the extent that they learn the relevant statistical associations. This is consistent with the conclusions in the previous section, where we described the rational analysis approach to reading and suggested that any process model of reading is likely to be successful just to the extent that it implements the appropriate statistically optimal or adaptively rational processing.

Thus, psychological mechanisms can be explicated and tested using formal approaches in a way that may not be possible at a purely psychological level of explanation. In many cases, it is only through simulation that the behavior of the system as a whole can be examined. We next examine the role of connectionist models of reading for understanding paradoxical findings in examinations of developmental dyslexia.

CONNECTIONISM—RESOLVING A PARADOX IN DYSLEXIC READING

In this section we show how the use of connectionist models can enable us to understand experimental data that have proved difficult or impossible to explain within the standard psychological account of the phonological deficit in developmental dyslexia. More specifically, computational modeling techniques can be used to examine the consequences, for the reading of nonwords and different types of word, of providing a learning system with different types of phonological and orthographic representations. It is clear that dyslexic reading development represents a departure from optimality, in the sense of "optimality" characterized earlier. However, such a departure could, in terms of the statistical approach described previously, be due to one of two very different reasons. It could be that disabled-reading development represents an inability to acquire or make use of statistically optimal linkages between normal input and output representations (representing a word's orthography and phonology respectively). Alternatively, it could be that dyslexics are reading in a statistically optimal fashion *given that they possess impaired representations* and are hence simply unable to represent orthography and phonology at a level of specificity that enables optimal generalization.

Before describing how we examined the consequences of impaired phonological representations in a connectionist network, we briefly describe the phonological deficit account of developmental dyslexia. The aim is to show that the observed pattern of empirical findings, taken as a whole, cannot easily be explained within the standard framework.

A central question has been whether the reading impairment in dyslexic children reflects the use of word recognition strategies that are qualitatively *different* from normal language processing, or, rather, the use of strategies that are normal but simply *delayed*. According to the phonological deficit account of dyslexia, a specific deficit in the phonological processing domain prevents the normal development of a spelling-to-sound translation routine that is assumed to make use of sublexical phonological processes. Thus, the phonological deficit account assumes that reading is indeed deviant rather than delayed, in that the adoption of the "normal" reading strategy is prevented. We call this the "strong" version of the phonological deficit account, to distinguish it from a "weak" version. According to the latter, deficient phonological processing leads merely to a delay, rather than to the adoption of abnormal alternative reading strategies.

The hypothesis that deficits in phonological processing are *causally* related to reading problems in dyslexia can, of course, only be tested by an empirical examination of the task of reading itself. Unfortunately, however, tests of this hypothesis have led to mixed results. The assumption of the phonological deficit account—that spelling-to-sound translation ability will be selectively impaired in dyslexia—leads to two critical predictions. We deal with each of these in turn, for different results have emerged from each.

One prediction is that there will be reduced effects of spelling-to-sound regularity in dyslexia. Many words in English have "irregular" or "exceptional" pronunciations (e.g., *pint*; cf. *mint, hint, tint,* etc.). These can be contrasted with "regular" or "consistent" words such as *pill* (cf. *mill, hill, till,* etc.). Thus, sublexical spelling-to-sound correspondences can be used to derive the correct pronunciations for regular words, but not for irregular words. The use of a sublexical spelling-to-sound translation routine will therefore lead to an advantage (faster or more accurate reading) for regular over irregular items. However, if no sublexical spelling-to-sound translation procedure is available, there is no reason to expect any difference in performance on regular and irregular items. Therefore, the presence or absence of spelling-to-sound regularity effects can be used as a "marker" for the use of sublexical spelling-to-sound translation. This has been used to test the phonological deficit account of reading, because if it is indeed the case that deficient phonological processing prevents or impairs the use of sublexical reading strategies, spelling-to-sound effects should be reduced or absent in dyslexic subjects, even if they are able to read words at the same level as younger normal readers.

Normal children and adults do have more difficulty processing words with irregular or exceptional pronunciations, reflecting the use of sublexical spelling-to-sound translation. In adults, word naming latency is generally slower for words with irregular or inconsistent pronunciations (e.g., Seidenberg et al., 1984; Szeszulski & Manis, 1987; Taraban & McClelland, 1987; Waters & Seidenberg, 1985), with further evidence that the spelling-to-sound correspondences used by skilled adults when they are reading words (as opposed to nonwords) are mainly those between orthographic and phonological rimes (Treiman et al., 1995). In children, regularity or consistency effects have been observed in error rates or single word reading times (e.g., Laxon, Masterson, & Coltheart, 1991; Laxon, Masterson, & Moran, 1994; Waters et al., 1984). There is, therefore, ample evidence that effects of spelling-to-sound regularity can be reliably observed in both children and adults. It is therefore possible to test the central prediction of the phonological deficit account that dyslexic reading should be associated with reduced or absent regularity effects.

As reviewed in Brown (in press), the majority of studies that have addressed this question have failed to find any evidence of reduced or absent effects of spelling-to-sound regularity in dyslexic subjects (Baddeley, Logie, & Ellis, 1988; Brown, in press; Holligan & Johnston, 1988; Seidenberg, Bruck, Fornarolo, & Backman, 1985; Szeszulski & Manis, 1987; Treiman & Hirsh-Pasek, 1985; Watson & Brown, 1992). A similar conclusion has emerged from the study of poor readers whose disability was defined in terms of a reading performance cutoff, rather than on the basis of a discrepancy between an intelligence measure and performance on a reading test (Backman, Bruck, Hebert, & Seidenberg, 1984; Siegel & Ryan, 1988; Stanovich, Nathan, & Zolman, 1988; Szeszulski & Manis, 1987). Although some studies have claimed to find evidence for smaller regularity effects associated with dyslexia (Beech & Awaida, 1992; Frith & Snowling, 1983; Snowling, Stackhouse, & Rack, 1986), the overwhelming majority of evidence fails to support the prediction of the phonological deficit model; that is, the prediction that spelling-to-sound regularity or consistency effects should be absent in dyslexia, reflecting an impaired sublexical routine.

On the basis of these studies, there might seem little evidence to support the strong version of the phonological deficit account; that is, the claim that the online reading performance of dyslexic children is a result of an absent or deviant sublexical routine. At best, it might seem possible to maintain a belief in the weak phonological deficit account. However, such a conclusion would be premature, because the search for reduced or absent regularity effects in development dyslexia is only one of two predictions of the strong version of the phonological deficit hypothesis. The second prediction has led to results more consistent with the strong version of the phonological deficit hypothesis, and it is to the alternative methodology used to evaluate this hypothesis that we now turn.

For the same reasons that impaired spelling-to-sound translation ability should lead to reduced regularity effects, a specific impairment on nonword reading is also predicted. Because a nonword (e.g., *blint*) has no lexical representation, it can be pronounced only by using sublexical spelling-to-sound correspondences. Therefore, the strong version of the phonological deficit account predicts that dyslexics should have a specific nonword reading problem. A test of this prediction is a comparison between nonword reading for dyslexic and normal readers who can read words equally well.

In a recent meta-review, Rack, Snowling, and Olson (1992) carefully examined the large number of experimental studies that have addressed this question (see also Ijzendoorn & Bus, 1994). On the basis of their analysis, they concluded that there is substantial experimental evidence for a selective nonword processing deficit in dyslexia. This observation has been taken as support for the phonological deficit account, according to which the specific nonword reading difficulties arise due to impaired spelling-to-sound translation ability.

There is, therefore, a paradoxical pattern of findings in the experimental literature. How can this be explained? Brown (in press) addressed this question using connectionist models, by examining the effects of providing models with impaired phonological representations. In order to explain what would constitute an impaired phonological representation for this model, we need to first consider how the phonological and orthographic forms of words can be represented in a connectionist network (as the network's inputs and outputs).

For ease of presentation, we consider the case of the orthographic representation, although similar considerations apply in both the phonological and orthographic domains. One widely used method involves dedicating a unit to the representation of every ordered triple of letters or phonemes contained in the word. The orthographic form of a word such as *have*, for example, contains the four triples _ha + hav + ave + ve_ (where the _ character signifies a word boundary). One input unit could be used to represent each of the triples necessary to represent all words in English. This type of scheme was used, with modification, by the model of reading developed by Seidenberg and McClelland (1989). A simple design of a one-to-one correspondence between a unit and a specified triplet is not feasible, because too many units would be required (except for very small vocabularies). The actual implementation, therefore, makes use of distributed representations, in which each unit participates in the encoding of many different triples. Each triple is therefore represented as a pattern of activity over many different units. We also note that triples of phonetic features, rather than phonemes themselves, were used in the Seidenberg and McClelland (1989) model's phonological (output) representations.

It turns out that a model using triple-based representations of the type described previously is successful at learning to read irregular and regular words, but does less well at reading nonwords (Besner et al., 1990). In contrast, models in which *individual* phonemes and graphemes have their own unique representations tend to do better at reading nonwords, while still exhibiting good performance on regular and irregular words (see Brown, in press; Bullinaria, in press; Coltheart, Curtis, Atkins, & Haller, 1993; Norris, 1994; Phillips, Hay, & Smith, 1993; Plaut et al., 1996; Seidenberg, Plaut, Petersen, McClelland, & McRae, 1994; Sejnowski & Rosenberg, 1987).

This is strong evidence that there is a relationship between the type of representations used by a computational learning model, and the model's eventual (i.e., after training on a corpus of words) nonword performance. The reason that a triple-based model will show relatively poor nonword reading performance appears to be because of what Plaut et al. (1996) termed the *dispersion problem*, which arises when the same spelling-to-sound correspondence must be learned in several different contexts (effectively reducing the value of training). In a triple-based representation, graphemes (and phonemes) effectively are assigned a different representation according to where in a triple they occur. Thus, the letter *A* at the beginning of a triple has, for the model, nothing in common with an *A* occurring at the end of a triple; the representation does not encode the fact that these are the same letter, and they will effectively be treated as different letters by the model. This impairs the ability of the model to learn generalizations between graphemes and phonemes.

Because of this, Brown (in press) suggested that the triple-based representations used in the original Seidenberg and McClelland (1989) model, with its selectively impaired nonword reading performance, could be seen as analogous to impaired representations in dyslexic children. Dyslexics' impaired performance on tasks that involve the implicit or explicit manipulation of phonemes may, it has been suggested, reflect the lack of, or impairment of, appropriate representations at the level of individual phonemes (e.g., Fowler, 1991; Hulme & Snowling, 1992; Metsala, 1997a, 1997b). This psychological account of the phonological deficit may be viewed as computationally analogous to the problems experienced by the Seidenberg and McClelland model. In the model, individual phoneme type-identities are not efficiently represented, because any given phoneme representation is context specific in that it is uniquely represented when it is either the first, middle, or last segment of a triple. Thus, the triple-based models can be seen as having impaired phoneme–level representations, and we follow Plaut et al. (1996) and others in suggesting that this is causally related to their difficulty with nonword reading.

Although the connectionist work that we have briefly reviewed may permit an understanding of how and why it is that impaired phonological representations cause particular problems for nonword reading, the computational consequences of the impaired representations for spelling-to-sound regularity effects have not been examined. We therefore carried out an investigation of this question (Brown, in press). Specifically, the ability to read regular and irregular words and nonwords was examined in (a) a connectionist model of reading with impaired phonological representations (in the sense characterized previously), and (b) a connectionist model with relatively "unimpaired" phonological representations (this model adopted the scheme used by Plaut et al. [1996], in which individual graphemes and phonemes are explicitly and uniquely represented). Performance was assessed in terms of the "error score" produced by the network. This provides a measure of the divergence between the "target" (i.e., correct) pronunciation of a given orthographic string, and the output that is actually produced by the network.

Based on results from previous connectionist implementations, we expected that the model with the impaired representations would perform badly on nonwords relative to words. However, of more interest was the relative performance of the two models on regular and irregular words. Recall that the purely psychological account of dyslexia—the phonological deficit hypothesis—predicted both impaired nonword reading and reduced or absent effects of spelling-to-sound regularity. However, behavioral data from dyslexic children indicates a nonword reading deficit in the company of preserved effects of spelling-to-sound regularity. The test, therefore, was to see if a computational instantiation of impaired phonological representations simulated this behavioral data—on the basis of previous connectionist models, it was not possible to determine in advance whether our connectionist interpretation of the phonological deficit would lead to preserved regularity effects.

In fact, the outcomes were very clear. The model with impaired phonological representations led to reduced performance overall (on both regular and irregular words, and on nonwords), and thus we scaled the results such that the two models performed equally well on regular words (analogous to a reading-level-match control). The relative performance of both models on irregular words and nonwords was then examined. The results are summarized in Fig. 12.2 (see Brown, in press, for more details of the implementation and results).

It can be seen from the figure that the relative increase in error scores (i.e., the relative *reduction* in performance) on irregular over regular words was approximately equal for the two different versions of the model (preserved regularity effects). Regarding nonword reading, however, the pattern was rather different. The error score to nonwords was higher than for either regular or irregular words in both versions of the model, but the increase in error score was substantially greater for the model with impaired phonological representations.

These simulation results help us understand the consequences, for learning, of providing a system with impaired representations. In this demonstration, we defined *impaired* representations to be representations that make it difficult to learn the position-independent systematic relationships between graphemes and phonemes (i.e., the triple-based representation scheme used in one version of the model). The results we have described demonstrate that use of such representations leads to a model that, after learning, exhibits (in relative terms) normal effects of spelling-to-sound regularity, but is particularly impaired on nonword reading. This is, of

12. FORMAL MODELS OF READING DEVELOPMENT 249

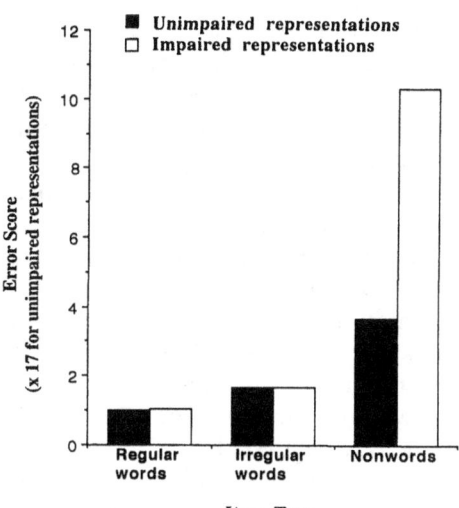

FIG. 12.2. Pattern of summed squared error scores to regular and irregular words, and nonwords, in connectionist models with impaired and unimpaired representations.

course, just the paradoxical pattern of reading that is observed in developmental dyslexic children—preserved effects of spelling-to-sound regularity, in combination with a selective impairment on nonword reading.

We therefore suggest that the computational approach resolves a paradox in the literature, and lends support to the claim of the phonological deficit hypothesis—that phonological processing deficits in dyslexia lead to a specific impairment in the spelling-to-sound translation routine. This claim need not, as has previously been assumed, predict that effects of spelling-to-sound regularity will be reduced or absent in developmental dyslexia. In computational terms, the reason for the particular sensitivity of nonword reading to phonological problems appears to be due to the need to use low-level units (graphemes and phonemes) in spelling-to-sound translation if such items are to be read correctly. If the available representations do not easily permit the learning of low-level regularities of this type, nonword reading performance will be particularly impaired. The reading of words, in contrast, can be achieved on the basis of higher-level spelling-to-sound correspondences. We also suggest that these results from computational modeling support the more specific claim that the phonological deficit in dyslexia is a consequence of abnormal or impaired phonological representations.

THE DEVELOPMENT OF PHONEMIC REPRESENTATIONS

The performance of connectionist models on reading, as outlined previously, are affected by the form of representations with which the model is provided. Thus, better generalization (i.e., nonword reading) was observed in models that use relatively more fine-grained input and output representations. A further important role for formal models of normal and dyslexic reading, we suggest, will therefore be to explicate the development of phonological representations. Central to current psychological accounts of reading acquisition is the role of phonological representations that are brought to the process of learning to read. The nature and properties of these representations have particular relevance given the significance of phonological processes in cognitive accounts of dyslexia. We next review a psychological account of the development of phonological representations, and discuss possible mechanisms for the abnormal representations that may underlie dyslexia. One formal approach to understanding developmental changes in the task facing the listener is reviewed, and some future directions in using simulations to explicate the psychological model are suggested.

Adult models of spoken word recognition employ segmental or phonemic representations (i.e., sequences of discreet speech sounds) for the task of discriminating amongst lexical alternatives (for a review of empirical work leading to these models, see Pisoni & Luce, 1987). This view of the phonemic form of lexical items in adults' long-term memory provides the goal state for developmental models of spoken word recognition (e.g., Halle, 1990).

There are two alternative hypotheses concerning the development of phoneme-based representations in lexical memory. First, phonemic segments may be present initially and form the basis of spoken word recognition throughout development. Vocabulary development within this model would involve the addition of lexical items and the growing familiarity of individual words. The second hypothesis has been referred to as the "developmental" or "emergent" position (e.g., Metsala & Walley, in press). According to this view, young children's lexical representations are initially more holistic and may undergo developmental changes into the early school years (e.g., Fowler, 1991; Metsala, 1997a; Treiman & Breaux, 1982; Walley, 1987, 1988, 1993; Walley, Smith, & Jusczyk, 1986). Because words are the primary unit of meaning, the word may constitute the initial level of linguistic contrast for young children (Aslin & Smith, 1988; Walley, Michela, & Flege, 1994). That is, children beginning to talk may be preoccupied with isolating words from the speech stream and building correspondences between words and their meaning.

The developmental task in speech perception, according to this emergent position, involves learning to perceive stimulus words as complexes of segments. A primary concern in understanding this developmental task is delineating the developmental time course of, and the factors driving, segmental restructuring of lexical representations. One hypothesis is that vocabulary growth, in terms of both familiarity of lexical items and the number of items in the listener's lexicon, with the concomitant need to discriminate between an increasing number of similarly sounding lexical alternatives, drives this lexical restructuring process (e.g., Metsala, 1997a; Metsala & Walley, in press; Walley, 1993). In essence, children will encode the distinctions that are necessary for word recognition. As the number of lexical items increases, and similarly sounding words are added to the child's lexicon, representations will need to become more fine-grained. Before discussing ways in which such a process could be explored using formal analysis and modeling techniques, we describe some of the relevant empirical evidence.

There has been little evidence bearing on spoken word recognition in early to middle childhood, and few developmental investigations have systematically examined the effects of word characteristics (e.g., Cole, 1973, 1981; Cole & Perfetti, 1980; Elliott, Hammer, & Evan, 1987; Walley, 1987, 1988; but see Elliott, Clifton, & Servi, 1983; Fox & Koenigsknecht, 1989; Walley & Metsala, 1990, 1992). On the basis of currently available empirical evidence, however, it appears that children do engage in more holistic processing of spoken words than adults. First, young 3-, 4-, and 5-year-old children's productions and perceptions of CVC syllables and individual phonemes are more influenced by coarticulatory factors than is perception in 7-year-olds and adults (Nittrouer & Studdert-Kennedy, 1987; Nittrouer, Studdert-Kennedy, & McGowan, 1989). Second, adults' speech perception was found to be most disrupted by segments replaced by noise in the beginning of words, whereas children's perception was not affected by the position of the replaced segment. It seems that children's attention is more evenly distributed throughout the word (Walley, 1988). Third, younger children are less able to use single segments in making phonetic similarity judgments than are older children and adults (e.g., Treiman & Breaux, 1982; Walley, Smith, & Jusczyk, 1986) and perform more poorly on phonemic manipulation tasks (e.g., Stanovich, Cunningham, & Cramer, 1984). Finally, younger children have been found to need more of the bottom-up input from word onset to recognize a word in speech gating tasks than older children and adults (Elliott, Hammer, & Evan, 1987; Fox & Koenigsknecht, 1989; Metsala, 1997a; Walley, 1988).

These findings suggest that young children's lexical representations are more holistic, with distinguishing information distributed across the entire word. For adults, online matching of input to internal segmentalized representations enables words to be recognized on the basis of less bottom-up input—several word-initial segments may suffice for adult recognition.

Therefore, there is increasing empirical support for the developmentally protracted holistic hypothesis (but see Gerken et al., 1995). This process is protracted in terms of the degree and number of lexical items that are segmentally represented over early childhood. Restructuring is not proposed to be an all or none, systemwide phenomenon; rather, words that have many similar-sounding alternatives in the listener's lexicon may be the first to undergo segmental restructuring (Metsala, 1997a; Walley, 1993). Therefore, at any one point in development, there will be differences in the degree of segmental structure between words (and possibly within different parts of the same word). For example, recognizing the word *big* will require a more detailed representation if the child's vocabulary also includes such items as *bag, bug, bit, dig,* and *wig,* than if these similarly sounding alternatives are not part of the child's lexical base.

Recently, we examined children's spoken word recognition for words in different functionally defined areas of the mental lexicon (Metsala, 1997a). Seven- and nine-year-old children required more of the bottom-up input from word onset to recognize words with few similarly sounding neighbors in the child's lexicon than did 11-year-olds and adults. For words that are heard frequently and have many neighbors, young children's recognition was based on the same amount of bottom-up input as for older children and adults; for these words, children displayed a degree of segmental processing equivalent to adult's speech recognition. These developmental comparisons support the developmentally protracted holistic hypothesis. Also, these data provide evidence for idea that structural properties of the listener's lexicon, such as sound similarity relations, influence the ability for segmental processing in recognition. Taken together, these empirical studies support the idea that more holistic representations may underlie young children's spoken word recognition and that these representations may change as a function of an increasing vocabulary base. We next examine formal approaches in the study of spoken word recognition, because these may shed light on these developmental findings.

FORMAL APPROACHES TO SPOKEN WORD RECOGNITION

Analyzing the structural properties of computerized lexicons has been one formal approach that has shed light on the observations from adult speech recognition, and this has led to models of developmental change in lexical representations. Luce (1986) analyzed the structural properties (e.g., neighborhood density) of individual words, using a computerized version of *Webster's Pocket Dictionary.* He defined a "neighbor" as a word that can be transformed into the target word by a one-phoneme addition, substitution, or deletion. Using this neighborhood similarity metric, he calculated words' neighborhood densities; that is, the number of neighbors for a given word. Luce (1986) developed the Neighborhood Activation Model (NAM), which includes neighborhood structure, word frequency, and neighborhood frequency in a formal metric. This model accounted for statistically significant variance in adults' spoken word recognition latencies and accuracy in a series of perceptual experiments.

Analyses of the structural properties of computerized lexicons corresponding to various developmental ages has helped to evaluate the plausibility of the developmentally protracted holistic hypothesis. Charles-Luce and Luce (1990) found that words in the lexicons of 5- and 7-year-olds had fewer neighbors than the same words in adult lexicons. These developmental differences were not fully accounted for by the larger absolute number of items in the adult lexicon. Charles-Luce and Luce (1990, 1995; see also Dollaghan, 1994) demonstrated the usefulness of the neighborhood similarity metric as a formal approach to comparing the structural properties between child and adult lexicons. These computational comparisons inform our understanding of developmental differences in the task facing the listener. On the basis of their observations, these investigators suggested that representations in children's lexicons may differ substantially from those in the adult lexicon. One hypothesis is that representations in the developing lexicon may not be sequentially represented or segmentally bundled to the same extent as the adult lexicon.

Logan (1992) also used the neighborhood similarity metric to examine structural properties of computerized lexicons corresponding to language samples collected from children between 18 months and 5 years of age and adults. He found relatively small neighborhoods for words in young children's lexicons, and suggested that traditional segmental representations may not be necessary in order to specify a word uniquely in children's speech recognition. He further examined structural properties (i.e., neighborhood densities) resulting from the instantiation of a number of alternative representational systems (e.g., based on manner class). Logan (1992) found that such alternative representation systems yielded a search task comparable with that in the adult's phonemic-based neighborhoods. Thus, these formalized approaches to specifying the structural properties of the lexical basis for spoken word recognition have driven the development of new and more sophisticated psychological models, particularly in terms of the computational viability of the developmentally protracted holistic hypothesis. We next examine how developmental models of phonological representations might be usefully applied to help explain the phonological deficit in dyslexia.

THE LEXICAL RESTRUCTURING DEFICIT HYPOTHESIS

Phonological processing deficits in dyslexic children have been shown for diverse tasks. These include measures of short-term memory for verbal information (e.g., Brady, Shankweiler, & Mann, 1983; Liberman, Shankweiler, Liberman, Fowler, & Fischer, 1977; Siegel & Linder, 1984), categorical perception of individual phonemes (De Weirdt, 1988; Godfrey, Syrdal-Lasky, Millay, & Knox, 1981; Reed, 1989; Werker & Tees, 1987), identification of minimal contrast word pairs (Reed, 1989), and identification of words in noise and words with ambiguous onsets (Reed, 1989; Snowling, Goulandris, Bowlby, & Howell, 1986). These deficits have variously been attributed to less robust, underspecified, or degraded representations. The earlier-outlined developmental framework of phonological representations provides, we believe, a promising basis for explaining dyslexics' performance deficits on phonological tasks.

Specifically, we propose that phonemic restructuring of lexical items does not progress in a developmentally appropriate manner in reading disabled children; rather, lexical representations and processing of speech input may remain more holistically based throughout early and middle childhood (Metsala, 1997b). We call this the *lexical restructuring deficit hypothesis*. Thus, we are proposing that the phonological deficit in dyslexia can be operationalized in terms of more holistic (less segmental) phonological representations. In support of this hypothesis, we recently found that reading-disabled children in Grades 1 through 6 needed more of the bottom-up input from word onset to recognize words in sparse neighborhoods than did same-age peers (Metsala, 1997b). Furthermore, the amount of bottom-up information needed from word onset was predictive of individual differences in word and nonword reading beyond variance accounted for by vocabulary and phonemic awareness measures for young children. Reading-disabled children displayed this deviation in lexical processing even when matched for vocabulary size with nondisabled peers. This study provides evidence for a specific link between phonological *representations* and dyslexia (see also Hulme & Snowling, 1992).

The lexical restructuring deficit hypothesis is also congruent with Scarborough's (1990) finding that toddlers who later experienced reading problems displayed a deficit in receptive vocabulary at 2 years of age. This age corresponds to the onset of the vocabulary growth spurt, and a deficit in lexical restructuring could cause such an early vocabulary lag in these children. A protracted deficit in lexical restructuring, we suggest, would give rise to the phonological processing performance deficits observed in reading-disabled children (reviewed previously)—most notably to difficulties accessing and manipulating phonemes (phonemic awareness tasks) and ultimately to making links between phonemes and graphemes.

We believe there is a need for both empirical and computational work in order to further delineate both the form of phonological representations at different points of development and the deviant pathway that, we hypothesize, will characterize such development in dyslexic readers. The effects of impaired representations on learning to read in a connectionist

12. FORMAL MODELS OF READING DEVELOPMENT 255

model have been demonstrated—but how do those representations come to be impaired through children's early development? In order to provide a satisfactory answer to this question, we suggest that it will be necessary to gain a computational-level understanding of the mechanisms that drive the development of segmental representations. Current connectionist modeling techniques are ideally suited to such a task, because a considerable body of computational research has examined the ways in which simple learning algorithms can enable connectionist networks to develop internal representations that provide both an economical encoding of the redundancies in the input-output mapping that must be learned, and (relatedly) a representation of the distinctions that are most effective in achieving the desired input-output mapping (for discussion, see, e.g., Elman, 1988; Hanson & Burr, 1990).

Psychologically interesting representations may be constructed either in multilayer backpropagation architectures, of the type discussed earlier, or in competitive learning architectures. In the former case, the pressure to develop appropriate representations comes from the requirement of the network to make the most efficient use of the limited computational resources (number of units or connections) that it has at its disposal. In competitive architectures, which have proved useful in understanding many aspects of low-level organization in the brain, similar inputs are assigned similar representations in the network. Both of these architectures are likely to prove useful in understanding the development of increasingly segmentalized lexical representations as a network with limited storage capacity is required to represent an ever-greater number of lexical items, many of which are very similar to one another.

In summary, we suggest that connectionist modeling techniques will prove ideally suited to the development of models of both normal and disturbed progression toward segmentalized lexical representations. This will be a productive avenue for further exploration.

CONCLUSIONS

In this chapter we have argued for the utility and, perhaps, even the necessity, of formal approaches in understanding reading development, skilled reading, and developmental dyslexia. This position was developed through reference to several case studies of formal approaches. We demonstrated that a formal analysis of the statistical properties of the orthographic-to-phonological mappings in the English language can help us understand reading in a different way. Specifically, the nature of the statistically optimal strategy for this mapping system was defined, independent of considerations of the mechanisms that might give rise to reading. We described work suggesting that an optimal reading approach indeed provides a good fit to observed effects of spelling-to-sound consistency in skilled adult reading (for detail, see Brown, 1997). These effects are precisely those that connectionist models have been found to account for well, suggesting that reading and its development can usefully be viewed as a task that involves the representation of the statistical pattern of associations between orthographic and phonological representations. We suggested that connectionist models will account for behavioral data in skilled adult reading just insofar as they implement the statistically optimal computations calculated by this formal approach.

We have argued that in order to derive unambiguous predictions about human behavior from a model, a computational approach is necessary. That is, given the complexity of psychological models, there exists no alternative methodology to ensure that predictions about the behavior of the model as a whole are correct. We demonstrated this potential danger of purely psychological models in the case of the phonological deficit account of developmental dyslexia. Specifically, the cognitive level of explanation, that a deficit in the spelling-to-sound routine in dyslexia, led to two predictions; that dyslexic readers should demonstrate (a) a nonword reading deficit and, (b) a reduced regularity/consistency effect. When behavioral data were inconsistent with these predictions, dismissal of the strong version of the phonological deficit account seemed imminent. However, we demonstrated that under conditions congruent with the phonological deficit (i.e., impaired phonological representations) a connectionist model's reading of regular, irregular, and nonwords was consistent with the behavioral data from dyslexic subjects (Brown, in press). Thus, on the basis of the purely psychological model, an erroneous prediction of the model's behavior was derived.

In an approach similar to that used to examine the structural properties of spelling-to-sound mappings in English, we reviewed the work of investigators analyzing the task of spoken word recognition in English (e.g., Charles-Luce & Luce, 1990; Logan, 1992; Luce, 1986). Luce's (1986) similarity metric for examining the number of similarly sounding words in a listener's lexicon (neighbors) accounted for behavioral data on adult spoken word recognition, and was used in analyzing structural properties of lexicons corresponding to the vocabulary base of differing chronological ages. This type of formal approach to spoken word recognition has played an important role in testing the plausibility of the developmentally protracted holistic hypothesis (the suggestion that representations underlying spoken word recognition are substantially different from the phonemic representations of adults, and that the restructuring from more holistic to segmentally based representations extends through early childhood). Indeed, Charles-Luce and Luce (1990) and Logan (1992) concluded, from structural analysis of child and adult computerized lexicons, that children's neighborhoods are structurally different, and recognition of spoken words may be supported by more holistic representations in the young listener's lexicon. We have suggested that further computational work will be important in demonstrating exactly how it is that the process of lexical growth leads to the development of increasingly segmentalised lexical representations.

We next offered a link between developmental perspectives of phonological representations underlying spoken word recognition and reading acquisition. We suggest that this link will be essential if we are to gain an understanding that moves beyond present accounts of the phonological deficit. Specifically, the lexical restructuring deficit hypothesis was proposed as a causal relation between phonological processing deficits and reading deficits in dyslexia. This view, according to which the underlying phonological representations in reading-disabled children remain holistically encoded for longer than normal, may be able to explain difficulties in the learning of spelling-to-sound mapping regularities. This is a further area in which computational investigation and analysis may enable us to understand the mechanisms that normally drive the development of segmental representations, and may also enable us to understand how such mechanisms can go wrong.

REFERENCES

Anderson, J. R. (1990). *The adaptive character of thought.* Hillsdale, NJ: Lawrence Erlbaum Associates.

Anderson, J. R., & Milson, R. (1989). Human memory: An adaptive perspective. *Psychological Review, 96,* 703–719.

Anderson, J. R., & Schooler, L. J. (1991). Reflections of the environment in memory. *Psychological Science, 2,* 396–408.

Aslin, R. N., & Smith, L. B. (1988). Perceptual development. *Annual Review of Psychology, 39,* 435–473.

Backman, J., Bruck, M., Hebert, M., & Seidenberg, M. S. (1984). Acquisition and use of spelling-sound correspondence. *Journal of Experimental Child Psychology, 38,* 114–133.

Baddeley, A. D., Logie, R. H., & Ellis, N. C. (1988). Characteristics of developmental dyslexia. *Cognition, 29,* 197–228.

Bechtel, W., & Abrahamsen, A. A. (1991). *Connectionism and the mind: An introduction to parallel processing in networks.* Cambridge, MA: MIT Press/Bradford Books.

Beech, J. R., & Awaida, M. (1992). Lexical and non-lexical routes: A comparison between normally achieving and poor readers. *Journal of Learning Disabilities, 25,* 196–206.

Besner, D., Twilley, L., McCann, R. S., & Seergobin, K. (1990). On the association between connectionism and data: Are a few words necessary? *Psychological Review, 97,* 432–446.

Brady, S., Shankweiler, D., & Mann V. (1983). Speech perception and memory coding in relation to reading ability. *Journal of Experimental Child Psychology, 35,* 345–367.

Brown, G. D. A. (1987). Resolving inconsistency: A computational model of word naming. *Journal of Memory and Language, 26,* 1–23.

Brown, G. D. A. (1997). *A rational analysis of reading: Spelling-to-sound translation is optimal.* Manuscript submitted for publication.

Brown, G. D. A. (in press). Connectionism, phonology, reading and regularity in developmental dyslexia. *Brain and Language.*

Brown, G. D. A., & Deavers, R. P. (1997). *Evidence for task-dependence in children's and adults' reading strategies.* Manuscript submitted for publication.

Brown, G. D. A., & Loosemore, R. L. (1994). Computational approaches to normal and impaired spelling. In G. D. A. Brown & N. C. Ellis (Eds.), *Handbook of spelling: Theory, process and application* (pp. 319–335). Chichester, England: Wiley.

Bullinaria, J. D. (in press). Neural network models of reading without wickelfeatures. To appear in J. Levy, D. Bairaktaris, J. Bullinaria, & D. Cairns (Eds.), *Connectionist models of memory and language.* London: UCL Press.

Charles-Luce, J., & Luce, P. A. (1990). Similarity neighborhoods of words in young children's lexicon. *Journal of Child Language, 17,* 205–215.

Charles-Luce, J., & Luce, P. A. (1995). An examination of similarity neighborhoods in young children's receptive vocabularies. *Journal of Child Language, 22*(3), 727–735.

Cole, R. A. (1973). Listening for mispronunciations: A measure of what we hear during speech. *Perception and Psychophysics, 1,* 153–156.

Cole, R. A. (1981). Perception of fluent speech by children and adults. *Annals of the Academy of Sciences, 379,* 92–109.

Cole, R. A., & Perfetti, C. A. (1980). Listening for mispronunciations in a child's story: The use of context by children and adults. *Journal of Verbal Learning and Verbal Behavior, 19,* 297–315.

Coltheart, M., Curtis, B., Atkins, P., & Haller, M. (1993). Models of reading aloud: Dual-route and parallel-distributed-processing accounts. *Psychological Review, 100,* 589–608.

Coltheart, V., & Leahy, J. (1992). Children's and adults' reading of nonwords: Effects of regularity and consistency. *Journal of Experimental Psychology: Learning, Memory and Cognition, 18,* 718–729.

De Weirdt, W. (1988). Speech perception and frequency discrimination for good and poor readers. *Applied Psycholinguistics, 9,* 163–183.

Dollaghan, C. A. (1994). Children's phonological neighborhoods: Half empty or half full? *Journal of Child Language, 21,* 257–271.

Elliott, L. L., Clifton, L., & Servi, D. (1983). Word frequency effects for a closed-set word identification task. *Audiology, 22,* 229–240.

Elliott, L. L., Hammer, M. A., & Evan, K. E. (1987). Perception of gated, highly familiar spoken monosyllabic nouns by children, teenagers, and older adults. *Perception and Psychophysics, 42,* 150–157.

Elman, J. L. (1988). *Finding structure in time* (CRL Technical Report 8801). San Diego: University of California.

Fowler, A. E. (1991). How early phonological development might set the stage for phonological awareness. In S. Brady & D. Shankweiler (Eds.), *Phonological processes in literacy: A tribute to Isabelle Y. Liberman* (pp. 97–117). Hillsdale, NJ: Lawrence Erlbaum Associates.

Fox, R., & Koenigsknecht, R. (1989, November). *The effect of cohort size one gated word recognition.* Paper presented at the American Speech and Hearing Association Meeting.

Frith, U., & Snowling, M. (1983). Reading for meaning and reading for sound in autistic and dyslexic children. *British Journal of Developmental Psychology, 1,* 329–342.

Glushko, R. J. (1979). The organization and activation of orthographic knowledge in reading aloud. *Journal of Experimental Psychology: Human Perception and Performance, 5*(4), 674–691.

Godfrey, J. J., Syrdal-Lasky, A. K., Millay, K. K., & Knox, C. M. (1981). Performance of dyslexic children on speech perception tests. *Journal of Experimental Child Psychology, 32,* 401–424.

Halle, M. (1990). Phonology. In D. N. Osherson & H. Lasnick (Eds.), *Language: An invitation to cognitive science* (pp. 43–68). Cambridge, MA: MIT Press.

Hanson, S. J., & Burr D. J. (1990). What connectionist models learn: Learning and representation in connectionist networks. *Behavioral and Brain Sciences, 13*, 471–518.

Holligan, C., & Johnston, R. S. (1988). The use of phonological information by good and poor readers in memory and reading tasks. *Memory & Cognition, 16*(6), 522–532.

Hulme, C., & Snowling, M. (1992). Deficits in output phonology: A cause of reading failure? *Cognitive Neuropsychology, 9*, 47–72.

Ijzendoorn, M., & Bus, A. (1994). Meta-analytic confirmation of the nonword reading deficit in developmental dyslexia. *Reading Research Quarterly, 29*, 266–275.

Jared, D., McRae, K., & Seidenberg, M. S. (1990). The basis of consistency effects in word naming. *Journal of Memory and Language, 29*, 687–715.

Laxon, V., Masterson, J., & Coltheart, V. (1991). Some bodies are easier to read: The effect of consistency and regularity on children's reading. *Quarterly Journal of Experimental Psychology, 43A*, 793–824.

Laxon, V., Masterson, J., & Moran, R. (1994). Are children's representations of words distributed? Effects of orthographic neighbourhood size, consistency and regularity of naming. *Language and Cognitive Processes, 9*, 1–27.

Liberman, I. Y., Shankweiler, D., Liberman, A. M., Fowler, C. A., & Fischer, F. W. (1977). Phonetic segmentation and recoding in the beginning reader. In A. S. Reber & D. L. Scarborough (Eds.), *Toward a psychology of reading* (pp. 207–223). Hillsdale, NJ: Lawrence Erlbaum Associates.

Logan, J. S. (1992). *A computational analysis of young children's lexicons* (Research on Spoken Language Processing, Technical Report No. 8). Bloomington, IN: Department of Psychology, Speech Research Laboratory.

Luce, P. A. (1986). *Neighborhoods of words in the mental lexicon* (Research on Speech Perception, Technical Report No. 6). Bloomington, IN: Department of Psychology, Speech Research Laboratory.

Marcus, G. F. (1995). The acquisition of the English past tense in children and multilayered connectionist networks. *Cognition, 56*, 271–279.

Metsala, J. L. (1997a). An examination of word frequency and neighborhood density in the development of spoken word recognition. *Memory & Cognition, 25*(1), 47–56.

Metsala, J. L. (1997b). Spoken word recognition in reading disabled children. *Journal of Educational Psychology, 89*(1), 159–169.

Metsala, J. L., & Walley, A. C. (in press). Spoken vocabulary growth and the segmental restructuring of lexical representations: Precursors to phonemic awareness and early reading ability. In J. L. Metsala & L. C. Ehri (Eds.), *Word recognition in beginning literacy*. Mahwah, NJ: Lawrence Erlbaum Associates.

Nittrouer, S., & Studdert-Kennedy, M. (1987). The role of coarticulatory effects in the perception of fricatives by children and adults. *Journal of Speech and Hearing Research, 30*, 319–329.

Nittrouer, S., Studdert-Kennedy, M., & McGowan, R. S. (1989). The emergence of phonetic segments: Evidence from the spectral structure of fricative-vowel syllables spoken by children and adults. *Journal of Speech and Hearing Research, 32*, 120–132.

Norris, D. (1994). A quantitative model of reading aloud. *Journal of Experimental Psychology: Human Perception and Performance, 20*, 1212–1232.

Phillips, W. A., Hay, I. M., & Smith, L. S. (1993). Lexicality and pronunciation in a simulated neural net. *British Journal of Mathematical and Statistical Psychology, 46*, 193–205.

Pisoni, D., & Luce, P. (1987). Acoustic–phonetic representations in word recognition. *Cognition, 25*, 21–52.

Plaut, D. C., McClelland, J. L., Seidenberg, M. S., & Patterson, K. E. (1996). Understanding normal and impaired word reading: Computational principles in quasi-regular domains. *Psychological Review, 103*(1), 56–115.

Prince, A., & Pinker, S. (1988). Wickelphone ambiguity. *Cognition, 30*, 189–190.
Pylyshyn, Z. W. (1984). *Computation and cognition: Toward a foundation for cognitive science.* Cambridge, MA: MIT Press/Bradford Books.
Rack, J. P., Snowling, M. J., & Olson, R. K. (1992). The nonword reading deficit in developmental dyslexia: A review. *Reading Research Quarterly, 27*(1), 29–53.
Reed, M. A. (1989). Speech perception and the discrimination of brief auditory cues in reading disabled children. *Journal of Experimental Child Psychology, 48*, 270–292.
Rumelhart, D. E., & McClelland, J. L. (1986). On learning the past tenses of English verbs. In J. L. McClelland & D. E. Rumelhart (Eds.), *Parallel distributed processing: Explorations in the microstructure of cognition* (Vol. 2, pp. 216–271). Cambridge, MA: MIT Press/Bradford Books.
Scarborough, H. S. (1990). Very early language deficits in dyslexic children. *Child Development, 61*, 1728–1743.
Seidenberg, M. S. (1985). The time course of phonological activation in two writing systems. *Cognition, 19*, 1–30.
Seidenberg, M. S., Bruck, M., Fornarolo, G., & Backman, J. (1985). Word recognition processes of poor and disabled readers: Do they necessarily differ? *Applied Psycholinguistics, 6*, 161–180.
Seidenberg, M. S., & McClelland, J. L. (1989). A distributed, developmental model of word recognition and naming. *Psychological Review, 96*(4), 523–568.
Seidenberg, M. S., Plaut, D. C., Petersen, A. S., McClelland, J. L., & McRae, K. (1994). Nonword pronunciation and models of word recognition. *Journal of Experimental Psychology: Human Perception and Performance, 20*, 1177–1196.
Seidenberg, M. S., Waters, G. S., Barnes, M. A., & Tanenhaus, M. K. (1984). When does irregular spelling influence word recognition. *Journal of Verbal Learning and Verbal Behavior, 23*, 383–404.
Sejnowski, T. J., & Rosenberg, C. R. (1987). Parallel networks that learn to pronounce English text. *Complex Systems, 1*, 145–168.
Shepard, R. N. (1987). Towards a universal law of generalization for psychological science. *Science, 237*, 1317–1323.
Siegel, L. S., & Linder, B. A. (1984). Short-term memory processes in children with reading and arithmetic learning disabilities. *Developmental Psychology, 20*(2), 200–207.
Siegel, L. S., & Ryan, E. B. (1988). Development of grammatical-sensitivity, phonological, and short-term memory skills in normally achieving and learning disabled children. *Developmental Psychology, 24*(1), 28–37.
Snowling, M. J., Goulandris, N., Bowlby, M., & Howell, P. (1986). Segmentation and speech perception in relation to reading skill: A developmental analysis. *Journal of Experimental Child Psychology, 41*, 489–507.
Snowling, M. J., Stackhouse, J., & Rack, J. P. (1986). Phonological dyslexia and dysgraphia: A developmental analysis. *Cognitive Neuropsychology, 3*, 309–339.
Stanback, M. L. (1992). Syllable and rime patterns for teaching reading: Analysis of a frequency-based vocabulary of 17,602 words. *Annals of Dyslexia, 42*, 196–220.
Stanovich, K. E., Cunningham, A. E., & Cramer, B. R. (1984). Assessing phonological awareness in kindergarten children: Issues of task comparability. *Journal of Experimental Child Psychology, 38*, 175–190.
Stanovich, K. E., Nathan, R. G., & Zolman, J. E. (1988). The developmental lag hypothesis in reading: Longitudinal and matched reading-level comparisons. *Child Development, 59*, 71–86.
Szeszulski, P. A., & Manis, F. R. (1987). A comparison of word recognition processes in dyslexic and normal readers at two reading-age levels. *Journal of Experimental Child Psychology, 44*, 364–376.
Taraban, R., & McClelland, J. L. (1987). Conspiracy effects in word pronunciation. *Journal of Memory and Language, 26*, 608–631.

Treiman, R., & Breaux, A. M. (1982). Common phoneme and overall similarity relations among spoken word syllables: Their use by children and adults. *Journal of Psycholinguistic Research, 11,* 581–610.

Treiman, R., & Hirsh-Pasek, K. (1985). Are there qualitative differences in reading behavior between dyslexic and normal readers? *Memory & Cognition, 13,* 357–364.

Treiman, R., Mullennix, J., Bijeljac-Babic, R., & Richmond-Welty, E. D. (1995). The special role of rimes in the description, use, and acquisition of English orthography. *Journal of Experimental Psychology: General, 124,* 107–136.

Walley, A. C. (1987). Young children's detections of word-initial and -final mispronunciations in constrained and unconstrained contexts. *Cognitive Development, 2,* 145–167.

Walley, A. C. (1988). Spoken word recognition by young children and adults. *Cognitive Development, 3,* 137–165.

Walley, A. C. (1993). The role of vocabulary development in children's spoken word recognition and segmentation ability. *Developmental Review, 13,* 286–350.

Walley, A. C., & Metsala, J. L. (1990). The growth of lexical constraints on spoken word recognition. *Perception and Psychophysics, 47,* 267–280.

Walley, A. C., & Metsala, J. L. (1992). Young children's age-of-acquisition estimates for spoken words. *Memory & Cognition, 20*(2), 171–182.

Walley, A. C., Michela, V. L., & Flege, J. E. (1994, December). *The development of speech perception: Beyond infancy.* Paper presented at the Acoustical Society of America, Austin, TX.

Walley, A. C., Smith, L. B., & Jusczyk, P. W. (1986). The role or phonemes and syllables in the perceived similarity of speech sounds for children. *Memory & Cognition, 14,* 220–229.

Waters, G. S., & Seidenberg, M. S. (1985). Spelling-sound effects in reading: Time course and decision criteria. *Memory & Cognition, 13,* 557–572.

Waters, G. S., Seidenberg, M. S., & Bruck, M. (1984). Children's and adults' use of spelling-sound information in three reading tasks. *Memory & Cognition, 12,* 293–305.

Watson, F. L., & Brown, G. D. A. (1992). Single word reading in college dyslexics. *Applied Cognitive Psychology, 6,* 263–272.

Werker, J. F., & Tees, R. C. (1987). Speech perception in severely disabled and average reading children. *Canadian Journal of Psychology, 41*(1), 48–61.

Chapter 13

The Origin and Functions of Phonological Representations in Deaf People

Jesus Alegria
Université Libre de Bruxelles

The role of phonological representations in mental activities has been well documented in cognitive psychology. Phonological codes, for instance, are central to theories of short-term memory (STM). Conrad (1962, 1964) showed that a considerable proportion of errors observed in STM experiments are similar to those made when listening in noise, even if the memory items consist of drawings. These results have been extended by demonstrating that memory span is affected by the phonological similarity between items: It is easier to remember series of items that differ phonologically from each other than rhyming items. It has also been shown that series of short words are easier to remember in order than are series of long words. In order to account for these data, models of STM have proposed a rehearsal device that works by reactivating the phonological representations of items held in memory (Baddeley, 1981; Baddeley & Hitch, 1974; Baddeley & Lewis, 1981).

Short-term memory experiments have revealed another phenomenon. Typically, the recall of items presented at the end of a list is better than recall of those in the middle of the list (the recency effect). This effect is more marked for spoken than for written materials (the modality effect). Early theories of the modality effect linked it to the mechanisms responsible for speech processing. The precategorical acoustic store (PAS) proposed by Crowder and Morton (1969) supposed that a raw copy of the acoustical message is briefly stored prior to phonological categorization for subsequent lexical processing (Baddeley & Hitch, 1974). More recently, it has been shown that items presented in lip-reading, that is to say without any acoustical information, produce a recency effect similar to heard materials (Campbell, 1987a; Campbell & Dodd, 1980; Crowder, 1986; Spoehr & Corin, 1978). This shows that an interpretation of the modality effect in terms of sensory input, visual versus auditory, must be incorrect. A more abstract code, common to both hearing and lip-reading but not involved in reading nor in identifying objects or pictures, seems necessary to explain such effects. This code is probably involved in online speech processing. This idea is examined in more detail in this chapter because it is central to understanding the phonological skills of deaf people.

It is argued that models of STM must include at least two different phonological codes to deal with all the data. The first one supports rehearsal. It is independent of the input modality and is related to speech production processes. This code is responsible for phonological errors in STM, and for the effects of rhyme and word length. The second device is related to speech processing from both auditory and lip-read sources, and is responsible for the recency and modality effects.

The phonological codes that underlie STM are submitted to time constraints. Word-length effects in short-term memory can be thought of as reflecting two different time constraints. First, the length of time a phonological code can be held in memory before it decays if it is not thus reactivated by rehearsal, and second, the rate of rehearsal. It is reasonable to argue that activities such as reading and speech, understanding which depend in part on STM, will be constrained by the duration of the phonological codes involved. If phonological codes were deficient or simply absent (as some people have argued they might be in profoundly deaf persons), the consequences for oral and written language processing would be considerable. However, STM processes not supported by phonological codes are perfectly conceivable. An example is given by deaf persons whose mother tongue is sign language. In STM tasks it appears that these people utilize a rehearsal processes that involves the reactivation of internal representations of the lexical units of sign language (Bellugi, Klima, & Siple, 1975).

It is not surprising that STM tasks were among the first used to explore the operation of phonological coding in the deaf (Conrad, 1970, 1972, 1979). Conrad (1979) gave all deaf school leavers in England and Wales in 1975–1976 a STM task involving two conditions defined by the type of words to be retained: phonologically similar but orthographically different (*do, few, true, through,* etc.) and phonologically different but orthographically similar (*bare, have, farm,* etc.). A subject was assumed to use phonological codes if he or she made more errors in the first than in the second condition. In the other case the subject was assumed to use visuoorthographic codes. The results showed that some deaf subjects used each type of code. Moreover, a strong correlation was found between phonological coding and both, speech intelligibility, and reading ability. These correlations remained significant and substantial, even if the effects of hearing loss were controlled.

The Stroop color–word interference task has been used with deaf children in a similar theoretical context (Leybaert & Alegria, 1993; Leybaert, Alegria, & Fonck, 1983). A number of experiments with hearing people have demonstrated that Stroop interference is considerably greater when the subject has to name the color than when he or she has to push a key that corresponds to the color presented according to a preestablished code (Pritchatt, 1968). It has been hypothesized that, while processing the color name, the written word is automatically identified. Consequently both phonological codes, one resulting from processing of the written word and the other from the color input, are activated and interfere with each other. It is supposed that the competition of these two codes accounts for the greatest part of the Stroop interference in the color-naming condition. In the manual response condition however, the interference is weaker because the phonological code evoked by the identification of the written word does not interfere (or not so much) with the color-naming task (Lupker & Katz, 1981). One experiment (Leybaert et al., 1983) examined the interference in a manual and in a naming Stroop task in two groups of orally trained deaf subjects, one having good speech intelligibility and the other poor speech intelligibility, and in a group of hearing controls. The interference in the manual task evaluated by the difference between the interfering condition (i.e., *bleu* written in red) and the control one (i.e., series of consonants written in red) was significant and almost identical in all of the three groups. A substantial increase in interference was observed in the naming task, but only in the hearing and in the good-speech-intelligibility deaf groups. The increase in interference in the poor-speech-intelligibility group was smaller and unreliable. All of the deaf subjects in the experiment were profoundly deaf. Thus, as in Conrad's short-term memory study, the intelligibility differences cannot be explained in terms of hearing loss. These results indicate that word and color identification do not automatically evoke the corresponding phonological output code in the deaf who have not developed intelligible speech.

A third source of evidence concerning phonological coding in the deaf that is worth mentioning in the present context is spelling (Leybaert & Alegria, 1995). Words whose spelling was directly derivable from their surface phonology (e.g., in French: *bleu, cartable*, etc.) were compared with words that were opaque from this point of view (in French: *pull, attention*, etc.). The results showed an important effect of phonological transparency at all of the ages considered. This effect, although highly reliable, was considerably weaker than the one obtained with groups of hearing children matched with the deaf groups, for their performance in either the opaque condition or the phonological condition. This demonstrates that deaf children possess the phonological representations of the words they know, and use it in order to write them. If their spelling mechanisms were based exclusively on the orthographic representations of words, an advantage for the phonological over the opaque condition would not be observed. The results also showed that the role played by phonology increases with age in the deaf subjects, suggesting that the accuracy of phonological word representations and/or the accuracy of their translation into orthography improves with age. It remains, however, far below the level demonstrated by the group of hearing controls (for converging evidence obtained with deaf adults, see Hanson, Shankweiler, & Fischer, 1983).

More than 90% of the errors in the group of normally hearing children were an acceptable transcription of the surface phonology of the target word. This proportion was considerably smaller in the deaf children. In accordance with previously reported data and speculation, however, it depended on the deaf children's speech intelligibility. In the poor-speech-intelligibility group, the proportion of spelling errors that were phonologically acceptable transcriptions was about 20%, and did not increase with age. In the good-speech-intelligibility group, however, this proportion reached 50% in the oldest group of children.

The three experimental paradigms considered thus far—STM, the Stroop color–word interference task, and the analysis of spelling performance—show a striking convergence. In each case, individual differences depend on the intelligibility of speech production of the subjects. In the first two cases, the activation of phonological codes has detrimental effects on performance (this is particularly strong in the Stroop case, in which the subjects were totally aware of the negative effects of their tendency to pronounce the word's name). The fact that phonological codes affect performance in those conditions shows that their activation is automatic in the deaf, just as in hearing subjects. It is important to add that the phonological codes revealed in these experiments are exclusively postlexical. One cannot infer from this that the deaf possess prelexical phonological codes.

Many models of written word identification involve a mechanism that translates orthographic strings into phonological ones. The phonological assembler proposed by Patterson and Morton (1985) is a good example of this kind of device. The importance of this mechanism is that it provides the possibility of phonological access to the lexicon. Evidence concerning the activity of the phonological assembler comes from experiments combining factors such as frequency or lexicality of the item on the one hand, with factors like length and spelling-to-sound regularity on the other hand. The basic assumption is that factors determining the contribution of the phonological assembler to word identification should interact with word frequency and/or lexicality which determine direct access. The notion of identification does not apply to pseudowords for obvious reasons. In the latter case, assembling a phonological code necessarily depends on the activity of the phonological assembler.

With this theoretical background, a group of 19 deaf adolescents aged from 14 to 20 years was tested in a series of tasks of reading aloud isolated items (for a more extended report of these data, see Leybaert, 1993). The items were presented one by one on the screen of a computer, and the latency of the response was measured from the stimulus presentation to the beginning of the subject's response. The oral response was also recorded in order to analyze its accuracy. Adequate precautions were taken to separate genuine reading errors from articulatory ones.

Numerous aspects of the results demonstrate that the reading of the deaf involves phonological assembly. The most obvious evidence was their correct pronunciation of many pseudowords, which shows that they can translate strings of letters into their corresponding strings of phonemes. Performance on pseudowords derived from words by changing one letter (e.g., *tur* from *dur* [hard]) was poorer than the performance for the corresponding words. This was also true in the control group of hearing subjects. It is important to emphasize that this effect of lexicality was not exclusively due to the fact that it is easier to articulate familiar words (e.g., *dur*) than unfamiliar pseudowords (e.g., *tur*). This potential explanation of the data has been excluded with a condition including two kinds of pseudowords: pseudohomophones on the one hand, and the corresponding control pseudowords on the other. The pseudohomophones were pronounced like words (e.g., *maizon* and *wazau*, which are pronounced like the French words *maison* [house] and *oiseau* [bird]), so a lexical facilitation at response level could be detected. The results show that the effect of lexicality was still present with pseudohomophones, but it was significantly smaller than the one obtained with the control pseudowords. These data reveal the activity of the phonological assembler when pronouncing pseudowords.

To further explore the activity of the phonological assembler in word identification, a comparison was made between frequent and rare words made of four, six, or eight letters (e.g., *seul* [alone], *soleil* [sun], and *souvenir* [memory, recollection] vs. *scie* [saw], *surnom* [nickname], and *salsifis* [salsify]). Frequency affected the latency and accuracy of the responses in the deaf as well as in the normally hearing groups of subjects. As expected, the effects of length were weaker for the frequent than for the infrequent words in both groups of subjects. This indicates that the deaf as well as hearing subjects have developed an assembly procedure that contributes to the identification of infrequent words to a greater extent.

This conclusion depends on data from the pronunciation of pseudowords and infrequent words, some of which were probably unknown to the deaf children. To check that the assembly procedure actually participates in the identification of familiar words, the reading of irregular words was considered. The application of an assembly procedure in this case produces regularizations (e.g., reading /fem/ instead of /fam/ for *femme* [woman]) that can interfere with the pronunciation stored in the lexicon. Special precautions were to be taken because sometimes deaf children produced the regularized response not only when presented with the written version of some words, but also in picture naming or when spontaneously pronouncing the words. This is because the phonology associated with lexical items comes sometimes from an orthographic representation of the word (data on a rhyme decision task examined later in this chapter are a good example of this). To eliminate this artifact, the subjects were asked to name a drawing of each of the irregular words used in the experiment. Only those words correctly pronounced in this case were considered. This control guarantees that the words were known by the subject and that he possessed the correct phonological code for the words. The results show a small but reliable effect of regularity with frequent words (the percentage of errors was 17% and 25% for regular and irregular words, respectively) and a stronger one with rare words (17% and 43%, respectively).

The evidence reviewed here leads to the conclusion that word reading in deaf children is not limited to visuoorthographic recognition, but that these children possess and use a device that generates prelexical phonological codes that may support recognition (for a more detailed discussion on this point, see Leybaert, 1993). Hence, the deaf may access the lexicon by using a phonological code. Together with the results of experiments on STM, Stroop interference in a color-naming task, and with the analysis of spelling production, it seems that a substantial proportion of the deaf population possess language representations that are accessible from a phonological code. Besides this, the access to one particular item in the lexicon automatically evokes the corresponding phonological code.

LIP-READING AND SPEECH PERCEPTION IN DEAF AND HEARING PEOPLE

The role assigned to lip-reading was, until the mid-1970s, rather modest, although it was recognized that lip-reading improves speech understanding in poor hearing conditions (Binnie, Montgomery, & Jackson, 1974; Erber, 1969, 1974; Sumby & Pollack, 1954). The fact that the visual component of the speech signal is not necessary for speech understanding seemed a sufficient reason to consider its role as quite limited. Indeed, hearing subjects understand radio programs and phone calls, and children born blind develop normal speech comprehension ability. More recently, the benefits of lip-reading have been extended to cases where the auditory signal was easy to hear but the message difficult to understand; for example, listening to an unfamiliar language or a difficult text (Reisberg, McLean, & Goldfield, 1987).

In all of these cases the results can be interpreted without giving lip-reading any role at the level of phonological processing. A possible interpretation of the experimental results was that lip-reading facilitates speech perception by drawing the listener's attention to the moments when important acoustic events could happen. This notion is incompatible with data reported by Summerfield (1991), who showed that fluorescent lips in the dark improve speech comprehension but a circle whose diameter is modulated by the lips' gap doesn't. The last stimulus preserves the temporal pattern given by the lips, but apparently this is not the relevant input.

A common idea implicitly adopted by virtually all models was that lip-read information is optional; that is to say that it can be exploited if the subject feels that it could be useful, and ignored otherwise. Data collected during the last 20 years, however, have shown that when the listener sees the speaker's face, he or she cannot ignore the lip-read information. The visual information accompanying speech production inevitably integrates into an audiovisual compound that is identified as a speech sound that can differ from the auditory signal. McGurk and McDonald (1976) showed that seeing a face pronouncing the syllable /ga/ while simultaneously hearing /ba/ produces an intermediate percept /da/. Similarly, a visual /ka/ combined with an auditory /pa/ produces a "heard" /ta/. If auditory and visual stimuli are inverted, that is, when the visual stimulus presents a bilabial feature, /ba/ or /pa/, this feature is inevitably included in the subject's impression, which sounds /bga/ or /bda/ (or /pka/–/pta/). These results have been confirmed, and their consequences for speech processing theories were developed by Massaro (1987, 1989). Their main point is that they convincingly demonstrate that speech processing must be considered as an audiovisual phenomenon.

Human beings, from birth, often see the face of a talking person: They are presented with highly correlated audiovisual speech. It might then be reasonable to imagine that the speech processing system progressively unites the lip-read information with auditory information from the speech signal. Studies concerning the McGurk effect on children have shown that it is present in 4- to 6-year-olds (Massaro, 1987; McGurk & McDonald, 1976). At those ages the connection between both events has had plenty of time to establish itself. Similar results have been obtained using the preference paradigm with infants. Dodd (1977) showed that 10- to 16-week-old infants devoted more attention to speech when sound and lip movements were synchronized than when they were out of synchrony by 400 msec. In a similar vein, Kuhl and Meltzoff (1982) and McKain, Studdert-Kennedy, Spieker, and Stern (1983) demonstrated that 4- to 6-month-old infants presented with two faces preferred to look at the face executing the articulatory gesture corresponding to the stimulus simultaneously presented through audition. As a matter of fact, the results obtained cannot be interpreted in terms of a simple sensitivity to audiovisual synchronization, because both visually presented syllables were synchronized with the auditory one. These results indicate that the visual lip-read information was processed in a linguistically relevant manner. Impressive as they are, these data do not prove that lip-reading is integrated into a hard-wired speech module, and it is possible that the connection between heard and seen speech becomes established during the first weeks of life. Two facts are compatible with this hypothesis. First is the infant's ability to imitate facial gestures, most of them involving the mouth, soon after birth (Field, Woodson, Greenberg, & Cohen, 1982; Meltzoff & Moore, 1977). Second is the delicate sensitivity to phonologically relevant auditory contrasts that can be observed at the age of 3 or 4 weeks (Bertoncini, Bijeljac-Babic, Jusczyk, Kennedy, & Mehler, 1988; Eimas, Siqueland, Jusczyk, & Vigorito, 1971).

In the context of the present discussion of phonological representations in the deaf, it would be extremely important to determine the origin of the correlation between auditory and visual information in speech perception. If exposure to massive, highly correlated, audiovisual speech was not the mechanism that creates an integrated speech processor, then we would have to conclude that the speech processor is prewired to treat lip-read information. In that case it would be conceivable that exposure to lip-reading alone, as in the case in deaf infants, would be sufficient to activate the speech processor.

The notion that lip-read information is integrated into the speech perception device forces to admit the existence of abstract speech representations common to both the auditory and the visual speech signals (see Summerfield, 1987, 1991, for a thorough discussion concerning the form that this common metric must possess; and Liberman & Mattingly, 1985, for a revision of the motor theory of speech perception). Thus, the phonological codes that are involved in a number of mental activities also have a visual lip-read dimension, at least in normally hearing individuals. From the perspective of the deaf this is as good news, insofar as it draws their phonological representations closer to those of normally hearing subjects. The main problem in their case is that lip-reading alone is insufficient to deliver much useful speech because of its intrinsic ambiguity. To take an example from the earliest referential items, French words like *papa* (/papa/) and *maman* (/mamã/) correspond to identical lip-read forms.

The next section examines the possible effects of an important reduction of this ambiguity.

CUED SPEECH (CS): A MANUAL AID TO LIP-READING

Blind children develop language in a basically normal manner, whereas deaf children don't. This is because, for speech, visual information alone is far more ambiguous than auditory information. Lexical development requires relatively systematic relationships between referents and the corresponding phonological forms (words) and lip-reading cannot reliably supply them. However, lip-reading does account for most of deaf children's phonological development (Dodd, 1976). At the same time, the deaf rarely develop useful speech from lip-reading alone. This situation has frequently led speech therapists and teachers of the deaf to add systematic signals, usually visual but sometimes tactile, to lip-reading in order to reduce its ambiguity. A good illustration of this idea, taken from studies of normally hearing subjects, is the demonstration that the understanding of speech dramatically improves if an auditory buzzer modulated by the vocal fold activity is added to lip-reading. The vocal fold activity gives essential information about voicing, a basic phonological feature that is totally absent in lip-reading (Rosen, Fourcin, & Moore, 1981). It is interesting to note that the buzzer alone conveys nothing of speech. This suggests that in some special contexts speech and nonspeech information can combine in a meaningful way.

This section deals with a system called cued speech (CS), which was developed to help deaf children to understand speech by eliminating the ambiguity of lip-read (Cornett, 1967; see also Périer, 1987, for a comparison of CS with some other similar systems). In CS, the speaker holds one hand near the mouth while speaking so that the listener can see the lips and the hand at the same time. In the French version of CS, the hand can adopt eight shapes and five different positions around the mouth. Hand shapes are for disambiguating consonants, and hand positions for disambiguating vowels. Consonants and vowels have been independently grouped into sets of two or three items, and each set has its specific hand shape or hand position. Shapes and positions are assigned to groups of consonants and vowels in such a way that items sharing the same hand shape or hand position are easy to discriminate by lip-reading, whereas items that are difficult to discriminate belong to different groups. Thus, a particular hand shape is shared by /p, d, ʒ/, a different one by /b, n, w/, a third one by /f, t, m/, and so on. For the vowels, one position is shared by /i, ɔ̃, ã/, a second one by /a, o, ə/, and so on. As a result of this organization, each time the speaker produces a "cue" (a particular, hand shape at one specific position) while pronouncing a CV syllable, he or she is giving unambiguous phonological information about this structure. Syllabic structures like VC, CCV, CVC, and so on, include additional cues to reveal the supplementary phones. (This question is not considered in this report. For a thorough examination of it, see Alegria, Charlier, & Mattys, submitted.) The whole system appears at first sight somewhat complex and artificial. In fact, it is relatively easy to learn and, with some practice, normally hearing adults succeed in using it with little slowing from their normal rate of speaking.

It is worth contrasting CS with other systems sharing similar aims. One well-known system is finger spelling. This system differs from CS in that it consists of an alphabetic representation of speech using hand shapes for letters, whereas CS represents speech at phonetic level: items are coded as they are pronounced. In a number of other systems, the hands (or other devices accompanying speech like tactile cues) give phonetic information in a direct way, often at a subphonetic level. A typical case is that in which particular signs are used to indicate that an item is voiced, nasal, or presents some other phonetic feature. This is radically different from CS, in which hands alone don't give any direct phonetic information: There is no hand shape or hand position that can be interpreted as a phonetic feature without taking the lips into consideration.

The intrinsic ambiguity of lip-read information is, as stated earlier, an obstacle to referential clarity and to speech understanding and speech development. CS is a system that, in principle, eliminates all of these ambiguities. Let one suppose that this were the only obstacle. In that case, nothing essential would distinguish deaf children raised in a family using CS to communicate from their normally hearing peers. An interesting situation has arisen from the fact that some schools, including one in Brussels, have adopted CS, and some parents have adopted it to communicate with their deaf children from the very beginning. This situation constitutes a real challenge for studies of the cognitive development of the deaf. Can words made of a sequence of lip postures accompanied by a systematic sequence of hand shapes and positions be processed, interpreted, stored, retrieved, and used in cognitive activities in a way equivalent to audiovisual speech? The a priori answer of Cornett was *yes*. We next present some empirical studies that allow us to go further.

Speech Processing and Cued Speech

Nicholls (1979) and Nicholls and Ling (1982) reported systematic data concerning speech understanding with CS. The experiment was done in a school in Australia where CS had been introduced about 10 years before. Eighteen deaf children aged from 9 to 16, who had been exposed to CS for at least 4 years, were presented with sentences for lip-reading alone or accompanied by CS. Their task was to identify the last word in the sentence. The percentage of correct responses increased from 40% in lip-reading to 95% in CS conditions.

Similarly, in our studies, a group of 55 deaf students aged from 5 years, 11 months to 16 years, 1 month were given a sentence comprehension task (Charlier, Hage, Alegria, & Périer, 1990; a preliminary report with a group of 24 students was published in Périer, Charlier, Hage, & Alegria, 1987). Fourteen used CS at home (the "home" group), and the others used it exclusively at school (the "school" group). The subjects were presented with sentences to lip-read with and without CS. Their task was to choose the one drawing out of a set of four that corresponded to the sentence. The results showed that CS brought significant improvements in the critical condition in both groups. The improvement, however, was weaker in the school group than in the home one. Correct responses in the most difficult condition (the most ambiguous from a lip-reading point of view) increased from 37% correct to 53%, with CS in the school group. The corresponding results in the home group were 39% and 72%. It is suggestive that the age at which the child had been exposed to CS was significantly and negatively correlated with the gain allowed by CS: The earlier children were exposed to CS, the greater was the observed improvement. This variable, however, was confounded with the total duration of the exposure to CS. A reanalysis of the data aimed at exploring this question was performed. Subgroups of home and school children paired for the duration of their exposure to CS were considered. The former subgroup was obviously younger than the latter: 8 years, 6 months and 12 years, 1 month, respectively. However, the improvement observed when CS was present was still greater in the home than in the school group, despite the fact that the home group was younger.

The extent to which CS improves the lip-reading of spoken items in deaf schoolchildren has been further explored in a third experiment (Alegria et al., submitted). One of the main aims of this experiment was to study the possible effects of the age at which children had been exposed to CS. Two groups were considered: early and late. The former group ($n = 7$) was aged from 8 years, 6 months to 12 years, 0 months (mean 10 years, 9 months). These children had started using CS with their parents at home before the age of 2 as the ordinary way to communicate. The mean duration of their exposure to CS was 9 years, 5 months. The "late" group ($n = 24$) was aged 11 years, 8 months to 19 years, 10 months (mean 15 years, 9 months). Their exposure to CS had begun later in their lives (usually at 6), and with two exceptions they used it exclusively at school (the two exceptions corresponded to cases where the parents adopted CS after their children reached the age of 2, and used it in a rather unsystematic way). The mean duration of exposure to CS in this group reached 6 years, 5 months. The task consisted in identifying words and phonologically paired pseudowords in lip-reading with and without CS. All of the items had four phonemes grouped into two syllables. Pseudoword material was included to obtain a clearer measure of how CS contributes to the perception of phonological strings without any lexical contribution. For this reason, separate blocks were run for words and pseudowords.

Figure 13.1 shows the percentage of correct responses for each group and condition. The performance of early and late groups overall was similar: 47% and 39% of correct responses, respectively. It is important to remember, however, that the late group was considerably older than the early group (15 years, 9 months and 10 years, 9 months, respectively). In order to obtain a better control of the age effects, a subgroup of the six youngest children from the late group was considered. This subgroup was still older than the early group but their ages were more similar (from 11 years, 8 months to 12 years, 11 months, mean 12 years, 4 months). The data presented in Fig. 13.1 show that when this age control is done, the difference between the early and late groups is considerable. The gain induced

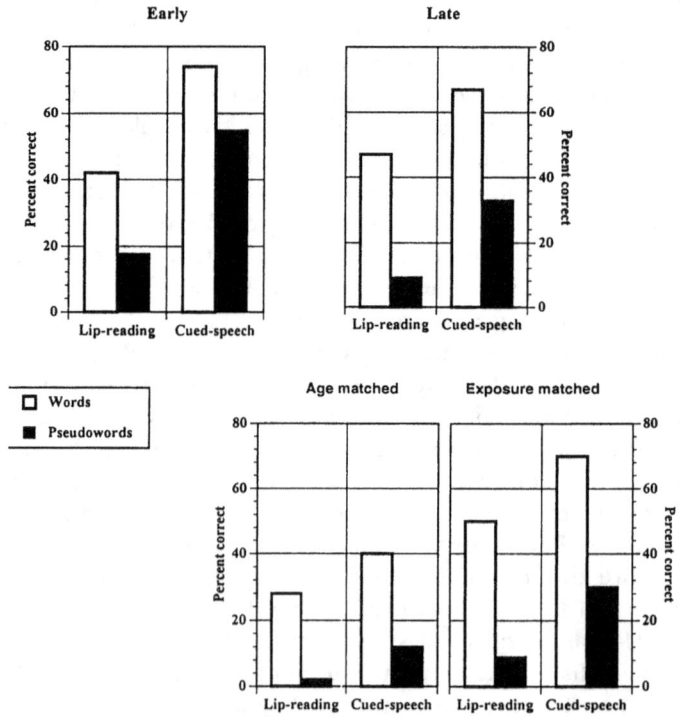

FIG. 13.1. Mean percentage of correct responses in the Phonological Strings Identification task per condition and group of subjects.

by CS was significantly greater in the early than in the late group, even if the age factor was not controlled. It is important to add that the group by lexicality interaction was also significant, indicating that although the groups did not differ from each other in word identification, a reliable difference favouring the early group appeared in pseudoword processing.

The differences observed between early and late groups of children cannot be directly attributed to how early the children had been exposed to CS, because children given earlier exposure had also received CS for longer overall. To evaluate the possible effects of the age at which exposure to CS began, controlling for exposure to CS duration, a subgroup of children from the late group was paired one by one with those of the early group on the bases of the duration of the exposure to CS (mean duration 9 years, 5 months, and 9 years, 1 month in early and late groups, respectively). The latte group was obviously older than the early group (15 years, 0 months and 10 years, 9 months, respectively). The results of this subgroup appear in Fig. 13.1. The results showed that the main difference between groups failed to reach a significant level, whereas group by cueing and group by lexicality interactions were both significant. This indicates that CS processing as well as pure nonlexical, phonological processing depended more strongly on how early children began to use CS than on the total length of time in which they had been using it.

These results show that CS reduces the ambiguity of lip-read information. This effect is particularly strong in deaf children who have been exposed to CS at an early age. This suggests that CS information could be a basic element of speech development and speech representation. Two projects are exploring some aspects of this question. The first concerns the development of morphological and syntactic items that are poorly represented in lip-read speech: CS might be expected to be especially important for learning these forms. The second concerns the role played by CS in the lexical representations of deaf people.

The first problem has been tackled by considering the capacity of deaf children, who had learned CS, to deal with French grammatical gender. This question was chosen for several reasons. First, derivational and grammatical morphology is quite poor in the deaf (see Swisher, 1976, for an examination of their performance on the classical Brown's 14 first English morphemes [Brown, 1973], see also a study in Italian by Taeschner, Devescovi, & Volterra, 1988; showing delays and in some cases deviations in gender morphology), whereas it has been demonstrated that normally hearing French-speaking children have productive control of gender morphology by three years (Karmiloff-Smith, 1979). Second, gender is phonologically marked at noun endings in a way that is not totally systematic: Nouns that end with /ɛt(ə)/ are almost certainly feminine words and those that end in /o/ masculine, whereas /wa/ endings are unmarked, that is to say that there exist as many words ending with /wa/ that are feminine as are masculine. To develop productive competence in gender morphophonology, the subject has to relate noun endings with other gender-marks such as articles, pronouns, and adjectives. This task is difficult for the deaf, because articles and pronouns are often short and usually unstressed.

The experiment involved asking subjects to classify drawings of common and unfamiliar objects in feminine and masculine categories (Hage, 1994; Hage, Alegria, & Périer, 1991). In the first experiment, nine subjects that had had intensive CS practice (three at school only for at least 8 years, and the six others at school and at home since before the age of 2) were considered. Their mean age was 10 years, 11 months (from 4 years, 6 months to 21 years, 0 months). The experimenter showed each drawing to the subject while pronouncing its name using CS. The subject had to orally repeat the name preceded by the corresponding article. The results for common names were rather good for marked as well as unmarked items (90% and 94% correct, respectively). For the unfamiliar unmarked nouns, the percentage of correct responses was exactly 50% (chance level), thus showing that the subjects didn't know these infrequent nouns. The score reached 75% correct for the unfamiliar marked items, significantly better than the chance level. These results indicated that subjects intensively exposed to CS were able to derive the grammatical gender of an unknown word based solely on its phonological properties at an exceptionally good level for the deaf.

The previous experiment did not include a control group of deaf subjects for technical reasons. To deal with this problem a new experiment was done with a number of deaf subjects with different family and school histories (Hage, 1994). Two groups of children were considered, one who had had CS at home and another group intensively trained by oral methods that did not include CS. The children in both groups were matched for vocabulary knowledge and lip-reading ability. The CS group was of 32 children, mean age 11 years, 3 months (from 6 years, 11 months to 17 years, 8 months). The classic oral group was of 21 children, mean age 13 years, 8 months (from 6 years, 11 months to 17 years, 8 months). The oral training of this group had begun at home at an age between 3 and 30 months. It was expected that, at equivalent levels of lexical ability, CS children would do much better than children in the purely oral group in dealing with grammatical gender. This is because grammatical gender understanding involves the ability to manipulate short and inconspicuous phonological strings, like word endings and articles, and CS would be expected to convey this tenuous phonological information more effectively than would classical oral methods.

The results showed that both groups were rather good on the common words task (above 80% correct). The groups differed, however, on the unfamiliar words: 66% and 48% for CS and oral groups, respectively, with unmarked words, and 76% and 61% with marked ones. The difference observed between groups at attributing grammatical gender to unmarked unfamiliar words indicated that the CS group knew more about these items than the oral group. So the difference between groups in improvement observed from unmarked to marked words could not be unambiguously interpreted.

To deal with this question, subjects of both groups matched on their results with unfamiliar, unmarked words were considered. The new CS group was of 14 deaf children aged between 6 years, 11 months and 14 years, 11 months (mean 10 years, 8 months) and the matched oral group was of 10 children, aged between 10 years, 11 months and 17 years, 8 months (mean 14 years, 10 months). Figure 13.2 represents the results obtained by these groups. The effect of marking on unfamiliar words was now reliably greater in the CS than in the oral group. Thus, children selected because they had had intense and precocious oral training, as well as for their exceptional success at lexical comprehension assessed by vocabulary knowledge, were nevertheless worse than those who had had CS when tested on subtle morphophonological information. The advantage of the CS group probably results from the efficiency of CS in revealing aspects of morphophonology usually hidden in lip-reading.

The second issue mentioned earlier was the possible effect of lip-reading combined with CS in the development of the phonological representations of lexical items. Two experimental situations were used to examine this question: short-term memory and a rhyme decision task (Charlier, 1994; Leybaert & Charlier, 1996). As previously mentioned, the results of numerous experiments on short-term memory demonstrate that a variety of memory codes are used by the deaf: phonological, visuoorthographic, dactylic, and sign language based, partially depending on their linguistic and

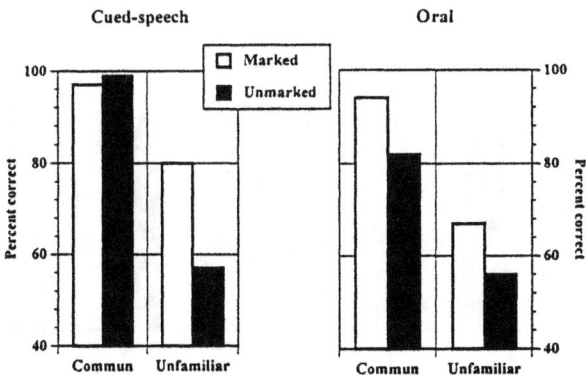

FIG. 13.2. Mean percentage of correct responses in the Grammatical Gender Attribution task per condition and group of subjects.

school background. Deaf subjects were divided in two groups: the "early" group ($n = 12$, age from 5 years, 8 months to 11 years, 0 months, mean age 8 years, 8 months) had adopted and used CS at home before the age of three, and the "late" group of children ($n = 14$, age from 8 years, 0 months to 13 years, 0 months, mean age 10 years, 9 months) were attending schools that had adopted methods of communication including "signed French," dactylology, and CS. A control group of hearing children was also included ($n = 30$, age from 8 years, 5 months to 11 years, 0 months, mean age 8 years, 4 months). Three series of eight drawings each were used. In the control condition the names of the drawings were monosyllabic (*chat* [cat], *feu* [fire], *banc* [bench], etc.). In the rhyming condition, the names of the drawings rhymed (*dé* [dice], *nez* [nose], *thé* [tea], etc). In the length condition, the names were of three or four syllables (*crocodile, télévision, portemanteau*, [coat rack], etc.). The experimenter showed a certain number of cards, one at a time, for about 2 seconds, while pronouncing its name. Then she put them in a row, face down. As soon as the last card had been presented, the experimenter put a strip of cardboard on the table on which the eight cards from the condition appeared. The child was asked to push each of the face-down cards in front of the corresponding ones on the strip. The number of cards was individually determined in the control condition in order to reach a performance slightly greater than 50% correct. The mean number of cards adopted was 5.2 (from 4 to 6), 4.9 (from 4 to 5), and 5.2 (from 4 to 7) in the early, late, and hearing groups, respectively.

The results are summarized in Fig. 13.3. The children from the early group and the normally hearing controls presented a very similar pattern of results, whereas the late group showed no differences in recall between conditions. Both early CS and hearing controls showed marked sensitivity to rhyme and to spoken word-length in their recall. If anything, the effects

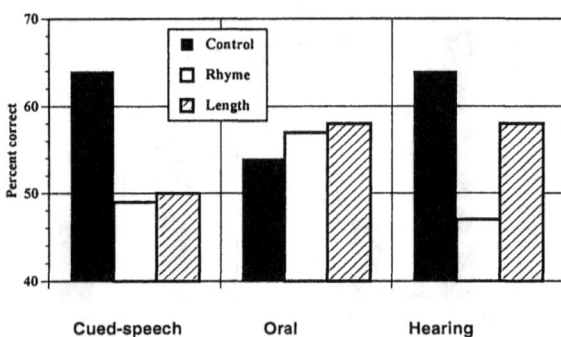

FIG. 13.3. Mean percentage of correct responses in the Short Term Memory task per condition and group of subjects.

of lengthening the words and introducing rhymes impaired the performance of the early CS children more than that of the hearing children. As a matter of fact, the length effect was significant in early subjects but failed to reach significance in the hearing group. There could be several explanations for this. The most likely is that hearing children rehearsed more quickly by using shortened version of the words ("croco" for *crocodile*, "tévé" for *télévision*, etc.).

Charlier (1994) and Leybaert and Charlier (1996) considered a second task to explore the nature of speech representations in deaf children. The subjects' task was to decide whether two items rhymed or not. The items were presented as pairs of drawings, and half of the pairs rhymed. In the case of rhyming items two conditions were considered: rhyming–orthographically similar (*pain–train* [bread–train]) and rhyming–orthographically different (*tasse–glace* [cup–ice]). The nonrhyming items were also divided into two conditions: nonrhyming but similar at lip-reading level (*train* /tRɛ̃/–*pied* /piɛ/; the items' endings are identical for lip-reading, /ɛ̃/ and /ɛ/, respectively); and nonrhyming differing in lip-reading (*robe* /Rɔb/–*bale* /bal/). The subjects were drawn from three groups according to the same criteria as in the previous (STM) experiment. The results are shown in Fig. 13.4.

In the orthographically similar rhyming condition as well as in the lip-reading different nonrhyming condition, all of the groups approached ceiling performance. In the rhyming but orthographically different condition, however, the late group fell to 74% correct "yes" responses, whereas the other two groups remained at more than 90% correct. Thus, when items rhyme but do not have similar orthographic endings, subjects trained exclusively at school with CS were often induced into false negative responses. It must be borne in mind that the items were presented as draw-

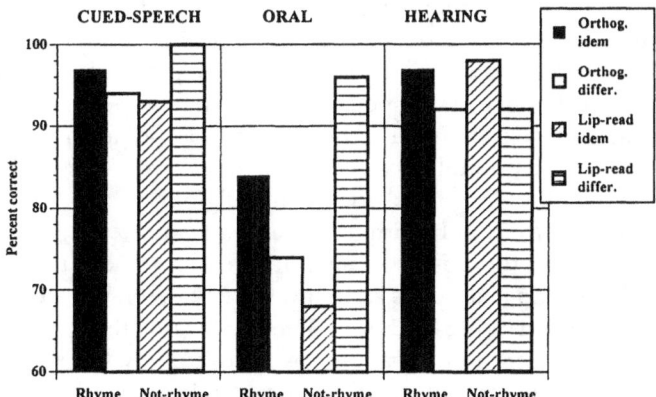

FIG. 13.4. Mean percentage of correct responses in the Rhyme Decision task per condition and group of subjects.

ings, and hence the experiment itself did not induce orthographically based responses. One possible interpretation for these errors is that some classically orally trained subjects derive the phonology of words from their orthographic representation. It is important to notice, however, that the score reached by this group clearly demonstrated that their rhyme judgments were not exclusively based on orthographic information (see Campbell & Wright, 1988; Hanson & Fowler, 1987; Hanson & McGarr, 1987, for partially contrasting results). The fact that the early CS group and hearing subjects were not influenced by orthography suggests that their phonological representations are sufficiently accurate and complete to support their rhyme judgments. The results in the nonrhyming but similar lip-reading condition also revealed differences among groups that are worth considering. The late group's performance decreased to 68% correct, whereas the other two groups remained above 90% correct. This confirms the findings and speculations of Dodd and Hermelin (1977) and Dodd (1987) that lip-reading constitutes the main input for phonological development in the deaf. The present results reveal that some deaf children tended to consider as homophones items that are identical on lip-reading. In contrast, the results of the early CS group indicate that the precocious use of CS allows the development of phonological contrasts between words whose distinguishing features are not visible on the lips.

SUMMARY AND QUESTIONS FOR FURTHER RESEARCH

The starting point of this chapter was the idea that phonological representations are crucial to many cognitive activities and that the development of these representations is critically dependent on the integrity of the auditory system. The question, then, is to understand how some deaf children apparently develop and use a phonological system. The results obtained by deaf youngsters in different experimental tasks (STM, Stroop color–word interference, and spelling) show that some of them possess phonological representations with the same properties as those of hearing people. The use of phonological codes in cognitive tasks in the deaf is closely related to these subjects' speech intelligibility.

These data, however, only address the role of postlexical phonology. In the case of the deaf, there is no compelling reason to admit the existence of prelexical phonological codes as an interface between the auditory signal and the lexical word representation. The analysis of the mechanisms involved in written word identification was motivated by the search for evidence for the existence of a phonological code used in lexical access. Numerous aspects of the results produced by deaf children educated in a classical oral tradition show that they carry out phonological assembly as hearing children do. The conclusion is that the deaf, like the hearing, do use a phonological code to access the lexicon.

Because deaf children clearly do possess phonological representations, we must consider their origins. One obvious source of phonology is lip-reading. Dodd (1976) argued convincingly that the development of a phonological system in the deaf child can be easily understood by assuming that lip-reading is its main source. Some aspects of our data on spelling (Leybaert & Alegria, 1995) as well as on the rhyme decision task (Charlier, 1994) reveal that lip-reading visibility has quite massive effects on the phonological representations of words.

Cued speech, which is designed to help eliminate the ambiguity of lip-read cues, was examined in this context. Experiments comparing the perception of speech materials with and without CS conclusively demonstrated improvements when CS was added to lip-reading, especially in children exposed to CS from an early age. These children were also more sensitive to word endings related to French grammatical gender that have low phonological salience.

The short-term memory and the rhyme decision tasks revealed notable differences between children precociously exposed to CS at home and children who have had a classic oral training including CS at school. In the latter group, the representations of words were mainly based on lip-reading, possibly improved by orthographic knowledge. The subjects in the former group, however, have phonological representations of words indistinguishable from those of hearing children. It seems reasonable to admit that, for them, CS has allowed the establishment of phonemic contrasts that are invisible in lip-reading.

The data discussed so far demonstrate that CS participates both in speech processing and in the creation of the speech representations used in memory tasks. A question for future studies is to determine how lip-reading and CS combine with each other to produce a unique speech percept. Two extreme models are possible. One supposes that the CS–lip-reading compound is perceived phonemically. The phoneme is the minimal speech unit allowing meaning distinctions. It is an abstract unit, hence there is no logical obstacle to the idea of CS and lip-read information combining to specify phonemic contrasts. The second interpretation supposes that both classes of clues—the lips and hands ones—are processed hierarchically, the former providing the core phonological information and the latter intervening afterward to solve the remaining ambiguities.

In the hierarchical view, the role of CS in speech perception is rather superficial: It works as an additional source of information in a kind of problem-solving task. In contrast, in the phonemic view, CS is thought of as one of the inputs to an automatic speech processing device. An obvious objection to the phonemic view would be that the speech processing device cannot handle artificial inputs, like the hand shapes and hand positions of CS. However, Rosen et al. (1981) demonstrated that the addition of an auditory nonspeech signal (a buzzer modulated by the pitch contour of the speaker's voice) to lip-reading substantially improves speech perception. This suggests that an artificial nonspeech stimulus can be integrated with natural lip-reading in speech processing. Campbell (personal communication) mentioned that, after some training, the subjects in this task reported that they experienced the introduction of the buzzer as if "the sound was added to the TV images." In a similar vein, Fowler and Dekle (1991) showed that acoustic syllables are integrated with synchronously presented haptic information (the subject places his or her fingers on the lips of the model pronouncing a syllable), producing a McGurk-like effect.

These examples suggest that the speech processing system can accept a variety of signals as if they possessed a phonetic value. However, the cues used in CS cannot be likened directly to the buzzer or haptic cues because the subjects in those experiments were normally hearing adults who possessed representations of the cues given by the buzzer or by the felt lips. It is certainly not obvious that a 5- or a 6-year-old deaf child who does not have phonological representations of some phonetic contrasts (e.g., voicing), can use CS to distinguish /p/ from /b/, and /ʒ/ from /ʃ/. But this may be different when CS is used as a way to communicate between infant and parents. The question in this case is not whether CS could participate in the perception of phonemic contrasts, but rather in the development of these contrasts. This probably depends on the early use of CS. Indeed, the results showing that children exposed to CS intensively and from an early age possess speech representations indistinguishable from those of normally hearing children supports this hypothesis. It is possible that children given early exposure to CS may use it directly in the creation of phonemic representations of speech, whereas children only given CS later may only be able to use it in a limited, problem-solving way. It is hard to go further in this discussion without evidence to constrain speculation; however, the question is an important one, because it involves basic questions about the operation of the speech processing device. If it could be demonstrated that CS is indeed incorporated into this device in some deaf children, as lip-reading clearly is in hearing subjects, we would have evidence in the domain of speech for "hearing" lips and hands as well as voices.

ACKNOWLEDGMENTS

This word was supported by a grant (no. 3.4571.94) from the Belgium F.R.S.M. (Fonds de la Recherche Scientifique Medicale). I wish to thank my "old" colleagues Olivier Périer and Jacqueline Leybaert, and even more specially my "new" ones, Brigitte Charlier and Catherine Hage, whose recent doctoral theses are the hard core of this chapter.

REFERENCES

Alegria, J., Charlier, B. L., & Mattys, S. (submitted). The role of lip-reading and Cued-Speech in the processing of phonological information in French-educated deaf children.
Baddeley, A. D. (1981). The concept of working memory: A view of the current state and probable future development. *Cognition, 10*, 17–23.
Baddeley, A., & Hitch, G. S. (1974). Working memory. In G. H. Bower (Ed.), *The psychology of learning and motivation* (Vol. 8, pp. 47–90). New York: Academic Press.
Baddeley, A., & Lewis, V. J. (1981). Inner active processes in reading: The inner voice, the inner ear, and the inner eye. In A. M. Lesgold & C. A. Perfetti (Eds.), *Interactive processes in reading* (pp. 107–129). London: Lawrence Erlbaum Associates.
Bellugi, U., Klima, E.S., & Siple, P. (1975). Remembering in signs. *Cognition, 3*, 93–125.
Bertelson, P., Vroomen, J., Wiegerad, G., & de Gelder, B. (1994). Exploring the relation between McGurk interference and ventriloquism. *Proceedings of the 1996 Conference of Spoken Language Processing*, Yokohama, Japan, Vol. 2, 559–562.
Bertoncini, J., Bijeljac-Babic, R., Jusczyk, P. W., Kennedy, L., & Mehler, J. (1988). An investigation of young infants' perceptual representations of speech sounds. *Journal of Experimental Psychology: General, 117*, 21–33.
Binnie, C. A., Montgomery, A. A., & Jackson, P. L. (1974). Auditory and visual contributions to the perception of consonants. *Journal of Speech and Hearing Research, 17*, 619–630.
Brown, R. (1973). *A first language: The early stages*. Cambridge, MA: Harvard University Press.
Campbell, R. (1987a). The cerebral lateralization of lip-reading. In B. Dodd & R. Campbell (Eds.), *Hearing by eye: The psychology of lip-reading* (pp. 215–226). London: Lawrence Erlbaum Associates.
Campbell, R. (1987b). Lip-reading and immediate memory processes on thinking impure thoughts. In B. Dodd & R. Campbell (Eds.), *Hearing by eye: The psychology of lip-reading*. London: Lawrence Erlbaum Associates.
Campbell, R., & Dodd, B. (1980). Hearing by eye. *The Quarterly Journal of Experimental Psychology, 32*, 85–99.
Campbell, R., & Wright, H. (1988). Deafness, spelling and rhyme: How spelling supports written word and picture rhyming skills in deaf subjects. *The Quarterly Journal of Experimental Psychology, 40A*, 771–788.
Charlier, B. L. (1994). *Le développement des représentations phonologiques chez l'enfant sourd: Étude comparative du Langale Parlé Complété avec d'autres outils de communication* [The devilment of phonological representations in deaf children: A comparison between Cued-Speech with other communication tools]. Unpublished doctoral dissertation, Laboratory of Experimental Psychology, University of Brussels.
Charlier, B. L., Hage, C., Alegria, J., & Périer, O. (1990). Evaluation d'une pratique prolongée du LPC sur la compréhension de la parole par l'enfant atteint de déficience auditive [An evaluation of long lasting exposure to Cued-Speech on speech understanding in hearing impaired children]. *Glossa, 22*, 28–39.
Conrad, R. (1962). An association between memory errors and errors due to acoustic masking of speech. *Nature, 193*, 1314–1315.
Conrad, R. (1964). Acoustic confusions in immediate memory. *British Journal of Psychology, 55*, 75–84.

Conrad, R. (1970). Short-term memory processes in the deaf. *British Journal of Psychology, 81*, 179–195.
Conrad, R. (1972). Speech and reading. In J. F. Kavanagh & I. G. Mattingly (Eds.), *Language by ear and by eye* (pp. 205–240). Cambridge, MA: MIT Press.
Conrad, R. (1979). *The deaf school child.* London: Harper & Row.
Cornett, O. (1967). Cued speech. *American Annals of the Deaf, 112*, 3–13.
Crowder, R. G. (1986). Auditory and temporal factors in the modality effect. *Journal of Experimental Psychology: Learning Memory and Cognition, 12*, 269–279.
Crowder, R. G., & Morton, J. (1969). Precategorical acoustic storage (PAS). *Perception and Psychophysics, 5*, 365–373.
Dodd, B. (1976). The phonological system of deaf children. *Journal of Speech and Hearing Disorders, 41*, 185–198.
Dodd, B. (1977). Lip reading in infants: Attention to speech presented in- and out-of-synchrony. *Cognitive Psychology, 11*, 478–484.
Dodd, B. (1987). Lip-reading, phonological coding and deafness. In B. Dodd & R. Campbell (Eds.), *Hearing by eye: The psychology of lip-reading* (pp. 177–189). London: Lawrence Erlbaum Associates.
Dodd, B., & Hermelin, B. (1977). Phonological coding by the prelinguistically deaf. *Perception and Psychophysics, 21*, 413–417.
Eimas, P. D., Siqueland, E. R., Jusczyk, P. W., & Vigorito, J. (1971). Speech perception in infants. *Science, 171*, 303–306.
Erber, N. P. (1969). Interaction of audition and vision in the recognition of oral speech stimuli. *Journal of Speech and Hearing Research, 12*, 423–424.
Erber, N. P. (1974). Visual perception of speech by deaf children. Recent developments and continuing needs. *Journal of Speech and Hearing Research, 39*, 178–185.
Field, T. M., Woodson, R., Greenberg, D., & Cohen, D. (1982). Discrimination and imitation of facial expressions by neonates. *Science, 218*, 179–181.
Fowler, C. A., & Dekle, D. J. (1991). Listening with eye and hand: Cross-modal contributions to speech perception. *Journal of Experimental Psychology: Human Perception and Performance, 17*, 816–828.
Hage, C. (1994). *Développement de certains aspects de la morpho-syntaxe chez l'enfant à surdité profonde: Rôle du Langage Parlé Complété* [The development of some aspects of morpho-syntax in profoundly deaf children: Role played by Cued-Speech]. Unpublished doctoral dissertation, Laboratory of Experimental Psychology, University of Brussels.
Hage, C., Alegria, J., & Périer, O. (1991). Cued speech and language acquisition: The case of grammatical gender morphophonology. In D. S. Martin (Ed.), *Advances in cognition, education, and deafness* (pp. 395–399). Washington, DC: Gallodet University Press.
Hanson, V. L., & Fowler, C. A. (1987). Phonological coding in word reading: Evidence from hearing and deaf readers. *Memory & Cognition, 15*, 199–207.
Hanson, V. L., & McGarr, N. (1987). Rhyme generation by deaf adults. Haskins Laboratories, *Status Report on Speech Research, SR-92*, 137–158.
Hanson, V. L., Shankweiler, D., & Fisher, F. W. (1983). Determinants of spelling ability in deaf and hearing adults: Access to linguistic structure. *Cognition, 14*, 323–344.
Karmiloff-Smith, A. (1979). *A functional approach to child language.* Cambridge, England: Cambridge University Press.
Kuhl, P. K., & Meltzoff, A. N. (1982). The bimodal perception of speech in infancy. *Science, 218*, 1138–1141.
Leybaert, J. (1993). Reading ability in the deaf: The roles of phonological codes. In M. Marschark & D. Clark (Eds.), *Psychological perspectives on deafness* (pp. 269–309). Hillsdale, NJ: Lawrence Erlbaum Associates.
Leybaert, J., & Alegria, J. (1993). Is word processing involuntary in deaf children? *British Journal of Developmental Psychology, 11*, 1–29.

Leybaert, J., & Alegria, J. (1995). Spelling development in deaf and hearing children: Evidence for use of morpho-phonological regularities in French. *Reading and Writing: An Interdisciplinary Journal, 7,* 89–109.

Leybaert, J., Alegria, J., & Fonck, E. (1983). Automaticity in word recognition and word naming by the deaf. *Cahiers de Psychologie Cognitive, 3,* 255–272.

Leybaert, J., & Charlier, B. (1996). Visual speech in the head: The effects of Cued-Speech on rhyming, remembering, and spelling. *Journal of Deaf Studies and Deaf Education, 1,* 234–248.

Liberman, A. M., & Mattingly, I. G. (1985). The motor theory of speech perception revised. *Cognition, 21,* 1–36.

Lupker, S. J., & Katz, A. N. (1981). Input, decision and response factors in picture-word interference. *Journal of Experimental Psychology: Human Learning and Memory, 7,* 269–282.

MacKain, K. S., Studdert-Kennedy, M., Spieker, S., & Stern, D. (1983). Infant intermodal speech perception is a left hemisphere function. *Science, 219,* 1347–1349.

Massaro, D. W. (1987). Speech perception by ear and eye. In B. Dodd & R. Campbell (Eds.), *Hearing by eye: The psychology of lip-reading* (pp. 53–83). London: Lawrence Erlbaum Associates.

Massaro, D. W., (1989). Multiple book review of: Speech perception by ear and eye: A paradigm for psychological inquiry. *Behavioral and Brain Sciences, 12,* 741–794.

McGurk, H., & McDonald, J. (1976). Hearing lips and seeing voices. *Nature, 264,* 746–748.

Meltzoff, A. N., & Moore, K. M. (1977). Imitations of facial and manual gestures by human neonates. *Science, 198,* 75–78.

Nicholls, G. H. (1979). *Cued speech and the reception of spoken language.* Unpublished master's thesis, McGill University, Montreal.

Nicholls, G. H., & Ling, D. (1982). Cued speech and the reception of spoken language. *Journal of Speech and Hearing Research, 25,* 262–269.

Patterson, K. E., & Morton, J. (1985). From orthography to phonology: An attempt at an old interpretation. In K. E. Patterson, J. C. Marshall, & M. Coltheart (Eds.), *Surface dyslexia: Neuropsychological and cognitive studies of phonological reading* (pp. 335–359). Hillsdale, NJ: Lawrence Erlbaum Associates.

Périer, O. (1987). L'enfant à audition déficiente: Aspects médicaux, éducatifs, sociologiques et psychologiques [The auditory impaired child: Medical, educational, sociological, and psychological questions]. *Acta Oto-Rhino-Laryngologica Belgica, 41,* 129–420.

Périer, O., Charlier, B., Hage, C., & Alegria, J. (1987). Evaluation of the effects of prolonged Cued Speech practice upon the perception of spoken language. In I. G. Taylor (Ed.), *The education of the deaf: Current perspectives* (Vol. 1, pp. 616–625). Beckenham, England: Croom Helm.

Pritchatt, D. (1968). An investigation into some of the underlying associative verbal processes of the Stroop colour effect. *The Quarterly Journal of Experimental Psychology, 20,* 351–359.

Reisberg, D., McLean, J., & Goldfield, A. (1987). Easy to hear but hard to understand: A lip-reading advantage with intact auditory stimuli. In B. Dodd & R. Campbell (Eds.), *Hearing by eye: The psychology of lip-reading* (pp. 97–113). London: Lawrence Erlbaum Associates.

Rosen, S. M., Fourcin, A. J., & Moore, B. C. J. (1981). Voice pitch as an aid to lip-reading. *Nature, 291,* 150–152.

Spoehr, K. T., & Corin, W. S. (1978). The stimulus suffix as a memory code phenomenon. *Memory & Cognition, 6,* 583–589.

Sumby, W., & Pollack, I. (1954). Visual contributions to speech visibility in noise. *Journal of the Acoustic Society of America, 26,* 212–215.

Summerfield, Q. (1987). Some preliminaries to a comprehensive account of audio-visual speech perception. In B. Dodd & R. Campbell (Eds.), *Hearing by eye: The psychology of lip-reading* (pp. 3–51). London: Lawrence Erlbaum Associates.

Summerfield, Q. (1991). Visual perception of phonetic gestures. In I. G. Mattingly & M. Studdert-Kennedy (Eds.), *Modularity and the motor theory of speech perception* (pp. 117–137). Hillsdale, NJ: Lawrence Erlbaum Associates.

Swisher, L. (1976). The language performance of the oral deaf. In H. Whitaker & H. A. Whitaker (Eds.), *Studies in neurolinguistics* (Vol. 2, pp. 59–93). New York: Academic.

Taeschner, T., Devescovi, A., & Volterra, V. (1988). Affixes and function words in written language of deaf children. *Applied Psycholinguistics, 9*, 385–401.

Chapter **14**

The Role of Letter Learning in Developing Phonemic Awareness Skills in Preschool Children: Implications for Explanations of Reading Disorders

Rhona S. Johnston
University of St. Andrews, Fife, Scotland

There is considerable evidence that there is a close association between phonological awareness and reading ability. One of the best correlates of later success at reading is preschool phonological awareness ability (e.g., Bradley & Bryant, 1983; Lundberg, Olofsson, & Wall, 1980, Share, Jorm, Maclean, & Matthews, 1984; Stanovich, Cunningham, & Cramer, 1984; Stuart & Coltheart, 1988). Phonological awareness is, therefore, seen as an important precursor of literacy skills. It is also proposed that some children are so deficient at acquiring phonological awareness skills that they have difficulty in becoming competent readers (Bradley & Bryant, 1978, 1983). Support for the idea that poor readers' problems are phonological in nature comes from the fact that studies have found poor readers to have difficulty in using a phonological approach to reading (i.e., they have problems in reading nonwords), and that they have deficient phonological or phonemic awareness skills for reading level (e.g., Baddeley, Ellis, Miles, & Lewis, 1982; Bradley & Bryant, 1978; Holligan & Johnston, 1988, 1991; Olson, Wise, Conners, & Rack, 1990; Snowling, 1981).

Not all studies, however, show poor readers to have deficient nonword naming or phonemic awareness skills for reading age (e.g., Baddeley, Logie, & Ellis, 1988; Beech & Harding, 1984; Johnston, Rugg, & Scott, 1987; Szeszulski & Manis, 1987; Treiman & Hirsh-Pasek, 1985). Such apparently aberrant findings have been attributed to methodological weaknesses in these studies, such as failure to match poor readers adequately on verbal

IQ to their reading age controls, or failure to use nonwords of sufficient complexity (Rack, Snowling, & Olson, 1992).

In this chapter, I propose to reconsider first the idea that preschool phonological awareness ability develops prior to and independently of literacy skills, and that preschool phonological awareness by itself is the causal factor behind success at starting to learn to read. Second, I also reconsider the evidence for the view that most poor readers' problems stem from an underlying phonological dysfunction.

WHAT ARE THE ORIGINS OF PRESCHOOL PHONOLOGICAL AWARENESS?

Although many studies show that phonological and phonemic awareness skills measured prior to formal reading tuition are predictive of later reading competence (e.g., Bradley & Bryant, 1983; Lundberg, Olofsson, & Wall, 1980; Share, Jorm, Maclean, & Matthews, 1984; Stanovich, Cunningham, & Cramer, 1984; Stuart & Coltheart, 1988), there is also an important literature that shows that learning to read in itself enhances phonemic awareness. It has been found that adult illiterates have difficulty in performing phoneme deletion tasks, such as taking the *c* from *cat* and saying what is left, but that adults from a similar background who have started to learn to read are much better at these tasks (e.g., Morais, Bertelson, Cary, & Alegria, 1986; Morais, Cary, Alegria, & Bertelson, 1979). Such findings have led to the conclusion that there is a reciprocal relationship between phonemic awareness and learning to read. It is argued that learning to read in an alphabetic language enhances phonemic awareness ability, and that training in phonemic awareness enhances reading skill (Bryant & Goswami, 1987; Morais, Alegria, & Content, 1987). One problem with the latter view, however, is that phonemic awareness training on its own rarely leads to an enhancement of reading skill; most studies show that such programs are only effective if alphabetic stimuli are used in the training (e.g., Bradley & Bryant, 1983; Fox & Routh, 1984; Hatcher, Hulme, & Ellis, 1994).

Goswami and Bryant (1990) argued that preschool children have little *phonemic* awareness, the small amount there is being confined to knowledge of the onsets of words (e.g., *c*at), which often coincide with a phoneme. They conclude that the progress children make in the early stages of reading is therefore unlikely to be due to their sensitivity to phonemes, and that it is awareness of the intrasyllabic units, the onset and rime in words (e.g., *c-at*), that plays a causal role in children's success at reading. However, there is evidence that preschool children are aware of more than just onset phonemes. Content, Kolinsky, Morais, and Bertelson (1986) asked preliterate children to say what a word would sound like if the initial or final consonant was removed; they found that the children actually performed better when asked to remove the *final* sound from words.

Given that preschool children do have some awareness of the phonemic structure of the spoken word, it is important to find out how this awareness arises. Clearly, it cannot develop through formal reading experience, given the care taken in preschool studies to exclude children who are able to read in normal print. Research in this area tends to assume that literacy starts when the child can read in normal print. It has been pointed out, however, that preschool children can have considerable environmental print reading ability, and that they often know quite a few letters of the alphabet (Barron, 1991). It is possible, therefore, that phonemic awareness is triggered off in preschool children through their knowledge of the alphabet and their ability to read environmental print.

In a recent study we examined the phonemic awareness skills of 49 4-year-old children who were unable to read in normal print (Johnston, Anderson, & Holligan, 1996). They had all failed to read any items on the Clay Ready to Read Word Test (Clay, 1979) or the British Abilities Word Reading Test (Elliott, Murray, & Pearson, 1977). Although overall levels of phonemic awareness were found to be low in this sample, some children showed considerable knowledge of the phonemic structure of the spoken word. The children were asked to say what the sounds were in two- and three-phoneme words, using the Yopp-Singer Phoneme Segmentation Task (Yopp, 1988). In response to three-phoneme words, although only 23.5% of the initial phonemes were correctly segmented, some nonreaders got all of the items correct. Performance on medial and final phonemes was even lower (mean performance being 5.8% and 6.1% correct, respectively), but again scores in these conditions were as high as 75% correct for medial phonemes and 100% correct for final phonemes for individual children. A similar pattern of performance was found with two phoneme words, with the first phoneme being identified significantly better than the final phoneme. Because some of these prereaders were found to have very high levels of phonemic awareness, this would seem to undermine the argument that these skills are largely due to learning to read. The overall pattern of performance on the phoneme segmentation task, however, supports Goswami and Bryant's (1990) view that onset phonemes are special, and that children find it easier to give the sounds of phonemes when they are in the initial position of words.

We also measured phoneme deletion skills, using Rosner's (1975) Test of Auditory Analysis skills. Here we found that deletion of the final phoneme in spoken words (e.g., ga*me*) was significantly better than that of initial phoneme deletion (e.g., *co*at), as did Content et al. (1986). Overall performance levels were low (2.0% correct for initial phonemes, 16.3%

for final phonemes), but again some children scored 100% correct in deleting initial or final phonemes. The relative ease of initial phoneme segmentation and final phoneme deletion suggests that the beginning parts of words are easier to pronounce.

How had these high levels of phonemic awareness arisen in some of the prereaders? Although the children could not read in normal print, it is evident that children of this age have some knowledge of the alphabet and can be very good at reading environmental print. We hypothesized that some of the children had become aware of the phonemic structure of the spoken word through learning some letters of the alphabet and relating that to their knowledge of environmental print.

We measured alphabet knowledge by asking the children to give the name and the sound for each letter of the alphabet, and to write each letter to dictation. The children could read on average 19.2% of the letters of the alphabet (names or sounds); however, some of them knew as much as 85% of the alphabet. The children could also write on average 16.1% of the letters to dictation. We combined the scores for the reading and writing of the alphabet to produce an overall measure of alphabet knowledge. The alphabet measure was found to be significantly correlated with phoneme segmentation and phoneme deletion ability. We also administered a measure of environmental print knowledge, asking the children if they could tell us the names on the wrappers of everyday items such as sweets; the names were cut out of the wrappers so that only the product name appeared. Alphabet knowledge was found to be significantly correlated with this measure. We also devised a measure of rhyme ability, asking the children to generate rhymes for a list of words; this measure correlated with alphabet knowledge as well.

Given that there was a close association between alphabet knowledge and phonemic awareness ability, it was of interest to try to determine the nature of the association. Although it is not possible to answer causal questions in a cross-sectional study, evidence was found that alphabet knowledge emerged prior to the development of explicit phonemic awareness skills. We divided the sample first into those children who knew some letters of the alphabet and those who knew none. The next stage was to divide the sample again into those who showed phonemic awareness ability and those who did not. We found that 17 children knew some letters of the alphabet but were unable to segment or delete phonemes. Six children knew no letters of the alphabet and had no phonemic awareness ability; only one child showed phonemic awareness skills in the absence of alphabet knowledge, but he had refused to carry out the alphabet tasks. Finally, 25 children knew some letters of the alphabet and could segment and delete phonemes. A chi-square analysis showed that there was a significant association between alphabetic knowledge and phonemic awareness ability.

Multiple regression analyses were carried out to see which variables were the best predictors of phoneme segmentation, phoneme deletion, and product name reading ability. The only significant predictor in all cases was knowledge of the alphabet; it predicted 24.3% of the variance in phoneme segmentation skills, 17.1% of the variance in phoneme deletion ability, and 25.6% of the variance in product name reading knowledge.

It has been proposed that preschool rhyme ability is a major factor in later success at reading (Bradley & Bryant, 1983; Goswami & Bryant, 1990). We found that rhyme ability was also correlated with alphabet knowledge, product name reading ability, and phoneme segmentation skills. Fixed-order regression analyses were carried out to determine the relative importance of alphabetic knowledge and rhyme skills to phoneme segmentation, phoneme deletion, and product name reading ability. Verbal IQ was entered first, followed by rhyme skills. Ability to carry out rhyme tasks accounted for a significant proportion of the variance in the phoneme segmentation and product name reading tasks, but not phoneme deletion ability. When alphabet knowledge was entered at the third step, however, it accounted for further variance in all three areas. Another analysis was carried out, in which, after entering verbal IQ, alphabet knowledge was entered at the second step. This measure accounted for a significant proportion of the variance in phoneme segmentation, phoneme deletion, and product name reading ability. When rhyme skills were entered at the third step, no further variance was accounted for in any of these tasks. Thus, rhyme skills made no independent contribution to phonemic awareness ability over and above that accounted for alphabet knowledge.

It seems unlikely that learning the alphabet would by itself trigger off phonemic awareness in preliterate children. Although such children are well aware of letters through television programs such as *Sesame Street*, through the activities of older siblings, and from their parents, who often teach them to write their names, letters by themselves are not likely to generate a great amount of interest. Environmental print awareness, however, can be very rewarding for children, because it enables them to identify products of considerable interest to them, such as sweets. We hypothesized that the association we found between letter knowledge and product name reading ability might be an important factor in developing phonemic awareness. Children may recognize some of the letters in environmental print and see that the sounds of the letters correspond to the sounds in the spoken word. It has been suggested that onsets are particularly salient for young children (Goswami & Bryant, 1990). It is possible that the child who can recognize "Kit Kat" may learn the name or the sound of the letter *k* and then realize that the word starts with the *k* sound. If this is the case, then it would be predicted that the relationship between alphabet knowledge and overall phonemic awareness ability might be largely due to an association between letter knowledge and awareness of the initial phoneme.

A further multiple regression analysis was carried out, looking at the extent to which alphabet knowledge, product name reading ability, and rhyme skills were predictive of knowledge of initial and final phonemes. As far as phoneme segmentation ability was concerned, alphabet knowledge predicted 33.4% of the variance in initial phoneme segmentation ability, and product name reading ability predicted 10.5% of the variance in final phoneme segmentation ability, no other factors being significant. For the phoneme deletion task, alphabet knowledge predicted 23.5% of the variance in initial phoneme deletion ability, with product name reading ability predicting a further 6.9%; none of the factors entered predicted final phoneme deletion ability. This supports the idea that the association between alphabet knowledge and overall phonemic awareness ability is largely mediated by the relationship between letter knowledge and awareness of the initial phoneme in words.

We concluded from this study that some prereaders have considerable knowledge of the phonemic structure of the spoken word, but that these skills cannot have been derived from learning to read in normal print. There is evidence, however, that their phonemic awareness is closely tied to *early literacy experiences*—their knowledge of the alphabet and their ability to recognise environmental print. This extends Morais et al.'s (1979) view that learning to read has a major impact on the development of phoneme deletion skills by showing that the early literacy skills of prereaders may have a causal role in the emergence of phonemic awareness.

It is necessary to consider, therefore, the well-established association between preschool phonological awareness skills and later reading ability (e.g., Bradley & Bryant, 1983). Other preschool skills have also been found to be predictive of reading ability, such as alphabet knowledge (e.g., Tizard, Blatchford, Burke, Farquhar, & Plewis, 1988). What do we know of the relative importance of these two skills for later reading ability? Share et al. (1984) carried out one of the few studies in which alphabet knowledge and phoneme segmentation ability were both measured early in the child's school career; in their study, phoneme segmentation skills and alphabetic knowledge measured at the start of Kindergarten were correlated to a similar extent with later reading ability. We recently studied our sample at the end of their first year at school. Phoneme segmentation and deletion skills at age 4 were indeed correlated with reading at age 5 ($r = 0.32$, $p < .05$, and $r = 0.33$, $p < .05$, respectively), as was rhyme ability ($r = 0.41$, $p < .01$); alphabet knowledge, however, was more highly correlated ($r = 0.64$, $p < .01$). When all of our measures of performance at age 4 were entered into a stepwise multiple regression analysis, alphabet knowledge accounted for 40% of the variance in reading ability at the age of 5, and product name reading ability accounted for a further 5%; phonemic awareness and rhyme skills did not enter into the equation. Thus, the well-documented correlations between phonemic awareness ability and later reading skill may be mediated by their associations with other factors (i.e., knowledge of the alphabet and emergent print reading ability).

When children who have an above-average knowledge of the alphabet enter school and start to learn to read in an alphabetic language, they are already orientated toward paying attention to the letters in words. Such children may never take a logographic or visual cue approach to reading, and may proceed directly to an alphabetic or cipher approach (Ehri, 1992; Frith, 1985) whereby there is sequential conversion of graphemes into phonemes. This means that such children are likely to be better readers than those who have not learned much of the alphabet prior to school entry, as they will have a head start in decoding unfamiliar words from themselves. However, the precocious phonemic awareness skills of children who have learned the alphabet as preschoolers are also likely in themselves to be a significant asset in learning to read; hence the reciprocal relationship between reading and phonemic awareness ability (Bryant & Goswami, 1987; Morais et al., 1987).

If phonemic awareness skills emerge due to learning the letters of the alphabet and relating that knowledge to environmental print, there may well be implications for the understanding of reading disorders.

ARE THE PROBLEMS EXPERIENCED BY POOR READERS DUE TO DEFICIENT PHONEMIC AWARENESS SKILLS?

Poor readers' problems are often examined by assessing whether their performance on reading and reading-related tasks is appropriate for their level of reading skill. In order to do this, normal younger readers are studied who have the same level of reading ability and similar IQ levels as the poor readers. If the poor readers show appropriate levels of performance for their reading age, it is concluded that they are progressing along the same path of reading development as normal readers, but at a slower rate. If, on the other hand, they are found to have a level of performance that is impaired for their reading age, then it is argued that this deficiency has implications for the cause of their disorder (e.g., Bryant & Goswami, 1986).

Across the last 15 years there has been growing evidence that poor readers have various phonological difficulties for their reading age. Bradley and Bryant (1978), for example, found that poor readers were impaired for reading age in the odd-word-out task, in which the child has to detect the odd item in a sequence such as "*bud, bun, bus, rug.*" Poor readers have also been found to have difficulty with tasks requiring more explicit phoneme segmentation (e.g., Olson et al., 1990). As far as reading tasks are concerned, poor readers have been found to be impaired in reading nonwords for their reading age, showing that they have difficulties with the phonological aspects of reading (Baddeley et al., 1982; Holligan & Johnston, 1988; Manis, Szeszulski, Holt, & Graves, 1988; Snowling, 1981).

So far the evidence would seem to lead to a clearcut conclusion—poor readers have impaired phonemic awareness ability, which leads to difficulty with the phonological aspects of reading. Children who have difficulty in reading nonwords will, therefore, make slow progress in word reading because they will be less able to decode unfamiliar items and thus will be slow to develop a store of rapidly accessible words. A problem with this view, however, is that not all studies find poor readers to have phonological deficits for reading age. Beech and Harding (1984) found that not only did their poor readers show appropriate odd-word-out performance for reading age, their nonword naming skills were appropriate for their level of word reading skill as well. Furthermore, many of the researchers who have found nonword naming deficits in some samples have failed to find them in others (e.g., Baddeley et al., 1988; Johnston et al., 1987; Szeszulski & Manis, 1987).

Rack et al. (1992) suggested that the failure to find nonword naming deficits in these studies may be due to a number of methodological weaknesses. They argued that poor readers may only have difficulty in reading complex nonwords, and proposed that many of the null results reported may be due to researchers not including nonwords of sufficient difficulty in their stimuli. They also argued that the studies that find nonword naming problems in poor readers have samples that are well matched on verbal IQ, whereas the studies that fail to find the deficit have an inadequate IQ match. They conclude that most dyslexics have a specific deficit in using a phonological approach to reading, and that the development of their word recognition skills is held back by their poor phonological decoding skills.

An analysis we carried out of individual differences in poor readers showed, however, that nonword naming ability varied according to level of visual segmentation skill (Johnston, Anderson, & Duncan, 1991). We found that one group of poor readers had difficulty in reading two-syllable nonwords whereas a second group read these items well for reading age; this was despite the fact that the two groups had similar levels of phonological segmentation ability. What differentiated the groups was the fact that the poor readers who had difficulty in reading nonwords performed well on a test of visual segmentation ability, whereas the ones who read nonwords well performed poorly on the visual task. It was found for the whole sample of poor readers ($n = 25$) that visual segmentation ability correlated positively with the use of a visual approach to reading (as indexed by the extent to which irregular words were read better than regular ones). It was proposed that the difficulty that the high visual segmentation ability that poor readers had in reading nonwords was due to the adoption of a visual approach to reading, rather than to a deficit in phonological segmentation ability. Visual segmentation ability was also found to correlate positively with IQ, so it seemed likely that brighter poor readers would have higher visual segmentation skills and therefore poorer nonword naming ability than would less able ones.

Stanovich (1988), in fact, proposed that higher-IQ poor readers are more likely to show a phonological deficit in reading. We therefore undertook a larger-scale study to examine the extent to which nonword naming problems in poor readers could be accounted for by levels of IQ and visual segmentation skill rather than phonemic awareness ability. We studied 80 10-year-old poor readers in the IQ range 74–136 (Johnston & Anderson, submitted); the poor readers were compared with 76 reading-age controls and 69 chronological-age controls. The poor readers were matched with the former group on the basis of IQ and reading ability, and with the latter group on IQ and chronological age.

In order to assess phonemic awareness skills, the subjects carried out two tasks—an odd-word-out task (similar to that of Bradley & Bryant, 1978) and a phoneme deletion task in which the children had to say, for example, what sound was left if you took the *f* from *flat*. The children also read two lists of nonwords; one list contained four- to five-letter nonwords designed to test knowledge of vowel and consonant digraphs (e.g., *smeak, nard*), and the other list contained a mixture of short and long nonwords (e.g., *hig, minlan*). Overall, the poor readers did not have difficulty with the phonemic awareness tasks; their odd-word-out and phoneme deletion skills were found to be appropriate for their reading age. Furthermore, they also read the four- to five-letters nonwords as well as their reading-age controls. They did have difficulty, however, with the list of short and long nonwords; here, performance was significantly worse than that of their reading-age controls. This is difficult to account for, however, if problems in reading nonwords are seen as stemming from an underlying phonemic awareness deficit.

In order to examine the influence of IQ on nonword reading ability, we divided our sample of poor readers and reading-age controls into three IQ bands. It was found that poor readers with IQs below 99.9 read nonwords as well as did their IQ-matched reading-age controls. However, the poor readers in the two higher-IQ bands (IQ 100 to 114.9, and IQ 115 upwards) read nonwords significantly less well than did their IQ-matched reading-age controls. It was found that performance on the phoneme deletion task did not vary with IQ level, and that both groups of higher-IQ poor readers performed as well as their IQ-matched reading-age controls on this task. The difficulty the brighter poor readers had in reading nonwords could not, therefore, be attributed to deficient phonemic awareness skills.

How could the varying patterns of performance by IQ level be accounted for, given that the poor readers were matched on IQ with their reading-age controls? Although it is the general practice to match poor readers with reading-age controls on IQ, this does not control for absolute levels of ability. The procedure merely ensures that if the poor readers are of average IQ for their age, then their reading-age controls are also of average IQ for their age. Thus, despite the match on age standardized scores, the child of 10 who is matched on verbal and/or performance IQ with an 8-year-old will have higher raw scores on these tests. In many domains poor readers will, in fact, have skills that are appropriate for chronological age, and that therefore exceed those of their reading-age controls.

We took the view that the age-appropriate skills exhibited by poor readers may have an impact on the approach they take to reading. In order to look at these influences, we calculated the children's raw score performance on the WISC-R IQ test (short form, Maxwell, 1959). When the effects of the raw scores were controlled for in an analysis of covariance, the poor readers' nonword reading skills were still deficient for their reading age. A new measure was then calculated by subtracting the phoneme deletion score from the IQ score of each poor reader and reading age control. When this new measure was controlled for in an analysis of covariance, it was found that the poor readers no longer showed a nonword naming deficit for their reading age. Thus, it was found that there was a complex association among IQ raw scores, phonemic segmentation skill, and nonword naming ability.

It seemed unlikely that a general measure such as IQ could be directly associated with nonword reading problems. Therefore, we looked more closely at the impact of the children's visual segmentation skills on their reading. Visual segmentation ability was measured by administering Witkin, Oltman, Raskin, and Karp's (1971) Children's Embedded Figures Test. In this test, the child has to find, for example, a triangle embedded in a clown's face. The poor readers performed appropriately for their chronological age on this task, and performance for all of the groups was found to be associated with IQ. Covarying out the effects of visual segmentation ability did not equate poor readers and reading-age controls on nonword naming ability. A measure of visual advantage was then calculated by subtracting the phoneme deletion score from the visual segmentation score of each child. When the effect of this measure was controlled for in a covariance analysis, the poor readers in the study no longer showed a nonword naming deficit for reading age. Thus, those poor readers who had better visual than phonological segmentation ability were more likely to show a nonword naming deficit for their reading age. The earlier small-scale study of individual differences in poor readers (Johnston et al., 1991) had suggested that there might be a direct association between visual segmentation skills and level of nonword reading, but the larger-scale study showed that it was the disparity between visual and phonological segmentation ability that accounted for the nonword reading deficit statistically.

How might the relative superiority of visual versus phonological segmentation ability in poor readers influence their nonword naming ability? We think it likely that those poor readers whose visual skills greatly exceed their phoneme deletion skills adopt a more visual approach to reading than that of their reading-age controls. A further task carried out by our poor readers supports the idea that they had superior visual reading skills; it was found that they performed as accurately as their chronological-age controls when they had to search for and delete the letter *e* in a list of words. In a number of studies, Olson (Olson, Kliegl, Davidson, & Foltz, 1985; Olson, Wise, Connors, Rack, & Fulker, 1989) also showed that poor readers can develop a more visual orthographic approach to reading than that of their reading-age controls. Olson proposed that a visual approach to reading develops in compensation for difficulty in reading unfamiliar stimuli such as nonwords.

Our explanation of the origin of the visual orthographic approach to reading in such poor readers differs, however, from Olson's. We argue that the adoption of a visual orthographic approach to reading by some poor readers is due to the high levels of visual skill that they have for their reading age; the use of this approach then leads to difficulty in reading nonwords. This visual orthographic approach may not be an abnormal compensation; instead, it may be appropriate for chronological age. Such poor readers may in fact be taking a more mature approach to reading than that of their reading age controls. Those poor readers who prematurely adopt a visual orthographic approach to word reading may be able to use a grapheme-to-phoneme conversion approach when reading fairly short nonwords, but the skill may break down when they are asked to read long polysyllabic items. Such poor readers may not persevere with grapheme-to-phoneme conversion when faced with long nonwords because they do not read words in this way and thus are less practiced at this approach. This may explain why the poor readers in our study were also impaired in reading simple three-letter nonwords when these items were included in the same list as the long items, despite their competence at reading more complex monosyllabic nonwords in a separate list.

The tendency to adopt a visual approach would be most pronounced in the bright poor readers, who would have higher levels of visual segmentation ability and therefore a greater disparity between their visual and phonological segmentation skills. This disparity would also increase with age, as poor readers' visual skills would develop in line with chronological age, whereas phonemic awareness ability would lag behind with reading ability. Thus, brighter and older poor readers would be more likely to show a nonword naming deficit.

Although it is difficult to explain the nonword naming problems experienced by the poor readers in our study in terms of deficient phonemic awareness skills, in other studies there is no such difficulty. Olson et al. (1990), for example, found adolescent poor readers to have difficulties with both phoneme segmentation and nonword reading. These differences between studies may be accountable for in terms of heterogeneity of reading disorders, such that some samples contain a large number of children suffering from deficient phonemic awareness skills. However, another possibility is that in prematurely adopting an orthographic approach to reading, some poor readers may not only become less adept at reading nonwords, they may also have difficulty in carrying out phonemic awareness tasks. Bruck (1993) studied adult dyslexics whose reading had become reasonably accurate, but who had very poor phonemic awareness skills for their reading age. She suggested that one possible explanation of this was that they may have been so poor at using a grapheme-to-phoneme conversion approach to reading that they failed to gain the metacognitive insights necessary for carrying out phonemic awareness tasks. This is in accord with the idea that there is a reciprocal relationship between reading and phonemic awareness, such that not only does phonemic segmentation ability aid the development of a phonological approach to reading, but that reading itself develops phonemic awareness skills (Morais et al., 1987; Perfetti, Beck, Bell, & Hughes, 1987). However, it may be that levels of phonemic awareness ability vary not only as a function reading skill, but also according to *how* an individual reads.

CONCLUSION

It is apparent that it is very difficult to disentangle the cause of reading disorders in cross-sectional studies of poor readers. Unfortunately, there is a dearth of studies that examine the performance of poor readers before they learn to read (i.e., before there is any indication that they will have severe literacy problems when they attend school). Although cross-sectional studies give a mixed picture as to whether poor readers have deficient phonemic awareness and nonword naming skills for their reading age, the idea that reading problems are phonological in origin has derived much support from the fact that preschool phonological awareness skills are highly predictive of later reading ability. The argument is that if phonological awareness skills are established prior to the development of reading, and if these skills are found to be deficient in poor readers, then they must have played a causal role in the reading disorder.

However, if preschool phonological awareness knowledge, particularly of phonemes, develops because of children's early literacy experiences, then it may be necessary to reconsider the phonological deficit explanation of reading disorders. If phonemic awareness develops initially through alphabetic knowledge, poor readers' slowness to gain the insight that the spoken word consists of phonemes may be due to difficulty in learning the names and sounds of the letters of the alphabet. This seems very likely to be a problem for them, given the evidence that poor readers are slow to acquire the names of visually presented stimuli (Jansky & de Hirsch, 1972; Share et al., 1984). Poor readers' deficient phonemic awareness skills may therefore stem from difficulty in learning the alphabet, and from being slow to detect letters in environmental print. Such a view is supported by the fact that in our longitudinal study it was preschool knowledge of the letters of the alphabet, rather than phonemic awareness ability, that was the main predictor of the children's reading skills at the end of their first year of schooling.

This schematization of the relationship between phonemic awareness and reading ability leads to the prediction that poor readers should show phonemic awareness skills that are appropriate for their reading age. However, as was discussed earlier, some poor readers may develop a visual or orthographic approach to reading; they may thus make little use of the visual–phonological approach to reading outlined by Ehri (1992) as being essential for normal reading development. Failure to use a visual–phonological approach effectively might lead to both impaired nonword reading and phonemic awareness skills for reading level. This may explain why in some studies nonword reading and phoneme segmentation skills are found to be impaired in poor readers even for reading age.

ACKNOWLEDGMENTS

The research described in this chapter was supported by grants from the Wellcome Trust, and the Medical Research Council, U.K.

REFERENCES

Baddeley, A. D., Ellis, N. C., Miles, T. R., & Lewis, V. J. (1982). Developmental and acquired dyslexia: A comparison. *Cognition, 11*, 185–199.
Baddeley, A. D., Logie, R. H., & Ellis, N. C. (1988). Characteristics of developmental dyslexia. *Cognition, 29*, 197–228.
Barron, R. (1991). Protoliteracy, literacy, and the acquisition of phonological awareness. *Learning and Individual Differences, 3*, 243–255.
Beech, J. R., & Harding, L. M. (1984). Phonemic processing and the poor reader from a developmental lag viewpoint. *Reading Research Quarterly, 19*, 357–366.
Bradley, L., & Bryant, P. E. (1978). Difficulties in auditory organisation as a possible cause of reading backwardness. *Nature, 271*, 746–747.

Bradley, L., & Bryant, P. E. (1983). Categorizing sounds and learning to read—a causal connection. *Nature, 301,* 419–421.

Bruck, M. (1993). Word recognition and component phonological processing skills of adults with childhood diagnoses of dyslexia. *Developmental Review, 13,* 258–268.

Bryant, P. E., & Goswami, U. (1986). Strengths and weaknesses of the reading level design: A comment on Backman, Mamem and Ferguson. *Psychological Bulletin, 100,* 101–103.

Bryant, P. E., & Goswami, U. (1987). Phonological awareness and learning to read. In J. R. Beech & A. M. Colley (Eds.), *Cognitive approaches to reading* (pp. 213–243). New York: Wiley.

Clay, M. M. (1979). *The early detection of reading difficulties.* London: Heinemann.

Content, A., Kolinsky, R., Morais, J., & Bertelson, P. (1986). Phonetic segmentation in prereaders: Effect of connective information. *Journal of Experimental Child Psychology, 42,* 49–72.

Ehri, L. C. (1992). Reconceptualizing the development of sight word reading and its relationship to decoding. P. B., Gough, L. C., Ehri, and R. Treiman (Eds.), *Reading acquisition* (pp. 107–143). Hillsdale, NJ: Lawrence Erlbaum Associates.

Elliott, C. D., Murray, D. J., & Pearson, L. S. (1977). *The British ability scales.* Windsor, England: NFER Nelson.

Fox, B., & Routh, D. K. (1984). Phonemic analysis and synthesis as word attack skills: Revisited. *Journal of Educational Psychology, 76,* 1059–1064.

Frith, U. (1985). Beneath the surface of developmental dyslexia. In K. Patterson, J. Marshall, & M. Coltheart (Eds.), *Surface dyslexia* (pp. 301–330). London: Lawrence Erlbaum Associates.

Goswami, U. C., & Bryant, P. E. (1990). *Phonological skills and learning to read.* Hove, England: Lawrence Erlbaum Associates.

Hatcher, P. J., Hulme, C., & Ellis, A. W. (1994). Ameliorating early reading failure by integrating the teaching of reading and phonological skills: The phonological linkage hypothesis. *Child Development, 65,* 41–57.

Holligan, C., & Johnston, R. S. (1988). The use of phonological information by good and poor readers in memory and reading tasks. *Memory & Cognition, 16,* 522–532.

Holligan, C., & Johnston, R. S. (1991). Spelling errors and phonemic segmentation ability: The nature of the relationship. *Journal of Research in Reading, 14,* 21–32.

Jansky, J., & de Hirsch, K. (1972). *Preventing reading failure.* New York: Harper & Row.

Johnston, R. S., & Anderson, M. (submitted). Phonological and orthographic reading skills in poor readers: The effects of IQ and visual segmentation ability.

Johnston, R. S., Anderson, M., & Duncan, L. G. (1991). Phonological and visual segmentation skills in poor readers. In M. Snowling & M. Thomson (Eds.), *Dyslexia: Integrating theory and practice* (pp. 154–164). London: Whurr.

Johnston, R. S., Anderson, M., & Holligan, C. (1996). Knowledge of the alphabet and explicit awareness of phonemes: The nature of the relationship. *Reading and Writing, 8,* 217–234.

Johnston, R. S., Rugg, M. D., & Scott, T. (1987). The influence of phonology on good and poor readers when reading for meaning. *Journal of Memory and Language, 26,* 57–68.

Lundberg, I., Olofsson, A., & Wall, S. (1980). Reading and spelling skills in the first school years predicted from phonemic awareness skills in kindergarten. *Scandinavian Journal of Psychology, 21,* 159–173.

Manis, F. R., Szeszulski, P. A., Holt, L. K., & Graves, K. (1988). A developmental perspective on dyslexic subtypes. *Annals of Dyslexia, 38,* 139–153.

Maxwell, A. E. (1959). A factor analysis of the Wechsler Intelligence Scale for Children. *British Journal of Educational Psychology, 29,* 237–241.

Morais, J., Alegria, J., & Content, A. (1987). The relationships between segmental analysis and alphabetic literacy: An interactive view. *Cahiers de Psychologie Cognitive, 7,* 415–438.

Morais, J., Bertelson, P., Cary, L., & Alegria, J. (1986). Literacy training and speech segmentation. *Cognition, 24,* 45–64.

Morais, J. Cary, L., Alegria, J., & Bertelson, P. (1979). Does awareness of speech as a sequence of phones arise spontaneously? *Cognition, 7,* 323–331.

Olson, R. K., Kliegl, R., Davidson, B. J., & Foltz, G. (1985). Individual and developmental differences in reading disability. In G. E. MacKinnon & T. G. Waller (Eds.), *Reading research: Advances in theory and practice* (Vol. 4, pp. 1–64), Orlando, FL: Academic.

Olson, R., Wise, B., Conners, F., & Rack, J. (1990). Organization, heritability, and remediation of component word recognition and language skills in disabled readers. In T. H. Carr & B. A. Levy (Eds.), *Reading and its development: Component skills approaches* (pp. 261–322). San Diego, CA: Academic.

Olson, R. K., Wise, B., Conners, F. A., Rack, J., & Fulker, D. (1989). Specific deficits in component reading and language skills: Genetic and environmental influences. *Journal of Learning Disabilities, 22,* 339–348.

Perfetti, C. A., Beck, I., Bell, L. C., & Hughes, C. (1987). Phonemic knowledge and learning to read are reciprocal: A longitudinal study of first grade children. *Merrill-Palmer Quarterly, 33,* 289–319.

Rack, J. P., Snowling, M. J., & Olson, R. K (1992). The nonword reading deficit in developmental dyslexia: A review. *Reading Research Quarterly, 27,* 28–53.

Rosner, J. (1975). *Helping children overcome learning difficulties.* New York: Walker and Company.

Share, D. L., Jorm, A. F., Maclean, R., & Matthews, R. (1984). Sources of individual differences in reading acquisition. *Journal of Educational Psychology, 76,* 1309–1324.

Snowling, M. J. (1981). Phonemic deficits in developmental dyslexia. *Psychological Research, 43,* 219–234.

Stanovich, K. E. (1988). Explaining the difference between the dyslexic and the garden variety poor reader: The phonological-core-variable-difference model. *Journal of Learning Disabilities, 21,* 590–612.

Stanovich, K. E., Cunningham, A. E., & Cramer, B. B. (1984). Assessing phonological awareness in kindergarten children: Issues of task comparability. *Journal of Experimental Child Psychology, 38,* 175–190.

Stuart, M., & Coltheart, M. (1988). Does reading develop in a sequence of stages? *Cognition, 30,* 139–181.

Szeszulski, P. A., & Manis, F. R. (1987). A comparison of word recognition processes in dyslexic and normal readers at two reading-age levels. *Journal of Experimental Child Psychology, 44,* 364–376.

Tizard, B., Blatchford, P., Burke, J., Farquhar, C., & Plewis, I. (1988). *Young children at school in the inner city.* London: Lawrence Erlbaum Associates.

Treiman, R., & Hirsh-Pasek, K. (1985). Are there qualitative differences in reading behavior between dyslexics and normal readers? *Memory & Cognition, 13,* 357–364.

Witkin, H. A., Oltman, P. K., Raskin, E., & Karp, S. A. (1971). *Children's Embedded Figures Test.* Palo Alto, CA: Consulting Psychologists Press.

Yopp, H. K. (1988). The validity and reliability of phoneme awareness tests. *Reading Research Quarterly, 23,* 159–177.

Chapter **15**

Fixed Reference Eye and Reading Disability: Is There a Connection?

Nata K. Goulandris
University College London

Ann McIntyre
Moorfields Eye Hospital, London

Margaret Snowling
University of York

The most widely accepted view of developmental dyslexia is that it is the consequence of an underlying verbal deficit (Vellutino, 1979), and a substantial body of research has stressed the pervasiveness of phonological impairments that prevent children from acquiring adequate reading and spelling skills (Snowling, 1987; Stanovich, 1988). In contrast, the role of visual deficits in developmental dyslexia has not been established. Despite the popular assumption that reading difficulties must be the consequence of visual deficits because reading is visible language, the involvement of visual factors in reading disability has not received consistent empirical support (see Willows, Corcos, & Kirk, 1993, for reviews). Nevertheless, there is currently a resurgence of interest in the role of visual deficits (Livingstone, Rosen, Drislane, & Galaburda, 1991; Lovegrove, Martin, & Slaghuis, 1986; Stein & Fowler, 1985), and it has been proposed that visual anomalies may be implicated in reading difficulties.

One influential theory proposed by Stein and Fowler (1980, 1985) is that dyslexics have anomalies of ocular-motor integration and vergence control that are particularly apparent when dyslexics are obliged to follow small targets, as in reading. Stein and Fowler (1982) consider that there is defective feedback between the retina and the ocular-motor system that precludes adequate focusing on small targets and, consequently, exacerbates reading difficulties. They emphasize that, because of poor vergence control, dyslexics have difficulty correctly locating letter sequences and that they appear "to lose their place on the page; letters and words seem to blur, move around and jump over each other so that they (dyslexics) misidentify and missequence them" (Stein, Riddell, & Fowler, 1987, p. 162). In terms of clinical management they suggest that dyslexic children's abnormalities of visuomotor integration can be diagnosed using the Dunlop reference eye test (Dunlop, 1976), and that monocular occlusion for reading and other types of close work results in improvement in vergence control with ensuing amelioration of reading ability.

Stein and Fowler and their colleagues undertook several studies to examine this hypothesis. When they compared the performance on the Dunlop test of 80 children with reading difficulties referred to the Ophthalmology Department of the Royal Berkshire Hospital to that of 80 normal readers matched for chronological- and IQ age-level controls whose reading age was almost 18 months in advance of their chronological age, they found that 63% of the dyslexics had unfixed reference eyes compared to 1% of the above-average readers (Fowler & Stein, 1980). In another study of 148 9-year-old dyslexic children (Stein & Fowler, 1985), 68% were found to have no fixed reference eye as compared to fewer than 20% reported by the same researchers for a normative sample of 9-year-old children (Stein, Riddell, & Fowler, 1986).

In a further study, Stein, Riddell, and Fowler (1988) also recorded the vergence eye movements of 39 dyslexic children using an infrared eye movement recording system during synoptophore tests. The targets were either large (7°) or were the macular-sized fusion targets slides (2.5°) used for the Dunlop test. Sixty-four percent of the dyslexics had disordered vergence control when presented with the macular-sized fusion targets, although they performed adequately with the larger targets. Their performance was compared to that of 24 normal readers matched for age and IQ and the 14 dyslexics who had had no difficulties with vergence control on both types of stimuli.

A more recent study (Sparks & Waddingham, 1993) examined 300 reading-disabled children who were referred to the Birmingham and Midland Eye Hospital for the Dunlop test. All subjects underwent a thorough orthoptic investigation. No ocular defects were found in 43%, but previously undiagnosed ocular anomalies were found in 26% of the sample. An additional 23% had unfixed reference and were diagnosed as having "visual dyslexia" in line with the terminology suggested by Stein and Fowler. The authors argued that even if some ocular defects do not cause reading difficulties, they may exacerbate the child's reading problems and should therefore be diagnosed and treated.

However, the incidence of unstable Dunlop test responses among normal readers and dyslexics remains controversial, as is the interpretation of the relationship between unfixed reference eye and reading ability. Bishop, Jancey, and Steel (1979) administered the Dunlop test to 147 8-year-old children. Approximately one third of their sample had unfixed reference. The group with stable vergence control was significantly better at reading than the group with unfixed reference, but this difference was attributed to the fact that the group with unfixed reference had a lower mean IQ. When the effects of IQ were partialed out, there was no longer a significant difference between the reading ability of the two groups. Thus, IQ appears to be an important variable that should be considered when designing experiments.

Newman, Karle, et al., (1985) reported that, in a sample of 323 children with a mean age of 8.5 years and WISC-R IQs above 90, an almost identical proportion of advanced readers (46%) who were reading 18 months or more in advance of their mental age had unfixed reference eyes as the proportion of backward readers (51%), whose reading age was 18 months or more below their performance mental age. Thus, similar rates of binocular instability were found in both the advanced and poor reader groups. Moreover, children classified according to fixed or unfixed reference eye did not differ in reading and spelling ability, chronological age, or mental age. Both the Bishop et al. (1979) and the Newman et al. (Newman, Karle, et al., 1985; Newman, Wadsworth, Archer, & Hockley, 1985) studies demonstrate that a substantial number of normal developing readers do not have a fixed reference eye, and suggest that fixed reference may not be a crucial component of competent reading.

The purpose of this study was:

1. To examine the hypothesis that dyslexic children have impairments of visual processing, especially unstable control of vergence eye movements, by comparing their performance on a battery of orthoptic tests and the Dunlop test to that of both chronological- and reading-age controls.
2. To determine whether a routine orthoptic assessment would reliably identify children with reading difficulties and help to elucidate the nature of those reading difficulties.
3. To examine the hypothesis that children with visual impairments, as identified by the Dunlop test, would perform differently on reading and spelling tests than would dyslexic children who had a fixed reference eye and no anomalous vergence control.

Stein and Fowler also listed more specific anomalies that came to light in the course of their investigations. Because stereoacuity depends on accurate binocular fixation and vergence control, children who have unfixed reference eye should have reduced stereoacuity (Fowler, Munco, Richardson, & Stein, 1989; Stein et al., 1987). Second, dyslexics should be more susceptible to the effects of peripheral distractors or "crowding" than should controls (Stein, 1991).

Twenty dyslexics, 20 chronological-age, and 20 reading-age controls participated in the study. The dyslexics formed a cohort of children whose progress was being followed over a 2-year period (see Snowling, Goulandris, & Defty, chap. 10, this volume). There was a discrepancy of 18 months or more between their attainment on reading and spelling tests and their chronological age, and they were all of average or above-average intelligence as measured on the Wechsler Intelligence Scale for Children or WISC-R (Wechsler, 1974). In addition, their first language was English and none had specific language impairments. Because an extensive battery of IQ, phonological, visual, reading, and spelling tests had been undertaken, the orthoptic tests were included to see if they were useful adjuncts in the assessment of reading difficulties.

The dyslexic group consisted of 18 boys and 2 girls whose mean chronological age was 11 years, 7 months; mean reading age was 8 years, 9 months; and mean verbal IQ on the Wechsler Intelligence Scale for Children–Revised (WISC-R) was 105. The mean chronological age of the chronological-age controls was 11 years, 5 months; their mean reading age was 11 years, 11 months; and their mean verbal IQ (BPVS) 100. The reading-age controls had a mean chronological age of 8 years, 7 months; a reading age of 8 years, 8 months; and a verbal IQ (BPVS) of 103. There was no significant difference between the groups' IQs, no significant difference between the chronological ages of the dyslexics and their chronological-age controls, and no significant difference between the reading ages of the dyslexics and their reading-age controls.

Because the dyslexic subjects came from many different regions, they were referred directly to Moorfields Eye Hospital through their general practitioner, with their parents arranging an appointment on a convenient date. All the chronological- and reading-age-matched controls were tested by the same orthoptists as the dyslexics, but in their own schools.

The British Ability Reading Test (Elliott, Murray, & Pearson, 1983), a single-word reading test, was administered to all the children. In addition, a verbal IQ test was given. For the dyslexics, the Verbal Scale of the Wechsler Intelligence Test for Children–Revised was used. In the case of the controls, either a short form of the WISC-R consisting of the Similarities and the Vocabulary subtests, or the British Pictures Vocabulary Scale (Dunn, Dunn, Whetton, & Pintilie, 1982), a test in which spoken words have to be matched to one of four pictures, was used.

Two orthoptists from Moorfields Eye Hospital performed the assessments. The orthoptist who administered the Dunlop test was blind to the nature of the experiment and the composition of the different groups. Following normal practice at Moorfields Eye Hospital, all experimental subjects received a fundus and media examination by a consultant strabismus surgeon

15. FIXED REFERENCE EYE AND READING DISABILITY 307

to exclude ocular pathology. The orthoptic assessment and the criteria to detect abnormality are detailed later in the chapter. Cutoffs were made on the basis of clinical experience with reference to the literature.

Because the dyslexics were accompanied by a parent a full case history was taken, but this was not possible in the case of the controls who were seen during a normal school day. All subjects were asked the following questions: Did they have any particular problems with their vision when reading? Did they find that words tended to move on the page? Had they ever attended an eye clinic?

Tests of visual acuity for both distance and near vision were undertaken. For distance visual acuity, the Cambridge crowding cards were used at a distance of 3 metres. This is a multiple-letter test in which the center letter must be named or selected from choices on a display card. These peripheral distractors cause crowding effects, rendering correct identification more difficult. According to Stein (1991), crowding causes particular difficulties in cases in which fixed ocular reference eye has not yet been established. A criterion of 6/9 was adopted for this test, because clinical experience using this test (AMcI) suggested that it is harder to achieve 6/6 with crowding than using the conventional Snellen's chart. To test near visual acuity, the Snellens Vision Chart, reduced for test distance of 33 cms, was administered on the RAF rule (a measure resembling a ruler on which the stimuli are presented). A criterion of 6/9 was also adopted for near visual acuity.

Accommodation is the ability to keep a near object in focus, and it is reduced in adults. When testing accommodation, the orthoptist is evaluating the extent to which the eyes can change focus ranging from the near point to the far point. Accommodation was tested at near point using "N series print" (times roman) on the RAF rule under conditions of binocular vision. A criterion of clear abnormality was set at $<N5$ or $N5$ at <10 cms. If size of print was larger than $N5$, this was considered in the abnormal range.

Convergence—the ability to maintain binocular fixation on an approaching target—was assessed for near point on the RAF rule. The ability to focus accurately on an approaching target is needed for single binocular vision, and brings retinal images to corresponding points. The level of effort required was also taken into account as a separate item.

The Cover Test is used to investigate whether one of the eyes is misaligned in respect of the other (a manifest deviation) or whether there is a significant tendency for one eye to deviate (a latent deviation). The subject is required to maintain steady fixation on a detailed target while a cover is placed over one eye. Two alternative procedures were administered. In the Cover-Uncover procedure, the behavior of the uncovered eye is observed to determine whether there is any manifest deviation, and then the behavior of the previously covered eye is examined to reveal any latent deviation. The Alternate Cover Test is then used, in the absence of a manifest deviation, to detect the effect of increased disassociation on any latent deviation. Both tests were administered at 1/3 and 6 meters. If a significant degree of deviation was identified, the Prism Cover test was also used; this test enables the clinician to measure the deviation in prism diopters.

The extent and quality of smooth pursuit ocular movement was assessed in each direction of gaze. Ocular movements should be smooth and fluid.

Stereoacuity—the ability to appreciate depth—was tested using the TNO stereotest, in which the eyes are dissociated by red and green filters and no monocular cues are present. If subjects performed badly, the Titmus test (which provides some monocular cues) was added. Only the results of the TNO were used in the analyses. Failure to perceive a disparity of 120 was recorded as abnormal. Stereoacuity is often reduced if visual acuity or binocular vision is poor.

Motor fusion tests evaluate the ability to maintain fused images while the eyes are converged or diverged. The strength of prism prior to that which induced diplopia (double vision) was recorded.

The Dunlop Test of Ocular Reference assesses whether a subject has a fixed reference eye. The *reference eye* is defined as the preferred eye in binocular situations and can be contrasted to the dominant eye, which is the eye preferred in monocular situations (such as looking through a telescope). Unfixed reference eye is said to cause visual confusion, contributing to letter reversals and misordering of letters within words and between lines (Stein & Fowler, 1993).

The test is administered on a synoptophore. The subject looks at two macular-fusion slides. The slide seen by the right eye depicts a house with a small tree to the left of the front door, whereas the slide seen by the left eye depicts the same house with a large tree to the right of the door. The child is asked to look at the front door and to adjust a knob until the two images fuse. When the slides are fused the subject sees a house with a large tree to the left of the door and a small tree to the right of it. The tubes of the synoptophore are then separated, with the subject's eyes diverging to retain fusion while maintaining central fixation on the door. Prior to the onset of diplopia (double vision) when fusion is no longer possible, movement of one or both of the trees may be observed. When this occurs, subjects are asked to report whether either or both trees appeared to move toward the door, or if no movement was detected. The slides are exchanged randomly to ensure that subjects will not be able to guess. Following the procedure adopted by Stein and Fowler, a subject is considered to have a fixed reference eye if he or she consistently reports the same eye on 8/10 trials.

Three different analyses were undertaken. First, the performance of the three groups on the orthoptic battery was compared. Second, all the subjects were pooled and regrouped according to whether they had passed or failed the Dunlop test, and their comparative performance on the visual battery was evaluated. Finally, the attainments of two small groups of dyslexics who had either passed or failed the Dunlop test were compared on a battery of reading, spelling, visual-memory, and phonological tasks.

First, we wished to ascertain whether dyslexics performed worse than chronological- and reading-age controls on the tests in our orthoptic battery, and to identify which tests differentiated the groups. The number of individuals who had reached criterion levels were calculated for each of the orthoptic tests, and chi-square tests performed. There were no significant differences between the three groups on any of the other tests, including the Dunlop test, apart from fusional divergence. On this test there was no significant difference between the groups at 12 diopters, but when the criterion of 10 dioptres was adopted, dyslexics performed significantly worse than age-matched peers but were comparable to reading-level controls. To examine the result more precisely, an analysis of variance was performed on each individual's fusion divergence score in prism dioptres. No significant difference was found between the three groups when the results were analyzed in this manner.

The orthoptic assessment was not, therefore, able to distinguish between the groups of poor readers and able readers in any meaningful way. There was some indication that fusion divergence was less well developed in dyslexics than in age-matched readers, but they were no less skilled than younger children whose reading age was equal to their own. Two possible interpretations of this result are possible. The first is that fusion divergence does indeed pose a problem for some children with reading difficulties. However, another, more plausible explanation is that the ability to maintain fused images while the eyes are being diverged is a skill that develops as a result of reading experience. If this were so, it would not be surprising that dyslexics performed at the same level as their reading-age-matched controls but were less proficient than children of the same age who were much more proficient readers.

Because we were interested in learning whether the Dunlop test was a good indicator of other visual anomalies, we reclassified all the subjects according to whether they had passed (fixed reference eye) or failed (unstable reference eye) the Dunlop test. If the dominant eye was consistent on 8 of the 10 trials, the subject was deemed to have a fixed reference eye (Stein & Fowler, 1982). The number of children who passed and failed the Dunlop test can be seen in Table 15.1. It is evident that many subjects in each of the original three groups had not yet acquired ocular dominance, despite the fact that the children in the two control groups were average or above-average readers.

TABLE 15.1
Number of Subjects With Fixed and Unfixed
Reference Eye When Tested on Dunlop Test

	Chronological Age	Reading Age	Passed	Failed
Dyslexics	11 years, 6 months	8 years, 9 months	6	14
CA controls	11 years, 5 months	11 years, 11 months	10	10
RA controls	8 years, 7 months	8 years, 8 months	6	14

Although the chronological-age controls performed better than the dyslexics and the reading-age-matched readers, this difference was not significant. A comparison of the test results on the visual test battery showed that there were no significant differences between the performance of the children who passed and those who failed the Dunlop test on *any* of the tests in the battery. Both intragroup and intergroup comparisons were undertaken. This suggested that the Dunlop test itself did not subdivide the children in a manner that drew attention to other underlying visual deficits.

READING AND SPELLING PERFORMANCE

The critical experimental question is whether dyslexics who give consistent responses to the Dunlop test differ in reading and spelling performance from dyslexics who give inconsistent responses. We therefore decided to test the following hypothesis: Dyslexic children who fail the Dunlop test will be subject to "visual dyslexia" and will differ from dyslexic children who have not failed the Dunlop test on reading and spelling tasks. We matched five dyslexic subjects who failed the Dunlop test with five dyslexics who passed the Dunlop test for reading age on the British Ability Scales Word Reading Test (Elliott et al., 1983). We then compared their performance on a number of experimental reading, spelling, and visual tests.

To assess lexical skills, each dyslexic was asked to read 31 irregular words (e.g., *bread, tongue, island, sausage*; Snowling, Stackhouse, & Rack, 1986). To evaluate phonological recoding ability, they were asked to read 22 one- and two-syllable nonwords (e.g., *lep, baltrid*). To examine spelling ability, they were asked to spell 40 regular words of increasing syllable length, ranging from one to four syllables (e.g., *pet, puppy, membership, geography*). The children also spelled 32 one- and two-syllable nonwords to evaluate their use of phonological strategies when attempting to spell unfamiliar words.

There was no difference in the scores attained on the reading and spelling tests when the children were subdivided according to their per-

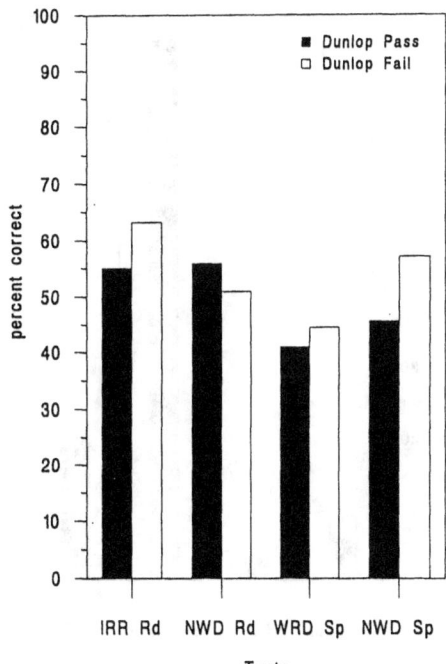

FIG. 15.1. Dyslexics' scores (% correct) on reading and spelling tests according to performance on the Dunlop test.

formance on the Dunlop test (see Fig. 15.1). Contrary to prediction, the children who did not have a fixed reference eye were somewhat better at reading irregular words, spelling by syllable length, and nonword spelling than were those who had a fixed reference eye, although these differences were not statistically significant. In addition, there was substantial variability within the groups, suggesting that performance on the Dunlop test was not dividing the dyslexics into cohesive subgroups. The fact that the two subgroups did not differ in their ability to read irregular words was particularly informative. If the group that failed the Dunlop test had visual problems that prevented them from focusing accurately on the letters in words when reading, one would have expected that their irregular word recognition would be seriously impaired. This was not the case.

VISUAL MEMORY

We also asked the children to undertake a number of visual memory tasks, reasoning that the visual dyslexic subgroup who had poor vergence control might also have difficulties recalling visually presented shapes or unfamiliar alphabetic material. We also included the Children's Embedded Figures

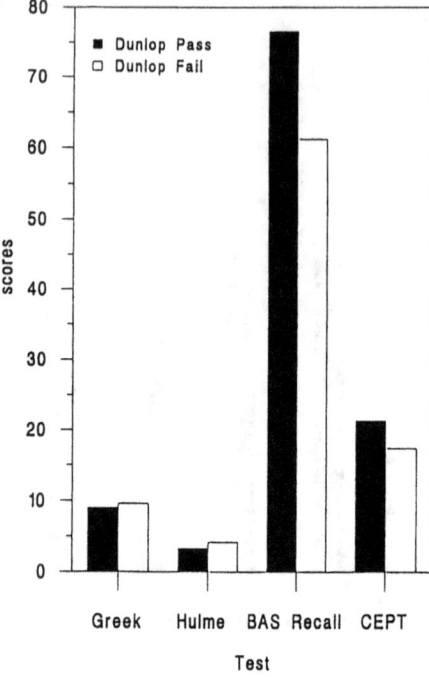

FIG. 15.2. Dyslexics' scores on visual memory tests according to performance on the Dunlop test.

test. Three visual memory tests were administered: the British Abilities Test Recall of Designs; the Greek Visual Memory Test (after Goulandris, 1989), a test requiring memory for abstract forms (after Hulme, 1981); and the Children's Embedded Figures test (Witkin, Oltman, Raskin, & Karp, 1971). The British Abilities Recall of Designs is a standardized test in which children are asked to examine a drawing of a series of geometrical shapes for 10 seconds and then reproduce them. The Greek Visual Memory Test is a visual–sequential memory test requiring recognition and correct sequencing of a series of Greek letters. The Hulme Memory Test (1981) is a test of recall consisting of 14 complex geometric shapes that are difficult to code verbally and thus depend primarily on visual memory. A random selection of between two and seven items is presented, with two consecutive trials for each number of items. The Children's Embedded Figures Test (CEFT) evaluates the ability to distinguish figure from ground. Two alternative shapes, either a tent or a house, are embedded in increasingly complex figures, and the subject is instructed to find the shape and to indicate its perimeter.

As can be seen in Fig. 15.2, there were no significant differences between the subgroups of dyslexics on any of the visual memory tests, suggesting that there is no link between performance on the Dunlop test and performance on the visual tests reported here.

DISCUSSION

Our results did not confirm that there is a relationship between performance on the Dunlop test and reading disability. Although a high proportion of the dyslexic children failed to achieve 8 out of 10 consistent responses required as evidence of fixed reference eye on the Dunlop test, so did many controls. The dyslexics did not differ from the controls on stereoacuity, and were no more susceptible to crowding than were the controls. In addition, the presence or absence of a reference eye did not indicate which children suffered from other visual disorders. When all the subjects were regrouped according to whether they did or did not have fixed reference, there was no significant difference in the reading ability of the two groups. In fact, the unstable group's reading age was marginally higher than that of the stable group. Therefore, there is no evidence in our data that children with unstable reference are poorer readers than those who have acquired stable reference. Moreover, a comparison of a small group of dyslexics with stable and unstable reference revealed very similar profiles on measures of reading, spelling, and visual memory processing.

Our finding that 70% of the dyslexics gave unstable responses on the Dunlop test was in line with the 68% reported by Stein and Fowler (1985) and the 64% reported by Stein, Riddell, and Fowler (1988). However, our controls found the task much more difficult than did the normal readers tested by Stein and his colleagues. For example, Stein, Riddell, and Fowler (1987) reported that none of their reading-age controls had unstable binocular control, whereas only 30% of our 8-year-old reading-age controls and only 50% of the 11-year-old age-matched controls performed consistently on the Dunlop test.

In our experiment, each dyslexic was matched as closely as possible to a chronological- and a reading-age-matched control to enable us to determine whether fixed ocular dominance was associated with physical maturity or with reading ability. Our groups were also closely matched for verbal IQ, eliminating the possibility that poor performance on the Dunlop test arose from differences in levels of mental ability. This methodology may have been different from that adopted by Stein et al. (1987), but is unlikely to account for the substantial discrepancy between our results. On the other hand, our results resemble those reported by other researchers. Newman, Karle, et al. (1985) reported that approximately 50% of their sample had unstable ocular dominance, and that the stable and unstable groups did not differ on age, intelligence, reading, or spelling. When we collapsed all the subjects regardless of initial group, we found that 63% had unstable binocular control. This is a very high rate of failure but one that cannot be attributed to an inexperienced orthoptist, because the orthoptist in question had been fully trained by the principal orthoptist at

Moorfield's hospital and was experienced at administering the test. In addition, neither Bishop (1989), Newman, Wadsworth, et al. (1985), nor this study found evidence that there was an association between reading and spelling and performance on the Dunlop test.

As Stein and Fowler (1993) already indicated, the general consensus among researchers is that a high proportion of dyslexics have unstable ocular dominance, but there is as yet no consensus on the incidence of unstable reference in the normal population. Although norms are available indicating the incidence of stable binocular control at different ages, unfortunately there are currently no norms relating stable reference to reading age.

Our data indicate that dyslexics perform in line with reading-age controls but are inferior to age-matched controls, and suggest that learning to read may contribute to the development of stable binocular control and that reading experience is the crucial factor (Bishop, 1989; Bruck, chap. 9, this volume). It is plausible that as children learn to read they become more proficient at focusing on letters and letter strings and at detecting distinguishing features. Thus, reading may serve as a catalyst for the development of visual skills, including the development of stable binocular control.

In conclusion, if some reading-disabled children do have underlying visual impairments, these do not appear to be identified by the usual battery of orthoptic tests administered in this experiment. Orthoptic tests are an invaluable resource for detecting children with frank visual anomalies of binocular vision, enabling orthoptists to recommend appropriate therapy. However, the results of this experiment do not support the view that the traditional battery and, in particular, the Dunlop test can differentiate children with reading disability from normal readers.

ACKNOWLEDGMENTS

This research was supported by Grant G8801538 from the Medical Research Council of Great Britain. We thank Jane-Michelle Bethel and Dr. John Lee for their assistance. We also wish to thank the staff and children at St. Matthew's School and Westminster City School for their participation.

REFERENCES

Bishop, D. V. M. (1989). Unstable vergence control and dyslexia—a critique. *British Journal of Ophthalmology, 73,* 223–245.

Bishop, D. V. M., Jancey, C., & Steel, A. M. (1979). Orthoptic status and reading disability. *Cortex, 15,* 659–666.

Dunlop, P. (1972). Dyslexia: The orthoptic approach. *Austrian Journal of Orthoptics, 12,* 16–20.

Dunn, L. M., Dunn, L. M., Whetton, C., & Pintilie, D. (1982). *British Picture Vocabulary Scale.* Windsor, England: NFER-Nelson.

Elliott, C. D., Murray, D. J., & Pearson, L. S. (1983). *The British Ability Scales*. Windsor, England: NFER-Nelson.
Dunlop, P. (1976). The changing role of orthoptics in dyslexia. *British Orthoptic Journal, 33*, 22–28.
Fowler, M. S., Munco, N., Richardson, A., & Stein, J. F. (1989). Vergence control in patients with lesions of the posterior parietal cortex. *Journal of Physiology, 417*, 92.
Fowler, M. S., & Stein, J. F. (1980). Visual dyslexia. *British Orthoptic Journal, 37*, 11–15.
Goulandris, A. M. (1989). *Emergent spelling: The development of spelling strategies in young children*. Unpublished doctoral thesis, University of London.
Hulme, C. (1981). *Reading retardation and multisensory learning*. London: Routledge & Kegan Paul.
Livingstone, M. S., Rosen, G. D., Drislane, F. W., & Galaburda, A. M. (1991). Physiological and anatomical evidence for a magnocellular defect in developmental dyslexia. *Proceedings of the National Academy of Sciences USA, 88*, 7943–7947.
Lovegrove, W. J. (1991). Is the question of the role of visual deficits as a cause of reading disabilities a closed one? Comments on Hulme. *Cognitive Neuropsychology, 8*, 435–441.
Lovegrove, W., Martin, F., & Slaghuis, W. (1986). A theoretical and experimental case for a visual deficit in specific reading disability. *Cognitive Neuropsychology, 3*, 225–267.
Newman, S. P., Karle, H., Wadsworth, J. F., Archer, R., Hockley, R., & Rodgers, P. (1985). Ocular dominance, reading and spelling: A reassessment of a measure associated with specific reading difficulties. *Journal of Research in Reading, 8*, 127–138.
Newman, S. P., Wadsworth, J. F., Archer, R., & Hockley, R. (1985). Ocular dominance, reading and spelling ability in schoolchildren. *British Journal of Ophthalmology, 69*, 228–232.
Snowling, M. J. (1987). *Dyslexia: A cognitive developmental perspective*. Oxford, England: Blackwell.
Snowling, M. J., Stackhouse, J., & Rack, J. P. (1986). Phonological dyslexia and dysgraphia: A developmental analysis. *Cognitive Neuropsychology, 3*, 309–339.
Sparks, J. A., & Waddingham, P. E. (1993). Incidence of ocular anomalies in children referred for a Dunlop Test. *British Orthoptic Journal, 50*, 22–24.
Stanovich, K. E. (1988). Explaining the differences between the dyslexic and the garden variety poor reader: The phonological-core variable difference model. *Journal of Learning Difficulties, 21*, 590–612.
Stein, J. F. (1991). Vision and language. In M. Snowling & M. Thomson (Eds.), *Dyslexia: Integrating theory and practice* (pp. 31–43). London: Whurr.
Stein, J. F., & Fowler, M. S. (1982). Diagnosis of dyslexia by means of a new indicator of eye dominance. *British Journal of Ophthalmology, 66*, 332–336.
Stein, J. F., & Fowler, M. S. (1985). Effect of monocular occlusion on visuomotor perception and reading in dyslexic children. *Lancet, 1384*, 69–73.
Stein, J., & Fowler, S. (1993). Unstable binocular control in dyslexic children. *Journal of Research in Reading, 16*, 30–45.
Stein, J. F., Riddell, P. M., & Fowler, M. S. (1986). The Dunlop test and reading in primary school children. *British Journal of Ophthalmology, 70*, 317–320.
Stein, J. F., Riddell, P. M., & Fowler, M. S. (1987). Fine binocular control in dyslexic children. *Eye, 1*, 433–438.
Stein, J. F., Riddell, P. M., & Fowler, M. S. (1988). Disordered vergence control in dyslexic children. *British Journal of Ophthalmology, 72*, 162–166.
Vellutino, F. R. (1979). *Dyslexia: Theory and research*. Cambridge, MA: MIT Press.
Wechsler, D. (1974). *Wechsler Intelligence Scale for Children–Revised*. New York: Psychological Corporation.
Willows, D. M., Kruk, R. S., & Corcos, E. (1993). *Visual processes in reading and reading disabilities*. Hillsdale, NJ: Lawrence Erlbaum Associates.
Witkin, A., Oltman, P. K., Raskin, E., & Karp, S. A. (1971). *Manual to the Embedded Figures Tests*. Palo Alto, CA: Consulting Psychologists Press.

Part **III**

READING COMPREHENSION

Research on children's reading has paid far more attention to the development of decoding skills than to the development of reading comprehension. This might be seen as unfortunate, because it is indisputable that the aim of reading is to comprehend meaning. However, an important limiting factor in reading comprehension is the level of decoding skill. This link between decoding and comprehension skill is well captured by Gough and Tunmer's "simple model." According to this model, reading is the product of decoding and comprehension or $R = D \times C$. This model captures the obvious point that if you cannot decode you cannot possibly comprehend. The model also captures another less obvious idea, which is that once decoding has occurred the processes of comprehension in reading are probably more or less synonymous with those of language comprehension.

The chapters in Part III explore the nature and limits on children's reading comprehension skills. The studies reported by Joshi, Williams, and Wood (chap. 16) can be considered as quite direct applications of the logic of the simple model. They explore the relationship between reading comprehension and listening comprehension in children of different ages. They find high correlations between listening comprehension and reading comprehension. They also show that decoding skill, as assessed by nonword reading ability, accounts for additional variance in reading comprehension after the effects of listening comprehension are controlled. The measures used by Joshi et al. appear to offer considerable promise in the diagnosis of specific reading difficulties, for which it was suggested that listening comprehension might be a better measure of the cognitive skills relevant to reading comprehension than IQ tests, which are typically used for this purpose.

Chapter 17 by Cain and Oakhill and chapter 18 by Oakhill, Cain, and Yuill both consider cognitive factors that are associated with reading comprehension difficulties in children. Cain and Oakhill report a study of inferential skills in children with reading comprehension difficulties. They compare the ability of children to answer literal questions about a text, or to answer questions requiring inferences. One type of inferential question merely requires the child to combine two separate pieces of information provided in the story, whereas a second type requires the child to combine what has been read with some aspect of general knowledge. Cain and Oakhill found that children with reading comprehension difficulties were particularly poor at making inferences requiring the of use general knowledge. They suggest that children with reading comprehension difficulties have a deficit in inference making, which is one plausible cause of their difficulties.

Oakhill, Cain, and Yuill consider inferences in the context of a number of other deficiencies that are associated with children's reading comprehension difficulties. They distinguish between deficiencies in processes, such as inference making and working memory skills, and deficiencies in knowledge, including knowledge of word meanings and general knowledge. They document the fact that children with reading comprehension problems show deficiencies on a wide variety of tasks tapping both processes and knowledge. They argue that deficits in working memory provide a plausible explanation for these children's reading problems and their difficulties on a range of other cognitive tasks.

Chapter 16

Predicting Reading Comprehension From Listening Comprehension: Is This the Answer to the IQ Debate?

R. Malatesha Joshi
Oklahoma State University

Katherine A. Williams
Langston University

Jackie R. Wood
Cameron University

Specific reading disability, or developmental dyslexia, has been defined as "a disorder manifested by difficulty in learning to read despite conventional instruction, adequate intelligence, and socio-cultural opportunity. It is dependent upon fundamental cognitive abilities which are frequently constitutional in origin" (Critchley, 1970, p. 5). This definition has led to diagnosing dyslexia on the basis of the discrepancy between a subject's IQ scores and his or her reading achievement scores. However, diagnosing reading disability on the basis of an IQ–achievement discrepancy has been criticized for several reasons. The validity of the assumptions that underlies the use of IQ scores in defining reading disabilities has been questioned (Siegel, 1989). For instance, IQ scores are not able to account for more than 20% to 25% of variance seen in reading performance, particularly in young children. Stanovich, Cunningham, and Feeman (1984) reviewed studies of the relationship between reading achievement and IQ scores at different grade levels, and although the correlation coefficients were around 0.6 and 0.7 for children aged 14 and above, the coefficients were around 0.4 for the first three grades. A more serious but pragmatic problem is that diagnosis based on IQ scores does not lead to recommendations regarding remediation, instruction, and management of reading problems. For these reasons it has been argued that defining reading disabilities on

319

the basis of a discrepancy between IQ and achievement is untenable (e.g., Joshi, 1995; Joshi & Leong, 1993; Stanovich, 1991).

These arguments have prompted researchers to search for alternative assessment procedures for identifying children with specific reading disabilities (dyslexia). One measure of ability that is often recommended as an alternative to IQ scores is listening comprehension (Aaron, 1991; Spring & French, 1990). As a diagnostic tool, listening comprehension does not have many of the limitations of IQ tests. The advantages of using listening comprehension are that it is an integral component of the language process; a test of listening comprehension is easy to administer; and, more important, the diagnostic findings based on this procedure can lead to recommendations regarding corrective instruction.

The idea of using listening comprehension to predict reading comprehension is not a new one. Several decades ago, Ladd (1970) noted that listening comprehension is an important indicator of reading ability, and Carroll (1977) was explicit in advocating the use of listening comprehension as a predictor of reading ability. Durrell and Hayes (1969) considered listening comprehension to be more directly related to reading than most measures of intelligence. Spring and French (1990) suggested that identifying children with specific reading disability on the basis of discrepancy between their reading comprehension and listening comprehension is more appropriate than using the discrepancy between reading achievement and IQ scores. The validity of using listening comprehension measures for the diagnosis of different forms of reading disabilities was recently documented by Aaron (1991).

There is an impressive body of literature to support the notion that apart from the modality of input, reading comprehension and listening comprehension are mediated by the same cognitive mechanism (Townsend, Carrithers, & Bever, 1987). Duker's (1965) review of 23 studies comparing reading comprehension and listening comprehension, and another review of an additonal 12 studies (Kennedy, 1971), report correlation coefficients that range from 0.45 to 0.82. In yet another review, Danks (1980) reported similar data. Stanovich et al. (1984) compared the reading performance of children from Grades 1, 2, and 5 with measures of intelligence, listening comprehension, and decoding skill. At all levels, listening comprehension was found to be a better predictor of reading achievement than were measures of intelligence.

Wood, Buckhalt, and Tomlin (1988) obtained an impressive correlation coefficient of 0.78 between reading and listening comprehenison for groups of children classified as learning disabled or mildly mentally handicapped. In a review of this topic, Trabasso (1981) noted that studies suggest it matters little as far as comprehension is concerned whether the material is read or heard. Kintsch and Kozminsky (1977) administered reading and listening tasks to college students and found surprisingly small differences in the comprehension of structural elements and propositions, which led them to conclude that reading and listening involve identical comprehension skills. In a study of college students, Palmer, McCleod, Hunt, and Davidson (1985) obtained a correlation coefficient of 0.82 between reading comprehension and listening comprehension, which led them to conclude that reading comprehension can be predicted almost perfectly by a listening comprehension measure.

Even though listening comprehension appears to be a better predictor of reading than IQ, many of the studies reviewed here have limitations. They have often used very small numbers of children, and some have not used well-standardized listening comprehension tests, because such tests have not been available until recently. These limitations led Stanovich (1991) to caution that the use of listening comprehension scores as a means of estimating reading potential needs further examination.

STUDY 1

This study was designed to determine the relationship between reading comprehension and listening comprehension by administering standardized reading comprehension and listening comprehension tests to a large group of subjects of different ages. A total of 273 children from Grades 3 through 6 were tested (see Table 16.1). A majority of the subjects were White and came from middle-income families. These subjects were from regular classrooms, and none of them had repeated a grade.

Procedure

The Passage comprehension subtest from Form G of the Woodcock Reading Mastery Test–Revised (WRMT-R; Woodcock, 1987) was used to assess reading comprehension. Listening comprehension was measured by ad-

TABLE 16.1
Correlations Between Reading and Listening Comprehension at Different Ages, as Assessed by WRMT-R

Grade Levels	r Between Listening and Reading Comprehension
Grade 3 ($n = 78$)	0.68
Grade 4 ($n = 68$)	0.61
Grade 5 ($n = 75$)	0.65
Grade 6 ($n = 52$)	0.75
Mean	0.67

ministering the passage comprehension subtest from Form H of the WRMT-R as a test of listening comprehension. In this case, the experimenter read each sentence to the subjects who were then asked to supply the missing word. Because the two forms (G and H) of the test are equated for difficulty level and length, they provide directly comparable measures, the difference being the mode of presentation. This form of listening comprehension measure has a test/retest reliability of 0.67, and correlates 0.63 with the WISC-R comprehension subtest (Aaron, 1991). The two tests were administered individually to all the subjects. The administration and the scoring procedures followed were the ones recommended in the manual, and the raw scores were converted to standard scores to compute the correlation between reading comprehension and listening comprehension. The results are shown in Table 16.1.

As can be seen in Table 16.1, the mean correlation coefficient for the four grades is 0.67, which can therefore account for nearly 45% of the variance seen in reading comprehension. The correlation coefficient of 0.67 is higher than the ones usually obtained between IQ scores and reading comprehension scores.

STUDY II

The previous study used a cloze format to assess comprehension, wherein the subject supplies the missing word from a sentence. Another common method used for assessing comprehension is to require the subject to answer a set of questions after reading a passage. The Wechsler Individual Achievement Test (WIAT; Wechsler, 1991) is a standardized test that utilizes this procedure. Yet another way of assessing comprehension is to require the subject to match a written sentence with a picture that represents the idea contained in the sentence. The Peabody Individual Achievement Test–Revised (PIAT-R; Markwardt, 1989) utilizes this method. Would listening and reading comprehension assessed by these different methods yield similar-sized correlations between reading and listening comprehension? The second study was intended to answer this question by administering the WRMT-R, Wechsler Individual Achievement Test (WIAT; Wechsler, 1992), and the PIAT-R. The WIAT has separate reading comprehension and listening comprehension measures. The reading comprehension subtest of WIAT has a validity coefficient ranging from 0.79 to 0.84 at different grade levels, and a reliability coefficient of about 0.90. The listening comprehension subtest of WIAT has a validity coefficient of 0.75 and a reliability coefficient of 0.95.

The PIAT-R does not have a standardized listening comprehension subtest. Therefore, we followed the procedure used by Spring and French

TABLE 16.2
Correlations Between Three Parallel Tests
of Reading and Listening Comprehension

	WIAT	WRMT-R	PIAT-R
Grade 3 ($n = 60$)	0.40	0.60	0.69
Grade 5 ($n = 60$)	0.49	0.65	0.90

(1990) to measure listening comprehension with this test: Odd items from the reading comprehension subtest of the PIAT-R were read to the subjects for assessing listening comprehension, whereas even items were administered as reading comprehension measure. As in Study I, reading comprehension subtest from Form H of the WRMT-R was presented as a test of listening comprehension. Reading comprehension was measured by the following three instruments: WIAT (reading comprehension subtest), odd items taken from the reading comprehension subtest of the PIAT-R, and the reading comprehension subtest from Form G of the WRMT-R. These tests were administered to 60 children from Grade 3 and 60 children from Grade 5. The correlations are shown in Table 16.2.

As in Study 1, the correlations obtained between reading comprehension and listening comprehension are quite impressive, often exceeding those between IQ and reading achievement. Listening comprehension can account for greater variance seen in reading at the fifth-grade level than at the third-grade level in all of the tests. Furthermore, PIAT-R, as a test of listening comprehension, is a better predictor of reading comprehension than are WIAT and WRMT-R. Approximately 47% and 81% of the variance seen in reading comprehension can be accounted for by listening comprehension as measured by PIAT-R at the third and fifth grades, respectively.

STUDY III

Although listening comprehension has been recommended as an alternate measure to IQ as a predictor of reading ability (Aaron, 1991; Spring & French, 1990), it does not account for all the variability seen in reading achievement. In the first two studies, the unaccounted variance in reading comprehension ranges from 20% to 60%, depending on the test.

Experimental, neuropsychological, and developmental studies of reading suggest that the two major components of reading are comprehension and decoding. According to the simple view of reading (Gough & Tunmer, 1986; Hoover & Gough, 1990; Tunmer & Hoover, 1993), reading (R)

equals the product of decoding (D) and comprehension (C). That is, $R = D \times C$. It follows, then, that if $D = 0$, then $R = 0$; and if $C = 0$, then $R = 0$. Thus, a student whose decoding skill is extremely deficient will also have very limited reading comprehension skill; similarly, a student who has severe language comprehension problems will also have very low reading comprehension scores. It is therefore possible that decoding skills can account for a substantial portion of the unaccounted variance seen in reading comprehension. Decoding, also referred to as *phonological recoding skill*, is often measured by a nonword reading task. Because the reader has not encountered these "words" before, they tap the reader's ability to decode, that is to generalize from their knowledge of spelling–sound correspondences to generate a pronunciation for these novel items. A list of 36 pronounceable nonwords based on increasingly complex spelling-to-sound correspondences (Ehri, 1991; Venezky, 1976; Wijk, 1966) was constructed. Subjects were asked to read the list of nonwords aloud. Responses were recorded for later analysis.

The contribution of decoding skill to reading comprehension was assessed by administering the decoding task, as well as a reading comprehension and a listening comprehension task, to 65 normal readers from fourth grade. Their reading achievement was measured by Gates-MacGinitie Reading Test (MacGinitie & MacGinitie, 1989), which is a "silent test" of vocabulary and comprehension. The intellectual ability of these subjects was measured by administering the Standard Progressive Matrices (Raven, 1986). Form G of the WRMT-R was used to assess reading comprehension, and Form H of the WRMT-R was used to assess listening comprehension, as was done in the previous two studies. The means and standard deviations of these tests are shown in Table 16.3. Correlations were computed between reading comprehension and IQ scores, between reading comprehension and listening comprehension, and multiple coefficient of correlation among reading comprehension and listening comprehension and decoding together. The results are shown in Table 16.4.

As in Studies I and II, the correlation between reading comprehension and listening comprehension (0.62) was higher than the correlation be-

TABLE 16.3
Means and Standard Deviations for Reading, Listening
Comprehension, and the Standard Progressive Matrix Tests ($n = 65$)

	Mean	*SD*
Gates-MacGinitie	4.59	1.91
IQ scores (SPM)	98.96	13.00
WRMT-R (G)	6.12	2.77
WRMT-R (H)	6.51	2.36
Decoding (NWR) task	26.73	7.19

TABLE 16.4
Correlations Between Scores on Reading, Listening, Decoding,
and Standard Progressive Matrix Tests

r between reading comprehension (R.C.) & IQ	0.36
r between reading comprehension and listening comprehension (L.C.)	0.62
r between reading comprehension and listening comprehension + nonword reading	0.79

tween reading comprehension and IQ (0.36). When nonword reading ability is added to listening comprehension, the multiple correlation increases to 0.79. That is, the combination of decoding and listening comprehension accounts for more than 62% of the variance seen in reading comprehension among fourth-grade children. A regression formula was derived for predicting reading comprehension from listening comprehension and nonword reading scores. The formula was:

$$\text{Reading comprehension} = 10.00 + 0.45 \text{ (Listening comprehension + Nonword reading)}$$

GENERAL DISCUSSION

We began by considering the problems inherent in using the discrepancy between IQ and reading ability in defining cases of reading difficulty. An alternative to this approach that has often been advocated but little explored is to use listening comprehension rather than IQ as a predictor of reading disability. To date, however, few studies have explored the fruitfulness of this approach. The studies we have reported here show that this approach has considerable promise. Listening comprehension proves to be comparatively easy to measure, and it is a very good predictor of individual differences in reading comprehension skill. We also found that listening comprehension is a better predictor of reading comprehension among older (fifth grade) than younger (third grade) children. This suggests that decoding skills may be relatively more important in accounting for variation in reading comprehension in younger children. This finding is in agreement with those of other investigators (Aaron, Joshi, & Williams, manuscript under review; Chall, Jacobs, & Baldwin, 1990) and deserves further investigation in future studies of reading development.

REFERENCES

Aaron, P. G. (1991). Can reading disabilities be diagnosed without using intelligence tests? *Journal of Learning Disabilities, 24,* 178–186.

Aaron, P. G., Joshi, R. M., & Williams, K. *Not all reading disabilities are alike.* Manuscript under review.

Carroll, J. B. (1977). Developmental parameters in reading comprehension. In J. T. Guthrie (Ed.), *Cognition, curriculum, and comprehension* (pp. 25–51). Newark, DE: International Reading Association.

Chall, J. S., Jacobs, V. A., & Baldwin, L. E. (1990). *The reading crisis: Why poor children fall behind.* Cambridge, MA: Harvard University Press.

Critchley, M. (1970). *The dyslexic child.* London: Heinemann.

Danks, J. (1980). Comprehension in listening and reading: Same or different? In J. Danks & K. Pezdek (Eds.), *Reading and understanding* (pp. 25–40). Newark, DE: International Reading Association.

Duker, S. (1965). Listening and reading. *Elementary School Journal, 65,* 321–324.

Durrell, D. D., & Hayes, M. (1969). *Durrell listening-reading series: Manual for listening and reading tests.* New York: Psychological Corporation.

Ehri, L. C. (1991). Development of the ability to read words. In R. Barr, M. L. Kamil, P. Mosenthal, & P. D. Pearson (Eds.), *Handbook of reading research* (2nd ed., pp. 383–417). New York: Longman.

Gough, P. B., & Tunmer, W. E. (1986). Decoding, reading, and reading disability. *Remedial and Special Education, 7,* 6–10.

Hoover, W. A., & Gough, P. B. (1990). The simple view of reading. *Reading and Writing: An Interdisiciplinary Journal, 2,* 127–160.

Joshi, R. M. (1995). Assessing reading and spelling skills. *School Psychology Review, 24,* 361–375.

Joshi, R. M., & Leong, C. K. (Eds.). (1993). *Reading disabilities: Diagnosis and component processes.* Dordrecht, The Netherlands: Kluwer.

Kennedy, D. K. (1971). *Training with the cloze procedure visually and auditorily to improve the reading and listening comprehension of third grade underachieving readers.* Unpublished doctoral dissertation, Pennsylvania State University, University Park.

Kintsch, W., & Kozminsky, E. (1977). Summarizing stories after reading and listening. *Journal of Educational Psychology, 69,* 491–499.

Ladd, E. M. (1970). More than scores from tests. *The Reading Teacher, 24,* 305–311.

MacGinitie, W. H., & MacGinitie, R. K. (1989). *Gates-MacGinitie Reading Tests.* Chicago, IL: Riverside.

Markwardt, F. C. (1989). *Peabody Individual Achievement Test–Revised.* Circle Pines, MN: American Guidance Services.

Palmer, J., McCleod, C., Hunt, E., & Davidson, J. (1985). Information processing correlates of reading. *Journal of Memory and Language, 24,* 59–88.

Raven, J. C. (1986). *Standard progressive matrices.* London: Lewis.

Siegel, L. S. (1989). IQ is irrelevant to the definition of learning disabilities. *Journal of Learning Disabilities, 22,* 469–479.

Spring, C., & French, L. (1990). Identifying children with specific reading disabilities from listening and reading discrepancy scores. *Journal of Learning Disabilities, 23,* 53–58.

Stanovich, K. (1991). Discrepancy definitions of reading disability: Has intelligence led us astray? *Reading Research Quarterly, 26,* 7–29.

Stanovich, K., Cunningham, A., & Feeman, D. J. (1984). Intelligence, cognitive skills and early reading progress. *Reading Research Quarterly, 38,* 175–190.

Townsend, D. J., Carrithers, C., & Bever, T. G. (1987). Listening and reading processes in college- and middle-school age readers. In R. Horowitz & S. J. Samuels (Eds.), *Comprehending oral and written language* (pp. 217–242). New York: Academic.

Trabasso, T. (1981). Can we integrate research and instruction on reading comprehension? In C. M. Santa & B. L. Hayes (Eds.), *Children's prose comprehension* (pp. 30–45). Newark, DE: International Reading Association.

Tunmer, W. E., & Hoover, W. A. (1993). Components of variance models of language-related factors in reading disability: A conceptual overview. In R. M. Joshi & C. K. Leong (Eds.), *Reading disabilities: Diagnosis and component processes* (pp. 135–173). Dordrecht, The Netherlands: Kluwer.

Venezky, R. (1976). *Theoretical and experimental base for teaching reading.* The Hague: Mouton.

Wechsler, D. (1991). *Wechsler Individual Achievement Test.* San Antonio, TX: Psychological Corporation.

Wijk, A. (1966). *Rules of pronunciation for the English language: An account of the relationship between English spelling and pronunciation.* London: Oxford University Press.

Wood, T. A., Buckhalt, J. A., & Tomlin, J. G. (1988). A comparison of listening and reading performance with children in three educational placements. *Journal of Learning Disabilities, 8,* 493–496.

Woodcock, R. W. (1987). *Woodcock Reading Mastery Tests–Revised.* Circle Pines, MN: American Guidance Services.

Chapter 17

Comprehension Skill and Inference-Making Ability: Issues of Causality

Kate Cain
Jane Oakhill
Sussex University, England

Inference making is an important component in text processing. Different sentences and ideas in a text have to be connected in order to build up a fully integrated and coherent representation of the text. Yet many details of these connections are not explicitly mentioned. Therefore, the reader (or listener) must infer these links and fill in missing material from general knowledge. Studies investigating inferential ability in skilled, adult readers demonstrate that they readily make inferences as and when necessary (see Garnham, 1985; Singer, 1994; van den Broek, 1994, for reviews of such work). What is less clear is when and how young children make inferences.

A series of studies by Paris and colleagues has demonstrated that the ability to make inferences is a skill that develops between the ages of 6 and 12. For instance, Paris and Upton (1976) found that 6-year-olds were much poorer at answering questions about a story in which the correct response required an inference to be computed, as opposed to ones that required simple recall of verbatim information. Although the 10-year-olds were also better at the questions accessing given information, the difference between their performance on this type of question and those relying on inferences was much smaller. This finding suggests that, with age, inferential skill had developed to a greater extent than general question-answering ability. This relation has been demonstrated using cued recall techniques as well. Paris, Lindauer, and Cox (1977) presented children with sentences such as "Mary dropped the vase of flowers" either with or without their implied consequence—"and broke it," for this example. The implied consequence was later used as a recall cue. Eleven-year-olds were equally good at sentence recall with this cue, whether it had been mentioned explicitly in the text or not. However, 8-year-olds were much poorer at recalling sentences that had not been presented with their consequence. Paris and Lindauer (1976) found the same pattern of data for verbs and their implied instruments.

These studies demonstrate that younger children do not make as many inferences as older children. This is not because they are incapable of making such inferences: When required to generate a story from the target sentence, younger children could infer the correct consequence (Paris et al., 1977), and when required to act out the action in the sentence, young children used the target instrument (Paris & Lindauer, 1976). Thus, lack of general knowledge about likely instruments or consequences is an inadequate explanation for the poorer inferential skills of young children.

Another factor that may account for the improvement in inferential skill that is found with age is memory. In the study mentioned earlier, Paris and Upton (1976) found that memory for the text improved with age. However, better memory for the stories could not wholly account for the greater inferential performance by the older children: The relation between age and inferential skill remained after the effects of memory for explicit textual details had been controlled for. Using a more stringent check of memory, Omanson, Warren, and Trabasso (1978) found similar results. They measured children's memory for the particular story information considered sufficient and necessary to make the inferences. After controlling for differences in retention of this given information, they found that 8-year-olds still made more inferences than did 5-year-olds; that is, the older children's superior inferential skill was independent of their ability to remember the text.

These studies show that changes in inferential ability are not wholly attributable to the improvements in memory capacity or general knowledge that come with age. Young children are capable of generating inferences, yet they do not seem to do so spontaneously.

Although the measures of inferential skill used in these studies are considered a measurement of comprehension for the text, these developmental studies did not address precisely how the two skills are related. A series of studies that did address the relation between comprehension skill and inference making was conducted by Oakhill and Yuill (e.g., Oakhill, 1982, 1983, 1984; Yuill & Oakhill, 1988; see Yuill & Oakhill, 1991, for a review of this work). Two groups of children participated in these studies: fluent readers with a specific comprehension deficit (less-skilled comprehenders), and same-age fluent readers with normal reading comprehension (skilled comprehenders). In general, Oakhill and Yuill found that children with good reading comprehension skills are more likely to make inferences than are less-skilled comprehenders.

Oakhill (1982) investigated the extent to which comprehension skill was related to the ability to draw inferences from information given explicitly in the text. Short passages were read out to the children followed by a recognition test. An example of the sort of passage is: "The car crashed into the bus. The bus was near the crossroads. The car skidded on the ice." Better comprehenders were more likely to falsely recognize sentences such as "The car was near the crossroads," which they had not previously heard but which could be inferred from the text. This result suggests that the poor comprehenders were less likely to engage in the constructive processing of text, connecting up ideas within it.

Another study (Oakhill, 1984) explored a different sort of inference: ones in which the information is only implicitly mentioned in the text. In this study, the children read short stories and were required to answer a series of questions about each one. Some of the questions did not require an inference to be made to answer them; they simply tapped information that was explicitly given in the text. The other sort of questions required an inference to be made by incorporating general knowledge with information given in the text to fill in missing details. For instance, in one story the protagonist cycles to school. Although the bicycle is never mentioned explicitly in the text, it is implied by key phrases and words such as "pedalling as fast as he could." To assess whether children could make such an inference they were asked "How did John [the character] travel to school?" The less-skilled comprehenders were worse than the skilled comprehenders at answering both sorts of questions: those tapping given information and those requiring inferences. Both groups' performance on both types of question improved when given back the passage to look over, but the less-skilled comprehenders' performance on the inference questions was still worse than that of the skilled comprehenders.

These studies demonstrate that although less-skilled comprehenders are capable of making inferences and indeed do make some, they do not make enough to ensure adequate comprehension. In addition, the differences between the two comprehension groups cannot simply be due to differences in their memory for the text. In the recognition study there were no group differences for original story sentences, and in this later study the differences on inferential questions persisted when the text was in front of the subjects. The study described in this chapter was designed to explore further the relation between comprehension skill and inferential ability. There were two aims. The first was to assess the direction of the relation between inference making and comprehension skill: Is inferior inference-making skill a more likely cause or consequence of comprehension difficulties? The second aim was to explore possible sources of inferential failure. The ways in which the experimental design addressed each of these aims is presented next, followed by a discussion of the findings.

Investigating the Direction of the Relation Between Comprehension Skill and Inference-Making Ability

In order to explore the direction of the relation between comprehension ability and inferential skill, the performance of the less-skilled comprehenders was compared to two groups: same-age skilled comprehenders (as in Yuill & Oakhill's work) and a comprehension-age-match group. The reason for using these two comparison groups is essentially the same as that underlying the use of chronological-age and reading-age matches in the work on phonological skills and reading ability (see Goswami & Bryant, 1990, for a review). This design can help us to determine the direction of the relation between comprehension ability and inference skills. If same-age skilled and less-skilled comprehenders differ in their inferential ability, we can assume this to be an important variable in reading comprehension, because other factors related to comprehension ability, such as decoding skill and vocabulary, are being held constant between the two groups. However, there are at least two alternative explanations for the direction of this relation. The difference could be the *result of* the comprehension differences between the two groups: It may be that the skilled comprehenders' greater experience of reading and understanding stories has resulted in more proficient inference generation and/or a greater understanding of when inferences should be made. Alternatively, any differences between the two groups on this task could be *causally* related to their comprehension differences: It may be that the less-skilled comprehenders' poorer ability at making inferences has (in part) caused their poorer text comprehension.

The comparison with the younger comprehension-age match group can help us to determine which of these two explanations is the more plausible. If the less-skilled comprehenders are less accurate at answering questions requiring an inference than are those in the comprehension-age match group, it is difficult to say that the younger group's superior inferential skills arise because of extensive good reading comprehension experience, because it is unlikely that the younger group will have had greater experience than the older less-skilled comprehenders. Therefore, we can rule out the first possibility—that good inferential skills are merely a product of reading experience. Instead, this result suggests that deficient inferential skill is a possible cause of comprehension failure.

The three groups who participated in this work—less-skilled comprehenders, skilled comprehenders, and the comprehension-age match group—were selected as follows. The children were all British schoolchildren who were native speakers of English. Two tests were used in the selection process: the *Gates-MacGinitie Primary Two Vocabulary test* (Gates & MacGinitie, 1965) and the *Neale Analysis of Reading Ability–Revised British Edition* (Neale, 1989). The Gates-MacGinitie is a test of sight vocabulary, in which children have to select one of four words that goes best with an accompanying picture. The Neale Analysis consists of a series of short self-contained stories, graded in difficulty, that children read aloud. After each story they are asked a series of questions about the story. Testing stops after the child has made a prescribed number of reading accuracy errors. The Neale Analysis provides separate age-equivalent scores for both reading accuracy (based on the number of word pronunciation errors that a child makes) and reading comprehension (based on the number of questions about the stories that the child answers correctly).

The characteristics of each group are shown in Table 17.1: There were 29 less-skilled comprehenders, 24 skilled comprehenders, and 27 children in the comprehension-age match group. The less-skilled comprehenders all had age-appropriate reading accuracy ability, but their comprehension ages were at least 6 months below reading accuracy. The skilled comprehenders also had age-appropriate reading accuracy, but their comprehension scores were at or above that predicted by their reading accuracy age. Because we were interested in looking at higher-level reasons for comprehension failure, the two groups of skilled and less-skilled comprehenders were matched for reading accuracy and sight vocabulary, well-established lower-level causes of comprehension failure. The important difference was in comprehension skill: Whereas the skilled group's comprehension level was comparable with their decoding skill, the less-skilled group's comprehension level was at least 6 months below their decoding ability. Thus, it was assumed that the less-skilled comprehenders had a specific comprehension deficit in the absence of other reading-related problems.

TABLE 17.1
Sample Statistics for Each Skill Group. Where Appropriate, Scores Are Given as Reading Ages in the Format Years; Months and Standard Deviations (in Parentheses) Are Expressed in Months

	Skill Group		
Measurement	Less-Skilled Comprehenders (n = 29)	Skilled Comprehenders (n = 24)	Comprehension-Age Match (n = 27)
Chronological age (years; months)	7;8 (3.81)	7;8 (3.27)	6;8 (4.02)
Reading accuracy age (years; months)	7;11 (7.44)	7;10 (5.28)	6;8 (4.67)
Reading comprehension age (years; months)	6;7 (3.94)	8;2 (5.97)	6;8 (3.45)
Number of stories read	3.31 (0.66)	3.33 (0.64)	2.37 (0.49)
Sight vocabulary (max = 48)	37.14 (3.46)	37.88 (2.92)	33.59 (3.60)

The two groups were also matched on the number of stories from the Neale Analysis that they had read. Testing on the Neale Analysis stops after a prescribed number of reading accuracy errors, so this matching was to ensure that the skilled group's higher comprehension scores were not simply an artifact of having read more stories. If that had been the case, they would have been asked more questions, which would give them a greater chance of obtaining a higher comprehension score than the less-skilled group. The comprehension-age match group was comprised of younger children, progressing normally in reading accuracy and reading comprehension for their age, matched to the less-skilled group for comprehension level. This group is referred to as the *comprehension-age match group* (CAM group). For further details on the selection procedure, see Cain and Oakhill (submitted).

Investigating Possible Sources of Poor Inferential Skill

The stories and questioning procedure used in this study were designed to investigate possible sources of poor inference-making ability. The children read aloud one practice and four experimental stories. After each story they were asked six questions. For four of these an inference was required in order to correctly answer the question. There were two gap-filling and two intersentence connecting inferences for each story. The intersentence inferences were similar to the sort used in the recognition study discussed earlier (Oakhill, 1982). These inferences, necessary to establish cohesion between sentences in a text, can be derived from information explicitly provided in the text. The other type of inference, a gap-filling inference, was like those used by Oakhill (1984), in which general knowledge must be applied in order to make sense of information that is implicit in the text. In addition, there were two questions tapping literal information from the story. An example of an experimental story and questions is given in Table 17.2.

One possible explanation for poor comprehenders' poor inferential skills is lack of general knowledge (Yuill & Oakhill, 1991). In the light of the developmental findings outlined earlier, it seems unlikely that lack of general knowledge is a major contributory factor to the poor comprehenders' difficulties. In addition, Oakhill (1983) found that although better comprehenders were more likely to instantiate the most contextually appropriate meaning of a category noun, such differences were not due to general knowledge differences. To investigate the role of general knowledge differences in this work, the following procedure was adopted. First, the child was told that his or her answer was incorrect and was told to look at the story again to find the right answer. If the child still gave an incorrect answer, the experimenter would direct him or her to the relevant

TABLE 17.2
Sample Story and Questions

Debbie was going out for the afternoon with her friend Michael. By the time they got there they were very thirsty. Michael got some drink out of his duffle bag and they shared that. The orange juice was very refreshing. Debbie put on her swimming costume, but the water was too cold to paddle in, so they made sandcastles instead. They played all afternoon and didn't notice how late it was. Then Debbie spotted the clock on the pier. If she was late for dinner her parents would be angry. They quickly packed up their things. Debbie changed and wrapped her swimming costume in her towel. She put the bundle in her rucksack. They set off for home pedalling as fast as they could. Debbie was very tired when she got home, but she was just in time for tea.

Questions
Given Information
  Why didn't Debbie paddle in the water?
  Where was the clock?
Intersentence Inference
  Where did Michael get the orange juice from?
  Where did Debbie put her towel when she packed up her things?
Gap-Filling Inference
  Where did Debbie and Michael spend the afternoon?
  How did Debbie and Michael travel home?

---

part of the text and say that there was a clue in that part of the story. If the child was still having problems after this prompt, further questions were asked that directly assessed the child's ability to draw these inferences and to assess the child's general knowledge (a full account of these questions is provided in Cain & Oakhill, in preparation). Thus, if errors on gap-filling questions persist when the passage is available, it indicates that inadequate memory is not the primary source of inferential failure. However, if the children are unable to explain the key words and phrases when these are pointed out to them, it is reasonable to conclude that a lack of the relevant general knowledge is one possible reason for not making the inferences.

The second possible source of poor inferential skill that was investigated in this study is that the less-skilled comprehenders do not realize when it is appropriate to make inferences (Yuill & Oakhill, 1991). There are (at least) two possible reasons for this: They may not realize how particular inferences are cued (e.g., anaphoric relations) and, in addition, they may not know when it is permissible to draw on general knowledge to make sense of a passage. The difference between two types of inferences used in this study was exploited to address this issue. When the text is available, less-skilled comprehenders may be better able to draw intersentence inferences that are made directly from the text, cued by mapping an instance of a nonspecific noun to a later more specific referent (e.g., *drink* → *orange juice*). They may still have difficulty with gap-filling inferences, because there is no explicit cue to indicate what parts of the text to combine. Instead, the children must relate textual and real-world knowledge, and they may not realize when it is appropriate to do so, or how use of this knowledge should be constrained. If this is the case, it is reasonable to expect that difficulties with gap-filling inferences should persist when the text is available for consultation, in the absence of difficulties with the other type of inference. An ability to make such inferences in the absence of general knowledge deficits (as tested previously), suggests that these children are unaware of how and when to bring this knowledge to bear on their story understanding.

EXPERIMENTAL FINDINGS

The first data concern children's performance when the questions were first asked and the text was covered (see Table 17.3). These data were analyzed in a two-way analysis of variance.

There was a main effect of skill group: $F(2, 77) = 16.33$, $p < .0001$: The skilled comprehenders were better than the two other groups at all question types. In addition, there was a significant effect of question type $F(2, 154) = 32.33$, $p < .0001$. This effect arose because all groups found the questions tapping given information to be the easiest, and those requiring gap-filling inferences to be the most difficult. Finally, there was a significant interaction between the two factors, skill group and question type, $F(4, 154) = 3.24$, $p < .015$. The interaction occurred because whereas group performance on the questions tapping given information was comparable, group differences were apparent on the inference questions. Although the skilled comprehenders and the comprehension-age match group performed comparably on questions requiring intersentence inferences to be made, the less-skilled comprehenders were much poorer on these sorts of questions than both comparison groups. In addition, all groups found the gap-filling inference questions harder, and the less-skilled comprehenders and CAM

TABLE 17.3
Mean Percentage of Correct Responses for Each Skill Group for First-Time Answers (When Text Covered)

	Skill Group		
Question Type	Less-Skilled Comprehenders ($n = 29$)	Skilled Comprehenders ($n = 24$)	Comprehension-Age Match ($n = 27$)
Given information	72.4	80.7	75.0
Intersentence inference	59.9	83.3	76.9
Gap-filling inference	52.6	70.3	58.3

TABLE 17.4
Mean Percentage of Correct Responses for Each Skill
Group After Text Is Available to Refer to (Undirected)

Question Type	Skill Group		
	Less-Skilled Comprehenders ($n = 29$)	Skilled Comprehenders ($n = 24$)	Comprehension-Age Match ($n = 27$)
Given information	94.4	99.0	95.8
Intersentence inferences	94.0	97.9	97.7
Gap-filling inferences	67.7	82.3	73.6

group were poorer on these than were the skilled comprehenders. These group differences were confirmed by planned comparisons.

Once the children could look back at the text, performance between the groups was comparable on the intersentence inference questions (see Table 17.4). However, although all groups improved their performance, the difference between the skilled comprehenders and the other two groups persisted for gap-filling inferences. Children who had not answered the question correctly at this point were directed to the relevant part of the story and told that there was a clue in that part. The data revealed that the less-skilled comprehenders and CAM group were still worse on the gap-filling inferences than was the skilled group: Percentage of correctly answered questions was 95.8% for the skilled, 87.0% for the CAM, and 84.9% for the less-skilled children. However, when the children who had not previously made the gap-filling inferences were asked questions to directly assess their general knowledge and ability to draw such inferences, they answered them correctly.

DISCUSSION

In this section we discuss the findings in relation to the two experimental aims: We evaluate the likely direction of the relation between inference-making skill and comprehension ability, and assess possible sources of poor inferential skill.

Was There Any Evidence to Suggest That Inference-Making Skill Was a Likely Cause of Comprehension Failure?

Evidence relating to this question comes from the children's performance when the questions were first asked and the text was covered. We found that the less-skilled comprehenders not only made fewer inferences than the same-age skilled comprehenders, but they also made fewer inferences than the comprehension-age match group. These results indicate that poor inferential skill is more likely a cause of comprehension failure than a result of it. Absolute comprehension level cannot be the reason for these poorer skills, because the less-skilled comprehenders were making fewer inferences than were children of equivalent comprehension skill, (i.e., they were not making as many inferences as would be expected for their level of comprehension skill). It is also unlikely that the comprehension-age match group would have had more overall experience of reading and understanding stories, which resulted in their superior inferencing skill. This is an important finding. If further work supports this direction of causality, it suggests that problems with inferential skill must be dealt with, in order to improve the comprehension problems of these children.

Possible Sources of Inferential Failure

When a question was answered incorrectly, the questioning procedure described previously enabled us to investigate some possible reasons for inferential failure. These reasons are discussed next, in relation to the data.

Memory for the Text. One reason for poorer inferential skill might be poorer memory for the text in general. The scores indicated that the less-skilled comprehenders were worse at questions tapping literal information than were the skilled comprehenders. This finding is in line with Oakhill's (1984) finding, although the difference in the present study was not significant. Oakhill suggested, following Paris and Upton (1976), that the reason that the skilled comprehenders were better at both literal and inferential questions might be because they made more inferences and, therefore, had a more durable and cohesive representation of the text. In contrast, Omanson et al. (1978) found that making more inferences did not facilitate recall. Furthermore, in the present study the less-skilled comprehenders remembered an amount of literal information similar to that of the comprehension-age match group, but were still poorer than them on at least one type of inference (the intersentence inferences). These data therefore suggest that memory for the texts was not a significant contributory factor in the differences found in inferential performance.

Reading Strategies. Once the children could look back at the text, performance between the groups was comparable on the intersentence inference questions. As mentioned previously, memory for the wording of the text cannot wholly account for the initial group differences. Why, then, are the less-skilled comprehenders initially poorer at these sorts of inferences, when they appear to be able to make them when the text is available? It may be that the less-skilled comprehenders adopt a different approach and strategy to reading that results in them processing text differently. One suggestion is that they do not see reading as an active, constructive process: It is only when their incorrect answer and therefore inadequate understanding is brought to their attention, and they are required to search the text for some information, that these children make such links as frequently as do the skilled comprehenders and younger children. This suggestion requires further investigation, because it is not clear from this data whether the differences arose during reading or when retrieving information to answer questions.

Despite the general improvement with the text available, the difference between the skilled comprehenders and the other two groups persisted for gap-filling inferences. A similar pattern of data was found by Oakhill (1984), in which the less-skilled comprehenders were still poorer at such inferences, even when they had the text in front of them. We know that the less-skilled comprehenders are capable of making these sorts of inferences but, for whatever reason, they do not make them as often as do the skilled comprehenders or even the comprehension-age match group, in contrast to performance on the other sort of inference. It cannot simply be that children of lower comprehension ability are particularly poor at scanning the text for the appropriate information, because their performance on the literal questions and other sort of inference was near perfect when the text was available for consultation.

The answer may lie in the different sorts of information required to make the two types of inference. As mentioned before, all of the information necessary to make an intersentence inference is provided explicitly in the text (e.g., establishing that a particular instance such as *orange juice*, is coreferential with a category word, such as *drink*). The other sort of inference requires the reader to relate general knowledge to clues given in the text, in order to make sense of a description. An example of this sort of inference is using given information such as the presence of a pier and making sandcastles, to infer that the children spent the day on the beach, even though this destination was not explicitly stated in the text. The fact that the less-skilled comprehenders were particularly poor at this sort of inference, even when the textual information was in front of them, suggests that they are not as aware as are the skilled comprehenders of when it is appropriate to use general knowledge to aid inferential skill. They were also slightly poorer than the CAM group in this respect.

General Knowledge Deficits. In this study we tested whether general knowledge deficits were the basis for lack of one type of inference, gap-filling inferences. When children were unable to answer questions requiring these inferences, even after being directed to the relevant part of the text, they were asked questions to directly assess the general knowledge on which these inferences were based. These questions revealed that all of the children had the requisite knowledge, which rules out general knowledge as a source of these particular differences.

The Role of Working Memory. Finally, memory ability must be reconsidered. The poorer inference performance by the less-skilled comprehenders cannot simply be due to poorer memory per se, because their scores for given information were comparable with other groups. However, differences in functional memory capacity might provide a more satisfactory explanation. The less-skilled comprehenders may have limited working memory processes that make it more difficult for them to combine different sorts of information, a skill necessary for inference making, either when reading or at a later retrieval stage. Yuill, Oakhill, and Parkin (1989) found a relation between functional memory capacity and comprehension skill, and related it to such text-processing requirements. The working memory capacity of a subset of the children who participated in this study was similarly assessed. However, these data did not support the memory capacity explanation for the present findings. Although the less-skilled comprehenders had reduced working memory capacity compared to the skilled comprehenders, their ability to concurrently store and process information was not significantly different from that of than the comprehension-age match children. Stothard and Hulme (1992) reported a similar pattern of data. Therefore, although working memory deficits may provide part of the explanation for the less-skilled comprehenders' poor inferential skill, other factors must also be involved.

SUMMARY AND CONCLUSIONS

This study set out to investigate the most likely direction of the relation between inferential skill and comprehension ability and, in addition, to narrow down the possible sources of less-skilled comprehenders' failure to make as many inferences as did skilled comprehenders. We found that children with reading comprehension difficulties demonstrated a specific deficit in answering questions about stories they had just read. Their performance was comparable to two comparison groups on questions requiring recall of verbatim detail from the story. However, they were poorer on questions tapping implicitly given information than were a group of skilled comprehenders matched for chronological age and reading accuracy and another group matched for comprehension ability. These findings identify deficient skill at drawing inferences as a candidate cause of poor comprehension. In addition, memory for the text and general knowledge deficits were ruled out as the source of these problems. Instead, our findings indicated that knowing when and how to relate such general knowledge to the text, in order to fill in missing details, was a more likely source of problems that requires further investigation. One way to evaluate the proposed relation between comprehension skill and inference-making ability is to train children in making inferences when reading (e.g., by teaching them how to relate general knowledge to a text). If we found that such a program aided less-skilled comprehenders more than their skilled peers, we would have additional support for the claim made here, that poor inference-making ability is more plausibly a cause than a result of poor reading comprehension skill. Another way to test the proposed relation between these two skills is to map their development over several years. We have recently embarked on a longitudinal study, which will include such measures and should enable a more robust evaluation of the issues raised in this chapter.

ACKNOWLEDGMENTS

This work was conducted while the first author was in receipt of a studentship from the Economic and Social Research Council. We would like to thank the staff and pupils from the Brighton schools who participated in this work.

REFERENCES

Cain, K., & Oakhill, J. (submitted). *Inference-making ability and its relation to comprehension failure.*
Garnham, A. (1985). *Psycholinguistics: Central topics.* London: Methuen.
Gates, A. I., & MacGinitie, W. H. (1965). *Gates-MacGinitie Reading Tests.* New York: Columbia University Teachers' College Press.
Goswami, U., & Bryant, P. (1990). *Phonological skills and learning to read.* Hove, England: Lawrence Erlbaum Associates.
Neale, M. D. (1989). *The Neale Analysis of Reading Ability–Revised.* Windsor, England: NFER-Nelson.
Oakhill, J. V. (1982). Constructive processes in skilled and less-skilled comprehenders' memory for sentences. *British Journal of Psychology, 73,* 13–20.
Oakhill, J. V. (1983). Instantiation in skilled and less-skilled comprehenders. *Quarterly Journal of Experimental Psychology, 35A,* 441–450.
Oakhill, J. V. (1984). Inferential and memory skills in children's comprehension of stories. *British Journal of Educational Psychology, 54,* 31–39.
Omanson, R. C., Warren, W. M., & Trabasso, T. (1978). Goals, inferential comprehension and recall of stories by children. *Discourse Processes, 1,* 337–354.
Paris, S. G., & Lindauer, B. K. (1976). The role of inference in children's comprehension and memory for sentences. *Cognitive Psychology, 8,* 217–227.
Paris, S. G., Lindauer, B. K., & Cox, G. L. (1977). The development of inferential comprehension. *Child Development, 48,* 1728–1733.
Paris, S. G., & Upton, L. R. (1976). Children's memory for inferential relationships in prose. *Child Development, 47,* 660–668.

Singer, M. (1994). Discourse inference processes. In M. A. Gernsbacher (Ed.), *Handbook of psycholinguistics* (pp. 479–515). San Diego: Academic Press.

Stothard, S. E., & Hulme, C. (1992). Reading comprehension difficulties in children: The role of language comprehension and working memory skills. *Reading and Writing: An Interdisciplinary Journal, 4,* 245–256.

van den Broek, P. (1994). Comprehension and memory of narrative texts: Inferences and coherence. In M. A. Gernsbacher (Ed.), *Handbook of psycholinguistics* (pp. 539–588). San Diego: Academic Press.

Yuill, N., & Oakhill, J. (1988). Effects of inference awareness training on poor reading comprehension. *Applied Cognitive Psychology, 2,* 33–45.

Yuill, N., & Oakhill, J. (1991). *Children's problems in text comprehension: An experimental investigation.* Cambridge, England: Cambridge University Press.

Yuill, N. M., Oakhill, J. V., & Parkin, A. J. (1989). Working memory, comprehension skill and the resolution of text anomaly. *British Journal of Psychology, 80,* 351–361.

Chapter 18

Individual Differences in Children's Comprehension Skill: Toward an Integrated Model

Jane Oakhill
Kate Cain
Nicola Yuill
University of Sussex, England

In this chapter, we concentrate on our own research with children who have comprehension difficulties, although we outline other theoretical perspectives and discuss how they relate to our work. The focus of our interest has been on young children who have developed good word recognition and can understand sentences and read aloud apparently fluently, but who have only a poor grasp of the meaning of what they have read.

Such children have been shown to be deficient in a number of skills relative to children of the same age and single-word reading ability who have good comprehension skills. Perfetti (1996) listed six general sources of comprehension problems, which he categorized into two main classes: processes and knowledge. These are shown below:

1. Processes:
   Lexical processes
   Inference making
   Comprehension strategies
   Working memory limitations
2. Knowledge:
   Word meanings
   Domain knowledge

Our own work has tended to catalogue the areas in which poor comprehenders are deficient, with, so far, only a tentative attempt to assess the relative influences and interactions of these skill deficiencies, and to assess the underlying cause or causes of comprehension problems. In this chapter, by drawing on Perfetti's classification and by taking examples from our own work, we suggest how process and knowledge factors might be incorporated into a more integrated model of comprehension, its development, and comprehension deficits. Before we discuss our own work and how our findings might be integrated within such a model, we first briefly outline the way in which we select subjects for our experiments.

The children we have studied have a *specific* comprehension problem, in that their single-word reading and vocabulary is normal for their age, but their ability to understand a text they have just read is considerably behind what would be predicted from their chronological age and word reading accuracy. In our studies, we have compared the performance of such children with that of skilled comprehenders of the same age and word recognition ability. Typical groups of subjects are shown in Table 18.1. The groups are selected using the Neale Analysis of Reading Ability and the Gates-MacGinitie Vocabulary Test. The Neale Analysis provides measures both of reading accuracy (word recognition in context) and comprehension (assessed by ability to answer a series of questions about short passages). The Gates-MacGinitie test requires the child to select one of four written words to go with a picture. Thus, it acts as a measure of silent word recognition, without context, and provides an index of the child's reading vocabulary. In all our studies, the groups of skilled and less-skilled comprehenders were matched for word recognition ability (Neale Accuracy and Gates-MacGinitie) and chronological age, but differed in Neale Comprehension scores. In general, all children were above average at word recognition; one group was also very good at comprehension, whereas the other group was poor at comprehension, particularly with respect to their ability to recognize words.

In this chapter, we outline studies to support our view that comprehension deficits are, in many cases, related to deficits in the *processes* that are involved in constructing a representation of a text, rather than *knowledge* about the text domain or of word meanings. Our view is that poor comprehenders often have difficulties at the level of inference and integration in text comprehension: In other words, they fail to build adequate *mental models* of

TABLE 18.1
Characteristics of Groups of Skilled and Less-Skilled Comprehenders

	Chronological Age (Years and Months)	*Accuracy Age* (Years and Months)	*Comprehension Age* (Years and Months)	*Gates-MacGinitie* (Score/48)
Less skilled	7 years, 9 months	8 years, 4 months	7 years, 3 months	38.0
Skilled	7 years, 9 months	8 years, 4 months	9 years, 1 month	38.3

texts (for a review, see Yuill & Oakhill, 1991). The categories suggested by Perfetti provide a convenient framework for discussing this work, except that we include some of our own findings that do not fit neatly within his processes/knowledge division. This is our work on children's ability to produce structured and coherent stories, where we use their productions to index both their knowledge about story structure and conventions, and the processes of establishing cohesion and causal links in stories. Here, we discuss this work under the heading of *Processes*, because we believe that children's ability to produce coherent stories is limited by the same factors that limit other processes in comprehension, but we also refer to this work in the briefer section on knowledge at the end of this chapter.

In the next section, we focus on these five areas of processing (lexical and semantic processes, inference making, understanding text structure, comprehension strategies, and working memory limitations), and consider how they might interact in an integrated model of comprehension and comprehension failure. We do not wish to imply that poor comprehenders might not have difficulties in other areas, but these are the ones we have focused on in our research. We say relatively little about the first area (inferential skills): Poor comprehenders' difficulties in this area are well established, and our own work in this area is already published. We instead concentrate on the other areas, particularly metacognitive skills and story structure, concerning which we present new data.

PROCESSES

Lexical and Syntactic Processes

Some theories of poor comprehension, for example that of Perfetti (e.g., 1985, 1988), have proposed that comprehension problems stem from difficulties in the operation of lower-level processes such as lexical access and parsing. Perfetti put particular emphasis on lexical processes in this "verbal efficiency" theory because "These processes are the most likely candidates for becoming uniformly high in efficiency" (1988, p. 121). Such assumptions, he argued, can be extended to the semantic information associated with the words. Because word decoding accuracy and comprehension are generally highly correlated, it is likely that many poor comprehenders will also have difficulties at the level of single words. However, proponents of this perspective argue that *accuracy* of word recognition is not sufficient for good comprehension: Recognition must also be fast and automatic so that, in a limited-capacity system, the lower-level (word recognition) processes do not use up the resources needed for higher-level (comprehension) processes. Perfetti and Hogaboam (1975), for example, found large differences in time to name words between third- and fifth-grade good and poor comprehenders. Although their groups were not selected to be matched for decoding skill, the results could not be explained simply in terms of word recognition accuracy, because the poor comprehenders had longer naming times for even very common words, almost all of which were identified correctly by both groups of subjects. However, although there is a tendency for fast decoding and good comprehension to go together, there is no evidence for a direct causal link between the two.

In our studies, we have excluded children who might have comprehension difficulties associated with word recognition problems because we are interested in looking at children who have a *specific* comprehension problem, rather than some more general reading deficit. We have, therefore, matched the good and poor comprehenders who participate in our studies for word recognition ability. Moreover, we have found no differences between groups as selected in decoding speed or automaticity (see Yuill & Oakhill, 1991). Thus, although we do not deny that such factors are likely to lead to comprehension problems in some children, we maintain that poor comprehenders exist who do not have difficulties at the word level.

Another possibility is that poor comprehenders have difficulties at the sentence level, failing to understand certain syntactic constructions. The idea that poor comprehenders fail to make use of the syntactic constraints in text has been explored extensively by Cromer and his colleagues (e.g., Cromer, 1970; Oakan, Wiener, & Cromer, 1971; Steiner, Wiener, & Cromer, 1971). They found that, rather than using information about semantic and syntactic groupings in a text, poor comprehenders tended to read word by word: They did not use the sentence and text structure to guide their comprehension. This reading style is similar to the listlike intonation that Clay and Imlach (1971) described poor readers as using. More recently, Shankweiler (1989) suggested that comprehension suffers because of parsing problems that are, in turn, related to having poor phonological coding skills. However, we have found no evidence to support this hypothesis when the poor comprehenders are selected as described previously (see Oakhill, Yuill, & Parkin, 1986).

One of the experimental groups used in Cromer's studies had comprehension difficulties, even though their vocabulary and decoding skills were commensurate with those of good comprehenders of the same age. Thus, these poor comprehenders were very similar to the less-skilled comprehenders used in our own experiments. However, when we tested the children's syntactic skills using Dorothy Bishop's *Test for Reception of Grammar* (1982), we found no differences between the groups.

Inference Making

To understand the full meaning of a text readers need to go beyond what is explicitly stated, both to link up ideas within the text and to bring their general knowledge to bear on their understanding of it. Authors necessarily leave some of the links and expansions of a text implicit. A fully explicit text would not only be very long and boring, but it would destroy the reader's pleasure in imposing meaning on the text—making it "their own." However, skilled readers need to assess which inferences are needed, and not let their inferential machinery run wild!

One persistent finding is that poor comprehenders are not skilled at making inferences. We have several lines of evidence that good and poor comprehenders differ in inference skills. One early concern in our research was whether the less-skilled comprehenders' poorer performance on questions about a text is simply a memory problem. To explore this issue, Oakhill (1984) asked children questions about short stories in two conditions. In the first, the children had to answer a series of questions from memory; in the second, they could reread and look back over the texts to find, or check, their responses to the questions. The questions were of two types: Some were "literal" in that they simply asked about information that was explictly stated in the text; the others were "inferential" in that they required the children to go beyond what was explicitly stated, to make plausible, very simple inferences from it. For instance, an inference question for one of the texts asked how a boy traveled to school. Although it was not stated explicitly that he traveled by bike, there were several clues in the text: He "pedaled" and he ran over some broken glass and had to walk the rest of the way (presumably because the tires on his bike were punctured). The particularly interesting aspect of these results was that, although the good and poor comprehenders were equally able to answer the literal questions when the text was available for them to refer to, the poor comprehenders performed significantly worse on the questions requiring an inference. These findings indicate that the poor comprehenders' difficulties cannot simply be attributed to poor memory; even when a text is available for them to look over, they are still unable to answer a high proportion of the questions that require them to infer information that is not explicit in the text.

There are several reasons for this result, some of which are taken up later in this chapter. First, poor comprehenders might simply lack the general *knowledge* to make the inferences. Such an explanation seems unlikely (we would expect a 7-year-old to know that a creature that flaps its wings is likely to be a bird) and, indeed, has been ruled out in a later study in which similar differences were shown, even though the poor comprehenders had the relevant knowledge available to them (Cain, 1994). A second possibility may be that poor comprehenders do not realize that inferences are necessary or even permissible—perhaps they focus too much on getting the literal meaning from the text. Third, poor comprehenders may realize that inferences are legitimate, but may have difficulty accessing relevant knowledge and integrating it with what is in the text, because of processing limitations. We argue later that there is some evidence that both the second and the third of these possible explanations may be correct.

Further support for the conclusion that poor comprehenders' inferences are not limited simply by their knowledge base comes from an experiment by Oakhill (1982). This study showed that poor comprehenders make fewer constructive inferences when they listen to short texts. It is notable that, in this experiment, there was no requirement to refer to general knowledge: All the information on which the inferences were based was given in the texts. In a recognition memory test, the good comprehenders were not significantly better at remembering the exact wording of short texts, but made more recognition errors than did the poor group on sentences that invited inferences from the text, but had not, in fact, been presented. These data were interpreted as showing that the good comprehenders were more likely to make integrative inferences, to bring together the ideas in the text as a whole, whereas the poor comprehenders tended to derive a more superficial, literal interpretation of the text.

A third area in which we have shown poor comprehenders to have trouble making inferences is in their ability to infer more specific meanings for words, based on the particular context in which the words occur (Oakhill, 1983). For instance, skilled adult readers, on reading a sentence like "The fish attacked the swimmer," would infer that the fish in this context was a shark or some other sort of dangerous and aggressive fish, a process that has been termed *instantiation*. We have found that children who are good comprehenders instantiate to a greater extent than do poor comprehenders, even though the children in both groups have similar levels of knowledge about suitable instantiations.

These studies demonstrate that, compared with good comprehenders, poor comprehenders have difficulties in making inferences of various types. In this section, we have been concerned with the processes required for fairly local understanding and integration of texts. In the next section, we turn to understanding of the structure of texts more globally.

Understanding Text Structure

Readers need to understand the structure of a text. In the case of stories, this might include identifying the main character(s) and their motives, following the plot, and extracting the main theme of the text. Now we turn to another aspect of our research that illustrates some of the difficulties that good and poor comprehenders have with text structure, but also, incidentally, illustrates the generality of their comprehension difficulties.

It is a reasonable hypothesis that children's knowledge about story structure and coherence will help them in understanding stories that they read or hear. There is now a good deal of research detailing how a child's concept of a story becomes refined with age (e.g., Applebee, 1978; Peterson

& McCabe, 1983; Stein & Glenn, 1979, 1982), but little is known about how comprehension skill relates to such knowledge.

Some of our work (see Yuill & Oakhill, 1991) has shown that skilled and less-skilled comprehenders differ in important ways in their storytelling abilities. We asked children to retell a story from a picture sequence that was narrated to them by the experimenter. We found that although the children from both groups were equally likely to reproduce the connectives presented in the original story, the skilled comprehenders included additional connectives. A further experiment, which required the children to plan and narrate their own stories prompted only by picture sequences, showed that the less-skilled comprehenders were less consistent in their use of causal connectives, and were more likely to use referential ties (such as pronouns) ambiguously or repetitiously. These studies indicate that the less-skilled children's problems are probably an aspect of a more general comprehension deficit. However, because these studies were not designed to investigate specific aspects of story knowledge, such as how stories are structured and what conventions are typically used, we do not know whether the differences arose primarily because of differences in ability to use cohesive links (perhaps because of processing limitations), or whether differences in knowledge about story conventions and story concepts underlay these differences.

The purpose of the studies described in this section was twofold. First, we wanted to see whether comprehension skill is related to story knowledge and, if so, how. A production task was used to assess how the concept of a story as a sequence of linked events was related to comprehension skill. The second aim was to explore the relation between good comprehension and story knowledge: Does story knowledge promote good comprehension skills, or is it a by-product of being a good comprehender? This issue was addressed in the design of the studies. We compared the performance of poor comprehenders with that of two control groups: same-age skilled comprehenders (as in the studies outlined earlier) and younger children whose comprehension skill was similar to that of the older poor comprehenders, but was commensurate with the younger children's age and word-reading ability (the "comprehension-age match"—CAM). The latter comparison can help to address the issue of whether poor comprehenders are just experiencing a developmental lag, or whether their comprehension skills are qualitatively different from those of other children. It can also help to rule out certain causal possibilities. If poor comprehenders are worse on certain measures than are younger children with the same comprehension skill (CAM), we can infer that the differences do not arise from less experience of reading, because it is the younger children who would be expected to have less experience than older poor comprehenders. Thus, a causal link is a possibility, although of course not proven. The characteristics of the three groups of subjects who participated in this study are shown in Table 18.2.

Two different prompt types were used to elicit stories. One was a sequence of six pictures that "told a story," and the other was a topic title (e.g., "Pirates") about which the children were asked to tell a story. The children were asked to tell three stories using each prompt type. The two prompt types were used in different sessions, and order of sessions was counterbalanced within groups. There was one practice story at the beginning of each session. We expected that poor comprehenders might produce more poorly structured stories in general, and that the topic prompts might lead to poorer stories than the picture prompts, because the story structure and plot were, essentially, provided in the picture condition. Moreover, we expected that there might be a larger difference between the skill groups in the topic than in the picture prompt condition, with the poor comprehenders performing particularly poorly in the topic prompt condition. In addition, if the ability to produce well-structured and coherent stories is causally linked to comprehension skill and not just a by-product of its development, then we might expect the younger CAM group to produce better stories than the older poor comprehenders, at least in the topic prompt condition.

The stories were tape recorded, transcribed, and scored by two independent raters, who agreed on over 90% of cases on classifications. Any disagreements were resolved by discussion. Each story was scored in two ways: for the occurrence of story conventions and for the quality of the event structure.

The four story conventions that we looked for were conventional openings and endings, such as "once upon a time," "one day," "the end," "and

TABLE 18.2
Sample Means for Groups Who Participated in the Narrative Production Study (Where Appropriate, Ages Are Given in Years and Months. The Sight Vocabulary Scores Are the Mean Raw Scores From the Gates-MacGinitie Vocabulary Test. Reading Accuracy and Comprehension Scores Are the Age Equivalent Scores Provided in the Neale Analysis of Reading Ability)

	Less-Skilled Comprehenders (n = 16)	Skilled Comprehenders (n = 12)	Comprehension-Age-Match Group (n = 15)
Age	7 years, 9 months	7 years, 9 months	6 years, 10 months
Gates-MacGinitie vocabulary	36.94	38.33	34.13
Neale accuracy	7 years, 10 months	7 years, 8 months	6 years, 8 months
Neale comprehension	6 years, 6 months	8 years, 3 months	6 years, 8 months

they all lived happily ever after"; and character setting information, such as "There was a mum, a dad, and a little girl," and scene-setting information, such as "This boy was at the circus."

An analysis of these data showed no differences between the groups in their use of any of these conventional features. The conventions were used very frequently by the children in all three groups. The only effect of prompt type was on the inclusion of conventional endings—these were less frequent in the picture than in the topic prompt condition.

The event structure of each story was classed in one of three categories, which aimed to capture the extent to which causality between events was signaled and the story as a whole cohered. The three categories, with an example from each, are shown in the following list:

1. Nonstories: These narratives were either totally incoherent, or lacked any obvious sequence of events. Some such nonstories comprised only an opening and character and/or scene setting information, but nothing else. For example: "Once upon a time there was a girl and she went on holiday" (topic prompt: The Holiday).

2. Intermediate stories: These narratives contained a sequence of events, but the main events were not causally linked to each other. For example: "It was a lovely day. The family decided to go down to the seaside. They saw lots of people there. The baby was making a sandcastle, the older children were playing in the sea, the mum and dad had their last swim before they went home" (topic prompt: The Seaside).

3. Complete stories: Narratives that related an integrated sequence of events, with the main events causally related. An example is: "There was once a girl who had scruffy hair. Her mum said she had to have her hair cut, but she didn't like to have her hair cut, she thought she might have the wrong haircut. So she went in mum's . . . her mum's room and got her hair scissors and she cut her hair short so . . . and she looked in the mirror and she didn't like the hair cut she did, so her mum came in the room and gave her a hat, so it didn't show her fringe. The end" (picture sequence prompt: The Haircut).

The stories were scored by awarding points from 0 to 2 depending on the category to which the story was allocated. Thus, each child obtained a score out of 6 for each prompt type. The mean scores are shown in Table 18.3.

An analysis of these data showed a main effect of group: The poorer comprehenders produced less well-structured stories overall: $F(2,40) = 8.15$, $p < .002$. There was also a main effect of prompt type: As predicted, the picture prompts elicited better-structured stories: $F(1,40) = 11.01$, $p < .002$. Although the interaction between comprehension skill and type of prompt

TABLE 18.3
Mean Scores for Story Structure in the Narrative Production Task
(the Maximum Possible for Each Prompt Type Is 6)

Prompt Condition	Less-Skilled Comprehenders	Skilled Comprehenders	Comprehension-Age-Match Group
Topic	2.94	4.92	4.27
Picture	4.31	5.33	4.80
Difference	1.37	0.41	0.53

did not reach significance, planned comparisons (using Bonferroni's t'), were conducted to test the specific predictions outlined previously. These comparisons showed that, in the topic prompt condition, the skilled comprehenders produced significantly better-structured stories than did the less-skilled group, $t' = 5.09$, $p < .01$, and the CAM also produced significantly better stories than the less-skilled comprehenders, $t' = 3.59$, $p < .01$. In the picture-prompt condition, the skilled comprehenders were, once more, better than the less-skilled group, $t' = 3.79$, $p < .01$, but the less-skilled group and CAM group did not differ significantly. In neither prompt condition was there any difference between the performance of the skilled comprehenders and the CAM group.

These results show no evidence of a relation between comprehension skill and the knowledge of conventional, formulaic features of stories. Thus, even poorer comprehenders and younger readers have this *knowledge* about story conventions. There were, however, differences among the groups in their ability to produce internally well-structured stories. The picture sequence prompt was easier overall, and the difference between the prompt conditions was particularly marked for the poor comprehenders—this group, in particular, needed the picture sequence in order to produce stories with a reasonably coherent event structure. The group differences were particularly marked in the topic prompt condition in which the poor comprehenders performed more poorly than either of the control groups. This result is especially interesting because it rules out the conclusion that the ability to produce a well-structured story is simply the result of extensive experience of reading (which the older children, and the older good comprehenders in particular, would be expected to have more of) and suggests, instead, an alternative explanation: Such knowledge might be causally linked to comprehension skill. There are two main reasons for coming to this conclusion. First, the less-skilled comprehenders produced less-well-structured stories than did the CAM group in the generally more-difficult topic prompt condition (i.e., two groups of equivalent comprehension skill performed differently on this task, and, importantly, the older children were *worse*). Thus, the results suggest that the ability to produce well-structured stories is not a consequence of reading comprehension skill, because the two groups are matched for comprehension. Second, the less-skilled comprehenders produced stories of equivalent quality to those of the CAM group when a picture sequence was provided as a prompt. This suggests that it was this structural framework that the poor comprehenders were lacking in the topic prompt condition, and that one of the reasons for poor story production and comprehension might be lack of ability to keep track of the event structure of a text. This inability to produce a well-structured and coherent event structure may be related to the children's working memory skill, a point to which we return shortly.

Comprehension Strategies

The third main area that we mentioned in the introduction was comprehension monitoring. Readers need to monitor their own comprehension, but poor comprehenders may not realize that they don't understand a particular text, or portion of text, and may not know what to do about their poor understanding even if they do realize.

In an initial experiment (Yuill, Oakhill, & Parkin, 1989) to explore whether good and poor comprehenders differ in their ability to keep track of their own comprehension, we used an anomaly resolution task (adapted from Ackerman, 1984). The children were read short stories describing an adult's apparently inconsistent response to a child's action. Information to resolve the inconsistency was contained somewhere within the story. There were other types of story: consistent ones and unresolved ones, which acted as controls. An example story is one in which a mother praises her son for refusing his brother a turn on his bike.

The apparent inconsistency was either preceded or followed by the resolving information (in the previous example, that the brother had a sprained ankle, and was not supposed to ride on bikes). We expected that resolving information that followed an inconsistency would be harder to use because it would require retrospective resolution. The difficulty of using the resolving information was manipulated by varying the distance between the anomaly and its resolution. After each story had been read, the children were asked three types of questions. First, they were asked about whether the adult in the story should have acted as he or she did, and why. This question could only be answered correctly if the anomaly had been correctly resolved. Second, they were asked a question to test their memory for a crucial aspect of the story. Third, they were asked a question about the rule on which the inconsistency was based (e.g., in the previous case, "Would people usually be praised or blamed for not giving their brother a turn on their bike?"). If children answered this question incorrectly, it would indicate that they did not agree with the behavioral norms and should not find the story inconsistent. Very few children in either skill group answered the memory and rule questions incorrectly. The ability of the children to resolve the anomalies in the inconsistent, resolving condition is shown in Table 18.4.

An analysis of variance showed a very marked interaction between comprehension skill and the memory demands of the task: The groups were equally good at resolving the inconsistencies when the inconsistency and the resolving information were in adjacent sentences, but very much worse when the two pieces of information were separated in the text. This is an interesting finding, because it demonstrates that the poor comprehenders do not have any general deficit in this aspect of comprehension monitoring. They are highly competent at the task when the memory demands are small. Both groups found it harder to use resolving information when it followed, rather than preceded, the inconsistency, and this difference was slightly, but not significantly, larger for the less-skilled comprehenders.

The experiment described earlier tested for ability to integrate information in text, and did not test comprehension monitoring directly. We now turn to some more recent (as yet unpublished) work on monitoring that uses more traditional monitoring tasks. In this study (Oakhill, Hartt, & Samols, 1996), slightly older children (9- to 10-year-olds) were used than in the experiments described previously, because they are more likely to be able to notice problems in texts and comment on them sensibly. The children were selected in the same way as described previously.

In this study, comprehension monitoring was assessed using an error detection paradigm, similar to that used by Markman (e.g., 1977). The errors were internal inconsistencies within the text (i.e., contradictory statements). This procedure had the advantage of allowing us to manipulate the intrinsic memory load of the task: The inconsistencies were either in adjacent sentences, or were separated by several sentences. An example passage is shown in Table 18.5. The children were presented with two passages in each of the memory load conditions. They were also asked to read and make judgements about two passages without any inconsistencies, so that we could make sure that they really could discriminate between passages with problems and those without.

The children read the passages aloud at their own pace, and were asked to identify any problems with them ("something that doesn't make sense")

TABLE 18.4
Percentages Correct in Anomaly Resolution Task

	Near	Far
Less skilled	72.2	16.7
Skilled	66.7	66.7

TABLE 18.5
Example Passage From Comprehension-Monitoring Experiment

Gorillas are clever animals that live together in groups in Africa.
Gorillas sleep on the ground on a bed of leaves and they like to eat different types of fruit.
They are shy and gentle and they hardly ever fight with each other.
Gorillas have flat noses and a very poor sense of smell but their eyesight is very good.
They move about the ground on their hands and feet.
*

Gorillas sleep in trees and they often build a shelter out of leaves above them, to keep the rain out.

___ This passage makes sense, it does not need to be changed.
___ This passage does not make sense, it needs to be changed.

Note. In the adjacent condition, the italicized sentence occurred in this position.

by underlining it. They were shown an example of the sort of blatant inconsistency that occurred in the test passages. At the end of each passage, they were asked to indicate their overall assessment of the passage (as shown in Table 18.5). If they had indicated a problem, they were asked to explain it. In the case of passages with inconsistencies, if the child did not immediately identify a problem, he or she was told that there was a problem and was given another chance to find it. If the child still failed to do so, the experimenter underlined the two inconsistent sentences and asked the child if they made sense together.

For each of the inconsistent passages, each child obtained a minimum score of 0 (if he or she did not identify a problem, despite all prompting) and a maximum of 3 (if the child ticked the correct option on first reading and correctly identified the problem). The mean scores for the groups, in the two conditions, are shown in Table 18.6. An analysis of these data showed that the skilled comprehenders were better overall: $F(1,20) = 7.29$, $p < .025$. There was also an effect of distance: $F(1,20) = 13.62$, $p < .01$. The inconsistencies were harder to detect when they were separated by several sentences. In adddition, there was an interaction between the distance and the skill variables: The less-skilled comprehenders were more affected by the distance manipulation than were the skilled ones, $F(1,20) = 7.66$, $p < .025$. Performance on the nonproblematic passages was uniformly high.

TABLE 18.6
Mean Scores on Detection Task (Max = 6)

	Condition	
	Adjacent	Distant
Less skilled	4.3	3.2
Skilled	5.2	5.0

Working Memory Limitations

This work on comprehension monitoring and our work on anomaly detection and inferences suggest that the integration of information from different parts of a text is very much harder for poor comprehenders. Such problems may well be related to working memory. We argue that working memory should not be regarded as simply another process with which poor comprehenders have problems, but might perhaps be an underlying *cause* of other processing difficulties (we come back to the direction of the link between working memory and comprehension processes in more detail later). Many recent models of reading emphasize the importance of various aspects of memory. Short-term memory is needed for temporary storage and integration of information; long-term memory for more permanent storage and as a source of background knowledge (e.g., in making inferences). Both, therefore, play an important part in comprehension, but in this section we focus on short-term and working memory.

Studies of the relation between short-term memory and comprehension skills have produced mixed results (e.g., Perfetti & Goldman, 1976; Perfetti & Lesgold, 1979; Torgeson, 1978–1979). Several studies have shown that, where good and poor readers do differ on memory span tasks, these differences can largely be accounted for by differences in the efficiency of phonological coding in working memory (see Stanovich, 1986; Wagner & Torgeson, 1987). Some of our own work has addressed the issue of whether children with a specific comprehension problem, as opposed to some more general reading problem, have deficiencies in short-term memory (see Oakhill, Yuill, & Parkin, 1986). Although we did not find any differences between good and poor comprehenders in their propensity to rehearse, or in their use of phonological coding in short-term memory tasks, the tests we used were primarily tests of storage capacity.

Oakhill, Yuill, and Parkin (1988) suggested that good and poor comprehenders might differ on a task that makes heavier demands on *working memory* (i.e., a task that makes concurrent storage and processing demands). Many studies of adults have shown that comprehension skill is related to performance on tests of working memory (for a review, see Daneman, 1987). Daneman and Carpenter (e.g., 1980, 1983) showed that various aspects of skilled comprehension (remembering facts, detecting inconsistencies, resolving pronouns) are related to a verbal test of working memory (the sentence span task). This task requires the subjects to read and understand a series of sentences (the processing requirement) while simultaneously trying to remember the final word in each (the storage requirement). Because reading and understanding sentences is a task at which the skilled comprehenders might be at an advantage, we developed an analogous task using digits rather than words. The children were presented with lists of numbers to read aloud (the processing requirement) and had to remember the final digit in each group (storage requirement). The memory load was varied by increasing the number of sets of digits (and, therefore, the number of final digits to be recalled): two, three, or four. Thus, for example, in a two-digit case, the child might read the sets 7-4-2 and 1-3-9 and then have to recall 2 and 9. Although there was no difference between the groups in the easiest version (two-digit recall), there were differences in the three- and four-digit versions of the task. We have replicated this finding several times, with both 7- to 8-year-olds and 9- to 10-year-olds. Thus, one obvious suggestion is that skilled comprehenders are better at making inferences, monitoring their understanding, interpreting anaphors, and deriving the structure of stories *because* they have more efficient working memories. Indeed, the idea of a working memory deficit fits in nicely with our studies of anomaly detection and comprehension monitoring, described earlier, in which we showed that it was only when the crucial pieces of information were nonadjacent in the text that the less-skilled comprehenders had particular difficulties.

This pattern of results—that the poor comprehenders are able to integrate information and detect inconsistencies at short distances, but not over longer distances—indicates that they are able to connect up information in text to some extent. The findings are consistent with the hypothesis that poor comprehenders are able to build adequate representations of parts of a text, but fail to relate and integrate these partial representations to produce a model of the text as a whole. Such a hypothesis would explain why they are able to appreciate anomalies and inconsistencies when the information on which this appreciation depends is not close together in the text. It can also explain why they have difficulty in making inferences that do not just depend on information that is locally available in the text, but on the integration of information from different parts, and perhaps the conjunction of that information with relevant background knowledge as well. We suggest that the poor comprehenders' more limited working memories are sufficient to support some local integration of text, but that they cannot support the integration of the text as a whole.

There are two major problems with this analysis, however. First, as yet, we have no data that addresses the issue of the direction of the link. It may be the case, as Tunmer (1989) suggested, that practice at reading with understanding increases working memory capacity, rather than the reverse.

Second, even if working memory were found to be causally linked to comprehension skill, it is very unlikely to be a complete explanation of individual differences in skill. We have found that even brief periods of training to raise children's awareness of the need to make inferences, and to go beyond the literal information in a text, were very successful in improving the poor group's performance on a standardized comprehension test, at least in the short term (for a review, see Oakhill & Yuill, 1991). It is highly unlikely that an incidental outcome of such training was that it also improved the children's working memory *capacity*. However, the two sets of findings—that the poor comprehenders have deficient working memories and that their comprehension can be improved by short periods of training—are not entirely incompatible. It may be the case that the training we gave the children provided them with strategies that helped them to circumvent their memory problems, rather than enabled them to process text as good comprehenders do. Perhaps the training strategies enabled them to link up the ideas in the texts and, thus, to utilize their available working memory resources more efficiently.

KNOWLEDGE

As we stated at the beginning of this chapter, we have relatively little to say in this section, because our research to date has very little bearing on the issue of knowledge in text comprehension. However, for completeness, we provide a very brief overview of these areas, and suggest how the process and knowledge components of the comprehension model might be integrated within a working memory framework.

Word Meanings

It is fairly obvious that a reader who does not know the meanings of more than a small proportion of the words in a text is going to have trouble understanding it. In most cases, vocabulary size in children is a good indicator of reading comprehension skill (for a review, see Rosenshine, 1980), perhaps because both knowledge of word meanings and comprehension depend, at least to some extent, on general linguistic skills and experience. The difficulty of the vocabulary in a text affects comprehension directly, and Beck, Perfetti, and McKeown (1982) showed that children find texts easier to recall if they know the meanings of the words in them. Beck et al. also demonstrated that comprehension can be improved by instruction that increased vocabulary, although other research on vocabulary instruction (Pany, Jenkins, & Schreck, 1982) has shown only limited effects. In any case, as Perfetti himself pointed out (1985), inadequate knowledge of word meanings can only, at best, be a partial explanation of comprehension problems, because children can fail to understand texts with only very familiar words in them. Daneman (1988) outlined a number of hypotheses to explain the strong correlation between vocabulary knowledge and reading comprehension. Her conclusion was that the most theoretically interesting and empirically persuasive of these hypotheses is what she called the *learning-from-context hypothesis*. She summarized it as follows: "According to the learning-from-context hypothesis, vocabulary and comprehension are correlated because vocabulary tests and comprehension tests both reflect the individual's ability to learn or acquire new information from context" (1988, p. 150).

Although it cannot be denied that vocabulary knowledge is linked closely to reading comprehension skill, in our own studies we have matched children for vocabulary as well as word recognition and shown that, nevertheless, they differ markedly on a number of measures of comprehension skill (for a review, see Yuill & Oakhill, 1991). More recent work (Cain, 1994) suggests, however, that the vocabulary test we used might not have been sufficiently sensitive to detect differences between the groups. When Cain tested such groups on the BPVS, she found small, but consistent, group differences. However, perhaps we were misguided in trying to control for group differences in vocabulary skill. It may be impossible to control adequately for this factor when comprehension and vocabulary knowledge are so intimately interrelated. What is needed, rather, is research to assess in more detail how each influences the other.

Once more, working memory might play a role. For instance, Gathercole and Baddeley (1989) concluded that the phonological storage component of working memory is involved in the acquisition of new vocabulary in children. In addition, there are no data that directly address the question of whether having a good vocabulary aids comprehension, or vice versa, although there is some convincing evidence that those who read avidly tend to improve their vocabularies. For instance, Anderson, Wilson, and Fielding (1988) found that the time spent reading books out of school (diary estimates) predicted vocabulary knowledge of fifth graders, even when previous (second grade) reading performance was taken into account. Anderson et al. used the time spent reading at home and reading rate measures to judge the amount read by the children. They estimated that a child at the 90th percentile for book reading would come across nearly 6.5 times as many words in a year as a child at the 50th percentile: 1,823,000 words/year versus 282,000. Thus, the possibilities of learning new vocabulary are very much larger for children who read more. Cunningham and Stanovich (1991) showed that a measure of exposure to print (their "Title Recognition Test") accounted for a significant proportion of unique vocabulary knowledge in fourth and fifth graders, even when age and IQ (Raven's matrices) were entered into the regression first.

Most convincing of all is a study by Stanovich (reported in Stanovich, 1993) in which he compared individuals who were low in print exposure but got high scores on Raven's matrices (LoPrint/HiAbility) with subjects who were high in print exposure, but got low scores on the Raven (HiPrint/LoAbility) test. What was particularly interesting is that the HiPrint/LoAbility group performed better on a number of measures, Peabody Picture Vocabulary Test (PPVT) performance among them. Perhaps even more striking was the finding of a mismatch between print exposure and reading comprehension skill itself—although good comprehenders usually read more avidly than poor ones, the correlation between comprehension skill and print exposure is not perfect, and Stanovich was able to capitalize on this fact to divide the sample according to performance on a comprehension test, and print exposure. The numbers of subjects in each group were smaller than in the above analysis but, nevertheless, he was able to find a substantial number of subjects who were low in print exposure but who performed well on the comprehension test (LoPrint/HiComp), or who were high on print exposure but performed more poorly on comprehension (HiPrint/LoComp). Although the LoPrint/HiComp group performed better on nonverbal cognitive abilities (Raven's matrices), the HiPrint/LoComp group were better on other measures, including, once again, the PPVT. This study provides striking evidence that it might be possible for print exposure to compensate for modest levels of cognitive ability.

Domain Knowledge

There are several sources of evidence that knowledge of a particular domain will facilitate understanding of a text in that domain—it is easier to understand a text if you have the relevant background knowledge. For example, a reader with a rich background knowledge of the rules of football, and of the teams playing, will find an account of a football match easier to understand and will give it a fuller interpretation than one who lacks that knowledge. The effects of such knowledge on comprehension and memory have been illustrated by Voss and his associates (Chiesi, Spilich, & Voss, 1979; Spilich, Vesonder, Chiesi, & Voss, 1979). They presented adults who had either high or low knowledge of baseball with a passage about a baseball match, and asked them to recall it. Not only did the high-knowledge group recall more of the passage, but they tended to recall more significant information. They remembered the order of events better, and integrated the events in the passage more successfully. The low-knowledge subjects tended to recall peripheral information, such as what the weather was like during the match.

There are also several studies that demonstrate the importance of prior knowledge in children's comprehension. In fact, prior knowledge about the topics of passages was found to be a better predictor than comprehension skill in fourth graders' ability to draw inferences from and elaborate on the information in the texts (Marr & Gormley, 1982). Pearson, Hansen, and Gordon (1979) chose two groups of second graders who were matched for IQ but differed in their knowledge of spiders. The children read a passage about spiders, and answered both explicit and implicit questions about it. The answers to the explicit questions could be found in the text, whereas the implicit ones necessitated the integration of prior knowledge and information from the text. The group who knew more about spiders performed better overall, mainly because of their superior performance on the implicit questions. In this study, as in the studies of adults cited previously, all of the subjects had *some* relevant background knowledge, but the extent and quality of their knowledge determined how well the texts were understood. Beck and McKeown (1986) suggested that insufficient background knowledge may be a major factor in reading failure, and that "Teachers need to be on the alert for knowledge problems masquerading as reading problems" (p. 133).

Fortunately, it seems that the provision of relevant background knowledge immediately prior to reading can facilitate comprehension. A series of studies by Graves and his colleagues (e.g., Graves, Cooke, & LaBerge, 1983; Graves & Palmer, 1981) showed that short previews that provided relevant background knowledge, introduced key story elements, and attempted to engage the children's interest improved their performance on a number of comprehension measures. The results held for both high- and low-ability children in the fifth and sixth grades, and for low-ability seventh- and eighth-grade children. Beck, Omanson, and McKeown (1982) showed that such procedures can also be effective for children as young as third graders.

It seems, therefore, that the provision of background knowledge may improve comprehension, although in the studies cited previously, the children in the experimental groups were provided with additional aids, other than just background knowledge. Some recent work by Barnes and Dennis (1996) is highly relevant to this issue. Her work is particularly interesting, because she provided the children with made-up information (about a make-believe world) and could, therefore, manipulate the knowledge that they had very precisely. Barnes compared average and poor comprehenders. The groups were taught a series of facts (the "knowledge base") about an imaginary world to criterion. There was no difference in the literal comprehension of the two groups. However, the poor comprehenders performed more poorly than the good ones at drawing both necessary and elaborative inferences from their knowledge base, despite the fact that prior testing had established that both groups knew all the facts on which the inferences were based. Thus, these findings demonstrate that deficits in inferencing cannot be fully explained by knowledge base differences.

Of course, although it is clear that lack of relevant knowledge is causally implicated in poor comprehension, there is almost certainly a causal link in the opposite direction: Good comprehenders probably read more than poor comprehenders, by definition understand more of what they read, and are able therefore to increase their knowledge base through reading. Once again, it may be possible that working memory is implicated in the acquisition and use of knowledge in comprehension. First, those with more efficient working memories are likely to be better at integrating newly acquired pieces of knowledge (whatever their source) within the relevant knowledge framework. Similarly, they are more likely to be successful in retrieving and integrating relevant background knowledge with the information presented in a text.

Whatever the precise nature of the relation between background knowledge and comprehension, domain-specific knowledge is typically assumed to be an additional component, and not an intrinsic part of comprehension. For instance, Perfetti (1989) argued for the concept of a general language comprehension ability that is knowledge independent. On this account, differences in domain knowledge could never be a central explanatory factor for differences in comprehension skill.

We have done very little work on the effects of domain-specific knowledge in text comprehension, and the little that we have done has already been mentioned. We showed that poor comprehenders often fail to make straightforward inferences based on general knowledge, even when they have such knowledge available to them. To some extent, this failure might result from their inability to integrate the knowledge (as our studies of working memory might suggest), or because they do not realize the importance of making inferences and bringing in relevant world knowledge when trying to understand a text. Our remediation studies, mentioned briefly, suggest that this latter possibility might be part of the explanation for failure to make inferences.

This section has been concerned with domain-specific knowledge (i.e., knowledge about the topic[s] of a text), but we have not, thus far, considered another aspect of knowledge in text comprehension: knowledge of how texts are structured. The story production experiment reported in the earlier section on text structure showed that less-skilled comprehenders produce less-coherent and more poorly integrated stories than do skilled comprehenders. We suggested that their poor ability might be related to working memory limitations. However, the ability to produce well-structured, coherent stories might also be influenced by knowledge about how stories are typically structured: not the superficial knowledge about conventional turns of phrase that we explored earlier, but more fundamental knowledge about story frameworks. Stein and Glenn's work on the development of a story concept (e.g., Stein & Glenn, 1979, 1982) was based on the assumption that skilled adult readers possess a "grammar" for stories that details the different elements of a story and how they fit together. This "schematic knowledge is used to guide the encoding and retrieval of story information" (Stein & Glenn, 1982, p. 256). Within this framework, knowledge as well as process variables can affect performance on story-related tasks, particularly in the case of young children who are still developing their grammar. Stein and Trabasso (1981) proposed that story grammar rules may be used to guide the construction of a text macrostructure: An incomplete grammar would therefore restrict both the planning of and processing of stories. Story grammars have been criticized as inadequate accounts of text processing (e.g., Garnham, 1983). However, such criticisms do not mean that a less-rigid and prescriptive type of story knowledge could not affect children's ability to produce and understand stories. It may be that the less-skilled comprehenders experience difficulties because they are less aware that there is a simple format that underlies the sorts of stories with which they are familiar. They may be less aware that stories comprise a sequence of causally related events within a fairly rigidly defined framework. Fitzgerald and Spiegel (1983) found that training children who had poor story knowledge improved both their story production and comprehension skills. Whether such effects could be found for less-skilled comprehenders remains to be seen.

CONCLUSIONS AND FUTURE DIRECTIONS

In this chapter, we hope to have made clear that it is easy to find skills on which good and poor comprehenders differ (although the precise nature of the differences might depend on how the subjects are selected). Now that we have a good deal of information about these differences, we need to move toward a more dynamic model of the processes that contribute to comprehension, and their interactions during development. We hope that this chapter provides some pointers in that direction.

The comprehension processes discussed here all make demands on working-memory resources, and it is reasonable to suppose that a child (or, indeed, an adult) who has a low working-memory capacity might find them difficult. The evidence so far suggests that working memory constrains the comprehension of children at least by limiting their ability to build mental models of texts. These constraints might arise because working memory is occupied with lower-level (lexical and syntactic) processing, or because it is generally inefficient. Poor comprehenders can, perhaps, build models of parts of the text, but fail to integrate these submodels into a coherent whole. We have argued that working memory deficits could readily explain the less-skilled comprehenders' problems in making inferences, understanding story structures, and monitoring and repairing their comprehension.

We have assumed that because we showed a relation between a nonverbal working memory test and children's comprehension, poor comprehenders have a general deficiency (rather than a specifically verbal deficiency) in working memory skills. However, we did not test the children on a verbal working memory test, so it may be the case that verbal working memory is an even better predictor of comprehension skill in children than the test we used. We are currently developing a variety of working memory tests (verbal, numerical, and spatial) for use with children, and hope to explore these issues and also to see how the relation between working memory and comprehension changes with age.

Patterns of causality between working memory skills and text comprehension have yet to be established, and it seems likely that—as has proved to be the case with the relation between phonological skills and reading development—the patterns of causality may turn out to be both subtle and complex. As Tunmer argued, it is feasible that working memory improves through practice at reading and understanding text, rather than working memory being causally linked to comprehension skill (although, of course, it may well be the case that there are causal links in both directions). In any case, a deficient working memory seems very unlikely to be a complete explanation of the less-skilled children's problem because inference skills can be trained, and one would not expect working memory to be susceptible to training. The training might increase children's awareness of the need to make inferences, but is unlikely to improve their working memory. One possibility that reconciles these two sets of findings is that less-skilled comprehenders do have a basic deficit in working memory *capacity* that affects their comprehension, but that they can be taught strategies that help them to circumvent their memory limitations, perhaps by improving the *efficiency of use* of memory resources.

In a further project, we intend to look at possible patterns of causality between the skills and abilities outlined in this chapter, and comprehension ability. If there is a difference between good and poor comprehenders on some measure (inferences, metacognitive skills), the poor comprehenders' lower performance might be either a cause or a consequence of their poor comprehension. For example, poor comprehenders might not adequately understand a text because they do not make the right inferences, or they might fail to make inferences because they have had less experience of reading text and, therefore, less practice at making inferences. Thus far our studies, with a few exceptions, have not addressed the issue of causality. We intend to do this in two main ways. The first way is by making further use of the "comprehension age match" (discussed previously). The other way in which we intend to investigate causal factors is by exploring, in a longitudinal study, how well various skills that have been identified as problematic for poor comprehenders (e.g., inference making, working memory, verbal IQ, metacognitive skills) predict comprehension at a later age, and compare that with how well comprehension predicts performance on tasks that measure those skills at a later age. The relative strengths of these relations will throw light on the direction of causal links between comprehension skill and the other variables and, we hope, will enable us to develop a better model of comprehension skill and its breakdown.

Thus far, we have considered children with comprehension problems to be a relatively homogenous population. However, it may well be the case that different individuals show different patterns of deficits. Indeed, some recent work by Cornoldi, de Beni and Pazzaglia (1996) showed that seven children with severe reading comprehension difficulties showed very different profiles of performance on a battery of tests that measured oral comprehension, metacognition, working memory, and general abilities. These data suggest strongly that we should be sensitive to individual differences *within* a population of poor comprehenders.

REFERENCES

Ackerman, B. P. (1984). The effects of storage and processing complexity on comprehension repair in children and adults. *Journal of Experimental Child Psychology, 37*, 303–334.

Anderson, R. C., Wilson, P. T., & Fielding, L. G. (1988). Growth in reading and how children spend their time outside of school. *Reading Research Quarterly, 23*, 285–303.

Applebee, A. N. (1978). *The child's concept of story: Ages two to seventeen.* Chicago: University of Chicago Press.

Barnes, M. A., & Dennis, M. (1996). Reading comprehension deficits arise from diverse sources: Evidence from readers with and without developmental brain pathology. In C. Cornoldi & J. Oakhill (Eds.), *Reading comprehension difficulties: Processes and intervention.* Mahwah, NJ: Lawrence Erlbaum Associates.

Beck, I. L., & McKeown, M. G. (1986). Instructional research in reading: A retrospective. In J. Orasanu (Ed.), *Reading comprehension: From research to practice* (pp. 113–134). Hillsdale, NJ: Lawrence Erlbaum Associates.

Beck, I. L., Omanson, R. C., & McKeown, M. G. (1982). An instructional redesign of reading lessons: Effects on comprehension. *Reading Research Quarterly, 17*, 462–481.

Beck, I. L., Perfetti, C. A., & McKeown, M. G. (1982). Effects of long-term vocabulary instruction on lexical access and reading comprehension. *Reading Research Quarterly, 17*, 462–481.

Bishop, D. (1982). *Test for reception of grammar.* Manchester, England: Chapel Press.

Cain, K. (1994). *An investigation into comprehension difficulties in young children.* Unpublished doctoral thesis, University of Sussex.

Chiesi, H. L., Spilich, G. J., & Voss, J. F. (1979). Acquisition of domain-related information in relation to high and low domain knowledge. *Journal of Verbal Learning and Verbal Behavior, 18*, 257–274.

Clay, M. M., & Imlach, R. H. (1971). Juncture, pitch and stress as reading behavior variables. *Journal of Verbal Learning and Verbal Behavior, 10*, 133–139.

Cornoldi, C., de Beni, R., & Pazzaglia, F. (1996). Profiles of reading comprehension difficulties: An analysis of single cases. In C. Cornoldi & J. Oakhill (Eds.), *Reading comprehension difficulties: Processes and intervention* (pp. 113–136). Mahwah, NJ: Lawrence Erlbaum Associates.

Cromer, W. (1970). The difference model: A new explanation for some reading difficulties. *Journal of Educational Psychology, 61*, 471–483.

Cunningham, A. E., & Stanovich, K. E. (1991). Tracking the unique effects of print exposure in children: Associations with vocabulary, general knowledge and spelling. *Journal of Educational Psychology, 83*, 264–274.

Daneman, M. (1987). Reading and working memory. In J. R. Beech & A. M. Colley (Eds.), *Cognitive approaches to reading* (pp. 57–86). Chichester, England: Wiley.

Daneman, M. (1988). Word knowledge and reading skill. In M. Daneman, G. MacKinnon, & T. G. Waller (Eds.), *Reading research: Advances in theory and practice* (pp. 145–175). San Diego: Academic.

Daneman, M., & Carpenter, P. (1980). Individual differences in working memory and reading. *Journal of Verbal Learning and Verbal Behavior, 19,* 450–466.

Daneman, M., & Carpenter, P. A. (1983). Individual differences in integrating information between and within sentences. *Journal of Experimental Psychology: Learning Memory and Cognition, 9,* 561–584.

Fitzgerald, J., & Spiegel, D. L. (1983). Enhancing children's reading comprehension through instruction in narrative structure. *Journal of Reading Behavior, XV,* 1–17.

Garnham, A. (1983). What's wrong with story grammars? *Cognition, 15,* 145–154.

Gathercole, S. E., & Baddeley, A. D. (1989). Evaluation of the role of phonological STM in the development of vocabulary in children: A longitudinal study. *Journal of Memory and Language, 28,* 200–213.

Graves, M. F., Cooke, C. L., & LaBerge, M. J. (1983). Effects of previewing difficult short stories on low ability junior high school students' comprehension, recall and attitudes. *Reading Research Quarterly, 18,* 262–276.

Graves, M. F., & Palmer, R. J. (1981). Validating previewing as a method of improving fifth and sixth grade students' comprehension on short stories. *Michigan Reading Journal, 15,* 1–3.

Markman, E. (1977). Realizing that you don't understand: A preliminary investigation. *Child Development, 48,* 986–992.

Marr, M. B., & Gormley, K. (1982). Children's recall of familiar and unfamiliar text. *Reading Research Quarterly, 18,* 89–104.

Oakan, R., Wiener, M., & Cromer, W. (1971). Identification, organization and reading comprehension in good and poor readers. *Journal of Educational Psychology, 62,* 71–78.

Oakhill, J. V. (1982). Constructive processes in skilled and less-skilled comprehenders. *British Journal of Psychology, 73,* 13–20.

Oakhill, J. V. (1983). Instantiation in skilled and less-skilled comprehenders. *Quarterly Journal of Experimental Psychology, 35A,* 441–450.

Oakhill, J. V. (1984). Inferential and memory skills in children's comprehension of stories. *British Journal of Educational Psychology, 54,* 31–39.

Oakhill, J. V., Hartt, J., & Samols, D. (1996, August). *Comprehension monitoring and working memory in good and poor comprehenders.* Paper presented at the XIVth Biennial ISSBD Conference, Quebec City.

Oakhill, J. V., & Yuill, N. M. (1991). The remediation of reading comprehension difficulties. In M. J. Snowling & M. Thomson (Eds.), *Dyslexia: Integrating theory and practice* (pp. 215–235). London: Whurr.

Oakhill, J. V., Yuill, N. M., & Parkin, A. J. (1986). On the nature of the difference between skilled and less-skilled comprehenders. *Journal of Research in Reading, 9,* 80–91.

Oakhill, J. V., Yuill, N. M., & Parkin, A. J. (1988). Memory and inference in skilled and less-skilled comprehenders. In M. M. Gruneberg, P. E. Morris, & R. N. Sykes (Eds.), *Practical aspects of memory* (Vol. 2, pp. 315–320). Chichester, England: Wiley.

Pany, D., Jenkins, J. R., & Schreck, J. (1982). Vocabulary instruction: Effects of word knowledge and reading comprehension. *Learning Disability Quarterly, 5,* 202–215.

Pearson, P. D., Hansen, J., & Gordon, C. (1979). The effects of background knowledge on young children's comprehension of explicit and implicit information. *Journal of Reading Behavior, 11,* 201–209.

Perfetti, C. A. (1985). *Reading ability.* Oxford, England: Oxford University Press.

Perfetti, C. A. (1988). Verbal efficiency in reading ability. In M. Daneman, G. MacKinnon, & T. G. Waller (Eds.) *Reading research: Advances in theory and practice* (pp. 109–143). San Diego: Academic.

Perfetti, C. A. (1989). There are generalized abilities and one of them is reading. In L. Resnick (Ed.), *Knowing, learning and instruction: Essays in honor of Robert Glaser* (pp. 307–335). Hillsdale, NJ: Lawrence Erlbaum Associates.

Perfetti, C. A. (1996). Sources of comprehension failure: Theoretical perspectives and case studies. In C. Cornoldi, & J. Oakhill (Eds.), *Reading comprehension difficulties: Processes and intervention* (pp. 137–165). Mahwah, NJ: Lawrence Erlbaum Associates.

Perfetti, C. A., & Goldman, S. R. (1976). Discourse memory and reading comprehension skill. *Journal of Verbal Learning and Verbal Behavior, 15*, 33–42.

Perfetti, C. A., & Hogaboam, T. (1975). Relationship between single word decoding and reading comprehension skill. *Journal of Educational Psychology, 67*, 461–469.

Perfetti, C. A., & Lesgold, A. M. (1979). Coding and comprehension in skilled reading and implications for reading instruction. In L. B. Resnick & P. Weaver (Eds.), *Theory and practice of early reading* (Vol. 1, pp. 57–84). Hillsdale, NJ: Lawrence Erlbaum Associates.

Peterson, C., & McCabe, A. (1983). *Developmental psycholinguistics: Three ways of looking at a child's narrative*. New York: Plenum.

Rosenshine, B. V. (1980). Skill hierarchies in reading comprehension. In R. J. Spiro, B. C. Bruce, & W. F. Brewer (Eds.), *Theoretical issues in reading comprehension* (pp. 535–559). Hillsdale, NJ: Lawrence Erlbaum Associates.

Shankweiler, D. (1989). How problems of comprehension are related to difficulties in decoding. In D. Shankweiler & I. Y. Liberman (Eds.), *Phonology and reading disability: Solving the reading puzzle* (pp. 35–68). Ann Arbor: University of Michigan Press.

Spilich, G. J., Vesonder, G. T., Chiesi, H. L., & Voss, J. F. (1979). Text processing of domain-related information for individuals with high and low domain knowledge. *Journal of Verbal Learning and Verbal Behavior, 18*, 275–290.

Stanovich, K. E. (1986). Cognitive processes and reading problems of learning-disabled children: Evaluating the assumption of specificity. In J. K. Torgeson & B. Wong (Eds.), *Psychological and educational perspectives on learning disabilities* (pp. 87–131). New York: Academic.

Stanovich, K. E. (1993). Does reading make you smarter? Literacy and the development of verbal intelligence. In H. Reese (Ed.), *Advances in child development and behavior* (Vol. 24, pp. 133–180). New York: Academic.

Stein, N. L., & Glenn, C. G. (1979). An analysis of story comprehension in elementary school children. In R. O. Freedle (Ed.), *New directions in discourse processing* (Vol. 2, pp. 53–120). Norwood, NJ: Ablex.

Stein, N. L., & Glenn, C. G. (1982). Children's concept of time: the development of a story schema. In W. J. Friedman (Ed.), *The developmenal psychology of time* (pp. 255–282). New York: Academic.

Stein, N. L., & Trabasso, T. (1981). What's in a story: An approach to comprehension and instruction. In R. Glaser (Ed.), *Advances in the psychology of instruction* (Vol. 2, pp. 213–267). Hillsdale, NJ: Lawrence Erlbaum Associates.

Steiner, R., Wiener, M., & Cromer, W. (1971). Comprehension training and identification for good and poor readers. *Journal of Educational Psychology, 62*, 506–513.

Torgeson, J. K. (1978–1979). Performance of reading disabled children on serial memory tasks: A selective review of recent research. *Reading Research Quarterly, 14*, 57–87.

Tunmer, W. E. (1989). The role of language-related factors in reading disability. In D. Shankweiler and I. Y. Liberman (Eds.), *Phonology and reading disability: Solving the reading puzzle* (pp. 91–131). Ann Arbor: University of Michigan Press.

Wagner, R., & Torgeson, J. K. (1987). The nature of phonological processing and its causal role in the acquisition of reading skills. *Psychological Bulletin, 101*, 192–212.

Yuill, N. M., & Oakhill, J. V. (1991). *Children's problems in text comprehension: An experimental investigation*. Cambridge, England: Cambridge University Press.

Yuill, N. M., Oakhill, J. V., & Parkin, A. J. (1989). Working memory, comprehension ability and the resolution of text anomaly. *British Journal of Psychology, 80*, 351–361.

Part IV

SPELLING

When children learn to read, at the same time they also learn to spell. Almost universally, the first spelling learned by a child is his or her own name. Spelling is more difficult than reading; it develops more slowly, and difficulties in spelling are usually regarded as less serious than difficulties in reading. Perhaps because of this, less research has been devoted to spelling than reading. Nevertheless, as the chapters in Part IV show, we have made considerable progress in understanding the process of learning to spell and the origins of children's difficulties in this area.

In chapter 19, Treiman gives an interesting historical perspective on studies of spelling before going on to describe some of her own recent studies in the area. Her studies demonstrate beautifully that the early stages of learning to spell involve children in a creative process of generating spellings from their knowledge of the sounds of words and the names of letters. Armed with this idea, Treiman shows how some otherwise rather bizarre errors in young children's spelling are actually lawful and can seem sensible.

In chapter 20, Lennox and Siegel examine the differences between good and poor spellers. They find that poor spellers have difficulty in learning the associations between letters and sounds and that they tend to rely more on a visual strategy for spelling. In chapter 21, Aaron, Wilczynski, and Keetay analyze what processes may support a "visual" approach to spelling. They do this in a novel way, by investigating the spelling and memory abilities of congenitally and profoundly deaf children. Their deaf subjects could not use phonology effectively, as witnessed by their inability to write words with a common pronunciation but different spelling pattern (*here–hear*). However, when asked to memorize written nonwords, these same deaf children were highly sensitive to their orthographic legality (the extent to which the nonwords followed the spelling patterns of English words). Both the deaf children and hearing children of the same reading age found orthographically legal nonwords much easier to remember than orthographically illegal ones. It seems that visual memory for spelling patterns, even in subjects who do not have access to a phonological code, is highly dependent on knowledge of the rulelike aspects of the spelling patterns of the language. Such knowledge is better described as orthographic than as visual.

Another critical issue in the study of spelling, as in reading, is the extent to which the spelling of different kinds of words depends on different mechanisms or different forms of knowledge. Traditionally, in both reading and spelling, dual-route models have argued for a separation between lexical processes that involve the direct retrieval of information for particular words and nonlexical or rule-governed processes. In the case of reading, there is growing evidence against the viability of this approach; some of this evidence was reviewed in Part II. A similar pattern is also emerging in the study of spelling, where increasingly it appears that single-route "connectionist" models are gaining influence. In chapter 22, Leong reports data from a large-scale study of spelling skills in 9- to 12-year-old children that question the viability of trying to separate lexical from rule-based spelling strategies. A similar conclusion is endorsed by Nation and Hulme in chapter 23. They report studies inspired by Goswami's earlier work on the role of analogies in spelling development. They find that even young children benefit from analogies between words they know and new words they are trying to spell. Nation and Hulme's interpretation of the findings is in terms of a one-route connectionist model of spelling, in which children abstract relationships between variously sized units in the orthographic and phonological representations of words.

Chapter 19

Beginning to Spell in English

Rebecca Treiman
Wayne State University

In comparison to the large body of research on reading, the study of spelling has been somewhat neglected. This chapter is designed to redress this neglect by reviewing recent work on how children learn to spell in English. The chapter focuses on beginning spellers—children in first grade and even younger. Part of the motivation for studying such young children is that if children can get off to a good start with writing and reading, many later difficulties can be avoided. Most of the research to be discussed deals with American English, although implications for other dialects and other languages are mentioned. To set the stage, the first section of the chapter discusses early ideas about how children learn to spell in English. The following sections review more recent research, including research done by me and my colleagues. This research has examined young children's misspellings, seeking to uncover the reasons for their errors. The results suggest that children bring their knowledge of the sound structure of the language and their knowledge of the names of letters to the spelling task. Certain common spelling errors that might otherwise be difficult to explain make sense when this knowledge is taken into account.

EARLY RESEARCH ON CHILDREN'S SPELLING IN ENGLISH

It has often been thought that learning to spell in English primarily involves memorizing the letters in printed words. This view of spelling as rote visual memorization is based on the assumption that the English writing system is complex, irregular, and illogical. If there is no reason for the *a* in *health* or the *e* in *give*, how can children spell these words but through rote memorization?

A good deal of research during the first two thirds of this century was interpreted to support the idea that visual memorization plays an important role in children's spelling. For example, Radaker (1963) found that as little as 2 weeks of training in visual imagery improved the spelling scores of fourth graders. However, it is hard to separate the cognitive effects of training from the increased motivation to learn to spell that it may have given the children. Gates and Chase (1926) discovered that deaf children spelled surprisingly well in comparison with their other linguistic abilities and in comparison with hearing children of similar reading levels. The deaf children's excellent performance, Gates and Chase suggested, reflected their keen visual perceptual abilities. Hearing children, the researchers argued, should follow the example of the deaf by relying less on sound-to-spelling translation and more on visual memorization.

The view of spelling as memorization reflected not only prevailing ideas about the nature of the English writing system but also widely held views about learning. During the middle part of this century, experimental psychologists studied how people memorize meaningless strings of items such as lists of unrelated letters or lists of digits. They discovered that learners did well on items at the beginning of a list—the primacy effect—and items at the end of a list—the recency effect. Items in the middle of a list were harder to remember. Some experimental psychologists became interested in spelling because it seemed to be a real-life example of the laboratory learning task. Researchers found a serial position effect such that letters at the beginnings and ends of words were spelled more accurately than letters in the middles of words (Jensen, 1962; Kooi, Schutz, & Baker, 1965; Mendenhall, 1930). The similar effects of serial position in spelling and in rote learning suggested to these verbal learning psychologists that spelling is a form of serial learning.

The idea that rote visual memorization plays a central role in learning to spell has influenced society's views about spelling and how it should be taught. Some well-educated adults seem almost proud to admit that they are poor spellers. They are too busy and too creative, they imply, to have taken the time to laboriously memorize a large number of irregular spellings. Spelling instruction in many American schools has been largely confined to copying words (Cronnell & Humes, 1980). Children have been given lists of words to memorize with little or no instruction about how to go about learning them (Peters, 1985).

Beginning in the 1960s, views of language and learning began to change. These changes led ultimately to a reconsideration of how children approach the task of spelling. One important alteration was in views of the

English writing system. Chomsky and Halle (1968) claimed that the English writing system, far from being irregular and illogical, is a "near optimal system for the lexical representation of English words" (p. 49). The *a* of *health* reveals the relationship in meaning between *health* and *heal*; the *e* of *courageous* reveals its link to *courage*. In these and other cases, Chomsky and Halle claimed, spelling reflects the underlying meanings of words. Venezky's (1970) description of English orthography also helped to rationalize some of its apparent peculiarities. For example, *e* is added after what would otherwise be a final *v* or *u*, as in *give* and *glue*. When a suffix beginning with *e, i,* or *y* is added to a word ending in *c*, a *k* is normally inserted after the *c*, as in *picnicking*. There are a number of such regularities in the English writing system, even though they are relatively complex.

Influenced by new work in linguistics, the fields of psycholinguistics (e.g., Fodor, Bever, & Garrett, 1974) and developmental psycholinguistics (e.g., Brown, 1973) emerged. Developmental psycholinguists studied children's acquisition of spoken language by means of detailed analyses of their speech. Researchers in this tradition stressed the rule-governed nature of children's errors. For example, young children may say "goed" rather than "went" or "gooses" rather than "geese." The children appear to have internalized rules governing the formation of the past tense and the plural, and to have overgeneralized these rules to cases in which they do not apply.

Within psychology, the cognitive revolution of the 1960s led researchers away from studies of serial learning and rote memorization. People were now seen as being strategic learners, actively searching for meaning and structure in the material with which they were confronted. Interested in how people perform real-life tasks, cognitive psychologists began to examine the processes involved in reading (e.g., Gibson & Levin, 1975) and spelling (e.g., Frith, 1980). Although there was much less research on spelling than on reading, the dominant view was that spellers use sound-to-spelling translation rules as well as rote visual memorization. Use of sound–spelling rules was thought to yield "phonetic" errors on irregular or exception words, such as PLAD for *plaid*. (Spelling errors are indicated in upper case throughout this chapter.) Regular words such as *trap* and *plant* were thought to be easier to spell.

The new views of language and learning came together in the work of Read (1975). Whereas cognitive psychologists focused on spelling in older children and adults, Read (1975) studied the earliest beginners. His major source of data, as in the case of the developmental psycholinguists studying the acquisition of spoken language, was children's spontaneous productions. After collecting the writings of 32 children who began to write on their own as preschoolers, Read carried out detailed analyses of their spellings. The results suggested that learning to spell, like learning to talk, is a creative process. The children studied by Read approached the task of spelling primarily by trying to symbolize the sounds that they heard in words rather than by trying to reproduce memorized strings of letters. They made errors such as CHRIE for *try* and CAT for *can't*, which were not strictly phonetic in the traditional sense but were nonetheless attempts to symbolize the children's phonological representations of words. Read's focus on children's implicit phonological knowledge as a motivation for their spelling was a major strength of his work. A potential weakness (Gibson & Levin, 1975) was that, because the children in his study began to write much earlier than average, their results may not generalize to normal children.

RECENT RESEARCH ON CHILDREN'S SPELLING IN ENGLISH

My own research on children's early spelling has been influenced by Read's (1975). Like Read, I have gathered large collections of children's writings and have performed detailed, linguistically based analyses of their spellings. To extend and complement the naturalistic data, my colleagues and I have carried out numerous experiments with children of preschool age and older, a research strategy also adopted by Read. In the following sections I review this work, together with related work of other investigators, and discuss its implications for views of spelling development.

My naturalistic study (Treiman, 1993) differed from Read's (1975) in that it examined first graders who were learning to read and write at school rather than children who started to write before they began school. The children in my study were not precocious or advanced. Instead, they happened to be assigned to a teacher who was an advocate of the whole-language approach (e.g., Goodman, 1986). School policy dictated that the children be given some instruction in phonics. However, the teacher put most stress on independent writing. At the beginning of the school year, some children spent their morning writing time drawing pictures and writing their names. As the school year progressed, the children began to write sentences and sometimes longer texts. Print began to occupy more space on their papers, and pictures less. The teacher believed that children should figure out the spellings of words on their own. Thus, she did not tell children the spelling of a word even if they asked. After children had finished writing, they brought their work to the teacher or teacher's aide and read aloud what they had written. The adult wrote the child's words on the paper, using conventional spelling, and also wrote the date. Through the teacher's kind cooperation, I was able to collect the writings of 43 children who were in her first-grade class during 2 successive school years. There were 5,617 spellings in the collection.

The naturalistic data allow us to observe the spellings produced by children engaged in meaningful writing in the classroom. Sometimes, however, children do not choose to spell a large number of words of a linguistically critical type. The words that they do spell differ in a number of ways, making it hard in some cases to pinpoint the reasons for the errors. In an attempt to overcome the weaknesses of the naturalistic data, my colleagues and I have conducted a number of experiments (e.g., Bruck & Treiman, 1990; Treiman, 1985c, 1985d, 1991, 1994; Treiman, Berch, Tincoff, & Weatherston, 1993; Treiman, Berch, & Weatherston, 1993; Treiman, Cassar, & Zukowski, 1994; Treiman, Weatherston, & Berch, 1994; Treiman, Zukowski, & Richmond-Welty, 1995; Treiman, Goswami, Tincoff, & Leevers, 1997). In the experiments, we asked young children to spell words or nonwords of particular types or to perform other tasks related to spelling. By combining the naturalistic data and the experimental data, we hope to draw stronger conclusions about spelling development than we could by using a single type of data.

Three phenomena are discussed in the following sections. The first concerns errors that, although not phonetically correct in the sense of PLAD for *plaid*, accurately reflect certain aspects of words' sounds. For example, the substitution of *ch* for *t* before *r* is motivated by the properties of /t/ when it precedes /r/. A second phenomenon to be discussed concerns omissions of consonants. Children may leave out the *n* of *can't* or of *snow*, producing CAT and SO. I argue that these omissions reflect the position of the consonant in the spoken syllable. For children, /sn/ may be a unit rather than a sequence of individual sounds. Finally, I discuss certain spelling errors that reflect children's knowledge of letter names. For example, young children may spell /w/ as *y* because the name of the letter *y* contains the sound /w/. In all of these cases, children create spellings for words based on their knowledge of spoken language and their knowledge about print. They do not simply reproduce memorized spellings.

"Phonetic" Errors

Misspellings like PLAD for *plaid* are often called *phonetic errors*. Phonetic errors are typically defined as those in which each sound is symbolized with a letter or group of letters that may represent that sound in conventional English. Such errors, which are common in skilled adult spellers (e.g., Baron, Treiman, Wilf, & Kellman, 1980), are thought to mean that spellers use a sound-based translation strategy in addition to or instead of rote visual memorization. In contrast, nonphonetic errors such as PAD for *plaid* are thought to mean that spellers are not successfully using spelling-to-sound translation.

Read (1975) observed that some of children's errors, although not phonetic in the traditional sense, nevertheless represented aspects of words' sounds. For example, some of the children in his study wrote *try* as CHRIE or *truck* as CHRAC. As well as symbolizing /t/ before /r/ as *ch*, some children spelled /d/ before /r/ as *g* or *j*, as in JRAGIN for *dragon* and GRADL for *dreidel.* These errors are not phonetic in the usual sense; the phoneme /t/ is never spelled as *ch* in English. However, the errors make sense given that /t/ before /r/ is pronounced similarly to the initial sound of *chick*, /tʃ/.[1] Specifically, when /t/ occurs before /r/, the place of articulation moves back in the mouth and the closure is released slowly rather than quickly, giving /t/ a degree of frication. Likewise, /d/ becomes similar to the /dʒ/ of *jack* when it occurs before /r/. Errors such as CHRIE and JRAGIN are reasonable errors that reflect the sound properties of words. Table 19.1 shows the number and proportion of these errors in Read's naturalistic study.

Importantly, the errors discovered by Read (1975) are not confined to precocious spellers. Spellings such as CHRAP for *trap* and JRAD for *drowned* also occurred in my study of first graders' classroom writings (Treiman, 1993), as Table 19.1 shows. These spellings were also found in an experiment reported by Read (1975) in which first graders were asked to write words and nonwords with initial /tr/. In addition, the same errors emerged when children were asked to orally name the first letters of syllables such as /tro/ and /dri/ (Treiman, 1985c). Because this task is easier than producing the full spellings of words, we could use it with kindergartners as well as first graders.

As Table 19.1 shows, the nonstandard spellings of /t/ and /d/ before /r/ generally formed well under 20% of the total, even among children who had relatively little experience with conventional spelling. However, there are good reasons to believe that these are not just random errors. The same errors were found in several independent studies. Spellings such as *ch* for /t/ primarily occurred when /t/ was followed by /r/; they were less common when /t/ occurred in other contexts (Treiman, 1985c, 1993). This finding indicates that the errors are based on sound rather than on some general tendency to replace *t* with *ch*. Further support for the idea that sound is crucial is that children who made the errors for /tr/ tended to do the same for /dr/ (Treiman, 1985c).

Errors like CHRAP for *trap* are not the only case in which children represent sounds in unconventional but plausible ways. Another case involves stop consonants after /s/. English has two series of stop consonants: the voiceless stops /p/, /t/, and /k/; and the voiced stops /b/, /d/, and /g/. At the beginnings of words, the two types of stops contrast with one another. Thus, English speakers distinguish *cot* from *got*. After initial /s/,

---

[1] Key to notation: /tʃ/ as in *chick*, /dʒ/ *jack* /ŋ/ *sing*, /θ/ *think*, /ʃ/ *ship*, /o/ *boat*, /i/ *beet*, /ɪ/ *bit*, /e/ *bait*, /ɛ/ *bet*, /a/ *bar*.

TABLE 19.1
Children's Spellings of /t/ and /d/ Before /r/

Study	Type of Data	Children Involved	Number and Percentage of Spellings	
			/t/ Before /r/ With c, h, or ch	/d/ Before /r/ With g or j
Read, 1975	Naturalistic, real words	Precocious spellers	17% (6/36)[a]	18% (3/17)
Treiman, 1993	Naturalistic, real words	First graders	9% (4/45)	13% (1/8)
Read, 1975	Experimental, words and nonwords	First graders	<11% (<66/600)[b]	Not tested
Treiman, 1985c	Experimental, mainly nonwords	Kindergartners	7% (18/244)	13% (32/244)
Treiman, 1985c	Experimental, mainly nonwords	First graders	6% (12/200)	21% (42/200)

[a]The data reported by Read are for c and ch spellings; the number of h spellings, if any, was not reported.
[b]Read reported that 11% of the responses, including ch, j, and f, reflected the frication of the /t/ in this context. He did not separately report the number of c, h, and ch responses.

however, voiced and voiceless stops are not distinguished. The English writing system assumes that stops are voiceless in this context, and thus *Scot* is spelled with *c* rather than *g*. In terms of certain phonetic properties, however, the second sound of *Scot* is more similar to /g/ than to /k/ (Klatt, 1975; Lotz, Abramson, Gerstman, Ingemann, & Nemser, 1960; Reeds & Wang, 1961). Correspondingly, young children sometimes symbolize stops after /s/ with letters that are appropriate for the voiced stops /b/, /d/, and /g/ rather than with letters that are appropriate for the voiceless stops /p/, /t/, and /k/. For example, one first grader in the classroom that I studied wrote *sky* as SGIE (Treiman, 1993).

As Table 19.2 shows, spellings of stops after /s/ with letters that are commonly used for voiced stops were not very frequent in my naturalistic study (Treiman, 1993). The first graders more often represented stops after /s/ in the conventional manner or omitted them altogether—a common error on the second consonants of initial clusters, as discussed later. However, voiced spellings of stops after /s/ were also observed in two experiments with first graders and kindergartners (Treiman, 1985d). The errors were particularly common among kindergartners, occurring as often as 42% of the time in a forced-choice task in which children chose between a voiced spelling and a voiceless spelling to represent the second consonant of a syllable such as /spo/ (Treiman, 1985d). The children selected for this latter study were able to choose *l* over *f*, say, as a spelling for the second consonant of /sli/. That is, these children could spell the second consonant of a cluster in the conventional manner when the identity of the consonant was unambiguous. Thus, some children who have little experience with the conventional English writing system appear to symbolize sounds in nonstandard but phonetically reasonable ways. This holds for stop consonants after /s/ as well as for /t/ and /d/ before /r/.

Yet a third case in which children spell sounds in an unconventional but plausible manner involves syllabic /r/. In most varieties of American English, the word *her* does not contain a separate vowel as it is pronounced. Rather, the /r/ takes the place of the vowel and is said to be syllabic. Similarly, the second syllable of *brother* contains a syllabic /r/. The syllabic /r/ of *brother* is unstressed, in comparison to the stressed syllabic /r/ of *her*. As Table 19.3 shows, the children in the naturalistic studies of Read (1975) and Treiman (1993) often omitted the vowels in these contexts, producing errors such as HR for *her* and BRUTR for *brother*. Indeed, the precocious spellers studied by Read (1975) and the kindergartners studied by Treiman et al. (1993) omitted the *er* of words like *her* and *brother* more often than they included them—the first case, of those examined so far, in which the sound-based errors occurred more than half the time. Even the first graders in the study of Treiman et al. (1993), who were average to above-average readers and who had surely seen common words such as

TABLE 19.2
Children's Spellings of Stop Consonants After Word-Initial /s/

Study	Type of Data	Children Involved	Number and Percentage of Spellings			
			Voiced	Voiceless	Omitted	Other
Treiman, 1993	Naturalistic, real words	First graders	3% (3/89)	60% (53/89)	34% (30/89)	3% (3/89)
Treiman, 1985d, Exp. 1	Experimental, mainly nonwords	Kindergartners	26% (114/432)	54% (232/432)	—[a]	20% (86/432)
Treiman, 1985d, Exp. 1	Experimental, mainly nonwords	First graders	12% (70/594)	79% (471/594)	—[a]	9% (53/594)
Treiman, 1985d, Exp. 2	Experimental, mainly nonwords	Kindergartners	42% (118/280)	58% (162/280)	—[b]	—[b]
Treiman, 1985d, Exp. 2	Experimental, mainly nonwords	First graders	15% (31/210)	85% (179/210)	—[b]	—[b]

[a]Children in this experiment chose from 1 of 10 letters to represent the consonant; they did not have the opportunity to omit it.
[b]Children in this experiment chose between the conventional voiceless spelling and the corresponding voiced spelling to represent the consonant; they did not have the opportunity to pick another spelling or to omit the consonant.

TABLE 19.3
Children's Spellings of Stressed and Unstressed Syllabic /r/

			Number and Percentage of Spellings in Which No Vowel Was Included	
Study	Type of Data	Children Involved	Stressed Syllabic /r/	Unstressed Syllabic /r/
Read, 1975	Naturalistic, real words	Precocious spellers	53% (62/116)	60% (163/270)
Treiman, 1993	Naturalistic, real words	First graders	45% (56/125)	65% (127/196)
Treiman, Berch, Tincoff, & Weatherston, 1993	Experimental, real words	Kindergartners	57% (60/105)	Not tested
Treiman, Berch, Tincoff, & Weatherston, 1993	Experimental, real words	First graders	33% (33/100)	52% (99/192)
Treiman, Berch, Tincoff, & Weatherston, 1993	Experimental, real words	Second graders	4% (4/100)	5% (9/176)
Treiman, Berch, Tincoff, & Weatherston, 1993	Experimental, nonwords	Kindergartners	66% (69/105)	Not tested
Treiman, Berch, Tincoff, & Weatherston, 1993	Experimental, nonwords	First graders	42% (42/100)	Not tested
Treiman, Berch, Tincoff, & Weatherston, 1993	Experimental, nonwords	Second graders	16% (16/100)	Not tested

her, work, and *mother,* omitted the vowel between one third and two thirds of the time when spelling syllabic /r/. Children were less likely to omit the vowels of words like *war* (which have a true vowel in the middle) than of words like *her* (which have a syllabic /r/). Thus, the problem on words like *her* does not stem from an across-the-board failure to include vowels in spellings or from a general tendency to omit the middle letters of words. It reflects the particular sound properties of words like *her.*

Errors like HR for *her* deviate from conventional English in that they do not include a vowel. Although kindergartners and first graders are beginning to learn about the kinds of letter sequences that occur in English words (Treiman, 1993), children often fail to honor the orthographic conventions of English in the case of syllabic /r/. American children's many errors like HR for *her* suggest that they consider the spoken form of *her* to contain a consonant followed by a type of /r/ rather than a consonant-vowel-consonant sequence such as found in *war.* Interestingly, children who speak dialects of English in which *her* is pronounced without a final /r/ (as in most parts of England) appear to consider this word a consonant-vowel syllable and sometimes spell it accordingly (Treiman et al., 1997).

How are we to explain errors such as CHRAP for *trap,* SGIE for *sky,* and HR for *her?* On one view, some young children mistakenly believe that spelling is meant to reflect low-level phonetic details of pronunciation. No current or past writing system represents speech at such a low level (DeFrancis, 1989); thus, on this view children fundamentally misunderstand the nature of writing. However, other findings fail to support the idea that children attempt to represent the phonetic level of speech when they spell. For example, the vowel of *bat* is about two thirds the length of the vowel of *bad;* vowels are shorter when they precede voiceless stops, such as /t/, than when they precede voiced stops, such as /d/ (Klatt, 1973; Lehiste, 1975; Peterson & Lehiste, 1960). If children considered spelling to represent low-level differences in sound, they would be expected to omit the vowel of *bat* more often than the vowel of *bad.* Yet they do not appear to do so (Treiman, 1993). This and other evidence (Treiman, 1993; Treiman, Cassar, & Zukowski, 1994; Treiman et al., 1995) suggests that children represent levels of language deeper than the surface phonetic level when they spell.

Another possible explanation for errors such as CHRAP, SGIE, and HR is that they reflect the children's own conceptions of phonemic structure. Some children may classify the first sound of *trap* as belonging to the /tʃ/ phoneme rather than to the /t/ phoneme; some may classify the second phoneme of *sky* as /g/ rather than /k/. Similarly, children who do not yet know how to read and write may consider *her* to be a two-phoneme word like *hi* rather than a three-phoneme word like *war.* Thus, the phonemic systems of preliterate children may differ in some ways from those of literate adults. Learning to read and write may shape children's conceptions of language, causing fundamental changes in their classification of certain potentially ambiguous sounds.

Whichever interpretation turns out to be correct, errors such as CHRAP, SGIE, and HR have some important implications. The results show that certain misspellings that are not phonetically correct in the sense of errors like PLAD for *plaid* nevertheless reveal children's fine sensitivity to the sounds of spoken words. We would miss this sensitivity if we categorized errors like CHRAP for *trap* as nonphonetic on the grounds that /t/ is never symbolized as *ch* in English. Thus, the division between phonetic and nonphonetic errors that forms the basis of many schemes of classifying spelling errors (e.g., Boder, 1973; Bruck & Waters, 1988; Finucci, Isaacs, Whitehouse, & Childs, 1983; Nelson, 1980) can be misleading when applied to young children.

Sound-based errors further show that, for young children, spelling is to a large extent a process of symbolizing the linguistic structure of spoken words. It is not only or not primarily a process of reproducing memorized letter sequences. If children had a general tendency to omit the middle letters of words or to replace *t* with *ch*, we could not explain why omissions of the vowel of *her* are so much more common than omissions of the vowel of *war*, or why *ch* substitutions for *t* are more common before *r* than in other contexts.

Finally, certain spelling errors may arise because children's implicit classifications of speech sounds sometimes differ from adults'. These errors may occur even on words that are completely regular for adults, such as *trap*. Thus, at least when regularity is defined according to an adult viewpoint, regular words are not necessarily easy for children to spell. Although the irregularity of the English writing system is often blamed for children's difficulties in grasping the system, consistent sound–spelling correspondences would not necessarily be a panacea during the early stages of learning to spell. It would be interesting to examine the early spellings of children in languages with highly regular alphabets to determine whether children learning those languages, like children learning English, make systematic errors on regularly spelled words.

Syllable Position and Spelling

To a literate adult, the spoken forms of *nose, pant,* and *snow* all share the /n/ sound. Correspondingly, *n* appears in the printed forms of all four words. Young children, however, sometimes leave out the *n*s when spelling *pant* and *snow*. Omissions are very uncommon for the *n* of *nose*. As I discuss in this section, one important factor that affects children's tendency to omit consonants in spelling is the position of the consonant in the syllable.

Children sometimes fail to represent consonants when they are the first element of a syllable-final cluster, as in *pant*, or the last element of a syllable-initial cluster, as in *snow*.

Consonants in Final Clusters

Read (1975) discovered that children who began to write before they started school often failed to symbolize the nasal consonants /m/, /n/, and /ŋ/ when they occurred as the first phoneme of a final consonant cluster. For example, some children left out the *n* of *and*, spelling it as AD. Likewise, children sometimes failed to symbolize the /m/ of *stamps* with a separate letter, producing STAPS. Overall, the children in Read's study omitted nasals 30% of the time when they occurred before stop consonants. The omissions varied with the phonological makeup of the cluster, being more common if the following stop consonant was voiceless, as with the cluster /nt/, than if the stop was voiced, as with /nd/.

The omissions observed by Read (1975) do not reflect an across-the-board failure to spell *m, n,* and *ng*. Children usually included these letters in other contexts, such as at the beginning of a word. Nor do the omissions reflect only a general tendency to leave out the middle letters of words. Although there are serial position effects in spelling (Jensen, 1962; Kooi et al., 1965; Mendenhall, 1930; Treiman, Berch, & Weatherston, 1993), serial position alone cannot explain why *n* is more susceptible to omission before letters such as *t*, which stand for voiceless stops, than before letters such as *d*, which stand for voiced stops. To explain errors such as STAPS for *stamps*, Read focused on the sound properties of nasals in final clusters. He pointed out that nasals are very short before final consonants, especially if the consonants are voiceless (Malécot, 1960). Read implied that omissions of consonants in final clusters are largely specific to nasals.

The first graders in my naturalistic study (Treiman, 1993) made the same kinds of nasal omission errors as Read's (1975) preschoolers. For example, they spelled *think* as THEECK and *stand* as STAD. Importantly, however, the first graders' omissions of consonants in final clusters were not restricted to nasals. The liquids /r/ and /l/ were also omitted, as in HOS for *horse* and OD for *old*. Other omissions involved obstruents such as /t/ and /s/, as in LAS for *lets* and FORET for *forest*. (Obstruents include stop consonants such as /t/, fricatives such as /s/, and affricates such as /tʃ/.) As these examples show, children tended to omit the interior phonemes of final consonant clusters. With two-consonant final clusters such as /rs/ and /ld/, the first consonant was omitted 25% of the time and the second consonant was omitted at less than half that rate. With three-consonant final clusters such as /mps/, the first and second consonants of the cluster both had omission rates of 25% or more. The final consonant was omitted much less often.

To further examine the breadth of the consonant omission phenomenon, we carried out a series of experiments with first graders (Treiman et al., 1995). In these studies, children were asked to spell nonwords whose final clusters varied in their phonological makeup. As expected from the previous work, the sound properties of the cluster influenced how it was spelled. Nasals were frequently omitted before voiceless obstruents, with omission rates ranging from 57% to 81%. Given that the first graders were reading at grade level and had surely seen words such as *went*, it is striking that they left out nasals before voiceless obstruents more often than they included them. Nasals before voiced obstruents were omitted at lower but still substantial rates, from 42% to 51%. Importantly, omissions of the first consonants of final clusters were not confined to nasals. When liquids were the first phonemes of final clusters, they were omitted at rates comparable to or even higher than those for nasals before voiced obstruents, between 40% and 63%. Omission rates for obstruents as the first elements of final clusters were lower than those for nasals and liquids, ranging from 13% to 23%. It should be noted that children in this study repeated the nonwords before spelling them, allowing us to analyze their spellings in relation to any repetition errors that they made. In general, failures to spell consonants did not reflect failures to pronounce them.

Given that misspellings such as AT for *ant* do not normally reflect mispronunciation, why do they occur? One possibility is that children analyze certain spoken syllables differently than literate adults do. They consider the spoken form of *ant* to contain two units of sound—a nasalized vowel followed by a final /t/. Such an analysis is more likely for *ant* (a word with a nasal + voiceless obstruent final cluster) than for *and* (a word with a nasal + voiced obstruent final cluster), because the duration of the nasal segment is shorter in *ant* than in *and* (Malécot, 1960). Similarly, many children may consider *born* to contain three units of sound—an initial /b/ followed by an /r/-colored vowel followed by /n/—rather than the four units of sound assumed by the conventional English writing system. Because children consider /r/-ness to be a quality of the vowel rather than a separate unit, they do not use the letter *r* in their spelling, producing BON. With *lets*, in contrast, the obstruent /t/ is less likely to be grouped with the vowel and is more likely to be spelled. Treiman et al. (1995) provided some evidence consistent with this view from a task in which children were asked to pronounce the individual sounds of syllables with various types of final clusters while putting down one token for each sound. Children often used three tokens for nonwords such as /morl/, saying that the sounds in this syllable were /m/, /or/, and /l/. These same children performed the phoneme counting task very accurately with syllables such as /θɪʃ/ and /ko/.

For literate adults, words such as *ant* and *born* are perfectly regular. Their regularity (at least regularity from an adult viewpoint) does not necessarily make them easy for children to spell, however. Misspellings such as AT for *ant* and BON for *born* are common among young children. These errors would be classified as nonphonetic according to commonly used phonetic/nonphonetic classification schemes. Nevertheless, the errors have a basis in sound that is belied by the nonphonetic label. This is the same phenomenon that was observed earlier for words like *trap*.

Consonants in Initial Clusters

The findings just reviewed show that the omissions of nasals in final clusters discovered by Read (1975) are not specific to nasals. Omissions of consonants in final clusters occur for non-nasal consonants as well. Nor are the omissions specific to final clusters. Young children also omit consonants when they occur in initial clusters. In my study of first graders' classroom spellings, children omitted the second consonants of two-consonant syllable-initial clusters almost 25% of the time (Treiman, 1993). Examples include SAK for *snake*, AFAD for *afraid*, and SET for *sweat*. The first consonants of initial clusters were omitted much less often, a rate of less than 1%. With three-consonant initial clusters, both the second and the third consonants were omitted at rates of 25% or higher. Thus, the interior phonemes of initial consonant clusters, like the interior phonemes of final clusters, are more susceptible to omission than the exterior phonemes.

Table 19.4 summarizes the results for two-consonant initial clusters from my naturalistic study (Treiman, 1993) and several other studies. The second consonants of initial clusters were omitted as often as 37% of the time in one study of kindergartners (Miller & Limber, 1985). The errors occurred at lower rates in studies involving first graders and older children, although there were a few children who frequently omitted the second consonants

TABLE 19.4
Children's Omissions of Consonants in Two-Consonant Initial Clusters

			Consonant Omission Rates	
Study	Type of Data	Children Involved	First Consonant	Second Consonant
Treiman, 1993	Naturalistic, real words	First graders	1% (4/423)	25% (104/423)
Miller & Limber, 1985	Experimental, nonwords	Kindergartners	< 1% (1/588)	37% (215/588)
Treiman, 1991, Study 2	Experimental, mainly nonwords	Kindergartners	0% (0/420)	17% (72/420)
Treiman, 1991, Study 2	Experimental, mainly nonwords	First graders	0% (0/441)	19% (85/441)
Bruck & Treiman, 1990	Experimental, words and nonwords	First and second graders	2% (10/660)	6% (38/660)

of initial clusters (Treiman, 1991). As discussed earlier, omissions of consonants in final clusters vary with the phonological makeup of the cluster. However, I detected no such influence for initial clusters (Treiman, 1991, 1993). For all types of syllable-initial clusters, the interior phonemes were more likely to be omitted than the exterior phonemes.

Among normal children, failures to spell consonants in initial clusters do not reflect failures to pronounce these consonants. Bruck and Treiman (1990) administered an articulation test to screen out children who had difficulty pronouncing initial clusters. As might be expected, given that the participants were first and second graders, none of the children had such difficulty. For similar reasons, Treiman (1991) had children repeat the syllables before spelling them and corrected any repetition errors. Failures to spell the second consonants of words like *snake* and *blows* do not just reflect serial position effects either. Children are much more likely to omit the *l* of *blows* than the *l* of *along*, even though *l* is the second letter in both words (Treiman, 1985b).

Earlier, I argued that omissions of consonants in final clusters as in BON for *born* reflect children's implicit categorizations of sounds. Specifically, children make these errors because they tend to group the first consonant of certain types of final clusters, such as those beginning with /r/, with the preceding vowel. In the case of initial consonant clusters, it appears that children group the two consonants of the cluster, treating them as a single unit. Thus, children may consider *snow* to contain the initial consonant unit /sn/ followed by the vowel /o/. Indeed, there is evidence that initial consonant clusters or onsets form cohesive units for both children and adults (Treiman, 1985a, 1989, 1992). Young children may symbolize the onset /sn/ with a single letter, the letter that is appropriate for /s/, rather than analyzing the onset into two units of sound and symbolizing each unit with a separate letter.

Conclusions About Syllable Position and Spelling

A parent or teacher seeing the spellings PAT and SO would probably assume that the child meant to write *pat* and *so*. As I have discussed, however, the intended words could well be *pant* and *snow*. The errors do not reflect the child's lack of knowledge that *n* makes the sound /n/. Children who produce PAT and SO usually spell /n/ with the appropriate letter when the sound occurs at the beginning of a word or the beginning of a syllable within a word. Thus, extra drill on letter–sound correspondences will probably not suffice to eliminate the errors. Nor do the errors reflect problems in pronouncing the words. Kindergarten and first-grade children with no apparent difficulties in articulating clusters produce misspellings such as PAT for *pant* and SO for *snow*. Repeating the word or having the child say the word again will not eliminate the misspellings.

Errors like PAT for *pant* and SO for *snow*, rather than reflecting ignorance of sound–letter relationships or mispronunciation, probably reflect children's conceptions of sounds. Some young children apparently believe that *pant* contains three units of sound (initial /p/, nasalized vowel, final /t/) and that *snow* contains two units of sound (initial /sn/, final /o/). These children need to learn that the sound they consider to be a single nasalized vowel can be analyzed as a vowel followed by a nasal consonant and spelled accordingly. Similarly, children need to learn that the complex onset /sn/ consists of /s/ followed by /n/ and is spelled as such.

How can children achieve these insights? One way is through exposure to conventional print. By seeing that *snow* begins with *sn* rather than just *s*, children are led to divide the onset of the spoken word into /s/ followed by /n/. By seeing that *pant* is spelled with *n*, children come to realize that its spoken form may be analyzed as containing the phoneme /n/. However, learning through exposure to print is fairly slow and does not at first generalize to new words. Supporting this point, some first graders who had surely seen words such as *went* and *stop* frequently deleted consonants in clusters when spelling nonsense words, words whose printed forms the children had never before seen. Children with spelling difficulties may continue to make these errors beyond the first grade (Marcel, 1990; Snowling, 1982).

Perhaps a faster and more efficient way to get children to revise their analyses of words like *pant* and *snow* is through direct teaching. Games with spoken words could lead children to the insight that the spoken form of *snow* begins with two consonants and that the spoken form of *pant* ends with two consonants. For example, children could learn a secret language in which words are said without their first consonants. Thus, *sat* becomes *at* and *Ned* becomes *Ed*. Given a word like *snow*, children's first response is likely to be *oh*, as documented by Bruck and Treiman (1990). Children could be taught that *no* is actually a better answer. This and other enjoyable games could help children learn to analyze initial and final clusters. Such teaching, even though it does not require children to be shown any printed words, should result in improved spelling. This would be a specific instance of the general finding that training in phonemic skills benefits spelling (e.g., Ball & Blachman, 1991; Lundberg, Frost, & Petersen, 1988).

English, with its large variety of initial and final consonant clusters, has more clusters than many other languages of the world. This characteristic of the spoken language could be one factor that makes learning to spell difficult for young English speakers. In future research, it will be important to examine beginning spelling in other languages that also have many consonant clusters. Caravolas and Bruck (1993) made a start in this direction by studying Czech. Their results suggest that Czech children, like English-speaking children, are more likely to omit the interior phonemes of consonant clusters than the exterior phonemes.

The Role of Letter Names in Beginning Spelling

Middle-class American children are usually familiar with the names of letters when they enter kindergarten. They have learned about letters from their parents, from alphabet books, and from television programs such as *Sesame Street*. Once children enter school, letter names play an important role in teaching. For example, adults tell children that *cat* is spelled /si/, /e/, /ti/, using the names of the letters. Just as children bring their phonological knowledge to the task of learning to spell, so they bring their knowledge of letter names. As I discuss in this section, some of children's errors make sense given their letter-name knowledge.

The names of many English letters suggest their sounds. A child who does not know or has forgotten how to spell the sound /b/ can search for a letter name that contains /b/ and can use this letter to spell the phoneme. Here and in many other cases, this approach will be successful. The only English letter name that contains /b/ is that of *b*; *b* is in fact the typical spelling of /b/. Likewise, /t/ occurs in the name of the letter that is usually used to spell this sound (*t*), and /l/ occurs in the name of the letter that is usually used to spell that sound (*l*). Certain phonemes, however, do not occur in the name of any letter. Two examples in American English are /g/ and /h/. If children use the names of letters to figure out their sounds, they should have more difficulty spelling /g/ and /h/ than phonemes such as /b/, /t/, and /l/. The results of my naturalistic study and of a follow-up experiment are consistent with this claim (Treiman, 1993; Treiman, Weatherston, & Berch, 1994).

A few English letter names suggest the wrong spellings for sounds. For example, the phoneme /w/ occurs in the name of the letter *y* but /w/ is never spelled as *y* in English. If children use the names of letters to suggest spellings for phonemes, they may misspell /w/ as *y*. As Table 19.5 shows, the first graders studied by Treiman (1993) hardly ever made such errors, nor did the precocious spellers studied by Read (1975). For these children, exposure to common words like *went* and *was*, where the link between /w/ and *w* is embodied in the salient initial position of the word, or direct teaching that /w/ is spelled with *w*, may have already had an effect. The kindergartners and preschoolers studied by Treiman, Weatherston, and Berch (1994), however, spelled /w/ as *y* between 17% and 18% of the time. For example, some kindergartners spelled *wet* as YAT (the use of *a* for /ɛ/ is common among young children; Read, 1975; Treiman, 1993) and *work* as YRK. In another study in which preschoolers and kindergartners were asked to orally produce the first letters of syllables such as /wo/, children sometimes responded with *y* (Treiman, Weatherston, & Berch, 1994).

It appears that children do not learn the links between sounds and letters in a rote, paired-associate manner. Rather, children who know the names of letters use this knowledge to help learn sound–spelling corre-

TABLE 19.5
Children's Spellings of /w/ as y

Study	Type of Data	Children Involved	Percent y Spellings
Read, 1975	Naturalistic, real words	Precocious spellers	< 1% (3/332)
Treiman, 1993	Naturalistic, real words	First graders	< 1% (1/447)
Treiman, Weatherston, & Berch, 1994, Study 1	Experimental, real words	Kindergartners	17% (18/105)
Treiman, Weatherston, & Berch, 1994, Study 1	Experimental, real words	First graders	3% (3/100)
Treiman, Weatherston, & Berch, 1994, Study 1	Experimental, real words	Second graders	0% (0/100)
Treiman, Weatherston, & Berch, 1994, Study 2	Experimental, mainly nonwords	Preschoolers	17% (15/90)
Treiman, Weatherston, & Berch, 1994, Study 2	Experimental, mainly nonwords	Kindergartners	18% (16/90)

spondences. For English, in which the names of letters are not always good guides to the letters' sounds, this strategy can lead to errors like YRK for *work*. Languages in which letters' names are more reliable guides to sound, such as Korean, may therefore have an advantage as compared to English. Moreover, English-speaking children in cultures in which letter names are not stressed in early education to the extent that they are in America, such as England, may not make some of the errors that American children do.

Another way in which letter-name knowledge can affect early spelling is exemplified by errors such as FRMMR for *farmer* and LEFIT for *elephant* (Treiman, 1993). In these cases, first graders use a single consonant letter to symbolize all of the phonemes in the letter's name. For example, the first r of FRMMR apparently stands for the two sounds /ɑ/ and /r/, which together constitute the name of the letter r. In LEFIT, l represents the sequence /ɛl/, the name of the letter l.

Several researchers had noted the existence of such letter-name spellings among young children (e.g., Chomsky, 1979; Ehri, 1986; Gentry, 1982; Read, 1975). According to Gentry, whenever beginning spellers encounter a phoneme or sequence of phonemes that matches the name of an English letter, they spell it with the corresponding letter. My results indicate that letter-name spellings do occur for some letters. In the study of first graders' classroom writings, children sometimes used the consonant letters r, l, m, and n to spell their names (Treiman, 1993). Errors such as BL for *bell* (which contains the letter-name sequence /ɛl/) were more common than errors such as BL for *ball* (which does not contain a letter-name sequence). Letter-name spellings did not occur at above-chance levels for letters such as *b* and *d*, however. For example, an error such as BT for *beat* (which contains the letter-name sequence /bi/) was no more common than an error such as BT for *boat* (which does not contain a letter-name sequence). Such a difference would be expected if children used the letter *b* to symbolize both /b/ and /i/.

To verify that letter-name spellings do not occur equally often for all consonants, I carried out a series of experiments in which children ranging from preschool to first grade spelled syllables (predominantly nonsense syllables) that contained various types of letter-name sequences (Treiman, 1994). For example, children were asked to spell /vɑr/, /zɛl/, and /biv/, as well as syllables that did not contain consonant letter-name sequences. For kindergartners and first graders, letter-name spellings were significantly more common for *r* than for other letters. Spellings such as VR for /vɑr/ occurred at rates of between 6% and 50% for first graders, the wide variation in the rate of these errors apparently reflecting the children's spelling levels and the nature of the spelling task. The errors occurred even more frequently for kindergartners than they did for first graders. Some kindergarten and first-grade children *never* included a vowel when spelling syllables like /vɑr/. Letter-name spellings were next most frequent for *l*, as in ZL for /zɛl/. The errors were lower in frequency for other consonant letters, such as *b* and *s*. For example, /biv/ was not commonly spelled as BV.

How can we explain the observed differences among consonant letters in their susceptibility to letter-name spellings? These differences may reflect the sound properties of the letters' names (Treiman, 1993, 1994). To spell a word such as *far*, children attempt to divide the spoken word into individual sounds or phonemes and to represent each phoneme with a letter. However, the /ɑr/ sequence in this word is difficult to segment. As I argued earlier, children tend to group vowels and following /r/s, treating them as a single unit. Given this fact, and given the strong association that children have between /ɑr/ and *r*, they may spell *far* as FR. In contrast, the /b/ and the /i/ of *beat* do not form a strong unit. The phoneme /b/ is the onset of the syllable and the /i/ is part of the remainder or rime. Thus, children will probably divide the spoken word into /b/, /i/, and /t/. Even though children associate /bi/ with *b*, they do not often use *b* to symbolize the sequence /bi/ because the sounds /b/ and /i/ are not closely linked in the word's spoken form. Thus, some letter names form stronger units than others from a phonological point of view. These differences affect children's tendency to use the names as guides to spelling.

SUMMARY AND CONCLUSIONS

For young children, spelling is a creative linguistic process rather than a learned habit involving rote visual memorization. Young children create spellings for words based on their knowledge of language and their knowledge of print. They do not simply memorize letter sequences. Many of children's common misspellings make sense when we take into account the knowledge that they bring with them to the spelling task. These misspellings include CHRAP and CHAP for *trap*, SGIE for *sky*, BON for *born*, HLP for *help*, and YRK for *work*.

Traditionally, errors such as those just listed would be classified as nonphonetic. For example, /t/ is never spelled as *ch* in conventional English and /y/ is never spelled as *w*. The term *nonphonetic* implies that the errors do not reflect the sound form of words, that they are random or unmotivated. As we have seen, however, this is far from true. Even if an error looks strange to an uninitiated adult, it may have a reasonable explanation. Even if an error matches one word when read aloud, it may represent a child's attempt to write a different word. To understand the processes that children employ in spelling, we must go beyond the simple classification of errors as phonetic or nonphonetic that has been employed in a good deal of spelling research.

The English writing system has shouldered most of the blame for children's difficulties in learning to spell. Although the system may be less irregular than commonly believed, there are a number of true irregularities. Eliminating these irregularities would be of some benefit to children and adults. For example, PLAD for *plaid* would no longer be an error if the word were spelled in the expected way. However, young children would still sometimes misspell the word as PAD. Indeed, many of young children's most common mistakes would not be eliminated through spelling reform.

ACKNOWLEDGMENTS

Preparation of this chapter was supported by NSF Grant SBR-9020956. I thank Victor Broderick, Marie Cassar, and Ruth Tincoff for their comments on a draft of the chapter.

REFERENCES

Ball, E. W., & Blachman, B. A. (1991). Does phoneme awareness training in kindergarten make a difference in early word recognition and developmental spelling? *Reading Research Quarterly, 26*, 49–66.
Baron, J., Treiman, R., Wilf, J. F., & Kellman, P. (1980). Spelling and reading by rules. In U. Frith (Ed.), *Cognitive processes in spelling* (pp. 159–194). London: Academic.
Boder, E. (1973). Developmental dyslexia: A diagnostic approach based on three atypical reading–spelling patterns. *Developmental Medicine and Child Neurology, 15*, 663–687.
Brown, R. (1973). *A first language: The early stages*. Cambridge, MA: Harvard University Press.
Bruck, M., & Treiman, R. (1990). Phonological awareness and spelling in normal children and dyslexics: The case of initial consonant clusters. *Journal of Experimental Child Psychology, 50*, 156–178.

Bruck, M., & Waters, G. (1988). An analysis of the spelling errors of children who differ in their reading and spelling skills. *Applied Psycholinguistics, 9,* 77–92.

Caravolas, M., & Bruck, M. (1993). The effect of oral and written language input on children's phonological awareness: A cross-linguistic study. *Journal of Experimental Child Psychology, 55,* 1–30.

Chomsky, C. (1979). Approaching reading through invented spelling. In L. B. Resnick & P. A. Weaver (Eds.), *Theory and practice of early reading* (Vol. 2, pp. 43–65). Hillsdale, NJ: Lawrence Erlbaum Associates.

Chomsky, N., & Halle, M. (1968). *The sound pattern of English.* New York: Harper & Row.

Cronnell, B., & Humes, A. (1980). Elementary spelling: What's really taught. *Elementary School Journal, 81,* 59–64.

DeFrancis, J. (1989). *Visible speech: The diverse oneness of writing systems.* Honolulu: University of Hawaii Press.

Ehri, L. C. (1986). Sources of difficulty in learning to spell and read. In M. L. Wolraich & D. Routh (Eds.), *Advances in developmental and behavioral pediatrics* (Vol. 7, pp. 121–195). Greenwich, CT: JAI.

Finucci, J. M., Isaacs, S. D., Whitehouse, C. C., & Childs, B. (1983). Classification of spelling errors and their relationship to reading ability, sex, grade placement, and intelligence. *Brain and Language, 20,* 340–355.

Fodor, J. A., Bever, T. G., & Garrett, M. F. (1974). *The psychology of language: An introduction to linguistics and generative grammar.* New York: McGraw-Hill.

Frith, U. (Ed.). (1980). *Cognitive processes in spelling.* New York: Academic.

Gates, A. I., & Chase, E. H. (1926). Methods and theories of learning to spell tested by studies of deaf children. *Journal of Educational Psychology, 17,* 289–300.

Gentry, J. R. (1982). An analysis of developmental spelling in GNYS AT WRK. *Reading Teacher, 36,* 192–200.

Gibson, E. J., & Levin, J. (1975). *The psychology of reading.* Cambridge, MA: MIT Press.

Goodman, K. S. (1986). *What's whole in whole language.* Portsmouth, NH: Heinemann.

Jensen, A. R. (1962). Spelling errors and the serial-position effect. *Journal of Educational Psychology, 53,* 105–109.

Klatt, D. H. (1973). Interaction between two factors that influence vowel duration. *Journal of the Acoustical Society of America, 54,* 1102–1104.

Klatt, D. H. (1975). Voice onset time, frication, and aspiration in word-initial consonant clusters. *Journal of Speech and Hearing Research, 18,* 686–706.

Kooi, B. Y., Schutz, R. E., & Baker, R. L. (1965). Spelling errors and the serial-position effect. *Journal of Educational Psychology, 56,* 334–336.

Lehiste, I. (1975). Some factors affecting the duration of syllable nuclei in English. In G. Drachman (Ed.), *Salzburger Beiträge zur Linguistik* [Contributions to linguistics from Salzburg] (pp. 81–104). Tübingen, Germany: Verlag Gunter Narr.

Lotz, J., Abramson, A. S., Gerstman, L. J., Ingemann, F., & Nemser, W. J. (1960). The perception of English stops by speakers of English, Spanish, Hungarian, and Thai: A tape-cutting experiment. *Language and Speech, 3,* 71–77.

Lundberg, I., Frost, J., & Petersen, O.-P. (1988). Effects of an extensive program for stimulating phonological awareness in preschool children. *Reading Research Quarterly, 23,* 263–284.

Malécot, A. (1960). Vowel nasality as a distinctive feature in American English. *Language, 36,* 222–229.

Marcel, T. (1980). Phonological awareness and phonological representation: Investigation of a specific spelling problem. In U. Frith (Ed.), *Cognitive processes in spelling* (pp. 373–403). London: Academic.

Mendenhall, J. E. (1930). The characteristics of spelling errors. *Journal of Educational Psychology, 21,* 648–656.

Miller, P., & Limber, J. (1985, October). *The acquisition of consonant clusters: A paradigm problem.* Paper presented at the Boston University Conference on Language Development, Boston.

Nelson, H. E. (1980). Analysis of spelling errors in normal and dyslexic children. In U. Frith (Ed.), *Cognitive processes in spelling* (pp. 475–493). London: Academic.

Peters, M. L. (1985). *Spelling, caught or taught?: A new look.* London: Routledge & Kegan Paul.

Peterson, G. E., & Lehiste, I. (1960). Duration of syllable nuclei in English. *Journal of the Acoustical Society of America, 32,* 693–703.

Radaker, L. (1963). The effect of visual imagery upon spelling performance. *Journal of Educational Research, 56,* 370–372.

Read, C. (1975). *Children's categorization of speech sounds in English* (NCTE Research Report No. 17). Urbana, IL: National Council of Teachers of English.

Reeds, J. A., & Wang, W. S.-Y. (1961). The perception of stops after s. *Phonetica, 6,* 78–81.

Snowling, M. J. (1982). The spelling of nasal clusters by dyslexic and normal children. *Spelling Process Bulletin, 22,* 13–18.

Treiman, R. (1985a). Onsets and rimes as units of spoken syllables: Evidence from children. *Journal of Experimental Child Psychology, 39,* 161–181.

Treiman, R. (1985b). Phonemic analysis, spelling, and reading. In T. Carr (Ed.), *New directions for child development: The development of reading skills* (Vol. 27, pp. 5–18). San Francisco: Jossey-Bass.

Treiman, R. (1985c). Phonemic awareness and spelling: Children's judgments do not always agree with adults'. *Journal of Experimental Child Psychology, 39,* 182–201.

Treiman, R. (1985d). Spelling of stop consonants after /s/ by children and adults. *Applied Psycholinguistics, 6,* 261–282.

Treiman, R. (1989). The internal structure of the syllable. In G. Carlson & M. Tanenhaus (Eds.), *Linguistic structure in language processing* (pp. 27–52). Dordrecht, The Netherlands: Kluwer.

Treiman, R. (1991). Children's spelling errors on syllable-initial consonant clusters. *Journal of Educational Psychology, 83,* 346–360.

Treiman, R. (1992). The role of intrasyllabic units in learning to read and spell. In P. B. Gough, L. Ehri, & R. Treiman (Eds.), *Reading acquisition* (pp. 65–106). Hillsdale, NJ: Lawrence Erlbaum Associates.

Treiman, R. (1993). *Beginning to spell: A study of first-grade children.* New York: Oxford University Press.

Treiman, R. (1994). Use of consonant letter names in beginning spelling. *Developmental Psychology, 30,* 567–580.

Treiman, R., Berch, D., Tincoff, R., & Weatherston, S. (1993). Phonology and spelling: The case of syllabic consonants. *Journal of Experimental Child Psychology, 56,* 267–290.

Treiman, R., Berch, D., & Weatherston, S. (1993). Children's use of phoneme–grapheme correspondences in spelling: Roles of position and stress. *Journal of Educational Psychology, 85,* 1–12.

Treiman, R., Cassar, M., & Zukowski, A. (1994). What types of linguistic information do children use in spelling?: The case of flaps. *Child Development, 65,* 1310–1329.

Treiman, R., Goswami, U., Tincoff, R., & Leevers, H. (1997). Effects of dialect on American and British children's spelling. *Child Development, 68,* 211–227.

Treiman, R., Weatherston, S., & Berch, D. (1994). The role of letter names in children's learning of phoneme-grapheme relations. *Applied Psycholinguistics, 15,* 97–122.

Treiman, R., Zukowski, A., & Richmond-Welty, E. D. (1995). What happened to the "n" of sink? Children's spellings of final consonant clusters. *Cognition, 55,* 1–38.

Venezky, R. L. (1970). *The structure of English orthography.* The Hague: Mouton.

Chapter 20

Phonological and Orthographic Processes in Good and Poor Spellers

Carolyn Lennox
Peel Board of Education
Mississauga, Ontario, Canada

Linda S. Siegel
Ontario Institute for Studies in Education

In this chapter we examine the skills and processes used by good and poor spellers as they learn to spell. More specifically, there is a need to determine whether good and poor spellers use similar or different processes in spelling, and the nature of these processes. A related question involves the nature of the cognitive abilities and skills in average and poor spellers.

We examine these issues in the context of the development of spelling. The integration of several skills is necessary for good spelling. Such skills include grammatical and semantic, phonological, as well as analogy with other words in visual memory and other orthographic rules (Bradley & Bryant, 1981; Bruck & Treiman, 1990; Henderson & Templeton, 1986; Marsh, Friedman, Welch, & Desberg, 1980; Siegel & Heaven, 1986; Siegel & Ryan, 1988; Snowling, 1994; Stanovich & West, 1989; Wagner & Torgesen, 1987; Waters, Bruck, & Malus-Abramowitz, 1988). According to the dual-route theory, these skills are mediated by two different processes. The first is a phonological process in which spellers learn how the sounds of the language correspond to letters in a spelling, by translating the graphemic code into a phonemic code. The second process involves direct lexical access without intermediate phonological processing. The application of orthographic rules is considered to involve direct lexical access as it relies on word-specific information. Through this process, spellers learn the distinctive visual representation of words.

Although the dual-route model has been useful in conceptualizing the development of spelling (see Brown & Ellis, 1994), there have been some challenges to the model. As Brown and Ellis (1994) suggested, the model fails to incorporate all of the data on spelling. For example, recent data has been collected that suggests the necessary integration between the two for successful spelling (Snowling, 1994). Goswami (1988) provided evidence that phonological decoding may rely, at some stages, on orthographic analogies with familiar words in visual memory, and discussed reading development as an interactive process in which phonological knowledge brought to the learning situation changes as orthographic knowledge is gained (Goswami, 1994). Reading or spelling by analogy and encoding orthographic structures depends both on orthographic skills as well as knowledge of spelling–sound relationships. Goswami (1988) demonstrated that teaching children to spell a word helped them to later spell analogous words (words incorporating similar spelling patterns). Snowling (1994) showed that children as young as 8 years old were able to use preexisting orthographic knowledge in their spellings.

Brown and Ellis (1994) also suggested that there are important conceptual links between a dual-route approach and stage theories. For example, models of the development of spelling have generally relied on the dual-route theory and have posited stages of emergence of spelling skills (Brown, 1990; Frith, 1985; Henderson & Templeton, 1986; Marsh et al., 1980). These models share the notion that children learn to spell in a series of stages characterized by either a phonological or an orthographic strategy. For example, Marsh et al. (1980) suggested that children switch from a strategy based on phonological analysis to a strategy based on analogy with visual characteristics of the word at around Grade 5. We (Lennox & Siegel, 1993) examined the spelling errors of 420 children between the ages of 6 and 16. There were 105 children at each age level. The results of this research indicate that both phonological and orthographic skills develop from the early years of learning to spell, and suggest that emergence of skill in discrete stages does not occur. We did not find evidence for stages in which only one procedure was used. However, we did see changes in the *relative* use of strategies, perhaps as a result of exposure to print (Stanovich & West, 1989) and knowledge of spelling words on which to base analogies for spelling of new words. Snowling (1994) conceptualized the demands of the spelling task in information processing terms. Her research, like our own, suggests that children draw on phonological and visual strategies from the beginning.

In summary, recent data suggest that the development of spelling is an interactive process including phonological and orthographic knowledge, and that the development of orthographic knowledge is dependent on well-specified phonological representations. The dual-route theory suggests two possible routes by which children could learn to read, whereas more recent spelling data has given rise to connectionist models postulating a unitary route, integrating phonological and orthographic skill (Hulme, Snowling, & Quinlan, 1991; Rack, Hulme, Snowling, & Wightman, 1994). However, a question that remains concerns the balance between component skills in literacy development at various stages of development in good and poor spellers.

ARE PROCESSES USED BY GOOD AND POOR SPELLERS SIMILAR OR DIFFERENT?

This issue can best be evaluated by a spelling-level-match comparison, in which a group of poor spellers is compared with a group of younger good spellers, matched according to spelling level. Comparison of these groups provides an indication of the skills attained by older poor and younger good spellers who have attained the same level of spelling. A developmental lag is posited when good and poor spellers, matched according to spelling level, make similar kinds of errors. The finding of no differences between good and poor spellers, matched according to spelling level, suggests that younger poor spellers catch up to older good spellers when they are older. On the other hand, if there are differences between the groups when they are matched according to spelling level, a different approach to spelling or deviant pattern in learning to spell can be posited. Different routes are used by the two groups to attain the same spelling level.

An analysis of the misspellings of these groups can be conducted to investigate strategies used in spelling. For example, misspellings can be examined to determine the relative extent to which information pertaining to sound–symbol association rules and to the visual characteristics of the word is used when the child approaches a difficult word. If the error sounds like the spelling word, then the child is said to have made a phonological error and thus successfully uses, to some extent, phonological rules. Alternatively, the error may look like the word, and thus the child may primarily use information about letters, their sequence, and the shape of the word. If this is the case, the child is said to have made a visual error, and primarily relies on visual cues.

Research comparing good and poor spellers at the same spelling grade indicates a similar *pattern* (or sequence) of phonological errors. For example, Bruck (1988) and Rohl and Tunmer (1988) found that both good and poor spellers made more errors on irregular than regular words. Bruck and Treiman (1990) found that both groups made more errors on CCV than CVC words. Similarly, Invernizzi and Worthy (1989) investigated the prevalence of error types such as ambiguous consonants and consonant digraphs, and Moats (1983) studied variables such as consonant doubling and positional constraints. Both researchers found no differences between good and poor spellers in pattern of error. However, Bruck (1988), Bruck and Treiman (1990), and Rohl and Tunmer (1988) found that poor spellers, when compared with good spellers, demonstrated an inadequate use of spelling–sound information to spell both familiar and unfamiliar words. Thus, the research is consistent in finding that poor spellers have more difficulty using basic sound–symbol association rules than do good spellers, although a similar sequence of the development of sound–symbol association rules is noted.

Phonological ability is not a unitary phenomenon, but, in fact, can be thought of in terms of subskills. For example, phonological awareness can include awareness of individual phonemes and awareness of phonological strings (Goswami & Bryant, 1990). We (Lennox & Siegel, 1993; 1996), using a system devised by Bruck and Waters (1988), categorized children's spelling errors according to two different types of phonological error: one based on rudimentary sound symbol association rules, and one based on the knowledge of sound–symbol association rules that included positional constraints (the knowledge of how sounds change according to position). When good and poor spellers matched according to spelling grade were compared, no differences were found in terms of the proportion of phonological errors that included knowledge of positional constraints. Good spellers produced more phonological unconstrained errors. This measure reflected the use of rudimentary sound–symbol association rules. The groups differed significantly on this measure, with good spellers producing more unconstrained errors than did poor spellers. These results are similar to the findings of several researchers who investigated the prevalence of error types and patterns of phonological error (Bruck, 1988; Bruck & Treiman, 1990; Invernizzi & Worthy, 1989; Moats, 1983). In summary, when they approached a difficult word, good spellers used rudimentary sound–symbol association rules to a greater extent than did grade-matched poor spellers. However, good and poor spellers used their orthographic knowledge of spelling rules to the same extent—rules that include knowledge of how sounds change according to position.

The importance of phonological skills in the development of literacy has been stressed, sometimes to the exclusion of visual memory skills. We (Lennox & Siegel, 1993, 1996) scored errors according to the visual accuracy of the spelling error. We used the system designed by Bruck and Waters (1988), and found, like Bruck and Waters, that good spellers produced more visual errors than did age-matched poor spellers; that is, the errors were closer visual matches to the target word. When we matched the children according to spelling level, however (Lennox & Siegel, 1996), we found that poor spellers at Grades 3 and 5 produced more accurate visual matches than did good spellers. No differences were found at the other spelling grades.

Our results indicate that poor spellers: use phonological rules involving positional constraints as well as good spellers, use their visual memory skills as well as or better than good spellers, and experience difficulty with rudimentary sound–symbol association rules (which letter stands for which sound). It is interesting to hypothesize about the nature of the phonological-constrained measure used in our studies. The measure focuses on the child's knowledge of how the sounds of letters change as a function of position of a letter in a word. Knowledge of legalities of word order and knowledge of what letter combinations can and cannot result in a particular sound in English are needed. Such rules represent the intersection between orthography and phonology. As Wagner and Barker (1994) suggested, measures of spelling skill vary in the degree to which they tap component skills, rather than being pure measures of a particular skill.

To determine whether in fact poor spellers *primarily* use one strategy over the other, we (Lennox & Siegel, 1996) conducted a direct comparison of error types by transforming each of the phonological and visual scores to a standard score. The results of an ANOVA on the standard scores indicated that poor spellers, matched with good spellers according to spelling grade, more frequently used a visual approach, whereas good spellers more frequently used a phonological approach. To more directly investigate this relationship, difference scores between the visual and phonological scores were computed. For both the visual–phonological constrained and the visual–phonological unconstrained measures, poor spellers more frequently used their visual memory skills and good spellers more frequently used their phonological skills (see Fig. 20.1).

In summary, the results of spelling-grade-match studies indicate that poor spellers attain the same spelling level as do good spellers by using their good visual memory skills. Poor spellers use different spelling strategies from good spellers. The spelling error comparison indicated that poor spellers produced more visual than phonological errors, and that the reverse pattern was true for good spellers. Investigation of the percentage of visually accurate matches in the spelling errors of good and poor spellers revealed that good and poor spellers were equally as proficient, whereas at some grade levels poor spellers made more visually accurate matches than did good spellers. Examination of the prevalence of phonological errors indicated that good spellers more frequently used phonological knowledge, whereas no group differences were found for rule-based orthographic conventions.

WHAT IS THE PATTERN OF COGNITIVE ABILITIES IN GOOD AND POOR SPELLERS?

The research to date suggests that phonological skills are deficient in poor readers and spellers, but that visual memory skills are equivalent or better than in the average population (Bruck & Waters, 1988; Lennox & Siegel,

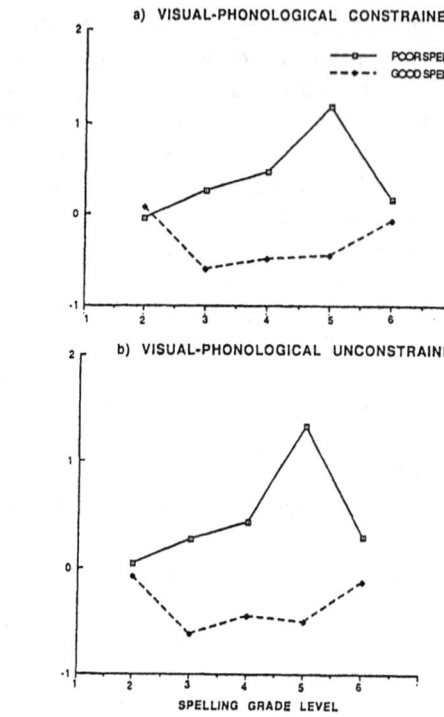

FIG. 20.1. This figure shows the difference between z scores at each of the spelling-grade levels for the visual–phonological scores. Higher scores represent higher visual as opposed to phonological scores. The top panel presents the data for the visual–phonological constrained scores, whereas the bottom panel shows the data for the visual–phonological unconstrained score.

1996; Olson, Kliegl, Davidson, & Foltz, 1985; Pennington et al., 1986; Siegel, 1994; Siegel, Geva, & Share, 1990; Siegel, Share, & Geva, 1994). The fact that some studies report equivalent visual memory skills in these groups, whereas others suggest superior visual skills in poor readers and spellers may be due to the different measures used. For example, orthographic skills have been measured through the knowledge of word-specific information (Bruck & Waters, 1988; Lennox & Siegel, in press; Olson et al., 1985). These studies have found that children with reading and spelling difficulties performed as well as grade-matched normal readers and spellers.

However, an alternate way of measuring orthographic ability, unconfounded with word-specific knowledge, involves the ability to recognize legal and illegal orthographic combinations of English letters (Pennington et al., 1986; Siegel, 1994; Siegel et al., 1990, 1994). In the task developed by Siegel et al. (1990), children were shown 17 pairs of pseudowords, one containing a bigram that never occurs in an English word in a particular position and the other containing a bigram that occurs in English. Examples are *filv–filk* and *vism–visn*. Studies that have used this task to measure orthographic skills (Siegel, 1994; Siegel et al., 1990, 1994) have shown that children with reading and spelling difficulties perform at a *higher* level than do children with average scores in reading and spelling. In a similar vein, Pennington and his colleagues (1986) found that adults with reading disabilities and their spelling-level-matched controls performed similarly on a measure of simple orthographic accuracy. The subjects with reading disabilities, however, were significantly *better* than spelling level controls on a measure of complex orthographic knowledge.

Orthographic ability or orthographic activation—the ability to retrieve and use knowledge about the orthographic representation of the word—was discussed by Barron (1994). He noted the necessary integration between orthography and phonology in the development of literacy skills. Research on the orthographic skills of poor readers and spellers have focused on word recognition tasks. The results have suggested that poor readers and spellers are more sensitive to the visual aspects of printed stimuli than are normal readers. For example, Rack (1985) presented reading disabled and normal readers with four lists of words to learn. The words were either orthographically similar and rhyming (*bull–pull*), orthographically similar and not rhyming (*bull–dull*), orthographically dissimilar and rhyming (*bull–wool*), and orthographically dissimilar and nonrhyming (*bull–sand*). The results indicated that orthographic similarity improved the performance of reading-disabled children more than that of normal readers. Reading-disabled children remembered more orthographically similar targets and fewer rhyming targets. Holligan and Johnston (1988) also found that poor readers and spellers tended to choose orthographically similar pairs in a recognition memory task. Snowling (1980) found that children with a reading disability were more accurate than were normal readers of the same reading level on a task involving selecting the visual form of an orally presented pseudoword.

The suggestion has been made that orthographic sensitivities develop as a compensatory mechanism in children with difficulties in acquiring literacy skills (Holligan & Johnston, 1988). However, there is no direct evidence to indicate that this superior ability arises to compensate for deficient phonological abilities. It may be, in fact, that children who have difficulty with literacy skills also have superior orthographic skills and deficient phonological abilities because of their neurological characteristics. Obviously, further research in this area is needed.

It is clear that the successful acquisition of literacy skills depends on the integration of phonological and orthographic skills. In fact, to account for data that indicate the overlap and integration of these skills, connectionist or unitary models of spelling development were developed. Goswami (1988) presented data concerning reading and spelling by analogy, and suggested that it is the relationship between orthography and phonology that forms the basis for analogy. The ability to use these two skills together requires meta-cognitive or higher-level cognitive skills to provide a coordinating function. Further research is needed to determine the exact nature of these processes, and how to encourage their development so that remedial strategies can be developed.

CONCLUSION

In conclusion, children learning to spell use all the strategies available to them throughout their development. Phonological and orthographic skills interact in a reciprocal manner throughout development. Good spellers successfully use both phonological and visual cues to a greater extent than do age-matched poor spellers. However, the results of the spelling-grade-level comparisons reveal that when poor spellers approach difficult words, they will more likely rely on their well-developed visual memory skills, whereas good spellers will more likely rely on their well-developed phonological skills.

ACKNOWLEDGMENTS

The research reported in this chapter was supported by a grant from the Natural Science and Engineering Research Council of Canada to L. S. Siegel. The authors wish to thank Letty Guirnela for secretarial assistance. Correspondence concerning this chapter should be addressed to L. S. Siegel, Applied Psychology, Ontario Institute for Studies in Education, 252 Bloor Street West, Toronto, Ontario, Canada M5S 1V6.

REFERENCES

Barron, R. W. (1994). The sound-to-spelling connection: Orthographic activation in auditory word recognition and its implications for the acquisition of phonological awareness and literacy skills. In V. W. Berninger (Ed.), *The varieties of orthographic knowledge I: Theoretical and developmental issues.* (Vol. 1, pp. 219–242). Dordrecht, The Netherlands: Kluwer.

Bradley, L., & Bryant, R. E. (1981). Visual memory and phonological skills in reading and spelling backwardness. *Psychological Research, 43,* 193–199.

Brown, A. (1990). A review of recent research in spelling. *Educational Psychology Review, 2,* 365–397.

Brown, G. D. A., & Ellis, N. (1994). Issues in spelling research: An overview. In G. D. A. Brown & N. Ellis (Eds.), *Handbook of spelling: Theory, process and intervention* (pp. 3–25). Toronto: Wiley.

Bruck, M. (1988). The word recognition and spelling of dyslexic children. *Reading Research Quarterly, 23,* 51–69.

Bruck, M., & Treiman, R. (1990). Phonological awareness and spelling in normal children and dyslexics: The case of initial consonant clusters. *Journal of Experimental Child Psychology, 50,* 156–178.

Bruck, M., & Waters, G. (1988). An analysis of the spelling errors of children who differ in their reading and spelling skills. *Applied Psycholinguistics, 9,* 77–92.

Frith, U. (1985). Beneath the surface of developmental dyslexia. In K. E. Patterson, J. C. Marshall, & M. Coltheart (Eds.), *Surface dyslexia* (pp. 301–330). London: Routledge & Kegan Paul.

Goswami, U. (1988). Children's use of analogy in learning to spell. *British Journal of Developmental Psychology, 6,* 21–33.

Goswami, U. (1994). Reading by analogy: Theoretical and practical perspectives. In C. Hulme & M. Snowling (Eds.), *Reading development and dyslexia* (pp. 18–30). London: Whurr.

Goswami, U., & Bryant, P. (1990). *Phonological skills and learning to read.* London: Lawrence Erlbaum Associates.

Henderson, E. H., & Templeton, S. (1986). A developmental perspective of formal spelling instruction through alphabet, pattern, and meaning. *The Elementary School Journal, 86,* 305–316.

Holligan, C., & Johnston, R. S. (1988). The use of phonological information by good and poor readers in memory and reading tasks. *Memory & Cognition, 16,* 522–532.

Hulme, C., Snowling, M. J., & Quinlan, P. (1991). Connectionism and learning to read: Steps towards a psychologically plausible model. *Reading and Writing: An Interdisciplinary Journal, 3,* 159–168.

Invernizzi, M., & Worthy, J. (1989). Spelling errors of learning disabled and normal children across 4 grade levels of spelling achievement. *Reading Psychology, 10,* 173–188.

Lennox, C., & Siegel, L. S. (1993). Visual and phonological spelling errors in subtypes of children with learning disabilities. *Applied Psycholinguistics, 14,* 473–488.

Lennox, C., & Siegel, L. S. (1996). The development of phonological rules and visual strategies in average and poor spellers. *Journal of Experimental Child Psychology, 62,* 60–83.

Marsh, G., Friedman, M., Welch, V., & Desberg, P. (1980). The development of strategies in spelling. In U. Frith (Ed.), *Cognitive processes in spelling* (pp. 339–353). Toronto: Academic.

Moats, L. D. (1983). A comparison of the spelling errors of older dyslexic and second-grade normal children. *Annals of Dyslexia, 33,* 121–139.

Olson, R., Kliegl, R., Davidson, B. J., & Foltz, G. (1985). Individual developmental differences in reading disability. In T. G. Waller (Ed.), *Reading research: Advances in theory and practice* (Vol. 4, pp. 1–64). New York: Academic.

Pennington, B., McCabe, S. D., Lefly, D. L., Bookman, M. O., Kimberling, W. J., & Lubs, H. A. (1986). Spelling errors in adults with a form of familial dyslexia. *Child Development, 57,* 1001–1013.

Rack, J. P. (1985). Orthographic and phonetic coding in developmental dyslexia. *British Journal of Psychology, 76,* 325–340.

Rack, J. P., Hulme, C., Snowling, M., & Wightman, J. (1994). The role of phonology in young children's learning to read words: The direct-mapping hypothesis. *Journal of Experimental Psychology, 57,* 42–71.

Rohl, M., & Tunmer, W. E. (1988). Phonemic segmentation skill and spelling acquisition. *Applied Psycholinguistics, 9,* 335–350.

Siegel, L. S. (1994). Phonological processing deficits as the basis of developmental dyslexia: Implications for remediation. In G. Humphries & J. Riddoch (Eds.), *Cognitive neuropsychology and cognitive rehabilitation* (pp. 392–400). Hove, England: Lawrence Erlbaum Associates.

Siegel, L. S., Geva, E., & Share, D. (1990). *The development of orthographic skills in normal and disabled readers.* Unpublished manuscript.

Siegel, L. S., & Heaven, R. K. (1986). Categorization of learning disabilities. In S. J. Ceci (Ed.), *Handbook of cognitive, social and neuropsychological aspects of learning disabilities* (Vol. 1, pp. 95–121). Hillsdale, NJ: Lawrence Erlbaum Associates.

Siegel, L. S., & Ryan, E. B. (1988). Development of grammatical sensitivity, phonological, and short-term memory skills in normally achieving and learning disabled children. *Developmental Psychology, 24,* 28–37.

Siegel, L. S., Share, D., & Geva, E. (1994). *Evidence for superior orthographic skills in dyslexics.* Unpublished manuscript.

Snowling, M. J. (1980). The development of grapheme–phoneme correspondence in normal and dyslexic readers. *Journal of Experimental Child Psychology, 29,* 294–305.

Snowling, M. J. (1994). Toward a model of spelling acquisition: The development of some component skills. In G. D. A. Brown & N. C. Ellis (Eds.), *Handbook of spelling: Theory, process and intervention* (pp. 111–128). Toronto: Wiley.

Stanovich, K., & West, R. (1989). Exposure to print and orthographic processing. *Reading and Research Quarterly, 24,* 402–433.

Wagner, R. K., & Barker, T. (1994). The development of orthographic processing ability. In V. W. Berninger (Ed.), *The varieties of orthographic knowledge I: Theoretical and developmental issues.* (pp. 243–276). Dordrecht, The Netherlands: Kluwer.

Wagner, R. K., & Torgesen, J. K. (1987). The nature of phonological processing and its causal role in the acquisition of reading skills. *Psychological Bulletin, 101,* 192–212.

Waters, G. S., Bruck, M., & Malus-Abramowitz, M. (1988). The role of linguistic and visual information in spelling: A developmental study. *Journal of Experimental Child Psychology, 45,* 400–421.

Chapter 21

The Anatomy of Word-Specific Memory

P. G. Aaron
Susan Wilczynski
Victoria Keetay
Indiana State University

A number of recent investigations that have studied the acquisition of spelling in children indicate that, during early stages, spelling reflects an attempt to represent the sounds of the words, rather than an effort to visually memorize the sequence of letters in words (Gentry, 1982; Read, 1973; Treiman, 1993). However, reliance on phonology alone does not lead ultimately to accurate spelling, because the constituent letters of many English words do not have a one-to-one relationship with pronunciation. This inconsistent relationship between spelling and pronunciation is due to the fact that the spelling of many words in the English language is influenced not only by phonology but also by etymological, morphemic, and syntactic conventions. The definition of *spelling pattern* (also referred to as *orthography*) as the "visual pattern of the written language as it relates to the graphemic, phonological, and semantic features of the language" (Henderson, 1984, p. 1) succinctly paraphrases this view. Consequently, far from being a literal phonetic transcription of speech, spelling is governed by complex phonemic, syntactic, and semantic conventions. Therefore, acquiring proficiency in spelling requires a knowledge of the semantic and syntactic features of the language, in addition to phonology. For this reason, mastery of spelling is said to be dependent on a mastery of morphophonemic knowledge.

Although morphophonemic knowledge may be essential for spelling, it may not represent a sufficient condition; some aspect of visual memory also might play a role in spelling. This statement could be supported by rational arguments alone. For instance, phonological and semantic knowledge cannot be helpful in choosing the correct spelling between a pair of heterographic homophones (e.g., *meet/meat; threw/through*). Similarly, a literal phonological transcription of heterophonic homographs (e.g., *minute* referring to time vs. *minute* referring to small size) would lead to incorrect spelling. It would appear that some form of visual memory is necessary to spell these words correctly.

The two-route model of spelling tries to resolve this problem by proposing that spelling involves two strategies: a phoneme–grapheme rule-based strategy for spelling "consistent" words, and a lexical strategy for spelling "inconsistent" words (cf. Barry, 1994; Nelson, 1980; Sterling, 1992). In a recent paper, Kreiner and Gough (1990) described this view as "rule idea" and "memory idea," respectively. The rule idea holds that the speller has access to a set of correspondences that maps the phonemes in the language onto the graphemes that represent them. The memory idea proposes that the speller has a store of memory for the spellings of words and draws on this store when necessary. These two processes imply that in the former case, spellings of words are "assembled" or "generated" with the aid of phoneme–grapheme rules, whereas in the latter case, spellings are "addressed" and "retrieved" from the memory store as single units. The latter form of lexical memory from which the spellings of words are retrieved as units is also referred to as *word-specific memory*.

However, Kreiner and Gough (1990), who have examined the validity of this hypothesis, noted that the primary appeal of the word-specific memory idea has been the insufficiency of the rule idea; if phonological rules are inapplicable for generating the spellings of inconsistent words, then word-specific memory has to be invoked; if word-specific memory is unavailable, as may be the case with unfamiliar or novel words, then rules are used. This view is similar to the frequency–regularity interaction effect reported by McCusker, Hillinger, and Bias (1981) and Seidenberg (1985), which proposed that high-frequency words are processed lexically whereas low-frequency words and novel words are processed by applying grapheme–phoneme rules. Kreiner and Gough also pointed out some disadvantages in positing word-specific memory as the sole mechanism that underlies spelling. One difficulty is that it is uneconomical, because word-specific memory would require an enormous amount of memory capacity; in addition, word-specific memory cannot account for our ability to spell novel words and pseudowords. Moreover, it also cannot explain the observed fact that more "regular" words are spelled correctly than are "irregular" words; if spellings are retrieved as individual units from word-specific memory and not generated with the aid of rules, both types of words should be equally easy or difficult to spell.

For these reasons, it appears that word-specific memory plays only a limited, albeit crucial, role in spelling. But what exactly are the parameters of its role in spelling? In spite of the apparent psychological reality of word-specific memory, its nature and composition are not entirely clear. A wide variety of descriptions of word-specific memory have been proposed, ranging from memory for the whole word to memory for the constituent letters within the word. For example, Sloboda (1980) discounted the possibility that proficient spelling is a rule-governed procedure and, instead, proposed that spelling involves rote memory for individual words and their constituent letters. Ehri (1980) proposed that spelling includes a memory for visual configuration of words. Wing and Baddeley (1980) noted that spelling may involve a serial recall of the constituent letters in a word. A more flexible approach was taken by Nelson (1980), for whom specific information pertaining to the spelling of an individual word has a lexical entry, and this information could be the whole written word or a part of the word.

There is yet one other possibility about the nature of word-specific memory that should be taken into account: Even though it is believed that word-specific memory is used only when phoneme–grapheme rules are not applicable (Kreiner & Gough, 1990), the possibility that some sort of rule, other than the ones based on grapheme–phoneme association, could still contribute to word-specific memory has to be considered. This is particularly true if visual memory for sequences of letters within words is considered part of word-specific memory. Just as words within a sentence are governed by syntactical rules, strings of letters within words can have systematic relationship with each other. Such predictable occurrences result in probability information and are described as *stochastic memory* (Peters, 1992). As Gibson and Levin (1975) observed, spelling can be thought of as a kind of grammar for letter sequences that generates permissible combinations without regard to sound. Thus, word-specific memory may be viewed as a rule-governed stochastic process.

Resolution of the uncertainty of the nature of word-specific memory is not only a matter of theoretical interest, but could also be a source of practical information that can be useful in teaching children how to spell. In order to understand the nature of word-specific memory, the following two questions were raised and addressed: Does word-specific memory entail memory for the entire word, or is it memory for frequently occurring intraword letter patterns? Is word-specific memory rote visual memory for words, or is it a rule-based memory?

As noted earlier, rule-based stochastic memory is conceived to be made up of a set of conventions that are abstracted as a result of repeated exposure to recurring letter patterns. These letter patterns are not random in nature but instead are predictable, because they conform to certain contingencies. Examples of these stochastic rules are the knowledge that "If the letter q is present, it will always be followed by the letter u; if the letter t is present, the probabilities are very high that it will be followed by the letter *h*." In addition, stochastic memory includes knowledge of constraints such as "the letter *q* is not followed by the letter *e*," and three or more consonants usually do not occur at the beginning of words. Spellings that violate these conventions are considered orthographically illegal. These conventions not only help generate orthographically acceptable spellings, but also prevent misspellings such as *qestion* for *question* and *theese* for *these* from occurring. Assink and Kattenberg (1994) referred to this knowledge as "implicit knowledge of orthographic structure" (p. 119). In the present chapter, conceptualizing stochastic memory as rule-based memory sets it apart from rote visual memory for an entire word.

It has to be noted that stochastic rules, on the basis of which spellings are generated, are distinct from the rules that specify phoneme–grapheme relationships. However, separating the contribution of stochastic memory to spelling from that of phoneme–grapheme rules is not easy. This is because orthography (spelling patterns from which stochastic rules are derived) and phonology are closely interrelated and developmentally become amalgamated (Ehri, 1980). The tangled relationship of orthography and phonology is apparent in the fact that orthographically illegal words are difficult to pronounce and contain bigram and trigram letter patterns that are seldom seen. These nonpronounceable words are also not encountered in written language.

One possible solution to this impasse is to study the performance of subjects who are not proficient in the use of phonological codes. Individuals who are born without hearing and are profoundly deaf could be expected not to have access to phonological codes and, therefore, they must rely for spelling, on pure visual memory or rule-governed stochastic memory for intraword letter sequences, or a combination of the two. By comparing deaf subjects' performance in spelling lists of nonpronounceable nonwords (which contain combinations of bigrams and trigrams that are seldom seen) with their performance in spelling pronounceable nonwords (which contain many frequently occurring letter patterns), the contribution of pure visual memory to spelling could be isolated from the contribution of stochastic memory. Because the deaf subjects involved in the present study did not seem to utilize phonology for word processing, both sets of words had to be reproduced by using some nonphonological strategy. If pure visual memory for words plays a decisive role in spelling, deaf subjects would be expected to spell both pronounceable and nonpronounceable nonwords equally well. If, in contrast, bigram and trigram frequency (i.e., stochastic memory) plays an important role in spelling, deaf subjects could be expected to spell pronounceable nonwords better than nonpronounceable nonwords.

Although the expectation that profoundly deaf individuals have no access to phonology would appear to be logically plausible, it is only an assumption. There is good reason to subject this assumption to test, because some investigators have reported evidence that the deaf subjects whom have studied use phonology. Campbell, Burden, and Wright (1992), for example, reported that deaf children, similar to hearing children, commit more errors in spelling irregular words than regular words. Campbell et al. interpreted this "word effect" as evidence of the use of phonology by the deaf children. In a series of studies of deaf college students, Hanson and her associates (Hanson, 1989; Hanson & Fowler, 1987; Hanson, Goodell, & Perfetti, 1991; Hanson & McGarr, 1989; Hanson, Shankweiler, & Fischer, 1983) also reported evidence for the utilization of phonological code by deaf students. The evidence for the utilization of phonology by congenitally and profoundly deaf subjects, however, is equivocal. For instance, Dodd (1980), who compared the performance of deaf and hearing children in the spelling of regular words and irregular words, reported that hearing children misspelled more irregular words than regular words, but there was no difference in the performance of deaf children on these two categories of words. Waters and Doehring (1990) and Beech and Harris (1992) also failed to observe this regularity effect in their deaf subjects. Moreover, the deaf subjects studied by Hanson and her associates were college students with reasonably good reading skills; these subjects, therefore, may not be representative of typical deaf subjects. Furthermore, children studied by Campbell et al. (1992) were taught English through oral methods and received instructions during testing by reading lips. These subjects, therefore, could have relied on visual and kinesthetic cues to spell words. There remains a possibility, therefore, that congenitally and profoundly deaf subjects who have not received their education exclusively through oral methods and have not reached college level of reading skills may not be able to utilize phonology for word processing.

PURPOSE OF THE PRESENT STUDY

The present study was designed to investigate the nature of word-specific memory. In order to accomplish this task, two questions were raised: Does word-specific memory entail memory for the entire word or is it memory for frequently occurring intraword letter patterns? Is word-specific memory rote visual memory for words, or is it a rule-based memory?

In order to answer these questions, a group of profoundly deaf students of elementary and high school age and a reading-age-matched control group of hearing children from Grade 3 were studied. The investigation was based on the expectation that these deaf students do not have access to phonological code for processing the written language. However, for reasons stated earlier, it became necessary to test this assumption first. The immediate purpose of the study was, therefore, to examine if the deaf subjects involved in the study showed any evidence of an ability to utilize phonological codes, and to exclude from the study those deaf subjects who did show such evidence.

SUBJECTS

The deaf subjects involved in the screening were attending a school for the deaf, and were enrolled in Grades 5 through 12. The school from which the deaf subjects came is located in a large city in the Midwest and follows a total communication philosophy of instruction. As ascertained from the school records, all the deaf students were profoundly and congenitally deaf, defined in terms of pure tone averages of 90dB HL or poorer, bilaterally. Deaf children who (according to the school records and teacher reports) were mentally or physically handicapped were not included in the study. Of the 36 deaf subjects studied, the speech quality of three could be considered normal or near normal, and the speech of five subjects was fairly easy to understand. The remaining 28 subjects either did not use speech for communication or their speech was ineffective as a means of communication.

The hearing children came from an elementary school in a Midwestern town. The schools from which the deaf subjects and hearing children came were comparable in their composition for ethnic and socioeconomic backgrounds.

Deaf subjects and children in the control group were selected by matching the two groups for reading age. The deaf students had been administered Stanford Achievement Tests by the school at the beginning of the year, and their raw scores had been converted into scaled scores, percentiles, and grade equivalents by using the hearing-impaired norms developed by the Center for Assessment of Demographic Studies, Gallaudet University. The hearing-impaired norms were developed by linking the test to the eighth-grade level of hearing children. For this reason, a deaf subject who scores at the thirteenth-grade level is reading at a level comparable to a hearing student in the thirteenth grade who obtains a reading score equivalent to thirteenth-grade level on material designed for Grade 8. Even though this normalizing procedure could yield somewhat inflated figures, no other standardized test for the deaf is available.

Reading comprehension and word-attack skills of the hearing children were assessed by administering the Woodcock Reading Mastery Tests and their listening comprehension with the aid of Wechsler Individual Achievement Test. Only those children whose achievement scores in the reading comprehension, word-attack, and listening comprehension tests were within a standard score of 100 ± 1 standard error of measurement were included in the control group.

21. THE ANATOMY OF WORD-SPECIFIC MEMORY 411

TABLE 21.1
Psychometric Information About the Deaf and Control Groups

Groups	Deaf	Control
N	36	31
Mean age	14.3	9.51
Age range	9.1–20.2	8.1–10.2
Grade range	5.3–12.3	3.3
Reading comprehension (GE)	3.27	3.55
Reading comprehension (SD)	2.8	0.98
Reading comprehension (SS)	—	98.2
Word attack (decoding; GE)	—	3.72
Listening comprehension (SS)	—	102.4

GE, SD, and SS refer to grade equivalent, standard deviation, and standard scores, respectively. The standard scores have a mean of 100 and a standard deviation of 15. The two groups do not differ significantly from each other on reading comprehension.

In order to secure a reasonable match, those who had extremely deviant reading comprehension scores were not included in the study. This criterion excluded several deaf students who read below Grade 2 level and a few hearing children from Grade 3 who were overachievers. This process resulted in 36 deaf students and a reading-age-matched control group of 31 children. Psychometric information about the groups of subjects is shown in Table 21.1.

STUDY 1: DETERMINATION OF THE EXTENT TO WHICH THE DEAF SUBJECTS USED PHONOLOGY FOR WORD PROCESSING

Method

All the tasks and tests described in this chapter were administered to the deaf students by their own teachers. When instructions were given, at least one teacher who was competent in the use of American Sign Language (ASL) was present. The teachers used several modes of communication to impart instruction to deaf students. This included, in the order of importance, ASL, signed English, pidgin, and oral communication. A sufficient number of examples were given so as to ensure that the students understood the nature of the task. Every task also had two sample items that the subjects had to complete. The teachers checked the responses to the sample items to ensure that the students understood the nature of the task. Hearing students were given oral instruction by their teachers with the assistance of two graduate students.

Task 1: Production of Homophones for Which Phonology Is Not Obligatory

Procedure. This task was designed to ensure that the vocabulary knowledge of deaf subjects was comparable to that of the children in the control group and that they were able to understand the nature of the experimental tasks. Task 1 required the production of orthographically dissimilar homophones in a sentence context. It consisted of pairs of sentences with one word missing in each sentence; the subjects were required to fill in the missing words by writing them down (e.g., Clouds are white, but the sky is b_____; Last fall, the wind b_____ away the leaves). The time limit was 5 minutes. Unlike in Task 2 (described in the next section), homophones could be generated in the present task by relying on multiple cues such as orthography, semantics, and context without accessing phonological cues.

Results and Discussion. In this task, the deaf subjects produced an average of 7.5 responses and the hearing subjects an average of 7.2 responses. The difference between the two groups was not statistically significant (see Table 21.2). It would, therefore, be safe to conclude that the deaf subjects were able to understand experimental instructions and that their vocabulary knowledge was equal to that of the subjects in the control group.

Even though the two groups did not differ from each other in the number of responses produced, when these responses were analyzed for spelling accuracy, it was found that deaf subjects spelled more words correctly than did control subjects (mean 5.1 vs. 4.0). The difference between the two groups was statistically significant ($t = 2.6$; $p < .05$). The initial impression that deaf subjects are better spellers than hearing subjects, however, had to be tempered by the fact that many of the responses of the deaf subjects, even though correct in terms of spelling, were not semantically correct answers. In other words, the deaf subjects drew from a pool of words they knew how to spell, even though they were not the appropriate words. As a result, a majority of the words spelled correctly

TABLE 21.2
Heterographic Homophones Produced Under Conditions When Phonology Was Obligatory and When It Was Not

Group	Deaf	Hearing	t	p
N	33	31		
Homophone pairs produced when phonology was not obligatory	7.5	7.2	1.23	> .10
N	36	31		
Homophone pairs produced when phonology was obligatory	0.98	4.92	11.44	< .001

(42%) were four-letter high-frequency words such as *that, this,* and *what.* Nearly 31% of the words spelled correctly were five-letter high-frequency words (e.g., *there, where*), and 16% were three-letter words. There were very few six-letter words (11%). These observations do not allow us to unequivocally conclude that deaf subjects are better spellers than hearing subjects. Nevertheless, the fact that many four- and five-letter words could be produced without phonology is noteworthy. As noted earlier, because the deaf subjects investigated in this study did not show evidence of using phonology, their spelling accomplishment could be attributable either to pure visual memory or to stochastic memory or a combination of the two. But which one of these three possibilities was correct?

Task 2: Production of Homophones for Which Phonology Is Obligatory

Procedure. Subjects were asked to write down as many pairs of words as they could, that are pronounced alike but spelled differently (e.g., *hear/here; right/write*). The time limit was 5 minutes. This task was extremely difficult for many deaf students to comprehend; consequently, the teachers had to repeat the instructions several times and provide additional examples. Successful performance on this task required the use of phonological information; reliance on visual information alone would lead to incorrect answers. Because no prompts or cues were available, the subjects were forced to produce individual words without relying on context cues or any semantic information.

Results and Discussion. The data obtained on this task are shown in Table 21.2. The deaf subjects performed very poorly on this task, and the difference between the two groups was highly significant ($t = 11.44$, $p < .001$). As noted earlier, this task was extremely difficult for deaf students who, as a group, could produce no more than a single pair of orthographically dissimilar homophones. One deaf student produced six pairs of words; another two students produced three pairs; six students produced two pairs; the remaining 33 students produced either one or none. (The data obtained from the three deaf students who produced six and three pairs of homophones were excluded from subsequent studies.) The present finding, which could not find strong evidence of phonological processing by deaf subjects, is in contrast to the one reported by Hanson and McGarr (1989), who found that congenitally deaf college students could generate almost half as many orthographically dissimilar rhyming words as orthographically similar rhyming words. The discrepancy between the Hanson-McGarr study and the present one could be due to the fact that the subjects in their study were college students whose overall reading achievement was between ninth- and tenth-grade levels, which is much higher than the average reading level of about Grade three of the deaf subjects tested in the present study.

After excluding the three subjects who showed some evidence of phonological processing, a group of deaf subjects who did not demonstrate the ability to utilize phonological cues for word processing remained. By studying this group of subjects, it was possible to investigate the nature of word-specific memory without the confounding effects of phonology.

STUDY II: DETERMINATION OF THE RELATIVE CONTRIBUTION OF PURE VISUAL MEMORY TO SPELLING

Task 3: Recall of Visually Presented Pronounceable and Nonpronounceable Nonwords

The previous two tasks assessed the extent to which deaf and hearing subjects rely on phonology to spell words. It was concluded that there is little evidence to indicate that the deaf subjects involved in the present study relied on phonology for processing words. This leaves two memory mechanisms as possible strategies that deaf subjects may have used for processing words. One is rote visual memory for entire words; the other is memory for intraword letter patterns, also referred to as *stochastic memory*. Rote visual memory for words operates at the surface level and is memory for the constituent letters of a word with no regard to letter contingencies. Stochastic memory, on the other hand, is memory for letter patterns based on contingencies. It operates at an abstract level in the sense the probabilities of letters occurring in certain sequences are remembered as the reader becomes sensitized to these patterns. A knowledge of this form of computational probabilities can form the basis of rules for generating acceptable spellings.

The relative roles of these two forms of memory can be assessed with the help of nonpronounceable nonwords and pronounceable nonwords. Nonpronounceable nonwords do not conform to phonologic conventions; such "words," therefore, have to be recalled or reproduced by relying on some process that does not utilize phonology. Pronounceable nonwords, on the other hand, can be remembered by utilizing phonological information, orthographic information, or pure visual memory. Because the deaf subjects involved in the present study did not appear to utilize phonology, their recall of pronounceable nonwords could be attributable to pure visual memory, stochastic memory, or a combination of the two—but not to phonological memory. The performance of deaf subjects in reproducing nonpronounceable nonwords, on the other hand, could be attributable only to pure visual memory—but not to phonology or to stochastic memory, because these stimuli contain few recurring letter patterns. The performances of the deaf subjects on these two forms of stimuli could, therefore, be compared with each other, and a subtractive process could be utilized to isolate the contribution of pure visual memory to the spelling of these words. If pure visual memory were an efficient mechanism for spelling, a significant difference in the recall of these two types of words by the deaf subjects would not be seen. If, however, a difference in favor of pronounceable nonwords were seen, this difference could be attributed to stochastic memory.

Procedure. The current task used two types of four-letter nonwords: pronounceable and nonpronounceable. The nonpronounceable nonwords were constructed by scrambling the letters in the pronounceable nonwords. It was ascertained that the first two and three letters in the nonpronounceable nonwords had very low bigram-frequencies, as determined by the tabulation published by Solso, Barbuto, and Juel (1980). Pronounceable and nonpronounceable nonwords (e.g., *doof, doal, kram* and *dfoo, dloa, rmka,* respectively) were photographed and the slides were projected on the screen. Each slide had either six pronounceable nonwords or six nonpronounceable nonwords. There were five slides in each of the two categories of words. After showing a pair of sample slides, each of the five slides from the two categories of nonwords was exposed, in an alternating fashion, for approximately a minute. After the presentation of each slide, subjects wrote down what they had just seen. Subjects were told that the order of recall of words was unimportant and that what they were going to see were not real words.

If pure visual memory is a reliable mechanism for spelling, deaf subjects could be expected to recall as many nonpronounceable nonwords as pronounceable nonwords.

Results and Discussion. Results of the analysis are shown in Table 21.3. The data presented in Table 21.3 show that both deaf and hearing subjects reproduced correctly more pronounceable nonwords than nonpronounceable nonwords, the difference between these two types of words being statistically significant. The two groups did not differ significantly from each other in reproducing either kind of nonwords. These results are interpreted as evidence that rote visual memory does not play an important role in spelling, but that stochastic memory for intraword letter patterns possibly facilitates the spelling of nonwords.

If rote visual memory can be effectively used to remember the spelling of words, deaf subjects should have reproduced as many nonpronounceable nonwords as pronounceable nonwords. The deaf subjects, however, reproduced significantly fewer nonpronounceable nonwords than pronounce-

TABLE 21.3
Performance of Deaf and Hearing Subjects in Reproducing
Pronounceable and Nonpronounceable Nonwords

Group	N	Mean Number of Words Correct		Statistical Analysis
		Pronounceable Nonwords	Nonpronounceable Nonwords	
Deaf subjects	33	7.02	4.13	$t = 5.14, p < .001$
Hearing subjects	31	7.62	3.67	$t = 4.84, p < .001$
Statistical analysis		$t = 0.66$ $p > 0.10$	$t = 0.90$ $p > 0.10$	

Note. Maximum number of words possible = 30.

able nonwords. Their ability to reproduce more pronounceable nonwords than nonpronounceable nonwords could therefore be attributable to two factors: stochastic memory for intraword letter patterns, because pronounceable nonwords contain many more high-frequency bigrams and trigrams than nonpronounceable nonwords contain; or phonological processing. However, the deaf subjects studied in the present project appear not to have been able to utilize phonology for word processing. This left stochastic memory for intraword letter frequency as the major means of their better recall of pronounceable nonwords. This interpretation is further confirmed by the findings of a qualitative analysis of the spelling errors committed by the two groups of subjects in the first two tasks, in which they were required to generate real words. Analysis showed that there was a qualitative difference between the spelling errors of the two groups. The errors committed by the hearing group were predominantly phonological in nature (e.g., *lauh, wach, truk, befour*), whereas those of the deaf subjects were due to transposition or intrusion of bigram and trigram letter units (e.g., /th/ = *lauth, laugth,* for *laugh*; /ght/ = *laught, trght,* for *laugh* and *truck*).

These findings also indicate that pure visual memory has limitations in reproducing even four-letter nonwords. It also may mean that the visual memory of deaf subjects for the spellings of nonwords is not better than that of hearing third-grade children.

CONCLUSIONS

The present study investigated the nature of word-specific memory for spelling. The conventional view of word-specific memory is that it is relied on when phoneme–grapheme rules cannot be used for generating spelling. Not being rule based, word-specific memory is thought to be rote in nature.

Described this way, word-specific memory can be equated with rote visual memory for entire words.

Two questions were raised in the present study: Does word-specific memory entail memory for the entire word, or is it memory for frequently occurring intraword letter patterns? Is word-specific memory rote visual memory for words, or is it a rule-based memory?

Analysis of the performance of the subjects shows that word-specific memory is likely to be memory for intraword segments within the word, particularly bigrams and trigrams. This is in agreement with the finding by Zhang and Simon (1985) that visual memory capacity for orthographic representation is limited to two or three items. This form of stochastic memory, although limited, is sufficient to override most of the potential spelling errors caused by inconsistencies between pronunciation and spelling (e.g., *come* vs. *cum*; *pint* vs. *pynt*). These subword units may very well be the visual component that is thought to be essential for reading and spelling (Geva & Willows, 1994; Holmes & Ng, 1993).

The observation that the performance of deaf subjects is better in spelling pronounceable nonwords than nonpronounceable nonwords suggests that word-specific memory, which is defined traditionally as rote visual memory, may not be totally rule free. The rule-based component of word-specific memory is likely to be memory for bigrams and trigrams; it can be the product of the frequency of their occurrence in print.

In conclusion, the question of what the nature of word-specific memory is can be answered as follows: Word-specific memory is a memory for intraword letter patterns conditioned by the frequency of their occurrence in print.

ACKNOWLEDGMENTS

We gratefully acknowledge the assistance provided by the following individuals and thank them. Ms. Mary Ann Stansfield, principal; Mr. Greg Ernst, executive director; Mr. Ron Keller, director of development; and the teachers of St. Rita School for the Deaf. Additionally, we thank Mrs. Patricia Fouty, principal, and the teachers of Dixie Bee elementary school, Mary Boyd, Shan Palmetier, and Julie Wacks, for help in data collection and analysis.

This project was supported by a grant from the Blumberg Center for Studies in Special Education and the Research Committee, Indiana State University.

REFERENCES

Assink, E., & Kattenberg, G. (1994). Higher-order linguistic influences on development of orthographic knowledge: Illustrations from spelling problems in Dutch. In V. W. Berninger (Ed.), *The varieties of orthographic knowledge* (pp. 111–136). Dordrecht, The Netherlands: Kluwer.

Barry, C. (1994). Spelling routes or roots, or rutes. In G. D. Brown & N. C. Ellis (Eds.), *Handbook of spelling: Theory, process and intervention* (pp. 27–49). New York: Wiley.

Beech, J. R., & Harris, M. (1992). The prelingually deaf young reader: A case of logographic reading? Cited in M. Marschark, *Psychological development of deaf children* (p. 211). New York: Oxford University Press.

Campbell, R., Burden, V., & Wright, H. (1992). Spelling and speaking in prelingual deafness: Unexpected evidence for isolated alphabetic spelling skills. In C. M. Sterling & C. Robson (Eds.), *Psychology, spelling and education* (pp. 185–199). Philadelphia: Multilingual Matters.

Dodd, B. (1980). The spelling abilities of profoundly pre-lingually deaf children. In U. Frith (Ed.), *Cognitive processes in spelling* (pp. 423–442). New York: Academic.

Ehri, L. C. (1980). The development of orthographic images. In U. Frith (Ed.), *Cognitive processes in spelling* (pp. 311–338). New York: Academic.

Gentry, J. R. (1982). An analysis of developmental spelling in GNYS AT WRK. *The Reading Teacher, 36*, 192–200.

Geva, E., & Willows, D. (1994). Orthographic knowledge is orthographic knowledge is orthographic knowledge. In V. W. Berninger (Ed.), *The varieties of orthographic knowledge* (pp. 359–380). Boston: Kluwer.

Gibson, E. J., & Levin, H. (1975). *The psychology of reading*. Cambridge, MA: MIT Press.

Hanson, V. L. (1989). Phonology and reading: Evidence from profoundly deaf readers. In D. Shankweiler & I. Y. Liberman (Eds.), *Phonology and reading disability: Solving the reading puzzle* (pp. 69–90). Ann Arbor: University of Michigan Press.

Hanson, V. L., & Fowler, C. A. (1987). Phonological coding in word reading: Evidence from hearing and deaf readers. *Memory & Cognition, 15*, 199–207.

Hanson, V. L., Goodell, E. W., & Perfetti, C. (1991). Tongue-twister effects in the silent reading of hearing and deaf college students. *Journal of Memory and Language, 30*, 319–330.

Hanson, V. L., & McGarr, N. S. (1989). Rhyme generation by deaf adults. *Journal of Speech and Hearing Research, 32*, 2–11.

Hanson, V. L., Shankweiler, D., & Fischer, F. W. (1983). Determinants of spelling ability in deaf and hearing adults: Access to linguistic structure. *Cognition, 14*, 323–344.

Henderson, L. (1984). Writing systems and reading processes. In L. Henderson (Ed.), *Orthographies and reading* (pp. 1–5). Hillsdale, NJ: Lawrence Erlbaum Associates.

Holmes, V., & Ng, E. (1993). Word-specific knowledge, word-recognition strategies and spelling ability. *Journal of Memory and Language, 32*, 230–257.

Kreiner, D. S., & Gough, P. B. (1990). Two ideas about spelling: Rules and word-specific memory. *Journal of Memory and Language, 29*, 103–118.

McCusker, L., Hillinger, M., & Bias, R. (1981). Phonological recoding and reading. *Psychological Bulletin, 89*, 217–245.

Nelson, H. E. (1980). Analysis of spelling errors in normal and dyslexic children. In U. Frith (Ed.), *Cognitive processes in spelling* (pp. 475–494). New York: Academic.

Peters, M. L. (1992). Towards spelling autonomy. In C. M. Sterling & C. Robson (Eds.), *Psychology, spelling and education* (pp. 220–223). Philadelphia: Multilingual Matters.

Read, C. (1973). Children's judgments of phonetic similarities in relation to English spelling. *Language Learning, 23*, 17–38.

Seidenberg, M. S. (1985). The time course of phonological code activation in two writing systems. *Cognition, 19*, 1–30.

Sloboda, J. A. (1980). Visual imagery and individual differences in spelling. In U. Frith (Ed.), *Cognitive processes in spelling* (pp. 231–250). New York: Academic.

Solso, L. R., Barbuto, P. F., & Juel, C. L. (1980). Bigram and trigram frequencies and versatilities in the English language. *Behavior Methods and Instrumentation, 12*, 297–343.

Sterling, C. (1992). Introduction to the psychology of spelling. In C. M. Sterling & C. Robson (Eds.), *Psychology, spelling, and education* (pp. 1–14). Philadelphia: Multilingual Matters.

Treiman, R. (1993). *Beginning to spell*. New York: Oxford University Press.

Waters, G., & Doehring, D. G. (1990). The nature and role of phonological information in reading acquisition: Insights from congenitally deaf children who communicate orally. In T. Carr & B. A. Levy (Eds.), *Reading and its development: Component skills approaches* (pp. 192–228). New York: Academic.

Wing, A. M., & Baddeley, A. D. (1980). Spelling errors in handwriting: A corpus and a distributional analysis. In U. Frith (Ed.), *Cognitive processes in spelling* (pp. 251–286). New York: Academic.

Zhang, G., & Simon, H. A. (1985). STM capacity for Chinese words and idioms: Chunking and acoustical loop hypothesis. *Memory & Cognition, 13*, 193–201.

Chapter 22

Strategies Used by 9- to 12-Year-Old Children in Written Spelling

Che Kan Leong
Department for the Education of Exceptional Children,
College of Education,
University of Saskatchewan, Canada

Research on the cognitive processes involved in children's spelling shows that two main strategies are used: a rule-based strategy and a lexical strategy (Ehri, 1986; Kreiner, 1992; Kreiner & Gough, 1990). The rule-governed nature of English spelling is emphasized by a number of linguists (e.g., Chomsky, 1970; Chomsky & Halle, 1991; Hanna, Hanna, Hodges, & Rudorf, 1966; Read, 1986) and psychologists (e.g., Frith, 1985). The *rule strategy* refers to the mapping of phonemes onto graphemes to represent them. These rules are *probabilistic* in nature. For example, for the word *cab* the phoneme /k/ can be represented by the grapheme <c> as in *cat*, or <k> as in *king*, or <ch> as in *chord*, or even <kh> as in *khaki*. The most probable phoneme to grapheme correspondence for initial /k/ is that of <c> according to the computer analysis of over 17,000 words by Hanna et al. (1966). *Graphemes* are defined as minimal lexical contrastive units in writing and are analogous to, but not entirely parallel with, phonemes in spoken language (Hanna et al., 1966; Henderson, 1985; Venezky, 1970). A grapheme may have one or more than one letter such that the letter or letter cluster is usually pronounced as one phoneme. Thus, *cheap* should be parsed as three graphemes <ch> + <ea> + <p>, or *deaf* as <d> + <ea> + <f> /dəf/.

Graphemes can assume different forms in different orthographic environments analogous to phonemes having different phonetic realizations in varying phonological environments. The digraph <sh>, for example, is usually associated with the /š/ sound. But /š/ corresponding to <sh> holds true only about 25% of the time (Hanna et al., 1966), and the most

421

common sound is the palatalized <t> as in <nation> according to the palatalization rule (Chomsky & Halle, 1991). Word features such as stress and morpheme boundaries may affect spelling–sound regularity especially with inconsistent vowels (Venezky, 1970). An example from Venezky and Massaro (1987) is the grapheme <d>, which is viewed as regular in *indian* but could be considered as irregular in not palatalizing to /ǰ/ as in *educate* or *cordial*. For these and other reasons, Barry and Seymour (1988) preferred the term sound–spelling *contingencies* over *regularities*, and these researchers distinguished between high-contingency (commonly occurring) and low-contingency (rarely occurring) spelling patterns. The main point is that the probabilistic rule-mapping strategy minimizes the load on memory storage, and provides an effective and powerful means to spell "regular" words and novel words according to phoneme-to-grapheme correspondence rules.

The *lexical strategy*, in contrast to the rule-based strategy, emphasizes orthographic knowledge and word-specific memory, and has been considered important for "irregular" or exception words. For example, the silent word-final <ue> following <g> in an exception word like *tongue* occurs in only a few words, such as *catalogue, dialogue, league,* and *plague*. The evolution of <tongue> from Old English <tunge> to Middle English <tonge, tounge> is neither etymological nor phonological, and is only in a small degree historical. Exception words such as *tongue* and *vague* are best learned with the lexical strategy.

Both Strategies Are Necessary

Early educational and psychological studies of spelling tended to emphasize the rule and lexical approaches as discrete, whereas current cognitive and psycholinguistic studies suggest that they are continuous and interrelated (Treiman, 1993). Both probabilistic rules and word-specific lexical strategies are necessary for spelling, and neither approach by itself seems sufficient to explain spelling proficiency and spelling difficulties (Kreiner, 1992; Kreiner & Gough, 1990).

This joint influence of phonologic and orthographic knowledge buttressed by working memory has been shown to vary developmentally in young children as revealed by their spelling of pronounceable nonwords (Stage & Wagner, 1992). If rules are important, we would expect the correlation between the spelling of pseudowords and regular words to be greater than that between regular and exception words. Furthermore, the children's spelling errors could be expected to vary according to the degree of transparency and opacity of the morphophonemic representation of these words. If the lexical strategy is important, we would expect spelling to be related to printed frequency and the degree of irregularity of the words. Both rule-based and lexical-based strategies reinforce each other and operate on knowledge of the language system to promote spelling proficiency.

The present study with tasks involving different kinds of words was designed to examine the role of lexical- and rule-based strategies in the spelling of Grade 3 to Grade 6 students. Multiple regression analyses provided an estimate of the contribution of these strategies as sources of variation in these children's spelling.

METHOD

Subjects

The subjects were a total of 150 elementary-school children from two schools in Davidson in Saskatchewan, Canada. There were 42 Grade 3, 38 Grade 4, 43 Grade 5, and 27 Grade 6 students. The average (and standard deviations) of these children's ages in months were: 108.71 (3.33), 120.79 (3.67), 132.51 (6.29), and 142.85 (3.00). Their mean general ability scaled scores and the standard deviations on the British Ability Scales (BAS) Matrix task were, respectively: 91.62 (10.56), 94.82 (13.41), 97.26 (13.74), and 111.82 (11.63). On the Wide Range Achievement Test–Revised (WRAT-R; Jastak & Wilkinson, 1984) mean spelling performance scores and standard deviations were, respectively: 101.12 (13.67), 100.53 (12.22), 101.56 (12.64), and 108.96 (13.83); and mean reading performance scores and standard deviations were, respectively: 101.62 (13.60), 102.92 (13.42), 102.84 (18.50), and 110.22 (11.84). The children were also given a vocabulary test from the Canadian Tests of Basic Skills (CTBS; King, 1982), and a short-term memory task involving the recall in the correct serial order of 12 sets with four items each of phonemically confusable monosyllabic words (STMPHON; e.g., *man, mad, mat, pan*) as an index of short-term memory span. As well, another 12 sets with four items each of semantically confusable monosyllabic words (STMSEM; e.g., *key, hot, cow, pen*) were administered. Both the STMPHON and the STMSEM tasks were based on the work of Baddeley (1986). The means and standard deviations of these tasks are shown in Tables 22.1 and 22.2.

Tasks

In Task 1 (S1), the 150 children (divided into small groups of about 8 to 10) were asked to spell 40 irregular or exception words embedded in short sentence frames. (The terms *regular* and *exception* are used here in a relative sense. It is recognized that in English orthography there is no clear di-

TABLE 22.1
Means and Standard Deviations (in Parentheses) of Chronological Age, British Ability Scales (BAS) Matrix Task, Wide Range Achievement Test–Revised (WRAT-R) Reading and Spelling, and Vocabulary Subtest of Canadian Test of Basic Skills (CTBS) for Grades 3, 4, 5, and 6

	Grade 3 n = 42	Grade 4 n = 38	Grade 5 n = 43	Grade 6 n = 27	Total Four Grades N = 150
Chronological age (CA) in months	108.71 (3.33)	120.79 (3.67)	132.51 (6.29)	142.85 (3.00)	124.74 (13.13)
BAS matrix scaled score	91.62 (10.56)	94.82 (13.41)	97.26 (13.74)	111.82 (11.63)	97.68 (14.17)
WRAT-R (reading)	101.62 (13.60)	102.92 (13.42)	102.84 (18.50)	110.22 (11.84)	103.85 (13.44)
WRAT-R (spelling)	101.12 (13.67)	100.53 (12.22)	101.56 (12.64)	108.96 (13.83)	102.51 (13.28)
CTBS vocabulary	19.12 (6.18)	24.29 (5.56)	24.49 (7.71)	31.26 (7.21)	24.15 (7.77)

TABLE 22.2
Means and Standard Deviations (in Parentheses) for Spelling Tasks: Two Levels of Exception Words (S1), Three Levels of Words Graded in Phonology–Orthography Relationship (S2), Two Levels of Derived Pseudowords (S4), Pseudowords Varying in "Orthographic Friendliness" (S5 & S6), and Two Kinds of Short-Term Memory Tasks (STMPHON & STMSEM) for Grades 3, 4, 5, and 6

	Grade 3 (n = 42)	Grade 4 (n = 38)	Grade 5 (n = 43)	Grade 6 (n = 27)
S1L1 (20 items)	9.83 (4.61)	10.92 (5.01)	13.58 (3.83)	17.10 (2.20)
S1L2 (20 items)	3.19 (2.92)	4.97 (3.80)	7.51 (4.42)	12.63 (4.64)
S1 total (40 items)	12.79 (7.23)	15.66 (8.18)	21.07 (8.00)	33.33 (6.33)
S2L1 (12 items)	5.36 (2.57)	6.82 (2.44)	8.61 (2.29)	10.70 (2.09)
S2L2 (12 items)	2.52 (2.31)	3.58 (2.56)	4.54 (3.03)	7.44 (2.91)
S2L3 (12 items)	1.33 (1.48)	2.11 (1.69)	2.79 (1.79)	4.85 (2.25)
S2 total (36 items)	9.21 (5.28)	12.24 (6.25)	15.93 (6.40)	23.00 (7.02)
S4A (15 items)	6.10 (2.62)	7.63 (2.84)	8.00 (2.66)	9.07 (2.88)
S4B (15 items)	5.67 (3.63)	7.05 (2.67)	8.65 (2.96)	10.30 (3.24)
S4 total (30 items)	11.50 (5.23)	14.68 (4.79)	16.42 (5.28)	19.44 (5.62)
S5 (40 items)	18.69 (6.26)	22.32 (5.47)	23.21 (5.79)	23.93 (5.68)
S6 (40 items)	16.17 (6.92)	18.92 (4.59)	21.37 (5.15)	18.59 (5.62)
STMPHON (12 sets)	56.57 (14.72)	64.13 (13.78)	63.40 (15.09)	68.52 (12.26)
STMSEM (12 sets)	87.81 (10.37)	92.42 (4.39)	91.72 (6.71)	92.26 (7.89)
STM total (24 sets)	145.21 (22.57)	156.53 (17.21)	156.28 (19.33)	160.63 (17.30)

chotomy between regular [major correspondence] and exception words.) The task was based on the test of children's "sight vocabulary" by Adams and Huggins (1985) and refined by Leong (1992) after item analysis with the Rasch model. The 40 exception words were divided into two levels of 20 items each, according to printed frequency (Carroll, Davies, & Richman, 1971) and orthographic irregularity. Examples of these exception words and the embedding sentence frames were: "The ship sailed across the *ocean*" (Level 1) and "The horse drank from the *trough*" (Level 2). The mean printed frequencies for the two levels of 20 exception words each were, respectively, 326.9 and 73.3.

In Task 2 (S2) the same 150 children in the same small groups were asked to spell a total of 36 decontextualized regular words equally divided into three levels, ranging from the more transparent to the more opaque in their phonology–orthography relationship. The task was modified from that originally used by Fischer, Shankweiler, and Liberman (1985) in their study of spelling proficiency of undergraduate good and poor spellers. Examples of the more transparent Level 1 words are *mask, zebra*; examples of the intermediate Level 2 words are *knock, thigh*; and examples of the more opaque Level 3 words are *thinned, sobbing*.

It should be noted that the mean printed frequencies for the three groups of 12 words each (26.8, 70.5, 38.7, respectively) may not be a good indication of linguistic depth of complexity as shown in the gradation of phonology–orthography relatedness. Level 3 words, for example, require implicit understanding of the consonant twinning rule and lexicalization of plurals (e.g., *omitted, echoes*) and contrast with the shallower *diplomat, pianos*. On this view, there is a gradation of phoneme-to-grapheme correspondence complexity of the three levels of 36 words, and this gradation should be reflected in both error rates and error patterns. Proficiency on Task 2 shows a subject's sensitivity to probabilistic morphophonemic rules in spelling (Fischer et al., 1985).

In Tasks 3 and 4 (S5 & S6) the 150 children in the same small groups were required to write 40 pseudowords with many friendly orthographic/phonologic neighbors (S5) such as <wull>, <slare>; and another 40 pseudowords with few orthographic/phonologic neighboring friends (S6) such as <woln>, <wrolk> (see Treiman, Goswami, & Bruck, 1990). Both Tasks 3 and 4 were modified from the lists of friendly nonwords and unfriendly nonwords used by Laxon, Coltheart, and Keating (1988) in their study of children's reading and spelling. The variation in orthographic friendliness of these pseudowords takes into account Glushko's (1979) consistency effect in reading and Henderson's (1982) lexical pooling model in emphasizing the probabilistic process of phonologic–orthographic correspondence. The accepted pronunciation of these items follows the principles suggested by Wijk (1966).

In addition, the children in the same small groups were also asked to attempt another pseudoword task (S4) modeled after the work of Waters, Bruck, and Malus-Abramowitz (1988). This task aimed at assessing the children's sensitivity to orthographic and morphological aspects of language, and consisted of two sets (S4A & S4B) of a total of 30 pronounceable orthographic or morphological pseudowords embedded in short sentence frames. The sentences were dictated to the children, and they were asked to write just the pseudowords to complete the sentence frames, which were also shown. An example of an orthographic pseudoword from S4A is "My rug is very *groit*," and an example of a morphological pseudoword is "Bob likes stamanics. He is very *stamanical*."

These tasks were administered in the previously mentioned order. The means and standard deviations for these tasks and the short-term memory tasks are shown in Table 22.2.

After a lapse of about 3 weeks, the 150 children were asked to read the 40 exception words (S1), and the 80 pseudowords varying in levels of association with many or few orthographic/phonologic friendly neighbors (S5 & S6).

RESULTS AND DISCUSSION

Relations in Spelling Pseudowords, Regular Words, and Exception Words

In line with the logic suggested by Treiman (1984), if the children used rules to spell regular words and if they differed in their use of rules, then the correlation between the friendly and unfriendly pseudowords (Tasks S5 & S6) and regular words (Task S2) should have been higher than the correlation between the same sets of pseudowords (Tasks S5 & S6) and exception words (Task S1). The correlation coefficients between S5 and S2 and S6 and S2 were 0.59 and 0.46. The corresponding correlation coefficients of S5 with S1 and S6 with S1 were 0.49 and 0.39.

These results suggest that the spelling of pseudowords and the spelling of regular words require many rulelike processes, whereas the spelling of exception words involves slightly different processes. It goes without saying that correlation does not necessarily mean causation, but the absence of covariation, or low correlation, rules out any presaging effects. The present results do not imply that children do not use word-specific associations to spell regular words. The high correlation of 0.89 between spelling exception words (Task S1) and regular words (Task S2) suggests that rulelike associations and lexical knowledge may both be used, although the latter may be less important for pseudowords.

These correlation coefficients between the spelling of different kinds of words parallel the relationship of the reading variables used in the study by Leong (1993). The first-order correlation for the 150 children between the WRAT-R reading and the reading of exception words (R1 from S1) is 0.68; the correlations between WRAT-R reading and the set of pseudowords with many friendly neighbors (R5 from S5) and the pseudowords with few friendly neighbors (R6 from S6) are 0.74 and 0.71, respectively. The correlations between the reading of exception words (R1) and of the sets of pseudowords (R5 & R6) are respectively 0.72 and 0.65, whereas the correlation of the two sets of pseudowords is 0.84.

These correlation coefficients between reading different kinds of words and pseudowords parallel the correlations reported by Gough and Walsh (1991) in their study of 93 first to third graders reading regular, exception, and nonsense words. Although reading pseudowords and exception words may require different kinds of subskills, the present results from both reading and spelling seem to bear out the view of Gough and Walsh that rulelike associations and word-specific knowledge may both derive from the same underlying representation, which they term "knowledge of the cipher." Reading and spelling for 9- to 12-year-old children are not disjunctive activities; they likely develop concurrently. This view of the concurrent development of the related activities over considerable individual differences was also emphasized by Shankweiler and Lundquist (1992).

Multiple Regression Analyses

To assess the relative contribution of the rule strategy and lexical strategy to spelling, a number of stepwise multiple regression analyses were carried out separately for spelling and reading with the standardized WRAT-R spelling and WRAT-R reading as criterion variables. These component tasks as described previously were used as "predictor" variables: spelling of exception words (S1), regular words (S2), morphologic pseudowords (S4), orthographic pseudowords with many or few "friends" (S5 & S6 respectively); reading of the same exception words (S1 as R1), orthographic pseudowords (S5 & S6 as R5 & R6); BAS Matrix, vocabulary, memory span for phonemically confusable words (STMPHON), chronological age (CA), and grade level.

It was reasoned that if the children relied more on their sensitivity to the phoneme-to-grapheme correspondence rules, then we would expect reading of the 36 words varying in their regularity to contribute more to individual variation in spelling performance. According to this logic, there seems to be some evidence for the preference of the rule strategy over the lexical strategy. Using the WRAT-R spelling as the criterion variable, stepwise multiple regression results show that the different levels of orthographic–phonologic transparency to opacity spelling task (S2) to be the most predictive with a multiple R of 0.76, accounting for 58% of the variation, which is considerable. Chronological age accounts for an additional 13%, the spelling of exception words (S1) a further 5%, and the reading of pseudowords with unfriendly orthographic and/or phonologic neighbors (R6) another 2% of the variation.

In contrast, when WRAT-R reading was the criterion variable, it was the 40-item friendly pseudoword reading task with many friendly orthographic/phonologic neighbors (R5) that explains most of the variation with a multiple R of 0.74, accounting for some 55% of the variance. The contribution of the other component tasks is in this order: spelling of exception words S1 (8%), chronological age (9%), vocabulary (4%), and spelling of regular words (2%), making a total conjoint contribution of 78%. This pattern of pseudoword reading predicting 55% of the variance is of some significance. Pseudoword reading is also a good indication of the person's productive knowledge of the orthography to enable the reader to read new words.

Analyses of the children's spelling errors suggest the conjoint effects of phonological and orthographic processing in spelling. Space limitation does not permit detailed elaboration here; suffice it to say that although knowledge of phoneme–grapheme correspondence is important, explicit morphological analysis seems to be just as important, especially for older learners (Ehri, 1986; Rohl & Tunmer, 1988; Treiman, 1993). Take the spelling of the word *answering* as an example. The corresponding /s/ = <sw> occurs only in *sword* and *answer*. This is because of the tendency of /w/ to be dropped from a weakly stressed syllable when it is between a preceding consonant and a vowel, especially the liquid /r/. Another example is *listening*, in which /s/ assumes <st> as in *listen, glisten, fasten, hasten,* and *moisten*. A third example is *thigh*, with <gh> lengthening the preceding short /i/ to create <igh>, as in *high* and *sigh*.

The results of the error analyses are in line with the earlier psycholinguistic findings of Fischer et al. (1985)—that spelling is most accurate where the underlying morphophonemic structure corresponds more closely to the phonetic realizations of the word. This position was further restated by Shankweiler and Lundquist (1992, p. 182): "The evidence supports the expectation that both phonologic and morphologic aspects of linguistic awareness are relevant to success in spelling and reading."

The mapping of phoneme–grapheme correspondences, as in the previous examples, is explainable by vowel/consonant alternation rules in the orthographic system, which cut through the orthographic complexity. A powerful theoretical position (from a linguistic perspective) on the item-process approach to morphophonemics was provided by Bybee (1985). In her functionally and typologically oriented treatise, Bybee argued for the interaction of morphologic, phonologic, and semantic connections to enhance lexical "strength" in acquiring lexical items.

Making Connections

It is a daunting task to make even passing reference to the connectionist approach to spelling and reading. Detailed and lucid accounts were provided by Quinlan (1995) and Brown and Loosemore (1995). Quinlan discussed the pros and cons of the traditional functional roles of lexical entries and the distributed representations of connectionist models at the levels of implementation and computation. Brown and Loosemore demonstrated the learnability of connectionist models in spelling and reading regular and exception words, and their simulation results paralleled those of the learning of the same words by children. Another powerful theoretical model is the restrictive-interactive (R-I) model of Perfetti (1992). This model emphasizes the use of multiple sources of information in parallel for both reading and spelling (Perfetti, 1997). All these models suggest the need to incorporate explicit training in phonologic and orthographic structures for children, as advocated by Seymour (1992) and others, to enhance the connections between phonemic and orthographic segments of words that must be learned in order to read and spell effectively.

ACKNOWLEDGMENTS

I acknowledge the assistance provided by the Social Sciences and Humanities Research Council of Canada through SSHRC Research Grants No. 410-89-0128 and No. 410-96-0186 and the University of Saskatchewan President's Social Sciences Research Fund. I thank the Davidson schools for their participation in the study, K. Sarich for assistance in administering the tasks, and W. K. Lai in analyzing the data.

REFERENCES

Adams, M. J., & Huggins, A. W. F. (1985). The growth of children's sight vocabulary: A quick test with educational and theoretical implications. *Reading Research Quarterly, 20,* 262–281.

Baddeley, A. D. (1986). *Working memory.* New York: Oxford University Press.

Barry, C., & Seymour, P. H. K. (1988). Lexical priming and sound-to-spelling contingency effects in nonword spelling. *The Quarterly Journal of Experimental Psychology, 40A,* 5–40.

Brown, G. D. A., & Loosemore, R. P. W. (1995). A computational approach to dyslexic reading and spelling. In C. K. Leong & R. M. Joshi (Eds.), *Developmental and acquired dyslexia: Neuropsychological and neurolinguistic perspectives* (pp. 195–219). Dordrecht: Kluwer.

Bybee, J. L. (1985). *Morphology: A study of the relation between meaning and form.* Amsterdam: John Benjamins.

Carroll, J. B., Davies, P., & Richman, B. (1971). *The American heritage word frequency book.* Boston: Houghton-Mifflin.

Chomsky, C. (1970). Reading, writing, and phonology. *Harvard Educational Review, 40,* 287–309.
Chomsky, N., & Halle, M. (1991). *The sound pattern of English* (2nd printing). Cambridge, MA: MIT Press. (Original work published 1968)
Ehri, L. C. (1986). Sources of difficulty in learning to spell and read. In M. Wolraich & D. K. Routh (Eds.), *Advances in developmental and behavioral pediatrics: A research manual* (Vol. 7, pp. 121–195). Greenwich, CT: JAI Press.
Fischer, F. W., Shankweiler, D., & Liberman, I. Y. (1985). Spelling proficiency and sensitivity to word structure. *Journal of Memory and Language, 24,* 423–441.
Frith, U. (1985). Beneath the surface of developmental dyslexia. In K. E. Patterson, J. C. Marshall, & M. Coltheart (Eds.), *Surface dyslexia: Neuropsychological and cognitive studies of phonological reading* (pp. 301–330). London: Lawrence Erlbaum Associates.
Glushko, R. J. (1979). The organization and activation of orthographic knowledge in reading aloud. *Journal of Experimental Psychology: Human Perception and Performance, 5,* 674–691.
Gough, P. B., & Walsh, M. A. (1991). Chinese, Phoenicians, and the orthographic cipher of English. In S. A. Brady & D. P. Shankweiler (Eds.), *Phonological processes in literacy* (pp. 199–209). Hillsdale, NJ: Lawrence Erlbaum Associates.
Hanna, P. R., Hanna, J. S., Hodges, R. E., & Rudorf, E. H., Jr. (1966). *Phoneme–grapheme correspondences as cues to spelling improvement.* Washington, DC: U.S. Government Printing Office.
Henderson, L. (1982). *Orthography and word recognition in reading.* New York: Academic.
Henderson, L. (1985). On the use of the term "grapheme." *Language and Cognitive Processes, 1,* 135–148.
Jastak, S., & Wilkinson, G. S. (1984). *The Wide Range Achievement Test–Revised: Administration manual.* Wilmington, DE: Jastak Associates.
King, E. M. (1982). *Canadian Tests of Basic Skills: Multilevel edition/levels 9–12/forms 5 & 6.* Toronto: Nelson.
Kreiner, D. S. (1992). Reaction time measures of spelling: Testing a two-strategy model of skilled reading. *Journal of Experimental Psychology: Learning, Memory, and Cognition, 18,* 765–776.
Kreiner, D. S., & Gough, P. B. (1990). Two ideas about spelling: Rules and word-specific memory. *Journal of Memory and Language, 29,* 103–118.
Laxon, V. J., Coltheart, V., & Keating, C. (1988). Children find friendly words friendly too: Words with many orthographic neighbors are easier to read and spell. *British Journal of Educational Psychology, 58,* 103–119.
Leong, C. K. (1992). Cognitive componential modeling of reading in ten- to twelve-year-old readers. *Reading and Writing: An Interdisciplinary Journal, 4,* 327–364.
Leong, C. K. (1993). Towards developing a framework for diagnosing reading disorders. In R. M. Joshi & C. K. Leong (Eds.), *Reading disabilities: Diagnosis and component processes* (pp. 85–131). Dordrecht: Kluwer.
Perfetti, C. A. (1992). The representation problem in reading acquisition. In P. B. Gough, L. C. Ehri, & R. Treiman (Eds.), *Reading acquisition* (pp. 145–174). Hillsdale, NJ: Lawrence Erlbaum Associates.
Perfetti, C. A. (1997). The psycholinguistics of spelling and reading. In C. A. Perfetti, L. Rieben, & M. Fayol (Eds.), *Learning to spell: Research, theory and practice across languages* (pp. 21–38). Mahwah, NJ: Lawrence Erlbaum Associates.
Quinlan, P. T. (1995). Connectionism and the new alexia. In C. K. Leong & R. M. Joshi (Eds.), *Developmental and acquired dyslexia: Neuropsychological and neurolinguistic perspectives* (pp. 175–193). Dordrecht: Kluwer.
Read, C. (1986). *Children's creative spelling.* London: Routledge & Kegan Paul.
Rohl, M., & Tunmer, W. E. (1988). Phonemic segmentation skill and spelling acquisition. *Applied Psycholinguistics, 9,* 335–350.

Seymour, P. H. K. (1992). Cognitive theories of spelling and implications for education. In C. M. Sterling & C. Robson (Eds.), *Psychology, spelling and education* (pp. 50–70). Clevedon, Avon, England: Multilingual Matters.

Shankweiler, D., & Lundquist, E. (1992). On the relations between learning to spell and learning to read. In R. Frost & L. Katz (Eds.), *Orthography, phonology, morphology, and meaning* (pp. 179–192). Amsterdam: North-Holland.

Stage, S. C., & Wagner, R. K. (1992). Development of young children's phonological and orthographic knowledge as revealed by their spellings. *Developmental Psychology, 28,* 287–296.

Treiman, R. (1984). Individual differences among children in spelling and reading styles. *Journal of Experimental Child Psychology, 37,* 463–477.

Treiman, R. (1993). *Beginning to spell: A study of first-grade children.* New York: Oxford University Press.

Treiman, R., Goswami, U., & Bruck, M. (1990). Not all nonwords are alike: Implications for reading development and theory. *Memory & Cognition, 18,* 559–567.

Venezky, R. L. (1970). *The sound structure of English orthography.* The Hague: Mouton.

Venezky, R. L., & Massaro, D. W. (1987). Orthographic structure and spelling–sound regularity in reading English words. In A. Allport, D. G. Mackay, W. Prinz, & E. Scheerer (Eds.), *Language perception and production: Relationships between listening, speaking, reading, and writing* (pp. 159–179). New York: Academic.

Waters, G. S., Bruck, M., & Malus-Abramowitz, M. (1988). The role of linguistic and visual information in spelling: A developmental study. *Journal of Experimental Child Psychology, 45,* 400–421.

Wijk, A. (1966). *Rules of pronunciation for the English language.* London: Oxford University Press.

Chapter 23

The Role of Analogy in Early Spelling Development

Kate Nation
Charles Hulme
University of York, England

The hypothesis that early reading development may be characterized by the use of analogy has been well documented during recent years (Goswami, 1986, 1993; Goswami & Bryant, 1990). Reading by analogy involves using the spelling–sound pattern of a familiar word to assist the pronunciation of a similarly spelled unfamiliar word; for example, using the pronunciation of *beak* to read *bead* or *peak*. Although much research attention has focused on the importance of analogies in reading development, less attention has been paid to the possible role of analogies in spelling development. In this chapter, we outline two experiments concerned with young children's use of analogy when spelling and go on to consider the relationship between spelling by analogy and phonological awareness.

THE ROLE OF ANALOGIES IN SPELLING DEVELOPMENT

Traditionally, it has been thought that when children first begin to spell novel words, they use phoneme–grapheme correspondence rules to assemble a plausible spelling. In Frith's (1985) stage model of literacy acquisition, following a period of logographic spelling, children move into the alphabetic stage. This is characterized by the strict use of sequential phoneme–grapheme rules. It is only after extensive reading and spelling experience that children move into the orthographic stage of development. It is in this stage that children begin to use lexical analogies when spelling.

This stage theory is consistent with experimental work showing a developmental increase in the number of analogies made when spelling nonwords. Marsh, Friedman, Welch, and Desberg (1980) asked 7- and 10-year-old children, as well as college students, to spell novel words such as /wɛnθ/. Plausibly, this may be spelled according to phoneme–grapheme rules (producing the spelling *wenth*) or by analogy to the word *length* (producing the spelling *wength*). Marsh et al. found that the 7-year-old children made no analogies, the 10-year-old children produced 33% of analogy responses, whereas the college students produced 50% of analogy responses. In a similar vein, Campbell (1985) reported that the nonword spelling of young children was not influenced by lexical priming. Lexical priming is an experimental technique in which subjects hear a mixed list of words and nonwords and are asked to ignore the words but attempt to spell the nonwords. Campbell found that when adults and children with a reading age of greater than 11 years heard the word *brain*, they were likely to spell the nonword /preɪn/ *prain*. If however, they had previously heard the word *crane*, they were likely to spell /preɪn/ as *prane*. Because the younger 7-year-old children failed to show any effect of lexical priming, Campbell argued that children are not able to use lexical knowledge to assist nonword spelling until later in development.

A major problem with these studies is that it is not clear whether the younger children were familiar with the spelling of the words on which the nonwords were based. It is highly likely that many 7-year-olds would be unable to spell the words *length*, *brain*, or *crane* correctly. Therefore, it is not surprising that they fail to make analogies to similar-sounding nonwords. In order to get an accurate measure of young children's use of analogy, it is clearly important to ensure that the children are familiar with the relevant spelling patterns.

Goswami (1988) developed a technique well designed to measure young children's ability to make analogies when spelling. Six-year-old children were asked to spell a set of target words. They were then presented with a clue word (e.g., *beak*), told its pronunciation, and that it may help them to spell some other words. The clue word remained in full view while the children were again asked to spell the set of target words. If children can make analogies, then they should spell more target words correctly when the clue word is present. Goswami reported that this was indeed the case. In particular, children were able to make analogies if the target word shared a rime unit with the clue word (e.g., *peak*). Analogies were also made when the clue and the target shared a common consonant + vowel (CV) unit (e.g., *bean*). However, analogies were not made when the clue and the target shared three common letters (e.g., *lake*). From this, Goswami argued—contrary to the proposals offered by stage models—that young children can make analogies from the earliest stages of spelling development.

Furthermore, she argued that analogies are based on large subsyllabic units, especially the rime unit. Because analogies were not made in the common-letter condition, she argued that young children are unable to make analogies based on shared phoneme–grapheme correspondences.

One possible criticism of Goswami's experiment concerns her choice of stimuli in the common-letter condition. Although *lake* shares three letters with the clue word *beak*, it does not share three phoneme–grapheme correspondences: Although graphemic similarity was maintained, phonemic similarity was not. Therefore, we cannot conclude that analogies are not made on the basis of common phoneme–grapheme correspondences. One other limitation of Goswami's experiment is that the clue word remains in view. It is not clear whether 6-year-old children would make analogies in a more realistic setting using their stored knowledge rather than the spelling pattern contained in a visible clue word. It may be the case they do not make analogies in their spontaneous spelling until later in development. Two experiments are now described that were designed to address these issues.

EXPERIMENT 1: CAN YOUNG CHILDREN MAKE ANALOGIES WHEN SPELLING WORDS SHARING ONLY A SINGLE PHONEME–GRAPHEME CORRESPONDENCE?

This experiment used Goswami's clue-word paradigm in order to assess whether—when appropriate target words are included—young children can make analogies between words that share a single phoneme–grapheme correspondence.

Subjects

Twelve primary year 2 children (mean age = 6 years, 11 months) participated in this experiment. Each child was tested individually in a quiet room adjacent to the main classroom. The experiment consisted of two sessions: a pretest and an analogy test.

Materials

Four types of target word were used. As in Goswami's (1988) study, some of the targets shared either a CV (*corn–cord*), a rime unit (*corn–born*), or three common letters with the clue word (*corn–cone*). In addition, a common vowel condition was devised in which the vowel sound *and* spelling was shared. For example, the target word *port* shares the vowel /ɔ/ and its spelling *or* with the clue word *corn*. Eight target words of each type were used in this experiment, making a total of 32 items.

Procedure

Pretest. As with Goswami's study (1988), the pretest was designed to establish prior spelling knowledge of the test words. All of the target words were spoken aloud by the experimenter, both in isolation and sentence context. The words were presented in a random order so that the common sound and letter patterns would not be obvious. The children were asked to write each word and were encouraged "to have a guess" if they were unsure of how to spell any of the items.

Analogy Test. This was administered at least 1 day after the pretest. The children were shown a clue word, told its pronunciation, and advised that the clue word might help them to spell some of these other words (although no indication of *how* it might help was offered). The clue word was left in full view while the children were asked to spell the analogous and control target words. This procedure was then repeated for the other clue words.

Results

The mean scores for each condition are summarized in Fig. 23.1. An analysis of variance showed that significantly more words were spelled correctly at analogy test than at pretest ($F(1, 11) = 15.9$, $p < .01$). This effect also interacted with clue-word type, however. Planned comparisons show that this interaction was caused by significant improvement between pretest and analogy test for CV, rime, and vowel words only (all $ps < .01$). The difference between

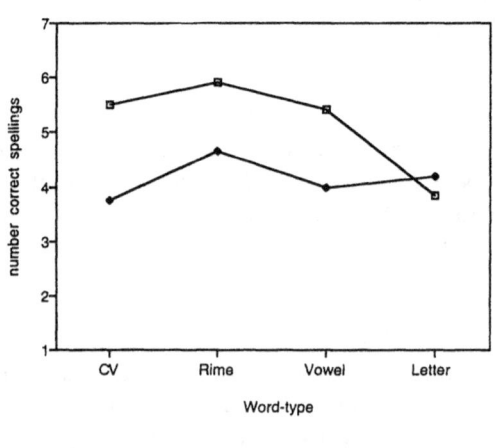

FIG. 23.1. Graph showing mean number of words spelled correctly in Experiment 1.

pretest and analogy test was not significant in the common-letter condition ($F = .15$, $p > .7$). Further planned contrasts revealed no significant difference between the number of analogies made in the CV and rime conditions ($F = .25$, $p > .6$), the CV and vowel conditions ($F = .01$, $p > .9$), or the rime and vowel conditions ($F = .14$, $p > .7$).

A second analysis of variance was run using the number of subjects correctly spelling each word in each condition as the dependent variable. This analysis produced an identical pattern of results as in the by-subjects analysis, thus indicating that the effects generalize across materials.

Discussion

This experiment provides good evidence that 6- and 7-year-old children are able to use the spelling pattern of a clue word to help them spell a similar-sounding target word. This is not consistent with stage models of spelling development, which propose that an analogical strategy does not become available until children are around 10 years of age. Goswami (1988) also found that young children can make analogies when spelling. However, she argued that the children's use of analogy was limited to those words sharing a large, subsyllabic unit, particularly a rime unit, and that analogies may not be made on the basis of phoneme–grapheme correspondences until later in development. In our experiment, however, young children were equally likely to make analogies based on common vowels as analogies based a common CVs or common rime units. This difference is due to the differences in stimuli used: Whereas Goswami controlled only for *graphemic* similarity, here both *graphemic* and *phonemic* similarity were maintained. Thus, even 6- to 7-year-old children are able to make analogies based on a single phoneme–grapheme correspondence when appropriate stimuli are used.

Although these results are interesting, they do not address the issue of whether or not such young children can make analogies when spelling spontaneously. It may be the case—as stage models suggest—that spontaneous analogies are not made until later in development. This idea was investigated in the following experiment by examining whether or not 6- to 7-year-old children make analogies using their stored knowledge of familiar spellings.

EXPERIMENT 2: CAN YOUNG CHILDREN MAKE ANALOGIES WHEN THE CLUE WORDS ARE NOT VISIBLE?

One way to measure whether young children are able to use their stored knowledge of familiar words to spell similar-sounding novel words is to use a priming technique. If children are able to use their stored knowledge, we predict that hearing a familiar word should influence their spelling of a subsequent similar-sounding nonword. Campbell (1985) found that young children's spelling was not influenced by lexical priming. However, it is not clear whether her subjects were familiar with the spelling of the prime words. In our experiment, care was taken to select prime words whose spelling patterns would be familiar to the children. In addition, Campbell's study only examined priming effects when prime and target shared a rime unit. Because our previous experiments indicated that children are equally able to make analogies between words sharing a rime unit, a CV, or a common vowel, we decided to investigate whether children's nonword spelling is influenced by a lexical prime sharing either a rime, a CV, or a common vowel.

Subjects

Fifteen primary year 2 children (mean age = 6 years, 8 months) took part in this experiment. All of the children were pretested to make sure that they were able to spell at least four of the eight prime words. The mean number of primes correctly spelled was 6.09 (S.D. = 1.69).

Materials and Procedure

Eight prime words were selected from the children's reading materials. For each prime, three nonwords were constructed, making a total of 24 items. For example, for the prime word *green*, the nonwords /grib/ (CV), /pim/ (vowel), and /trin/ (rime unit) were chosen. The nonwords and corresponding prime words were randomly allocated to three lists, with the limitation that two nonwords based on the same prime word should not appear in the same list. In addition, a number of word and nonword filler items were included so that the relationship between primes and nonwords would not be obvious. The experiment consisted of two parts: unprimed and primed spelling.

Unprimed Spelling. The children were asked to spell all 24 nonwords in isolation. This provided a baseline measure of nonword spelling.

Primed Spelling. The following day, children were presented with the first primed test. They were told that they would hear a mixed list of words and nonwords, and that they should place a tick on the response sheet when they heard a word. When they heard a nonword, they were told to attempt to spell it. On the following 2 days, the other two primed tests were administered. The three primed tests were administered in three different orders, with one third of the sample completing the tests in each order.

Results

In this experiment, the dependent measure was the number of times the critical spelling pattern was used (i.e., whether the nonword was spelled using the same pattern as in its prime word). Each child contributed six scores: the number of times the critical spelling pattern was used to spell the CV, rime unit, and common vowel nonwords in both the unprimed and the primed conditions. Mean scores are shown in Fig. 23.2.

An analysis of variance showed that children used the critical spelling pattern more often in the primed than in the unprimed condition ($F(1,12)$ = 32.70, $p < .001$). However, neither the main effect of prime type ($F(2,24)$ = 2.71, $p > .2$) nor the interaction between prime type and test session ($F(2,24) = 1.54$, $p > .2$) were significant, showing that the type of prime—whether it shares a CV, a rime unit, or a vowel—does not influence critical spelling pattern use.

Two other analyses of variance were run to assess the robustness of these findings. First, the data were analyzed by items. Exactly the same pattern of results as in the by subjects analysis emerged, thus demonstrating that the effects generalize across materials. Second, an analysis was performed in which only those items based on the prime words spelled correctly at pretest were included. Not all of the children were able to spell all eight prime words (mean = 6.09). If a particular child spelled only six prime words at pretest, only the data based on those six prime words were considered; the nonwords based on the two prime words incorrectly spelled

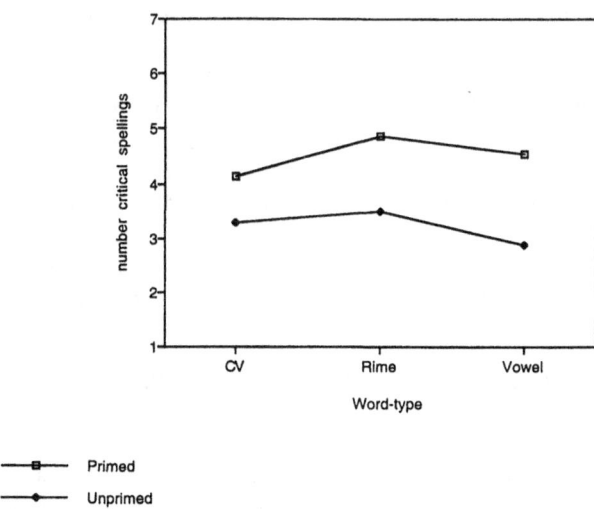

FIG. 23.2. Graph showing mean number of words spelled with the critical spelling pattern in Experiment 2.

were not included in the analysis. These scores were converted to proportions and were subjected to an angular transformation before an analysis of variance was computed. This yielded an identical pattern of results as in the previous analyses, confirming that priming occurred equally across all three word types.

Discussion

Because the children in this experiment did not see the prime words (cf. Experiment 1), these results provide good evidence that children can make analogies when spelling: Even children aged between 6 and 7 years old are able to use their *stored* lexical knowledge to assist their spelling of new words. Furthermore, the extent of lexical priming was not dependent on the size of the unit shared by the prime and target: An equal analogy effect was observed regardless of whether the prime and target shared a CV, a rime unit, or a common vowel.

Recently, Goswami (1993) proposed an integrated model of *reading* in which development is seen as the product of an increasingly refined use of analogy "underpinned" by increasingly refined phonological awareness. Briefly, her theory argued that, in the earliest stages of reading development, children are not sensitive to phonemes. They do, however, show awareness of larger phonological units, especially of onset and rime. Therefore, they can use this knowledge to read by analogy those words that share common rime units. As phonological awareness develops and children become sensitive to phonemes, they also become able to make analogies based on smaller units, such as common phoneme–grapheme correspondences.

In both the experiments we have discussed so far, there is no evidence to suggest that children are especially likely to use rime units when spelling by analogy. This stands in stark contrast to Goswami's work showing that shared rime units form the basis for analogies in the earliest stages of *reading* development. However, it is generally believed that awareness of phonemes is more crucial to beginning spelling than to beginning reading (Frith, 1980, 1985). It may well be the case, then, that young children make analogies based on common phoneme–grapheme correspondences when spelling *before* they are able to make them when reading.

SPELLING BY ANALOGY AND PHONOLOGICAL AWARENESS

Although the relationship between phonological awareness and spelling has been studied far less than the relationship between phonological awareness and reading, it is widely accepted that awareness of the sound structure of language is essential to attaining the alphabetic principle (Liberman,

Shankweiler, & Liberman, 1989; Snowling & Hulme, 1991). Rather than presenting a general discussion concerning the importance of phonological awareness to spelling per se, in the remainder of this chapter we focus on the interesting question concerning the relationship between phonological skills and the use of analogy when spelling.

Goswami and Bryant (1990) and Goswami and Mead (1992) presented data suggesting a special relationship between phonological awareness and reading by analogy. In particular, the relationship between rhyming skills (as measured by tasks such as Bradley & Bryant's [1983] sound categorization test) and the ability to make rime unit analogies has been stressed. Using multiple regression, Goswami demonstrated that performance on the Bradley and Bryant (1983) sound categorization task predicted the number of rime unit analogies made when reading. Measures of phoneme-level awareness, however (such as phonemic segmentation or phoneme deletion), failed to predict the use of analogy.

To our knowledge, no study has examined the relationship between phonological awareness and spelling by analogy. It may be the case that the relationship between phonological awareness and spelling is different to that between phonological awareness and reading. Because in our own experiments we found that 6-year-old children can make analogies when the clue and target word share only a single common phoneme, we were particularly interested in investigating the relationship between phoneme-level awareness and spelling by analogy.

We decided to use multiple regression to examine whether the scores obtained from various different phonological measures are able to predict individual differences in the extent to which children spell by analogy. We performed several hierarchical regressions comparing the effect of entering different phonological awareness measures in different orders. The advantage of using this type of analysis is that it enabled us to examine the amount of unique variance predicted by one variable after all other variables have been controlled statistically.

The data used for the regression analysis were obtained from a training study that had been designed to examine the influence of training 5-year-old children to spell by analogy. Three groups of nine children took part in the experiment, all closely matched for age, reading ability, and spelling ability. One group was trained to make analogies based on common CVs (*corn–cord*), one was trained to make analogies based on common vowels (*corn–port*), and the third group was trained to make analogies based on common rime units (*corn–born*). Consistent with the experiments outlined earlier in this chapter, all three groups learned to make analogies to an equal extent: The rime-trained group showed no advantage over the other groups, either in terms of speed of learning or extent of generalization. However, because all of the children were asked to complete various phonological awareness tasks, it was possible to investigate the relationship between phonological skill and spelling by analogy. The measure of analogy was the amount of generalization shown to nonwords that shared spelling patterns with the training words. The measures of phonological awareness used were two sound categorization tasks (rhyme and alliteration oddity, similar to Bradley & Bryant's odd-one-out tasks) and two measures of segmentation (segmenting spoken nonwords into phonemes or onset-rime units).

Table 23.1 shows the results of four hierarchical multiple regressions. In all cases, the dependent variable was nonword generalization and the first step entered was standardized spelling scores as measured by the Vernon graded spelling test (Vernon, 1977). The phonological awareness measures were entered in Steps 2 through 5. The order of entry differed for each different regression. As can be seen from Table 23.1, the only phonological measure to account for a significant portion of unique variance was phonemic segmentation. Thus, those children with good phonemic awareness were more likely to make analogies when spelling than were children with poorer phonemic awareness skills, even when the variance associated with Vernon spelling and other phonological skills was statistically controlled.

In contrast to the finding that reading by analogy is strongly related to rime-level phonological awareness (Goswami & Mead, 1992), it appears

TABLE 23.1
Results of Multiple Regression Predicting Nonword Generalization

Step	Variables Entered	R^2 Change	F	p
1	Vernon	.327	11.21	< .003
2	Alliteration	.0004	.014	ns
3	Rhyme	.026	.802	ns
4	Onset rime	.015	.478	ns
5	Phonemic	.143	5.55	< .03
1	Vernon	.327	11.21	< .003
2	Rhyme	.02	.705	ns
3	Alliteration	.004	.138	ns
4	Onset rime	.015	.478	ns
5	Phonemic	.143	5.55	< .03
1	Vernon	.327	11.21	< .003
2	Onset rime	.019	.644	ns
3	Phonemic	.105	4.01	< .05
4	Alliteration	.0009	.034	ns
5	Rhyme	.06	2.26	ns
1	Vernon	.327	11.21	< .003
2	Phonemic	.124	4.95	< .05
3	Onset rime	.0004	.017	ns
4	Alliteration	.0009	.034	ns
5	Rhyme	.06	2.26	ns

that spelling by analogy is more closely related to phonemic–level phonological awareness. This is consistent with many studies showing a relationship between spelling ability and phoneme awareness (see, e.g., Griffith, 1991; Perin, 1983; Rohl & Tunmer, 1988). It also fits well with our observations that even children in the earliest stages of spelling development (recall that these children were aged between 5 and 6 years) can make analogies when spelling based on a single common phoneme–grapheme correspondence.

GENERAL DISCUSSION AND CONCLUSIONS

Although traditional stage models assert that analogies are not made until fairly late in development, the two experiments outlined in this chapter show that children between ages 6 and 7 years are able to make analogies when spelling. Furthermore, because analogies were made between words sharing only a common vowel, the use of analogy does not seem to be limited to those words that share rime units. Clearly, neither traditional stage models nor analogy models that emphasize the importance of the rime unit can accommodate these findings.

In our view, a better way in which to conceptualize spelling development is within a framework based on connectionist models. The advantage of these models is that it is not necessary to propose different mechanisms or algorithms to represent different stages or strategies. In Seidenberg and McClelland's (1989) model of reading development or Brown and Loosemore's (1994) model of spelling development, for example, developmental change and apparent stagelike behavior emerge as natural properties of the networks. What causes developmental change in these models is simply a change in the knowledge base of the model. In the early stages of training, a network such as these will not generalize to any great extent, because it will not have encoded the statistical relationship between inputs (phonology) and outputs (orthography). However, because such a network is exposed to more words, it will begin to extract statistical regularities relating input to output. This knowledge can then be used to make effective generalization to novel stimuli possible. Similarly, children appear to make more analogies as they get older. Previously, this has been interpreted as evidence for the use of qualitatively different strategies at different stages of development. We suggest that a better interpretation—and one in keeping with the present results—is that analogies may be made from the earliest stages of spelling development so long as children are familiar with the relevant sound–spelling patterns.

The finding that an equal analogy effect is observed regardless of whether the transfer is based on shared rime units, shared CVs, or shared vowels also fits well with a model of development based on a connectionist framework. In a connectionist system, information is represented in a distributed fashion: It is not the case that a single unit codes uniquely for a word, rime, letter, or phoneme. The finding that children are able to pick up on and use the regularities that exist between the beginnings, middles, or endings of words is therefore entirely consistent with the predictions from such models.

A final conclusion to be drawn concerns the relationship between spelling by analogy and phonological awareness. Whereas early reading by analogy is related to awareness of rhyme and not phoneme awareness (Goswami & Mead, 1992), our analyses show that spelling by analogy is more closely related to phonemic awareness. Young children are able to make analogies when spelling, not only between words sharing rime units but also to words that share a single phoneme–grapheme correspondence. Furthermore, their ability to do this is closely related to their phoneme-level awareness, even in the earliest stages of spelling development.

REFERENCES

Bradley, L., & Bryant, P. E. (1983). Categorising sounds and learning to read—a causal connection. *Nature, 301*, 419–421.

Brown, G. D. A., & Loosemore, R. P. W. (1994). Normal and dyslexic spelling: A connectionist approach. In G. D. A. Brown & N. C. Ellis (Eds.), *Handbook of spelling research: Theory, process and intervention* (pp. 319–335). Chichester, England: Wiley.

Campbell, R. (1985). When children write nonwords to dictation. *Journal of Experimental Child Psychology, 40*, 133–151.

Frith, U. (1980). Unexpected spelling problems. In U. Frith (Ed.), *Cognitive processes in spelling* (pp. 495–516). London: Academic.

Frith, U. (1985). Beneath the surface of surface dyslexia. In K. E. Patterson, J. C. Marshall, & M. Coltheart (Eds.), *Surface dyslexia: Neuropsychological and cognitive studies of phonological reading* (pp. 301–330). London: Routledge & Kegan Paul.

Goswami, U. (1986). Children's use of analogy in learning to read: A developmental study. *Journal of Experimental Child Psychology, 42*, 73–83.

Goswami, U. (1988). Children's use of analogy in learning to spell. *British Journal of Developmental Psychology, 6*, 21–33.

Goswami, U. (1993). Towards an interactive model of reading development: Decoding vowel graphemes in beginning reading. *Journal of Experimental Child Psychology, 56*, 443–475.

Goswami, U., & Bryant, P. E. (1990). *Phonological skills and learning to read.* London: Lawrence Erlbaum Associates.

Goswami, U., & Mead, F. (1992). Onset and rime awareness and analogies in reading. *Reading Research Quarterly, 27*, 153–162.

Griffith, P. L. (1991). Phonemic awareness helps first graders invent spellings and third graders remember correct spellings. *Journal of Reading Behaviour, 23*, 215–233.

Liberman, I. Y., Shankweiler, D., & Liberman, A. M. (1989). The alphabetic principle and learning to read. In D. Shankweiler & I. Y. Liberman (Eds.), *Phonology and reading disability: Solving the reading puzzle* (pp. 1–33). Ann Abor: University of Michigan Press.

Marsh, G., Friedman, M. P., Welch, V., & Desberg, P. (1980). The development of strategies in spelling. In U. Frith (Ed.), *Cognitive processes in spelling* (pp. 339–353). New York: Academic.

Perin, D. (1983). Phonemic segmentation skill and spelling. *British Journal of Psychology, 74,* 129–144.

Rohl, M., & Tunmer, W. E. (1988). Phonemic segmentation skill and spelling acquisition. *Applied Psycholinguistics, 9,* 335–350.

Seidenberg, M. S., & McClelland, J. L. (1989). A distributed, developmental model of word recognition and naming. *Psychological Review, 96,* 523–568.

Snowling, M., & Hulme, C. (1991). Speech processing and learning to spell. In W. Ellis & R. Bowler (Eds.), *Language and the creation of literacy* (pp. 33–39). Baltimore, MD: The Orton Dyslexia Society.

Vernon, P. E. (1977). *Graded word spelling test.* London: Hodder & Stoughton.

Part V

THE REMEDIATION OF READING PROBLEMS

One justification for research on reading development and its disorders is that it will help provide us with better methods of remedial teaching for poor readers. Such translation of research into practice is certainly happening, and a number of chapters in earlier sections of the book touched on these issues. The two chapters in Part V deal more directly with issues of remedial teaching.

In chapter 24, Juel reviews work that has looked at the effects of one-to-one tutoring for poor readers. In one of her early studies, university students (who were themselves poor readers) took on the role of tutoring children with reading difficulties. Most impressively, both the children and the tutors showed marked improvements in their reading skills as a result of participation in this program. A subsequent project that Juel describes has looked at the effects of volunteer tutors in helping first-grade children at risk of reading failure, once again with encouraging results. A number of components are thought to contribute to the success of these tutoring programs, including the use of explicit word study instruction and the rereading of books at an appropriate level of difficulty. As well as these technical factors, however, Juel emphasizes the importance of the quality of the relationship that develops between tutors and the individual children they help.

In chapter 25, Wise and Olson provide an overview of their computer-based teaching programs, which have grown out of the Colorado twin study of dyslexia. Here, computer-generated speech is used to turn the computer into a highly cost-effective and motivating tool for helping poor readers. In these programs, the child reads stories presented on the computer screen and is able to target words that cannot be read. The computer then pronounces the targeted word. The computer programs also allow for spelling practice, with the computer pronouncing the child's attempted spellings. One study of particular interest has combined computer-based remediation with exercises to develop the children's phonological skills using a method focusing on the articulatory gestures of speech (Lindamood & Lindamood, 1975). The results showed that this form of teaching was particularly effective. Such results are clearly highly consonant with the framework for considering the relation between speech skills and learning to read outlined by Liberman at the beginning of this volume. They also lend credence to the phonological linkage hypothesis (Hatcher, Hulme, & Ellis, 1994)—the idea that combining phonological training with the teaching of reading and spelling will be particularly effective for poor readers.

REFERENCES

Hatcher, P., Hulme, C., & Ellis, A. E. (1994). Ameliorating reading failure by integrating the teaching of reading and phonological skills: The phonological linkage hypothesis. *Child Development, 65,* 41–57.

Lindamood, C., & Lindamood, P. (1975). *Auditory discrimination in depth.* Columbus, OH: Macmillan/McGraw-Hill.

Chapter 24

What Kind of One-on-One Tutoring Helps a Poor Reader?

Connie Juel
University of Virginia

One-on-one tutoring of first-grade children who are struggling with reading has become very popular. The most famous tutoring program, Reading Recovery, was begun by Marie Clay in New Zealand. Reading Recovery has now been adopted in nearly every state in the United States, and a Spanish version of the program is spreading in Latin America. The benefits of Reading Recovery are well documented (DeFord, Lyons, & Pinnell, 1991); so, however, are its costs. A study by the San Diego (California) Unified School District (1992) found that the average cost per pupil served by Reading Recovery was $3,250. Reading Recovery teachers typically are assigned to the program for 50% of the school day, and tutor only four students at a time. The typical Reading Recovery teacher serves only eight children over the course of a school year.

Due to the high monetary and human cost of Reading Recovery, suggestions have been made to incorporate its activities into group instruction. Pinnell, Lyons, DeFord, Bryk, and Seltzer (1994) attempted to do just that, and reported more powerful effects of one-on-one Reading Recovery than small-group Reading Recovery. This latter finding is in line with the overall finding that one-on-one instruction is more effective than instruction given to small groups (Bloom, 1984; Cohen, Kulik, & Kulik, 1982; Glass, Cahen, Smith, & Filby, 1982; Wasik & Slavin, 1993).

Yet the reasons behind the powerful effects of one-on-one tutoring are not clear. For answers, one can look to the program, the tutor, the child, the environment, and to some combination of interactions among them.

Some researchers, for example, have suggested that the extensive training provided tutors, such as those in Reading Recovery, is at least partially responsible for success (Wasik & Slavin, 1993); yet other researchers have found that successful learning in one-on-one tutoring is not significantly related to the quantity of tutor training (Cohen et al., 1982).

One-on-one tutorials may simply heighten the engagement of the learner with both the materials and the learning process for longer periods of time than occurs in a typically bustling classroom. The attention-focusing nature of one-on-one instruction may be especially powerful for the younger learner. The immediate nature of individualized, contextual feedback provided in the tutorial may provide more effective cues to guide the fledgling reader toward useful reading strategies and away from nonproductive ones.

For several years I have been involved in tutoring programs for at-risk first-grade children. This chapter discusses two long-term projects. The first tutoring program evolved when I was at the University of Texas at Austin. It involved university students who were mostly poor readers themselves (most were also student athletes) tutoring first- and second-grade poor readers (Juel, 1991; Juel, 1996; Juel, 1996a). The second program I discuss is ongoing in the Charlottesville City Schools, one that my colleague Marcia Invernizzi and I developed (Invernizzi, Juel, & Rosemary, 1996/1997; Invernizzi, Rosemary, Juel, & Richards, in press). In the Charlottesville program, community volunteers are trained to tutor needy first-grade children in all six elementary schools in the city.

Drawing from data collected in these two tutoring programs, the three questions I focus on in this chapter are: What are the major stumbling blocks for the first-grade children that we have encountered? What verbal interactions between tutor and child seem to help them? What tutoring activities seem to help them?

WHAT ARE THE MAJOR STUMBLING BLOCKS FOR THE FIRST-GRADE CHILDREN THAT WE HAVE ENCOUNTERED?

Alphabet Knowledge

The literature is replete with studies indicating that the top two predictors of children's success in learning to read in first grade are alphabet knowledge and phonemic awareness (Adams, 1990; Share, Jorm, Maclean, & Matthews, 1984). At various points in time, debate has concerned why both have such predictiveness: They suggest a home in which attention has gone to literacy; they suggest a motivated or bright child; and they indicate that the basic knowledge necessary for word recognition and spelling are already in place and additional time will not need to be spent on them in school.

Children who do not know the letters of the alphabet well when entering first grade sometimes spend considerable time at the beginning of that grade in "reading readiness" activities, whereas their alphabet-aware peers are reading books right from the start. This often leads to "tracking," showing that the "readiness" children not only read considerably less in first grade, but never catch up as the tracking continues into subsequent grades (Cunningham & Allington, 1994; Juel, 1990, 1994).

It is invariably the case in the two intervention programs in which I have been involved that the majority of children we tutor are still struggling to recognize the majority of letters at the beginning of first grade. In one rather extreme case, we tutored a child in Charlottesville who had considerable phonemic awareness; she could easily sort picture cards into stacks according to their initial phonemes at the beginning of first grade. She had memorized some of the phonic rules taught in her first-grade classroom (e.g., she could tell people that the letter *m* says /m/). She could not write the word *me*, however, unless we let her copy the letter *m* from a chart (and it took her a while to be able to copy it because the strokes were unfamiliar)—even though she could tell us it started with an *m*. This lack of print knowledge had left her unable to engage in the invented spelling and message writing of her alphabet-savvy peers.

Each year in our interventions we seem to find an increasing number of children who do not know the alphabet when entering first grade. This is most likely a result of the "developmentally appropriate" movement. Proponents of this movement generally assume that academic skills like reading and writing do not belong in the child-centered kindergarten or preschool. McGill-Franzen (1992) suggested that although middle-class parents and private preschools often ignore such advice and provide direct instruction in written English, "In many publicly funded early childhood programs for poor children it is considered developmentally inappropriate to display the letters of the English alphabet or even to sing the alphabet song" (p. 57). The goals of many programs like Head Start are focused on developing self-esteem and socialization skills (McGill-Franzen, 1992; Rosemary, 1995).

The research of Goldenberg (1994) provides strong evidence of the benefits derived from "academic" kindergartens and the lack of any negative socioemotional effects to such instruction. Certainly my experience with tutoring children has made me concur with his statement: "Although I am not necessarily making a case for academic kindergartens, I *am* suggesting that the current, mainstream revulsion at teaching academic skills to 5-year-olds merits reexamination, particularly when there is evidence that children can benefit from such learning while suffering no adverse side effects" (p. 185).

Phonemic Awareness *and* Concept of Word

I have long been on the phonemic awareness bandwagon (Juel, 1986, 1988, 1991b, 1994; Juel, Griffith, & Gough, 1986). It wasn't until I became involved with the tutoring programs that I began to see how phonemic awareness initially plays a role in reading—and it wasn't in the way I had thought.

In both the Texas and Virginia tutoring programs we have made use of predictable text. These are texts with either all or most of the sentences being quite memorable based on repetition, rhyme, or picture clues. In *Cat on the Mat* (Wildsmith, 1982), for example, various animals join a cat on the mat, with text such as, "The cat sat on the mat," and "The goat sat on the mat," and "The elephant sat on the mat." Predictable texts are extremely popular as early reading material in classrooms today because the children can be instant "readers."

In watching children read predictable texts, however, I was reminded of the need for them to develop a "concept of word" (Morris, 1992a). In their attempts to finger-point to the words in print that they say, children frequently track the stress, beat, syllables, or letters, rather than the words. One child might point to the *e* in *the* as she read *sat* in, "The cat sat. . . ." Another child would do fine until encountering the word *elephant*, which she considered three words; this resulted in her pointing to *on* for the second syllable in *elephant*, *the* for the last syllable, and looking all around for more text to point to at the end of the sentence.

One of the reasons I now believe phonemic awareness is so important as a predictor of early reading acquisition is that it functions to help children identify where words exist on a page. Concept of word and phonemic awareness operate together like a radar device to allow the accurate tracking of words. Phonemic awareness assists children to track print when they can segment initial consonant sounds and connect these sounds to letters. Oddly, awareness of beginning consonant sounds and the letters that connect to these sounds *precedes* a firm concept of word (Ehri & Chun, in press; Ehri & Sweet, 1991; Morris, 1992a).

In the Texas tutoring program, we administered several assessments throughout the school year to the 49 tutored children. These included spelling and word recognition tests (Wide Range Achievement Test; WRAT), beginning consonant knowledge (Metropolitan Readiness Test; MRT), and *Stones— The Concept About Print Test* (Clay, 1979). The beginning consonant test assesses both phonemic awareness (e.g., "Mark the picture that starts with the same sound as *soap*") and initial consonant knowledge (e.g., "Listen to the sound at the beginning of *face*. Mark that letter"). We found that children could not accurately track the print on a memorized page of the *Stones* story until they did well on the beginning consonant assessments. Also, once they did well on the beginning consonant assessments, their spelling and word recognition began to soar.

During the 1992–1993 school year we administered several assessments to the 102 children we tutored in Charlottesville. Pre- and posttesting included measures of alphabet knowledge (upper- and lowercase recognition and production), concept of word (Morris, 1992b), phonemic awareness (beginning sound picture sort), spelling (counting number of phonemes correctly represented; Morris, 1992b), word recognition (WRAT), and contextual reading (*Little Bear*, Minarik, 1957). Factor analysis was used to identify the principal components within the pretest measures. Components were extracted and rotated to simple structure according to the varimax criterion. The rotated factors were interpreted as: alphabet knowledge, including upper- and lowercase alphabet recognition, and alphabet production; and an amalgamated factor of concept of word and phonemic awareness. It appears that children need to be helped to track print by coordinating beginning sounds with printed word boundaries in context (Juel, Invernizzi, & Johnston, 1994).

One of the earliest phonemic insights about words is distinguishing the onset (i.e, the initial phoneme, like /k/) and rime (e.g., *at*) (Treiman, 1992). The child who can do this at its simplest level could distinguish which words rhyme among *cat, fat,* and *dog*. At more advanced levels, which may require some print experience, the child can actually segment the rime and create new rhyming words with the phonogram. Once concept of word and awareness of initial consonant sounds are in place, then invented spelling and word recognition begins to blossom. The word unit now can be more accurately tracked, its sounds segmented, and these sounds connected to letters. Until a stable concept of word is developed, it is difficult for the child to advance in word recognition (e.g., it is hard to connect the first letter in *parrot* to /p/ when there is confusion as to where the word *parrot* is on a page). It is this connection of phonemic awareness to tracking print that seems to be how phonemic awareness initially operates in reading.

Unproductive Hypotheses

Children learn about printed language in much the same way they learn about spoken language: They are active hypothesis makers, and take in information (whether it be oral or print), ponder it, and form increasingly sophisticated hypotheses about its nature. Different children acquire aspects of language (e.g., grammatical morphemes or acquisition of negatives) in virtually the same order (Brown, 1973; Clark & Clark, 1977). Children at a given stage come up with oral creations that they have never heard an adult speak (e.g., *goed*). Similarly, different children's invented spellings look remarkably alike at set stages of development (Henderson, 1990). The same type of "rule" overgeneralizations that appear in language (e.g., *goed* and *broked*) are seen in children's spellings (e.g., *rain* spelled as *rane*, and *desks* spelled as *deskes*) (Juel, 1994; Juel, Griffith, & Gough, 1985). Just as in language development, apparent regressions occur (such as saying "broked" after earlier use of "broke" in oral language), or laboriously "sounding out" words that were formerly effortlessly read (Bissex, 1980; Söderbergh, 1977).

Written language is not, however, a biologically driven process like oral language (Liberman & Liberman, 1992). Human cultures exist without written language, and written language has evolved as a cultural—and not a biological—phenomenon. It is virtually inevitable that any child with the ability to hear will learn to speak. On the other hand, if we were to provide vast quantities of print to a child, there is no guarantee that that child will learn to read. The child's task in learning to read is much more difficult and unnatural, requiring more knowledge about the mechanics of the system than is required by the biologically driven process of learning to speak (Gough & Hillinger, 1980; Liberman & Liberman, 1992). Although the child approaches learning to read as an active hypothesis maker, he or she is much more likely to stumble and to fixate on unproductive hypotheses for lengthy periods of time (Ferreiro, 1986, 1990). One child in my longitudinal study of reading development continued to write words with only the letters in his own name well into second grade (Juel, 1994). Although explicit instruction may not instantly change a child's initial hypotheses, guidance may direct the child to enough exemplars and situations in which discussion can help him or her consider alternative hypotheses faster than if he or she were left without such assistance.

Once children understand that print in text carries meaning, when there is a growing concept of word and the understanding that a spoken word corresponds to a printed word, and when some letters are known, children begin to form their own hypotheses about how to use *the print* itself to create meaning. Usually such hypotheses focus on only one or two aspects of visual print (e.g., initial letters, distinctive letters, or length of words; Gates & Boeker, 1923; Gough & Juel, 1991). The child may remember the word *cat* because it starts with a *c*, the word *moon* because it has two "moons" in the middle of it, and the word *elephant* due to its length. Sometimes a letter might be chosen as a cue because it is associated with a word's sound, as in the *b* in *bee* (Ehri, 1991; Ehri & Wilce, 1985, 1987). Children who recall words in this manner are using classic paired-associate learning. Their selection of a distinctive cue to represent a word has been labeled the *selective-cue stage* of reading development (Gough & Hillinger, 1980; Gough & Juel, 1991; Juel, 1991).

Due to the selection of a particular cue, children in this stage misread and misspell words in distinctive ways. Their focus on one particular cue in a word (e.g., the first letter) leaves them clueless as to the rest of the word (Gough, Juel, & Griffith, 1992). In reading, children in the selective-cue stage will substitute an originally recalled word for a new word that shares the cue used for recall. Hence, *cow* is read as *cat*, *good* is read as *moon*, or *armadillo* is read as *elephant* (Gough & Juel, 1991). Because it is difficult to recall these random cues, it is common for children to seem to know a printed word at one moment and not the next. Spelling reflects the use of distinctive cues too, but a misspelling may not result in a recognizable word. *Cat* may be written as *c*, *moon* as *xoop*, or *elephant* as *albe2kz* (Juel, Griffith, & Gough, 1985).

It is at the selective-cue stage that frustration can set in. With every new word that needs to be learned, it becomes more difficult to find a distinguishing cue that will differentiate it from old words (e.g., initial *c* for *cat* won't work when *can* is encountered). It is at the selective-cue stage that many of the first- and second-grade children whom we tutor appear to be stuck. The child at the selective-cue stage is most likely to advance and learn a more reliable way to identify words through interaction with others (Mason, 1980). The more reliable way will, of course, include taking advantage of the spelling–sound relationships found in an alphabetic written language like English (e.g., initial *c* for /k/) and entering what is sometimes called the *spelling–sound* stage (Juel, 1990, 1991; Söderbergh, 1977).

WHAT VERBAL INTERACTIONS BETWEEN TUTOR AND CHILD SEEM TO HELP?

In the current reading literature there is an increasing emphasis on a social constructivist or sociocognitive view of reading (Hiebert, 1991; Hiebert & Raphael, 1996). Learning is viewed largely as coming about through social contexts and interactions. The work of Vygotsky (1978) is frequently cited as providing support for this view. The metaphor used for instruction is often that of "scaffolding" based on Vygotsky's (1978) idea of the "zone of proximal development"—the distance between what the novice can do alone and what can be done in collaboration with a more skilled individual. Vygotsky, in fact, emphasized that this collaboration is highly social and interactive in nature. The adult's role in scaffolding was not particularly developed by Vygotsky, but has been elaborated on by others (Anderson, 1989; Wertsch, 1984; Wood, Bruner, & Ross, 1976).

According to Langer (1991):

> A sociocognitive view means two things for instruction. First, more attention is paid to the social purposes to which the literacy skills are being put—students learn best when they are trying to accomplish something that is per-

sonally and socially meaningful. Second, more attention is paid to the structure as well as content of tasks that we ask students to undertake so that direct instruction in needed skills will be provided as part of the task, at points where it is needed. In this way students will have a better chance of understanding how the new skills and knowledge relate to the activities that are being completed." (pp. 18–19)

The emphasis on scaffolding is clear in Reading Recovery, although this program was not explicitly developed from Vygotsky's theory (Clay & Cazden, 1990; Gaffney & Anderson, 1991). Teachers first receive extensive training (30 hours) and then weekly ongoing training to become Reading Recovery teachers. The training emphasizes how teachers help children develop self-improving strategies to facilitate reading *within the context* of reading (Clay, 1985).

A typical Reading Recovery lesson includes the rereading of familiar little books (often predictable text) and the introduction of a new book. In both instances the teacher provides just enough scaffolding to facilitate the child's own reading. In the teacher's orientation to a new book, for example, the teacher may purposely refer to vocabulary that may be new or difficult for the child as he or she flips through the pages (e.g., "Look at what Santa brought the child—a skateboard"). Such scaffolding sets up the child's eventual "reading" (i.e., of the word *skateboard* when the child comes to that page). If the child pauses when reaching the word *skateboard*, the teacher might refer back to previous conversations ("What did we say Santa brought"), the picture cue on the page, or the initial phoneme in *skateboard*. Reference to the initial phoneme is often made with the statement, "Get your mouth ready." If the child misreads *skateboard* as *rollerblades*, the teacher might prompt the child to consider what letter *rollerblades* begins with and whether that letter is seen at the beginning of *skateboard*. If the child self-corrects without teacher support (e.g., initially reads *skateboard* as *rollerblades* and then amends it to *skateboard*), the teacher will encourage the child to state how he or she "fixed" it—to verbalize his or her strategy so it will later be recalled (e.g., "How did you know that said *skateboard*?").

What this type of dialogue promotes is the use of productive hypotheses/strategies and the disuse of nonproductive ones. It is extremely difficult, if not impossible, to provide this type of individualized discussion *during reading*, in the context of a full classroom of children. It is this one-on-one interaction that appears to me to be one of the most significant reasons for the success of tutoring.

I am not convinced, however, that such interaction can come about only as the result of extensive training of tutors. There certainly seems evidence that mother–child interactions are naturally replete with scaffolding in conversations about the environment (Rogoff & Garner, 1984) or more specifically while reading storybooks (Wood, Bruner, & Ross, 1976).

In storybook reading mothers are frequently seen to "up the ante" as they reread books to their children. On first reading the mother might simply leaf through the book, commenting on the objects in the pictures. After that, she might ask the child what is going on in a particular picture. Next, attention might focus on a particular word beneath the picture by pointing to it and labeling it. Later, the child might engage in such finger pointing and recall of words and content to "read" the story. This is not to say that scaffolded interactions come naturally to all mothers, and that such interactions cannot be improved by watching others engage in them (Edwards, 1991). Still, scaffolding seems to be a somewhat natural human response to young children—especially when it occurs in an intimate, one-on-one setting. (A major task in teacher education is to help future teachers find ways to provide scaffolded instruction to large groups of children, that is, to children who are at different levels of development.)

In the Texas tutoring program, relatively untrained tutors worked with a first- or second-grade child who was having difficulty learning to read. The tutors were student athletes whose low scores on the Nelson-Denny Reading Test (Brown, Bennett, & Hanna, 1981) averaged at the ninth-grade level and indicated that they themselves would have difficulty reading college-level textbooks (Juel, 1991, 1996, 1996a). These student athletes tutored a child twice a week, for about 45 minutes each time, at a local elementary school. One evening a week all the tutors met at the university for a 2½-hour class. During this class we discussed possible tutoring activities, how literacy develops, books the tutors were reading (they were required to read self-selected novels for 4 hours a week and write about their reading in response journals), and books the tutors wrote for the children they tutored. The student athletes took my class instead of the two developmental reading classes they would normally have been required to take. One purpose of the class, then, was to help the tutors advance their own reading and writing skills.

At the end of the school year, the student athletes in the class scored statistically better than a control group of student athletes who had taken the regular developmental reading courses customarily provided to poor readers at the university. Whereas the tutors had a mean grade equivalent of 9.1 in August, they had a mean grade equivalent of 13.1 in May. In contrast, the control group has a mean grade equivalent of 11.5 in August, and a mean grade equivalent of 12.6 in May.

At the end of the school year, the tutored children were reading significantly better than was a control group of nontutored children on the Iowa Tests of Basic Skills (Hieronymous, Lindquist, & Hoover, 1983). The mean score of the 27 first-grade tutored children on the reading comprehension subtest was at the 41st percentile. The mean score of the 15 nontutored children was at the 16th percentile—despite the fact that these latter 15 children had begun first grade with considerably higher scores on the prereading composite of the Metropolitan Readiness Test (Nurss & McGauvran, 1976).

Fifteen of the tutored children scored above the 50th percentile on the IOWA, as well as read at at least an early second-grade level on the Spache oral reading passages (Spache, 1981). It was those particularly successful dyads that we intensively reviewed to see what might have contributed to their success. All tutoring sessions were either videotaped or tape recorded, and transcripts of sessions were made of these 15 most successful dyads. Videotapes and transcripts of the most effective tutors were independently viewed or read by four people (three graduate students and me). We looked for overlap in techniques and effective interactions. We did not share our observations with one another. Each wrote comments about specific clips in the tapes or spots in the transcripts. There was considerable overlap in the comments, and those features that were commented on by at least three of the four observers informed our understandings. The successful dyads shared obvious affection, bonding, and verbal and nonverbal reinforcement of children's progress; scaffolded reading and writing experiences; and explicit cognitive modeling of reading and writing processes by the tutor.

Affection, Bonding, and Reinforcement

Noted by all observers was the supportive relationship that developed between tutor and child. One observer said, "You just look at the videos and you see love." Another observer commented, "It looks like family." The special one-on-one feeling was reflected in the words of another tutor that were spoken to his child on the first tutoring day: "I'm going to come *just to see you.*" All observers noted the physical affection between the tutors and the children in the successful dyads. The pairs sat close together, the tutor often had an arm around the child, and they often held hands. The children frequently asked for, and received, hugs. Not uncommon were sessions ending with scenes such as the following:

Tutor: Did you like the session today?
Child: Yes.
Tutor: That's good. That's good. I'm glad you like it 'cause I like doing it too. Are you ready to go back to class?
Child: Could you take me in your lap?
Tutor: Yeah.

McDermott (1977) reminded teachers that trust, warmth, and caring are necessary for learning to flourish. The successful tutors certainly needed no reminder. Effective tutors wanted their children to feel like their sessions were a team effort. This may reflect their sports backgrounds, but it helped the child feel like one of the team of learners—not like an outsider. As one tutor wrote in his journal: "The reason I keep stressing 'we,' is because it's a team thing. I let my child know that I am in this as much as they are [sic]. It's a learning experience for the both of us."

The student athletes were especially concerned about building the self-confidence and self-esteem of the children they tutored. Many described in their journals how painful learning to read had been for them, and how they wanted to keep their children from feeling that pain. One way many of the tutors tried to keep their children feeling successful was to help them be aware of their learning and the progress they were making:

Tutor: Hum, so your teacher tells me that you be reading a lot. Is that true? Can you tell? Can you see the improvement in yourself?

Child: Yeah.

Tutor: How? How can you see that you've improved? Do you read faster now? Can you sound out words a little bit better than you did before?

Child: I can sound out words.

Tutor: I mean you just spelled *tape*. [I]t wasn't up on the board and you could spell it. You spelled it in your head. That's the hardest way to spell things. So that's improvement right there. You could do it without looking. You know all your sounds, now . . . so, you're getting better and better every day.

Have you been practicing? (Child nods.) See, that's why you're getting better and faster. The more you practice the faster you get.

Can't was a common word for the children when we began to tutor. Many of the children routinely said they couldn't read, couldn't write, couldn't spell, and so forth. The tutors noted this, and their comments illustrate how they helped the children realize they "could." Here's one example (from one tutor and one session) of the type of comments that many tutors made during the sessions:

Tutor: Do you know what you just did? You just read three pages!

Child: (Laughs.)

Tutor: I think you['re] telling stories, don't ya? "I can't read that." You know you can.

Later

Tutor: You read the whole page to me! How do you feel about that? Okay. Thumbs up! Thumbs up, dude! Way to go, guy!

Later

Tutor: Now you just read five pages and you told me that you can't read. Hum! So!

Later

Tutor: You've read six pages! I thought, I thought you couldn't read?

Scaffolded Reading and Writing Experiences

Of course the child was partly able to read in the previous example, because the tutor had scaffolded the experience. They were reading a text that had been read several times before, and with varying degrees of support. This time the child was on his own. Scaffolding seems to provide the context for success that builds self-confidence.

Here's an example of scaffolding during writing. The child was trying to write the word *bat* to go with the picture of a bat he had drawn. He was very interested in bats, because his father had taken him to see bats flying under a bridge the night before. (Austin, Texas, is the bat capital of the United States.) After the child wrote the word *bat* with his tutor's help, he requested help writing another word, *kid*.

Tutor: Here's some looong wings! Here's another picture in your book. Some day you can go back and say, "Hey, look at all this that I did. . . ." Why don't you write it? Baaaat.

Child: (writes a *B*) Now what?

Tutor: Do you hear the "aaaa" sound?

Child: (writes an *A*)

Tutor: What about the "tuh," "tuh," what is that?

Child: (writes a *T*) Now I want to write *kid*.

Tutor: How you spell it out? What sounds do you hear? (Slowly elongates each sound in *kid*, repeats "kid") What's the first sound you hear?

Child: (Not sure.)

Tutor: What about the beginning? /kkkkkkkkkk/

Child: K.

Tutor: K. What next?

Child: I don't know.

Tutor: Kid. Say it slow. Kiiiiiiiiiiid.

Child: Kid.

Tutor: You have the /k/, but the next one, kiiiiiiiiiii.

Child: /i/, /i/

Tutor: Hey, good job. So what letter does that . . . ?
Child: I, /i/, /i/.
Tutor: Hey, good job. Now we got KI, kiiiii, what word we trying to spell?
Child: Kid.
Tutor: So we got kiiii. What [do] we need to make it kiiiiidddd?
Child: D.
Tutor: That's the way!

It's hard to imagine this type of slow, step-by-step building of experiences that allows a child to write so successfully in the context of the larger classroom. In the classroom, the child might simply be told how to spell the word, and this would not necessarily help him or her learn strategies for elongating and spelling a different word. Even if the teacher does model sounding out and spelling, it is not as likely to be for a word that captures the interest and subsequent attention of an individual child.

Explicit Cognitive Modeling of Reading and Writing Processes

Effective tutors frequently informed their children about how reading and writing work. Often the tutors modeled how to sound out words for the child by talking the child through the process step by step. The tutors "walked" the children through the processes of word recognition and spelling, so that the tasks were clearer, more accessible, and less mysterious. Here is an example of word recognition using letter cards to make words.

Tutor: So whenever you see those two letters together, it sounds like "aaaaattt, aaaaaatttt." So what is that?
Child: "Aaaaattt."
Tutor: Right, so what word is that?
Child: At.
Tutor: Right. So you've got the "at." Let's put a sound on the front of it, okay? What's one of your favorite sounds? I know, it's "ssss."
Child: "S."
Tutor: Right. (Puts up the letter *s* in front of *at*.) So you go, "ssss"—"at," and put them together. What have you got? You see? You see how that works? "Ssss" plus "at" gives you "sat." What about "m" plus "at"? What does that give you? (replaces the letter *s* with *m*)
Child: "m."

Tutor: And what is the other part?

Child: "At."

Tutor: Put them together. What do you get? You got the "at." You got the "mmmmm" sound. You put them together and what do you get? "Mmmmmaaaaaaat."

Child: Mat.

Tutor: Good. (replaces *m* with *f*) So you got "f" and "at." Gives you what?

Child: (Laughs) Fat.

Tutor: Right. They come together. You have this word "fffffaaaat." Fat. What do you hear when you say that word *fat?*

Child: "Ffff."

Tutor: Right. And the last two?

Child: "At."

Tutor: Right. All we did was change the letters, and you change the sound. (Puts up appropriate letters) "at," then "sssat," then "mmmat," "fat." See? What about "b" plus the "at"?

Child: Buh. Bat.

Tutor: Right. You got it.

Once again, it is difficult to imagine this lengthy, step-by-step modeling occurring in a classroom. And, if it did happen, it is difficult to see it keeping the attention of an individual child.

One of the most effective techniques for modeling reading processes that one tutor devised, which quickly was adopted by other tutors, was role reversals. The tutors pretended to be the child; the child pretended to be the teacher. Through this role reversal, the tutor could model thought processes of how to approach an unrecognizable word, and so forth. Here's one example of a tutor pretending to be a child, slowly sounding out words. The tutor calls on his child for assistance.

Tutor: (Slowly reading) I like to play (he comes to the word *with* and hesitates). What sound does "w" make?

Child: "Wi," and you said it up here (pointing to already read text).

Tutor: "Wi," I know that.

The role reversals focused even the most distractible child's attention on the print. The children took particular delight in the role reversals, perhaps because the pressure to read was lifted off them, and perhaps also because they felt more grownup as they pretended to be the tutor.

It may be that because the tutors themselves had difficulty learning to read, they were more cognizant of some of the insights and steps that had helped them learn. They were also extremely patient in working with their children and modeling some of the step-by-step processes involved in reading and writing words. It is not surprising to me that cross-age tutoring programs are flourishing. Someone who has just been through the learning process—or even had a difficult time learning and therefore recalls the process well—may be able to help the beginner better than the expert. They may be more aware of the both of the type of scaffolding needed by the novice and how to provide it. As explained by one of my Texas tutors:

> I had a lot of difficulty in school. My parents were told I was learning disabled. I carry this with me to this day. I found early on that I could learn okay, but usually not in the classroom. I learned early on that my best teachers were my peers, the ones who had just been through the same stuff. They could always explain things better to me than anyone else. I even find this to be true in college.

WHAT TUTORING ACTIVITIES SEEM TO HELP?

In devising our current community volunteer tutoring program in Charlottesville, Marcia Invernizzi and I borrowed heavily from the successful tutoring programs of others. She drew extensively from the years of clinical experience in the McGuffey Reading Clinic. I leaned on what I learned from the student athletes in Texas. We both learned a lot from Reading Recovery and the Howard Street Tutoring Project of Darrell Morris (Morris, 1992b). We also learned from researching each year of the community volunteer program.

Background on the Charlottesville Tutoring Program

At the beginning of the school year, first-grade children are rank ordered by classroom teachers on the strength of their literacy proficiencies (e.g., alphabet knowledge, concept of word). Tutor assignments proceed from the bottom of the list as tutors become available (e.g., the most needy children are picked up first for tutoring). Tutors are solicited by a volunteer recruiter employed by the city schools. Tutors range in age from 20 to 79, and they vary in background from rock 'n' roll musicians to city council members to retired senior citizens. Tutors are initially trained by Marcia Invernizzi and me in a 2-hour session that includes videotapes of tutoring sessions. Once in the schools, the volunteers receive ongoing training and supervision from an onsite reading coordinator who is a current or former student of the University of Virginia's McGuffey Reading Center. These reading coordinators each supervise approximately 15 volunteer tutors and the 15 children they tutor. We expect that some of the outstanding volunteers will soon become the reading coordinators. Coordinators assess children for individual literacy needs, create individual lesson plans, and organize materials for each dyad.

The volunteers tutor the same child one on one all year, twice a week, 40 to 60 minutes each day. This is a teaching tutorial (not a reading to or meeting with children) session. The reading coordinators have the lesson plan and materials for each tutoring session planned and designed before the tutors arrive at their assigned school. A four-part lesson, made up of reading familiar material, word study and phonics, writing for sounds, and introduction of new books, is adhered to within each session. Tutors know what they're doing and why they're doing it. This does not, however, keep them from getting to know the children personally and having a good time with them.

To date, 229 at-risk children have been served. In 1992–1993, 86 first-grade children were served by six "Book Buddies" reading coordinators at four schools. In 1993–1994, nine reading coordinators were at work in all six elementary schools. A total of 143 at-risk first- and second-grade children were served. The cost per child was $568. This cost reflects all salaries paid to the Book Buddies reading coordinators, the salary of the CCS volunteer recruiter, and all materials and books. This cost is considerably less than alternative one-on-one interventions (e.g., The San Diego Unified School District [1992] found that the average cost per pupil served by Reading Recovery was $3,250).

Cost, however, is not the bottom line; successful intervention is. We have closely monitored the progress of the tutored children with several assessments (e.g., alphabet recognition, word recognition, spelling). During the first year of implementation (1992–1993), most volunteers did not begin tutoring until January. We found that first-grade children who had between 17 and 48 hours of tutoring during the year grew significantly more in word recognition and spelling than did children who received between 4 and 16 hours of tutoring. In fact, children who received between 33 to 48 hours of tutoring scored similar to nontutored children on our measures of word recognition and spelling, even though they began the year considerably behind in prerequisites like alphabet knowledge. Tutoring clearly had a significant impact. Nonetheless, only 32% of all the tutored children were reading on grade level by the end of first grade.

During the 1993–1994 school year, three changes occurred. First, we changed our lesson plan to include more word study instruction. Second, we started tutoring earlier in the school year, with most tutors beginning in October. Third, the majority of our tutors were returnees, and thus had a year of experience. At the end of last year, 72% of our tutored first-grade children who received 40 or more tutoring sessions were reading on grade level. Although this represents an exciting and substantial improvement over the prior year, our aim continues to be to have 100% of the children tutored reading at grade level. We recognize, however, that some children may need more than 1 year of tutoring to achieve this goal. We are encouraged by the fact that 50% of our tutors from last year have volunteered to tutor another child this year.

What Activities Seem to Work

Similar to Reading Recovery, we begin each tutoring session with the rereading of several familiar little books. These are often predictable texts like *Cat on the Mat* (Wildsmith, 1982). Unlike Reading Recovery, however, we have included some books with controlled vocabulary. The main one is called *My Book*. *My Book* is a "build-up" reader (Guszak, 1985). Build-up readers slowly introduce high-frequency vocabulary, as well as new words that contain common phonogram patterns. The first page in the first build-up reader had only one word, *run*, which was repeated many times in different formats (e.g., "Run, _____, run. Run, run, run, _____."). There were blanks where the child could tell the tutor, or could write on their own, what would "run." Each subsequent page in the build-up added another word.

Build-up readers were part of my program in Texas. Reading instruction at the Texas elementary school followed a traditional mode, with the children placed in basal readers and reading groups. The children we tutored were all struggling with the basal vocabulary. One problem with "pullout remediation" has been the lack of overlap between the materials and experiences in the child's classroom and those in the remedial situation (Johnston & Allington, 1991). By including the high-frequency basal vocabulary in the build-up readers, a link was created between the materials used in the tutoring and those used in the classrooms. Many of the classrooms in Charlottesville also use basal readers, and our current build-up readers include words from these basals.

We include the build-up readers as part of our current tutoring because they proved very effective in Texas. The tutors in Texas kept track of the time they spent doing various activities (e.g., reading the build-up reader, reading other books, doing letter-sound activities). Time spent reading *My Book* was statistically correlated with reading growth (as opposed to activities—e.g., that included time spent on drawing a picture to illustrate a favorite word—that were negatively correlated with reading growth). Additionally, the 15 most successful tutors in Texas tended to use *My Book* more than the other tutors.

My Book provides children with considerable exposure to the same words and word parts (i.e., high-frequency phonograms). It is the first thing from the tutoring project that the children's regular classroom teachers want copies of when they see the tutoring materials. This includes teachers who do not use a basal. The teachers (and children) like the instant success, the inclusion of the children's own words in the texts, and the learning of vocabulary that occurs. I must add, however, that children do not like reading *My Book* for very long. It is boring. In a sense, we have recreated readers like *Dick and Jane* (with, of course, more of a focus on word families than fictional families and Spot and Sally).

The increasing use of literature—or basals that are really anthologies of literature—in first-grade classrooms has signaled the end of controlled-vocabulary basal readers. An analysis of these new literature materials (which are used in about half of the schools in Charlottesville) shows that first-grade children are seeing fewer words overall in first grade, but considerably more unique (different) words (Hoffman et al., 1994). (Literature tends to have more pictures, less text, and certainly less repetition of the same words than do traditional basal readers.) Thus, on average, a child sees any particular word fewer times than in the past, but sees more different words. For the children we tutor, the build-up readers seem to provide the repeated exposure they need to the same high-frequency words—precisely the experience they are getting less of in their classrooms.

We are working in a school district that is committed to whole language. We are committed to making the predictable texts that are the mainstay of early books in this movement work in a way that the story is not just memorized, but words are learned. Predictable text, as previously discussed in this chapter, provides children with text they can read right from the start—or at least after it is read to them once or twice. The dissertation research of one of our students, Francine Johnston, examined first-grade children's learning of sight words while reading predictable text in three conditions: after repeated rereadings and dramatic activities that emphasized the meaning of the texts, after rereadings of the text and the reading of sentence strips from the text, and after rereadings of the text and readings of word cards that contained words from the story. Children learned and recalled considerably more words in the word card condition (Johnston, 1995).

Iversen and Tunmer (1993) found that the addition of explicit code instruction involving phonograms to the standard Reading Recovery tutorial lesson significantly increased the speed at which children learned to read. A considerable amount of evidence has accumulated in support of a specific type of code instruction, that is, word sorts (Barnes, 1989; Bear, Invernizzi, Templeton, & Johnston, 1996; Invernizzi, 1992; Morris, 1982). In brief, word sorts require children to sort words into categories based on orthographic features (i.e., all the words that start with /m/ or all the words that end in *at*). The increased use of word sorts in our tutorials was implemented in our second year of tutoring, and seems supported by the better results that year.

Our current tutorial lessons are still under scrutiny, although we are increasingly confident of the components. The first part of the lesson, the rereading of familiar books (often predictable text and sometimes build-up readers), concentrates on the development of reading strategies. In particular, at the beginning of the year we stress using initial consonants and context clues to figure out unknown words. The tutor models these strategies for the child. As the year advances we increasingly stress the use of orthographic clues to recognize unknown words.

After the rereadings of familiar texts, word cards are pulled from the back of one or two of the familiar books. The words cards are read by the child. The tutor copies known words on cards and adds them to the child's word bank. Unknown words are matched back to the text. Finally, words in the child's word bank are reviewed and a game played with them (e.g., "Pick up all the words that start with /s/").

Next, a picture sort or word sort occurs. For example, at the beginning of the year pictures may be sorted based on their initial phonemes. Then a child is asked to write the first letter of the words that are pictured. Later in the year, a child will sort words into categories based on their orthographic features, followed by a "writing sort" in which the tutor dictates words that were just sorted and the child writes each word under the correct spelling category (e.g., *at* words are written in a different column than *an* words).

The next activity is called *writing for sounds*. The tutor dictates a sentence or has the child compose a sentence (frequently the sentence is about the familiar books that were previously read in the lesson). A line is drawn on a blank sheet of paper for each word in the sentence. Then the tutor slowly says each word, elongating its sounds, and the child writes the word. The tutor models the process of how to elongate words into their component sounds and connect these sounds to letters. The child is only held accountable for letter sounds that have been taught; thus, invented spellings are accepted.

The last component of each tutoring session is the introduction of a new book. Early in the year the tutor first reads the book to the child; the pair enjoy its content, pictures, and discuss any difficult vocabulary. Then the tutor rereads the book with the child echo reading and pointing to the words. Finally the child reads the book alone. As the child's reading ability improves, the tutor provides less support or scaffolding. The tutor may simply flip through the book initially, stopping to briefly discuss the book's content. The child will then be asked to read the book, with support provided only as needed.

So, what kind of tutoring helps a poor reader? Tutor scaffolding of reading experiences, modeling of reading and writing processes, explicit word study instruction through word sorts and writing, and the very special relationship of caring and trust that can develop in one-on-one tutorials seem to function together to make them successful.

REFERENCES

Adams, M. J. (1990). *Beginning to read: Thinking and learning about print.* Cambridge, MA: MIT Press.
Anderson, L. M. (1989). Classroom instruction. In M. C. Reynolds (Ed.), *Knowledge base for the beginning teacher* (pp. 101–115). New York: Pergamon Press.
Barnes, W. G. (1989). Word sorting: The cultivation of rules for spelling in English. *Reading Psychology, 10,* 293–307.
Bear, D., Invernizzi, M., Templeton, S., & Johnston, F. (1996). *Words their way: Word study for phonics, vocabulary, and spelling instruction.* Boston: Merrill.
Bissex, G. L. (1980). *Gnys at wrk.* Cambridge, MA: Harvard University Press.
Bloom, B. S. (1984). The 2 sigma problem: The search for methods of group instruction as effective as one-to-one tutoring. *Educational Researcher, 13,* 4–16.
Brown, R. (1973). *A first language: The early stages.* Cambridge, MA: Harvard University Press.
Brown, J. I., Bennett, J. M., & Hanna, G. (1981). *The Nelson-Denny Reading Tests, forms E and F.* Chicago: Riverside.
Clay, M. M. (1979). *Stones—the concepts about print test.* Hong Kong: Heinemann.
Clay, M. M. (1985). *The early detection of reading difficulties* (3rd ed.). Portsmouth, NH: Heinemann.
Clay, M. M., & Cazden, C. B. (1992). A Vygotskian interpretation of reading recovery. In C. B. Cazden (Ed.), *Whole language plus* (pp. 114–135). New York: Teachers' College Press.
Clark, H. H., & Clark, E. V. (1977). *Psychology and language.* New York: Harcourt Brace Jovanovich.
Cohen, P., Kulik, J. A., & Kulik, C. (1982). Educational outcomes of tutoring: A meta-analysis of findings. *American Educational Research Journal, 19,* 237–248.
Cunningham, P. M., & Allington, R. L. (1994). *Classrooms that work: They can all read and write.* New York: HarperCollins.
Deford, D. E., Lyons, C. A., & Pinnell, G. S. (Eds.). (1991). *Bridges to literacy: Learning from Reading Recovery.* Portsmouth, NH: Heinemann.
Edwards, P. A. (1991). Fostering early literacy through parent coaching. In E. H. Hiebert (Ed.), *Literacy for a diverse society* (pp. 199–213). New York: Teachers' College Press.
Ehri, L. C. (1991). Development of the ability to read words. In R. Barr, M. Kamil, P. Mosenthal, & P. Pearson (Eds.), *Handbook of reading research* (Vol. II, pp. 383–417). New York: Longman.
Ehri, L. C., & Chun, C. (in press). How alphabetic/phonemic knowledge facilitates text processing in emergent readers. In J. Shimron (Ed.), *Literacy and education.* Cresskill, NJ: Hampton.
Ehri, L. C., & Sweet, J. (1991). Fingerpoint-reading of memorized text: What enables beginners to process the print? *Reading Research Quarterly, 26,* 442–462.
Ehri, L. C., & Wilce, L. S. (1985). Movement into reading: Is the first stage of printed word learning visual or phonetic? *Reading Research Quarterly, 20,* 163–179.
Ehri, L. C., & Wilce, L. S. (1987). Cipher versus cue reading: An experiment in decoding acquisition. *Journal of Educational Psychology, 79,* 3–13.

Ferreiro, E. (1986). The interplay between information and assimilation in beginning literacy. In W. H. Teale & E. Sulzby (Eds.), *Emergent literacy* (pp. 15–49). Norwood, NJ: Ablex.

Ferreiro, E. (1990). Literacy development: Psychogenesis. In Y. M. Goodman (Ed.), *How children construct literacy: Piagetian perspectives* (pp. 12–25). Newark, DE: International Reading Association.

Gaffney, J. S., & Anderson, R. C. (1991). Two-tiered scaffolding: Congruent processes of teaching and learning. In E. H. Hiebert (Ed.), *Literacy for a diverse society* (pp. 184–198). New York: Teachers' College Press.

Gates, A. I., & Boeker, E. (1923). A study of initial stages in reading by preschool children. *Teachers' College Record, 24,* 469–488.

Glass, G., Cahen, L., Smith, M. L., & Filby, N. (1982). *School class size.* Beverly Hills, CA: Sage.

Goldenberg, C. (1994). Promoting early literacy development among Spanish-speaking children. In E. H. Hiebert & B. M. Taylor (Eds.), *Getting reading right from the start* (pp. 171–199). Boston: Allyn & Bacon.

Gough, P. B., & Hillinger, M. L. (1980). Learning to read: An unnatural act. *Bulletin of the Orton Society, 30,* 179–196.

Gough, P. B., & Juel, C. (1991). The first stages of word recognition. In L. Rieben & C. A. Perfetti (Eds.), *Learning to read: Basic research and its implications.* Hillsdale, NJ: Lawrence Erlbaum Associates.

Gough, P. B., Juel, C., & Griffith, P. (1992). Reading, spelling and the orthographic cipher. In P. Gough, L. C. Ehri, & R. Treiman (Eds.), *Reading acquisition* (pp. 35–48). Hillsdale, NJ: Lawrence Erlbaum Associates.

Guszak, F. J. (1985). *Diagnostic reading instruction in the elementary school* (3rd ed.). New York: Harper & Row.

Henderson, E. H. (1990). *Teaching spelling* (2nd ed.). Boston, MA: Houghton Mifflin.

Hiebert, E. (Ed.). (1991). *Literacy for a diverse society.* New York: Teachers' College Press.

Hiebert, E., & Raphael, T. E. (1996). Psychological perspectives on literacy and extensions to educational practice. In D. C. Berliner & R. C. Calfee (Eds.), *Handbook of educational psychology* (pp. 550–602). New York: Macmillan.

Hieronymous, A. N., Lindquist, E. F., & Hoover, H. D. (1983). *Iowa Tests of Basic Skills, levels 7 & 8.* New York: Houghton Mifflin.

Invernizzi, M. (1992). The vowel and what follows: A phonological frame of orthographic analysis. In S. Templeton & D. R. Bear (Eds.), *Development of orthographic knowledge and the foundations of literacy: A memorial festschrift for Edmund H. Henderson* (pp. 105–136). Hillsdale, NJ: Lawrence Erlbaum Associates.

Invernizzi, M., Juel, C., & Rosemary, C. A. (1996/1997). A community volunteer tutorial that works. *The Reading Teacher, 50,* 304–311.

Invernizzi, M., Rosemary, C., Juel, C., & Richards, H. C. (in press). At-risk readers and community volunteers: A three-year perspective. *Scientific Studies in Reading.*

Iversen, S., & Tunmer, W. E. (1993). Phonological processing skills and the Reading Recovery program. *Journal of Educational Psychology, 85,* 112–126.

Johnston, F. (1995). *Enhancing the learning of words when using predictable text.* Doctoral dissertation, University of Virginia.

Johnston, P., & Allington, R. (1991). Remediation. In R. Barr, M. L. Kamil, P. B. Mosenthal, & P. D. Pearson (Eds.), *Handbook of reading research* (Vol. 2, pp. 984–1012). New York: Longman.

Juel, C. (1986). Support for the theory of phonemic awareness as a predictor in literacy acquisition. In J. A. Niles & R. Lalik (Eds.), *Solving problems in literacy: Learners, teachers, and researchers* (pp. 239–243). Rochester, NY: National Reading Conference.

Juel, C. (1988). Learning to read and write: A longitudinal study of fifty-four children from first through fourth grade. *Journal of Educational Psychology, 80,* 437–447.

Juel, C. (1990). Effects of reading group assignment on reading development in first and second grade. *Journal of Reading Behavior, 22,* 233–254.
Juel, C. (1991a). Cross-age tutoring between student-athletes and at-risk children. *The Reading Teacher, 45,* 178–186.
Juel, C. (1991b). Beginning reading. In R. Barr, M. L. Kamil, P. D. Pearson, & P. Mosenthal (Eds.), *Handbook of reading research* (Vol. 2, pp. 759–788). New York: Longman.
Juel, C. (1994). *Learning to read and write in one elementary school.* New York: Springer-Verlag.
Juel, C. (1996). Learning to learn from effective tutors. In L. Schauble & R. Glaser (Eds.), *Innovations in learning: New environments for education* (pp. 49–74). Hillsdale, NJ: Lawrence Erlbaum Associates.
Juel, C. (1996a). What makes literacy tutoring effective? *Reading Research Quarterly, 31,* 268–289.
Juel, C., Griffith, P. L., & Gough, P. B. (1985). Reading and spelling strategies of first grade children. In J. A. Niles & R. Lalik (Eds.), *Issues in literacy: A research perspective* (pp. 306–309). Rochester, NY: National Reading Conference.
Juel, C., Griffith, P. L., & Gough, P. B. (1986). Acquisition of literacy: A longitudinal study of children in first and second grade. *Journal of Educational Psychology, 78,* 243–255.
Juel, C., Invernizzi, M., & Johnston, F. (1994, April). *Alternative learning in first grade: Tutoring by community volunteers.* Paper presented at the meeting of the American Educational Research Association, New Orleans.
Langer, J. A. (1991). Literacy and schooling: A socio-cognitive perspective. In E. H. Hiebert (Ed.), *Literacy for a diverse society* (pp. 9–27). New York: Teachers' College Press.
Liberman, I. Y., & Liberman, A. M. (1992). Whole language versus code emphasis: Underlying assumptions and their implications for reading instruction. *Annals of Dyslexia, 40,* 51–78.
Mason, J. M. (1980). When do children begin to read: An exploration of four-year-old children's letter- and word-reading competencies. *Reading Research Quarterly, 15,* 203–227.
McDermott, R. (1977). Social relations as contexts for learning in school. *Harvard Educational Review, 47,* 198–213.
McGill-Franzen, A. (1992). Early literacy: What does "developmentally appropriate" mean? *The Reading Teacher, 46,* 56–58.
Minarik, E. M. (1957). *Little bear.* New York: Trumpet Club.
Morris, D. (1981). Concept of word. A developmental phenomenon in the beginning reading and writing processes. *Language Arts, 58,* 659–668.
Morris, D. (1982). "Word sort": A categorization strategy for improving word recognition ability. *Reading Psychology, 3,* 247–257.
Morris, D. (1992a). Concept of word: A pivotal understanding in the learning-to-read process. In S. Templeton & D. R. Bear (Eds.), *Development of orthographic knowledge and the foundations of literacy* (pp. 53–77). Hillsdale, NJ: Lawrence Erlbaum Associates.
Morris, D. (1992b). *Case studies in teaching beginning reading.* Boone, NC: Fieldstream.
Nurss, J. R., & McGauvran, M. (1976). *Metropolitan Readiness Tests, level II.* New York: Harcourt, Brace, Jovanovich.
Pinnell, G. S., Lyons, C. A., DeFord, D. E., Bryk, A. S., & Seltzer, M. (1994). Comparing instructional models for the literacy education of high-risk first graders. *Reading Research Quarterly, 29,* 9–39.
Rogoff, B., & Garner, W. (1984). Adult guidance of cognitive development. In B. Rogoff & J. Lane (Eds.), *Everyday cognition: Its development and social context* (pp. 95–116). Cambridge, MA: Harvard University Press.
Rosemary, C. A. (1995). *Coming to school, ready or not: An ethnographic study of the ecological factors that influence the early school experiences of six children from low-income families.* Doctoral dissertation, University of Virginia.

San Diego Unified School District, Planning, Research and Evaluation Division. (1992). *Review of data concerning the reading recovery, turning point, and Hispanic reading programs* (ED344189). San Diego, CA: Author.

Share, D. L., Jorm, A. F., Maclean, R., & Matthews, R. (1984). Sources of individual differences in reading achievement. *Journal of Educational Psychology, 76,* 1309–1324.

Söderbergh, R. (1977). *Reading in early childhood: A linguistic study of a preschool child's gradual acquisition of reading ability.* Washington, DC: Georgetown University Press.

Spache, G. D. (1981). *Diagnostic Reading Scales.* Monterey, CA: CTB/McGraw-Hill.

Treiman, R. (1992). The role of intrasyllabic units in learning to read and spell. In P. B. Gough, L. C. Ehri, & R. Treiman (Eds.), *Reading acquisition* (pp. 65–106). Hillsdale, NJ: Lawrence Erlbaum Associates.

Vygotsky, L. S. (1978). *Mind in society.* Cambridge, MA: MIT Press.

Wasik, B. A., & Slavin, R. E. (1993). Preventing early reading failure with one-to-one tutoring: A review of five programs. *Reading Research Quarterly, 28,* 179–200.

Wertsch, J. V. (1984). The zone of proximal development: Some conceptual issues. In B. Rogoff & J. V. Wertsch (Eds.), *Children's learning in the zone of proximal development* (pp. 7–18). San Francisco, CA: Jossey-Bass.

Wildsmith, B. (1982). *Cat on the mat.* Oxford, England: Oxford University Press.

Wood, D., Bruner, J. S., & Ross, G. (1976). The role of tutoring in problem solving. *Journal of Child Psychology and Psychiatry, 17,* 89–100.

Chapter 25

Studies of Computer-Aided Remediation for Reading Disabilities

Barbara W. Wise
Richard K. Olson
University of Colorado

Research from around the world reported in this volume confirms that the primary deficit in specific reading disability is in printed word recognition, caused mainly by underlying deficits in analytic language skills of phoneme awareness (reflecting on sounds within a syllable) and phonological decoding (translating print to sound). Phoneme awareness manifests in the ability to analyze and manipulate sounds within syllables (e.g., to count, delete, and reorder them). It is the strongest predictor of reading progress (Stanovich, Cunningham, & Feeman, 1984), it correlates with reading ability across grade levels (Calfee, Lindamood, & Lindamood, 1973), and it is the major cause of problems in phonological decoding (Wagner, Torgesen, & Rashotte, 1994). Group deficits in phoneme awareness and phonological decoding may have a neuropsychological basis (Hynd & Semrud-Clikeman, 1989; Larsen, Hoien, Lundberg, & Odegaard, 1989) and a significant genetic etiology (Olson, Forsberg, & Wise, 1994). Yet research suggests that they can be remedied with methods specifically designed to address them (Alexander, Anderson, Voeller, & Torgesen, 1991; Brady, Fowler, Stone, & Winbury, 1994; Kennedy & Backman, 1993; Truch, 1994; Wise, 1991; Wise & Olson, 1995).

In the last decade at the University of Colorado, we have developed and studied computer-based remediation focusing specifically on dealing with the previously mentioned deficits. Our Reading with Orthographic and Speech Segmentation (ROSS) programs use microcomputers equipped with high-quality synthetic speech (DECtalk; Wise & Olson,

1994a). Children read stories on the computer, gaining speech feedback and decoding assistance for any difficult word. Whenever children ask for help on a word by targeting it with a mouse, the program highlights and subsequently pronounces it, either as a whole, in syllables, or in subsyllable segments.

This chapter provides an overview of the research with the talking computers. The opening sections describe early studies of word segments, first in short-term studies with isolated words and then in long-term school studies with ROSS. The next section describes a study using spelling exploration with speech feedback for the development of phonological decoding. The following section covers a study using these programs in a home setting. The final review section presents the methods and results of our recent school studies that included computer-supported phonological-awareness training prior to, and in conjunction with, reading with the talking computers. The chapter closes with ideas for future research.

STUDIES OF WORD SEGMENTATION ON THE COMPUTER

Short-term training studies focused on different ways of segmenting orthographic and speech feedback for first and second graders' learning of words presented on the computer. One study compared two ways of segmenting syllables into subsyllable units (Wise, Olson, & Treiman, 1990) to see whether either would prove easier to blend and to remember than the other. An onset-rime segmentation condition divided syllables between the initial consonant cluster and the vowel-consonant group (e.g., *d/ish*, *cl/ap*), whereas a postvocalic split divided the syllable immediately following the vowel (e.g., *di/sh*, *cla/p*). Treiman (1983) showed that onset-rime units were easier than units based on postvocalic divisions for adults and children to use in spoken language. We hypothesized that these segments would also be more helpful in feedback for learning to read words. In three variations of an experiment, 40 first graders learned lists of 24 four-letter words more easily when the words were divided at the onset-rime boundary than when they were divided after the vowel.

Subsequently we compared 56 first and 56 second graders' short-term word learning of isolated words from feedback presented at four levels of segmentation: whole word (e.g., *reader*); *boss* type syllables (e.g., *read/er*; Taft, 1979); onset-rime subsyllables (e.g., *r/ead/er*); and grapheme phoneme units (e.g., *r/ea/d/er*; Wise, 1992). All conditions except grapheme–phoneme feedback were effective aids to short-term isolated word learning; thus, this condition was excluded from the long-term training studies, in which students decoded words in the context of meaningful stories.

READING WITH ORTHOGRAPHIC AND SPEECH SEGMENTATION (ROSS)

The first ROSS studies aimed to learn whether talking computers could provide a powerful remedial tool by providing speech feedback for difficult words while students read stories of interest to them. A second goal of the research was to learn whether different students would benefit more or less from ROSS depending on the type of segmentation in the orthographic and speech feedback for targeted words. Three different segmentation conditions included whole-word feedback, syllable feedback (based primarily on phonological considerations; e.g., *gar/den, plant/ing*; Spoehr & Smith, 1973), and onset-rime units as described in the previous paragraph (e.g., *pl/ant/ing*).

With ROSS, students read stories of interest to them. When a student targeted a word, the computer first highlighted it sequentially in segments. About every 10 pages, at convenient breaks in the stories, a multiple-choice comprehension question was presented. (In later versions of ROSS, if a child missed a comprehension question, the program highlighted the appropriate section in the story, reading it aloud if requested.) After the comprehension check, five targeted words appeared individually on the screen for review. Subjects scored themselves as correct or incorrect on independent days. When monitoring the child, the trainer scored their responses. In later versions of the program, all word checks were moved to the end of the session, to cause less disruption in reading the story.

Over five semesters of training, 138 second- to sixth-grade children with reading disabilities were randomly assigned to read with one of the feedback conditions or to be included in an untrained control group that continued instead with their usual reading program provided by the school. Children were pulled from their regularly scheduled language arts or reading instructional time to read for 30 minutes, 3 to 4 days per week on the computer. There were two computers present in a room, which had some adult nearby every day. Often the computers were placed in the school library, the computer lab, or a resource room. A trainer pretested the children and trained them to use the computers appropriately, targeting any word with which they had difficulty. After the first 2 weeks of training and testing, the trainer came to read with the children on 1 day per computer, and the children read independently on the other days. Thus, the trainer actually involved with the study was present in the room only 2 days per week.

Post-testing followed an average of 28 half-hour training sessions over a semester. Trained groups gained twice as much as control groups on word recognition (average of .6 vs. .3 grade levels) and four times as much on phonological decoding (average of 9.4 percentage points vs. 2.5 percentage points). Average gains did not differ significantly across the three segmentation conditions. Children also improved in attitude about reading from working with the programs.

In these studies, gains were similar whether feedback was whole or segmented (Olson & Wise, 1992). Apparently, ROSS subjects improved because they read more, and more accurately, than control children in class. The similar gains for the different segment types does not deny the importance of learning subword letter–sound associations (cf. Lovett et al., in press). It shows only that segmenting targeted words in story reading, without extra training or repetition, does not aid poor readers more than whole-word feedback.

A particularly important result in the early ROSS studies related to children's initial level of phoneme awareness, as measured by a phoneme deletion task. Across all conditions, pretest phoneme deletion skill correlated significantly with gains in phonological decoding and word recognition (Olson & Wise, 1992). Although trained students were generally low in this skill, subjects above the group mean in initial phoneme-awareness level averaged twice the gains in word recognition and phonological decoding compared to those below the mean. Thus, those children with the lowest phoneme awareness were not benefiting as well from the programs as we would have hoped.

SPELLING EXPLORATION PROGRAMS

There is much evidence that guided practice in spelling can significantly improve phonological decoding and phonological awareness (Ehri & Wilce, 1987; Uhry & Shepherd, 1993). Foorman, Francis, Novy, and Liberman (1991) reported that first graders' gains from the beginning to the end of the year in phonological awareness were linked to their gains in spelling but not word recognition.

We developed a spelling exploration program called Spello that took advantage of text-to-speech technology (Wise & Olson, 1992). Computers with synthetic speech can pronounce not only the correct word to be spelled, but can also pronounce any attempt of the student's. We conducted a short-term training study to examine benefits from spelling manipulations with synthetic speech to see whether continuously available speech feedback for correct or erroneous attempts would lead to benefits in learning phonological decoding. In the Spello program, the computer pronounced a word to spell. In the interactive speech version, the speech synthesizer pronounced any attempt typed in by students, so they could compare the sounds of spelling patterns as they changed letters, as in *bak* to *bake*. They could also request spelling feedback to learn which of their letters were in the correct word, and which were correctly placed. We compared this to a version that gave only orthographic feedback, but that could pronounce only the correct item, as a program with recorded or digitized speech could do.

Twenty-eight children in a summer clinic for students with reading disabilities participated in the study (Wise & Olson, 1992). All students scored at least 1 year behind national norms on the Wide Range Achievement Tests of Spelling (WRAT; Jastak, & Jastak, 1978), and all but three scored at least 1 year behind on the WRAT in reading. In Boulder, most average students score at least 1½ grades above national norms on these tests. Items from both the reading and the spelling tests of the WRAT were administered first as spelling and then as reading tests. A nonsense word reading test was constructed with items that shared rimes with single-syllable items (e.g., *edge, medge*) and shared syllables with multisyllable items (e.g., *collapse, unlapse*). The students studied 32 words each session, 16 that they had missed on the pretest and 16 that shared structure with the trained words (e.g., *edge, ledge*). Students spent one session learning their 32 words with interactive speech feedback and orthographic feedback for errors, and spent the other session learning another 32 words with orthographic feedback for errors but speech feedback only for the correct item. The results suggested that with speech feedback for errors, subjects showed greater gains than without speech feedback in phonological decoding of nonwords that were related in structure to the trained words.

HOME STUDY OF SEGMENTED AND WHOLE-WORD FEEDBACK

One recurring problem in the ROSS school reading studies had been limited training time, due to assemblies, field trips, achievement testing, and the difficulty of scheduling much time pulled out of class. In order to obtain more training hours, we decided to try a home setting. We hypothesized that with longer training, any unique benefits of segmented feedback might become evident, particularly for gains in phonological decoding. We also wanted to see if the previous school study's correlation between subjects' initial phoneme awareness and gains in phonological decoding and word recognition would replicate over a longer training time. Finally, we wanted to see if placing the computers in the twins' homes was practical and useful.

The 33 subjects who completed the study were twins who were initially tested in the Colorado Twin Study. Both twins were at least one standard deviation below the normal control-group mean on both word recognition and phonological decoding. Their average age was 10.3 years. Subjects were pretested on reading and language measures, including word recognition, phonological decoding, and spelling. The twin pairs were then semi-randomly assigned to the two feedback conditions (both members of a pair in the same condition), with the constraints that the feedback groups were initially balanced in age, word recognition, phonological decoding, and phoneme awareness.

Following pretesting, trainers worked with the children in their homes for five consecutive 45-minute sessions to ensure the subjects' understanding of the training conditions and their sensitivity to decoding errors while reading on ROSS. They continued reading independently in 3 to 5 sessions per week for an average of 3 hours weekly time. The trainer subsequently visited each pair of twins once a week to back up behavioral data from the ROSS program, to encourage the children, to monitor their reading and targeting behavior, and to raise or lower the difficulty level of their story directories. When the children had reached a total of 60 training hours, they were post-tested on the same measures they had as pretests.

Fourteen twins completed the 60 hours of whole-word training, and 19 completed the segmented training. Three twin pairs dropped out of the whole-word feedback condition. One twin did not complete the segmented feedback condition, which used onset-rime units for one-syllable words and syllabic feedback for multisyllable words.

Overall, we were pleased with the children's use of the computers in the home, and questionnaire data from both the children and the parents indicated a high level of satisfaction. However, we were disappointed by two main results. First, the favored hypothesis that the segmented feedback group would show greater gains in phonological decoding and word recognition was not confirmed. The group means were quite similar and the contrasts were not significant for a number of individual measures as well as combined measures. For example, the average percentage-point gains across two lists of nonwords were 11 for the whole-word group and 12.4 for the segmentation group.

The second disappointing result was that the nonword gains were not much different from the 9.4 percentage-point gains averaged across segmentation conditions in the previous school study with only 14 hours reading on ROSS. Similarly, the grade-level gains in PIAT word recognition of .83 for the segmentation group and .85 for the whole-word group were not much greater than the .64 grade-level gain in the previous school study. Grade-level gains in PIAT comprehension were .94 and .95, respectively. Even though the children and families were generally pleased with the results and the children seemed to have greater confidence in their reading skills, we had hoped for greater objectively measured improvement considering the much greater time on ROSS. Subjects' initial scores on a phoneme deletion test and phonological decoding (nonword) gains again correlated significantly with gains, after partialing on age and initial pretest scores.

PHONOLOGICAL AWARENESS TRAINING WITH ROSS

These results in both the school and home settings motivated us to try to improve children's phonological awareness with special exercises before and during reading with ROSS (Wise & Olson, 1995). Several well-designed studies with unselected populations of young children have confirmed that training phoneme awareness prior to or at the onset of early reading instruction improves later reading and spelling. Working on phoneme awareness solely in oral language can improve later reading and spelling (Lundberg, Frost, & Peterson, 1988). Not surprisingly, effects are much stronger when phoneme-awareness training is linked with letter–sound associations and merged with reading and spelling instruction to improve phonological awareness (Ball & Blachman, 1991; Bradley & Bryant, 1983; Byrne & Fielding-Barnsley, 1991, 1993; Cunningham, 1989; Uhry & Shepherd, 1993).

Three recent studies trained phonological awareness in children with reading disabilities using the Lindamood Auditory Discrimination in Depth program (ADD; Lindamood & Lindamood, 1975), a method that first encourages awareness of the articulation of speech sounds. Two studies used no control groups, but reported good progress for students who had made little progress with other programs (Alexander et al., 1991; Truch, 1994). The third study used matched groups ($n = 9$ each) of children with severe reading disability at a private school (Kennedy & Blackman, 1993). The control group received the school's well-reputed program, which included auditory training and strategies for encoding and decoding written symbols. The trained group spent 6 weeks learning ADD before merging it with the regular program. All children improved substantially by the end of the year. The ADD group did not gain significantly more than controls on standardized tests of reading and spelling, although trends favored the ADD group. Compared to controls, ADD children did make significantly greater improvement in the phonetic quality of their errors in spelling and nonsense word reading.

Besides being a well-structured phonemic-awareness program, the ADD approach holds theoretical interest because of its strong emphasis on developing concrete articulatory (speech-motor) representations to distinguish phonemic differences. The program includes associating articulatory labels, pictures, letters, and sounds, and using these articulatory concepts in phonological awareness work and manipulating letters and sounds in reading and spelling exercises.

Most children with reading disabilities falter in several basic phonological processes, such as articulatory awareness (Montgomery, 1981), short-term memory, lexical access, and articulatory speed and clarity (Snowling & Hulme, 1994; Wagner et al., 1994). Snowling and Hulme discussed how all these deficits may result from an underlying phonological representation that is somehow degraded or indistinct, making precise awareness of phonemes difficult and hindering all phonological processing. In fact, Snowling and Hulme believed that the low-level degraded representations are actually the root of reading and spelling problems, rather than the higher level metacognitive skill of phoneme awareness.

In examining the ADD program for our own purposes, we reanalyzed some unpublished data from a California first-grade training study run by the Lindamood–Bell Center. We wanted to look at the children most at risk for reading problems in this study (Wise, Olson, & Lindamood, 1993). A control class there had received the Ginn basal reading program, whereas an experimental class spent 4 months learning ADD before integrating it with the Ginn program. The at-risk lower 10% of children (based on pretest abilities in word recognition, spelling, and phoneme awareness) gained differently in the two classes. In the ADD class, at-risk children gained at least as much as better readers on reading and spelling, and more in nonsense word reading (phonological decoding). In contrast, at-risk children in the control classroom made the least progress on all measures.

We decided, therefore, to use a portion of ADD training as part of phonemic and phonological awareness training prior to and concurrent with ROSS reading (Wise & Olson, 1995). The aims of the study were to see whether phonological awareness training could be supported with computerized practice, and to see whether the correlation between initial phoneme awareness and reading progress in previous ROSS studies could be overcome. That is, would reading-disabled children with initially the lowest phonological awareness make gains as large as children with reading disabilities who had relatively higher phoneme awareness?

The trained control method was chosen because of another problem evident in previous ROSS studies, one of error detection. Although students had readily targeted words when they knew they needed help, extensive training had been needed to help them detect their errors (Wise & Olson, 1994a). ADD encourages detecting errors with a bottom-up, phonological awareness (PA) approach, in which students who have learned to associate mouth movements with letters will then notice when their mouth movements don't match the print on the page. The comparison training condition we chose was based on reciprocal teaching (RT; Palincsar & Brown, 1984). RT improves self-monitoring and error detection with top-down comprehension strategies, so that students notice when they lose clarity about what is going on in the text. Both methods are highly motivating and use a discovery, or teaching-by-questioning, approach. We hoped both experimental ADD and comparison RT methods would improve performance with ROSS, but in different component skills of reading.

We attempted to make small-group instruction equally interesting, motivating, and social in both conditions. Both groups received equal time in small-group and individualized computer instruction. However, an important, and planned, difference between the conditions was that PA children spent half their computer time in analytic PA exercises, and half reading stories with ROSS, using PA and decoding skills in context. The RT children, on the other hand, spent all their computer time reading stories on ROSS and had twice as much print exposure in this context as did the PA group.

Reciprocal teaching emphasizes trading teacher and student roles, with the teacher first modeling and students later leading discussions using the four comprehension strategies of prediction, question generating, clarifying, and summarizing. By taking over the role of teacher in a guided manner, students learn to monitor their own comprehension and evaluate what they need to do to maintain good comprehension. The RT and PA groups received equal time in small-group and individualized computer instruction, with each group receiving fourteen 30-minute group sessions, interspersed with individualized practice on the computer. In the RT group, trainers defined, discussed, and practiced the strategies with students using cartoons, stories read as a group with books and with ROSS, and stories read individually with ROSS. Every third day, the trainer and student read on ROSS together. They traded roles (using a wooden apple, as they had in the small groups, to designate who was taking the leader role), while trainers also monitored progress. On the two other days, children were encouraged to use the RT strategies independently while reading with ROSS.

The phonological awareness (PA) training began with speech-motor phoneme-awareness training in fourteen 30-minute small-group sessions based on the ADD method with its discovery approach (Lindamood & Lindamood, 1975). The first small-group sessions were interspersed with practice on computer programs in which students matched letters, sounds, and articulatory labels with animated mouth pictures for consonants and vowels with programs under development at the Lindamood–Bell Center.

As soon as consonant and vowel articulatory labels were learned with 80% accuracy, the PA students assembled and manipulated appropriate mouth pictures to represent syllables in two group sessions. They then proceeded with phonological decoding with talking-computer programs with DECtalk developed in Colorado. The first program let students manipulate letters and sounds in syllables. The program pronounced an item, and the child selected and ordered letter symbols with a mouse to match the item. For example, the computer would say, "Show me /iv/." Synthetic speech pronounced whatever the child assembled, and the child kept working until his or her string matched what the computer said. Next the computer would say, "If that is /iv/, show me /oov/," and the student inserted, deleted, or reordered sounds as needed. This program began with eight-item sets of consonant-vowel (CV) patterns, and advanced to more complex sets (up to CCCVCC) after 80% correct on two files in a row, or moved back for scores below 60%. Students could use mirrors to see their own mouth actions to help them construct the correct string.

Students also began two nonword reading programs at this point. One was developed at the University of Colorado. In it, students selected one of four printed nonwords to match what the computer pronounced. The items increased in difficulty, from CV items up to three-syllable nonwords. Each practice set contained eight items with three distractors a piece (e.g., <u>klem</u>, <u>kelm</u>, <u>klam</u>, <u>kloom</u>). The program changed levels based on performance. The other nonsense word program was developed by Lindamood–Bell Learning Processes. Students decided whether an animated mouth pronounced the nonsense word appearing on the screen, or analyzed how the pronunciation differed, in terms of additions, deletions, substitutions, or order changes. The program was lively and quite motivating. The trainer reassigned difficulty levels as the student improved.

The final PA program was Spello, described earlier in this chapter (Wise & Olson, 1992). This version of Spello was similar to the previous one in that it had interactive speech comparison of the correct word and the child's spelling attempts, as well as orthographic feedback up to three times. However, this version had the children study prescribed lists of real words that ranged from simple to complex and emphasized different spelling patterns, such as silent *e* or final *-le* syllables. The program changed students' levels as in all the Colorado PA programs, individualized by performance, moving children up or down in complexity depending on their accuracy with the programs. When students achieved 80% competence manipulating letter symbols and sounds in CVC patterns they began spending about half their time on ROSS reading and half on the phonological exercises.

Subjects included 103 second to fifth graders from the Boulder Valley Schools, recommended by teachers to be in the lower 10% on reading ability and screened and selected by us for low word recognition and verbal or performance IQ estimates of 90 or above. Students were assigned by age in sets of three (Wise & Olson, 1995). Sets were balanced on age, word recognition, and nonsense word reading, and randomly assigned to condition. Training groups did not differ on pretest measures. They also did not differ in the severity of their deficit, calculated as a ratio of PIAT word recognition pretest score over expected grade level (RT = .77, PA =

.75). Although a national ratio would be expected to be 1, the average ratio in the Boulder schools is about 1.25.

All subjects completed 7 hours group instruction in PA or RT. The RT group completed 18 more hours reading stories with ROSS, practicing their RT strategies individually and using the colors to help them sound out targeted words and obtain speech feedback. The PA children's computer time included almost 10 hours on PA exercises, and 8.4 hours applying PA strategies for difficult words while reading stories with ROSS.

The strategies practiced by the groups were designed to aid different component skills of reading, and the pattern of gains across the measures shows that they did that. The PA training was designed to help the children become at first very analytic and careful in decoding (print to sound) and encoding (sound to print). The hope was that these skills would become faster with practice with ROSS. When comparing gains, one must remember that PA children spent all their 7 small-group hours and more than half of their 18 computer hours on speech awareness and phonological decoding and encoding in analytic reading and spelling exercises. RT children, on the other hand, spent all their 18 individualized computer hours reading with speech and segmentation feedback in context. Even in the 7 small-group hours, RT children spent much of that time reading in context either in books or on the computer. The question is which type of work led to greater gains in which aspects of reading.

After one semester of training, the PA group gained more than the RT group on all tests of phoneme awareness and nonsense word reading, showing clear benefits for this kind of training for children with reading disabilities. The PA students showed significant advantages on all untimed tests of words studied, whether daily, monthly, or at the end of a semester. They showed a trend of an advantage on an untimed standardized test of word recognition, yet they performed worse than the RT children on a time-limited test of word recognition. The PA children's significantly more improved decoding skill apparently led to greater accuracy, but slower responses with difficult words, after one semester's training time. Children with training in reciprocal teaching performed better on comprehension, but only while reading with a trainer.

An encouraging result of this study was in the correlations with phoneme awareness. Initial phoneme awareness correlated with gains in phonological decoding and word recognition for the RT children, whose training was most like the earlier ROSS studies. However, in the PA group the correlation did not hold; children with initially low phoneme awareness gained as much as the children who began with relatively higher skills. This lack of correlation with initial phoneme awareness is encouraging for the possibility of negating "Matthew" effects, by which children with the lowest initial skills usually tend to get further and further behind in reading (Stanovich, 1986).

This study confirmed that phoneme awareness can be significantly benefited by PA training, as demonstrated by gains in a tape-recorded phoneme deletion task that bore little or no resemblance to any training tasks. The results confirm that the low phoneme awareness of children with reading disabilities can be significantly boosted with this type of training. Children with PA training gained strongly and significantly more in all three tests of phonological decoding (nonword reading), whether analyzed separately or together. This result was expected from the commonly found correlations between phoneme awareness and nonword reading. Thus, the PA children did benefit from their extensive training in reading nonwords and in manipulating sounds in phonological exercises.

In previous ROSS studies, children's initial phoneme awareness correlated with gains in word recognition and phonological decoding. This relation held in the RT condition, the one most like our previous studies, but not in the PA group. Children with initially lower phoneme awareness gained as much as the higher children with the PA training.

RT children comprehended better, but only while reading with the trainer. This suggests that the children's use of RT strategies was effective while trainers were there, but did not transfer to independent reading. There were no significant differences on comprehension on independent ROSS days, nor in end-of-semester gains on standardized tests of comprehension. A study in one of the schools found a significant advantage for the RT group in the ability to summarize a passage, again while reading with a trainer (Johnson, Wise, & Olson, 1994). In future, we will modify the structure of RT to encourage more use of the strategies in independent reading, by having students justify their use of strategies and record their use on independent days. Groups gained similarly on spelling, as in Kennedy and Backman (1993). Previous analyses of Spello indicated gains in phonological decoding and not in spelling (Wise & Olson, 1992); Spello included neither the memorization nor writing of specific word spellings that lead to gains in spelling (Wise & Olson, 1994b).

A comparison of the number of words targeted on independent compared to monitored days indicated that PA children detected recognition errors better than RT children. However, even the PA group targeted only 69% as much when reading independently as when reading with a trainer. This shows that many students were still misreading many words without correcting them in independent reading, which makes maintenance of gains uncertain without further training.

Follow-up testing was conducted on the 57 students of the PA/RT school study who were still in their elementary school 9 months after post-testing (Olson, Wise, Ring, & Johnson, in press). The PA students maintained a strong and significant advantage in phonological coding, even without further training. The group also maintained an advantage in phoneme deletion, significant in growth curve analyses. However, the groups had evened out in word recognition, and no differences remained on tests of word recognition, timed or untimed, after 1 year. The hypothesis is that with more training time, students can be brought to a higher level of error detection so that their decoding advantage will translate into stronger and more stable gains in word recognition.

It is important to note that children in *both* PA and RT groups improved significantly and impressively in word recognition and phonological decoding. In our previous one-semester school studies with ROSS, trained children averaged gains of .64 grade levels in PIAT word recognition (compared to .33 for untrained controls), 9.4 percentage points in phonological decoding (compared to 2.5 percentage points for untrained controls; Olson & Wise, 1992). Students in the most recent study gained about 1 year in PIAT word recognition and 15 (RT) or 27 (PA) percentage points in phonological decoding. The greater gains may have been partly due to improved attendance and more supervision, leading to more hours of reading with trainers present every day.

FUTURE RESEARCH

The most recent school study indicated clear benefits of training in phonological awareness, especially for children with initially lowest phoneme awareness. Our phonological awareness training included articulatory awareness as well as manipulation of sounds and symbols in real and nonsense words with computer-speech feedback. It is important to know if there are specific benefits of systematic training in articulatory concepts as part of phoneme-awareness training, beyond what good phonological awareness training can include with teaching letter–sound associations followed by exercises in manipulation, segmentation, and blending. Other studies have shown strong gains without systematic work on articulatory concepts (Ball & Blachman, 1991; Uhry & Shepherd, 1993), yet the studies of Truch (1994) and Alexander et al. (1991) suggest there may be special benefits for children with severe deficits from the articulatory training. The question holds theoretical significance, if articulatory awareness is particularly suited to improve underlying degraded phonological representations. It holds practical significance as well, as letter–sound-based phoneme awareness training requires less extensive training of teachers. Our computerized system is well-suited to studying this question of differential benefits from training with and without articulatory concepts, and future research is aimed at answering this question.

REFERENCES

Alexander, A., Anderson, H., Voeller, K., & Torgesen, J. (1991). Phonological awareness training and remediation of analytic coding deficits in a group of severe dyslexics. *Annals of Dyslexia, 31,* 193–207.

Ball, E., & Blachman, B. A. (1991). Does phoneme awareness training in kindergarten make a difference in early word recognition and developmental spelling? *Reading Research Quarterly, 26,* 49–66.

Bradley, L., & Bryant, P. (1983). Categorizing sounds and learning to read: A causal connection. *Nature, 301,* 419–421.

Brady, S., Fowler, A., Stone, B., & Winbury, N. (1994). Training phonological awareness: A study with inner-city kindergarten children. *Annals of Dyslexia, 24,* 26–59.

Byrne, B., & Fielding-Barnsley, R. (1991). Evaluation of a program to teach phoneme awareness to young children. *Journal of Educational Psychology, 83,* 451–455.

Byrne, B., & Fielding-Barnsley, R. (1993). Evaluation of a program to teach phoneme awareness to young children: A 1-year follow-up. *Journal of Educational Psychology, 85,* 104–111.

Calfee, R., Lindamood, P., & Lindamood, C. (1973). Acoustic-phonetic skills and reading: Kindergarten through twelfth grade. *Journal of Educational Psychology, 64,* 293–298.

Cunningham, A. (1989). Phonemic awareness: The development of early reading competency. *Reading Research Quarterly, 24,* 471–472.

Ehri, L. C., & Wilce, L. S. (1987). Does learning to spell help beginners learn to read words? *Reading Research Quarterly, 20,* 12–26.

Foorman, B., Francis, D., Novy, A., & Liberman, D. (1991). How letter-sound instruction mediates progress in first-grade reading and spelling. *Journal of Educational Psychology, 83,* 456–469.

Hewison, J., & Tizard, J. (1980). Parental involvement and reading attainment. *British Journal of Educational Psychology, 50,* 209–215.

Hynd, G., & Semrud-Clikeman, M. (1989). Dyslexia and brain morphology. *Psychological Bulletin, 24,* 447–482.

Jastak, J., & Jastak, S. (1978). *The Wide Range Achievement Test–Revised.* Wilmington, DE: Jastak Associates.

Johnson, M., Wise, B., & Olson, R. (1994, November). *Text comprehension in reading-disabled second to fifth graders: Phonological analysis versus reciprocal teaching.* Paper presented at the annual meeting of the Psychonomics Society, St. Louis, MO.

Kennedy, K. M., & Backman, J. (1993). Effectiveness of the Lindamood Auditory Discrimination in Depth program with students with learning disabilities. *Learning Disabilities Research and Practice, 8,* 253–259.

Larsen, J., Hoien, T., Lundberg, I., & Odegaard, H. (1989). *MRI evaluation of the size and symmetry of the planum temporale in adolescents with developmental dyslexia.* Stavanger, Norway: Center for Reading Research.

Lindamood, C., & Lindamood, P. (1975). *Auditory discrimination in depth.* Columbus, OH: Science Research Associates Division, Macmillan/McGraw-Hill.

Lovett, M., Borden, S., DeLuca, T., Lacerenza, L., Benson, N., & Brackstone. (in press). Treating the core deficits of developmental dyslexia: Evidence of transfer-of-learning following strategy and phonologically-based reading training programs. *Developmental Psychology.*

Lundberg, I., Frost, J., & Peterson, O. (1988). Effects of an extensive program for stimulating phonological awareness. *Reading Research Quarterly, 23,* 263–284.

Montgomery, D. (1981). Do dyslexics have difficulty accessing articulatory information? *Psychological Research, 43,* 235–243.

Olson, R. K., Forsberg, H., & Wise, B. W. (1994). Genes, environment, and the development of orthographic skills. In V. Berninger (Ed.), *The varieties of orthographic knowledge I.* Dordrecht, The Netherlands: Kluwer.

Olson, R. K., Wise, B. W., Ring, J., & Johnson, M. (in press). Computer-based remedial training in phoneme awareness and phonological decoding: Effects on the post-training development of word recognition. *Scientific Studies of Reading.*

Olson, R. K., & Wise, B. W. (1992). Reading on the computer with orthographic and speech feedback. *Reading and Writing, 4,* 107–144.

Palincsar, A. S., & Brown, A. L. (1984). Reciprocal teaching of comprehension-fostering and comprehension-monitoring activity. *Cognition and Instruction, 2,* 117–175.

Snowling, M., & Hulme, C. (1994). The development of phonological skills. *Philosophical Transactions of the Royal Society of London, B, 346,* 21–27.

Spoehr, K. T., & Smith, E. E. (1973). The role of syllables in perceptual processes. *Cognitive Psychology, 5,* 71–89.

Stanovich, K. (1986). Matthew effects in reading: Some consequences of individual differences in acquisition of literacy. *Remedial and Special Education, 5,* 11–19.

Stanovich, K., Cunningham, A., & Feeman, D. (1984). Intelligence, cognitive skills and early reading progress. *Reading Research Quarterly, 19,* 278–303.

Taft, M. (1979). Lexical access via an orthographic code: The Basic Orthographic Syllabic Structure (BOSS). *Journal of Verbal Learning and Verbal Behavior, 18,* 21–39.

Treiman, R. (1983). The structure of spoken syllables: Evidence from novel word games. *Cognition, 15,* 49–74.

Truch, S. (1994). Stimulating basic reading processes using Auditory Discrimination in Depth. *Annals of Dyslexia, 24,* 60–81.

Uhry, J., & Shepherd, M. (1993). Segmentation/spelling instruction as part of a first-grade reading program: Effects on several measures of reading. *Reading Research Quarterly, 28,* 218–233.

Wagner, R., Torgesen, J., & Rashotte, C. (1994). The development of reading related phonological processing abilities: New evidence of bi-directional causality from a latent variable longitudinal study. *Developmental Psychology, 30,* 73–87.

Wise, B. (1991). What reading disabled children need: What is known and how to talk about it. *Learning and Individual Differences, 3,* 307–321.

Wise, B. W. (1992). Whole words versus phonics for short-term learning: Comparisons on a talking-computer system. *Journal of Experimental Child Psychology, 54,* 147–167.

Wise, B. W., & Olson, R. K. (1992). Spelling exploration with a talking computer improves phonological coding. *Reading and Writing, 4,* 145–156.

Wise, B. W., & Olson, R. K. (1994a). Computer speech and the remediation of reading and spelling problems. *Journal of Special Education Technology, 12,* 207–220.

Wise, B., & Olson, R. (1994b). Using computers to teach spelling to children with learning disabilities. In D. Brown & N. Ellis (Eds.), *Handbook of spelling: Theory, process, and intervention.* Chichester, England: Wiley.

Wise, B., & Olson, R. K. (1995). Computer-based phonological awareness and reading instruction. *Annals of Dyslexia, 45,* 99–122.

Wise, B. W., Olson, R. K., & Lindamood, P. (1993, April). *Training phonemic awareness: Why and how in computerized instruction.* Paper presented at the annual meeting of the American Educational Research Association, Atlanta, GA.

Wise, B. W., Olson, R. K., & Treiman, R. (1990). Subsyllabic units as aids in beginning readers' word learning: Onset-rime versus post-vowel segmentation. *Journal of Experimental Child Psychology, 49,* 1–19.

Author Index

A

Aaron, P. G., 320, 322, 323, 325, *325*, 326
Abrahamsen, A. A., 241, *257*
Abramson, A. S., 378, *392*
Ackerman, B. P., 353, *365*
Adams, M. J., 33, 35, 36, 37, 41, 42, 43, 44, 50, 54, 62, *63*, 87, *109*, 113, 114, *124*, 142, *148*, 158, 160, *168*, 227, *232*, 426, *430*, 450, *468*
Alegria, J., 70, *85*, 129, 134, *149*, *151*, 154, 157, *168*, *171*, 265, 272, 273, 276, 279, 281, *283*, *284*, *285*, 288, *300*, *301*
Alexander, A., 473, 479, 485, *486*
Alford, J. A. Jr., 21, *31*, 182, *199*
Allington, R. L., 451, 465, *468*
Alvarez, C. J. 144, *149*
Anderson, H., 473, *486*
Anderson, J. R., 239, *257*
Anderson, L. M., 289, 294, *300*, 455, *468*
Anderson, R. C., 72, *84*, 359, *365*, 456, *469*
Andrews, S., 75, *83*
Angell, A. L., 159, *173*
Antonak, R. F., 158, *170*
Applebee, A. N., 348, *365*
Archer, R., 305, *315*
Aslin, R. N., 250, *257*
Assink, E., 408, *417*
Atkins, P., 21, *31*, 144, *149*, 183, *198*, 246, *258*
August, G., 188, *197*
Awaida, M., 245, *257*

B

Backman, J., 181, 184, *197*, *200*, 245, *257*, *260*, 473, 479, *486*

Baddeley, A. D., 208, 212, *216*, 245, *257*, 263, *283*, 287, 294, *299*, 359, *366*, 407, *419*, *430*
Baker, R. L., 372, *392*
Baldwin, L. E., 325, 326, *326*
Ball, E. W., 114, 122, *125*, 131, 140, *149*, 163, *168*, 387, *391*, 479, 485, *486*
Barbuto, P. F., 415, *418*
Barker, T., 399, *404*
Barnes, M. A., 238, *260*, 365, *365*
Barnes, W. G., 466, *468*
Baron, J., 24, *31*, 375, *391*
Barron, R. W., 82, *83*, 153, 159, 161, 162, 163, 164, 165, 166, 167, *168*, *171*, *172*, 289, *299*, 401, *402*
Barry, C., 406, *418*, 422, *430*
Beale, A. L., 144, *151*
Bear, D., 466, *468*
Bechtel, W., 241, *257*
Beck, I. L., 69, *85*, 195, *199*, 298, *301*, 358, 361, *365*
Beech, J. R., 202, *215*, 245, *257*, 287, 294, *299*, 409, *418*
Bell, L. C., 69, *85*, 195, *199*, 298, *301*
Bellugi, U., 264, *283*
Bennett, J. M., 457, *468*
Bentin, S., 131, *149*
Berch, D., 160, *172*, 375, 380, 383, 388, 389, *393*
Berry, D. C., 141, *149*
Bertelson, P., 128, 144, *149*, *151*, 154, 155, 157, 162, *168*, *169*, *171*, *283*, 288, *300*, *301*
Bertoncini, J., 270, *283*
Besner, D., 237, 246, *257*
Bever, T. G., 320, *326*, 373, *392*,
Bias, R., 406, *418*
Bijeljac-Babic, R., 73, *85*, 238, *261*, 270, *283*
Binnie, C. A., 268, *283*

Bishop, D. V. M., 304, 305, 314, *314*, 346, *365*
Bissex, G. L., 454, *468*
Biziot, E., 141, *150*
Bjaalid, I.-K., 160, *170*
Blachman, B. A., 114, 122, *125*, 131, 140, *149*, 163, *168*, 387, 479, 485, *486*
Black, R. S., 140, *149*
Blatchford, P., 292, *301*
Bloom, B. S., 449, *468*
Boder, E., 209, *215*, 382, *391*
Boeker, E., 454, *469*
Boettcher, W., 159, 160, *173*
Bond, G. L., 113, *125*
Bookman, M. O., 400, 403
Borden, S. L., 72, *84*
Bowey, J. A., 38, *64*, 108, *109*, 153, 156, 160, 163, 165, *168*, *169*, *170*, 195, *198*
Bowlby, M., 202, *216*, 254, *260*
Bradley, L. L., 38, *64*, 69, 70, 81, *83*, *84*, *85*, 114, *125*, 131, 143, 146, *149*, 154, 155, 156, 158, 160, 161, 163, *169*, *171*, 194, *198*, 202, 204, *215*, 287, 288, 291, 293, 295, *299*, *300*, 395, *402*, 441, *444*, 479, *486*
Brady, S., 77, *83*, 253, *257*, 473, *486*
Brannan, J., 188, *198*
Breaux, A. M., 250, 251, *261*
Breitmeyer, B., 186, *198*
Broadbent, D. E., 141, *149*
Brooks, L. 73, *83*
Brown, A. L., 81, *83*, 480, *487*
Brown, G. D. A., 74, *83*, 153, *169*, 237, 238, 239, 240, 245, 246, 247, 248, 256, *257*, *258*, *261*, 395, 396, *402*, 430, *430*, 433, 441, *444*, 479, *484*
Brown, J. L., 457, *468*
Brown, R., 275, *283*, 373, *391*, 453
Bruck, M., 75, 79, 82, *83*, *85*, 182, 142, *148*, 166, *169*, 179, 181, 183, 184, 187, 189, 190, 192, 194, 195, *198*, *199*, 200, 242, 245, *257*, *260*, *261*, 298, *300*, 314, 375, 382, 385, 386, 387, *391*, *392*, 395, 397, 398, 399, 400, *402*, *403*, *404*, 426, 427, *432*
Bruner, J. S., 455, 456, *471*
Bryant, P. E., 38, 39, 56, *64*, 65, 69, 70, 81, *83*, *84*, *85*, 97, *110*, 114, 121, 123, *125*, 131, 154, 155, 156, 158, 160, 161, 163, *169*, *170*, *171*, 194, 195, *198*, 202, 209, 210, 211, *215*, 287, 288, 289, 291, 293, 295, *299*, 332, 395, 398, *402*, *403*, 433, 441, *444*, 479, 484, *486*
Bryk, A. S., 449, *470*
Buckhalt, J. A., 320, *327*

Bullemer, P., 141, *152*
Bullinaria, J. D., 246, *258*
Burke, J., 292, *301*
Burr, D. J., 255, *259*
Bus, A. G., 159, *169*, 246, *259*
Bybee, J. L., 429, *430*
Byng, S., 209, *215*
Byrne, B., 95, *109*, 115, 122, *125*, 128, 139, 143, *149*, 153, 160, *169*, 180, *198*, 479, *486*

C

Cahen, L., 449, *469*
Cain, K., *341*, 347, 359, *365*
Calfee, R., 473, *486*
Campbell, R., 264, 280, *283*, 409, *418*, 434, 438, *444*
Caravolas, M., 195, *198*, 387, *392*
Cardoso-Martins, C., 155, *169*
Carlisle, J. F., 70, *83*
Carnine, D., 88, *109*
Carpenter, P. A., 356, *366*
Carreires, M., 144, *149*
Carrillo, M., 157, 162, *169*
Carrithers, C., 320, *326*
Carroll, J. B., 22, *31*, 41, *64*, 320, *326*, 426, *430*
Cary, L., 154, 157, *171*, 288, *301*
Cassar, M., 375, 381, *393*
Castles, A., 184, 185, *198*, 209, *215*
Castro, S. -L., 146, *149*
Cavanagh, P., 181, 187, *199*
Cazden, C. B., 456, *468*
Chafetz, J., 144, *152*
Chall, J. S., 88, *109*, 113, *125*, 325, *326*
Charles-Luce, J., 253, 256, *258*
Charlier, B. L., 272, 273, 277, 279, 281, *283*, *285*
Chase, E. H., 372, *392*
Chew, J., 106, *109*
Chiesi, H. L., 360, *365*, *367*
Childs, B., 179, *198*, 382, *392*
Chomsky, C., 389, *392*, 421, *431*
Chomsky, N., 373, *392*, 421, 422, *431*
Christophers, U., 116, *125*
Chun, C., 452, *468*
Cioffi, G., 158, *170*
Clark, E. V., 453, *468*
Clark, H. H., 453, *468*
Clay, M. M., 88, *109*, 158, *169*, 289, 346, *365*, 452, 456, *468*
Clifton, L., 251, *258*
Cluytens, M., 146, *149*
Cohen, D., 270, 284
Cohen, P., 449, *468*
Cole, R. A., 251, *258*

AUTHOR INDEX

Coleman, E. B., 36, *65*
Coltheart, M., 21, 23, *31*, 73, 74, 75, 82, *83*, *85*, 92, *109*, 144, *149*, 160, *172*, 183, 184, 185, *198*, 209, *215*, *258*, 287, 288, *301*
Coltheart, V., 74, 75, *83*, *84*, 238, 245, 246, *258*, *259*, 426, *431*
Compton, P., 144, *149*
Conners, F. A., 26, *32*, 194, *199*, 287, 297, *301*
Conrad, R., 263, 264, *283*, *284*
Content, A., 70, *85*, 134, 143, *150*, *151*, 154, 155, *168*, *169*, *171*, 288, 289, *300*
Cooke, C. L., 361, *366*
Cooper, F. S., 9, *17*
Corcos, E., 303, *315*
Corin, W. S., 264, *285*
Cornett, O., 271, *284*
Cornoldi, C., 365, *365*
Cossu, G., 128, 129, 132, 133, 134, 136, 137, 142, *149*, *150*
Cowie, C., 49, *64*
Cox, G. L., 329, *341*
Cramer, B. R., 69, *85*, 114, *125*, 155, *172*, 194, *200*, 251, *260*, 287, 288, *301*
Critchley, M., 319, *326*
Croft, C., 41, 42, 48, 49, *64*
Cromer, W., 346, *365*, *366*, *367*
Crone, D. A., 159, *173*
Cronnell, B., 372, *392*
Crossland, J., 154, 155, *169*
Crowder, R. G., 263, 264, *284*
Cuksts, B., 163, *171*
Cunningham, A. E., 19, 26, *31*, 38, *64*, *65*, 69, 85, 114, 122, *125*, 131, *149*, 154, 155, *169*, *172*, 194, *200*, 251, *260*, 287, 288, *301*, 319, *326*, 359, *365*, 473, 479, *486*, *487*
Cunningham, P. M., 72, 80, 81, 82, *84*, *86*, 451, *468*
Curtis, B., 21, *31*, 144, *149*, 183, *198*, 246, *258*
Custodio, R., 203, *216*
Cutler, A., 145, *151*

D

D'Alimonte, G., 129, *149*
Daneman, M., 356, 358, *365*, *366*
Danks, J., 320, *326*
Davidson, B. J., 27, *32*, 297, *301*, 400, *403*
Davidson, J., 321, *326*
Davies, P., 22, *31*, 41, *64*, 426, *430*
de Beni, R., 365, *365*

de Hirsch, K., 299, *300*
De Weirdt, W., 254, *258*
Deavers, R. P., 238, *258*
Defior, S., 131, 163, *169*
DeFord, D. E., 449, *468*, *470*
DeFrancis, J., 381, *392*
DeFries, J. C., 179, 181, *199*
Defty, N., 203, *216*
deGelder, B., 155, 162, *168*
Dekle, D. J., 282, *284*
Dennis, M., 361, *365*
Desberg, P., 73, *85*, 88, *111*, 395, *403*, 434, *445*
deVega, M., 144, *149*
Devescovi, A., 275, *285*
DiBenedetto, B., 50, 51, *65*, 227, *233*
Dijkstra, T., 146, 165, *169*
Dobrich, W., 159, *172*
Dodd, B., 264, 269, 271, 280, 281, *283*, *284*, 409, *418*
Doehring, D. G., 409, *419*
Doi, L., 184, *199*
Dollaghan, C. A., 253, *258*
Dommergues, S., 145, *150*
Downer, M. A., 72, *84*
Dozier, M. G., 156, *173*
Drislane, F. W., 189, *199*, 303, *315*
Drum, P. A., 94, *111*, 158, *171*
Duker, S., 320, *326*
Duker, T. G., 320, *326*
Duncan, L. G., 294, *300*
Dunlop, P., 304, *314*
Dunn, L. M., 306, *314*
Dunning, D. B., 159, *169*
Dupoux, E., 145, 146, *151*
Durrell, D. D., 320, *326*
Dykstra, R., 113, *125*

E

Edwards, P. A., 457, *468*
Ehri, L. C., 33, 35, 36, 63, *64*, 73, 81, 82, *83*, *84*, 87, 88, 90, 91, 92, 93, 94, 95, 96, 98, 101, 103, 104, 106, *109*, *111*, 123, *125*, 153, 158, 159, 160, 163, 165, 166, *170*, *171*, 207, *215*, 293, 299, *300*, 324, *326*, 389, *392*, 407, 408. *418*, 421, 429, *431*, 452, 454, *468*, *486*
Eimas, P. D., 146, 270, *284*
Elley, W., 41, 42, 49, *64*
Elliot, C. D., 116, *125*, 289, *300*, 306, 310, *314*
Elliott, L. L., 251, *258*
Ellis, A. W., 81, *84*, 114, 122, *125*, 131, 156, *171*, 288, *300*, 448, *448*

Ellis, N. C., 245, *257*, 287, *299*, 395, 396, *402*
Elman, J. L., 255, *258*
Epstein, J. N., 159, *173*
Erber, N. P., 268, *284*
Evan, K. E., 251, *258*
Evans, H. M., 70, *85*, 212, *216*

F

Farquhar, C., 292, *301*
Feeman, D. J., 38, *65*, 319, *326*, 473, *487*
Feitelson, D., 88, *110*
Felton, R. H., 181, 183, *198*, 219, 220, 221, 224, 231, 232, *232*, *233*
Ferguson, H. B., 181, *197*
Ferreiro, E., 158, *170*, , *284*, 454, *469*
Field, T. M., 270, *284*
Fielding, L. G., 359, *365*
Fielding-Barnsley, R., 95, 109, 115, 122, *125*, 160, *169*, 479, *486*
Filby, N., 449, *469*
Finucci, J. M., 179, *198*, 382, *392*
Firth, I., 19, *31*
Fischer, F. W., 254, *259*, 266, *284*, 409, *418*, 426, 429, *431*
Fitzgerald, J., 363, *366*
Flege, J. E., 250, *261*
Fletcher-Flinn, C. M., 138, 139, *152*
Fodor, J. A., 373, *392*
Foltz, G., 27, *32*, 163, *171*, 297, 400, *403*
Fonck, E., 265, *285*
Foorman, B. R., 143, 476, *486*
Forbes, J. E., 163, *171*
Fornarolo, G., 184, *200*, 245, *260*
Forsberg, H., 473, *487*
Fourcin, A. J., 271, *285*
Fowler, A. E., 38, *64*, *83*, 247, 250, *258*, 473, *486*
Fowler, C. A., 77, 254, *259*, 280, 282, *284*, 409, *418*
Fowler, M. S., 303, 304, 305, 308, 309, 313, 314, *315*
Fox, B., 69, *84*, 288, *300*
Fox, P. T., 144, *151*
Fox, R., 251, *258*
Francis, D. J., 143, 160, *169*, 195, *198*, 476, *486*
Frauenfelder, U. H., 145, 146, *151*, 165, *169*
Freebody, P., 143, *149*
French, L., 320, 322, 323, *326*
Friedman, M. P., 73, *85*, 88, *111*, 395, *403*, *434*
Frith, U., 73, *84*, 93, 96, *109*, 128, *151*, 202, *215*, 245, *258*, 293, *300*, 373, *392*, 396, *403*, 421, *431*, 433, 440, *444*
Frost, J., 69, *84*, 114, *125*, 130, *150*, 154, *171*, 387, *392*, 479, *486*
Fruchter, B., 221, *232*
Fulker, D., 26, *32*, 297, *301*

G

Gaffney, J. S., 456, *469*
Galaburda, A. M., 189, *199*, 303, *315*
Ganz, L., 186, *198*
García-Albea, J. E., 146, *149*
Garfinkel, B., 188, *197*
Garner, W., 456, *470*
Garnham, A., 329, *341*, 363, *366*
Garrett, M. F., 373, *392*
Garzia, R., 186, *199*
Gaskins, I. W., 72, *84*
Gaskins, R. W., 72, *84*
Gates, A. I., 143, *149*, 333, *341*, 372, *392*, 454, *469*
Gathercole, S. E., 208, 211, *216*, 359, *366*
Gentry, J. R., 389, *392*, 405, *418*
Gerstman, L. J., 378, *392*
Geva, E., 400, *403*, 404, 417, *418*
Gibson, E. J., 158, *170*, 373, 374, *392*, 407, *418*
Gillham, W. E. C., 116, *125*
Gilmore, A., 48, *64*
Gipstein, M., 77, *83*
Glass, G., 449, *469*
Glenn, C. G., 349, 362, *367*
Glushko, R. J., 21, *31*, 88, *110*, 238, *258*, 426, *431*
Godfrey, J. J., 254, *258*
Golden, J. O., 161, 168
Goldfield, A., 269, *285*
Goldman, S. R., 356, *367*
Golinkoff, R., 90, *110*
Goodell, E. W., 409, *418*
Goodman, K. S., 9, *17*, 21, *31*, 33, 34, *64*, 88, 90, *110*, 374, *392*
Goodman, Y. M., 9, *17*, 21, *31*, 34, *64*
Gordon, C., 360, *366*
Gormley, K., 360, *366*
Goswami, U. C., 21, *31*, 70, 71, 72, 73, 74, 75, 81, 82, *84*, *85*, *86*, 88, 97, 100, 101, *110*, *111*, 114, 121, 123, *125*, 154, 162, *170*, 192, 195, *198*, *200*, 288, 289, 291, 293, *300*, 332, *341*, 375, *393*, 396, 398, 401, *403*, 426, *432*, 433, 434, 435, 436, 437, 440, 441, 442, 444, *444*
Gottfredson, L. S., 179, *198*
Gough, P. B., 2, *3*, 19, 20, 21, 22, 24, *31*, 34, 36, 38, 40, 41, 42, 58, 63, *64*,

AUTHOR INDEX

88, 91, 96, 106, *111*, 143, 165, 181, 182, *199*, 219, *232*, 323, *326*, 406, 407, *418*, 421, 422, 428, *431*, 454, 455, *469*, 470
Goulandris, A. M., 202, 203, 210, 213, *216*, 254, *260*, 312, *315*
Graves, K., 194, *199*, 294, *300*
Graves, M. F., 361, *366*
Greenberg, D., 270, *284*
Griffith, P. L., 20, *31*, 88, 93, *110*, 165, *170*, 443, *444*, 454, *469*, 470
Groff, P., 40, 47, *64*
Grossenbacher, P., 144, *149*
Guilford, J. P., 221, *232*
Guszak, F. J., 465, *469*
Guttentag, R., 90, 91, *111*

H

Hage, C., 273, 276, *283*, *284*, *285*
Haines, L. C., 161, *168*
Haines, L. P., 80, 82, *85*, *168*
Haith, M., 90, 91, *111*
Halle, M., 250, *259*, 373, *392*, 421, 422, *431*
Haller, M., 21, *31*, 183, *198*, 246, *258*,
Hammer, M. A., 251, *258*
Hanley, J. R., 214, *216*
Hanna, G., 457, *468*
Hanna, J. S., 421, *431*
Hanna, P. R., 421, *431*
Hansen, J., 108, *109*, 156, *170*, 360, *366*
Hanson, S. J., 255, *259*
Hanson, V. L., 266, 280, *284*, 409, 413, *418*
Harding, L. M., 202, *215*, 287, 294, *299*
Harris, M., 409, *418*
Hartt, J., 354, *366*
Hastie, K., 214, *216*
Hatano, G., 145, *151*
Hatcher, P. J., 81, *84*, 114, 122, *125*, 131, 288, *300*, 448, *448*
Hay, I. M., 246, *259*
Hayduk, S., 181, 187, 189, *199*
Hayes, M., 320, *326*
Heaven, R. K., 395, *403*
Hebert, M., 245, *257*
Heese, K. A., 116, *125*
Henderson, E. H., 395, 396, *403*, 454, *469*
Henderson, L., 405, *418*, 421, 426, *431*
Hermelin, B., 280, *284*
Herriman, M. L., 35, *65*
Hiebert, E. H., 158, *170*, 455, *469*
Hieronymous, A. N., 457, *469*
Hill, T., 141, *150*

Hillinger, M. L. 2, *3*, 36, 40, *64*, 96, 106, *111*, *170*, 165, 406, *418*, 454, *469*
Hirsh-Pasek, K., 202, *217*, *261*, 287, *301*
Hitch, G. S., 263, *283*
Hockley, R., 305, *315*
Hodges, R. E., 421, *431*
Hoffman, H., 144, *151*
Hogaboam, T., 345, *367*
Hohn, W. E., 163, *170*
Høien, T., 160, *170*, 473, *486*
Holley-Wilcox, P., 182, *199*
Holligan, C., 245, *259*, 287, 289, 294, *300*, 401, *403*
Hollingshead, A. B., 221, *232*
Holmes, V., 417, *418*
Holt, L. K., 194, *199*, 294, *300*
Hoover, H. D., 457, *469*
Hoover, W. A., 19, *32*, 33, 35, 39, *65*, 323, *326*, 327
Howard, D., 203, *217*
Howell, P., 202, *216*, 254, *260*
Huggins, A. W. F., 33, 35, 36, 37, 41, 42, 43, 44, 50, 54, 62, *63*, 87, *109*, 227, *232*, 426, *430*
Hughes, C., 69, *85*, 195, *199*, 298, *301*
Hulme, C., 81, *84*, 95, *111*, 114, 122, 123, *125*, 131, 140, 153, 156, 207, 210, 214, 215, *216*, 247, 254, *259*, 288, *300*, 312, *315*, 340, *342*, 397, *403*, 441, *445*, 448, 480, *487*, 488
Humes, A., 372, *392*
Hummer, P., 159, 160, *173*
Hunt, E., 321, *326*
Hynd, G., 473, *486*

I

Ijzendoorn, M., 246, *259*
Imlach, R. H., 346, *365*
Impey, L., 209, 210, 211, *215*
Ingemann, F., 378, *392*
Invernizzi, M., 397, 398, *403*, 450, 453, 466, *468*, *469*, 470
Isaacs, S. D., 382, *392*
Iversen, S., 466, *469*

J

Jackson, P. L., 268, *283*
Jacobs, V. A., 325, *326*
Jancey, C., 304, *314*
Jansky, J., 299, *300*
Jared, D., 192, *199*, 238, *259*
Jastak, J., 477, *486*
Jastak, S., 158, 171, 423, *431*, 477, *486*
Jenkins, J. R., 358, *366*

Jensen, A. R., 372, 383, *392*
Johnson, D. J., 209, *216*
Johnson, M. B., 222, *233*, 484, *486*, 486
Johnston, F., 453, 466, *468*, *469*, 470
Johnston, P., 465, *469*
Johnston, R. S., 203, *216*, 245, *259*, 287, 289, 294, 296, *300*, 401, *403*
Jorm, A. F., 36, *65*, 183, 194, *199*, *200*, 287, 288, *301*, 450, *471*
Joshi, R. M., 320, 325, *326*
Juel, C. L., 20, 22, *31*, 36, *64*, *65*, 69, *84*, 88, 93, *111*, 165, 170, 415, *418*, 450, 451, 452, 453, 454, 455, 457, *469*
Jusczyk, P. W., 250, 251, *261*, 270, *283*, *284*

K

Kane, M. J., 81, *83*
Kaplan, N. E., 156, *173*
Karle, H., 305, 313, *315*
Karmiloff-Smith, A., 275, *284*
Karp, S. A., 296, *301*, *312*
Kattenberg, G., 408, *417*
Katz, A. N., 265, *285*
Kavanagh, J. F., 127, *150*
Kay, J., 214, *216*
Keating, C., 74, *84*, 426, *431*
Kellman, P., 375, *391*
Kennedy, D. K., 320, *326*
Kennedy, K. M., 473, 479, 484, *486*
Kennedy, L., 270, *283*
Kibby, M. W., 36, *65*
Kimberling, W. J., 400, *403*
King, E. M., 423, *431*
Kintsch, W., 320, *326*
Kirk, S. A., 116, *125*
Kirk, W. D., 116, *125*
Kirtley, C., 70, *84*, 158, *171*
Klatt, D. H., 381, *392*
Kliegl, R., 27, *32*, 297, *301*, 400, *403*
Klima, E. S., 264, *283*
Knox, C. M., 254, *258*
Koenigsknecht, R., 251, *258*
Kolinsky, R., 133, 146, 148, *149*, *151*, 155, *169*, 288, *300*
Kooi, B. Y., 372, 383, *392*
Kozminsky, E., 320, *326*
Kreiner, D. S., 406, 407, *418*, 421, 422, *431*
Kruk, R. S., 303, *315*
Kuhl, P. K., 270, *284*
Kulik, C., 449, *468*
Kulik, J. A., 449, *468*

L

LaBerge, M. J., 361, *366*
Labuda, M., 179, 181, *199*
Ladd, E. M., 320, *326*
Landerl, K., 74, *86*, 160, *173*
Langer, J. A., 455, *470*
Larsen, J., 473, *486*
Lavine, L. O., 158, *171*
Laxon, V. J., 74, *84*, 245, *259*, 426, *431*
Leahy, J., 74, 75, *83*, 238, *258*
Ledez, J., 180, *198*
Leevers, H., 375, *393*
Lefly, D. L., 400, *403*
Lehiste, I., 381, *392*, *393*
Lennox, C., 396, 398, 399, *403*
Leong, C. K., 320, *326*, 426, 428, *431*
Lesgold, A. M., 356, *367*
Leshem, H., 131, *149*
Levin, H., 158, *170*, 373, 374, *392*, *407*
Lewicki, P., 141, *150*
Lewis, S., 141, *151*
Lewis, V. J., 263, *283*, 287, *299*
Leybaert, J., 134, 143, *150*, *151*, 265, 267, 268, 277, 281, *284*, *285*
Liberman, A. M., 6, 9, 10, 13, 14, *17*, 254, *259*, 270, *285*, 441, *444*, 454, *470*
Liberman, D., 143
Liberman, I. Y., 6, 11, *17*, 127, 138, *150*, 157, *171*, 253, *259*, 426, *431*, 441, *444*, 454, 476, *486*
Limber, J., 385, *393*
Lindamood, C., 223, *233*, 448, 473, 479, *448*
Lindamood, P., 223, *233*, 448, *448*, 473, 479, 480, *487*
Lindauer, B. K., 329, 330, *341*
Linder, B. A., 254
Lindquist, E. F., 457, *469*
Ling, D., 272, *285*
Linortner, R., 160, *173*
Livingston, M. S., 303
Livingstone, M., 189, *199*, 315
Logan, J. S., 253, 256, *259*
Logie, R. H., 245, *257*, 287, *299*
Lomax, R. G., 159, *171*
Lonigan, C. J., 159, *171*
Loosemore, R. L., 153, *169*, 237, *258*, 430, *430*
Loosemore, R. P. W., 443, *444*
Lotz, J., 378, *392*
Lovegrove, W. J., 186, 187, 188, *199*, *200*, 303, *315*
Lovett, M. W., 72, *83*, 163, *171*
Lubs, H. A., 400, *403*
Luce, P. A., 250, 252, 253, 256, *258*, *259*

AUTHOR INDEX

Lundberg, I., 69, *84*, *85*, 114, *125*, 130, *150*, 154, 157, 160, 164, *170*, *171*, 194, 287, 288, *300*, 387, *392*, 473, 479, *486*
Lundquist, E., 428, 429, *432*
Lupker, S. J., 265, *285*
Lyons, C. A., 449, *468*, *470*

M

MacGinite, R. K., 324, *326*
MacGinite, W. H., 324, *326*, 333, *341*
MacKain, K. S., 270, *285*
MacLean, M., 38, *64*, 69, 70, *84*, *85*, 154, 155, 157, 158, 162, *169*, *171*, *285*, *301*
MacLean, R., 194, *200*, 450, *471*
Malécot, A., 383, *392*
Malus-Abramowitz, M., 190, *200*, 395, *404*, 427, *432*
Mamen, M., 181, *197*
Manis, F. R., *199*, 203, *216*, 244, 245, *260*, 287, 294, *300*, *301*
Mann, V. A., 157, *171*, 253, *257*
Marcel, T., 21, *32*, 387, *392*
Marcovitz Hornstein, S. B., 146
Marcus, G. F., 240, *259*
Markman, E., 354, *366*
Markwardt, F. C., 322, *326*
Marmurek, H. H. C., 161, *168*
Marr, M. B., 360, *366*
Marsh, G., 73, 88, *111*, 395, 396, *403*, 434, *445*
Marshall, J. C. 128, 132, 133, *149*, *150*, 209, *217*
Martin, F. R., 186, 187, *199*, 303, *315*
Mason, J. M., 94, *111*, 158, 159, *169*, *171*, 180, 455, *470*
Masonheimer, P. E., 94, *111*, 158, *171*
Massaro, D. W., 269, *285*, 422, *432*
Masterson, J., 74, *84*, 209, *215*, 245, *259*
Matthews, R., 194, *200*, 287, 288, *301*, 450, *471*
Mattingly, I. G., 10, 11, 12, 13, 14, *17*, 127, *150*, 270, *285*
Mattys, S., 272, *283*
Maxwell, A. E., 296, *300*
McBride-Chang, C., 184, *199*
McCabe, A., 349, 400, *403*
McCann, R. S., 237, *257*
McCarthy, J. J., 116, *125*
McClelland, J. L., 21, *32*, 144, *150*, *151*, 153, *172*, 185, 191, *199*, *200*, 236, 237, 238, 240, 241, 242, 244, 246, 247, *259*, *260*, 443, *445*
McCleod, C., 321, *326*
McConkie, G. W., 91, *111*

McCusker, L., 406, *418*
McKeown, M. G., 358, 361, *365*
McDermott, R., 458, *470*
McDonald, J., 269, *285*
McDougall, S., 156, *171*
McGarr, N. S., 280, *284*, 409, 413, *418*
McGauvran, M., 458, *470*
McGee, L. M., 159, *171*
McGill-Franzen, A., 451, *470*
McGowan, R. S., 251, *259*
McGurk, H., 269, *285*
McKelvie, S. J., 141, *151*
McKeown, M. G., 358, 361, *365*
McLean, J., 269, *285*
McRae, K., 192, *199*, 238, 246, *259*, *260*
Mead, F., 72, *84*, 100, 101, *111*, 162, *170*, 441, 442, 444, *444*
Mehler, J., 145, 146, *151*, 270, *283*
Meltzoff, A. N., 270, *284*, *285*
Mendenhall, J. E., 372, 383, *393*
Metsala, J. L., 247, 250, 251, 252, 254, *259*, *261*
Mewhort, D. J. K., 144, *151*
Meyer, D. E., 166, *171*
Michela, V. L., 250, *261*
Miles, T. R., 202, *216*, 287, *299*
Millay, K. K., 254, *258*
Miller, G. R., 36, *65*
Miller, P., 385, *393*
Milson, R., 239, *257*
Minarik, E. M., 453, *470*
Moats, L. D., 397, 398, *403*
Monk, A., 156, *171*
Montgomery, A. A., 268, *283*
Montgomery, D., 480, *486*
Moore, B. C. J., 271, *285*
Moore, K. M., 270, *285*
Morais, J., 70, *85*, *127*, 129, 133, 134, 142, 144, 146, 148, *149*, *151*, 154, 155, 157, *168*, *169*, *171*, 195, *199*, 288, 292, 293, 298, *300*, *301*
Moran, R., 245, *259*
Morris, D., 452, 453, 463, 466, *470*
Morton, J., 128, *151*, 263, 266, *284*, *285*
Mousty, P. 134, 143, 144, *151*
Mullennix, J., 73, *85*, 238, *261*
Munco, N., 305, *315*
Murphy, A., 184, *199*
Murray, B. A., 114, *125*, 153, 155, 156, 157, 162, *172*
Murray, D. J., 116, *125*, 289, *300*
Muter, V., 161, *171*
Myklebust, H., 209, *216*

N

Nathan, R. G., 245, *260*
Naylor, C., 181, *198*

Neale, M. D., 116, 119, *125*, 333, *341*
Nelson, H. E., 382, *393*, 406, 407, *418*
Nemser, W. J., 378, *392*
Nepomuceno, L., 133, *151*
Nesdale, A. R., 35, 38, 69, *86*, 166, *173*
Newman, S. P., 305, 313, 314, *315*
Ng, E., 417, *418*
Nicholls, G. H., 272, *285*
Nicholson, S., 186, *199*
Nicholson, T., 35, *65*, 90, *111*
Nissen, M. J., 141, *152*
Nittrouer, S., 251, *259*
Norris, D., 145, 237, 238, 246, *259*
Novy, D. M., 476, *486*
Nurss, J. R., 458, *470*

O

Oakan, R., 346, *366*
Oakhill, J. V., 330, 331, 334, 335, 338, 339, 340, *341*, *342*, 345, 346, 347, 348, 349, 353, 354, 356, 357, 359, *366*, *367*
Odegaard, H., 473, *486*
Olofsson, Å, 69, *85*, *125*, 114, 157, *171*, 287, 288, *300*
Olson, R. K., 26, 27, *32*, 79, 82, *86*, 102, *111*, 158, 163, *171*, *172*, 183, 194, *199*, 202, *216*, 219, *233*, 246, *260*, 287, 294, 297, 298, *301*, 400, *403*, 473, 474, 476, 477, 479, 480, 482, 484, 485, *486*, *487*
Oltman, P. K., 296, *301*, 312, *315*
Omanson, R. C., 330, 338, *341*, 361, *365*
Otake, T., 145, *151*

P

Palinscar, A. S., 480, *487*
Palmer, R. J., 321, *326*, 361, *366*
Pany, D., 358, *366*
Papagno, C., 134, *152*
Paris, S. G., 329, 330, 338, *341*
Parkin, A. J., 340, *342*, 346, 353, 356, *366*, *367*
Patel, R. K., 38, *64*
Paterson, R., 146, *152*
Patterson, K. E., 21, *32*, 153, *172*, 191, *199*, 237, *259*, 266, *285*
Payne, A. C., 159, *173*
Payton, P., 146, *150*
Pazzaglia, F., 365, *365*
Pearson, L. L. 166, 167, *171*, *172*
Pearson, L. S., 116, *125*, 289, *300*
Pearson, P. D., 360, *366*
Pelligrini, A. D., 159, *169*
Pennington, B., 400, 401, *403*

Perfetti, C. A., 69, 73, *85*, 87, 90, *111*, 153, *172*, 195, *199*, 251, *258*, 298, *301*, 345, 362, *365*, *366*, *367*, 409, *418*, 430, *431*
Périer, O., 271, 273, 276, *283*, *284*, *285*
Perin, D., 443, *445*
Peters, M. L., 372, *393*, 407, *418*
Petersen, A. S., 184, *199*, 246, *260*
Petersen, O. -P., 69, *84*, 114, *125*, 130, 150, 154, *171*, 387, *392*
Petersen, S. E., 144, *151*
Peterson, C., 348, *367*
Peterson, G. E., 381, *393*
Peterson, M. E., 80, 82, *85*
Phillips, W. A., 246, *259*
Pinker, S., 240, *260*
Pinnell, G. S., 449, *468*, *470*
Pintilie, D., 306, *314*
Pisoni, D., 250, *259*
Plaut, D. C., 21, *32*, 153, *172*, 191, 194, *199*, *259*, 237, 246, 247, *260*
Plewis, I., 292, *301*
Pollack, I., 268, *285*
Pollatsek, A., 87, *111*, 184, *199*
Pool, J., 74, *84*
Posner, M., 144, *149*
Prince, A., 240, *260*
Prinzmetal, W., 144, *151*
Prior, M., 209, *215*
Pritchatt, D., 265, *285*
Pylyshyn, Z. W., 240, *260*

Q

Quinlan, P., 153, *170*, 397, *403*, 430, *431*

R

Raban, B., 116, *125*
Rack, J. P., 26, *32*, 95, 96, 97, *111*, 123, *125*, 140, *151*, 153, 158, 160, 165, *172*, 183, 194, *199*, 202, *216*, *217*, 219, *233*, 245, 246, *260*, 287, 288, 294, 297, *301*, 310, *315*, 397, 401, *403*
Radaker, L., 372, *393*
Radeau, M., 144, 145, *151*, *152*
Raichle, M. E., 133, *151*
Ransby, M. J., 72, *84*
Raphael, T. E., 455, *469*
Rapp, B. C., 144, *151*
Rardin, D., 202, *216*
Rashotte, C. A., 160, *173*, 230, *233*, 473, *487*
Raskin, E., 296, *301*, 312
Raven, J. C., 324, *326*,
Rawson, M., 179, *199*
Rayner, K., 87, *111*

AUTHOR INDEX

Read, C. R., 160, *172*, 180, *199*, 373, 374, 375, 376, 377, 378, 380, 383, 385, 388, 389, *393*, 405, *418*, 421, *431*
Reber, A. S., 73, *85*, 127, 141, *151*
Reed, M. A., 254, *260*
Reeds, J. A., 378, *393*
Rego, L., 39, 40, 56, *65*
Reid, N., 48, *64*
Reisberg, D., 269, *285*
Reitsma, P., 73, 78, *85*, 87, 92, *111*, 145, *152*
Rho, S. H., 144, *151*
Richards, H. C., 450, *469*
Richardson, A., 305, *315*
Richardson, E., 50, 51, *65*, 227, *233*
Richman, B., 22, *31*, 41, *64*, 426, *430*
Richmond-Welty, E. D., 73, 160, *172*, 238, *261*, 375, *393*
Riddell, P. M., 304, 313, *315*
Riddoch, J., 209, *215*
Ring, J., 484, *487*
Robbins, C., 33, *64*, 81, 82, *84*, 98, 101, 103, 104, *110*
Rogoff, B., 456, *470*
Rohl, M., 397, 398, *403*, 429, *431*, 443, *445*
Roper-Schneider, D., 22, *31*
Rosemary, C. A., 450, 451, *469*, *470*
Rosen, G. D., 189, *199*, 303, *315*
Rosen, S. M., 271, 282, *285*
Rosenberg, C. R., 246, *260*
Rosenshine, B. V., 358, *367*
Rosinski, R., 90, *110*
Rosner, J., 227, *233*, 289, *301*
Ross, G., 455, 456, *471*
Ross, J., 202, *216*
Rossini, F., 128, *149*
Routh, D. K., 69, *84*, 288, *300*
Ruddy, M., 166, *171*
Rudorf, E. H. Jr., 421, *431*
Rugg, M. D., 203, *216*, *300*
Rumelhart, D. E., 88, *111*, 144, *150*, 240, 241, *260*
Rutter, M., 202, *216*
Ruyter, L., 180, *199*
Ryan, E. B., 38, 39, 48, *65*, 245, *260*, 395, *404*

S

Saevens, M., 144, *151*
Saltmarsh, J., 87, *110*
Samuels, D. P., 354, *366*
Sánchez-Casas, R. M., 146, *149*
Satz, P., 202, *216*
Scanlon, D. M., 69, *86*, 160, *173*
Scarborough, D. L., 127, *151*

Scarborough, H. S., 159, *172*, 254, *260*
Schmidt, H., 146, *152*
Schommer, M., 72, 84
Schneider, W., 74, *86*
Schonell, F. E., 116, *125*
Schonell, F. J., 116, *125*
Schooler, L. J., 239, *257*
Schreck, J., 358, *366*
Schrender, R., 165, *169*
Schutz, R. E., 372, *392*
Schvaneneldt, R. W., 166, *171*
Scliar-Cabral, L., 133, *151*
Scott, J. A., 95, 96, *111*
Scott, T., 203, *216*, 287, *300*
Sebastián-Gallés, N., 145, *151*
Seergobin, K., 237, *257*
Segui, J., 145, 146, *151*
Seidenberg, M. S., 21, *32*, 144, *151*, 153, 165, 166, *172*, 184, 185, 186, 191, 192, *199*, 200, 236, 237, 238, 240, 242, 244, 245, 246, 247, *257*, *259*, 260, 406, *418*, 443, *445*
Sejnowski, T. J., 246, *260*
Seldon, D. M., 161, *168*
Seltzer, M., 449, *470*
Semrud-Clikeman, M., 473, *486*
Servi, D., 251, *258*
Seyll, S., 129, *149*
Seymour, P. H. K., 70, *85*, 209, 210, 212, *216*, 422, *430*, *430*, *432*
Shanks, D. R., 141, *151*
Shankweiler, D. P., 6, 9, 11, *17*, 253, *257*, *259*, 266, *284*, 346, 367, 409, *418*, 426, 428, 429, *431*, *432*, *444*
Share, D. L., 36, *65*, 183, 194, *199*, 200, 287, 288, 292, *301*, 400, *403*, *404*, 450, *471*
Shepard, R. N., 239, *260*
Shepherd, M. J., 479, 485, *487*
Siegel, L. S., 38, 48, *65*, 181, *200*, 245, 254, *260*, 319, *326*, 395, 396, 398, 399, 400, *403*, *404*
Simon, H. A., 417, *419*
Singer, M., 329, *342*
Siple, P., 264, *283*
Siqueland, E. R., 270, *284*
Slaghuis, W., 186, 187, *199*, *200*, 303, *315*
Slavin, R. E., 449, 450, *471*
Sloboda, J. A., 407, *418*
Smith, A., 207, *216*
Smith, E. E., 475, *487*
Smith, F., 6, *17*, 33, *65*
Smith, L. B., 250, 251, *257*, *261*
Smith, L. S., 246, *259*
Smith, M. L., 449, *469*
Snowling, M. J., 69, *85*, 95, *111*, 123, *125*, 140, *151*, 153, 158, *170*, *172*,

183, *199*, 202, 203, 205, 207, 210, 213, 214, 215, *216*, *217*, 219, *233*, 245, 246, 247, 254, *258*, *259*, *260*, 287, 288, 294, *301*, 303, 310, *315*, *326*, *365*, *367*, 387, 395, 396, 397, *403*, 404, 441, *445*, 480, *487*
Snyder, A. Z., 144, *151*
Söderbergh, R., 454, 455, *471*
Solso, L. R., 415, *418*
Spache, G. D., 458, *451*
Sparks, J. A., 304, *315*
Spiegel, D. L., 363, *366*
Spieker, S., 270, *285*
Spilich, G. J., 360, *365*, *367*
Spoehr, K. T., 264, *285*, 475, *487*
Spring, C., 320, 322, 323, *326*
St. John, M. F., 141, *151*
Stackhouse, J., 205, 213, *216*, *217*, 245, *260*, 310, *314*
Staffod, C., 202, *217*
Stage, S. C., 422, *432*
Stahl, S. A., 114, *125*, 153, 155, 156, 157, 162, *172*
Stanback, M. L., 238, *260*
Stanovich, K. E., 19, 26, *31*, *32*, 35, 38, 46, 50, *64*, *65*, 69, *85*, 114, *125*, 154, 155, 157, 160, *170*, *172*, 181, 182, 194, *200*, 219, *233*, 245, 251, *260*, 287, 288, 295, 303, 319, 320, 321, 356, 363, 388, 395, 396, *404*, 473, 483, *487*
Steel, A. M., 304, *314*
Stein, J. F., 303, 304, 305, 307, 308, 309, 313, 314, *315*
Stein, N. L., 349, 362, 363, *367*
Steinbach, K. A., 163, *171*
Steiner, R., 346, *367*
Sterling, C., 406, *418*
Stern, D., 270, *285*
Stewart, J. P., 159, *169*
Stone, B., 473, *486*
Stothard, S. E., 340, *342*
Stuart, M., 73, *85*, 160, *172*, *259*, *285*, 287, 288, *301*
Studdert-Kennedy, M., 9, *17*, 251, *270*
Sumby, W., 268, *285*
Summerfield, Q., 269, 270, *285*, *286*,
Sweet, J., 452, *468*
Swisher, L., 275, *286*
Syrdal-Lasky, A. K., 254, *258*
Szeszulski, P. A., 194, *199*, 203, *216*, 244, 245, *260*, 287, 294, *300*, *301*

T

Taeschuer, T., 275, *286*
Taft, M., 145, *152*, 474, *487*

Tanenhaus, M. K., 165, 166, *172*, 238, *260*
Tangel, M., 140, *149*
Taraban, R., 238, 242, 244, *260*
Teale, W. H., 158, *172*
Tees, R. C., 254, *261*
Temple, C., 209, *217*
Templeton, S., 395, 396, *403*, 466, *468*
Thomas, J., 207, *216*
Thompson, G. B., 138, 139, *152*
Tincoff, R., 160, *172*, 375, 380, *393*
Tizard, B., 292, *301*
Tomlin, J. G., 320, *327*
Torgesen, J. K., *86*, 156, 157, 160, *173*, 230, *233*, 356, *367*, 395, *404*, 473, *486*, *487*
Townsend, D. J., 320, *326*
Trabasso, T., 320, *326*, 330, *341*, 363, *367*
Treiman, R., *31*, *32*, 69, 70, 73, 75, 79, 82, *83*, *85*, 97, 102, *111*, 144, *151*, *152*, 155, 160, *172*, 192, 194, 195, *198*, *200*, 202, *217*, 238, 244, 245, 250, 251, *261*, 287, 301, 374, 375, 376, 377, 378, 379, 380, 381, 383, 384, 385, 386, 387, 388, 389, 390, *391*, *393*, 395, 397, 398, *402*, 405, *419*, 422, 426, 427, 429, *432*, 453, *471*, 474, *487*
Treisman, A., 146, *152*, 187, 188, *200*
Truch, S., 473, 479, 485
Tucker, D. M., 144, *149*
Tudela, P., 131, 163, *169*
Tunmer, W. E., 19, *31*, 33, 35, 38, 39, *65*, 69, *86*, 166, *173*, 181, *199*, 219, 232, 323, 326, *327*, 357, *367*, 397, 398, *403*, 429, *431*, 443, *445*, 466, *469*
Twilley, L., 237, *257*

U

Uhry, J., 479, 485, *487*
Upton, L. R., 329, 330, 338, *341*

V

Vallar, G., 134, *152*
van Daal, V. H. P., 145, *152*
van den Broek, P., 329, *342*
van der Leij, A., 145, *152*
van der Lely, H., 203, *217*
van IJzendoorn, W. H., 159, *169*
van Wagtendonk, B., 202, *217*
Vellutino, F. R., 69, *86*, 160, *173*, 181, *200*, 303, *315*

AUTHOR INDEX

Venezky, R., 324, *327*, 373, *393*, 421, 422, *432*
Vernon, P. E., 442, *445*
Vesonder, G. T., 360, *367*
Vest, K., 144, *151*
Vicente, S., 146, *149*
Vigorito, J., 270, *284*
Voeller, K., 473, *486*
Volterra, V., 275, *286*
Voss, J. F., 360, *365*, *367*
Vygotsky, L. S., 455, *471*

W

Waddington, P. E., 304, *315*
Wadsworth, J. F., 305, 314, *315*
Wagner, R. K., 69, *85*, *86*, 156, 157, 160, 163, *173*, 230, *233*, 356, *367*, 395, 399, *404*, 422, *432*, 473, 480, *487*
Wall, S., 69, *85*, 157, *171*, 287, 288, *300*
Wallach, L., 107, *111*, 156, *173*
Wallach, M. A., 107, *111*, 156, *173*
Walley, A. C., 250, 251, 252, *259*, *261*
Walsh, M. A., 24, *31*, 36, 38, 58, 63, *64*, 143, 428, *431*
Walsh, S., 91, *111*
Wang, W. S. -Y., 378, *393*
Warren, W. M., 330, *341*
Warren-Chaplin, P. M., 72, *84*
Wasik, B. A., 449, 450, *471*
Waters, G. S., 182, 190, *198*, *200*, 238, 242, 244, 245, *260*, *261*, 382, *392*, 395, 398, 399, 400, *403*, *404*, 409, *419*, 427, *432*
Watson, F. L., 74, 245, *261*
Weatherstone, S., 160, *172*, 375, 380, 383, 388, 389, *393*
Wechsler, D., 115, 116, *125*, 306, *315*, 322, *327*
Welch, V., 73, *85*, 88, *111*, 395, *403*, 434, *445*
Well, A., 184, *199*
Wells, G., 158, *173*
Werker, J. F., 254, *261*
Wertsch, J. V., 455, *471*
West, R. F., 26, *32*, 395, 396, *404*
Whetton, C., 116, *125*, 306, *314*
White, T. G., 80, 81, 82, *86*
Whitehouse, C. C., 382, *392*
Whitehurst, G. J., 159, *173*
Wiener, M., 346, *366*, *367*
Wightman, J., 95, *111*, 123, *125*, 140, *151*, 153, *172*, 397, *403*

Wijk, A., 324, *327*, 426, *432*
Wilce, L. S., 88, 90, 91, 93, 94, 96, 98, 106, *110*, 160, 166, *170*, 454, *468*, *486*
Wildsmith, B., 452, 465, *471*
Wilf, J. F., 375, *391*
Wilkinson, G. S., 158, 423, *431*
Williams, J., 107, *111*, 131, *152*
Williams, K. A., 325, *326*
Williams, M., 188, *198*
Willingham, D. B., 144, *152*
Willows, D. M., 38, 39, *65*, 303, *315*, 417, *418*
Wilson, M. R., 19, *31*, 346
Wilson, P. T., 359, 365
Wimmer, H., 74, *86*, 159, 160, 162, *173*
Winbury, N., 473, *486*
Wing, A. M., 407, *419*
Wise, B. W., 26, *32*, 79, 82, *86*, 102, *111*, 163, *171*, 194, *199*, 287, 297, *301*, 473, 474, 476, 477, 479, 480, 482, 484, 485, *486*, *487*
Witkin, H. A. 296, *301*, 312, *315*
Wood, D., 455, 456, *471*
Wood, F. B., 181, *198*, 219, 220, 221, 224, 231, 232, *232*, *233*
Wood, T. A., 320, *327*
Woodcock, R. W., 158, *173*, 222, 223, *233*, 321, *327*
Wooden, P. E., 159, 160, *173*
Woodson, R., 270, *284*
Worthy, J., 397, 398, *403*
Wright, A. D., 38, *65*
Wright, H., 280, *283*, 409, *418*

Y

Yopp, H. K., 114, *125*, 155, 156, 157, *173*, 289, *301*
Yuill, N. M., 330, 334, 335, 340, *342*, 345, 346, 349, 353, 356, 357, 359, *366*, *367*
Yule, W., 202, *216*

Z

Zhang, G., 417, *419*
Zola, D., 91, *111*
Zolman, J. E., 245, *260*
Zukowski, A., 70, *86*, 375, 381, *393*

Subject Index

A

Activation value, 241
Alphabetic code, 36, 219, 272
  recode, 97
Alphabetic principle, 8, 122, 123, 440
  stage, 122, 433
  knowledge, 290, 291, 292, 299, 453, 464
Amalgamation, 35
Analogies, 71, 72, 78, 82, 82, 88, 97, 99, 101, 104, 105, 107, 108, 370, 395, 396, 401, 433, 434, 437, 438, 441, 442, 443
  interactive, 73
  rime-based, 81
Articulatory awareness, 480, 485

B

Binocular fixation, 305, 314
  vision, 314
Blind subjects, 271
BOSS type syllables, 474

C

Cipher readers, 106
Cognitive model, 235, 461
Comprehension
  inferential, 318, 329, 330, 332, 334, 335, 340, 341, 343, 345, 347, 361
  language, 177, 195, 317, 324, 362
  listening, 317, 318, 320, 321, 322, 323, 325
  literal, 318, 347, 361
  monitoring, 354
  passage, 22, 223, 230, 322, 362, 475
  problem, 344
  reading, 88, 90, 181, 317, 318, 320, 321, 322, 323, 325, 331, 332, 340, 341, 358, 359, 360, 410
  top-down, 480
Computational model, 176, 235, 236, 249
Computer-based remediation, 473
Connectionism, 240
Connectionist models/ systems/ approach, 40, 85, 186, 236, 241, 242, 243, 246, 247, 249, 254, 255, 370, 396, 430, 443, 444
Context cues, 88, 90
Cryptanalytic intent, 36
Cued speech (CS), 176, 271, 272, 273, 274, 275, 276, 277, 278, 279, 280, 281, 282

D

Dactylic, 277
Deaf subjects/individuals, 176, 177, 264, 267, 268, 271, 275, 276, 278, 280, 281, 370, 372, 408, 409, 410, 411, 412, 413, 414
Decoding, 19, 31, 71, 105, 143, 345, 346, 473, 474, 475, 476, 478, 479, 480, 484
Decoding skills, 2, 19, 98, 135, 143, 317, 324, 334, 346
  bottom up, 2
DECtalk, 164, 473, 481
  speech synthesizer, 163, 473, 482
Diplopia (double vision), 308
Discovery approach, 480, 481

501

Dispersion problem, 247
Domain knowledge, 343, 362
Down's syndrome, 134, 135
Dual-route hypothesis/model, 23, 82, 183, 195, 196, 236, 370, 395, 406
Dyslexia/reading disability
   adult, 175, 180, 181, 182, 184, 194, 195, 401
   college students, 183
   developmental, 175, 176, 177, 179, 186, 189, 195, 201, 209, 243, 255, 305, 310, 319
   phonological, 147, 185, 210, 211, 212, 213, 214, 215, 245, 248, 249, 253, 256
   surface, 147, 185, 210, 211, 212, 213, 214, 215
   visual, 304, 310

E

Eye
   fixed reference, 304, 305, 308, 313
   unfixed reference, 304, 305
Eye movements
   vergence, 304, 305

G

Garden variety poor readers, 219
Graphememe-phoneme correspondences (GPC), 35, 36, 72, 74, 76, 77, 82, 105, 107, 108, 115, 123, 124, 128, 129, 130, 138, 140, 144, 183
Grapho-phonemic cues, 34, 35, 47, 63, 98, 100, 105, 127, 128, 139
   information, 61, 62, 89, 90, 92

H

Howard Street Tutoring Project, 463

I

Information-processing, 235, 396
Instantiation, 348

K

Kinesthetic cues, 409

L

Learning-from-context hypothesis, 358
Lexical access, 91, 280, 343, 395, 480
Lexical analogies, 433
Lexical knowledge, 31, 251, 254, 267, 275, 310, 345, 427, 430, 434, 440
Lexical memory, 33, 87, 102, 406
Lexical pooling model, 426
Lexical priming, 434, 438, 440
Lexical processes, 370, 406
Lexical representation, 373
Lexical restructuring deficit hypothesis, 254
Lexical route, 183, 184, 185, 407
Lexicon
   computerized, 253, 257
   mental, 183, 184, 236, 251, 252
   phonological, 138, 268, 281
Lip reading, 176, 177, 264, 268, 269, 270, 271, 273, 274, 275, 277, 279, 280, 281, 282
Logographic spelling, 433
Logographic stage/phase, 72, 93, 122

M

Matthew Effect, 483
Memory
   functional, 340
   long-term, 356
   phonological, 414
   rule-based, 407, 409, 417
   semantic, 35
   short-term, 263, 264, 266, 268, 281, 356, 480
   stochastic, 407, 408, 413, 415
   tests, 132, 197, 208
   visual, 311, 312, 313, 370, 371, 372, 373, 390, 395, 396, 398, 399, 400, 402, 406, 407, 408, 409, 413, 414, 415, 416, 417
   working, 182, 318, 340, 343, 345, 356, 357, 358, 359, 361, 362, 363, 364, 365, 422
Metalinguistic operations, 39, 195, 204
Metaphonological tests, 128, 136
Metacognitive skills, 364, 365, 401
Modality effect, 263, 264
Models
   analogies, 236, 443
   formal, 236, 237
   integrated, 440
   mental, 344
   monocular occlusion, 304
   unitary, 401
   restrictive-interactive (RI), 430
   stage, 434, 437, 440, 443
Morphophonemic knowledge/representation, 405, 422, 429

SUBJECT INDEX

N

Neighborhood Activation Model (NAM), 252
Neural mechanisms, 1
Neural networks, 241

O

Ocular dominance, 313, 314
Ocular reference, 308
Ocular-motor integration, 303
Onsets, 2, 69, 70, 71, 72, 79, 97, 102, 104, 106, 114, 155, 157, 162, 163, 165, 194, 195, 288, 291, 386, 390, 453, 474, 475
Orthographic cipher, 20
Orthographic complexity, 429
Orthographic familiarity, 78
Orthographic knowledge, 37, 72, 73, 183, 396, 398, 401, 414, 422, 467
Orthographic mechanism, 24, 396
Orthographic neighbors, 203, 421, 426, 429
Orthographic processing, 26, 27
Orthographic representation, 35, 128, 146, 166, 186, 395, 401
Orthographic segment, 80
Orthographic stage, 433
Orthographic training, 430
Orthography, 71, 81, 138, 157, 162, 176, 191, 236, 243, 256, 279, 280, 298, 299, 397, 399, 400, 401, 405, 408, 412, 413, 429, 443
　artificial, 81
　Catalan, 145
　Czech, 387
　deep, 27, 131
　Dutch, 145
　English, 23, 69, 236, 238, 246, 256, 371, 373, 374, 376, 378, 381, 382, 387, 389, 421, 423, 451, 455
　French, 145, 146, 265, 275
　illegal, 370, 400, 408
　Italian, 275
　Japanese, 145
　Korean, 389
　legal, 370, 400
　opaque/opacity, 422, 429
　Portuguese, 146, 147
　shallow, 131, 219
　Spanish, 145
　transparent, 74, 107, 108, 422, 429
Orthoptic tests, 306, 309, 314

P

Phoneme, 2, 70, 108, 113, 129, 155, 156, 163, 165, 166, 167, 194, 229, 238, 239, 254, 288, 289, 298, 381, 389, 390
Phonemic awareness, 31, 70, 114, 115, 127, 128, 130, 131, 132, 133, 137, 142, 143, 147, 153, 154, 157, 161, 165, 195, 229, 287, 288, 289, 290, 291, 292, 293, 295, 298, 299, 398, 433, 440, 442, 443, 444, 450, 451, 452, 473, 476, 479, 481, 482, 483, 484
Phonetic cue reading, 94, 97, 100, 108, 414
Phonics method, 129, 130, 139, 140, 142, 374
　implicit, 138
Phonological representation, 35, 176, 191, 193, 194, 236, 250, 253, 256, 480
　in deaf, 263, 266, 270, 280, 282, 414
Phonological awareness, 5, 70, 71, 113, 114, 115, 116, 120, 121, 122, 123, 131, 155, 156, 157, 162, 163, 164, 166, 194, 202, 208, 231, 287, 288, 388, 440, 441, 442, 479
　compound, 114
　simple, 114
Phonological linkage hypothesis, 115, 122, 448
Phonological neighbors, 426, 429
Phonological processing, 26, 27, 180, 196, 201, 204, 206, 207, 210, 212, 213, 214, 220, 229, 232, 235, 265, 269, 480
Phonological recoding, 33, 38, 39, 40, 57, 58, 59, 61, 62, 63, 87, 90, 91, 95, 96, 98, 105, 106, 108, 324, 296, 484
Phonological route, 183, 184
Phonological skills, 1, 3, 72, 207, 332
　and reading, 1, 69, 187, 197
　and spelling, 370, 396, 397, 414, 415
Phonological/phonemic awareness training, 81, 298, 388, 430, 479, 480, 481, 483, 485
Phonology
　and the development of reading, 1, 175, 176, 203, 298, 401, 443
　development of spelling, 370, 399, 401, 414, 443
　and syntax, 6
　opaque, 265
　speech, 9, 11, 280, 381, 448
　surface, 265, 266

Polyphonic words, 20, 23
Prealphabetic phase, 93
Precategorical Acoustic Store (PAS), 263
Primary effect, 372
Proto-literate, 153, 159, 164, 165
 and phonological awareness, 161, 163

R

Reading
 an unnatural art, 2
 and speech, 15
 decoding skills, 19
 psycholinguistic guessing game, 9
 risk taking, 34
 selective cue stage, 454, 455
 visual approach, 294, 295
 visual processes, 186, 187, 188
 visual-phonological approach, 299
Reading Recovery, 449, 450, 456, 463, 465, 466
Reading and Orthographic and Speech Segmentation (ROSS) Programs, 473, 474, 475, 476, 477, 478, 479, 480, 481, 482, 483, 484
Recency effect, 263, 372
Reciprocal teaching, 263, 372
Rime-based training, 79, 80, 82
Rimes, 2, 69, 70, 71, 72, 75, 79, 82, 97, 102, 104, 106, 114, 155, 157, 162, 163, 166, 192, 194, 288, 390, 435, 436, 438, 439, 440, 442, 443, 453, 474, 475
 orthographic, 73, 238, 239
 phonological, 238

S

Scaffolding, 455, 456, 457, 460, 467, 468
Self-monitoring, 480
Sight word reading, 91
Sight acuity, 308
Sign language, 277
 and cued speech, 272
 and deaf children, 279
 and reading/writing, 5, 6, 13, 14
 perception, 14, 281
Segmentation, 195
Speech, 10, 13
Spelling, 15, 91, 93, 114, 122, 124, 128, 130, 143, 153, 158, 159, 160, 165, 166, 168, 176, 179, 183, 194, 195, 205, 214, 242, 281, 305, 306, 310, 313, 369, 370, 371, 373, 374
 contingencies, 422
 invented, 140, 451, 453
 lexical strategy, 421, 422, 423, 428
 nonphonetic errors, 375, 382, 391
 phonetic, 95, 96, 213, 399, 402, 405, 416
 phonetic errors, 375, 376, 382
 rule-based strategy, 421, 422, 423, 428
 serial position, 383, 386
 visual approach, 369, 370, 399
 visual, 95, 397, 399, 402, 405, 407
Spello program, 482, 484
Stroop task, 265, 266, 268
Sustained Pathway, 186, 187

T

Text domain, 344
Text processing, 329
Transient pathway, 186, 187, 189
Transient-sustained model, 186

U

Unstable ocular dominance, 177

V

Verbal deficits, 201, 303
Verbal efficiency theory, 345
Visible language, 303
Visual cue reading, 93, 409
Visuo-motor integration, 304
Visual-phonological, 399
Visuoorthographic codes, 264, 268, 277, 297
Visuoperceptual development, 201

W

Wernicke's aphasia, 147
Whole language, 8, 9, 34, 48, 63, 374, 466
Whole word method/training, 129, 142, 407, 478
Word family approach, 81, 82
Word recognition, 35, 36, 53, 61, 88, 130, 166, 180, 181, 182, 194, 196, 219, 250, 252, 256, 266, 280, 294, 343, 345, 401, 453, 464, 475, 476, 478, 484
Word-specific
 information, 400, 427
 knowledge, 31, 35, 37, 38, 47, 61, 63, 400
 memory, 406, 407, 414, 416, 417, 422

For Product Safety Concerns and Information please contact our EU representative GPSR@taylorandfrancis.com
Taylor & Francis Verlag GmbH, Kaufingerstraße 24, 80331 München, Germany

www.ingramcontent.com/pod-product-compliance
Lightning Source LLC
Chambersburg PA
CBHW071134300426
44113CB00009B/972